HANDBOOK ON THE ECONOMICS OF HAPPINESS

Handbook on the Economics of Happiness

Edited by

Luigino Bruni

Associate Professor of Economics, University of Milan-Bicocca, Italy

and

Pier Luigi Porta

Professor of Economics, University of Milan-Bicocca, Italy

Edward Elgar
Cheltenham, UK • Northampton, MA, USA

63705905

Published by
Edward Elgar Publishing Limited
Glensanda House
Montpellier Parade
Cheltenham
Glos GL50 1UA
UK

Edward Elgar Publishing, Inc.
William Pratt House
9 Dewey Court
Northampton
Massachusetts 01060
USA

A catalogue record for this book
is available from the British Library

Library of Congress Cataloguing in Publication Data
Handbook on the economics of happiness / edited by Luigino Bruni and Pier Luigi Porta.
    p. cm. — (Elgar original reference)
  Includes bibliographical references and index.
  1. Economics—Psychological aspects. 2. Happiness. I. Bruni, Luigino, 1966– II. Porta, Pier Luigi. III. Series.
  HB74.P8H372 2006 2007
  330.01'9—dc22
                                            2006042556

ISBN 978 1 84376 826 5

Printed and bound in Great Britain by MPG Books Ltd, Bodmin, Cornwall

Contents

Contributors

Stefano Bartolini Department of Political Economy, University of Siena, Italy.

Leonardo Becchetti Department of Economics and Institutions, University of Tor Vergata, Rome, Italy.

Marina Bianchi Department of Economics and Environment, University of Cassino, Italy.

Salvador A. Borrego Department of Management, University of Monterrey, Mexico.

Luigino Bruni Department of Political Economy, University of Milan-Bicocca, Milan, Italy.

Mark Chekola Department of Philosophy, Minnesota State University, Moorhead, USA.

Mario Cogoy Department of Economics, University of Trieste, Italy.

Donald Cox Economics Department, Boston College, USA.

Sergio Cremaschi Department of Humanistic Studies, University of Amedeo Avogadro, Vercelli, Italy.

Luca Crivelli Department of Economics, University of Lugano, University of Applied Sciences of Southern Switzerland, Switzerland.

Gianfranco Domenighetti Department of Health and Social Affairs, Canton Ticino, Health Economics and Management Institute, University of Lausanne, Switzerland.

Stravos Drakopoulos Department of Philosophy and History of Science, University of Athens, Greece.

Massimo Filippini Department of Economics, University of Lugano, Swiss Federal Institute of Technology, Zurich, Switzerland.

Nicole Christa Fuentes Department of Economics, University of Monterrey, Mexico.

Jose de Jesus Garcia Department of Economics, University of Monterrey, Mexico.

Gianluca Grimalda Centre for the Study of Globalisation and Regionalisation (CSGR), University of Warwick, Coventry, UK.

Marco E.L. Guidi Department of Economics, University of Pisa, Italy.

Monica Guillen Royo ESRC, University of Bath, UK.

Monica D. Gutierrez Department of Communications, University of Monterrey, Mexico.

Johannes Hirata Institute for Business Ethics, St Gallen University, Switzerland.

Julie R. Irwin Red McCombs School of Business, University of Texas, Austin, USA.

Anastasios Karayiannis Economics Department, University of Piraeus, Greece.

Silva Marzetti Dall'Aste Brandolini Economics Department, University of Bologna, Italy.

Amado Peiró Economics Department, University of Valencia, Spain.

Vittorio Pelligra Department of Economics, University of Cagliari, Italy.

Pier Luigi Porta Department of Political Economy, University of Milan-Bicocca, Milan, Italy.

Nattavudh Powdthavee Department of Economics, Warwick University, Coventry, UK.

Maurizio Pugno Economics Department, University of Cassino, Italy.

Rajagopal Raghunathan Red McCombs School of Business, University of Texas, Austin, USA.

Lorenzo Sacconi Department of Economics, University of Trento and EconomEtica (Inter-university Centre for Economic Ethics and Corporate Social Responsibility), University of Milano-Bicocca, Italy.

Marika Santoro Economics Department, University of Tor Vergata, Rome.

Roberto Scazzieri Institute of Advanced Studies, University of Bologna, Italy.

Oded Stark University of Klagenfurt, Austria; University of Bonn, Germany; University of Vienna, Austria; Warsaw University, Poland; ESCE Economic and Social Research Center, Cologne, Germany and Eisenstadt, Austria.

Alejandro Tapia Department of Psychology, University of Monterrey, Mexico.

Maarten Vendrik Department of Economics, Maastricht Univeristy, The Netherlands.

Gloria Vivenza Department of Economics, University of Verona, Italy.

Luca Zarri Department of Economics, University of Verona, Italy and School of Economics, University of East Anglia, Norwich, UK.

Introduction
Luigino Bruni and Pier Luigi Porta*

1. Economics and happiness: a new field with a long history

Many people focus on wealth when they pursue happiness, but research on social relationships suggests that they can be more important than material prosperity to subjective well-being. The word needs to be spread – it is important to work on social skills, close interpersonal ties, and social support in order to be happy. It is a mistake to value money over social relationships. (Diener and Seligman 2004)

After Rome had caught fire, it was probably 65 AD, Emperor Nero engineered to restore his reeling popularity by staging, in a surviving amphitheatre (before the Colosseum even existed), an immense gathering to watch a group of poor Christians be eaten up by fierce lions. As the stage opened – so the story goes – very soon after the first roaring hungry beast had dashed into the arena, one of those poor Christians, quite unexpectedly, sprang up toward the lion and somehow managed to mutter a few words in the lion's ear. Instantly the lion lost his mood, collapsed to the ground and lay still without any possible reaction. Breathless, the crowd looked at Nero. The Emperor immediately ordered a second lion, a fiercer one, to enter the stage. To no avail, however, and the same scene went on being repeated three or four times. The event definitely looked like a miracle. The Emperor, of course, was furious as the atmosphere was getting stormy. Two brutal soldiers got hold of the poor Christian, raised him to the Emperor's stalls and threw him at His Majesty's feet. 'What the hell did you say' – Nero raged – 'in the lion's ear?'. To which the man innocently replied 'I just said to him: "There will be speeches after dinner!"'.

The story looks plausible and it explains the inclination of a number of scholars who are, to the present day, so fiercely opposed to dinner speeches during Conferences. The same fate, unfortunately, sometimes extends to introductory chapters of collected papers or classics. Some editors may in fact sometimes be tempted to seize the opportunity and play Nero at the expense of their fellows, the proper authors. It will be up to the readers to judge if, in the present instance, we are able to escape our lot in that respect. Our introductory chapter presents a brief survey of the formative steps of the new and developing field of research on Economics and Happiness. We really trust this is not merely paying lip-service to a possibly disputed custom. To give a more precise idea of what it is all about, we further

xi

propose a discussion of the main interactions of the analysis on Economics and Happiness with old and new topics in contemporary Economics. We are going to touch on externalities, especially in consumption, Sen's idea of liberty, including his discussions on functionings and capabilities, and the recent developments on *civil* (rather than political) economy, characteristically emphasizing the role of interpersonal relations. All of these topics have some close relationships with the current developments of Ethical studies in Economics, as we shall see along the way. We shall also discuss some of the recent achievements in Cognitive or Behavioural Economics, which come as a fruit of the renewed Interactions of Economics and Psychology and are extremely relevant to our subject. A number of open questions concerning Happiness studies in Economics will then be touched upon in a third section: these concern issues on labour and satisfaction, problems of income distribution, the role of the market and, more particularly, of financial markets. We shall then finally give a summary outline of the present volume and try to weave a plausible thread linking the contributions to one another, thus offering an evaluation on the coverage in this volume of the fast expanding field of Happiness studies in Economics. We shall close with a number of indications for further reading in a brief survey of the recent literature in the field.

A great philosopher of music (Jankélévitch 1983), has made it part of his own philosophy and argued at some considerable length that it is a special character of musical experience that through music we are rewarded with an acceptable expression of something valuable if, and *only* if, we have not directly and possessively searched for it, so that it all comes to us as a gratuitous reward (ibid., pt III, § 2). A kind of serendipity is involved in the argument. Jankélévitch draws an interesting parallel with religious experience: in fact what he contends for the case of music is hardly new in the realm of events which are the result of *grace*. That we should probably *not* be inclined to think of music in the first place under that rubric, only means that, indeed, it can be rated as a discovery that the approach applies to both musical creation and musical experience, as Jankélévitch maintains.

Once we understand that as a discovery, we will probably find it quite natural to extend the result to the whole field of *poetical* creation. However, that would sound utterly implausible in economics, at least in so far as it is assumed that economics deals with actions where grace, and thereby *gratuity*, is excluded. The surprising discovery here, then, is that this is no longer self-evident once we enter the domain of happiness studies within economics. The main reason for this is that here we are led beyond the realm of action *per se* into the relatively unexplored territory of motivation. As we enter that territory we see immediately that current economic thinking is rather arbitrarily restricted to a narrow set of motivations to action and we are, therefore, forced to think in more general terms. It is in a context of this kind that we approach the idea that the notion of creation or ποιεσις – which means 'production' or 'creation' and from which also the word 'poetry' comes – has a very extensive domain for its application and that, indeed, had a not inconsiderable part historically in the shaping of the economic language. That this sounds odd today and require justification can be explained by the prevailing emphasis on exchange, rather than production, of much of the current imprinting of our current economic language. Of course production and exchange cannot possibly be entirely separated in economic reasoning; at the same time we get a very different view of the subject according as to whether we put the emphasis in our language on one or the other of the two terms. The dichotomy has often been stressed in the economic literature, albeit from different standpoints compared to the perspective chosen in our case.

A view of happiness which emphasizes creation has been called *eudaimonism* – a term which was popular in eighteenth-century philosophy, but which today forms the backbone of *one* current of thinking on happiness and well-being in economics. *Eudaimonism* – as explained, for example, by Deci and Ryan (2001, pp. 143–5) – conveys the belief that well-being consists of fulfilling or realizing one's *daimon* or true nature. In today's research *eudaimonism* parallels *hedonism* (to which we shall turn presently) as one of the two major approaches in the field of happiness studies in economics. The philosophical reference for the *eudaimonistic* approach is to be found in Aristotle, while Jeremy Bentham – not unexpectedly – still represents today the parent stem of the hedonic line of thinking and language in economics.[1]

It is proper here to dwell on two characteristics of *eudaimonia*, that are important also for the current debates on the paradoxes of happiness in economics, to which we shall come in due course. The first characteristic concerns the *civil* or political nature of *eudaimonia* leading to make friendship, as a form of fellow-feeling, an ingredient of it. This is stressed by Aristotle in his *Nichomachean Ethics*:

> Surely it is strange, too, to make the supremely happy man a solitary; for no one would choose the whole world on condition of being alone, since man is a political animal and one whose nature is to live with others. Therefore even the happy man lives with others; for he has the things that are by nature good. And plainly it is better to spend his days with friends and good men than with strangers or any chance persons. Therefore the happy man needs friends. (*Nic. Eth.*, IX, 9, 1169b)

In its highest expression friendship is a virtue and it is more important than wealth, according to Aristotle, because it is *part* of *eudaimonia* and, therefore, is an end in itself, while wealth is only a means to that end.

In the second place, as a further ingredient of *eudaimonia* as a conception of happiness, to Aristotle there is an *intrinsic value* in the commitment to participate in civil or political life, without which human life does not flourish. Although human life by its very nature is capable of autonomous flourishing, in the sense that it cannot be jeopardized by bad fortune, it is also true that some of the essential components of the good life are connected with our links to our fellows and with *interpersonal relationships*. Thereby participation in civil life, as much as having friends, loving and being loved are essential elements of a happy life. In this sense – this is what needs emphasis – *eudaimonia* involves a paradox of the invisible-hand type: it cannot be achieved *only* through instrumental means. Rather it is the indirect result of virtuous actions, carried out merely in view of their intrinsic value, without any further motive.

Because it is composed of actions and goods, who has the activity – we might say – will of necessity be acting. This is what Aristotle argues in his *Nichomachean Ethics* in which he defines that 'it is our actions and the soul's active exercise of its functions that we posit as being Happiness'. With that definition we have 'virtually identified happiness with a form of good life or doing well'; and 'virtue in active exercise cannot be inoperative – it will necessarily act, and act well' (*Nic. Eth.*, I, viii). We may translate Aristotle's words in the following message: civil life leads to *eudaimonia* by its very nature, that is, only if it is marked by sincere and gratuitous sentiments. Martha Nussbaum (1986, ch. 12) argues that friendship, love and political commitment are the three main *relational goods* that Aristotle had in mind. They have an intrinsic value, are part of *eudaimonia*, are gratuitous, and cannot be instrumental. Because they are *made of relationships*, relational goods can be enjoyed only in reciprocity and, also for this reason, they are said to be vulnerable and fragile.

2.   The paradox of happiness
The process of rediscovery of happiness in economics has been mainly a byproduct of a process that originated in psychology. In fact, the chapter published by Brickman and Campbell in 1971, under the telling title of 'Hedonic relativism and planning the good society', can rightly be considered the starting-point of the new studies on happiness in relation to the economic domain. In their study, the two psychologists extended the 'adaptation level' theory to individual and happiness, reaching the conclusion that bettering the objective conditions of life (income or wealth) bears no lasting effects on personal well-being. Such a thesis should have provoked a serious methodological storm about the nature and causes of the wealth of people. Yet it did not; the study remained practically unknown to mainstream economists for years.

Only a few years later, two economists, Richard Easterlin (1974) and Tibor Scitovsky (1976), were persuaded, however, that what was going on in that field of psychology could have something important to say to economic analysis. So, the 'paradox of happiness' entered economics, re-echoing economic science from its classical origins. In fact, the wealth–happiness nexus was central in the classical tradition – as we shall see in the core chapters.[2]

By utilizing empirical research on people's happiness, Richard Easterlin managed to open up the debate around the 'happiness paradox' – also today called the 'Easterlin paradox'. He made use of two types of empirical data. The first base was supplied by the responses to a Gallup-poll type of survey in which a direct question was asked – a question which is still at the basis of most of the empirical analyses on happiness: 'In general, how happy would you say that you are – *very* happy, *fairly* happy or *not very* happy?' (Easterlin 1974, p. 91, original emphasis). The other set of data Easterlin made use of came from more sophisticated research carried out in 1965 by the humanist psychologist Hadley Cantril (another forerunner of contemporary quantitative studies on happiness), concerning people's fears, hopes and satisfaction in 14 countries. The subjects interviewed were asked to classify their own satisfaction on a scale from 0 to 10^3 – in today's World Values Survey (WVS) questionnaires, happiness is ranked in 'qualitative' terms (from 'not very happy' to 'very happy'), whereas life satisfaction is still measured using a Cantril methodology (a scale from 1 to 10).

Both types of data, then, were based on a *subjective self-evaluation* of one's happiness or life satisfaction – this subjective definition of happiness is a crucial point in the whole debate, as we shall see.[4] They both produced, in Easterlin's seminal analyses, the same results. Within a single country, at a given moment in time, the correlation between income and happiness *exists and it is robust*: 'In every single survey, those in the highest status group were happier, on the average, than those in the lowest status group' (ibid., p. 100). In cross-sectional data among countries, instead, the positive association wealth–happiness, although present, *is neither general nor robust*, and poorer countries do not always appear to be less happy than richer countries. In other words: 'if there is a positive association among countries between income and happiness it is not very clear. . . . The results are ambiguous' (ibid., p. 108).[5] But the most interesting result came from the time-series analysis at the national level: in 30 surveys over 25 years (from 1946 to 1970 in the US) per capita real income rose by more than 60 per cent, but the proportion of people who rated themselves as 'very happy', 'fairly happy' or 'not too happy' remained almost unmodified.

The main drift of Easterlin's seminal paper was developed two years later by Scitovsky's *Joyless Economy* (1976), which – as we shall see – added an original contribution calling more on psychology. Hirsch (1977), Ng (1978), Layard (1980) and Frank (1985) all brought new insights into the explanations of the 'Easterlin paradox', which grew slowly but steadily. Today the debate on economics and happiness is gaining increasing attention among economists, psychologists, sociologists and the public.

The theoretical debate about the paradox of happiness is contentious. Almost all scholars, from different backgrounds, agree on the results over time, because there is evidence that 'over time and across OECD countries rises in aggregate income are not associated with rises in aggregate happiness. . . . At the aggregate level, there has been no increase in reported happiness over the last 50 years in the US and Japan, nor in Europe since 1973 when the records began' (Layard 2005, p. 148).[6]

The income–happiness relationship within a single country in a given moment in time is not controversial today among economists: almost all agree that a causal correlation running from income to happiness exists and is robust: 'Various studies provide evidence that, on average, persons living in rich countries are happier than those living in poor countries.' (Frey and Stutzer 2001).[7]

Psychologists do not deny this correlation, but, in general, are less optimistic about the importance of income on well-being:

> [T]he effects of wealth are not large, and they are dwarfed by other influences, such as those of personality and social relationships. . . . [W]hen the sciences of economics and of well-being come face-to-face, they sometimes conflict. If the well-being findings simply mirrored those for income and money – with richer people invariably being much happier than poorer people – one would hardly need to measure well-being, or make policy to enhance it directly. But income, a good surrogate historically when basic needs were unmet, is now a weak surrogate for well-being in wealthy nations. What the divergence of the economics and well-being measures demonstrates is that well-being indicators add important information that is missed by economic indicators. Economic development will remain an important priority, but policies fostering economic development must be supplemented by policies that will have a stronger impact on well-being. (Diener and Seligman 2004, p. 10)

Also among economists, however, the income–happiness correlation across countries is more controversial.[8] Easterlin in 1974 found, as we have seen, a not clear and evident correlation between happiness and income between different countries. Today most of the economists, using data coming from the WVS, agree that a correlation does exists: 'Various studies provide evidence that, on average, persons living in rich countries are happier than those living in poor countries' (Frey and Stutzer 2001).

Layard makes an important distinction in the cross-country analyses:

> [I]f we compare countries, there is no evidence that richer countries are happier than poorer ones – so long as we confine ourselves to countries with incomes over $15,000 per head. . . . At income levels below $15,000 per head things are

different, since people are nearer to the absolute breadline. At these income levels richer countries are happier than poorer ones. And in countries like India, Mexico and Philippines, where we have time series data, happiness has grown as income levels have risen. (2005, p. 149)[9]

These issues are relevant in economic theory: explaining the happiness paradoxes calls into question some of the basic tenets of contemporary economics – as we shall see.

Before continuing, however, it can be useful to explore more the concept of happiness, by comparing it with similar concepts.

3. What is happiness?

As Diener and colleagues correctly note, 'A widely presumed component of the good life is happiness. Unfortunately, the nature of happiness has not been defined in a uniform way. Happiness can mean pleasure, life satisfaction, positive emotions, a meaningful life, or a feeling of contentment, among other concepts' (Diener and Seligman 2004).

Economists do not even like the question: 'what is happiness?'. To them happiness is not a concept clearly distinct from pleasure, satisfaction or welfare. Ng (1997) defines happiness as 'welfare', for Oswald (1997) happiness means 'pleasure' or 'satisfaction', and Easterlin, is even too explicit: 'I use the terms happiness, subjective well-being, satisfaction, utility, well-being, and welfare interchangeably' (2001, p. 465). To Frey and Stutzer (2005): 'Happiness research in economics takes reported subjective well-being as a proxy measure for utility' (p. 116). The sociologist Ruut Veenhoven 'use[s] the terms "*happiness*" or "*life satisfaction*" for comprehensive judgment' (2005, p. 245, original emphasis). Happiness, by economists, is not generally *defined*, but empirically *measured*, on the basis of the answers to questionnaires that ask people: '*how* happy are you?'. The WVS questionnaires ask people about both happiness ('how happy are you?') and life satisfaction ('how satisfied are you with your life?'), both of which are also often used in academic analyses about people's happiness. The Eurobarometer of the European Commission measures Europeans' self-evaluation of life satisfaction, and these data are often used as synonymous of self-reported happiness in economic analyses (see Oswald 1997). Ronald Inglehart, the WVS coordinator, uses the Subjective Well-Being (SWB) Index which is a combination of the responses to 'happiness' and the responses to 'life-satisfaction' questions.[10]

Some economists (Frank 1997, 2005; Layard 2005) use the SWB category simply as a synonym of happiness, relying on psychologists for the definition. Actually, in psychological studies the story is more complex. In psychology, experimental studies on happiness began in the 1950s, and, in general, psychologists use the expression 'happiness' with more precision than economists. Psychologists distinguish among: (a) 'life satisfaction', which is a cognitive element; (b) 'affection', the affective component; and (c) SWB, defined as a 'state of general well-being, synthetic, of long duration, which includes both the affective and cognitive component' (Ahuvia and Friedman 1998, p. 153).

Ed Diener, for example, proposes on the basis of abundant empirical evidence an SWB hierarchical model whose four components are: (i) pleasant emotions (joy, contentment, happiness, love and so on); (ii) unpleasant emotions (sadness, anger, worry, stress and so on); (iii) global life judgement (life evaluation, fulfilment, meaning, success and so on); and (iv) domain satisfaction (marriage, work, health, leisure and so on).[11] In this approach, SWB comprises all these components, therefore, happiness is considered to be a *narrower* concept than SWB, and different from life satisfaction: life satisfaction and happiness are both considered to be *components* of SWB – as in the Senian capability approach where happiness is just *a* component of a 'good life'. In particular, life satisfaction reflects individuals' perceived distance from their aspirations (Campbell et al. 1976). Happiness results from a balance between positive and negative affect (Bradburn 1969).[12] SWB is instead defined as 'a general evaluation of a person's life' (Diener and Seligman 2004). In general, 'the term subjective well-being emphasizes an individual's own assessment of his or her own life – not the judgment of "experts" – and includes satisfaction (both in general and satisfaction with specific domains), pleasant affect, and low negative affect' (ibid.). For this reason, 'SWB is not a unitary dimension, and there is no single index that can capture what it means to be happy' (ibid.). In this approach to SWB, 'to be' happy is considered to be different from 'to feel' happy: SWB is a synonym of 'being happy', a concept close to the Aristotelian approach to happiness as *eudaimonia*, whereas concepts such as 'satisfaction' and 'happiness' belong to 'feeling' happy.

The result of the above discussion is that we should emphasize that in psychological studies of happiness we do find a tension between a '*hedonic*' idea of happiness and a '*eudaimonic*' one. In the *hedonic* approach, happiness is the result of avoiding pain and seeking pleasure; on the contrary, according to the *eudaimonic* approach, happiness arises as people function and interact within society, an approach that places emphasis on non-material pursuits such as genuine interpersonal relationships and intrinsic motivations (Deci and Ryan 2001).

More precisely, hedonism (Kahneman et al. 1999, 2003) reflects the view that *well-being consists of pleasure or happiness*: 'Hedonism, as a view of well-being, has thus been expressed in many forms and has varied from a relatively narrow focus on bodily pleasures to a broad focus on appetites and self-interests' (Deci and Ryan 2001, p. 144). In 1999, Kahneman et al.

announced the existence of a new field of psychology. The title of their book, *Well-being: The Foundations of Hedonic Psychology*, clearly suggests that, within their paradigm, the terms 'well-being' and 'hedonism' are essentially equivalent.[13]

The second view, (eudaimonism), both as ancient and as current, claims that well-being consists of more than just hedonic or subjective happiness: 'Despite the currency of the hedonic view, many philosophers, religious masters, and visionaries, from both the East and West, have denigrated happiness *per se* as a principal criterion of well-being' (Deci and Ryan 2001, p. 145). It lies instead in the actualization of human potential. Due to a close continuity with Aristotelian ethics, this view has been called '*eudaimonism*' conveying the belief that

> [W]ell-being consists of fulfilling or realizing one's *daimon* or true nature. The two traditions – hedonism and *eudaimonism* – are founded on distinct views of human nature and of what constitutes a good society. Accordingly, they ask different questions concerning how developmental and social processes relate to well-being, and they implicitly or explicitly prescribe different approaches to the enterprise of living. (Ibid., p. 143).

Ryff and Singer (1998, 2000), also drawing from Aristotle, describe well-being not in terms of attaining pleasure, but as 'the striving for perfection that represents the realization of one's true potential' (Ryff 1995, p. 100). Carol Ryff has even proposed the idea of psychological well-being (PWB) as distinct from subjective well-being: 'Whereas the SWB tradition formulates well-being in terms of overall life satisfaction and happiness, the PWB tradition draws heavily on formulation of human development and existential challenges of life' (Keyes et al. 2002, p. 1008).[14] Another, complementary, way of presenting this tension is to distinguish between an *ethical* approach to happiness (the Aristotelian) and a purely *subjectivist* one based on psychological experience (the hedonic). In fact, the philosophical reference point for the hedonistic approach is Bentham (or Epicurus), while Aristotle is the father of the *eudaimonic*/ethical one. Given the importance of Aristotle's theory of *eudaimonia* in the context of our research, it is worthwhile examining in greater depth, his theory which is what we shall do at the beginning of the historical analysis (Part I). The next section examines the main explanations offered today for the 'Easterlin paradox'.

4.   Explanations for the Easterlin paradox

Hedonic treadmill and set-point theory
We want to stress right from the beginning that the economists working today on the 'happiness paradox' are generally far from the *eudaimonistic*

tradition. As a matter of fact, if we want to spot an economist who is moving along a line of research very similar to the Aristotelian one, we should mention Amartya Sen. Although he cannot be considered a 'scholar of happiness',[15] in all his work he reminds economists that happiness, in order to be a proxy of a good life, must be translatable into human flourishing (*eudaimonia*), in terms of capabilities and functioning, human rights and freedom:

> If we have reasons to want more wealth, we have to ask: What precisely are these reasons, how do they work, on what are they contingent and what are the things we can 'do' with more wealth? In fact, we generally have excellent reasons for wanting more income or wealth. This is not because, typically, they are admirable general-purpose means for having more freedom to lead the kind of lives we have reasons to value. The usefulness of wealth lies in the things that it allows us to do – the substantive freedom it helps us to achieve. But this relation is neither exclusive (since there are significant influences on our lives other than wealth) nor uniform (since the impact of wealth on our lives varies with other influences). It is as important to recognize the crucial role of wealth determining living conditions and the quality of life as it is to understand the qualified and contingent nature of this relationship. (Sen 2000, p. 14)

As far as sociality is concerned, apart from a very few exceptions interpersonal relations, or sociality-as-relationality, is absent among the *key ingredients* of happiness. Sociality-as-positionality is very central, but such an idea of sociality is everything but Aristotle's *philia*. In fact – and in the final section of the introduction we shall provide evidence of this – in the explanations of the paradox of 'more income and less (or constant) happiness over time' there is an important missing link: the role of sociality seen as a direct source of happiness. The idea is that by concentrating on such crucial variables as income, wealth or consumption, economic science *neglects something relevant in the interpersonal domain*, which affects happiness or well-being. The aim of the following review, therefore, is to spot an *absence*: the lack in economics of a deep analysis of sociality for explaining the paradox of happiness, which is basically an introduction to both the historical and the theoretical analyses that will follow.

The first economist who attempted to explain the Easterlin paradox was Richard Easterlin himself, in his 1974 seminal paper. His explanation was based on Duesenberry's (1949) 'relative income' assumption. Many authors working on economics and happiness today still base their analyses on the relative income hypothesis: among them Robert Frank (1997, 1999), Yew K. Ng (1997), Heinz Höllander (2001) and Richard Layard (2005).

Before entering into the analysis of the most common explanations of the Easterlin paradox grounded on the relative consumption hypothesis (next section), it is important to examine other explanations, based on individual 'treadmills'.

While the relative consumption hypothesis can be considered an internal evolution of the *economic* tradition, the explanations of the paradox that make use of the treadmill effects have a clear origin in psychological research. Such psychological theories are based on 'hedonic adaptation' or 'set-point' theory. According to set-point theories there is a level of happiness that remains practically constant during the life cycle, because personality and temperament variables seem to play a strong role in determining the level of happiness of individuals. Such characteristics are basically innate to individuals. In other words, in the long run, we are fixed at hedonic neutrality, and our efforts to make ourselves happier by achieving good life circumstances are only short-term solutions. Therefore, life circumstances including health or income often account for a very small percentage of the variance in SWB: people initially do react to events, but then they return to baseline levels of well-being that are determined by personality factors (Argyle 2001; Lucas et al. 2002). Empirical research (Lykken and Tellegen 1996, among others), concluded that more than 80 per cent of the variance in long-term stable levels of SWB could be attributed to inborn temperament. On this basis, these psychologists have claimed that people have inborn SWB 'set points'.[16] The various shocks that occur during our lifetime affect our happiness only temporarily. We inevitably return to our *set point* after a brief period. As Daniel Kahneman writes: 'individuals exposed to life-altering events ultimately return to a level of well-being that is characteristic of their personality, sometimes by generating good or bad outcomes that restore this characteristic level' (1999, p. 14).

Many psychologists and economists today maintain that there is a 'hedonic treadmill' operating in the area of economic goods. The hedonic treadmill, a metaphor coined by Brickman and Campbell (1971) comes from 'set-point theory': we are running constantly and yet remain at the same place because the treadmill runs at the same pace – or even faster – but in the opposite direction.

Set-point theory is also popular today among economists (Easterlin 2005; Frey and Stutzer 2005). According to this theory, happiness is essentially a congenital matter that mostly depends on subjective elements such as character, genes, or the inherited capacity to live with and overcome life's hardships. In other words, there is a given level of happiness, around which the various experiences of life gravitate. This is a similar approach to that of Herrnstein and Murray (1994), who in *The Bell Curve* proclaimed the uselessness of social programmes on the basis that there is an innate level of intelligence that cannot be permanently changed by education.

Although in a quite different methodological line, Ruut Veenhoven (2005)[17] rejects the common perception that misery, handicaps and inequality in income distribution are the principal causes of people's unhappiness, and concludes that there is no 'paradox' of happiness (in the Easterlin meaning). In Veenhoven's *World Database of Happiness*,[18] Ghana and Columbia are ranked highest among all the nations classified according to their happiness level. France and Italy take a back seat to Guatemala.

Satisfaction treadmill

More recently, Kahneman has drawn a distinction between two types of treadmill effects, namely, the 'hedonic' treadmill and the 'satisfaction' treadmill. While the former depends on *adaptation*, the latter depends on *aspiration*, 'which marks the boundaries between satisfactory and unsatisfactory results' (1999, p. 14).

As their income increases, people are induced to seek continuous and ever-more intense pleasures in order to maintain the same level of satisfaction. The satisfaction treadmill works in such a way that a person's *subjective* happiness (self-evaluation) remains constant even when his/her *objective* happiness improves. In this case, while an individual's objective well-being, or happiness, receives a boost because he/she has bought a new car; the fact that the individual has had a rise in income has also increased his/her aspirations about the ideal car to own, so that his/her subjective satisfaction level remains the same. This is true even though the individual may be objectively more comfortable in his/her new car.[19]

Easterlin carried out an interesting experiment over a period of 16 years in which he periodically asked the same group of people the following questions:

1. We often hear people talk about what they want out of life. Here are a number of different things. [The respondent is handed a card with a list of 24 items.] When you think of the good life – the life you'd like to have, which of the things on this list, if any, are part of that good life as far as you personally are concerned?
2. Now would you go down that list and call off all the things you now have? (Easterlin 2005, p. 45)[20]

The first question aims at measuring the aspirations, while the second measures the means (income). The results showed that with an increase in material means (indicated by the first list), the things that were considered necessary for a happy life change (the second list). Thus, in the first phases of the life cycle, a summer home at the seaside and a second car were not indicated as being important for a good life, but they did feature as income increased. The ratio between possessed goods and desired goods remains practically constant over a life span, much as in a treadmill where means and aspiration run, more or less, at the same pace. Layard (2005) calls this the 'effect of habit':

> The process at work here is the basic human process of adaptation, whereby people adjust to a change in circumstances, be it upwards or downwards. This is for example the mechanism that explains the famous endowment effect, whereby people suffer more from losing something than they would gain from obtaining it. (p. 152)

This mechanism is also very close to one of the most important ideas in modern behavioural economics, the idea that preferences are *reference dependent* (Tversky and Kahneman 1991).

This idea is not completely new in the tradition of economics.

The social treadmill: relative consumption and positional competition
Explanations based on the relative consumption hypothesis can rightly be considered as a development of the satisfaction treadmill. The hedonic treadmill based on adaptation is essentially individual and a-social. The satisfaction treadmill is instead associated with social comparisons, although the satisfaction treadmill can apply even in isolation – that is, it can also occur on Robinson Crusoe's island when he tries to exceed his performance (in cultivation, fishing and so on). In other words, the hedonic treadmill does not necessarily require society for it to function; satisfaction occurs *normally* in society, but neither the hedonic nor the satisfaction treadmills *require sociality by necessity*. Rather, a '*pure social* treadmill' is the 'positional' one.

Even the relative consumption hypothesis is not new. Making use of his 'relative income' theory, we have already mentioned that Duesenberry was the first to introduce relative consumption theory explicitly in 1949. Duesenberry claimed that a person draws utility, or satisfaction, from his/her own level of consumption in relation or in comparison to the level of other people's consumption (1949, p. 32).

In other words, he basically said that we are constantly comparing ourselves to other people, and that what they buy influences the choices about what we want to buy. It is the old 'keeping up with the Joneses' scenario, where the consumption function is constructed upon the hypothesis that our consumption choices are influenced by the difference between our level of income and the level of income of others, rather than the absolute level. Therefore, the utility of a person's level of consumption depends not only on the *absolute* level but also on the *relative* one.

Without going as far back as the eighteenth century, where considerations about the social dimensions of consumption were prominent (we shall consider Adam Smith and Antonio Genovesi later), at the end of the nineteenth century Veblen (1899) treated consuming as a social issue, because

of the simple fact that the most significant acts of consumption are normally carried out under the public gaze. In recent times, Scitovsky (1976,
ch. 6) dealt with the relationship between consumption and status, and
Fred Hirsch (1977) coined the term 'positional good'. The basic element of
the contemporary positional theory is the concept of 'externality': conspicuous commodities share some characteristics of the 'demerit goods'
(private goods generating negative externalities), with the typical consequence of Pareto inefficiency:

> That many purchases become more attractive to us when others make them
> means that consumption spending has much in common with a military arms
> race. A family can choose how much of its own money to spend, but it cannot
> choose how much others spend. Buying a smaller-than-average vehicle means
> greater risk of dying in an accident. Spending less on an interview suit means a
> greater risk of not landing the best job. Yet when all spend more on heavier cars
> or more finely tailored suits, the results tend to be mutually offsetting, just as
> when all nations spend more on armaments. Spending less – on bombs or on per-
> sonal consumption – frees up money for other pressing uses, but only if every-
> one does it. (Frank 2005, pp. 83–4)[21]

Thus, relative consumption theory can also be described by using the
image of a treadmill: *something else* is running alongside our income or consumption: that is, the income of others. We shall return to the 'positional
explanation' of the happiness paradox later, where this theory is confronted
with a more relational approach to happiness.

To sum up. The theories reviewed above, which are the main explanations of the paradox of happiness in contemporary literature, take sociality into consideration mainly as a public good problem: a rise in aspirations
or positional competition generates negative externalities in consumption
that affect or 'pollute' individual utility. From this arises Layard's and
Frank's recipe: Pigouvian taxes. In other words, these theories do not deal
with the *direct* relationship between individual well-being and sociality-as-
relationality, or, the economic explanations of the 'Easterlin paradox' do
not refer to sociality as a source of happiness *per se*.

Mainstream economic literature, in fact, finds it hard to do this kind of
analysis: this book can be read as a study for comprehending *why* it is so
hard, and to put forward the methodological bases for a theory of happiness where relationality plays a key role.

5.   The present volume
This volume contains a number of recent contributions on the relationship of economics and happiness. This appears *prima facie* to be a comparatively new field of research for economists as it has experienced a
revival during the last 20–30 years and has only very recently attracted the

attention of the general economist. In March 2003, the editors of this volume had the privilege of organizing and hosting at the Bicocca University of Milan an International Conference on 'The Paradoxes of Happiness in Economics', gathering together for the first time some of the major contributors to the field in recent years. A number of the chapters in this volume are revised drafts of contributions first presented at the Bicocca 2003 conference.

The volume is divided into four parts, as follows.

Part I contains six chapters of a historical nature, highlighting the contributions that older philosophies made to the modern concept of economic happiness.

In Chapter 1, Gloria Vivenza examines some important contributions that the ancient Greek and Roman philosophies have made to the modern concept of economics, by resolutely denying any relationship between material welfare and happiness. Indeed in the ancient world, 'happiness' did not consist of material things; although welfare could be considered desirable and even necessary for living well, it was conceived mainly in terms of things to be possessed and *used*: for being independent, for devoting oneself to one's preferred activities, and for benefiting friends and the city.

Chapter 2, by Luigino Bruni, is a journey through the vicissitudes of happiness in economics; this critical and historical analysis aims to show that the contemporary approach to happiness in economics may be enriched by recovering some elements of the 'old' debate. In particular, this is true for two fields such as the theory of 'social capital' and development, related to both public happiness and 'civic virtues'. The main conception underlined here is that twentieth-century neoclassical economics finds it difficult to explain the paradox, because it did not pay enough attention to the 'technology of happiness' – that is, the transformation of wealth into well-being, the analysis of how and whether economic goods become happiness, well-being. This chapter therefore stresses the need for a new approach which takes adequately into account the role of interpersonal relationships in the transformation problem to fully open and look inside the 'black box' of the current theory of happiness, where the 'transformation problem' – the how and whether maximized wealth or income is transformed into well-being or happiness – still remains unknown.

In Chapter 3, Stravos Drakopoulos and Anastasios Karayiannis look at the history of economic ideas to get some further clues for a possible explanation of the paradox of happiness. The authors examine the ideas of some well-known pre-classical and classical economists concerning the relationship among basic goods, consumption and happiness. The main idea in this work is that, following the ancient theories, human needs are hierarchically structured so that basic needs, corresponding to basic goods, are more urgent and must be satisfied first. Therefore, since basic needs are more urgent and basic goods satisfy better these basic needs, basic goods might provide more happiness, while the subsequent satisfaction of secondary needs does not provide an equivalent increase in individual happiness and this may explain the observed gap between real income increases and increases in happiness level.

Marco E.L. Guidi (Chapter 4) undertakes a critical review of the theories of Jeremy Bentham, universally considered as the founding father of utilitarian ethics by philosophers and of rational choice theory by economists. Guidi considers that 'Bentham himself was clearly always more interested in quality than in quantity' and that the 'felicific calculus' continued to be for him an essential element both of moral and of legal theory. Nevertheless he was also conscious of the differences between individual sensibility to pain and the pleasures of different natures and he fought to establish the perfect substitutability between pleasure seeking and pain avoidance against a tradition that stressed the ephemeral nature of pleasure and the prevailing presence of pain in human life. Finally, and despite such substitutability, he discovered some asymmetries between pain and pain of loss, which were essential for the evaluation of individual happiness and social welfare and for the normative theory that was built upon it.

In Chapter 5, by Pier Luigi Porta and Roberto Scazzieri, the concept of *public happiness* is discussed and related to the definition of a constellation of enabling conditions based on a complex inter-play of cultural beliefs and social opportunities. *Civil society*, in turn, is introduced as a sphere of possible outcomes resulting from the 'horizontal' interactions of individuals (or social groups). It may be considered as a virtual setting in which individuals (or groups) 'take position' relative to one another in virtue of a particular structure of admissible events. The study attempts to construct an economic theory of public happiness by laying emphasis upon the *relational dimension* of happiness in the presence of social diversity. A 'mean distance' criterion is introduced and the ensuing discussion draws attention to the fact that, under specific social and historical circumstances (close to the characterising features of Adam Ferguson's civil society or of Adam Smith's commercial society), a synthetic measure of public happiness may be obtained.

Finally, in Chapter 6, Sergio Cremaschi aims at a revaluation of Immanuel Kant's thoughts on happiness. In fact, Kant is often thought to hold that happiness is not valuable, and even to have ignored it wholly in his ethics. Instead, to be virtuous, for Kant, is to be worthy of happiness and the perfect good requires that happiness is distributed in accordance with virtue. His highest good is presented as something different from happiness, indeed as the sum of happiness and virtue. In particular Cremaschi shows how Kant was aware that wealth is a very poor means to happiness and his own idea of a highest good (a good where material well-being and moral worth are joined together) and his 'real' idea of happiness is the idea of a state where man is both happy and deserving of happiness, that is the *summum bonum*, a state that includes both moral and non-moral elements.

The six chapters in Part II offer explanations of the income–happiness paradox, delving behind the economics factor in order to understand the paradox of happiness.

In Chapter 7, Marina Bianchi offers a critique to the economic theory of choice based on maximization of own satisfaction, utility or pleasure, which individuals pursue in their actions. Following the reasoning by the economist Tibor Scitovsky, Bianchi concentrates on the role that joyful and stimulating activities can play in making life pleasant, stressing the possible consequences in terms of social welfare configurations. The aim is therefore to underline how creative consumption represents a 'technology' of consumption that can give rise to increasing returns and the unhappiness that can arise when people privilege choices that lock them into defensive technologies that have lower returns: this trade-off between the two cannot be easily reconciled, because comfort consumption may also have high costs of exit.

In Chapter 8, Monica Guillen Royo analyses an alternative theoretical framework with respect to the traditional neoclassical consumption theory, where consumption is considered either to fulfil consumers' desires or to contribute to their happiness. Because goods and services may differ in their capacity to meet certain universal goals considered to be minimum requirements to enable an individual to flourish or even to give him/her the opportunity to strive for happiness, it is necessary to evaluate the current patterns of consumption, distinguishing among goods purchased. To this end, attention is drawn to the normative theories of 'functionings', capabilities or human needs developed by Sen, Nussbaum and Doyal and Gough; by providing a list of thresholds or basic needs that have to be fulfilled in every society they enable the evaluation of present patterns of consumption in terms of their suitability to meet needs or capabilities. Drawing from this theory of human needs, the process of consumption is evaluated, taking into consideration the goals pursued by society as a whole through its production system and consumption patterns. This also has some policy implications, not only for economic policies that do not provide for minimum levels of consumption evaluated negatively, but also for policies that foster unproductive or non-welfare-generating consumption.

Mario Cogoy, in Chapter 9, focuses on enjoyment as a contribution to happiness. A time-allocation approach is combined with a model of economic dynamics, based on the accumulation of human capital. Enjoyment is modelled as an activity, taking place in time, and using knowledge in order to improve the quality of life. The accumulation of knowledge improves both the efficiency of production and enjoyment activities, and technical progress is therefore extended to the realm of life enjoyment. This implies that knowledge and technology accumulated in the consumption sector directly affect welfare, and that the structure of preferences regarding time, consumption goods and consumption knowledge significantly determines the dynamics of the economy.

In Chapter 10, Maarten Vendrik and Johannes Hirata offer an alternative explanation to the paradox of happiness, in terms of rising aspirations and positional externalities. The new approach investigated here is the distinction between intrinsic and extrinsic goals. This approach points to a second kind of discrepancy between decision utility and experienced utility of income and implies that life satisfaction depends on absolute rather than relative income. It has some potential, but, in its present stage, it yields less-specific predictions with respect to the paradoxes than the theories of aspirations and positional externalities. On the other hand, in the case of top-down relations between life satisfaction and aspiration levels, the intrinsic/extrinsic-goals explanation seems more fundamental.

In Chapter 11, Rajagopal Raghunathan and Julie R. Irwin examine whether people's happiness with a product experience increases or decreases as a function of their happiness with past experiences in the same as opposed to other product contexts. In brief, they find that happiness with a product experience is enhanced when it follows inferior experiences in the same product category, and is diminished when it follows superior experiences in a different product category. Under circumstances where there is ambiguity about product category membership of the target, framing the target as belonging to the same (as opposed to a different) product category (such as that of the contextual stimuli) produce a conceptually similar pattern of results. These findings have straightforward implications for agents interested in the welfare of consumers: they suggest that consumption experiences should be arranged in an improving sequence over the life-span of consumers.

In Chapter 12, Mark Chekola offers a view of the nature of the happiness of a life that captures what it is we think is a happy life. The author refers to it as the realization of a 'life plan view of happiness' (one's higher-order desires) in terms of maintaining the status quo in the absence of serious felt dissatisfaction and an attitude of being displeased with or disliking one's life. This view of happiness sees a happy life as one in which a person's higher-order desires, the relatively more comprehensive, permanent and important desires the person has, are in the process of being realized. Two further conditions are also added. First, there can be serious felt dissatisfaction even where one's life is, objectively, going well, if someone suffers from depression and second, that there is a disposition to experience favourable feelings and attitudes associated with the realization of these higher-order desires.

The six papers of Part III are still centred on the explanations of the Easterlin paradox, but the emphasis is put on interpersonal relations, or 'relational goods', as the main theoretical tool.

In Chapter 13, Leonardo Becchetti and Marika Santoro suggest a theoretical interpretation for the paradox of happiness through a model explaining why and under which conditions a prisoner's dilemma in the production of relational leisure may arise, in so far as the opportunity cost of producing relational leisure gets higher. The authors' conclusions are that, for given intervals of productivity growth, rising productivity may make people wealthier, but not happier, if coordination failures dramatically reduce the production and consumption of relational goods.

Maurizio Pugno (Chapter 14) provides an explanation for the paradox by drawing heavily on the psychological and other literature. In fact, subjective well-being is largely influenced by close personal relationships which exhibit an unfortunate tendency to deteriorate. To capture these facts, relational goods are defined as a distinct input to subjective well-being, together with the usual economic goods; and individuals' aspirations for relational goods are explained as being tendentially greater than their realization, especially when individuals are young. Disappointing experiences with relational goods cumulate across generations, triggering a vicious circle because individuals unintentionally reduce their disposition towards others, while technical progress fosters materialistic growth.

The starting-point of Chapter 15, by Vittorio Pelligra, is Martha Nussbaum's well-known argument of the so-called 'fragility of goodness'. This conception states that bringing interpersonal relationships out of the control of the subject, and ultimately into others' hands, exposes one to the risk of opportunism. At the same time, it is implicitly assumed that such trustful behaviour does not in any way change the quality of the relationship. On the contrary, the author's point of view is that trustful actions tend to elicit trustworthy responses. That mechanism finds its roots in what Smith defined as an innate desire for the good opinion of another, which produces a tendency to fulfil certain expectations from a given class of behaviours. The author calls such a mechanism 'trust responsiveness' and supports this thesis by devising an experiment based on game theory ('the trust game') which shows, from the data obtained, that the principle of trust responsiveness or reciprocity emerges as the one that shows the widest consistency with all the classes of strategic interactions considered (altruism, inequity aversion, team thinking and reciprocity itself).

In Chapter 16, Luca Zarri provides a contribution to the understanding of the relationship between material and non-material determinants of individual happiness in the context of non-cooperative game theory. One of the major purposes of this methodological work is to shed light on the primitive concepts constituting two-player, simultaneous-move non-cooperative games in order to properly account for the crucial interplays taking place between 'preferences' and 'moral principles'. Zarri shows that non-cooperative game theory can deal with *some* moral principles through a proper respecification of individual payoffs. However, it is also clearly stated that 'non-preferential' moral principles, such as the Kantian principle of universalizability, cannot be satisfactorily modelled by simply respecifying players' payoffs: with regard to this set of moral principles, the author suggests taking a step forward by introducing non-utilitarian solution concepts. Under this last scenario, individual players are capable of obtaining results which are Pareto superior to the ones they would get within a classic, maximizing framework.

The theoretical issue of Chapter 17, by Stefano Bartolini, is to show that both the theory based on the idea that relative position is important in agents' preferences and the one based on GASP (growth as substitution process) models, according to which the empirical evidence can be explained by considering negative externalities as an engine of growth, may explain the empirical evidence that economic growth has largely betrayed its promises to increase leisure and happiness. In fact, the decrease in social and natural capital caused by negative externalities induces people to rely increasingly on private goods to prevent a decline in their well-being and productive capacities. According to the GASP models, the two broken promises of growth represent two sides of the same coin: people work hard because they must defend themselves against negative externalities by substituting free goods with costly ones; but an increase in their income does not increase their happiness because it is associated with a decrease in their access to free goods.

Finally, in Chapter 18, Donald Cox and Oded Stark deal with relational goods by claiming that parents provide help with housing downpayments in order to encourage the production of grandchildren, and that such a subsidization emanates from the 'demonstration effect': a child's propensity to provide its parents with attention and care can be conditioned by parental example. Parents who desire such transfers in the future have an incentive to make transfers to their own parents in order to instil appropriate preferences in their children. This generates a derived demand for grandchildren since potential grandparents will be treated better by their adult children if the latter have their own children to whom to demonstrate the appropriate behaviour. Empirical work indicates behaviour consistent with subsidization of the production of grandchildren and the demonstration effect.

Part IV contains both empirical and policy papers.

In Chapter 19, Jose de Jesus Garcia, Nicole Christa Fuentes, Salvador A. Borrego, Monica D. Gutierrez and Alejandro Tapia analyse the relationship between happiness and its determinants, devoting particular attention to the case of Latin America countries, characterized as countries of strong traditional values. Therefore, empirically exploring the relationship between happiness and its determinants in the northern Mexican city of Monterrey, among happiness determinants such as money income, health and personality, the authors particularly emphasize the role of personal values as one of the key variables. The main findings of their analyses confirm the paradox about the income effect on happiness, while with regard to non-monetary variables, people with higher social values tend on average to be happier.

In Chapter 20, Amado Peiró uses the World Values Survey conducted in 1995 and 1996, to examine self-reported happiness, financial satisfaction and life satisfaction of individuals from 15 countries, relatively diverse from a socioeconomic perspective, from five continents. The main results suggest the existence of two distinct spheres of well-being: happiness and satisfaction, with the first relatively independent of economic factors, and the second more strongly dependent, but both are affected in a similar way by social conditions. In fact, the estimations show that age, health and marital status are strongly associated with happiness and satisfaction, while unemployment and income does not appear to be associated with happiness, although it is clearly associated with satisfaction.

The main issue of the framework of Chapter 21, by Nattavudh Powdthavee, is to ask whether the happiness pattern is the same structurally between poor and rich countries, where there are significant differences in living standards. Using cross-sectional data from the SALDRU93 survey, the author shows that relationships between subjective well-being and some of the already identified socioeconomic variables have a similar structure in South Africa as in the developed countries. Well-being appears to rise with income. Unemployment, on the other hand, is detrimental to the perceived quality of life, both at the individual and the household levels. Living standard indicators such as durable assets ownership are equally as good determinants of happiness levels as income. The author also finds evidence that relative income matters in the evaluation of subjective well-being, once relative consumption in the environment is controlled.

In Chapter 22, Luca Crivelli, Gianfranco Domenighetti and Massimo Filippini investigate how changes in the health system in Switzerland, which does not have a National Health Service and where decision making is made by the separate cantons, may induce wide changes in citizens' well-being. In particular, the authors investigate the consequences of federalism and of the interregional inequalities in per capita health-care expenditure and in production capacity, on the willingness of Swiss citizens to foster more equity in the financing of health care; and to empirically test the willingness to pay more for collective interests – as in the case of a mandatory health insurance system increase as the income of individuals increases). Using micro data collected through a special survey carried out in 2002, where people participating in the survey gave their opinion on the basis of the general principle of promoting vertical equity through income-dependent health insurance premiums, the results of the econometric analysis reject the Margolis hypothesis of group-interest spending behaving as a superior good. Indeed, as household income increases, the likelihood of accepting a more equitable financing of health insurance decreases.

In Chapter 23, Silva Marzetti Dall'Aste Brandolini examines the consistency of some different economic welfare theories with the main values involved in sustainability: the 'classical' theory based on the utilitarian view; the new welfare economics based on the neo-Humean view; John Harsanyi's utilitarianism rule, based on Benthamism and the neo-Humean view; and John Maynard Keynes's theories. The main conclusions from this analysis are therefore that only Keynes's approach to welfare has strong sustainability; his point of view of goodness is the only one to accept all possible kinds of values, not only instrumental but also intrinsic. Recognizing that public good and private interest may compete, Keynes also accepts that there are situations in which it is morally acceptable that sacrifice is uncompensated. This has an important consequence on the behaviour of the present generation, whose sacrifice becomes unavoidable if we pursue sustainable development. Nevertheless, economic growth should be defined in terms of sustainable development, which in turn requires the recognition not only of the impossibility of fully substituting capital for the life support system, but also of what the author calls 'the paradox of sustainability', meaning that individuals should sacrifice themselves today in order to be happy in the future, to allow future generations to be happy and also to permit other, non-human life, to survive; therefore sacrifice is good.

Finally, in Chapter 24, Lorenzo Sacconi and Gianluca Grimalda provide an account of the emergence of non-profit enterprise based on a theory of motivations of the agents involved. Their main idea is that these are *ex post* motivated by both self-interest and a conditional willingness to conform to their *ex ante* accepted constitutional ideology, which are weighed up in a *comprehensive* utility function. For conformist preferences that depend upon expectations of reciprocal conformity to a normative principle, defined on social states in as much as they conform to an ideal, then the agents' model of choice demands the adoption of the *psychological games* approach, where payoff functions range over not only the players' strategies but also their beliefs. If the conformist prompt to action is sufficiently strong, then the outcome in which both the active agents perform an action improving the quality of the good with respect to the free market standard, thus maximizing the surplus of the consumers, results in a psychological Nash equilibrium of the game. The authors associate this outcome, and the corresponding norm of behaviour, with the constitution of the non-profit enterprise. They also show that the structure of the interaction is a coordination game, thus calling for the necessity of devices such as codes of ethics to solve the coordination problem.

We shall conclude this introduction by giving voice to an author who is not a contributor to this volume. This is the case of Amartya Sen, whose presence – albeit not physical – is pervasive through the issues touched on in the present volume. He has often repeated that although happiness (however we can define it) is very important in every human life, nevertheless there are things other than happiness that are also important and indeed come first: freedom, justice, or rights.

> It is quite easy to be persuaded that being happy is an achievement that is valuable, and that is evaluating the standard of living, happiness is an object of value (or a collection of object of value, if happiness is seen in a plural form). The interesting question regarding this approach is not the legitimacy of taking happiness to be valuable, which is convincing enough, but its *exclusive* legitimacy. Consider a very deprived person who is poor, exploited, overworked and ill, but who has been made satisfied with his lot by social conditioning (through, say, religion, political propaganda, or cultural pressure). Can we possibly believe that he is doing well just because he is happy and satisfied? Can the living standard of a person be high if the life that he or she leads is full of deprivation? The standard of life cannot be so detached from the nature of the life the person leads. (1991, pp. 7–8)

If happiness is interpreted as just self-reported well-being or life satisfaction, measured on an absolute scale, then Sen's criticism is fully justified. If, instead, happiness is intended as *relational* happiness – as many chapters in this volume argue – then his criticism is less severe but is still justified. Therefore, the relationship between subjective happiness and the 'objective' preconditions of human flourishing will be the natural continuation of our research project.

Notes

* We would like to thank Nazaria Solferino for her valuable help with the bibliographic work.

1. Martha Nussbaum (2005) gives a synthetic and very clear analysis both of Bentham's conception and of Aristotle's *eudaimonia*.
2. In general, however, these economists, and those who have followed them, are not aware of such an old tradition. Their reference points were far more recent: apart from psychology's influence, Duesenberry's (1949) social theories of consumption, or the American Institutionalist tradition (from Thorstein Veblen to John Kenneth Galbraith). In a parallel stream of research, the Dutch economist Bernard Van Praag, in his doctoral thesis (1968), showed an unusual and heterodox interest in investigating wealth and well-being amidst the almost complete indifference of mainstream economists.
3. This study also offered important considerations concerning the 'hopes' of people in different countries. For example, while Nigeria and the USA attributed the same value to health in relation to hope, for Nigeria, the economic factor was more important (90 versus 65), and, less obviously, Nigerians gave more weight to the family than the USA (76 versus 47).
4. In the following pages we shall discuss the differences between the concept of 'happiness' and 'life satisfaction'.
5. Cantril's data showed, for instance, that Cuba and Egypt were more satisfied than West Germany (1965, p. 258). He plotted satisfaction against the log of income and thus construed a lack of relationship.
6. A recent paper, Hagerty and Veenhoven (2003), challenges this thesis, claiming that growing GDP does go with greater happiness. Easterlin (2005) replied to this paper, defending his classical thesis. Earlier in 1991, Veenhoven had criticized Easterlin's thesis about international comparisons. He plotted the same data as Cantril, though using the same scale on both axes, and showed that the relationship follows a convex pattern of diminishing returns. A similar criticism has been put forward by Oswald (1997, p. 1817) and others, but the idea of a very low correlation between happiness and income growth is still the most accepted among economists working on happiness.
7. The same thesis is in Frank: 'When we plot average happiness versus average income for clusters of people in a given country at a given time . . . rich people are in fact a lot happier than poor people. It's actually an astonishingly large difference. There's no one single change you can imagine that would make your life improve on the happiness scale as much as to move from the bottom 5 percent on the income scale to the top 5 percent' (2005, p. 67). And Layard: 'Of course within countries the rich are always happier than the poor' (2005, p. 148).
8. Among psychologists the debate is more controversial. Some, on the basis of data different from those of the WVS, challenge the correlations (also when other variables are controlled for) between income and happiness in general (*among* countries, *within* a country and *over time*): for a review see Diener and Seligman (2004).
9. Obviously, the positive correlation between income and happiness among countries can derive from factors other than income: democracy, rights, health and so on. Current research on the WVS (Bruni and Stanca 2005) also show a robust correlation (other variables controlled for) between income and happiness among countries.
10. 'The subjective well-being index reflects the average between (1) the percentage of the public in each country that describes itself as "very happy" or "happy" minus the percentage that describes itself as "not very happy" or "unhappy" and (2) the percentage placing itself in the 7–10 range, minus the percentage placing itself in the 1–4 range, on the 10-points scale of life-satisfaction' (Inglehart 1996, p. 516).
11. Note the high role of marriage in this hierarchical model (Diener and Seligman 2004, pp. 21 ff.): in fact, marriage has been found to affect happiness in a significant and positive way (Diener 1984; Frey and Stutzer 2001).
12. On SWB, see also Diener and Lucas (1999), and Diener (1984).
13. Kahneman's approach to happiness is twofold: in some studies he follows explicitly a hedonistic approach (Kahneman et al. 1997, 2003), but in other research (such as that of Nickerson et al. 2003), he reaches a conclusion in line with the Aristotelian approach.
14. Ryff and others presented a multidimensional approach to the measurement of PWB that taps six distinct aspects of human flourishing: autonomy, personal growth,

self-acceptance, life purpose, mastery and positive relatedness. These six constructs define PWB (Ryff and Singer 1998). See also Keyes et al. (2002).

15. Recently, Sen has shown an increasing interest in this issue, see Sen (2005).
16. For a critical approach to this theory, see Lucas et al. (2002, p. 4).
17. Veenhoven's methodological position is different from set-point theory. In his 1991 paper, he argued that happiness does not depend on social comparison or culturally variable wants, but rather reflects the gratification of innate human 'needs'; and a few years later he rejected set-point theory altogether (1994).
18. See www.eur.nl/fsw/research/happiness/prologue.htm.
19. On the basis of the distinction between objective and subjective happiness, Kahneman maintains the individual and social importance of improving the *objective* conditions of happiness, even if such improvements are not felt *subjectively*. To drive more comfortable cars or eat better food is an expression of a higher quality of life ('objective happiness', in Kahneman's terms) although, because of the hedonic and satisfaction treadmills, there can be no increase in subjective terms.
20. Similar experiments have also been reported in Layard (2005).
21. Although the paradoxes of happiness are more relevant in high-income societies, they do not have the monopoly on positional or consumer competition. Anthropologists tell us that positional competition exists in all types of societies. Even the act of giving is often another way of showing off one's high consumer level in order to reinforce one's status. In *The Theory of the Leisure Class* (1899), Veblen blamed the depersonalization of social relations, typical of modern society, for the increase in conspicuous or positional consumption. While there are many ways to communicate one's social position in villages and small communities, consumption is the only way to say who we are in today's anonymous society. The tribe's witch-doctor earned respect for his family for generations, as did the mighty warrior, and also the person who taught our children to read. Now the big cars and homes tell our neighbours, whom we do not know, just who we are. Goods have become almost the only means to communicate status in anonymous societies.

References

Ahuvia, A.C. and D.C. Friedman (1998), 'Income, consumption, and subjective well-being: toward a composite macromarketing model', *Journal of Macromarketing*, **18**, 153–68.

Argyle, M. (2001), *The Psychology of Happiness*, New York: Taylor & Francis.

Aristotle (1980), *Nicomachean Ethics*, Oxford: Oxford University Press.

Bradburn, N.M. (1969), *The Structure of the Psychological Well-being*, Chicago: Aldine.

Brickman, P. and D.T. Campbell (1971), 'Hedonic relativism and planning the good society', in M.H. Apley (ed.), *Adaptation-level theory: A Symposium*, New York: Academic Press, pp. 287–302.

Bruni, L. and P.L. Porta (eds) (2005), *Economics and Happiness: Framing the Analysis*, Oxford: Oxford University Press.

Bruni, L. and L. Stanca (2005), 'Watching alone: TV, relational goods and happiness in WVS', mimeo, Milano-Bicocca.

Campbell, A., P.E. Converse and W.L. Rodgers (1976), *The Quality of American Life: Perceptions, Evolutions, and Satisfactions*, New York: Russell Sage Foundation.

Cantril, H. (1965), *The Pattern of Human Concerns*, New Brunswick, NJ: Rutgers University Press.

Deci, R.M. and E.L. Ryan (2001), 'On happiness and human potentials: a review of research on hedonic and eudaimonic well-being', *Annual Review of Psychology*, **52**, 141–66.

Diener, E. (1984), 'Subjective well-being', *Psychological Bulletin*, **95**, 542–75.

Diener, E. and R.E. Lucas (1999), 'Personality and subjective well-being', in Kahneman et al. (eds), pp. 213–29.

Diener, E. and M.E.P. Seligman (2004) 'Beyond money: toward an economy of well-being', *Psychological Science in the Public Interest*, **5** (1), 1–31.

Duesenberry, J. (1949), *Income, Saving and the Theory of Consumer Behavior*, Cambridge, MA: Harvard University Press.

Easterlin, R. (1974), 'Does economic growth improve the human lot? Some empirical evidence', in P.A. David and M.W. Reder (eds), *Nations and Households in Economic Growth: Essays in Honor of Moses Abramovitz*, New York and London: Academic Press, pp. 89–125.

Easterlin, R. (2001), 'Income and happiness: towards a unified theory', *Economic Journal*, **111**, 465–84.

Easterlin, R. (2005), 'Towards a better theory of happiness', in Bruni and Porta (eds).

Frank, R. (1985), *Choosing the Right Pond*, New York: Oxford University Press.

Frank R. (1997), 'The frame of reference as a public good', *Economic Journal*, **107**, 1832–47.

Frank, R. (1999), *Luxury Fever*, New York: Free Press.

Frank, R. (2005), 'Does absolute income matter?', in Bruni and Porta (eds).

Frey, B.S. and A. Stutzer (2001), 'Happiness, economy and institutions', *Economic Journal*, **110**, 918–38.

Frey, B. and A. Stutzer (2005), 'Testing theories of happiness', in Bruni and Porta (eds).

Hagerty, M.R. and R. Veenhoven (2003), 'Wealth and happiness revisited: growing national income does go with greater happiness', *Social Indicators Research*, **64**, 1–27.

Herrnstein R.J. and C. Murray (1994), *The Bell Curve: Intelligence and Class Structure in American Life*, New York: Free Press.

Hirsch, F. (1977), *Social Limits to Growth*, London: Routledge.

Höllander, H. (2001), 'On the validity of utility statements: standard theory versus Duesenberry's', *Journal of Economic Behaviour and Organization*, **45**, 227–49.

Inglehart, R. (1996), 'The diminishing utility of economic growth', *Critical Review*, **10**, 508–31.

Jankélévitch, V. (1983), *La musique et l'ineffable*, Paris: éd. du Seuil.

Kahneman, D. (1999), 'Objective happiness', in Kahneman et al. (eds).

Kahneman, D., E. Diener and N. Schwartz (eds) (1999), *Well-being: The Foundations of Hedonic Psychology*, New York: Russell Sage Foundation.

Kahneman, D., A.B. Krueger, D.A. Schkade, N. Schwarz and A.A. Stone (2003), 'A survey method for characterizing daily life experience: the day reconstruction method (DRM)', mimeo, Princeton University.

Kahneman, D., P.P. Wakker and R. Sarin (1997), 'Back to Bentham? Explorations of experienced utility', *Quarterly Journal of Economics*, **112**, 375–405.

Keyes, C.L.M., D. Shmotkin and C.D. Ryff (2002), 'Optimizing well-being: the empirical encounter of two traditions', *Journal of Personality and Social Psychology*, **82** (6), 1007–22.

Layard, R. (1980), 'Human satisfactions and public policy', *Economic Journal*, **90**, 737–50.

Layard, R. (2005), 'Rethinking public economics: the implications of rivalry and habit', in Bruni and Porta (eds).

Lucas, R.E., A.E. Clark, Y. Georgellis and Ed Diener (2002), 'Unemployment alters the set-point for life satisfaction', Working Paper 2002/17, Delta, Paris.

Lykken, D. and A. Tellegen (1996), 'Happiness is a stochastic phenomenon', *Psychological Science*, **7**, 186–9.

Ng, Y.K. (1978), 'Economic growth and social welfare: the need for a complete study of happiness', *Kyklos*, **31** (4), 575–87.

Ng, Y.K. (1997), 'A case for happiness, cardinalism, and interpersonal comparability', *Economic Journal*, **107**, 1848–58.

Nickerson, C., N. Schwartz, Ed Diener and D. Kahneman (2003), 'Zeroing the dark side of the American dream: a closer look at the negative consequences of the goal for financial success', *Psychological Science*, **14**, 531–6.

Nussbaum, M. (1986 [2001]), *The Fragility of Goodness: Luck and Ethics in Greek Tragedy and Philosophy*, Cambridge: Cambridge University Press.

Nussbaum, M. (2005), 'Mill between Aristotle and Bentham', in Bruni and Porta (eds), pp. 170–83.

Oswald, A.J. (1997), 'Happiness and economic performance', *Economic Journal*, **107**, November, 1815–31.

Ryff, C.D. (1995), 'Psychological well-being in adult life', *Current Directions in Psychological Science*, **4**, 99–104.

Ryff, C.D. and B. Singer (1998), 'The contours of positive human health', *Psychological Inquiry*, **9**, 1–28.

Ryff, C.D. and B. Singer (2000), 'Interpersonal flourishing: a positive health agenda for the new millennium', *Personality and Social Psychology Review*, **4**, 30–44.

Scitovsky, T. (1976), *The Joyless Economy: An Inquiry into Human Satisfaction and Consumer Dissatisfaction*, Oxford: Oxford University Press.

Sen, A.K. (1991), *The Standard of Living*, Cambridge: Cambridge University Press.

Sen, A.K. (2000), *Development as Freedom*, New York: A. Alfred Knopp.

Sen, A.K. (2005), 'Why Happiness is important but not uniquely so', paper presented at the workshop 'Capabilites and Happiness', Milano-Bicocca, 16–18 June.

Tversky, A. and D. Kahneman (1991), 'Loss aversion in riskless choice: a reference dependent model', *Quarterly Journal of Economics*, **106** (4), 1039–61.

Van Praag, B.M.S. (1968), *Individual Welfare Functions and Consumer Behavior: A Theory of Rational Irrationality*, PhD thesis, Amsterdam: North-Holland.

Veblen, T. (1899), *The Theory of the Leisure Class*, New York: Prometheus Books.

Veenhoven, R. (1994), 'Is happiness a trait? Tests of the theory that a better society does not make people any happier', *Social Indicators Research*, **32**, 101–60.

Veenhoven, R. (2005), 'Happiness in hardship', in Bruni and Porta (eds).

PART I

LESSONS FROM
THE PAST

1 Happiness, wealth and utility in ancient thought

Gloria Vivenza

1. Private and public in ancient economic thought

This chapter examines the relation between happiness and material goods, as illustrated by the ancient Greeks and Romans; I shall refrain from digressing about issues relating to the idea of happiness in general, which would be too long and complex to be dealt with here. It is generally recognized that ancient moral philosophy attributed an important role to the search for happiness; nevertheless the results were various and the concept of happiness itself differed greatly between one school and another.[1] Moreover, when the ancients speak of happiness they generally envisage it as the ultimate end in life, while in economics happiness is frequently interpreted within the framework of a means–ends relationship.[2]

Many concepts of philosophical origin (from the Socratic 'know thyself' to Stoic apathy, Sceptic ataraxy or Epicurean 'pleasure', so often misunderstood) have been considered as conditions of the mind and/or of the body conducive to happiness; but it is evident that we cannot discuss so wide a range of subjects in the framework of the main theme of this chapter.

We should obviously remember that here we are speaking about happiness for economists, and that before Pareto's optimality there was the famous 'greatest happiness for the greatest number' usually attributed to Jeremy Bentham but written down by Adam Smith's teacher, Francis Hutcheson, albeit traces of it can be found even earlier.[3] This kind of modern 'economic happiness' may still be compared with ancient philosophical theories which gave origin to medieval and modern perspectives, while the recent upsurge of research on the subject (say, from the 1970s onwards[4]) is obviously beyond the possibility of a rigorous comparative analysis, having to do with concepts which make sense only in a post-industrial world.

The relationship between economics and happiness is centred, it would seem, on the concept of welfare: I do not wish to go into specialized philosophical questions, but economics is notoriously associated with material prosperity rather than with spiritual happiness which, it is well known, may be possessed even by the most helpless, poor and unfortunate of people.

3

Obviously, the instruments for analysing this concept evolved in the course of time: the extension of happiness to the 'greatest number', although probably connected with the medieval and modern discussions about the common good, modifies in a certain way their basic assumption. It had been maintained for centuries that individual interest was detrimental to the common good, and that it had to be sacrificed to the latter in the case of need.

From the eighteenth century onwards there was a change in perspective: the preference now was to emphasize that attaining common good or public welfare implies reducing individual sacrifice to a minimum: this search for happiness is directed to the improvement of the highest possible living standard without anybody being sacrificed. It is therefore from the eighteenth century that we become familiar with the principle that the greatest happiness for the greatest number should be: (a) the measure of right and wrong; (b) the only reasonable and proper purpose of government; and (c) the foundation of morals and legislation, and other like formulations.[5] This obviously relates to concepts of public utility or general interest, and to a 'social' conception of common happiness as different from individual happiness: 'when man enters society he must surrender part of his happiness to the common happiness'.[6]

I think that this was a most important change, and that the main difference between ancient and modern thought was the shift from an individual to a collective concept of happiness, together with its commensurability, unknown to the classics but obviously suited to an economic concept.

Now what had been for centuries the object of philosophical enquiries, in the ancient world was personal happiness: concerns for the happiness of the community were not known. This may also seem too sweeping a statement. Hellenistic philosophies were mainly concerned with individual problems; whereas certainly Plato and Aristotle wanted to describe a happy community. As regards Aristotle, moreover, happiness for the individual and for the *polis* should coincide (*Pol.* 1324 a 5–8, see note 19, below). Note that this chapter offers simply a very broad outline of the subject and dwells only briefly on Aristotle's view on happiness, and only because one version of it explicitly includes external goods. Certainly political rulers used to say that they had at heart the well-being of all, but what they had in mind was the political entity of the *polis* in a rather abstract way, as a sound – or corrupt – organism, where the single individuals were functional to the state, not vice versa. We cannot go into the differences of the various political discourses, but a good example of a conservative utilitarian argument was Menenius Agrippa's famous apologue (*Liv.* II, 32, 8–12) and its analogy with the human body, which aimed to obtain that every part of society accepted its place without discussion. Clearly the poor were not happy, but they had to accept a bad lot in order to avoid even worse. This is, in a nutshell, the basis of many subsequent arguments about the common good in political economy: it was not said openly that many people were sacrificed to the well-being of the happy few, but it was maintained that, if the poor did not accept that order of things, a catastrophe would ensue and overthrow them together with the few lucky and rich.

Theories of an opposite character, namely orientated towards equality, were not absent in ancient political thought, and in Greek thought in particular. '*Isomoiria*' theories advocated the distribution of land in equal portions; theories that more than once found a concrete application in the ancient world, for instance in colonial policies.[7] It is impossibile to deny that this kind of political programme involved a problem of distribution – but Agrippa's apologue, on the other hand, also aimed at justifying unequal distribution. Supporters of both inequality and equality in property maintained that it was for the common good; however, such a point of view was never exclusively economic, and it is impossible to say that the target was the citizens' welfare or the city's opulence. It was rather a question of justice and of moral integrity of the political community. An economic reasoning of the (economic) consequences of the equal/unequal distribution of goods and property is not easily found, apart from the complaint of it not being just that the few possessed so much and the many so little.

We know from Aristotle that Phaleas of Chalcedon maintained that 'the citizens' estates ought to be equal' (*Pol.* 1266 a 39–40), while the town-planner Hippodamus of Miletus divided the land of his city into three parts corresponding to an analogous tripartite division of people and laws (ibid. 1267 b 22–39). Although these two authors may seem utopian to us, Aristotle distinguishes them from Plato, the true utopian author of a completely ideal picture of the city, as might be expected from a pure philosopher.[8] Aristotle himself, who does not accept the theories of any of the three, puts forward his own, also abstract, theory: as always, the theory centres on the concept of property, and the philosopher of Stageira declares himself against absolute equality in favour of a 'proportionate' equality. The latter concept obviously aims to prevent nobles (*aristoi*, the best) and people from being put on the same footing; we shall not discuss either principle (Aristotle's distinction is probably ethical more than hierarchical), or the difference between arithmetical and proportional equality, a long-debated issue which is connected with economic exchange also in *Nicomachean Ethics*.[9]

The perspective, however, is always ethical and political, as shown by Aristotle's persuasion that it is better 'to level men's desires than their properties' (*Pol.* 1266 b 29–30), and that the most dangerous inequality in the city is between virtue and vice, not between wealth and poverty (ibid. 1281 a 4–8).

Even certain rigid schemas which actually existed in ancient constitutions (the most famous example being that of Sparta) seem to have the same purpose as the ideal ones, namely to divide the population in such a way that one part produces the material goods which are needed for the survival of the other parts, which are thus free to devote themselves to other tasks. This kind of 'division of labour' had a functional character, and was not organized in order to secure the happiness of a part, or of the whole population, but to guarantee the good of the *polis* as a healthy and well-governed political entity. We may certainly suppose that, if the purpose was achieved, the final result was also the happiness of the city, but that was not the primary objective.

We shall not dwell on the fact that a true democratic experience was short-lived in ancient Greece, and was never known in Rome, or that aspirations of equality were greater in Hellenistic philosophies than in those of the classical period simply because by this time they were merely an ideal concept and could be nothing more than that.[10]

In general, Greek political theories held to the principle that wealth and opulence are not desirable objects in the life of the *polis*. We know of only two ancient works devoted to what today is called political economy: Xenophon's *Poroi* (revenues), and the second book of the Pseudo-Aristotle's *Oikonomikà*, a list of the various financial strategies of the different political organizations. Both authors make a similar study of the private economy: Xenophon was also author of the more renowned *Oeconomicus*, a handbook of instructions for administering the estate of a rich Athenian landowner; and the Pseudo-Aristotle's first book deals with the private economy. We must, however, recognize that this kind of literature had no great echo in the ancient world; if we look for a continuation of this 'literary genre' we have to refer to the Roman treatises *de re rustica*, which also teach how to manage (private) estates. On public economy the Romans did not write any systematic treatise – and, in any case, a relation between public economy and public happiness was not envisaged. In ancient literature there are sporadic suggestions about political–economic issues in historical narratives, or in the so-called 'mirror for princes' tradition,[11] but they are the exception rather than the rule.

What has to be stressed, above all, is that the most influential aspect of Greek philosophy, namely that part of it which left its stamp on western thought, denied resolutely any relationship between material welfare and happiness. Both Plato and Aristotle expounded the problem of the subsistence of the city-state in their (different) theories about government; but neither of them maintained that the city had to strive for something more than self-sufficiency. Plato was more resolute against personal wealth so he did not admit any sort of private ownership, while Aristotle, although criticizing his teacher on this point, also believed that it was not good for the *polis* to be rich.[12] His opinion against chrematistics is well known, together with his principle that economic activities of a commercial character should be practised only within the limits that guarantee the *polis'* economic independence. In short, Greek political thought as well as political regulations discriminated certain economic activities from citizenship: hired work, commerce and manufacturing had to be exercised by non-citizens (strangers or slaves).[13]

This ideal of restriction, so to speak, is also reflected in the principle that the city should not grow beyond certain limits (maximum ten thousand citizens), and this was also justified in terms of autarchy: the ideal city must not be so populous as to be difficult to rule, or so small that it cannot be self-sufficient (Aristotle, *Pol.* 1326 a 26–1326 b 25).[14]

On similar grounds the commercial, especially maritime, cities were criticized because they were exposed to the corrupting influence of contacts with strangers and dealers: presumably rich and dishonest people (Plato, *Leg.* 705 A–B; Aristotle, *Pol.* 1327 a 11–40).[15]

These were, obviously, moral arguments, of an intellectual character as usual in Greek thought: the city had to keep the 'measure', the golden mean; no concept of (economic) growth was considered acceptable. A good example of this is the activity that Aristotle defines as chrematistics and describes as an unending bent for acquiring wealth, whose main fault is that of being without limits (*Pol.* 1256 b 40–1257 b 40). For Aristotle, exchanges and commercial activities have the sole purpose of providing for the needs and self-sufficiency of the family and of the city – nothing more. When the shortage of material goods is over, so the activity of wealth-getting must finish. Sustained growth would be appreciated today: indeed we may find it paradoxical that Aristotle criticizes precisely its unlimited aspect; but I think that few things can illustrate so aptly the difference between ancient and modern feeling in relation to problems of this kind. Thus in the ancient world the activity of producing wealth is always instrumental to something else.

In recent years, the sharp divide between public and private in this field has softened. An appropriate starting-point ought to have been the principle that governing a state is the same as governing an *oikos* (house), only with a difference in size: a principle upheld by Socrates and Plato, but opposed by Aristotle (*Pol.* 1252 a 7–9). We may be justified in thinking that this 'enlarged' government should also have included economic issues for the state, as was the case for the household; however, the protagonists of the quarrel left things as they were and the argument was carried no further. It nevertheless formed the basis of most medieval and modern theories of the administration of the reign (and of the universe, too), which gave the *oikodespotes* (or *paterfamilias*: the head of the household) the role of paradigm for kingly (and divine) power.[16] Recent scholarship, however, has followed another path. Considerable effort has been devoted to connecting Aristotle's philosophy with modern economic thought, frequently with the addition of a more or less exhaustive excursus on the differently authoritative interpretations offered by Karl Marx, Karl Polanyi and Moses Finley.[17]

It is not my intention here to discuss efforts which have the principal merit of attracting attention to an author whose importance is beyond discussion, yet who is not widely read outside the faculties of classics and philosophy. At times I have had the impression that, having linked his name to the sort of 'catholic' books on which Jacob Viner wrote a meaningful sentence,[18] Aristotle shared the destiny of many great authors, namely of having almost everything attributed to themselves.

There is a point, however, where Aristotle says that the city and the individual are on equal footing: this point is happiness.

Aristotle parallels individual happiness with the happiness of the city-state (*Pol.* 1324 a 5–1325 b 32) and his conclusion is that happiness means well-doing for both man and city (ibid. 1325 b 14–16), but this 'doing' also means directing action by thought, which is the best character even of material activity. And the principle that well-doing has to be directed towards something different from the acquisition of external goods remains unshaken.[19]

2.   Wealth, virtue and happiness for Greeks and Romans

So, social or collective welfare, or happiness, was treated mainly with these kinds of argument; but there were, on the other hand, plenty of instructions on attaining personal or individual happiness, and this was the target of (moral) philosophy rather than of political thought.

It seems commonplace to say that, for the classics, happiness did not consist of material things. But what people should have, rather than wealth, was independence from 'material' necessities: this was the meaning of *scholé*, leisure in order to be able to devote oneself entirely to something different from earning one's living.[20]

From this point of view, therefore, welfare had an instrumental character, according to a well-known formulation by Aristotle: men begin to philosophize only when they have satisfied all their material requirements (*Met.* 982 b 19–24).

Welfare is therefore needed for the exercise of the 'superior' activities; but there is also the other side of the coin: this superior knowledge was not to be used for practical purposes. The philosopher loves knowledge for its own sake, not because he may gain any advantage from it. In short, true intellectual activity must be free even from the suspicion of an involvement in material things, that is, in the world of 'necessity' relating to the body.[21] It has been puzzling for modern scholars, unable to cope with this waste of economic potential, that the advanced scientific knowledge of the Greeks was never used for practical 'utilitarian' purposes but rather, sometimes, for creating theatrical mechanisms or toys.[22]

The practice of the 'superior' activities worthy of a freeman presupposed that the latter be exempt from whatever kind of dependence, which, in the ancient world, meant not exclusively servile labour, but also free labour: according to another Aristotelian saying, the only difference between a slave and a craftsman is that the first has only one master, while the second has many (*Pol.* 1278 a 11–13). We may observe here an analogy between public and private values: the city was allowed to trade in order to secure its independence and not to be in the power of other states, as it would be if it owed its livelihood to them; the individual must also prize his independence above all the rest, and must be free from whatever necessity, including that of earning his own living. The value of independence is enormously emphasized in both cases.

Greek morals, it has been frequently observed, had a strong intellectual character: knowledge was the first step towards the good, and it was conditioned by the possibility of consecrating time to speculation. Here we meet a well-known feature of Greek philosophy: the separation between theory and practice, which relegates all economic activities to the field of the latter, qualifying them as inferior to scientific, disinterested knowledge.

So, it was necessary to be (already) rich to give oneself up entirely to study, knowledge and contemplation which led to happiness: only wealth brought a command of one's own time. And we may suppose that it had to be considerable wealth: literary sources do suggest a sort of incompatibility between leisure and wealth, but this was not, as we would expect, because being idle one becomes quickly poor, but because 'a life spent in worries about the administration of one's possessions cannot be conducive to *scholé*'.[23] To be obliged to work was bad, but to bustle about becoming very rich was not good: in this case, survival was not at stake, but this behaviour was deemed to be inspired by greed. Besides, it meant a waste of time and energy, even intellectual energy: Socrates did not like the conversation of those who had made a fortune because they were unable to speak of anything else (Plato *Rep.* 330 C).

Certainly in everyday life wealthy men were respected, as has been the case since the world began; but philosophical theories asserted that one should not look for wealth because the true values are to be found elsewhere. Which ones? Happiness, I would say, namely personal realization through the pursuit of knowledge and virtue, not of money: and this is true both of men and of cities (Aristotle, *Pol.* 1323 b 21–31).

It would be necessary, however, to distinguish between the different authors and the various schools of thought: I am aware of the risk of giving too uniform a picture. There are different ways of answering questions about happiness in the Greek philosophies: for instance, Stoic indifference offers a marked contrast with Aristotle's persuasion that external goods are necessary for a good life; as a result, virtue alone is sufficient for the Stoics, but not so for Aristotle.[24]

The connection with virtue, however, is inescapable: the unending discussions about Aristotle's *eudaimonia* (see note 24) are ultimately grounded on the dualism theory/practice or – to put it another way – contemplation/activity, where the latter must obviously be virtuous activity.

We are also indebted to Aristotle, however, for a thorough treatment of 'other-regarding' virtues like justice, friendship and liberality in particular, which is, as observed by the Renaissance commentators, the only virtue connected with wealth, and which can be practised only by a rich man. But the rich man will not practise it for the sake of his own happines and self-satisfaction; rather to 'do good', and to secure a good reputation among his fellow citizens. There is much evidence, including epigraphic evidence, on the role of the good rich citizen: he was 'to benefit his friends and the city',[25] that is, to spend his money to help individuals (political supporters, frequently, but not only) and to offer splendid monuments or useful buildings to his city. These liberal donations of the most influential persons in the city were important: state intervention in public works had not the same importance as today.

We will not dwell on the fact that the liberal disposition, having been spontaneous at the beginning, became compulsory through time, especially in Athens. We should rather underline the link between wealth and the 'civic function', so to speak, of rich men: it is expected that they spend their money to help their fellow citizens and the city itself.

This may be a first paradox: ancient thinkers seem to have contemplated only inherited wealth, so to speak, since they looked down on acquisitive activities and on efforts to become rich. At the same time, as their model of behaviour was one of expenditure rather than of production, they seem to have scarcely realized that (inherited) wealth would soon be consumed. This is an oversimplified picture, naturally.

The Roman attitude, it would seem, was more pragmatic and less intellectual. E Gabba, in an article of 1981, pointed out that increasing the riches of the family by correct means was considered, in archaic Rome, a laudable enterprise. Rome had a less philosophical and more juridical–political attitude than Greece: the rights conferred to the richest citizens by its constitution based on the census had to be carefully preserved, because the loss of estate precluded access to a political career. The ancient Cato had severe words for the man who did not preserve or increase his estate (Plut. *Cat. mai*, 21).

It is true that senators were prohibited from conducting commercial activities on a large scale,[26] because these were considered, according to a controversial statement of Livy (XXI, 63, 3–4), harmful for their *dignitas*. The fact that prohibition was regularly eluded by means of men of straw clearly indicates that the Romans considered enrichment desirable, and did not think only of spending money. They, too, had an instrumental concept of wealth, but it was instrumental to the political career, rather than to the exercise of intellectual activities.

We should bear this in mind, in order to understand the extent to which Greek theories were received by Roman thought. After the Romans had conquered Greece and were in turn conquered by its culture, they were fascinated and subdued, but they did not change their nature.

In broad outline, the Greeks proposed a model of liberality and consumption,[27] a model which disapproved of attachment to money: money had to be freely given, if one had it.

The Romans, although deriving many of their ideas from Greece, adapted them to their own traditions. It is Cicero who says that certainly liberality is a virtue, but it must not be pushed as far as to waste one's estate (*De Off.* I, 44): evidence that he had fully grasped the relationship between expenditure and impoverishment. On the subject of 'public expenditure', Cicero portrays a politician who endows the city with useful, rather than merely representative, buildings (ibid. II, 60). Cicero is speaking in the framework of an analysis of virtues, but his *liberalitas*, although somewhat indebted to Aristotle's treatment of it, is less theoretical and more concrete. Aristotle describes liberality as a mean between prodigality and meanness: a simple juxtaposition between a virtue and two extremes.[28] His analysis, as so often, is applied to the origin of things or concepts. Men who are born rich, he affirms, are more liberal than those who have grown rich because they have not experienced necessity. On the other hand, it is difficult for a man with a generous temper to be rich, because he is clever neither at earning money, nor at keeping it (*NE* 1120 b 11–18). Aristotle's conclusion is that of a dispassionate observer: 'Hence people blame fortune because the most deserving men are the least wealthy. But this is really perfectly natural: you cannot have money, any more than anything else, without taking pains to have it' (ibid. 1120 b 17–20, Rackham's translation). What a difference from Cicero: 'those who wish to be more open-handed than their circumstances permit . . . do wrong to their next of kin; for they transfer to strangers property which would more justly be placed at their service or bequeathed to them' (*De Off.* I, 44, Miller's translation). Aristotle, too, opposed a foolish expenditure, but as being disproportionate and suited to immature minds (*frg.* 89, p. 90 Rose).

Cicero gives very detailed instructions about the best way for a man of goodwill (and trusted with political responsibilities) to accomplish his task by doing good to his fellow citizens, so opening the way for Seneca's *De Beneficiis*, where, among other things, we find the first allusion to the difference (not so obvious as we may think today) between gift exchange and market exchange.[29]

This aspect of exchange was a protagonist in anthropological studies.[30] Again in this case we cannot dwell on such a widely debated topic, although it would be interesting: classical studies could not ignore it, and indeed devoted many important works to the subject. Here I shall simply say that I do not intend to speak of 'gifts' in the sense made famous by Marcel Mauss's famous 'essay', and thoroughly elaborated later by studies on 'reciprocity',[31] but of the difference between a commercial relation which begins and ends with the transaction itself, and a relation involving other aspects besides the economic one, which cannot come to an end unless the relationship between the two persons ceases. The personal relation was important in ancient economic behaviour, even from a political point of view: both the liberal benefactors of Greek cities and the Roman politician portrayed by Cicero gave 'gifts' to the public which were the material expression of the link between themselves and the city.

3. Wealth, utility and morals

Cicero, again, was the first to establish with plenty of detail the antithesis between *utile* and *honestum*, that is, to envisage and theorize a clash between profit and morals.[32] We should emphasize that this conflict is mainly described from a political or juridical point of view; very seldom did he put it in terms of a problem connected with an exclusively economic profit,[33] but it was only a matter of time before this was the case. And from there, 18 centuries were needed to overturn the principle that to seek one's own advantage was something immoral, perceived as an attempt to damage others, or at least a dishonest attitude towards them. There was certainly a mix of Christian and pagan principles: for instance, Cicero's reference to the Stoic principle that to take away something from others in order to further one's own advantage is against nature (*De Off.* III, 21, 24) could easily be subsumed under the precept against theft, in defence of property.

Up to this point, we have dealt with what the ancients thought was the right attitude towards wealth and personal enrichment. But there was also a different attitude in ancient moral philosophy: the pursuit of happiness passed through a resolute reduction of needs. This position, of Cynical origin, prevails in Hellenistic doctrines, and was received in Roman philosophy through a certain influence that the Cynics had on Stoicism, at least in its initial form.[34] Wealth was, for the Stoics, among things 'indifferent', but faced with a choice it had to be considered preferable to poverty in so far as it could allow life according to nature.

Overall, almost none of the philosophical schools of the past (not only the ancients, I would say) allow wealth to constitute a source of happiness for individuals, or trouble themselves with problems concerning fair or just distribution among the different strata of society. Even Epicurus, considered the most 'hedonistic' of ancient philosophers, and the only one to be regarded as a 'utilitarian',[35] who did not consider wealth to be bad in itself, admitting that it was moderately sought after, maintained however that to the wise man very little was sufficient: he who had excessive or extravagant 'needs' was the victim of illusion, therefore he was not wise.[36] So, these philosophies recognized true happiness or satisfaction in being content with little material support, while attending to elevated and noble spiritual activities.

It is evident that Hellenistic theories concentrated on the single individual rather than on the citizen as a part of a community. The 'private' individual may be happy even without possessing anything other than his good conscience; but the 'public' man in the classical *polis* needs an economic basis to perform his function well. Certainly this point of view prevented egoistic representations of wealth: a frequently repeated principle was that we are not rich only for ourselves. External indigence was no obstacle to *eudaimonia* for the Stoics, but Aristotle, followed in this aspect by Cicero, gave greater responsibilities, and more important duties, to the man in high station.

In sum, there were different attitudes towards welfare and wealth in the ancient world. These could be considered desirable and even necessary for living well, but were conceived mainly as things to be possessed and used: for being independent, for devoting oneself to one's preferred activities, for benefiting friends and the city. We should remember that the etymological root of 'chrematistics' (from *chremata*, goods or riches) comes from the verb *chraomai*: to use. The man who is an important member of society, with a relevant role in the life of the city, will use his wealth generously in the service of others – and to avoid the reputation of being a miser, among other things. Concern about the way he has acquired his riches is not important from a 'public' point of view:[37] it is the private man, the *oikodespotes/ paterfamilias* who has the task of providing (and administering/preserving) his wealth.[38]

There were, on the other hand, different strategies, and perhaps more 'philosophical' ones: being contented with the minimum required for living brings the 'liberty' of not being a slave to external goods – another way of being rich, in that one has what is needed; or Plato's attempt to bring economic activities into the more important sphere of the communal bond, which leads him to annihilate the social institutions of family and property.[39]

It is obvious that there are different aspects of individual well-being, and different relationships of it with material goods. One of the characteristics of moral perfection, deemed to be the best path towards true happiness, was simply independence from material welfare, in the sense of not caring for it – and this could be achieved by both rich and poor man alike. Only Christian teaching will say that wealth is so incompatible with this kind of happiness that it should be eliminated by giving it to the poor; the classics never thought this, but much of their philosophy maintains that even the poorest of men (Diogenes) could easily attain happiness.

Now ancient moral philosophy is usually defined by modern scholars as eudemonistic, from the Greek word *eudaimonia*, to which we shall return later. The meaning of this modern definition is that ancient ethics was concerned with a search for happiness rather than for virtue – although we should note that frequently virtue was considered a means to reaching happiness. But virtue was not enough: Socrates' well-known principle was that knowledge was required to give a correct evaluation of everything including material goods. In the field of ethics, the two kinds of theoretical and practical knowledge must be connected, although usually ethics is characterized as a philosophy of practice, together with politics and economics. But it would be very strange to engage in practical activities and to exclude reasoning, awareness and knowledge: for instance, in the problem of choice, which was so important for the Stoics; or the adaptation of means to ends, vital for Aristotle and connected in later thought with the unbelievable 'fortune' of the virtue of prudence.

In our context, together with Socrates' renowned sentence that wrong behaviour is due to ignorance, it is appropriate to recall another well-known principle, namely that the wise man knows that the true values are not economic, therefore he does not care to become rich, even if he could. This principle is illustrated in the well-known anecdote about Thales who, as reported by Aristotle (*Pol.* 1259 a 5–18) was able to foresee, studying astronomical signs, an exceptionally good crop of olives and hired at the right time all the olive presses in the country, thus earning a lot of money with his 'monopolistic' position. The philosopher, concluded Aristotle, if he so desired, would even be able to become rich (Thales proved that he possessed this ability) – but this does not interest him.

So the individual could be happy only provided that he was able to correctly judge what was really good in life, and keep to it.

One basic difference with Christian ethics is that the latter deems the individual to be unable to reach this object by him/herself, needing the help of God. Moreover, happiness being reserved to the other world, it seems wrong to search for it in the present. In this life, we must strive to reach virtue, rather than happiness. This is the reason, I think, why the idea of 'eudemonistic ethics' is perceived in modern meaning as something blameworthy, in a certain sense, as if it were an egoistic search for personal worldly success void of whatever spiritual aspirations.[40] Moreover, it was arrogant in character, so to speak, with its 'autonomy' which was not likely to be appreciated by Christian thought, since the latter did not admit that individuals could reach virtue and happiness only by virtue of their strength.

If we look at the etymology of the word, which is always revealing, we see that even in ancient thought outside intervention was considered. The Greek happiness, *eudaimonia*, means literally 'to have a good *daimon*', that is a good lot or fortune, something untranslatable but somehow referring to the power controlling the destiny of individuals. All the Greek lexica give this meaning of lucky circumstances, connected with well-being, prosperity and perfect fulfilment of one's own best aspirations.[41]

If we add that also the corresponding Latin word, *felicitas*, has an analogous meaning of enjoying the favour of fortune,[42] we may conclude that this kind of happiness was (dangerously?) approaching the idea of success, and was therefore more or less connected with wealth. I do not maintain that *eudaimonia/felicitas* meant simply 'good luck',[43] it also implied an aspect of personal ability and moral character, but these alone were not sufficient: the favourable circumstances were also considered.

So there was an idea of happiness connected with material wealth and worldly success, but the truly 'philosophical' idea of happiness followed a different path and was considered independent from economic welfare. If one had wealth, so much the better; if not, the quality of life did not suffer because true values were to be found elsewhere. Notwithstanding the concreteness and realism of Roman political (and economic) choices, Cicero repeats over and over again that nothing can be really useful if it is not honest; and this principle was to spread all over Europe with the momentous diffusion during the Renaissance of the *De Officiis*, with its warning that virtue must take precedence over profit.

4.   Ancient and modern happiness

Now: what contribution have the ancient philosophies made to the modern concept of economic happiness? We have seen that the philosophers did not worry about the 'greatest number': their social sensibility was different from ours. But it has been possible to discover many 'anticipations', especially in Aristotle's writings, of modern economic concepts. To my mind, the most important contribution of the philosopher of Stageira should be recognized in the impetus that some of his analyses, discussed and commented upon, gave to the subsequent economic thought, obviously beginning with Scholastic philosophy, but also continuing later. Odd Langholm's works have demonstrated that certain economic principles beyond doubt originated in Aristotle's texts, and in the elaborate exegesis that was made of them in the medieval period.

Other scholars, in different ways, have found many opportunities for establishing relationships between Aristotle and modern economic theories. For instance, the Polanyi–Finley controversy centred on the fact that according to Polanyi, Aristotle did effect economic analysis by 'attacking the problem of man's livelihood with a radicalism of which no later writer on the subject was capable', while according to Finley he did not[44]; E. Kauder was persuaded that Aristotle anticipated the main principle of marginalism, namely the subjective aspect of utility in determining economic value;[45] also a close relationship between the Austrian school and the Aristotelian background has been demonstrated.[46]

All this may be accepted or rejected; but it is difficult to deny, I think, that the philosophical reflection upon economic subjects originated in Greek thought, although its development in abstract and systematic theorizing was to come later. I think it is important, however, to hold to a historical interpretation of the ancient doctrines, without being tempted by modern perspectives which could be misleading about the real meaning of the ancient text.[47] I shall merely recall a good article by Stephen Worland, who maintained that there is a relationship between Aristotle and neoclassical welfare economics, despite criticizing the basis on which this interpretation rested. It was a development of Werner Jaeger's commentary about the function of reason in human choices which led Max Weber and later Lionel Robbins to use Aristotle's concept of moral knowledge (in *Nicomachean Ethics*) as a philosophical basis for neoclassical welfare economics.[48] Worland does not agree with Jaeger's interpretation, and therefore he would be inclined to destroy the whole argument; but his reading of Aristotle leads him to the conclusion that there is, after all, a complementarity between the moral philosophy of Aristotle and neoclassical welfare economics. His argument is based on the concept of *eudaimonia* in Aristotle's work: according to whether it is perceived to be directed towards contemplation or action, Worland deduces that the quantity of exterior goods needed by the *eudaimon* man is different: a man of contemplation needs very little, a man of action much more, especially in the ancient world where the virtue of magnificence was inseparable from the man of excellence entrusted with political responsibilities.[49]

Although Worland's analysis is penetrating and very interesting, I do not agree that an ancient thinker, even a great mind like Aristotle's, could see things in this way. The ancients did not conceive things in a statistical way, so to speak: they probably never thought of lots of people working to produce the goods which were to support the few who did not produce; or of the whole product of a country as a stock to be divided among the inhabitants according to certain criteria; and it is well known that they lacked an abstract concept of labour, not to mention of the workforce. In the present case Worland, despite being familiar with Aristotle's passage concerning the beginning of philosophy quoted above, seems to interpret it the other way round. Aristotle's man of contemplation can philosophize because he is already rich, or at least supplied with all necessities, without being obliged to depend on anybody, as he should were he not self-sufficient.

Not being obliged to work, he has leisure: that is all. Worland takes leisure as a good, a commodity to be provided by the economic activity of others,[50] suggesting an awareness of this issue as a problem of social and economic organization and distribution, as if the ancients had asked themselves the question: 'how can we ensure that a certain number of philosophers, out of the whole of society, be provided with leisure and exempt from the necessity of earning their living?' – but it is probable that things were never perceived this way in the ancient world, although the very existence of a 'leisure class' was recognized and even theorized as we have seen.

Ancients and moderns differ mainly on this point of view: the ancients had not yet envisaged labour, leisure, time as commodities, and they did no calculations about them. When I read the article by Frey and Stutzer, 'What can economists learn from happiness research?', I found some sentences which could have been subscribed to by an ancient author, for example, 'individuals who prize material goods more highly than other values in life tend to be substantially less happy',[51] or 'their [positional goods] rely solely on not being available to others'.[52] Even the passages on freedom (at p. 423), despite referring to a different historical context, could easily have met the approval of the ancients, for whom freedom was the basis of happiness and who transmitted this ideal to the modern world. But interestingly, I found these analogies in the first and the last of the four sections in which the article is divided, namely, 'Effects of income on happiness', and 'Institutional effects on happiness'. I could completely disregard the two central topics ('Effects of unemployment' and 'Effects of inflation on happiness') because both these problems were ignored by ancient thought – although I am not saying that they did not affect personal happiness in everyday life.

Now let us draw some conclusions about ancient thought. The above-mentioned trends of thought tried to reach the same result by means of different approaches. As happiness does not consist of material things, it is necessary either (i) to have them already; or (ii) to be able to do without them.

The concept of happiness therefore was understood in the ancient world as 'freedom' in the sense of independence both from other men, and from material needs. Maybe another paradox was that they did realize that the two things were connected, but their connection was contrary to the modern one. In fact, since Adam Smith's *Wealth of Nations* at least, we have considered labour as the element which rids us of dependence, while for the ancients the opposite was true, and not only in the case of slave labour. The fact that the free labourer was paid counted for nothing because they considered that the man was obliged to work, and to work as an employee for another man. So he was not free, first, because he had a master, and second, because he could not devote himself to doing what he preferred. We must also bear in mind that because the world of 'necessity' was seen as inferior, the ancient philosophers generally refused to discuss it, and left little intellectual work on the issue. And what they did leave (for example, the concept of *utilitas*, so well exploited in Cicero's *De Officiis*), does not exactly correspond to the modern meaning.

So ancient thinkers did not emphasize the relationship between happiness and wealth, and would not have been puzzled, as the moderns seem sometimes to be, by the discovery that economic growth does not increase subjective happiness. Their utility, on the other hand, had nothing to do with rational choice and was rather connected with a concept of personal advantage that did not reflect common good, justice or solidarity.[53]

The most 'modern' contribution of ancient thought to the concept of happiness connected with economics was the idea of authority in the sense of decision making. The only economic literature of the ancient world, the treatises on the administration of the *oikos*, are a 'schooling in command'. The successful *paterfamilias* decides for himself and others. This is the 'classical' attitude, revived in modern thought, which transferred to the state the concept of good administration of the household, so creating the new discipline of political economy. In the classical world it did not exist: economic administration[54] was mainly a 'private' matter. Among the tasks of the head of the family there was also that of administering his property well; but this was not his most important function: his most relevant qualification was citizenship, a political quality. Man had to realize himself in all his qualities, but to be clever at earning money was not, usually, one of them: this activity could be entrusted to servants or strangers. Only certain philosophers[55] maintained that the head of a family should also be a good *oeconomus*, but simply because he had to be able to do well whatever activity was part of his role. Even the most famous administrator of ancient literature, Xenophon's Ischomachus, speaks about the management of his estate in terms of commanding an army, and defines the good housemaster as a 'royal' character.[56] So, if this kind of activity enjoyed a minimum respect it was because it reflected the authority of the chief of the household in one of his functions as a member of the community of citizens with full rights.

The Hellenistic approach was different: the man of tranquillity makes decisions only about himself and finds his serenity by ensuring that he is not under the power of others. So men tried to be masters of themselves and to maintain spiritual rather than material independence. This was especially the Stoic stance, with their 'arrogant' vindication of deciding for themselves about their own good, interest or happiness without recognizing any external authority. And here again I refer to Frey and Stutzer's observation: 'people whose goals are intrinsic, i.e., *those who define their values by themselves*, tend to be happier than those with extrinsic goals, i.e., those oriented towards some external reward'.[57] Why so? Because they are independent, an ancient philosopher would answer. This would seem the last frontier of an independence which no longer has political and civic relevance; nor is it related to a concept of authority over other persons (in the family and/or in the state).

So the first important characteristic of ancient happiness, namely independence from wealth, evolved into extreme individualism.

But during the Renaissance the important role of the ancient *paterfamilias* was (re)discovered. During the Middle Ages it was paralleled with the 'administrative' organizational role of the Deity in the universe, and of the King in the state. In modern times, therefore, leading qualities and power were stressed, but also a good end result was important, namely that the 'administered' people were prosperous and happy. Cicero's relationship between good and useful was read, in modern political philosophy, 'in terms of the needs of the public'[58] – so that the main justification of a politician was that of serving the common good, or public utility. This paved the way for the quest to achieve the greatest happiness for the greatest number.

Notes

1. For instance, there is a very long sequel of articles – begun in 1965 and not yet finished – about Aristotle's concept of happiness; see note 24, below.
2. Bruni (2004: 19–20).
3. Hruschka (1991: 165–8).
4. See Easterlin's 'Introduction' to Easterlin (2002).
5. Shackleton (1972: 1462, 1464, 1465).
6. Ibid.: 1468.
7. The original Greek distributions were always of equal allotments, by draw (Asheri 1966: 13), and theories about redistribution aimed at restoring the previous equality which had been lost through greed and injustice (ibid., 60–108).
8. Lana (1973: 216–17).
9. Vivenza (1999).
10. It has been supposed that *Eudemian Ethics* may be the work of another author rather than Aristotle just because it seems to reflect a more egalitarian perspective than *Nicomachean Ethics*, see Pakaluk (1998: 431–2).
11. The ancient sources have been singled out by Lowry (2001).
12. Cicero's political understanding, however, brought him to affirm that the citizens' wealth is a resource for the state (*Pro Sestio*, 103; *De Off.* III, 63).
13. Vegetti (1982: 594–600).
14. Bertelli (1982: 512).
15. Vegetti (1982: 592–4). The motif was taken up again by Cicero in *De Rep.* II, 7.
16. Lambertini (1985); Baeck (1998).
17. For example, Swanson (1992), and Meikle (1995).

18. 'Traces of every conceivable sort of doctrine are to be found in that most catholic book, and an economist must have peculiar theories indeed who cannot quote from the *Wealth of Nations* to support his special purpose' (Viner 1928: 126).
19. Individual and collective happiness come from the same source for Aristotle; he criticizes Plato (in *Pol.* 1264 b 15–17) for having deprived the Guardians of happiness, although maintaining that the lawgiver should make the whole city happy. It is interesting to observe that the sentence 'it is not possible for the whole to be happy unless most or all of its parts, or some of them, possess happiness' (ibid. 1264 b 17–19, Rackham's translation) is to some extent similar to Adam Smith's well-known opinion that 'No society can surely be flourishing and happy, of which the far greater part of the members are poor and miserable' (Smith, 1976, I.viii.36 x).
20. For happiness corresponding to *scholé*, see Aristotle, *NE* 1177 b 4. A recent analysis of Greek thought about the subject is Anastasiadis (2004).
21. Solmsen (1964: 205).
22. There is much literature on this subject; I shall only refer to the recent survey of Greene (2000).
23. Solmsen (1964: 202).
24. Annas (1993: 285). I would not dwell on the 'double theory' of Aristotle's *eudaimonia*, according to whether it was pure contemplation, or a crafty blend of virtues and external goods leading to virtuous activity. There have been (and are) strong debates about this since 1965; I shall only refer to the excellent summary of Natali (1989, 215 ff.), but the issue has been discussed further in recent years, for example, with Kenny (1991), Purinton (1998), Gardiner (2001), Yu (2001), Wielenberg (2004) and others. There is no point adding that 'contemplative' happiness is not connected with other-regarding virtues; the relation with external goods, however, is essential to both concepts of *eudaimonia*: they are needed in order to be able to practise theoretical or practical activities. I do not dwell on 'paradoxes' raised for the sake of argument (Gardiner 2001: 271 n.18) concerning the additions to happiness offered by an increase in economic goods. And I only hint at Diogenes Laertius VII 128, who attributes to some Stoics (Panaetius and Posidonius, in fact) the view that external goods are required for happiness: this is highly controversial because it goes against the orthodox Stoic doctrine.
25. Levy (1976: 245 and *passim*).
26. Gabba (1981: 545–6).
27. This refers to philosophical doctrines rather than specialized 'economic' treatises like Xenophon's *Oeconomicus*, on which we cannot dwell now, but which certainly taught the rules of a good administration.
28. See *NE* 1107 b 8–10, 1119 b 22–8 and 1121 a 10–15.
29. In *De Beneficiis* II, 18, 5, Seneca explains the difference between a relationship of benefit-gratitude, and a money transaction where the payment brings the relation to an end.
30. Polanyi's famous article (1965), arousing Finley's equally famous response (1970), were soon connected with the 'Buecher–Meyer' controversy about ancient economy (also revived by Finley); there is plenty of valuable work on the subject, for a recent example, see Mazza (2000).
31. I refer only to Seaford's recent work (1994 and 2004).
32. The antithesis derived from his source, the Stoic Panaetius; but it does not seem to have had a great impact on Greek thought: not comparable, at least, with Cicero's widespread treatment.
33. Although he did, in the famous example of the Alexandrine corn dealer, *De Off.* III, 50–53 – not by chance one of the most discussed passages in the work.
34. Perrotta (2003: 207). See also Schofield (2003, 233–5).
35. By Bentham, John Stuart Mill and Henry Sidgwick, see Long (1986: 287).
36. Perrotta (2003: 208–9).
37. As always, I am speaking of theoretical treatment in the literature; not of what we may read in the lawsuit speeches by the great Greek orators.
38. Natali (1995).
39. Vegetti (1982: 594–6); Fabris (1982).

40. For the 'egoistic' character attributed to Greek moral philosophy, and recent discussions of it, see Gill (1998). Also Annas (1993: 322–5).
41. The shortcomings of the English rendering of *eudaimonia* with 'happiness' are stressed by Cooper (1975: 89 n.1). Following G.E.M. Anscombe, he proposes the expression 'human flourishing' which is probably responsible for the spread of the word 'flourishing' in much recent English–American literature.
42. It was used, for instance, by the Roman dictator Sylla who attributed to himself the designation of *felix*, as the favourite of *Fortuna*.
43. For which there were other words, such as *tuche* and *fortuna*.
44. Polanyi (1965: 66); Finley (1970: 22).
45. Kauder (1953), see also Vivenza (2001: 143).
46. Smith (1990).
47. Aristotle, for instance, has become a fashionable author, and his thought is analysed in many different ways, some of which use principles which have only recently been formulated. It is impossible to discuss these kinds of work in a short chapter; see, for instance, van Staveren (2001).
48. Worland (1984: 113). See also the comment of Temple Smith (1986).
49. Worland (1984: 127–9).
50. '[T]he ultimate objective of social institutions and economic activity becomes that of providing minimal subsistence but ample leisure for a cultured class, the rest of the population being left as hewers of wood and drawers of water', (Worland 1984: 128).
51. Frey and Stutzer (2002: 410).
52. Ibid.: 412. See also Polanyi's renowned passage: 'They [the highest honours and the rarest distinctions] are scarce for the obvious reason that there is no standing room at the top of the pyramid . . . they would not be what they are if they were attainable to many', (Polanyi 1965: 77–8).
53. I am unfortunately unable to deal thoroughly with this subject here as I am still working on it.
54. S. Todd Lowry stressed the 'administrative tradition' in the whole of ancient Greek thought, see Lowry (1987, part one).
55. For example, the Stoic Zeno, see *SVF* I, 216.
56. Xenophon, *Oec.* VIII, 4 and XXI, 10. See also Baeck (1994: 57–8). Baeck opposes this 'kingly' character to the ascetic philosopher who practises a reduction of his needs.
57. Frey and Stutzer (2002: 410, italics added).
58. Miller (1994: 6).

References

Ancient authors
Aristotelis fragmenta (frg), ed. V. Rose, Leipzig: Teubner, 1886.
Aristotle, *Metaphysics (Met.)*, Cambridge, MA and London: Harvard University Press, 1990.
Aristotle, *Politics (Pol.)*, Cambridge, MA and London: Harvard University Press, 1990.
Aristotle, *Nicomachean Ethics (NE)*, Cambridge, MA and London: Harvard University Press, 1994.
Cicero, *De Officiis (De Off.)*, Cambridge, MA and London: Harvard University Press, 1968.
Cicero, *De Republica (De Rep.)*, Cambridge, MA and London: Harvard University Press, 1994.
Cicero, *Pro Sestio*, Cambridge, MA and London: Harvard University Press, 1966.
Diogenes Laertius, *Lives of Eminent Philosophers*, Cambridge, MA and London: Harvard University Press, 1991.
Plato, *The Laws (Leg.)*, Cambridge, MA and London: Harvard University Press, 1984.
Plato, *The Republic (Rep.)* Cambridge, MA and London: Harvard University Press, 1930–35.
Plutarchus, *Cato Maior (Cat. Mai.)* in *Vitae Parallelae*, rec. K. Ziegler, Monachii et Lipsiae, in aedibus K.G. Saur, 2000 (Biblioteca Scriptorum Graecorum et Romanorum Teubneriana, 1.1).

Seneca, *De Beneficiis*, Paris: Les Belles Lettres, 1961.
Stoicorum veterum fragmenta (SVF), ed. J. Von Arnim, Stuttgart: Teubner, 1978.
Titi Livii, *Ab urbe condita libri*, Oxford: E Typographeo Clarendoniano, 1914–19.
Xenophon, *Economique (Oeconomicus: Oec.)*, ed. Belles Lettres, 1971.

Modern literature
Anastasiadis, V.I. (2004), 'Idealized scholé and disdain for work: aspects of philosophy and politics in ancient democracy', *Classical Quarterly*, **54** (1), 58–79.
Annas, J. (1993), *The Morality of Happiness*, Oxford: Oxford University Press.
Asheri, D. (1966), *Distribuzioni di terra nell'antica Grecia*, Memorie dell'Accademia delle scienze di Torino, classe di Scienze morali storiche filologiche, IV serie n.10.
Baeck, L. (1994), *The Mediterranean Tradition in Economic Thought*, London and New York: Routledge.
Baeck, L. (1998), 'The Mediterranean trajectory of Aristotle's economic canon', *Revue Belge de Philologie et d'Histoire*, **76**, 5–30.
Bertelli, L. (1982), 'L'utopia greca', in L. Firpo (ed.), *Storia delle idee politiche, economiche e sociali*, Vol. I, Turin: UTET, 463–581.
Bruni, L. (2004), 'The "technology of happiness" and the tradition of economic science', *Journal of the History of Economic Thought*, **26** (1), 19–44.
Cooper, J.M. (1975), *Reason and Human Good in Aristotle*, Cambridge, MA and London: Harvard University Press.
Easterlin, R.A. (ed.) (2002), *Happiness in Economics*, Cheltenham, UK and Northampton, MA, USA: Edward Elgar.
Fabris, G. (1982), 'Economia di sussistenza, rapporti di scambio e istituzioni politiche. Un'indagine su Platone', in L. Ruggiu (ed.), *Genesi dello spazio economico*, Naples: Guida, 11–45.
Finley, M.I. (1970), 'Aristotle on Economic Analysis', *Past and Present*, **47**, 3–25.
Frey, B.S. and A. Stutzer (2002), 'What can economists learn from happiness research?', *Journal of Economic Literature*, **40**, 402–35.
Gabba, E. (1981), 'Ricchezza e classe dirigente romana fra III e I sec. a.C.', *Rivista storica italiana*, **93**, 541–58.
Gardiner, S.M. (2001), 'Aristotle's basic and non-basic virtues', *Oxford Studies in Ancient Philosophy*, **20**, 261–95.
Gill, C. (1998), 'Altruism or reciprocity in Greek ethical philosophy?', in C. Gill, N. Postlethwaite and R. Seaford (eds), *Reciprocity in Ancient Greece*, Oxford: Clarendon Press, pp. 303–28.
Greene, K. (2000), 'Technological innovation and economic progress in the ancient world: M.I. Finley re-considered', *Economic History Review*, **53**, 29–59.
Hruschka, J. (1991), 'The greatest happiness principle and other early German anticipations of utilitarian theory', *Utilitas*, **3**, 165–77.
Kauder, E. (1953), 'Genesis of the marginal utility theory: from Aristotle to the end of the eighteenth century', *Economic Journal*, **63**, 638–50.
Kenny, A. (1991), 'The Nicomachean conception of happiness', *Oxford Studies in Ancient Philosophy*, Suppl., 76–80.
Lambertini, R. (1985), 'Per una storia dell'oeconomica tra alto e basso Medioevo', in *Governo della casa, governo della città*, edited by M. Bianchini, D. Frigo and C. Mozzarelli, *Cheiron*, **2** (4), 45–74.
Lana, I. (1973), *Studi sul pensiero politico classico*, Naples: Guida.
Levy, E. (1976), *Athènes devant la défaite de 404. Histoire d'une crise idéologique*, Paris: Bibliothèque des écoles françaises d'Athènes et de Rome, 225.
Long, A.A. (1986), 'Pleasure and social utility – the virtues of being Epicurean', in *Aspects de la philosophie hellénistique*, Entretiens de la Fondation Hardt pour l'étude de l'antiquité classique, XXXII, Vandoeuvres/Geneva, 283–324.
Lowry, S.T. (1987), *The Archaeology of Economic Ideas*, Durham, NC: Duke University Press.

Lowry, S.T. (2001), 'The training of the economist in antiquity: the "mirror for princes" tradition in *Alcibiades Major* and Aquinas' *On Kingship*', in J.E. Biddle, J.B. Davies and S.G. Medema (eds), *Economics Broadly Considered, Essays in Honour of W.J. Samuels*, London and New York: Routledge, pp. 33–48.

Mauss, M. ([1923] 1950), *Essai sur le don*, Paris: Presses Universitaires de France.

Mazza, M. (2000), '*Was ist (die antike) Wirtschaftsgeschichte?* Teoria economica e storia antica prima di Buecher, Meyer e Rostovzeff', *Mediterraneo antico*, **3**, 499–547.

Meikle, S. (1995), *Aristotle's Economic Thought*, Oxford: Clarendon.

Miller, P.N. (1994), *Defining the Common Good. Empire, Religion and Philosophy in Eighteenth-century Britain*, Cambridge: Cambridge University Press.

Natali, C. (1989), *La saggezza di Aristotele*, Naples: Bibliopolis.

Natali, C. (1995), *Aristotele, L'amministrazione della casa, Introduzione*, Bari: Laterza.

Pakaluk, M. (1998), 'The egalitarianism of the *Eudemian Ethics*', *Classical Quarterly*, **48**, 411–32.

Perrotta, C. (2003), 'The legacy of the past: ancient economic thought on wealth and development', *European Journal of the History of Economic Thought*, **10**, 177–229.

Polanyi, K. (1965), 'Aristotle discovers the economy', in K. Polanyi, C.M. Arensberg and H.W. Pearson (eds), *Trade and Market in the Early Empires. Economics in History and Theory*, 2nd edn, New York: Free Press, pp. 64–94.

Purinton, J.S. (1998), 'Aristotle's definition of happiness (N.E. 1.7., 1098 a 16–18)', *Oxford Studies in Ancient Philosophy*, **16**, 259–97.

Seaford, R. (1994), *Reciprocity and Ritual: Homer and Tragedy in the Developing City-State*, Oxford: Clarendon Press.

Seaford, R. (2004), *Money and the Early Greek Mind. Homer, Philosophy, Tragedy*, Cambridge: Cambridge University Press.

Schofield, M. (2003), '*Stoic ethics*', in B. Inwood (ed.), *The Cambridge Companion to the Stoics*, Cambridge: Cambridge University Press, pp. 233–56.

Shackleton, R. (1972), 'The greatest happiness of the greatest number: the history of Bentham's phrase', *Studies on Voltaire and the Eighteenth Century*, **90**, 1461–82.

Smith, A. (1976), *An Inquiry into the Nature and Causes of the Wealth of Nations*, ed. by R.H. Campbell and A.S. Skinner, Oxford: Clarendon Press.

Smith, B. (1990), 'Aristotle, Menger, Mises: an essay in the metaphysics of economics', *History of Political Economy*, Suppl. **22**, 263–88.

Solmsen, F. (1964), 'Leisure and play in Aristotle's ideal state', *Rheinisches Museum 107*, 193–220.

Swanson, J.A. (1992), *The Public and the Private in Aristotle's Political Philosophy*, Ithaca, NY and London: Cornell University Press.

Temple Smith, R. (1986), 'Aristotle as a welfare economist: a comment, with a reply by Stephen T. Worland', *History of Political Economy*, **18**, 523–9.

van Staveren, I. (2001), *The Values of Economics. An Aristotelian Perspective*, London and New York: Routledge.

Vegetti, M. (1982), *Il pensiero economico greco*, in L. Firpo (ed.), *Storia delle idee politiche, economiche e sociali*, Vol. I, Turin: UTET, pp. 583–607.

Viner, J. (1928), 'Adam Smith and *laissez-faire*', in J.M. Clark, P.H. Douglas, J.H. Hollander, G.R. Morrow, M. Palyi and J. Viner (eds), *Adam Smith, 1776–1926*, Chicago: University of Chicago Press, pp. 116–55.

Vivenza, G. (1999), 'Translating Aristotle: at the origin of the terminology and content of economic value', in R. Rossini Favretti, G. Sandri and R. Scazzieri (eds), *Incommensurability and Translation*, Cheltenham, UK and Northampton, MA, USA: Edward Elgar, pp. 131–56.

Vivenza, G. (2001), *Adam Smith and the Classics*, Oxford: Oxford University Press.

Wielenberg, E.J. (2004), 'Egoism and *eudaimonia*-maximization in the *Nicomachean Ethics*', *Oxford Studies in Ancient Philosophy*, **26**, 277–95.

Worland, S.T. (1984), 'Aristotle and the neoclassical tradition: the shifting ground of complementarity', *History of Political Economy*, **16**, 107–34.

Yu, J. (2001), 'Aristotle on *eudaimonia*: after Plato's *Republic*', *History of Philosophy Quarterly*, **18** (2), 115–38.

2   The 'technology of happiness' and the tradition of economic science

*Luigino Bruni**

Truth, virtue and happiness are bound together by an unbreakable chain.
(Marquis de Condorcet)

1. Happiness is back

It is a matter of fact that happiness is once again one of the foci of interest for economists, the 'professors of the dismal science' (Carlyle 1850, p. 43). This is also the conviction of the editor of 'Controversy: economics and happiness' in the *Economic Journal* in 1997: 'Economists from different backgrounds . . . all believe that happiness must play a more central role in economic science once again' (Dixon 1997, p. 1812). Dixon's thesis is twofold: (a) 'once again': the reference is to the Neapolitan *pubblica felicità* (public happiness), developed by Antonio Genovesi and others in the mid-1700s. In fact, Dixon sees a link between the new interest in happiness by contemporary economists and the eighteenth-century debate on 'public happiness' in the Latin countries, and in Italy in particular, as he explicitly says in a footnote; (b) 'more central role' according to Dixon, is that happiness nowadays does not play a central role in economics.

In this chapter I shall show that it is possible to agree with Dixon on the second point, but disagree on the first, because the 'new' and the 'old' happiness have very little in common. The reasons for the new interest in the issue of happiness in economics is well expressed by one of the three authors of the articles of the 'Controversy' in the *Economic Journal*: 'The importance of the economic performance is that it can be a means for an end. The economic matters interest only as far as they make people happier' (Oswald 1997, p. 1815). The same concept is restated by Yew-Kwang Ng: 'We want money (or anything else) only as a means to increase our happiness. If to have more money does not substantially increase our happiness, then money is not so important, but happiness is' (1997, p. 1849). The special issue of the *Journal of Economic Behaviour and Organisation* (July 2001) on happiness and subjective well-being is also a sign that the interest in this topic is increasing.

After a long silence on happiness in the economics literature, interest in empirical analyses of the happiness of people began among economists nearly thirty years ago, thanks, on the one hand, to the pioneer works of

24

Richard Easterlin (1974) on the relationship between individual income and happiness, and on the other, to Tibor Scitovsky's *Joyless Economy* (1976), which brought to the attention of economists the conflict between comfort and stimulation and offered an explanation for why more wealth could not lead to more happiness. These works launched the so-called 'paradox of happiness'.

Income and wealth, in fact, are related to many positive goals in life (see Diener and Biswas-Diener 2002): wealthy people normally have better health, greater longevity, lower rates of infant mortality, fewer financial problems (a common cause of mental distress), have a higher social status and access to more goods and services, and so on (Frey and Stutzer 2002). Rich people then, should be substantially happier than others. However the paradox of happiness tells us something different. In particular, it refers to empirical data about two main issues:

1. *Income and happiness at a particular point in time and place (country)*: as underlined by Frey and Stutzer, 'As a robust and general result, it has been found that richer people, on average, report higher subjective well-being. The relationship between income and happiness, both in simple regressions and when a large number of other factors are controlled for in multiple regressions, proves to be statistically (normally highly) significant. In this sense, "income does buy happiness"' (Frey and Stutzer 2002, p. 10).
2. *Income and happiness over time*: Oswald (1997), in line with Easterlin's empirical research (although he partially criticizes him), reaches the conclusion that the available collected data 'do not encourage the idea that economic growth leads to greater well-being' (p. 1818), since the percentage of Americans, Europeans, or people from developing countries, who answered the questionnaires as 'very happy' is decreasing.[1] In other words, income has risen sharply in recent decades, whereas average happiness has stayed constant or has declined over the same period. The index of 'very happy' responses in US National Surveys in the 1946–90 period has decreased – or has not increased (in this case, from 7.5 to 7 per cent) while the GDP per capita has strongly increased (from 6,000 to 20,000 dollars).[2]

The expression 'paradox of happiness' refers to the contrast between these two points: why, along the life cycle, does happiness not depend on income (or depends negatively) while in every given moment income and happiness are highly related (Easterlin 2005)?

How do we explain this paradox? In looking for answers, economists are mostly focused on the 'comparative perspective' hypothesis – and as such, differ from psychologists.[3] Robert Frank is the reference point for the economists working in this area, and his theory is known as 'relative consumption'. Since the early 1980s, Frank has been working to show that consumption behaviours are full of social elements (Frank 1985, 1999, 2005), a thesis not completely new,[4] but interesting for the connections between consumption, interpersonal dimensions and happiness.

In his last book, *Luxury Fever*, Frank (1999) puts forward his analysis of the relationship between consumption and happiness. The central idea that inspires the book is built around a dilemma: what counts in terms of 'subjective well-being' (which for Frank is synonymous with happiness) is the *relative* (as opposed to *absolute*) position. This generates a zero-sum positional competition: 'smart for one, dull for all'. Therefore, the positional competition leads only to a redistribution of individual well-being but neither individual nor 'public' happiness increase, even if they do not actually diminish: 'the problem, of course, is that although any one person can move forward in relative terms, society as a whole cannot' (Frank 1999, p. 104).[5]

Some specific aspects of the debate are focused on showing that 'unemployed people are very unhappy' (Oswald 1997, p. 1822); married people are, *ceteribus paribus*, happier, because happiness depends on altruism, and there is a strong correlation between being altruistic and being married (Phelps 2001); and political participation and democratic procedures increase happiness (Lane 2000; Frey and Stutzer 2002).

Charles Kenny's (1999) paper is quite original in that after restating the 'classical' thesis that happiness depends on relative consumption (or income), he moves the fulcrum of the analysis to the issue of economic growth. He *inverts* the direction of the happiness/growth relation (he considers wealth as synonymous with economic development); his thesis, based on the dataset from the World Bank, is summarized as follows: 'The link between general happiness and a cooperative society provides the basis for asserting that happiness might, in fact, cause growth' (p. 9). The causal nexus is articulated in three stages: (i) happier people are more 'genuine' relationship makers, and they create 'relational goods' and *social capital*; (ii) it is an unquestioned fact that social capital is one of the key factors of economic development; and (iii) the increase of social capital, due to the actions of (relatively) happier people, *determines* economic development.[6] We shall see below that Genovesi had a similar theory of social development, with the important role of civic virtues related to happiness/*eudaimonia*.

In Kenny's study, the independent variable is happiness, and the dependent variable is economic development. In the studies on relative consumption in contrast, happiness is the dependent variable (the *explanandum*) and relative hypothesis the independent variable (the *explanans*). The same approach is followed by Charness and Grosskopf (2001), who tested the hypothesis that relatively (self-rated) happier people are less concerned with relative comparisons of payoff (show less 'inequality aversion'). They found that the correlation between happiness and concern for relative payoff is not strong, although they discovered that a willingness to lower another person's payoff below one's own (that is, comparative preferences) is correlated with unhappiness.[7]

The explanations of the paradox of happiness are many. There is, however, an idea present in all the theories: economics, focused on its focal variables (income, wealth, consumption), *neglects something important which affects people's happiness*. Without entering here into the rich and growing literature, what immediately emerges is that every theory spots this 'something important' in a forgotten dimension: stimulation and creativity (Scitovsky 1976), health (Lebergott 1993), political participation (Frey and Stutzer 2002), social aspiration (Easterlin 2001, 2002), freedom (Veenhoven 2000; Sen 2000), loss of altruism (Phelps 2001), the decrease of social capital (Putnam 2000; Lane 2000), and positional externalities (Frank 1997, 1999; Keely 2000). These different and sometimes conflicting theories agree on one point: the neglected 'something important' is, somehow, related to *interpersonal relationships*.

Another common characteristic of this debate is the loose use of the term 'happiness'. Although the prevalent meaning of happiness is the subjective well-being, almost every author has his/her own definition of happiness. Ng (1997) defines happiness as 'welfare'; for Oswald happiness means 'pleasure' or 'satisfaction'; and, last but not least, Easterlin says: 'I use the terms happiness, subjective well-being, satisfaction, utility, well-being, and welfare interchangeably' (2001, p. 465).

The role of interpersonal relationships in the search for happiness and the need for specifying the peculiarity of the concept of happiness with respect to other similar and familiar words, are the pillars of this chapter. After an outline of the contemporary debate on happiness and economics (Section 1), the chapter analyses the comparison between the classical Latin tradition of political economy, focused on 'happiness', and the Scottish-centred tradition focused on the 'wealth of nations' (Section 2). Neapolitan Antonio Genovesi's 'public happiness' and *eudaimonia* (Section 3), and Adam Smith's theory of 'deception' (Section 4) are the key themes around which the first part of the chapter is built. Section 5 is devoted to Marshall, showing his strict continuity with the classical tradition (both Latin and British), on the one hand, and his profound intuitions on well-being and happiness on the other. The main aim of the historical analysis is to show (Section 6) that the real breaking point in the history of happiness has been Bentham's utilitarianism, which later affected mainstream neoclassical

economics (Jevons in particular) with the reduction of happiness to pleasure, and the disappearance of the classical distinction between means
(wealth) and end (happiness). Section 7 shows that both the reductionism
and the absence of the distinction continue in the rational choice theory of
the twentieth century, to which the current emergence of the issue of happiness represents a profound challenge. Section 8 concludes.

The whole historical reconstruction is intertwined with a *methodological*
analysis in order to understand the reasons why mainstream leading economists (Smith, Malthus and Marshall) have decided to break away from
the analysis of happiness (as *eudaimonia*) within economics, choosing
instead to deal with wealth, welfare, utility, or preferences.

2.   'Wealth' or 'happiness' of nations?
Having finished this brief sketch of the current debate on happiness, we now
enter into the historical analyses. Modern political economy is supposed to
have been a byproduct of the desire to make the quest for wealth legitimate.
However, before Adam Smith published *The Wealth of Nations* in 1776, a
different approach had gained ground, and it was particularly in the French
and Italian traditions that this newly born 'political economy' was characterized by 'public happiness' as the direct object of its research. The first
author who used the expression *Pubblica felicità*, as the title of one of his
books was the Italian Ludovico Antonio Muratori (On public happiness),
in 1749. After this, the term 'happiness', that is, *felicità* (and more particularly *pubblica felicità*), appeared in the title of many books and pamphlets
by Italian economists of that time. Some examples are Giuseppe Palmieri's
Reflections on Public Happiness (1788), and Pietro Verri's *Discourse on
Happiness* (1781), among others. 'All our [Italian] economists, from whatever regional background, are dealing not so much, like Adam Smith, with
the wealth of nations, but with public happiness' (Loria 1893, p. 85).

It should also be noted that in Italy the theme of public welfare must
be coupled with the idea of *ben vivere sociale* (the social weal),[8] an association which had been characteristic of the Italian civic humanist tradition,
from Francesco Petrarca to Leon Battista Alberti and Lodovico Antonio
Muratori. A special Neapolitan echo of that tradition stayed alive in Naples,
thanks to Giambattista Vico, Pietro Giannone and Paolo Mattia Doria.

Some years later in France, philosopher–economists such as Rousseau,
Liguet, Maupertuis, Necker, Turgot, Condorcet and Sismondi, all gave a
place to happiness in their analyses, and the *félicité publique* was one of the
key ideas of the French Enlightenment movement: 'The mass of English
seems to forget, as do philosophers, that the increase in riches is not the
scope of the political economy, but the means by which to endeavour the
happiness to all' (Sismondi 1819, pp. 8–9).

Loria's and Sismondi's thesis has to be circumstantiated. In fact, if it is true that neither Smith nor David Ricardo accorded happiness a central place in their economic theories, nevertheless the issue of happiness was not totally absent in Great Britain in their time, as seen in utilitarianism. Having said that, we must recognize that English classical political economy did not choose public happiness for its inquiry but rather, the wealth of nations, its distribution, creation and growth. An important English author who believed this was T.R. Malthus. In his *Essay*, where the word 'happiness' is present in the title, he wrote:

> The professed object of Dr Adam Smith's inquiry is the nature and causes of the wealth of nations. There is another inquiry however perhaps even more interesting, which he occasionally includes in his studies and that is the inquiry into the causes which affect the happiness of nations . . . I am sufficiently aware of the near connection of these two subjects and that the causes which tend to increase the wealth of a state tend also, generally speaking, to increase happiness . . . But perhaps Dr Adam Smith has considered these two inquiries as still more nearly connected than they really are. (Malthus 1798, pp. 303–4)

From this paragraph we have the main elements to be able to understand the key points of Malthus's idea of happiness and his evaluation of Smith's position. To Malthus happiness is not wealth, but, in general, he agrees with Smith that more wealth leads to more happiness. According to Malthus, however, Smith was not sufficiently aware that the relationship between these two concepts is complex and worth being investigated on its own. In particular, Malthus belongs to those economists (Sismondi, Genovesi and many Italians) who thought that the 'happiness of the nations' is 'another inquiry, however, perhaps still more interesting' than that of wealth, as the modern theorists of happiness also think.

Malthus's wish to directly study happiness as the object of political economy however lasted only very briefly; in his later *Principles of Political Economy* there are no more references to happiness, and the object of his enquiries became *wealth*, as in Smith and the classical mainstream tradition of economics. There remains, however, in both traditions, the Latin and the English, the distinction between wealth (means) and happiness (the final end).

At this point a question comes to mind: apart from labels, is there really a substantial distinction between the English tradition focused on wealth, and the Latin one centred on happiness? If the answer is positive, what are the reasons for this (supposed) difference?

Classical historiography sees a *real* difference between the two traditions. We have already mentioned Loria, who however was leaning on older interpretations. A solid reference point for Loria was the historian Giuseppe

Pecchio, who in his very famous *History of Public Economy in Italy* (first published in 1829), in the chapter of the book dedicated to a 'comparison between Italian and English writers', wrote:

> One of the most distinctive features among economists of these two nations is the definition they give of public economy and how they deal with it. For the English it is an isolated science; it is the science of how to make nations wealthy, and that is the exclusive subject of their research. On the other hand, Italians regard it as a complex science, as the administrator's science and they treat it in all its relationships with ethics and public happiness. The English, always favourable to division of labour, seem to have applied this rule also to this science, which has been severed from all other sciences.[9]

A similar interpretation is evidenced by the (anonymous) reviewer of Nassau Senior's *Outline of Political Economy* who, in the *Edinburgh Review* (October 1837, pp. 73–102), wrote:

> The English writers, or chrysologists, as M. Cherbuliez would call them, or fol-lowers of Dr Smith (though his own definition of Political Economy differs widely from that of his successors), define their science as that of the laws which regulate the production and distribution of wealth. Their opponents say that it both inves-tigates those laws, and, moreover, directs the legislator as to how to regulate dis-tribution, so as to secure that proportion in the enjoyment of it which is most conducive to the general welfare. The foreign school (we term them so for conve-nience, although there are many English authors whose views assimilate to theirs) hold, that it is the office of the political economist to point out in what way social happiness may best be attained through the medium of national wealth. Our own writers reply, that this is the province, not of the economist, but of the politician . . . We contend that the study is purely a science: our opponents, that it includes the practical adaptations of the science to existing circumstances. (p. 77)[10]

Therefore, these two authors agree in acknowledging that the English school was more scientific, but this target has been obtained thanks to the elimination of important dimensions from the field of political economy, such as the relationships between wealth and ethics, and wealth and happi-ness. However, in order to answer the two questions introduced above, it is necessary to look more closely at the content of the thoughts of the main authors of this story.

3.   Antonio Genovesi: *pubblica felicità* and *eudaimonia*

The Neapolitan Antonio Genovesi (1713–69) is one of the last authorita-tive representative of the classical (Aristotelian–Thomistic) tradition of economic and social thought. While Smith taught moral philosophy at the University of Glasgow in Scotland – and began reflecting upon econom-ics – in 1754 Genovesi began to teach in Naples in the first-ever chair of economics.[11]

Genovesi's account of human nature and of human action uses some Newtonian motifs (such as the idea of equilibrium as a representation of the relationship between the passions), but in its fundamentals it belongs to the Latin tradition. Genovesi does not try to reduce human motivation to self-interest. In his *Diceosina* (1766), a treatise of moral philosophy, he argues that some passions are manifestations of self-love (*forza concentrativa*), but others reflect 'love of the species' (*forza diffusiva*). Love of the species is not altruism (that is, concern for the well-being of others); it is a matter of *relations* between people. Its most basic element is 'sociality' – the desire for relationships with our fellows. Sociality is 'an indelible feature of our nature', common to all social animals. We are 'created in such a way as to be touched necessarily, by a musical sympathy, by pleasure and internal satisfaction, as soon as we meet another man'; no human being not even the most cruel and hardened can enjoy pleasures in which no one else participates (Genovesi 1766, p. 42). Thus it is essential to Genovesi's theory that social relations are not just means by which, or constraints within which, we satisfy self-interest. So far, of course, there is not a qualitative difference between Genovesi and other classical economists (such as Smith, who was keenly aware of the ways in which human sentiments are responsive to interpersonal relationships). However, in Genovesi's work there is a much stronger sense that these relationships are valuable in their own right. For Genovesi, it seems, the chief advantage of society is not to be found in its production of material goods, but in the enjoyment of social relationships.

To Genovesi, economy is 'civil' only if it aims at public happiness. In this expression the adjective 'public' is very important, as one Ludovico Muratori, at the very beginning of his *pubblica felicità* season underlined: 'in us, the master desire, the father of many other desires, is our private good, our private happiness . . . More and more sublime, and of more noble origin, is another desire, that is the Good of Society, the Public Good, that of the Public Happiness. The former comes from the nature, the latter has virtues as mother' (Muratori 1749, preface).

The common good therefore, is not simply the unintended result of individual search for private interest: individual self-interest can be transformed into public happiness only within the laws and institutions of civic life. This idea was common to the whole Neapolitan tradition, in particular in Giovambattista Vico, who put the emphasis on the need for the presence of public trust and civic institutions in order to make the 'hand' work properly.[12]

Coming now to Genovesi's theory of happiness, what we note immediately is that his account of happiness is in strict continuity with the classical tradition, in particular with Aristotelian *eudaimonia*. We find in the first chapter of his *Lezioni di Economia civile*: 'every person has a natural obligation to be happy' (1765, I, p. 29). His theory of happiness in fact presents the typical key elements of the Aristotelian *eudaimonia*, embodied in particular in his *Nicomachean Ethics*. Let us see why. First of all, to Genovesi happiness is clearly distinguished from pleasure: happiness has to be evaluated along the entire life, although pleasure is a mental state of a moment (1766, p. 34).[13] To Genovesi, happiness is the *final end* of human conduct: 'there is no one so foolish . . . who doesn't search for happiness for all of his life rather than the happiness of only a moment of his life' (ibid.; see also 1765, I, pp. 24, 43).[14]

Furthermore, happiness can be reached only as a 'byproduct' of virtues (1765, I, p. 35): 'Only a savage can think that virtues don't lead to people's and the republic's happiness' (1765, I, pp. 241–2). In particular you can be happy only by means of being virtuous, by reasoning in a non-calculating way and doing actions that are right for their own sake.[15]

Furthermore, Genovesi was a priest, and virtues to him are Christian virtues (other important sources for Genovesi were the Christians, Thomas Aquinas and G. Vico). As a consequence, economic life is an exercise of virtues: the market is a place to put into practice the virtues, in particular the 'civic' virtues, such as the love of the common good and the control of individualistic passions: 'nothing is truer: the first spring of art, opulence, happiness of every nation is the good custom and virtue' (1765, I, pp. 245, 255). The market is the place where each agent is helping others to satisfy their wants. With this conception of economics, engagement in economic relations is an exercise of virtue (1765, I, p. 27).[16]

For Genovesi then, virtue is also an economic resource. The general aim of Genovesi's economic writing is to explain the role of virtue in promoting economic development by promoting trust and social capital. For Genovesi public trust (*fede pubblica*), which can be correctly translated in modern terms as 'social capital', consists of a common and mutually recognized commitment to the virtues of friendship and reciprocal assistance. Or perhaps we should say that social capital consists of a network of associations based on those virtues and that propagate them.

Also, to Genovesi happiness is *social* (where 'social' is different from 'political' in the Hegelian sense), because it can be reached only in 'genuine' (virtue–friendship) interpersonal relations.[17] Genovesi recommends (to his students) cultivating *sincere* friendships with one another, and the *will* to be useful to one another. The logic of his reasoning is to warn each individual that if he/she fails to cultivate the virtues of friendship, there will be adverse consequences for his/her happiness.[18] The logic of Genovesi's argument suggests that we should identify friendship with reciprocal assistance, reciprocity being understood in an individually non-instrumental, non-calculating way.

Finally, coming as a synthetic characteristic, happiness is paradoxical. There is an old common idea about happiness: to look for a happy life is the direct way towards unhappiness. This emerges, for instance, from a passage by John Stuart Mill:

> I never, indeed, wavered in the conviction that happiness is the test of all rules of conduct, and the end of life. But I now thought that *that end was only to be attained by not making it the direct end*. Those only are happy (I thought) who have their minds fixed on some other than their own happiness; on the happiness of others, on the improvement of mankind, even on some art or pursuit, *followed not as a means, but as itself an ideal end*. Aiming thus at something else, they find happiness by the way. (Mill 1874, p. 146, italics added)

The first philosopher who tried to conceptualize this general idea was Aristotle, for whom happiness can only be arrived at indirectly, as a byproduct of virtuous actions.

In a letter we find a very clear sentence synthesizing Genovesi's theory of happiness as *eudaimonia* and its paradox,

> [E]very man acts looking for his happiness, otherwise he would be less of a man . . . The more one acts for interest, the more, if he is not mad, he must be virtuous. It is a universal law that it is impossible to make our happiness without making others' happiness. (1764, p. 449)

Here it is affirmed that man acts according to his own 'interest'. Interest however means 'happiness', and one can only reach happiness/interest indirectly, by being virtuous. Virtue here is civic virtue, that is, other-orientated, genuinely social. Finally, happiness is a 'byproduct' of this virtuous/social behaviour.

Genovesi, too, has a theory of unintended consequences of an individual's actions: (i) human beings naturally look after their own interests; (ii) the true interest, however, is happiness; (iii) happiness, in the classical tradition, means *eudaimonia*, and therefore one can be happy only by means of virtues; and (iv) if all people look for happiness they will develop civic virtues (what today we call 'social capital') and, unintentionally, 'public happiness' will increase.

Now we have the elements for making Genovesi's public happiness consistent with the individual *eudaimonia*. Public happiness is, as Genovesi and the whole tradition of *pubblica felicità* say, the sum of individuals' happiness. Within a theory of happiness as *eudaimonia*, the more individuals behave virtuously, the more individual happiness increases, the more civic virtues (*buon costume* and *fede pubblica*) grow, the 'happier' the population (public happiness) is.

4.   Adam Smith on happiness

That Genovesi and the Neapolitan economists should be seen in continuity with the tradition of *civic humanism* does not seem odd.[19] Their vision of economic agency in fact considered the individual as a social entity, and the acknowledgement of the existence of the *ego* and of his/her rights and freedom was not seen in opposition to the existence, rights, and value of the others of the community.

In reading Adam Smith, contemporary historiography agrees that both his moral and economic theories are also in continuity with the tradition of civic humanism.[20] His *Theory of Moral Sentiments* is fraught with a relational approach to the human person, seen ontologically in relationship with others (Smith 1759, pp. 9, 113–14). People are fortunate if they receive consideration and unfortunate if they are indifferent to others (ibid., pp. 89–91). The entire relationship between others and us is mediated by how we look: how we are seen, considered, admired and imitated. For Smith, even riches and power are only the means for attracting an other's attention, for being 'recognized'.[21]

From this relational anthropology, most probably influenced by Rousseau (Todorov 1995), comes the idea that 'nothing pleases us more than to observe in other men a fellow-feeling with all the emotions of our own breast; nor are we ever so much shocked as by the appearance of the contrary' (Smith 1759, p. 13). Fellow-feeling can also be defined as 'mutual sympathy' or 'correspondence of sentiments' (ibid., p. 14), and for Smith it is the main source of human happiness.[22] Furthermore, wealth can be transformed into happiness or well-being, not automatically, but only under given conditions (mainly 'propriety') that allow wealth to become happiness, both individual and social (ibid., pp. 212 ff.).

In *The Theory of Moral Sentiments* we find the classical idea of happiness as the ultimate goal, '[t]he happiness of mankind, as well as other creatures, seems to have the original purpose intended by the Author of the nature, when he brought them into existence' (ibid., p. 166). According to Smith, it is not part of an individual's desires to be happy; the human being actually wants to be recognized and admired, also because of his wealth and fortune.

This happiness, which does not present a peculiar characteristic for human beings with respect to other creatures, under the Stoic influence is defined as 'tranquillity and enjoyment' (ibid., p. 149). It can be reached by the virtuous man (for Smith there is no happiness without the practice of virtues, another Aristotelian idea), and it is associated with the concept of 'pleasure', so much so that it is very difficult to distinguish between the two concepts. Even if the idea is present that men need others in order to be happy, happiness is not distinguished from pleasure, and pleasure is used as a primitive concept (ibid., 1759, pp. 296, 302). The idea that happiness is related to interpersonal relations is not emphasized, although his moral system is built on relational categories.

More generally, we can acknowledge that Smith's aim in *The Theory of Moral Sentiments* was not to write an ethical theory of *eudaimonia* – although he gives central importance to virtues (see Raphael and Macfie 1980). His main aim was different: '*The Theory of Moral Sentiments* is a study of spontaneous order' (Sugden 2001, p. 5). Nevertheless, the key idea in the relation between wealth and happiness is that *the former is instrumental to the latter* – wealth is just a means for being happy (Smith 1759, p. 166), a thesis not far away from the classical one.[23]

However, Smith's vision of happiness in relation to the economic field is more complex than the simple equivalence 'more wealth = more happiness'. The argument runs as follows. The emulation of wealth and greatness of the rich is the engine of both social mobility and economic development. So the 'poor man's son' submits 'to more fatigue of body and more uneasiness of mind . . . he labours night and day to acquire talents superior to all his competitors' (ibid., p. 181). This social engine however, is based upon a deception, namely the idea that the rich man is happier than the poor, or that he possesses 'more means for happiness' (p. 182). In reality this is not true. Smith brings many arguments in support of this thesis (the solitude and dissatisfaction of the old rich man, his anxiety and so on), recalling also the old proverb: 'the eye is larger than the belly', for physiological reasons (the capacity of the stomach and the limited duration of a healthy life), rich men 'consume little more than the poor' (p. 184).

At this point the invisible hand argument comes into play. Given the fallacy that more wealth brings more happiness, and the impossibility of consuming all the products of his industry, rich men:

> in spite of their natural selfishness and rapacity, though they mean only their conveniency, though the sole end which they propose from the labours of all the thousands whom they employ, be the gratification of their own vain and insatiable desires, they divide with the poor the product of all their improvements. They are led by an invisible hand to make nearly the same distribution of the necessaries of life, which would have been made, had the earth been divided into equal portion among all its inhabitants, and thus without intending it, without knowing it, advance the interest of society. (Ibid., pp. 184–5)

Smith sees in this mysterious fact the presence of Providence, which 'when it divided the earth among a few lordly masters, it neither forgot nor abandoned those who seemed to have been left out of the partition'. Nature then has designed the world with endogenous just mechanisms, which allow the equal distribution not of material means but of happiness: 'In what constitutes the real happiness of human life, they [the poor men] are in no respect inferior to those who would seem so much above them. In ease of body and peace of mind, all the different ranks of life are nearly upon a level, and the beggar, who suns himself by the side of the highway, possesses that security which kings are fighting for' (ibid., p. 185).[24]

So Smith the philosopher was aware that thinking that wealth, social recognition and fortune leads to happiness is a deception (ibid., pp. 182 ff.). Social dynamics, however, is providentially based on this deception. The individual desires to improve his material conditions, for his happiness, he thinks, is guided by an 'invisible hand' towards public happiness, despite the 'natural selfishness and rapacity' of the deceived individuals (ibid., p. 185). When a few years later he wrote the *Wealth of Nations*, the title itself defined the object of the newborn political economy. It deals with wealth not with happiness, even if in Smith's choice of the word 'wealth' instead of 'riches' one can rightly see the idea that wealth (weal, well-being) is more and different from simply possessing riches.

Given the very rich anthropology and theory of human agency present in the *Theory* and his theory of deception, Smith's political economy (and the whole classical paradigm) could have become something completely different: instead of being defined as the science of wealth, political economy could have been defined as the study of how and under which conditions riches could be transformed into happiness.

Nevertheless, the philosopher of the deception became an economist studying the wealth of nations. However, if wealth does not lead to happiness, if the wealth–happiness link is a deception that the philosopher points out, why would the philosopher study the ways of increasing wealth? Smith's probable answer to this question of happiness (as emerges in particular from *The Theory of Moral Sentiments*) could have been that it is produced by an active life and *modest* wealth, but not by idleness, luxury and *excessive* wealth. In general, the 'wealth of nations' is strictly linked to the happiness of nations, because only a tiny minority are in the idle class. The pursuit of (excessive) wealth is a deception; but it provides the motivational power for the economic system, which provides everyone with subsistence, and people's susceptibility to this deception is one of the mechanisms through which the invisible hand mechanism works. The tradition of economics after Smith, apart from the very few exceptions that we shall consider later on, forgot the very complex and slippery relationship between wealth and happiness, as the enthusiasm for the 'novelty' of contemporary paradox of happiness signals.

5.   Alfred Marshall: a continuation of the classical tradition

Marshall's economics is very interesting from the point of view of a history of happiness in economics. It is known that Marshall allowed room for altruism in his economics, denying that individualistic self-interest is an essential requisite of economic science. He wanted to study the 'man in flesh and blood', and therefore any human motivation can have, theoretically, space within economics (Marshall 1890, pp. 27 ff.). The only limitation in the economic domain is, for Marshall, the possibility of monetary measurement. Therefore economic goods are those that 'can be measurable by a money price' (ibid., p. 33).[25] It is a methodological operation very close to that performed by Malthus in shaping the boundaries of economic *wealth*.

Marshall's theory of human agency is in continuity with the classical philosophical tradition. A few pages back we examined Malthus's position on happiness. He saw a sharp distinction between happiness and wealth, but in his economic analyses he chose to deal with wealth and only indirectly with happiness. This approach, from the founder of the Cambridge tradition, was continued by Marshall and his school (Arthur Pigou in particular). Marshall in opening his *Principles* wrote the following:

> Political economy or economics is a study of mankind in the ordinary business of life; it examines that part of individual and social action which is most closely connected with the attainment and with the use of the material requisites of wellbeing. Thus it is on the one side a study of wealth; and on the other, and more important side, a part of the study of man. (Ibid., p. 1)

In this Marshall was really a 'neo' classical, his approach being fully in continuity with Smith and even more so with Malthus, his predecessor in the Cambridge chair. Given his moral approach to economics, partially influenced by John Ruskin and Thomas Carlyle,[26] and his concern for poverty, he was very aware of the complexity of the relationship between happiness and wealth. From that sentence, not by chance placed at the beginning of his *Principles*, we get the basic elements of Marshall's vision of economic agency:

1. Economics does not deal directly with 'well-being' (that to Marshall is a substitute for happiness) but with the 'material requisites' of it. We no longer find the word 'happiness' (which in England was linked to the utilitarian and hedonistic philosophy from which Marshall wanted to distance himself); there is however the expression 'well-being' (not completely new among economists of his time), later translated by his follower A.C. Pigou into 'welfare', the key category in his *Economics of Welfare*.
2. The 'material requisites' of well-being is 'wealth', in line with the English classical tradition.[27]

In the 'Introduction' to the *Principles* we also find the theoretical key to understanding Marshall's idea of the relationship between happiness and wealth:

> It is true that in religion, in the family affections and in friendship, even the poor may find scope for many of those faculties which are the source of the highest happiness. But the conditions which surround extreme poverty, especially in densely crowded places, tend to deaden the higher faculties. Those who have been called the Residuum of our large towns have little opportunity for friendship; they know nothing of the decencies and the quiet, and very little even of the unity of family life; and religion often fails to reach them. (1890, p. 2)

Happiness, to Marshall, depends largely on extra-economic factors that are not wealth in the usual economic sense, that do not pass through the market, such as religion and, mainly, genuine interpersonal relationships, such as family affections and friendship. We still find in Marshall the Aristotelian idea that happiness does not coincide with wealth, and also that happiness has a social nature. Nevertheless poverty, even if in itself it does not necessarily mean unhappiness, determines those objective conditions that render very difficult, if not impossible, the possibility of developing the dimensions of life and the interpersonal relationships on which happiness actually depends. Therefore to Marshall, the economists' role in society is very important. Studying the means of increasing wealth or reducing poverty is consistent with the general well-being or happiness[28] – a means for increasing directly the standard of life by also fostering the interpersonal dimensions of life.[29]

In this methodological choice there was, however, a gap, the analysis of the transformation of goods into well-being (happiness), subjectively and collectively. In fact, as the contemporary economy and economics show, economic goods do not always become welfare or well-being. In his *Principles*, however, there is also a suggestion of this possible inverse (and perverse) tendency. This can be found in his theory of the 'standard of life' in the last chapter of *Principles*.

First of all Marshall, in a full Aristotelian (and Senian) flavour, states that 'the true key-note of economic progress is the development of new activities rather than new wants' (1890, p. 688), specifying that the question that 'is of special urgency in our generation' is 'the connection between changes in the manner of living and the rate of earning' (p. 688).

In order to analyse this urgent question he distinguishes between two concepts: 'the standard of life' and 'the standard of comfort', where the 'standard of life is here taken to mean the standard of activity adjusted to wants' (p. 688), and 'the standard of comfort [is] a term that may suggest a mere increase of artificial wants, among which perhaps the grosser wants may predominate' (p. 690). Then he repeats his thesis that

> [i]t is true that every broad improvement in the standard of comfort is likely to bring with it a better manner of living, and to open the way to new and higher

activities; while people who have hitherto had neither the necessaries nor the decencies of life, can hardly fail to get some increase in vitality and energy from an increase of comfort, however gross and material the view which they may take of it. This rise in the standard of comfort will probably involve some rise in the standard of life. (p. 690)

But this is not always the case. The rest of the chapter, in fact, is an analysis, applied to the labour market and the 'burning question of the limitation of the hours of labour' (Edgeworth 1927, III, p. 14) and to the related issues of the minimum wage and redistribution of income, of the cases when rises in the standard of comfort bring to a fall the standard of life. A first application of this analysis is Marshall's recommendation for a general reduction of the hours of labour that is likely to cause a little net material loss and much moral good, a case where a reduction of income can lead to a higher standard of life (happiness). At the end of the chapter he goes on to explain:

> Even if we took account only of the injury done to the young by living in a home in which the father and the mother lead joyless lives, it would be in the interest of society to afford some relief to them also. Able workers and good citizens are not likely to come from homes from which the mother is absent during a great part of the day; nor from homes to which the father seldom returns till his children are asleep and therefore society as a whole has a direct interest in the curtailment of extravagantly long hours of duty away from home. (Marshall 1890, p. 721)

6. The 'other' story of happiness: from Bentham to rational choice theory and the neglect of the 'technology of happiness'

It is impossible to write a history of happiness without taking into account utilitarianism, built around the golden rule of 'the greatest happiness for the greatest number'. In fact, utilitarianism plays an important role in our reconstruction for the methodological turn it gave to the concept of happiness in economics. If we look carefully at Bentham's idea of happiness we immediately see that in his system happiness is equal to 'pleasure', as it comes straight from the very first lines of his *An Introduction to the Principles of Morals and Legislation* (1789): 'Nature has placed mankind under the governance of two sovereign masters, *pain* and *pleasure*' (italics added). Therefore with respect to happiness, he belongs to the hedonist tradition.

The Benthamite vision of happiness can therefore rightly be called 'psychological hedonism', having an individualistic nature; people are depicted as seekers of happiness–pleasure. This psychological feature is essential to the utilitarian programme in which social happiness is seen only as an aggregation, a sum of individual pleasures. J.S. Mill, who on happiness diverges deeply from Bentham and from his father James, explicitly states in his *Utilitarianism* that in their utilitarianism there was an identification between pleasure and happiness: 'By happiness is intended pleasure' (Mill 1861, p. 210).

The other keyword of Bentham is 'utility' (from which the term 'utilitarianism' came), and the 'principle of utility' (inherited from Beccaria's *Dei delitti e delle pene*) is stated appropriately in the first page of his *Principles of Morals and Legislation* as the 'foundation of the present work'. In all his works the words 'happiness', 'pleasure' and 'utility' are used interchangeably as different ways of expressing the same basic concept of 'utilitarianism'. In his *Introduction to the Principles of Morals and Legislation* he wrote that by utility he meant the propriety of every object by which it tends to make a benefice, advantage, pleasure, good or happiness (Bentham 1789).[30]

With Bentham the distinction between end (happiness) and means (wealth) disappeared, happiness also became the direct end of economic actions, and meant pleasure. Bentham's approach to happiness, therefore, is far from *both* Aristotle's (and Genovesi's) *eudaimonia, and* Smith and the classics who kept the distinction between happiness (the final end) and wealth. Bentham's methodological project, as is well known, nurtured economics thanks mainly to the works of Stanley Jevons and Edgeworth.

In classical political economy the emphasis was on objective elements. With marginalism the centre of interest became the subject, the agent, and his philosophy was hedonistic utilitarianism. This was not only the case for English neoclassicism; many of the heralds of the new economics (although not all – Carl Menger and Léon Walras cannot be considered hedonist) based their subjectivist approach to economics on a hedonistic philosophy. Although H.H. Gossen and Maffeo Pantaleoni are two remarkable (not English) economists strongly influenced by hedonism, the pivotal country for this methodological operation was England. In Edgeworth's early works up to *Mathematical Psychics* (1881), the utilitarian and hedonist philosophy had a great impact. To him happiness means pleasure, and maximizing happiness means maximizing pleasure (1881, pp. 7, 16).

W.S. Jevons (1871) defined economics as the science of utility, explicitly stating his acceptance of the utilitarian philosophy of Bentham (Robbins 1998, p. 262). 'Happiness' entered neoclassical economics fully identified with utility, the new subject of the new economics. Jevons not only states the old utilitarian thesis that happiness is related to utility, but also that economics is the 'calculus of pleasures and pain' (Jevons 1871, Introduction). To Jevons, pleasures are different 'only in degree, not in kind' (Schabas 1990, p. 39). Economics deals with the 'lowest' ones, and he does not exclude that men can renounce pleasures coming from the economic domain for the sake of ethical or superior pleasures. But, as with Bentham,

Jevons's ethical rule is to maximize the sum of pleasures, both individually and socially. In *The Theory of Political Economy* he states, 'The theory which follows is entirely based on a calculus of pleasure and pain and the object of economics is to maximise happiness by purchasing pleasure as it were, at the lowest cost of pain' (Jevons 1871, p. 91).

For English marginalist economists, economics became the science of happiness–pleasure. The domain of economics was no longer 'wealth' but happiness–pleasure directly. While the classical economists were dealing with objective, external aspects ('material prerequisites'), with Jevons and even more so with Edgeworth, economics comes back to a 'subjective' approach – the domain of economics is inside man's mind.

With Jevons, happiness–pleasure became the object of economics, therefore it is not true that happiness is not central in neoclassical economics. The reductionism of happiness/*eudaimonia* to utility/pleasure is the real breakpoint in this history of happiness in economics. The distinction between material prerequisites and happiness has been lost and whereas *eudaimonia* is not consequentialist (the action is performed because it is intrinsically good and, as a byproduct, happiness can arrive), utilitarianism (both act- and rule-) is. Furthermore, every connection with the non-instrumentality of the logic of happiness and its relation to virtues disappeared.

7. Back to the psychology of choice? The challenge of happiness to rational choice theory

The contemporary rational choice theory (based on the preference-satisfaction approach) is, from a methodological point of view, a continuation of the Benthamite approach: 'How well-off an individual is, is the same thing as how well satisfied an individual's preferences are. Orthodox normative economics consequently identifies welfare and preference satisfaction' (Hausman and McPherson 1996, p. 42). The analysis assumes that individuals maximize welfare as they conceive it (Becker 1996, p. 139).

Contemporary rational choice theory is far from the classical/neoclassical economists and very close to Bentham or Jevons (more than they thought if we consider John Hicks' and Paul Samuelson's battle against hedonism in economics in the 1930s). Why? Like Jevons, the domain of economics is 'maximizing' pleasure (preferences); second, the place of pleasure has been taken by preferences satisfaction, but the core elements of the utilitarian approach are still there:

1. The domain of economics is not more wealth or economic welfare (the material prerequisites) but to directly bring about happiness, which can be translated into concepts such as pleasure (old marginalists), ordinal utility or preferences (Hicks), or choices (Samuelson).

2.   The tools utilized for studying the 'means' (maximization, quantitative calculus, instrumental rationality) are now used for specifically studying 'happiness'.

Any reference to classical tradition of happiness has gone astray. Frey and Stutzer (1999) put forward the thesis that studying individual happiness means to challenge the standard utility theory. In fact the standard contemporary utility (and consumer) theory is based on observable individual choices:

> Individual utility only depends on tangible factors (goods and services), it is inferred from revealed behavior (or preferences), and is in turn used to explain the choices made . . . It rejects subjectivist experience (e.g., captured by surveys) as being 'unscientific,' because it is not objectively observable. It is assumed that the choices made provide all the information required to infer the utility of outcomes'. (Frey and Stutzer 1999, pp. 2–3)

Therefore happiness is different from utility and represents a challenge to standard (neo-positivist) economic theory. To revert to happiness (instead of utility) means to share the same methodology as that of the behavioural economics school, represented today by people such as Kahneman or Sugden, an approach that is critical towards rational choice theory, both for failing to explain the facts of real economic decision, and for making normatively indefensible claims about rationality. In particular, they argue that choice theory needs to abandon *a priora* about rationality, and to become empirical, experimental, and more related to behavioural psychology.

From the historical point of view (which is my main perspective here), recovering happiness in microeconomic theory means bringing back rational choice theory prior to Pareto. Originally, neoclassical economics was grounded on hedonist psychology, the assumption that there exists a one-dimensional, interpersonally comparable measure of mental states (pleasure) and the hypothesis that rational individual choice means maximization of this measure. In the twentieth century, economists abandoned these assumptions (because of the difficulties with measurement and because of a hostile attitude towards unobservables like pleasure), but retained most of the theoretical structure that had originally been derived from those assumptions. The new foundations were postulates about preferences, or about choices (revealed preferences).

Up to Pareto's shift to rational choice theory and the birth of the ordinal and not hedonistic utility theory, economists did revert to psychology; Edgeworth, as well as Jevons, Pantaleoni and all the hedonist economists of the first generation of marginalism did not abstain from psychological introspection in order to understand the reality behind curves and formulas.[31]

From the behavioural economics' point of view, the 'Paretian turn' in rational choice theory was where economics went wrong. Having started with a psychological theory and then found that this theory lacked support, economists (according to this school) should have looked for better psychological foundations (that is, conserve the question, look for the correct answer) instead of changing the interpretation of the foundations (that is, conserve the answer, look for a different question that will make it correct).

Pareto is generally regarded as the prime instigator of this switch, though recently some historians of thought suggest that there has been some later touching-up of the portrait and that the mathematical economists of the 1930s and 1940s, Hicks, Roy Allen, Samuelson and so on, wanted to find distinguished ancestors for their theoretical approach, and so reinterpreted Pareto to make him an exponent of their own neo-positivist and operationalist ideas.[32] The story is well known. Here it is enough to quote a passage from a letter that Pareto wrote to Pantaleoni in 1899, just after having re-founded rational choice theory on empirical and ordinalist new bases:

> Edgeworth and others start from the concept of the final degree of utility and *arrive* at the determination of the indifference curves (as in fact I have myself done in the article of the *Giornale*). I now completely leave aside the final degree of utility and *start* from the indifference curves. In this lies the whole novelty . . . Up to now the principles of pure economics have been founded on the final degree of utility, the *rareté*, the ophelimity, etc. Well! This is unnecessary. One can start from the indifference curves, *which are a direct result of experience*. (1899, II, pp. 287–93, italics added)

This is the new foundation on which, thanks to Hicks, Allen and Samuelson, the rational choice theory of the 1930s was based.

The hedonist marginalist economists had a completely different approach to choice. Let us take Edgeworth. He was the marginalist economist who most took seriously the findings of experimental psychology of his time. Already in 1877 in his *New and Old Methods of Ethics* he tried to found his economics on psychology, in particular on psychophysics developed in Germany a few years before (Weber, Fechner and Wundt in particular). To him the results of psychophysics offered the ground for building economics both on hedonism and experimental data.[33]

Edgeworth knew very well Pareto's new theory of choice, and at the same time he was aware that between his and Pareto's system there was no bridge. In his article 'Pareto' in the *Palgrave Dictionary of Political Economy*, he wrote:

> The *Manuale* is distinguished by the original idea of treating the laws of demand and supply, or rather the 'indifference curves', from which those may be deduced, as objective and capable of being ascertained by external observation without the psychological knowledge obtained through the sympathy. In short, the economist may be a *solipsist*. The conception has been criticised (cf. Pantaleoni, *Giornale degli Economisti*, January–February 1924, pp. 17 ss.) as a needless abandonment of one large source of information. (Edgeworth 1926, p. 711)

Of course, this criticism was not just Pantaleoni's. Pantaleoni, who more than anyone else appreciated Pareto's genius as an economist, was also very critical towards Pareto's refusal to return to psychology:

> How to distinguish economic acts from non economic ones looking at the sole choice, instead of the psychological motivation of choice, which is, like the choice, the object of observation and experience? . . . From the choice we cannot trace the motivation back, but from the motivation we can descend to the choice. The two logical operations are like the direct operations with respect to the inverse ones. The former have many solutions, the latter only one. (Pantaleoni 1924, pp. 355–6)

And in a paper in 1913 he wrote even more clearly:

> I cannot see the convenience of not utilising some laws regarding tastes and pains that we know to be the reasons of economic actions. It is a sterile aberration to insist on analysing human facts in the same manner in which we must analyse the phenomena of the dead nature. I cannot interrogate the clouds to know when, where and how much it will rain, and therefore I need a lot of observations . . . Men, however, if interrogated, answer! . . . As an economist I have no reason to look away from the evident ultimate reasons of economic phenomena, i.e. pleasures and pains, tastes or costs. (Pantaleoni 1913, I, pp. 8–10)

To 'interrogate' people and use psychological data is exactly what the modern scholars of happiness do. At the same time, it is worth noting that even 'this' happiness is not the 'classical' happiness but the utilitarian 'pleasure' (although called 'subjective well-being'). Therefore, the contemporary central role of happiness is closer to Bentham and Jevons than to Genovesi or Malthus.

8.   Conclusion

This journey through the vicissitudes of happiness in economics allows us to draw some conclusions. First of all, there are more histories of happiness potentially available in economics than is usually recognized. The three main lines are the classical (from Aristotle to Genovesi), the classical English, and the hedonist–utilitarian. The first two traditions are closer to each other and both are far removed from the third.

Historical analyses show that the contemporary debate on happiness is a return to the classic line (happiness is not wealth), but happiness remains individualistic and hedonistic: *eudaimonia* and *pubblica felicità* are the great absences here. This is a shame, because it is my conviction that economic (and social) theory can be enriched by a recovery of these elements of classical happiness. In particular, there are some fields that evidently can be nurtured by such an idea of happiness. The first is the theory of 'social capital', which is related to both public happiness and 'civic virtues'. A second is the idea of economic rationality; in the vital and rich debate on rationality there is a strong need to find alternative approaches in rational choice theory. 'We-rationality' (Hollis 1998; Sugden 2001), 'expressive rationality' (Hargreaves-Heap et al. 1994), and the Weberian 'axiological rationality' (Boudon 2000), all attempt to enrich the too simplistic portrait of human beings embraced by standard neoclassical economics. It is easy to imagine that the 'paradoxical' logic of *eudaimonia* and *pubblica felicità* can have new and important things to say in this promising field of research.

The whole theoretical building of modern economics has been grounded on the key idea that an increase in wealth will lead to an increase in well-being, or happiness. We have seen that this conviction was central and explicit not only in the Latin tradition but also in Smith, Malthus and Marshall. On this basis it has been possible to take away, rightly, the label of 'dismal science' from political economy. If, instead, having more economic goods does not lead to well-being but to bad-being, if 'goods' become 'bads' (because they make living unhappy, as the literature on the paradox of happiness is showing), then the very philosophical and social bases of the job of the political economist are called into question. For this reason these paradoxes – and in this chapter we have seen that they are many – can open a season of new questions and, hopefully, new answers for economic science. In this chapter I have also tried to show that in the history of thought there are previously held ideas, often forgotten, which deserve to be re-examined.

Twentieth-century neoclassical economics has become the science of the study of instrumental interactions among individuals, under the assumption that it would be (theoretically) possible to isolate the economic moment based on individualism, anonymity and instrumental rationality, from the wider social fact of the economic life. Every well-equipped economist was aware that economic goods were not all 'goods', and nor perhaps were they the most important things in life. Nevertheless, they chose 'wealth', goods, as the subject of this discipline in the division of labour among disciplines. In performing this choice, *per se* legitimate, there was, however, an important missing link: the analysis of how and if economic goods become happiness, well-being. And what we see today in the debate on economics and happiness is that the effort for augmenting material goods has systematic negative effects on the other components of wealth. In particular, less interpersonal relationships and more income can lead, as the growing literature on the paradox of happiness shows, to diminished well-being. We have seen that political economy has paid too little attention to the 'technology of happiness' – that is the transformation of wealth into well-being.

This work has attempted to show that this 'transformation problem', the how and if maximized wealth or income is transformed into well-being or happiness, still remains unknown. In this 'black box' that connects economic goods to well-being lie also the reasons for the absence of a theory of happiness in economics. Amartya Sen has done most in pointing out that the key variable to look at is not income or goods *per se*, but actually to look at how they are important when they become functionings and capabilities. But notwithstanding Sen's important contributions, the box is still black with respect to the role of interpersonal relationships in the transformation problem. Maybe the time has come to open the whole box and look into it.

Notes

*   I would like to thank Nicolò Bellanca, Benedetto Gui, Pier Luigi Porta, Robert Sugden and Stefano Zamagni with whom I discussed many of the theoretical passages of this chapter. First published in the *Journal of the History of Economic Thought*, and reprinted with the kind permission of the editor, Steve Madema.
1.   An interesting consideration Oswald reaches using statistical indicators supplied by the General Health Questionnaire Conclusion, is that 'the unemployed people are very unhappy' (Oswald 1997, p. 1822). From that Oswald concludes that economic growth should not be the main worry of governments (p. 1828), their primary worry should be instead the fight against unemployment.
2.   See Lane (2000, p. 5).
3.   For a good overview of the different theories in psychology, see Kahneman et al. (1999).
4.   Before Frank, few economists had the intuition of such a theory: Thorstein Veblen, John Maynard Keynes, James Duesenberry, Fred Hirsch and Scitovsky, to cite the best known.
5.   Other economists working on relative consumption hypothesis include, for example, Oswald (1997), Höllander (2001), Charness and Grosskopf (2001). The first step of Frank's analysis consists in re-stating the central thesis present in his previous studies on consumption, namely the strongly relational nature of many, and the most important, acts of consumption: peer pressure, status and relative position in the hierarchy in the workplace are all crucial factors for understanding the nature of the consumption. It is the 'relative level of consumption' between us and others close to us, not the absolute level, that increases or diminishes our well-being. For Frank it is the 'relative' level of income or consumption that matters in terms of individual happiness, not the 'absolute' one, as mainstream consumer theory says, that is, the difference between our level of income and that of our benchmark – if F_i is the happiness of individual i, and I is his/her income, this theory states that happiness depends on the difference between the absolute level of the individual (I_i) and the level of the reference point (I_m). The function of happiness is therefore $F_i = f(I_i; I_i - I_m)$, and the paradox has its explanation: if my per capita income increases but the income of reference (that is, that of my fellow colleagues) increases more, I can have more income and less happiness.

6. Another element present in Kenny's argument is the comparison between classical and modern authors with respect to happiness. He said that the classics (Adam Smith in particular) linked happiness to interpersonal relations, while moderns linked happiness to the 'relative income hypothesis' (Kenny 1999, p. 19). The analysis in this chapter can (partly) confirm that Kenny's intuition makes an important point, although not all the classics have attributed the same importance to the relational dimension with respect to happiness (for example, Bentham), although in some contemporary authors the emphasis on interpersonal interactions is also present (for example, Lane or Frank).

7. The empirical evidence on this issue is, nowadays, huge.

8. The phrase was used in a well-known book by Ludovico Bianchini (1845), one of Italy's early historians, as a hallmark of Italian economic thought.

9. Quoted in Vitale (2001, p. 130).

10. The anonymous reviewer is referring to a lively debate at that time in England. Emblematic is the dialogue between Senior and Cardinal Newman. Senior claimed that it was legitimate for economics to deal with wealth on the basis of the conviction, expressed in his opening lecture as Drummond Chair of Political Economy in 1827, that 'wealth [was] leading to virtue and true religion' (Oslington 2002, p. 831). By virtue of the same considerations, a few years later Alfred Marshall will reach a similar methodological position. Newman adopted a different position: 'given that wealth is to be sought, this and that is the method of gaining it. This is the extent to which the political economist has a right to go; he has no right to determine that wealth is at any rate to be sought, or that it is the way to be virtuous and happy' (quoted in Oslington 2002, pp. 836–7).

11. Bellamy (1987) gives the fullest English-language account of the intellectual milieu in Naples in which Genovesi wrote his work. See also, Pii (1984).

12. On 'civil economy' see Bruni and Porta (2003).

13. Also for Aristotle, happiness is not pleasure. One of the goals of Aristotle's ethics was to distinguish his *eudaimonia* from hedonism, that is, the philosophy that equates happiness with pleasure. The hedonist philosophy has a long history: from Aristippus, who taught that the end of life was to experience the maximum of happiness, and that happiness is the sum of one's hedonistic moments, to Maupertius (the modern main representative of hedonism, whose hedonistic idea of happiness came to Bentham through Beccaria (see Guidi 1999), to modern thinkers who believe that 'the terms well-being and hedonism are essentially equivalent' (Ryan and Deci 2001, p. 144). The modern hedonists see a double equivalence: happiness is the same as subjective well-being, subjective well-being, in the end, is pleasure (Ryan and Deci 2001). Therefore the economists who use happiness as subjective well-being endorse, knowingly or not, the hedonistic approach. Aristotle had a completely different idea of happiness/*eudaimonia*, which he linked with virtues. Today the neo-Aristotelian philosophers have the same ideas and in order to distinguish *eudaimonia* from pleasure and *similia*, they have translated *eudaimonia* as 'human flourishing'. Today many scholars (Elizabeth Anscombe, Martha Nussbaum and others) think that this translation is the best in order to give the original meaning of Aristotle's *eudaimonia*. According to the human flourishing tradition, pleasure is just a *signal* that the action is intrinsically good (is virtuous): pleasure is a sign of the activity's value, not its substance; it is *the effect* not the cause of a virtuous action.

14. To Aristotle happiness is the 'final end', the *summum bonum*; it is never sought after to the exclusion of other things, because it includes all possible final ends. It is never chosen as a means to something else: 'that which is always desirable in itself and never for the sake of something else ... Happiness ... no one chooses for anything than itself' (*Nicomachean Ethics* (*NE*), I.7, 1097 a 30, a 34).

15. Aristotelian *eudaimonia* cannot be reached *instrumentally* but only as a byproduct of actions done for their own sake because they are intrinsically good, *virtuous* actions (*NE*, II 4, 1005 a 17 ss.). This is particularly clear in his theory of friendship (*Philia*). Aristotle (as did Socrates and Plato) claims that true friendship is friendship for virtue (not the other two types: for advantage or for pleasure), wanted non-instrumentally but for the other's sake. Aristotle insists that virtue–friendship supplies the 'focal meaning' of

friendship. So friendship contributes to the agent's *eudaimonia* only if it comes from true and genuine concern for the friend's care: happiness from friends cannot be achieved instrumentally.

16. See Bruni and Sugden (2000).
17. It is well known that for Aristotle 'by self-sufficient we do not mean that which is sufficient for a man who lives a solitary life, but also for parents, children, wife, and in general for his friends and fellow citizens, since man is born for citizenship' (*NE* I.7, 1097 a 44–7). This last and very famous sentence shows that already in his thought, later developed by the Latin tradition, from Thomas Aquinas to Rousseau or Genovesi, *sociality was considered an essential feature of happiness*. This social nature of happiness present in the Latin tradition has been at least understated. By translating happiness into pleasure the individualistic dimension of happiness (also originally present) has overcome the social and its paradoxical logic. To Aristotle, *philia*, political participation and love are essential constituents of the flourishing of a human being (Aristotle, *Politics*, part II).
18. Genovesi is addressing his readers both individually and collectively. Individually each of us can best achieve happiness by being ready to form relations of friendship with others who are similarly inclined. Collectively, we can best achieve happiness by acting together in relations of friendship.
19. By the expression 'civic humanism' (Baron 1955; Pocock 1975) we refer to that period of Italian history, especially Florentine, characterized by a revaluation of civic life. Medieval thought, centred on the vertical (religious) dimension, had not considered sociality as a key element of its world view. So, with humanism, the need for a revaluation of the civic dimension, which only became evident by the Middle Ages, exploded thanks to the great political, economic and philosophical changes that began in the late twelfth century with the birth of urban civilization (*civiltà cittadina*) in the northern Italian *Comuni*.
20. See Winch (1978), Gualerni (2002), and, in particular, Hont and Ignatief (1983).
21. Also the role of 'emulation', both in *The Theory of Moral Sentiments* and in the *Wealth of Nations*, shows an idea of 'social self' underlying Smithian self-interest: the attainment of wealth and of success is always a means for achieving social approbation and recognition (see Guidi 1995).
22. Smith (1759, pp. 219–24) ascribes great importance to friendship as a source of happiness.
23. Also Smith's definition of wealth leaves room for interpersonal relationships as a form of wealth: 'Every man is rich or poor according to the degree in which he can afford to enjoy the necessaries, conveniences, and amusements of human life' (1776, I, p. 32). In the expression 'amusements' one can find all kinds of social activities. Smith develops this idea further a few lines later: 'Wealth, as Mr Hobbes says, is power' (p. 33). In fact Hobbes in his *Leviathan* (I, x) says that riches are power 'because it procureth friends'.
24. We find a similar thesis (Providence = invisible hand) in Gianbattista Vico, the Neapolitan philosopher and Genovesi's master (1764, p. 59).
25. The same thesis is presented in Pigou (1920, ch. 1). For Marshall and his school the domain of economics is determined by the *strength* of man's motives – 'not the motives themselves' – strength that 'can be approximately measured by the sum of money' (Marshall 1890, p. 15).
26. See Henderson (2000).
27. J.M. Keynes, another important representative of the Cambridge tradition of economics, has a similar approach to the relationship between wealth (material prerequisites) and happiness (the final end). This comes in particular from his writings on social philosophy (such as his paper on 'The economic possibilities of our grandchildren'). At the end of a speech at a dinner on the occasion of his retirement as editor of the *Economic Journal* in 1945 he refers to 'economists, who are the trustees, not of civilisation, but of the possibility of civilisation' (quoted in Harrod 1951, p. 194).
28. If one takes Sen's theory of the 'the standard of living' (1999) one finds a strong assonance between the two 'Cambridge' economists. Marshall's line of thought was followed

by his heir in Cambridgean A.C. Pigou, who moved the fulcrum of the issue at hand towards the other magic word in economics: 'welfare'. In his *Economics of Welfare* (1920, p. 16), he states that he deals only with the economic aspects of total welfare (which he calls 'economic welfare'), that part of total welfare that 'can be expressed, directly or indirectly, by a money measure'.

29. In the same way Marshall was the first to use, in the English language, the word 'good' for 'commodity' in his *Principles* (following the German writers).
30. Note that utility is a property of objects, whereas pleasure or happiness is related to individuals.
31. See Bruni and Sugden (2003).
32. See Bruni and Guala (2001).
33. Fechner's law was a way, which had little success in economics, of measuring stimulus and sensations; Jevons applied this law to measure pleasure and utility.

Bibliography

Ahuvia, Aron and Douglas C. Friedman (1998), 'Income, consumption, and subjective well-being: toward a composite macromarketing model', *Journal of Macromarketing* **18** (Fall): 153–68.

Aristotle (1980), *Nicomachean Ethics*, Oxford: Oxford University Press.

Aristotle, *Politics*, The Internet Classics Archive, http://classics.mit.edu/index.html.

Baron, H. (1955), *The Crisis of the Early Italian Renaissance*, Princeton, NJ: Princeton University Press.

Becker, Gary (1996), *Accounting for Tastes*, Cambridge, MA: Harvard University Press.

Bellamy, Richard (1987), '*Da metafico a mercatante*: Antonio Genovesi and the Development of a New Language of Commerce in Eighteenth-century Naples', in Anthony Pagden (ed.), *The Language of Political Theory in Early Modern Europe*, Cambridge: Cambridge University Press, pp. 277–99.

Bentham, Jeremy (1789, [1996]), *An Introduction to the Principles of Morals and Legislation*, edited by J.H. Burns and H.L.A. Hart, Oxford: Clarendon Press.

Bianchini, Ludovico (1845), *Della scienza del ben vivere sociale e della economia degli stati*, Palermo: Stamperia di Francesco Lao.

Boudon, Raymond (2000), *Études sur le sociologiques classiques*, Paris: Presses Universitaires de France.

Bruni, Luigino and Francesco Guala (2001), 'Pareto and the epistemological foundations of rational choice theory', *History of Political Economy* **33** (1): 21–49.

Bruni, Luigino and Pier Luigi Porta (2003), 'Economies in the age of Newton: natural science and political economy in the Italian Enlightenment', *History of Political Economy*, **35**, supplement: 361–85.

Bruni, Luigino and Pier Luigi Porta (eds) (2005), *Economics and Happiness: Framing the Analysis*, Oxford: Oxford University Press.

Bruni, Luigino and Robert Sugden (2000), 'Moral canals: trust and social capital in the work of Hume, Smith and Genovesi', *Economics and Philosophy* **16** (1): 21–45.

Bruni, Luigino and Robert Sugden (2007), 'The road not taken: two debates in economics and psychology', *Economic Journal*, **117**, forthcoming.

Carlyle, Thomas (1850 [1898]), *Letter-Day Pamphlets*, London: Chapman & Hall.

Charness, Gary and Brit Grosskopf (2001), 'Cheap talk, information and coordination – experimental evidence', University of California at Santa Barbara, Economics Working paper no 1046, Department of Economics.

Diener, Ed and R. Biswas-Diener (2002), 'Will money increase subjective well-being?', *Social Indicators Research* **57** (1): 119–69.

Dixon, Huw D. (1997), 'Controversy: economics and happiness', Editorial note, *Economic Journal* **107** (November): 1812–14.

Easterlin, Richard (1974), 'Does economic growth improve the human lot? Some empirical evidence', in P.A. David and M.W. Reder (eds), *Nations and Households in Economic Growth: Essays in Honor of Moses Abramowitz*, New York and London: Academic Press: 89–125.

Easterlin, Richard (1995), 'Will raising the incomes of all increase the happiness of all?', *Journal of Economic Behaviour and Organisation* **27** (1): 35–48.

Easterlin, Richard (2001), 'Income and happiness: towards a unified theory', *Economic Journal* **111** (July): 465–84.

Easterlin, Richard (ed.) (2002), *Happiness in Economics*, Cheltenham, UK and Northampton, MA, USA: Edward Elgar.

Easterlin, Richard (2005), 'Towards a better theory of happiness in economics', in Bruni and Porta (eds) (2005).

Edgeworth, Francis Y. (1877), *New and Old Methods of Ethics*, London: James Parker.

Edgeworth, Francis Y. (1881), *Mathematical Psychics*, London: Kegan.

Edgeworth, Francis Y. (1926), 'Pareto', *Palgrave Dictionary of Political Economy*, Vol. 3, London: Macmillan, pp. 711–12.

Edgeworth, Francis Y. (1927 [1970]), *Papers Related to Political Economy*, 3 vols, New York: Burt Franklin.

Frank, Robert (1985), *Choosing the Right Pond*, Oxford and New York: Oxford University Press.

Frank, Robert (1997), 'The frame of reference as a public good', *Economic Journal* **107** (November): 1832–47.

Frank, Robert (1999), *Luxury Fever*, New York: Free Press.

Frank, Robert (2005), 'Does absolute income matter?', in Bruni and Porta (eds) (2005).

Frey, Bruno and Alois Stutzer (1999), 'Maximising happiness?', Working paper no. 22, University of Zurich: Institute for Empirical Research in Economics.

Frey, Bruno and Alois Stutzer (2002), *Happiness in Economics*, Princeton, NJ: Princeton University Press.

Genovesi, Antonio (1753 [1962]), *Discorso sopra il vero fine delle lettere e delle scienze*, Milan: Feltrinelli.

Genovesi, Antonio (1764 [1962]), *Autobiografia e lettere*, Milan: Feltrinelli.

Genovesi, Antonio (1765 [1820]), *Lezioni di commercio o sia di Economia civile*, Milan: Silvestri.

Genovesi, Antonio (1766 [1973]), *Diceosina o sia della filosofia del giusto e dell'onesto*, Milan: Marzorati.

Genovesi, Antonio (1984), *Scritti economici*, Naples: Istituto Italiano per gli Studi Filosofici.

Gualerni, Giuseppe (2002), *L'altra economia e l'interpretazione di Adam Smith*, Milan: Vita e Pensiero.

Guidi, Marco E.L. (1995), 'Pain and human action: Locke to Bentham', Mimeo, University of Pisa.

Hargreaves-Heap, Shaun et al. (1994), *Rational Choice: A Critical Guide*, Oxford: Blackwell.

Harrod, Roy (1951), *The Life of J.M. Keynes*, London: Macmillan.

Hausman, Daniel and M.S. McPherson (1996), *Economic Analysis and Moral Philosophy*, Cambridge: Cambridge University Press.

Henderson, Willie (2000), *John Ruskin's Political Economy*, London: Routledge.

Hirschman, Albert O. (1977), *The Passions and the Interests*, Princeton, NJ: Princeton University Press.

Hobbes, T. (1651 [1954]), *Leviathan*, London: Dent & Son.

Höllander, H. (2001), 'On the validity of utility statements: standard theory versus Duesenberry's, *Journal of Economic Behaviour and Organization*, **45**, 227–49.

Hollis, Martin (1998), *Trust Within Reason*, Cambridge: Cambridge University Press.

Hont, Istvan and Michael Ignatief (1983), *Wealth and Virtue: The Shaping of Political Economy in the Scottish Enlightenment*, Cambridge: Cambridge University Press.

Jevons, Stanley (1871 [1970]), *The Theory of Political Economy*, New York: Penguin Books.

Kahneman, Daniel, Ed Diener and Norbert Schwarz (eds) (1999), *Well-being: The Foundation of Hedonic Psychology*, New York: Russell Sage Foundation.

Kelly, L.C. (2000), 'Why isn't growth making us happier?', Mimeo, Oxford University.

Kenny, Charles (1999), 'Does growth cause happiness, or does happiness cause growth?', *Kyklos* **52** (1): 3–26.

Lane, Robert (2000), *The Loss of Happiness in the Market Democracies*, New Haven, CT: Yale University Press.

Lebergott, S. (1993), *Pursuing Happiness*, Princeton, NJ: Princeton University Press.

Loria, Achille (1893 [1904]), *Verso la giustizia sociale*, Milan: Società Editrice Libraria.

Malthus, Thomas R. (1798 [1966]), *An Essay on the Principle of Population*, London: Macmillan.

Marshall, Alfred (1890), *Principles of Economics*, London: Macmillan.

Michels, Robert (1918), *Economia e felicità*, Milan: Vallardi.

Mill, John S. (1861), *Utilitarianism*. Reprinted as *The Collected Works of J.S. Mill*, Vol. X, edited by John M. Robson and Jack Stillinger, Toronto and London: University of Toronto Press and Routledge & Kegan 1963.

Mill, John S. (1874), *Autobiography and Literary Essays*. Reprinted as *The Collected Works of J.S. Mill*, Vol. X, edited by John M. Robson and Jack Stillinger, Toronto and London: University of Toronto Press and Routledge & Kegan, 1981.

Moore, G.E. (1903), *Principia Ethica*, London: Macmillan.

Muratori, Ludovico (1749), *Della pubblica felicità*, Lucca.

Ng, Y.K. (1997), 'A case for happiness, cardinalism, and interpersonal comparability', *Economic Journal* **107** (November): 1848–58.

Nussbaum, Martha (1986), *The Fragility of Goodness: Luck and Ethics in Greek Tragedy and Philosophy*, Cambridge: Cambridge University Press.

Oslington, Paul (2002), 'John Henry Newman, Nassau Senior, and the separation of political economy from theology in the nineteenth century', *History of Political Economy* **33** (1): 825–42.

Oswald, Andrew J. (1997), 'Happiness and Economic performance', *Economic Journal* **107** (November): 1815–31.

Palmieri, Giuseppe (1788), *Riflessioni sulla pubblica felicità relativamente al Regno di Napoli*, Milan: Pirotta & Maspero.

Pantaleoni, Maffeo (1913 [1925]), 'Definizione dell'economia. Una prolusione', in *Erotemi di economia*, I: 1–66, Bari: Laterza.

Pantaleoni, Maffeo (1924), 'In occasione della morte di Pareto: Riflessioni', *Giornale degli Economisti*, **64** (1): 1–19. Reprinted in Pantaleoni 1938.

Pantaleoni, Maffeo (1938), *Studi di finanza e statistica*, Bologna: Zanichelli.

Pareto, Vilfredo (1899), 'Letter to M. Pantaleoni', *Lettere a Maffeo Pantaleoni*, Vol. III, edited by G. De Rosa. Rome: Banca Nazionale del Lavoro.

Phelps, C. (2001), 'A clue to the paradox of *Happiness*', *Journal of Economic Behavior and Organization*, **45**, 293–300.

Pigou, Arthur C. (1920), *Economics of Welfare*, London: Macmillan.

Pii, Elugero (1984), *Antonio Genovesi: Dalla politica economica alla 'politica civile'*, Florence: Olschki.

Pocock, J.G.A. (1975), *The Machiavellian Moment: Florentine Political Thought and the Atlantic Republican Tradition*, Princeton NJ: Princeton University Press.

Putnam, Robert (2000), *Bowling Alone*, New York: Simon & Schuster.

Raphael, D.D and A.L. Macfie (1980), 'Introduction', in Adam Smith, *The Theory of Moral Sentiments*, Indianapolis, IN: Liberty Fund.

Robbins, Lionel (1998), *A History of Economic Thought: The LSE Lectures*, edited by Steven G. Medema and Warren J. Samuels, Princeton, NJ and Oxford: Princeton University Press.

Ryan, R.M. and E.L. Deci (2001), 'On Happiness and Human Potentials: A Review of Research on Hedonic and Eudaimonic Well-Being', *Annual Review of Psychology* **52**: 141–66.

Schabas, Margaret (1990), *A World Ruled by Numbers: William Stanley Jevons and the Rise of Mathematical Economics*, Princeton, NJ: Princeton University Press.

Scitovsky, Tibor (1976), *The Joyless Economy: An Inquiry into Human Satisfaction and Consumer Dissatisfaction*, Oxford: Oxford University Press.

Sen, Amartya (1991), *The Standard of Living*, Cambridge: Cambridge University Press.

Sen, A. (2000), *Development as Freedom*, New York: A. Alfred Knopp.

Sismondi, J.C. Simonde de (1819 [1974]), *Nouveaux Principes d'économie politique*, Italian edition, edited by P. Barocci, Milan: Isedi.

Smith, Adam (1759 [1980]), *The Theory of Moral Sentiments*, Indianapolis, IN: Liberty Fund.

Smith, Adam (1776 [1976]), *An Inquiry into the Nature and Causes of the Wealth of Nations*, Oxford: Clarendon Press.

Sugden, Robert (2002), 'Beyond sympathy and empathy: Adam Smith's concept of fellow-feeling', *Economics and Philosophy*, **18**: 63–87.

Todorov, Tzvetan (1995), *La vie commune: Essay d'antropologie générale*, Paris: Éditions du Seuil.

Veblen, Thorstein (1899 [1998]), *The Theory of the Leisure Class*, New York: Prometheus Books.

Veenhoven, R. (2000), *Freedom and Happiness: A Comparative Study in 44 Nations in the Early 1990s*, Mimeo, Oxford University.

Verri, Pietro (1763 [1964]), *Del piacere e del dolore ed altri scritti*, edited by R. De Felice, Milan: Feltrinelli.

Verri, Pietro (1781), *Discorsi sull'indole del piacere e del dolore, sulla felicità e sulla economia politica*, Milan: Giuseppe Marelli. Reprinted in Verri, 1964, pp. 1–260.

Vico, Gianbattista (1727 [1907]), *Principii di scienza nuova*, Bari: Laterza.

Vico, G.B. (1744 [1948]), *The New Science*, tr. Thomas Goddard Bergin and Max Harold Fisch, Ithaca, NY: Cornell University Press.

Vitale, Marco (2001), 'Starting again from Carlo Cattaneo', in Carlo Cattaneo (ed.), *Intelligence as Principle of Public Economy*, Milan: Scheiwiller, pp. 107–58.

Winch, Donald (1978), *Adam Smith's Policy*, Cambridge: Cambridge University Press.

3. Human needs hierarchy and happiness: evidence from the late pre-classical and classical economics

Stravos Drakopoulos and Anastasios Karayiannis

1. Introduction

In the last few years the concept of happiness has begun to interest economists seriously. The papers published in the *Economic Journal* in 1997, the special issue of the *Journal of Economic Behaviour and Organization* in 2001 and the 2003 Conference on the Paradoxes of Happiness in Economics are clear indications of the rising interest in the subject. However, this does not imply that there were no examples of older work of economists like Easterlin (1974) which had dealt with this issue. In the older and in the more recent literature one can discern a common empirical finding in many countries, that substantial increases in real per capita income do not correspond to equivalent increases of individual happiness. In fact, there are examples where a negative correlation between real income and happiness was observed (see, for instance, Easterlin 1974; Oswald 1997; Lane 2000; Wright 2000). These findings have puzzled many economists, some of whom have called the phenomenon the 'paradox of happiness' (for example, Bruni 2002).

As one would expect there have been a number of explanations regarding this paradox. One is based on the 'subjectivist' approach to utility, whereby variables which are considered by many economists to be non-economic, play an important role in individual utility functions and thus in the level of happiness (Frey and Stutzer 2002). Such variables can be emotions, social stimuli, goal completion and meaning, freedom and social capital (see Scitovsky 1976; Elster 1998; Loewenstein 1999; Putnam 2000; Veenhoven 2000). Another line of approach has to do with traditional economic concepts which if incorporated might be able to explain the paradox. Two of these are: the idea of relative income or relative consumption hypothesis (Duesenberry 1949; Frank 1985, 1999; Andrews 1991; Veenhoven 1991), and the level of inequality (Alesina, Tella and MacCulloch 2004). One can also observe here that the above ideas are not new in economic literature but have been around for a long time. For instance, the idea of 'conspicuous consumption' which is related to relative income, can be found in Rae (1834), Veblen (1899) and Keynes (1973). In addition, the idea of inequality level as a negative factor for social well-being is equally old in economic thought. Thus one might get some further clues for a possible explanation of the paradox by looking at the history of economic ideas. In this chapter we examine the ideas of some well-known pre-classical and classical economists concerning the relationship between basic goods, consumption and happiness.

More specifically, in the literature of the late mercantilist and classical period, one can find interesting ideas and arguments dealing with the distinction between basic and non-basic goods and their effect on the level of happiness. Furthermore, there are views supporting a hierarchical pattern of consumption, implying that individuals are concerned more with the acquisition of basic goods and this in turn implies that their effect on the level of happiness is much stronger than those of non-basic goods. The purpose of this chapter is to examine these ideas and to see whether they can contribute towards the explanation of the paradox of happiness. Section 2 will discuss the various views expressed on the distinction between basic and non-basic goods and the various causes which determine such a distinction. Section 3 traces the ideas concerning a hierarchical approach to consumption behaviour. Section 4 attempts to explain how the various goods classifications and the hierarchy of goods affect the level of human happiness. Finally, Section 5 links the findings with recent arguments.

2.   Basic and non-basic goods

The majority of the authors connected the distinction of basic and non-basic goods with the different economic classes of society. More specifically, Steuart (1767, p. 269) claimed that the rate of consumption was indicative of the rank of individual in the social climax-a dichotomy previously introduced by Turgot (1766, pp. 180–81). Steuart analytically described 'physical' and 'political' necessaries (1767, pp. 269–76): the first to be the 'able subsistence where no degree of superfluity is implied' (p. 269), and the second to be related to the fulfilment of desires which 'proceed from the affections of his mind, are formed by habit and education' (p. 270).[1]

Although the consumption of basic goods was of paramount importance for the living standard of the working class,[2] the existence and consumption of luxury goods[3] was stressed as a means for increasing employment, trade and production levels (for example, Mandeville 1724, pp. 68, 75; Steuart 1767, pp. 9, 282; see also Perrotta 1997). Thus there are indications that even before Smith's time, authors have distinguished various consumable goods according to different living standards and classes of men. Smith (1776, p. 842) adopted the differentiation of classes according to income and consumption,[4] and he differentiated between basic and non-basic goods. The first, which he calls 'necessary and conveniences', are mainly consumed by the working class and include: 'food, clothing and lodging' (pp. 178, 185) and 'household furniture, and what is called Equipage, [which] are the principal objects of the greater part of those wants and fancies' (p. 180).[5] The second category of goods are 'luxuries, without meaning by this appellation to throw the smallest degree of reproach upon the temperate use of them . . . Nature does not render them necessary for the support of life, and custom nowhere renders it indecent to live without them' (pp. 869–71). The distinction of goods also brings an effect on the satiety of men. Smith (1759, p. 184; 1776, p. 180) holds that the consumption of necessary goods is satiated while that of luxuries is non-satiated. He also (1776, p. 347) recognized the intergenerational alteration of the living standard. He holds that today's living standard of rich men will become tomorrow's conveniences of labourers.[6] In addition, he stressed (p. 93) that the level of real wage rate determines the living standard of the labourer and not the other way round.

With the above distinction of goods as a basis, Smith forms two conclusions: (a) the increase of luxury consumption is detrimental for the economy, and (b) permanent differences emerge between the market rate of prices and the natural cost of various goods. In relation to the first point, Smith (ibid., pp. 190, 208) described the conspicuous consumption behaviour, or the 'parade of riches' as he characterized it – as did Rousseau before him (1758, p. 152). Smith also recognized (1776, p. 686) that when luxury goods are widespread among the majority of citizens, 'idle consumers' start preferring a variety of goods. He was against luxury consumption and the behaviour of idle consumers because their short-run consumption pattern[7] would decrease the rate of capital accumulation (1762–63, p. 394), and would increase the rate of unproductive labour (1776, pp. 337–9, 349; see also Mason 1998).[8] Thus, Smith, as previously did Turgot (1766, p. 169), and contrary to Steuart, held that parsimony and not increased demand would be the main cause of the increased wealth of the nation. In regard to the second point, Smith (1776, p. 242) claimed that the rate of prices of fashionable goods would rise faster than their real cost,[9] and this would alter the natural exchange rate between various goods.[10]

Because of the above arguments, Smith opposed the taxation of necessary goods, considering it to be a tax on wages (ibid., p. 871), as also did Rousseau (1758, p. 149). Instead of such a tax, Smith proposed the taxation of luxury goods since it is paid by the consumers of such goods (1776, pp. 232, 872–3). Such a tax was also favoured by many scholars of the period such as Hume ('Of taxes', 1970, pp. 83, 85) and Rousseau (1758, pp. 134, 146–7, 152), for its usefulness in decreasing wealth inequality.[11]

In the middle of the classical period, Torrens defined the minimum accepted living standard of labourers to cover 'the necessaries and conveniences of life sufficient to preserve the labourer in working condition, and to induce him to keep up the race of labourers' (1834, pp. 11–12; see also pp. 13, 54 and 1815, pp. 84, 87).[12] However, he held that through technological progress this living standard would be increased by more and better goods and services (see Karayiannis 2000). Through such progress, new consumption habits will be adopted by the labourers and eventually, through custom, their minimum living standard would be advanced, as 'custom is a second nature, and things not originally necessary to healthful existence become so from habit' (Torrens 1834, p. 54).

At the same time, Senior (1827, p. 36) by strictly distinguishing between basic and non-basic goods, argued (1829, pp. 3–6; 1836, pp. 36–7) that the classification of goods into these categories is relevant in terms of customs and per capita income.[13] Generally speaking, he believed (1836, pp. 38–9, 161) that luxury consumption does not constrain the rate of wealth augmentation. On the contrary, he stated (p. 42) that the intergenerational articulation of the various kinds of goods[14] under the human motive of variety and distinction in consumption, is an indication of economic development (see Karayiannis 2001). Moreover, and contrary to Smith, Senior believed (1831, pp. 21, 25–7) that through the increased luxury consumption of the idle consumers, the rate of circulating capital rises and under the wage fund theory, the short-run employment level and/or wage of labourers also rises.[15]

The Scottish Canadian John Rae (1834, p. 267) writes about the passing from basic to non-basic goods under the influence of conspicuous consumption behaviour as a result of the 'principle of vanity' (see also Mason 2002). Rae stressed (1834, p. 270) that due to economic development, luxurious goods are consumed by all classes of citizens and thus the rich prefer a variety of such goods according to fashion – an argument already put forward by Smith.

Thus the gradual passing of the working class from the consumption pattern of consisting solely of basic goods to another which includes non-basic goods, was a well-recognizable sign of economic progress (see also Johnson 1813, pp. 27–60; Malthus 1820, pp. 224–7; Craig 1821, pp. 60–61; McCulloch 1825, pp. 332, 337; 1826, pp. 7, 34; Read 1829, pp. 143–4; Newman 1835, p. 289).[16] Such a passing may take place mainly when the rate of population increase is lower than the rate of income increase.[17] Malthus (1820, pp. 224–5) has shown analytically in what conditions the living standard of individuals proceeds from basic to non-basic goods. In the case that an increase in real wage rate is taking place, either the quantity of labour would be increased (by multiplying their number) or the living standard of the labourers would incorporate more comfortable and luxurious goods

(p. 226). The first effect, according to Malthus (pp. 226–7) takes place in societies where despotism, oppression and ignorance prevail. The second effect appears in societies where there is civil and political liberty, a good 'quality and prevalence' of education, and security of property rights.

3. Hierarchical consumption behaviour

As we have seen from the previous analysis, during the period from the late mercantilism to the classical school, the majority of authors have clearly distinguished between various goods corresponding to pressing and non-pressing needs. Furthermore, as will be seen, there are clear indications that some authors followed a hierarchical approach to consumption. This implies that there are basic needs which need to be satisfied first before non-basic needs come into the picture (see also Drakopoulos 1994; Drakopoulos and Karayiannis 2004).

In the beginning of the eighteenth century, the philosopher George Berkeley recognized the hierarchy of needs and the emergency in fulfilling the necessary ones. He questioned '[w]hether necessity is not to be hearkened to before convenience, and convenience before luxury?' (1735–37, query 58), and '[w]hether national wants ought not to be the rule of trade? And whether the most pressing wants of the majority ought not to be first considered?' (query 168). He believed that consuming luxury goods before necessary goods is a sign of irrational behaviour. Furthermore, he questions:

> Whether she would not be a very vile matron, and justly thought either mad or foolish, that should give away the necessaries of life from her naked and famished children, in exchange for pearls to stick in her hair, and sweetmeats to please her own palate? (query 175)

By following a more systematic approach, Cantillon (1755, p. 75) justified the hierarchy in consumption as a 'nobleman' cares more for his luxury than his necessary consumption because of his abundance of wealth to cover subsistence. In the same tone, Hume ('On public credit', 1970, p. 97), presented a hierarchy of the consumed goods according to the pressing needs that they fulfil. Moreover, he implicitly accepts a system of needs hierarchy by attributing certain goods to certain needs. In his discussion of the issue of revenue from taxation, he writes:

> In GREAT BRITAIN, the excises upon malt and beer afford a large revenue; because the operations of malting and brewing are tedious, and are impossible to be concealed; and at the same time, these commodities are not so absolutely necessary to life, as that the raising of their price would very much affect the poorer sort. (Ibid.)

Some members of the classical school recognized three broad categories of hierarchical consumption. Some of them identified this sort of behaviour as an immediate consequence of the increased rate of per capita income. Others connected it to the subjective theory of value and justified it in terms of utility rate. The third, and more general approach, explained such a hierarchy in terms of a response to different price and income elasticities of goods.

Smith developed the first justification of the hierarchy in consumption. In his early work, Smith (1759, pp. 50, 184–5) recognized such behaviour but he elaborated upon it mostly in his *Wealth of Nations*. He stressed (1776, pp. 287, 289, 405) that men fulfil first their more oppressive needs and then proceed to the consumption of the conveniencies and luxuries. Therefore,

> [A]s subsistence is, in the nature of things, prior to conveniency and luxury, so the industry which procures the former must necessarily be prior to that which ministers to the latter. The cultivation and improvement of the country, therefore, which affords subsistence, must, necessarily, be prior to the increase of the town, which furnishes only the means of conveniency and luxury. (p. 377)

That is, not only is the consumption of necessary goods first fulfilled but also the primary sector of economy is first advanced before the extension of the secondary and tertiary ones. This hierarchy of goods could take place, according to Smith (p. 96) when the total production was able to cover the subsistence of men and when the increased rate of nations' wealth cause an extension of luxurious living (pp. 199, 234).

This explanation of the hierarchical consumption in terms of per capita income was also adopted by some other authors. For example, Rae (1834, p. 203) made it explicit that by an increase to the propensity of saving, the consumer would first decrease the consumption of luxury and not of basic wants.[18]

J.B. Say (1803, pp. 397–8; 1821, p. 82) is closer to the second justification of hierarchical consumption since he recognized two main cases and causes of hierarchical consumption behaviour of individuals: the first is determined by the rate of urgency of needs and the utility of its satisfaction, and the second by the duration of the consumable good. The longer the duration, the more preferable that good is. Say also stressed (1803, pp. 4–5) that the demarcation criterion between necessary and luxury goods is an ever-changing one: 'For my own part, I am at a loss to draw the line between superfluities and necessaries' as its 'line of demarcation . . . shifts with the fluctuating conditions of society'.

Similarly, Lloyd (1833, p. 28) and Longfield (1834, p. 115) elaborated at greater length the idea of hierarchical consumption behaviour. In particular,

Lloyd (1833, p. 12) uses a mechanical parable in order to describe the hierarchy of consumption and the urgency of needs to be satisfied, namely:

> Each different kind, therefore, of human wants may like that of food, be compared to a spring; and, in the comparison, the different wants, according to their several differences, will be represented by a spring of different degrees of strength. For example, the wants which food can satisfy will be represented by a spring of great power. So also those to supply which water is required. For representing the wants of clothing and fuel, which are articles not so indispensably necessary to human existence, a spring of an inferior degree of power may suffice. Passing on to the artificial wants, we may represent them according to their intensities, by a lesser spring of various degrees of strength. (p. 13)

The imitation effect in consumption pattern, namely to 'keep up with Jones's', as a cause of the hierarchical behaviour has been identified by John Craig, who stated that: 'A young man will propose to maintain his family in the same style that his relations and acquaintances now live' (1821, p. 55), and 'It is not any particular degree of comfort that is requisite to self respect, but that degree of it which is enjoyed by reputable people of the same rank. If all be equally reduced, none can feel degraded' (p. 59). Similarly, Whately argued (1832, p. 51) that goods included in a consumption basket are socially determined. Therefore, 'an individual man is called luxurious, in comparison with other men, of the same community and in the same walk of life with himself' (p. 53).[19]

With reference to the third approach, according to which the hierarchy of goods is a consequence or a characteristic of the differential behaviour of consumers towards a change in the level of price, income and taxation, the following arguments were developed:[20] Lord Lauderdale (1804, pp. 71–2, 76, 95–6) specified that the hierarchy of the consumption of goods affects price, quantity and income elasticities. For instance, various goods fulfilling different wants such as necessaries and luxuries have a different rate. He used this idea for the hierarchy of consumption behaviour in examining 'the Effects of the Alteration in the Order of Expenditure occasioned by' the following circumstances: (a) 'a Diminution in the Quantity of any Commodity' (p. 81); (b) 'an increase of Demand for any Commodity' (p. 86); (c) 'an Increase in the Quantity of any Commodity' (p. 93); and (d) 'a Diminution of Demand for any Commodity' (p. 96). Thus by this method he explained the changes in the consumption pattern of individuals caused by some drastic changes in the state of demand and supply of various goods. In addition, he links (pp. 329, 342–3) his argument about the hierarchy of consumption to the distribution and production of goods. He held that the distribution of wealth caused an hierarchy and specific consumption behaviour among necessaries and luxury goods and thus determines the efficiency and the kind of production in various countries.

Ricardo (1817, pp. 237, 241, 343–4), elaborating on the issue of hierarchical behaviour, pointed out that there would be a different price and income demand elasticities after a change in the price of necessary and/or luxury goods. Such an idea was also adopted by some other authors like Torrens (1815, pp. 15, 278, 309), Senior (see Karayiannis 2000), Tucker (1837, p. 6) and J.S. Mill (1848, pp. 447, 596). Similarly, Malthus (1815, pp. 187–8) argued that there are different causes determining the price of necessaries (mainly the rate of supply) and conveniencies–luxuries (mainly the rate of demand) goods. Furthermore, other authors like Rogers (1822, pp. 39–40) and J.S. Mill (1848, pp. 806–7, 868) connected the hierarchical consumption of goods with the effects and incidence of taxation. (For a modern treatment of hierarchical consumption and elasticities, see Earl 1986.)

Thus we can see that there were approaches justifying the hierarchical consumption behaviour of individuals mainly upon: (a) the rate of per capita income, (b) social and psychological grounds, and (c) the responsiveness of demand to changes in the quantity and price of goods.

4.   Happiness and material consumption

Happiness in the period under examination, was mainly justified and measured on materialistic grounds.[21] For instance, Hume (1970, 'Of the jealousy of trade', p. 80; 'Of interest', p. 56) pointed out that happiness is increased by international trade through the possibility of consuming a variety of goods. However, Smith was the leading figure who connected happiness to the living standard of the labourers in an economy. He consciously related the dependence of general welfare to the living standard of the labourers:

> Is this improvement in the circumstances of the lower ranks of the people to be regarded as an advantage or as an inconveniency to the society? The answer seems at first sight abundantly plain. Servants, labourers, and workmen of different kinds, make up the far greater part of every great political society. *But what improves the circumstances of the greater part can never be regarded as an inconveniency to the whole.* No society can surely be flourishing and happy, of which the far greater part of the members are poor and miserable. It is but equity, besides, that they who feed, clothe, and lodge the whole body of the people, should have such a share of the produce of their own labour as to be themselves tolerably well fed, clothed, and lodged. (1776, p. 96, emphasis added)

He also claimed (pp. 91, 96) that the rate of labourers' standard of living was the effect not the cause of the wealth of nation.

Some years later, Bentham (1780, p. 2) following the same path but providing philosophical justification, linked happiness to material pleasure. Bentham assessed (p. 3) the various effects of economic policy in terms of increasing and/or decreasing the general welfare–happiness. According to Bentham (p. 24) the main scope of state policy is the increase of people's happiness that is, pleasure and security. This idea was followed up by many utilitarians such as Scrope (1833, pp. xii, 2, 58) and Senior (1852, p. 9).

Bentham's idea that the level of happiness depends on the material consumption of individuals, was also adopted and emphasized by many scholars, such as the American Alexander Johnson (1813, pp. 28–9), Raymond (1823, pp. 36, 117–18, 128, 133–4, 410, 416), Read (1829, p. 46) and Torrens (1834, p. 1). Furthermore, this analysis provided the justification of the material incentives for wealth accumulation (see, for example, Read, 1829, p. 143).

The same context was used in order to connect happiness with goods and needs. More specifically, Scrope (1833, pp. 50–51, 185) claimed that a labourer's happiness is directly determined by the rate of the real wage or the quality and affluence of material consumption. Furthermore, he believed that happiness should be a universal right: 'Happiness – all the happiness, at least, which is directly or indirectly derivable from an abundance of the necessaries and conveniences of life – ought to be within the easy reach of every individual, even of the lowest class, in every human society' (1833, pp. 293–4). In the same tone and implying a hierarchical consumption behaviour, Longfield (1834, pp. 44, 113) held that a higher rate of happiness is acquired by the consumption of necessary rather than of luxury goods. However, some other authors recognized that the consumption of luxury goods was an important element of human happiness. For example, Lloyd (1833, pp. 8–9) and Senior (1836, pp. 11–12), stressed that the 'love' for variety of consumption and distinction are motives not only for increasing the rate of consumption and production in an economy, but additionally to be important ingredients of human happiness (see also Karayiannis 2001).

There are also examples of authors who consider happiness to be the main scope of economics. Sismondi (1815, pp. 1, 100; 1826, p. 132) a radical of the classical period, seems to adopt such a thesis by connecting wealth to the rate of labourers' happiness and this is the main scope of political economy. Senior also linked happiness with the art of economics: 'If wealth be the object of Political Economy, and wealth include all that man desires, Political Economy, whether a science or an art, is the science or the art which treats of human happiness' (1852, p. 74). He also claimed (1831, p. 14) that 'a certain degree of leisure' as a component of happiness must be included in any estimation of wealth.

In general, for most authors happiness is clearly associated with material consumption. Furthermore, it seems that for many authors, happiness is more closely connected to the fulfilment of urgent needs than of luxurious wants.

5.   Conclusions

In this chapter, we found indications that many pre-classical and classical economists distinguished between basic and non-basic goods. Usually, this distinction was associated with different social classes. More specifically, the consumption of basic goods was mainly attributed to the working classes and the consumption of non-basic or luxury goods to the upper classes. Next, we found evidence that the idea of hierarchical behaviour was present in pre-classical and classical thought. This behaviour implies that human needs are structured and that basic needs are satisfied first. In other words, basic needs are viewed as more urgent than non-basic or secondary needs. Basic needs correspond to basic goods. Furthermore, it was seen that for a number of authors, happiness is closely associated with material consumption.

Given the above, one can argue that since basic needs are more urgent and that since basic goods satisfy better the basic needs, basic goods might provide more happiness. The association between basic goods, hierarchical behaviour and happiness might assist in explaining one aspect of the paradox of happiness. In particular, one can argue that the satisfaction of basic needs substantially increases individual happiness. However, taking into account the hierarchical structure of needs, the subsequent satisfaction of secondary needs does not provide equivalent increases in individual happiness. This can be an alternative explanation of the observed gap between real income increases and increases in happiness level.

Notes

1. One of the earlier distinctions between basic and non-basic goods was drawn by Locke (1691, pp. 244, 276) who characterized respectively the first type of goods as necessaries for life and the second as fashionable goods. Further, he argued (pp. 276–7) that through the conspicuous consumption behaviour the rate of price of fashionable goods is not determined by the cost of production but by the preference of rich consumers and the rate of demand.
2. Richard Cantillon defined necessary goods as 'the food, clothing, housing, etc' (1755, p. 87; see also p. 125). For Harris (1757, pp. 352–3) such a collection of consumable goods determines the level of subsistence wage.
3. One of the most descriptive definitions of luxury goods is given by Steuart: 'By LUXURY, I understand the consumption of any thing produced by the labour or ingenuity of man, which flatters our senses or taste of living, and which is neither necessary for our being well fed, well clothed, well defended against the injuries of the weather, or for securing us against every thing which can hurt us' (1767, pp. 43–4). In a similar tone and some decades later, Chalmers (1832, p. 42) defined luxury goods as 'every thing prepared by human labour, and which enters not into the average maintenance of labourers'.
4. Many authors of the classical school who mainly followed the cost of production or labour theory of value adopted such a classification of goods consumed by different classes of men in society. These authors, such as Ricardo (1817, pp. 48, 93, 118, 205, 236, 276), James Mill (1821, pp. 54–5), McCulloch (1825, p. 490; 1826, pp. 27, 34–5), Torrens (1834, pp. 5, 11–12) and J.S. Mill (1848, p. 68), distinguished between two different

classes of men consuming two different patterns of goods. Under the 'iron law of wages' they supposed that labourers are consuming only 'necessaries and conveniences of life', which are determined by economic, environmental and institutional (for example, habit) conditions. This strict distinction of consumable goods and services between the poor and rich was also adopted by the nineteenth-century radicals. For example, Simonde de Sismondi (1815, pp. 22, 24; 1826, pp. 127–8), Thompson (1824, pp. 198–9), Bray (1839, pp. 55, 96–7) and Hodgskin (1825, p. 310). Karl Marx introduced the separation in consumption patterns between proletariats and capitalists or poor and rich (see, for example, 1867, pp. 185, 208–9, 299–300, 486–7, 419).

5. McCulloch stated that the necessary rate of wages must include 'the cost of the food, clothes, fuel & c., required for the use and accommodation of labourers' (1825, p. 325). J.S. Mill (1848, pp. 689, 719) gave a full account of the normal and customary living standard of labourers.

6. Raymond observed (1823, pp. 74–5) that the distinction between basic and non-basic goods is rather arbitrary and is based upon the false assumption of interpersonal utility comparisons.

7. In a representative statement Smith wrote: 'With regard to profusion, the principle which prompts to expense is the passion for present enjoyment; which, though sometimes violent and very difficult to be restrained, is in general only momentary and occasional. But the principle which prompts to save is the desire of bettering our condition, a desire which, though generally calm and dispassionate, comes with us from the womb, and never leaves us till we go into the grave' (1776, p. 341).

8. For an extensive analysis of the Smithian argument about the relationship of productive (producing mainly basic wage goods) and unproductive labour (producing mainly luxury goods) and its effects on economic development and general welfare, see Myint (1948, ch. V).

9. Longfield analysed the effect of the distinction of goods on cost and wages. He holds (1834, pp. 101, 105–6) that the extensive division of labour on such productive activities destined for mass consumption (that is, necessary and comfort goods), cause a drastic decrease in the cost of production and the rate of prices. On the other hand, the volume of the production of luxury goods is very restricted. Thus the extent of the division of labour for its production is at a low level and thus their cost and prices are rather high.

10. By recognizing the conspicuous consumption behaviour, Smith noted the entrepreneurial strategy in promoting a relevant kind of goods by increasing their prices: 'By raising their price [i.e. of some non-necessary goods] they make [i.e. the merchants] an object of their [i.e. consumers'] desire, and such as good-fellowship requires them to press on their guests' (1762–63, p. 363).

11. During the reign of Edward IV (mid-fifteenth century) the so-called sumptuary law was established in England, prohibiting labourers from spending their income on luxury goods. Smith (1776, p. 262) turned against this policy, arguing that such laws not only restrained innovations in manufacture but also safeguarded the welfare of the labourers.

12. The distinction of basic and non-basic goods was the main characteristic of the described consumption pattern of the period in question (the majority of the classical writers after Smith included necessary and convenience goods in this category). However, an American economist, George Opdyke, developed a rather different classification. He considered that consumption goods and services must be classified under the following three categories: '1., in the augmentation of the productive forces' (mainly for labour such as necessaries and convenience goods), '2., in the gratification of the senses' (such as 'the sense of smell, for fragrant and pungent odors' and so on), and '3., in the satisfaction of mental desires' (such as benevolence, 'fitting guards for securing personal safety' and so on). However, the second and third categories of goods and services are mostly consumed by the rich and non-labouring classes (1851, pp. 114–15, 119).

13. Senior (1829, p. 6) also claimed that the characteristics of necessary goods do not alter as often as those of luxury goods.

14. Such an effect was clearly described by Poulet Scrope who wrote: 'A mode of dress which has gone out of fashion among the higher and wealthier ranks, will perhaps be

just introducing itself in the middle class, to descend, when the latter have worn it out, to the lower and more numerous' (1833, p. 187).

15. J.S. Mill (1848, pp. 68, 350) described how an increase of capital without being accompanied by a proportional increase in population would increase the real wage rate and the living standard of labourers, which would include not only necessaries but also luxury goods.

16. Similarly to Duesenberry (1949, p. 34), McCulloch argued that present consumption is determined by habit and past consumption schedule: 'were the supply of labourers suddenly diminished when wages fall, the fall would merely lessen their number, without having any tendency to degrade the habits or to lower the condition of those that survived' (1825, p. 333).

17. Or, as Read (1829, pp. 325–6) put it, when the desire for bettering the material conditions would be more intense than the desire for the multiplicity of their numbers.

18. By the same reasoning, the American Henry Vethake (1844, pp. 115–17) a follower of Ricardo, stressing the effects of general education in increasing the taste for luxury consumption, specified the hierarchy of goods and needs by commenting: 'in a certain country, the labourer can, by working nine hours in the day, obtain what constitute to him the necessaries of life, and that he can procure a certain amount of luxuries by working one hour in the day more' (1844, p. 125).

19. Whately also emphasized that a variety of consumption goods is desirable by all individuals (1832, pp. 94–5).

20. One of the early exponents of such an approach was Cantillon (1755, p. 173), who argued that the price elasticity of necessary goods would be low while the income elasticity of luxury goods would be high. He also used the hierarchy of goods in order to contradict the proportionality between the scarcity of silver and the level of prices advanced by Locke. Cantillon (pp. 179, 181) questioned such a proportionality, arguing that the consumption of various goods relates not only to its price and the income of the consumer, but furthermore to the importance of goods for his living and the hierarchy that the consumer grants to the various goods.

21. Since mercantilism, one can observe the connection between happiness with material well-being. For example, Davanzati (1588, para.13) as early as the end of the sixteenth century, defines happiness in terms of material well-being. Then, he argued that individuals' behaviour to achieve material happiness determines, together with custom and natural endowments, the rate of demand and value of various goods. In the same framework, Berkeley (1735–37, query 345) relates the general happiness to individual happiness and believed that its rate is influenced by economic policy – as stated later by Bentham.

References

Alesina, A., R.D. Tella and R. MacCulloch (2004), 'Inequality and happiness', *Journal of Public Economics*, **88**, 2009–42.

Andrews, F. (1991), 'Stability and change in levels and structure of subjective well-being: USA 1972 and 1988', *Social Indicators Research*, **25**, 1–30.

Bentham, J. (1780 [1907]), *An Introduction to the Principles of Morals and Legislation*, Oxford: Clarendon Press.

Berkeley, G. (1735–37), *The Querist*, Dublin,

Bray, J. (1839 [1968]), *Labour's Wrong and Labour's Remedy*, New York: A.M. Kelley.

Bruni, L. (2002), 'A history of happiness in economics', Paper presented to the ESHET (European Society for the History of Economic Thought) Conference, Crete, March.

Cantillon, R. (1755 [1964]), *Essay on the Nature of Trade in General*, Eng. trans. by H. Higgs, New York: A.M. Kelley.

Chalmers, T. (1832 [1968]), *On Political Economy in Connexion with the Moral State and Moral Prospects of Society*, New York: A.M. Kelley.

Craig, J. (1821 [1970]), *Remarks on Some Fundamental Questions in Political Economy*, New York: A.M. Kelley.

Davanzati, B. (1588 [1696]), *A Discourse Upon Coins*, Eng. trans. by John Toland, London: Printed by J.D. for Awnsham and John Churchill.

Drakopoulos, S. (1994), 'Hierarchical choice in economics', *Journal of Economic Surveys*, **8**, 133–53.

Drakopoulos, S. and A. Karayiannis (2004), 'The historical development of hierarchical behaviour in economic thought', *Journal of the History of Economic Thought*, **26**, 363–78.

Duesenberry, J. (1949), *Income, Saving, and the Theory of Consumer Behavior*, Cambridge, MA: Harvard University Press.

Earl, P. (1986), *Lifestyle Economics*, Brighton: Wheatsheaf Books.

Easterlin, R. (1974), 'Does economic growth improve the human lot? Some empirical evidence', in P.A David and M.W. Reder (eds), *Nations and Households in Economic Growth: Essays in Honor of Moses Abramovitz*, New York: Academic Press, 89–125.

Elster, J. (1998), 'Emotions and economic theory', *Journal of Economic Literature*, **36**, 47–74.

Frank, R. (1985), *Choosing the Right Pond*, Oxford and New York: Oxford University Press.

Frank, R. (1999), 'The frame of reference as a public good', *Economic Journal*, **107**, 1832–47.

Frey, B. and A. Stutzer (2002), 'What economists can learn from happiness research?', *Journal of Economic Literature*, **40**, 402–35.

Harris, J. (1757 [1966]), 'An essay upon money and coins', in J.R. McCulloch (ed.), *A Select Collection of Scarce and Valuable Tracts on Money*, 1856, New York: A.M. Kelley.

Hodgskin, T. (1825 [1969]) *Labour Defended against the Claims of Capital*, New York: A.M. Kelley.

Hume, D. (ed.) (1970), *Writings on Economics*, edited by E. Rotwein, Madison, WI: University of Wisconsin Press.

Johnson, A. (1813 [1968]), *An Inquiry into the Nature of Value and of Capital*, New York: A.M. Kelley.

Karayiannis, A.D. (2000), 'Robert Torrens on technological progress', *History of Economic Ideas*, **8** (2), 63–94.

Karayiannis, A.D. (2001), 'Behavioural assumptions in Nassau Senior's economics', *Contributions to Political Economy*, **20**, 17–29.

Keynes, J. (1973), *The General Theory of Employment Interest and Money*, London: Macmillan.

Lane, R. (2000), *The Loss of Happiness in the Market Democracies*, New Haven, CT: Yale University Press.

Lauderdale, J.M. (1804 [1966]), *An Inquiry into the Nature and Origin of Public Wealth and into the Means and Causes of its Increase*, New York: A.M. Kelley.

Lloyd, W.F. (1833 [1968]), 'A lecture on the notion of value as distinguished not only from utility, but also from value in exchange', in Lloyd, *Lectures on Population Value, Poor-Laws and Rent*, 1837, New York: A.M. Kelley.

Locke, J. (1691 [1991]), 'Some considerations of the consequences of the lowering of interest and raising the value of money', in P. Hyde Kelly (ed.), *Locke on Money*, Oxford: Clarendon Press.

Loewenstein, G. (1999), 'Because it is there: the challenge of mountaineering for utility theory', *Kyklos*, **52**, 315–43.

Longfield, M. (1834 [1971]), 'Lectures on political economy', in R.D. Collison Black (ed.), *The Economic Writings of Mountifort Longfield*, New York: A.M. Kelley.

Malthus, T.R. (1815 [1970]), 'An inquiry into the nature and progress of rent, and the principles by which it is regulated', in *The Pamphlets of Thomas Robert Malthus*, New York: A.M. Kelley.

Malthus, T.R. (1820 [1986]), *Principles of Political Economy Considered with a View to their Practical Application*, 2nd edn 1836, Fairfield: A.M. Kelley.

Mandeville, B. (1724 [1970]), *The Fable of the Bees*, Middlesex: Penguin Books.

Marx, K. (1867 [1954]), *Capital*, Vol. I, London: Lawrence & Wishart.

Mason, R. (1998), *The Economics of Conspicuous Consumption: Theory and Thought since 1700*, Cheltenham, UK and Lyme, USA: Edward Elgar.

Mason, R. (2002), 'Conspicuous consumption in economic theory and thought', in E. Fullbrook (ed.), *Intersubjectivity in Economics: Agents and Structures*, London and New York: Routledge, 85–104.

McCulloch, J.R. (1825 [1965]), *The Principles of Political Economy*, 5th edn 1864, New York: A.M. Kelley.
McCulloch, J.R. (1826 [1967]), *A Treatise on the Circumstances which Determine the Rate of Wages and the Condition of the Labouring Classes Including an Inquiry into the influence of Combinations*, 2nd edn 1854, New York: A.M. Kelley.
Mill, J. (1821 [1965]), *Elements of Political Economy*, 3rd edn 1844, New York: A.M. Kelley.
Mill, J.S. (1848 [1976]), *Principles of Political Economy*, 7th edn 1871, Fairfield: A.M. Kelley.
Myint, H. (1948 [1965]), *Theories of Welfare Economics*, New York: A.M. Kelley.
Newman, S. (1835 [1973]), *Elements of Political Economy*, Clifton: A.M. Kelley.
Opdyke, G. (1851 [1973]), *A Treatise on Political Economy*, Clifton: A.M. Kelley.
Oswald, A. (1997), 'Happiness and economic performance', *Economic Journal*, **107**, 1815–31.
Perrotta, C. (1997), 'The preclassical theory of development: increased consumption raises production', *History of Political Economy*, **29**, 295–326.
Putnam, R. (2000), *Bowling Alone*, New York: Simon & Schuster.
Rae, J. (1834 [1964]), *Statement of Some New Principles on the Subject of Political Economy*, New York: A.M. Kelley.
Raymond, D. (1823 [1964]), *The Elements of Political Economy*, Vol. I, New York: A.M. Kelley.
Read, S. (1829 [1976]), *Political Economy an Inquiry into the Natural Grounds of Right to Vendible Property or Wealth*, Fairfield: A.M. Kelley.
Ricardo, D. (1817 [1951]), *On the Principles of Political Economy and Taxation*, 3rd edn 1821, edited by P. Sraffa, M. Dobb: *The Works and Correspondence of David Ricardo*, Vol. I, Cambridge: Cambridge University Press.
Rogers, E. (1822 [1976]), *An Essay on Some General Principles of Political Economy on Taxes upon Raw Produce and on Commutation of Tithes*, Fairfield: A.M. Kelley.
Rousseau, J.J. (1758 [1973]), 'A discourse on political economy', in J.J. Rousseau, *The Social Contract and Discourse*, London: J.M. Dent & Sons.
Say, J.B. (1803 [1964]), *A Treatise on political economy, or The Production, Distribution and Consumption of Wealth*, Eng. trans. by C. Prinsep, 1821, New York: A.M. Kelley.
Say, J.B. (1821 [1967]), *Letters to Malthus*, New York: A.M. Kelley.
Scitovsky, T. (1976), *The Joyless Economy: An Inquiry into Human Satisfaction and Consumer Dissatisfaction*, Oxford: Oxford University Press.
Scrope, Poulet G. (1833 [1969]), *Principles of Political Economy deduced from the Natural Laws of Social Welfare and Applied to the Present State of Britain*, New York: A.M. Kelley.
Senior, N. (1827 [1966]), 'An introductory lecture on political economy', in *N. Senior: Selected Writings on Economics: A Volume of Pamphlets 1827–1852*, New York: A.M. Kelley.
Senior, N. (1829 [1966]), 'Two lectures on population with a correspondence between the author and T.R. Malthus', in *N. Senior: Selected Writings on Economics: A Volume of Pamphlets 1827–1852*, New York: A.M. Kelley.
Senior, N. (1831 [1966]), *Three Lectures on the Rate of Wages*, New York: A.M. Kelley.
Senior, N. (1836 [1965]), *An Outline of the Science of Political Economy*, New York: A.M. Kelley.
Senior, N. (1852 [1966]), 'Four introductory lectures on political economy', in *N. Senior: Selected Writings on Economics: A Volume of Pamphlets 1827–1852*, New York: A.M. Kelley.
Sismondi, J.C. Simonde de (1815 [1966]), *Political Economy*, New York: A.M. Kelley.
Sismondi, J.C. Simonde de (1826 [1966]), 'Preface to New Principles of Political Economy', in *J.C. Simonde de Sismondi: Political Economy and the Philosophy of Government*, New York: A.M. Kelley.
Smith, A. (1759 [1976]), *The Theory of Moral Sentiments*, edited by D.D. Raphael and A.L. Macfie, Oxford: Clarendon Press.
Smith, A. (1762–63 [1978]), *Lectures on Jurisprudence*, edited by R. Meek, D. Raphael and P. Stein, Oxford: Clarendon Press.
Smith, A. (1776 [1976]), *An Inquiry into the Nature and Causes of the Wealth of Nations*, edited by R.H. Campbell and A. Skinner, Oxford: Clarendon Press.
Steuart, Sir J. (1767 [1966]), *An Inquiry into the Principles of Political Economy*, edited by A. Skinner, Edinburgh: Oliver & Boyd.
Thompson, W. (1824 [1963]), *An Inquiry into the Principles of the Distribution of Wealth most Conductive to Human Happiness*, New York: A.M. Kelley.

Torrens, R. (1815 [1972]), *An Essay on the External Corn Trade*, new edn 1829, Clifton: A.M. Kelley.
Torrens, R. (1834 [1969]), *On Wages and Combination*, New York: A.M. Kelley.
Tucker, G. (1837 [1964]), *The Laws of Wages, Profits and Rent*, New York: A.M. Kelley.
Turgot, A.R. (1766 [1973]), 'Reflections on the formation and distribution of wealth', in R. Meek (ed.), *Turgot on Progress, Sociology, and Economics*, Cambridge: Cambridge University Press.
Veblen, T. (1899), *The Theory of the Leisure Class*, New York: Prometheus Books.
Veenhoven, R. (1991), 'Is happiness relative?', *Social Indicators Research*, **24**, 1–34.
Veenhoven, R. (2000), 'Freedom and happiness: a comparative study in forty-four nations in the early 1990s', in E. Diener and E. Suh (eds), *Culture and Subjective Well-Being*, Cambridge, MA: MIT Press, 257–88.
Vethake, H. (1844 [1971]), *The Principles of Political Economy*, New York: A.M. Kelley.
Whately, R. (1832 [1966]), *Introductory Lectures on Political Economy*, New York: A.M. Kelley.
Wright, R. (2000), *Nonzero: The Logic of Human Destiny*, New York: Pantheon Books.

4 Jeremy Bentham's quantitative analysis of happiness and its asymmetries
Marco E.L. Guidi

1. Introduction

Jeremy Bentham (1748–1832) is universally recognized among philosophers as the founding father of utilitarianism, and among economists as a forerunner of rational choice theory. However, his analysis is often judged primitive and naive. Among the main objects of this negative evaluation, the hedonistic content of his psychology and his cardinalist approach to the measure of value rank first. It is generally assumed that Bentham simplistically believed in the measurability of feelings, implying *inter alia* homogeneity and symmetry between pain and pleasure, perfect substitutability among pleasures of different kinds, interpersonal comparison of utility, and an additive social welfare function. Moreover, Bentham's emphasis on probability and remoteness as 'dimensions' of pleasure and pain and the central role attributed to expected utility in his theory of motivation are almost universally ignored.

In order to rescue Bentham from this reductive appraisal, some interpreters, including myself (Guidi 1991: 91), have argued that 'Bentham himself was clearly always more interested in quality than in quantity' (Harrison 1983: 149). It is also contended that Bentham was increasingly sceptical about the feasibility of the 'felicific calculus' (Dinwiddy 1989), whose features he had outlined in chapter 4 of *An Introduction to the Principles of Morals and Legislation* (hereafter *IPML*) (Bentham [1789] 1970), a work privately printed as early as 1780 and published in 1789. According to this interpretation, Bentham moved from quantity to a taxonomic approach applied to the species of pleasure and pain as 'motives' of action, which he did in a systematic way in *A Table of the Springs of Action*, printed in 1815 and published in 1817 (hereafter *Table*) (Bentham [1815] 1983). Some recent contributions (Lapidus and Sigot 2000; Sigot 2001), have suggested a different interpretation, according to which Bentham's mounting interest in the taxonomy of pleasures and pains did not imply mistrust of quantitative analysis: it was simply a sign of his refutation of cardinal utility, ending up in a very peculiar 'ordinalist' approach.

This chapter argues instead that Bentham's quantitative approach always remained cardinalist, and that he constantly considered it an essential element of the analysis of individual and collective happiness. Bentham's conception of happiness – from *IPML* to *Deontology*, a work he wrote from 1814 to 1831 (Goldworth 1983: xxi–xxii) – was based on a notion of 'well-being' as balance between pleasures and pains. This conception required a measure as exact as possible of all the 'psychological phenomena' belonging to what Bentham called 'mental pathology', although he was conscious of some important strictures of hedonistic calculation. But the central aim of this chapter is to show that Bentham's approach to the measure of happiness was based on an elaborate reflection on the problem of the *substitutability* and *symmetry* between pleasure and pain, which implied an answer to the question of the predominance of happiness or suffering in human life. This question was the object of lively debate among sensationalist philosophers in the seventeenth and eighteenth centuries. Bentham's answer was both speculative and practical, indicating the moral and political strategies that were apt to increase the balance of well-being.

Of course, the analysis provided by the present chapter does not exhaust all the aspects related to Bentham's conception of happiness. Questions concerning, for instance, the standard of evaluation (total utility versus the utility of the majority) and distributive issues (Kelly 1990) are largely outside the scope of this chapter.

As to its division, Section 2 examines Bentham's opposition between the notion of 'happiness' and that of 'well-being', a notion which implies a quantitative assessment of pleasure and pain. It also highlights Bentham's doubts on the feasibility of the 'felicific calculus', especially those connected with direct measurability and interpersonal comparison. Section 3 discusses Bentham's revision of the traditional view that considered pain as the fundamental motive of action, an approach which implied the conclusion that pain prevails in human life. Bentham more optimistically emphasized the role of pleasures of expectation and argued in favour of the perfect substitutability and symmetry between pleasure and pain. Section 4 shows, however, that Bentham himself discovered some asymmetries between pleasures and pains. Some pains, like the pain of loss, should be considered as more intense than the corresponding pleasures. These asymmetries challenged Bentham's optimistic views on happiness. Finally, the concluding remarks highlight some answers Bentham gave to this problem. On the one hand, the central role of legislation should consist in providing the security of expectations, while, on the other, the utilitarian 'deontologist' should encourage the exercise of virtues, especially of beneficence inspired by benevolence. These answers show that Bentham's fundamental problem, both in politics and in private morality, was that of the conciliation of interest with duty. This makes his utilitarian ethics coincide with a sophisticated and extended theory of rational behaviour.

2.   Well-being versus happiness: a quantitative approach

'Nature has placed mankind under the governance of two sovereign masters, *pain* and *pleasure*. It is for them alone to point out what we ought to do, as well as to determine what we shall do . . ... The *principle of utility* recognises this subjection, and assumes it for the foundation of that system, the object of which is to rear the fabric of felicity by the hands of reason and of law' (Bentham [1789] 1970: 11, original italics). These well-known statements put at the opening of *IPML* connect the fundamental rule of utilitarian ethics, the greatest-happiness principle, to a notion of good of which pleasure and pain are the only intrinsic content. Good – at an individual as well as at a social level – is therefore happiness, and happiness is a 'balance' between the sum of pleasures enjoyed by the individuals in question, and the sum of their pains.

When, towards the end of his life, Bentham writes his work on 'private' ethics entitled *Deontology*, it appears to him that the best way of emphasizing the exact quantitative nature of this hedonistic conception consists in coining a neologism – 'well-being' – opposed to the traditional notion of 'happiness':

> For clearness of discourse and conception, it is absolutely necessary to have some word by which the *difference* in *value* between the sum of the pleasures of all sorts and the sum of the pains of all sorts, which down to the point of time (suppose the end of his life) a man has experienced, may be designed. (Bentham [1814–1831] 1983: 130, original italics)

This term is 'the net amount of his well-being – or, more briefly, his clear well-being', if the difference is 'on the pleasure side of the account'. Otherwise, we may speak of 'ill-being' (ibid.). It is exactly this character of quantitative balance – 'this sort of economy', as Bentham significantly calls it (ibid.: 122) – that is wanting in the common-sense notion of 'happiness':

> Instead of *well-being*, the word 'happiness' will not be equally suitable to the purpose. It seems not only to lay pain in all its shapes altogether out of the account, but to give it to be understood that whatsoever have been the pleasures that have been experienced, it is in a high and as it were superlative degree that they have been experienced. (Ibid.: 130, original italics)

As Bentham maintains in chapter 4 of *IPML*, this relativistic notion of happiness immediately raises the question of the value of pleasures and pains. As is well known, the core of Bentham's theory of value is represented by the analysis of its 'elements' or 'dimensions' of pleasures and pains. In a short manuscript note of the early 1780s published by Elie Halévy ([1901–1903] 1995: I, 302), entitled 'Value of pain and pleasure', this connection is explicitly stated:

Body, to exist, must in like manner possess those things: length, breadth and thickness . . . . By them it is *measured*. Mathematicians call them its *Dimensions*. 'Dimension' comes form 'Dimetior', or 'to measure'.

Of Mathematicians then let us borrow the appellation: and let us begin with saying: Pleasure is comprised under two dimensions, *Intensity* and *Duration*. (Original italics)

The rest of this draft contains the list of dimensions of pleasure and pain that Bentham expounds both in *IPML* (Bentham [1789] 1970: 38–9) and in *Table* (Bentham [1815] 1983: 88–9): 'certainty or uncertainty', or 'probability', 'propinquity or remoteness', 'fecundity' (that is, 'the chance it has of being followed by sensations of the same kind'),[1] 'purity' (that is, 'the chance it has of not being followed by sensations of the opposite kind'),[2] and 'extent', that is, the number of persons involved (Bentham [1789] 1970: 39). After calculating the value of pleasures and pains at an individual level following these dimensions except the last, the total value of social happiness is derived as the linear sum of individual balances (ibid.: 39–40). This obviously implies a cardinal measure of value. In an early manuscript partially published by Halévy ([1901–1903] 1995: I, 300–308), and then integrally transcribed by David Baumgardt (1952: 554–66),[3] Bentham engages in a detailed analysis of the conditions required for measuring utility. Reasoning in arithmetic rather than infinitesimal terms, he first examines the continuity of the function of pleasure and pain, by considering the divisibility of intensity. 'The limit of the quantity of a pleasure in respect of intensity on the [var.: this] side of diminution – he argues – is a state of indifference [var.: insensibility]'. Bentham then defines as 'unity' such a 'degree of intensity possessed by that pleasure which is the faintest of any that can be distinguished to be pleasure' (ibid.: 555). Higher numbers represent higher degrees of intensity. He then repeats the same reasoning for duration and states that the limits of probability and remoteness are represented by certainty and presence, respectively, pointing out that 'the degrees of intensity and duration must be express'd by whole numbers: that of proximity and that of certainty by fractions' (ibid.: 556).

Bentham shows awareness of two connected problems: that of the unit in which utility can be measured, and that of decreasing marginal utility. Having stated that an 'instrument of pleasure' is any good or 'possession' in the hands of an individual, and that the value of goods is measured by 'their aptitude of producing pleasure', Bentham gets nearer to Marshall's notion of 'disposition to pay' by arguing that money is the unit of measure of such a value, 'being the pledge and representative of almost all the rest as a means of procuring them at any time' (ibid.: 558). Money is the 'direct' measure '[of] such pleasure . . . as is produced by the bestowal of money, and of such pain as is produced by the taking it away' (ibid.: 560), and an indirect measure 'of a pleasure or a pain produced by any other cause' (ibid.).[4]

Bentham then analyses the relationship between quantities of money and quantities of pleasure. His reconstruction of the notions of decreasing marginal utility and satiability is elaborate, albeit expressed in an arithmetic language:

> *One Guinea*, suppose, gives a man *one degree* of pleasure: it is not true by any means that a *million* of guineas given to the same man at the same time would give him a *million* of such degrees of pleasure. Perhaps not a thousand, perhaps not a hundred: who knows [var.: can say]? Perhaps not fifty. In large sums the ratio of pleasure to pleasure is in this way less than a ratio of money to money. There is no limit beyond which the quantity of money cannot go: but there are limits, and those comparatively narrow, beyond which pleasure cannot go. There are men whose pleasure the acquisition of a hundred guineas would carry to this utmost limit: [in margin: which borders upon distraction;] beyond which [var.: even with] is [var.: lies] pain: a hundred thousand could not carry it farther [var.: beyond]. (Baumgardt 1952: 559, original italics)

Unfortunately, Bentham sees satiability as an obstacle to the use of money as a measure of value, rather than a starting-point for elaborating a theory of value. For this reason, he resorts to the assumption that 'with respect to such proportions [var.: small quantities] as ordinarily occur, . . . *cæteris paribus* the proportion between pleasure and pleasure is the same as that between sum and sum' (ibid.). With this notable simplification, he recommends money as an instrument for a cardinal measure of pleasure and pain (ibid.: 559):

> The Thermometer is the instrument for measuring the heat of the weather: the Barometer the instrument for measuring the pressure of the Air. Those who are not satisfied with the accuracy of those instruments must find out others that shall be more accurate, or bid adieu to Natural Philosophy. Money is the instrument for measuring the quantity of pain and pleasure. Those who are not satisfied with the accuracy of this instrument must find out some other that shall be more accurate, or bid adieu to Politics and Morals. (Ibid.: 562)

As the above quotations suggest, Bentham is also aware of another difficulty related to interpersonal (and intertemporal) differences in the utility of money.[5] However, it is not clear whether this difference is simply due to comparative income – as Marshall ([1890] 1961: B. III; Ch. 3, 3) later assumed – or to a more radical difference in sensibility to pleasures and pains. In other works, though, Bentham discusses this problem from two different viewpoints: (i) quantitative differences in sensibility; and (ii) different sensibility to pleasures and pains of different qualities.

Let us first examine quantitative differences in sensibility. In a manuscript entitled *Considération d'un Anglais sur la composition des Etats généraux*, originally written in French in November 1788 as a response to the debate on the summons of the Etats généraux,[6] Bentham considers the 'relative degree of happiness of which different individuals are capable' (Halévy [1901–1903] 1995: I, 315). There may be differences both in the 'desire of happiness' and in the 'ability to judge what conforms to happiness' (ibid.: 316).[7] However, it is difficult 'to find some sign, or some evidence, whose probative quality be in this connection clear and manifest' (ibid.). And 'since no proof or measure of these differences can be provided, they cannot be taken into account' (ibid.). Therefore, 'we should start from the supposition that this degree is the same for all' (ibid.: 315). It is worth observing that Bentham draws from this 'supposition' the conclusion that every individual has in principle an equal right to vote. More in general, such an assumption is also preliminary to the calculation of collective utility:

> Assuming an operation whatsoever, whose character would consist in influencing the well-being of this society by adding to the collective mass of happiness that of a more or less considerable number of individuals who compose it, having to do with equal portions of happiness, the utility of this operation would be exactly proportional to this number. (Ibid.: 316)

But where Bentham gets closer to raising doubts on cardinal utility is in the analysis of interpersonal differences in sensibility to pleasures and pains of different species. In *Deontology*, Bentham ([1814–1831] 1983: 130) argues that: 'Quantity depends upon *general* sensibility, sensibility to pleasure and pain in general; quality upon *particular* sensibility: upon a man's being more sensible to pleasure or pain from this or that source, than to ditto from this or that other' (original italics). At an individual level the quality of one's own sensibility is known by introspection.[8] However, this is not so for interpersonal comparisons. In this case there is no direct evidence: only indirect evidence is available from 'countenance, gesture, deportment, contemporary conduct', and, to a lesser extent, from 'verbal account', which is, however, highly unreliable (ibid.). Bentham is therefore conscious that an external observer cannot guess exactly what is more conducive to the happiness of other individuals. Implicitly he also assumes that it is impossible to measure the exact quantity of satisfaction that different pleasures can afford to different individuals. This conclusion does not induce Bentham to dispose of the felicific calculus as an instrument for the evaluation of social welfare. However, it is evident that an aggregate cardinal measure of happiness is highly imperfect. As a consequence, he argues that there is at least a minimum level of non-interference that should be safeguarded: for Bentham it is an 'absurdity . . . in a case in which the agent himself were the only person whose well-being were in question [to] prescribe exactly the same line of conduct to be observed by every man' (ibid., p. 131). Generally speaking, 'every man is a better judge of what is conducive to his own well-being than any other man can be' (ibid.).

The latter conclusion seems to imply that a measure of aggregate happiness is necessary in extra-regarding matters. The fact that *A Table of the Springs of Action* contains many passages on the value of pleasures and pains shows that Bentham considered the classification of motives as an important step towards quantification. Making reference to his 'theory of fictions',[9] he explained that the names of motives are 'fictitious entities' that cannot be 'explained' through 'definition *per genus et differentiam*', since they have 'no superior genus'. Their meaning can be clarified only through the 'method of paraphrasis', that is, by reducing fictions to pleasures and pains, the only 'real entities' that are known to human minds (Bentham [1815] 1983: 74-9). The *Table* presents an attempt to reduce a whole world of 'psychological phenomena' (ibid.: 94) to a limited number of qualitatively different pleasures and pains. Moreover, as explained in *IPML* (Bentham [1789] 1970: 51-73), interpersonal differences in sensibility may be explained in terms of external and internal circumstances influencing sensibility.

But although these operations reduce the difficulty of interpersonal comparison, they do not remove the existence of different sensibilities to pleasures and pains. Bentham's approach to quantification is neither naively realistic nor dogmatic: admittedly, it is based on a set of simplifications, assumptions and 'axioms of mental pathology' that restrict human variability and provide the legislator and the 'deontologist' with a manageable albeit imperfect instrument for evaluating the consequences of their recommendations.[10]

3.   Symmetry restored: Bentham's criticism of Locke and Maupertuis
One of the pillars on which Bentham intended to build his quantitative approach was the perfect substitutability and full symmetry between pleasure-seeking and pain-avoidance against a tradition that stressed the ephemeral nature of pleasure and the prevalence of pain in human life.

The predominant versions of the sensationalist paradigm before Bentham were based on the assumption that every time a person receives an impulsion from an external force influencing his/her sensibility, that person cannot but feel pain. Pleasure is the limited sensation deriving from the re-establishment of psychological equilibrium, and human action is at one and the same time motivated and limited by this reaction to pain. Most human faculties – such as imagination – are only factors of instability, since they hint at pleasures that are unattainable by ordinarily constituted human beings; therefore, imagination must simply be repressed. A conclusion drawn by many authors was that humans should give up the unlimited pursuit of pleasures (especially those of the material kind) and cultivate more steady and satisfying 'pleasures of the mind', such as amity, goodwill and the love of science. Among the philosophers belonging to this tradition were John Locke, Etienne Bonnot de Condillac, Pierre Moreau de Maupertuis, Pietro Verri, Gianmaria Ortes and Antonio Genovesi (Guidi 1993, 1995).

Bentham's criticism was addressed especially to Locke and Maupertuis. According to Locke (1694: II, xx), sensations may be pleasurable, painful or indifferent. 'Good' is what increases pleasure or diminishes pain, while 'evil' is what diminishes pleasure or increases pain. Passions are but different modifications of simple sensations. One of these passions is uneasiness, the painful feeling experienced by individuals for the absence of some objects that are expected to be pleasurable. In the second edition of the *Essay on Human Understanding* (1694), uneasiness is indicated as the main spur to human action. Without the pain of privation, humans would make no effort to obtain what they desire, and they would languish in a state of inaction. This does not mean that individuals cannot achieve happiness. What is denied is the continuous and cumulative nature of this process: it is impossible to add pleasure to pleasure in an uninterrupted way, since a pain is always experienced before pleasure. Therefore – as Pietro Verri stressed in his 'Discorso sull'indole del piacere e del dolore' (1773, 2nd edn 1781) – every sensation of pleasure is as it were isolated, temporarily limited when not ephemeral, and interrupted by pains that it often provokes.

As Bentham himself recognizes (Baumgardt 1952: 557), Maupertuis's 'Essai de philosophie morale' played a decisive role in the history of felicific calculus. It is also remarkable that through Beccaria, Maupertuis influenced Bentham ([1829] 1983: 291). Maupertuis's definition of pleasure and pain was an extension of Locke's approach. Every painful sensation is the source of uneasiness and consequently of action. Conversely, pleasure is 'every perception in which [the mind] would like to persist, and during which it does not desire either to pass to another perception, or to sleep' (Maupertuis [1749] 1965: 201). Pleasure is therefore no more than 'a happy moment'. A consequence of this definition is that pleasure is considered as an undetermined and absolute sensation, unsusceptible of degrees. Moreover, since humans, while experiencing it, do not wish to pass to another sensation, they do not even desire greater pleasures.

With these definitions in mind, Maupertuis concluded that 'happy moments' are rare and short, and life is almost entirely dominated by pain. Unfortunately, humans try to rebel against this situation, and this rebellion makes their condition worse: a strong desire for everlasting happiness seizes their minds (ibid.: 202), and the fear of future distress governs their choices.

The expectation of pleasures is another cause of affliction, since it makes uneasiness border on frustration (ibid.: 222–4). Imagination is far from being a source of pleasure; on the contrary it dashes hope and drives humans to melancholy (ibid.: 227–8).

This analysis strongly oriented Maupertuis's ethical conclusions. Compared to the force of desires, Epicurean ethics is impossible: humans are not inclined to follow Epicure's precept to accept the greatest happiness they can achieve. Maupertuis preferred the Stoical suggestion to limit every unnecessary desire. But Stoical ethics was still a negative solution. A better suggestion consisted in discovering an object of desire that could limit frustration and produce, if not happiness, at least a permanent state of inner peace (Naudin 1975: 25): this was possible by replacing 'physical' with 'spiritual pleasures' deriving from 'the practice of justice' and 'the contemplation of truth' (Maupertuis [1749] 1965: 212–13). Christian uninterested love was a further degree of 'spiritual pleasure'. The 'sweetness' coming to the soul from this sentiment was the only medicine against melancholy.

Bentham's criticism of Locke and Maupertuis can be found in several passages of his work. The most suggestive among them are a page of an already mentioned early manuscript (Baumgardt 1952: 557), and a section of *Deontology* (Bentham [1814–1831] 1983: 130–33). Bentham refuses to consider the reduction of pain as the sole motive of individual efforts (ibid.: 132). This refusal also applies to uneasiness, the species of pain Locke had placed at the origin of human action. According to Bentham, pain is not a necessary condition for the emergence of pleasure. Individuals who are experiencing a pleasure can directly imagine another one and strive to attain it (ibid.: 133).

This conclusion was partially responsible for Bentham's decision to abandon the term 'happiness' in favour of 'well-being'. 'Happiness' could be intended as a 'superlative' degree of pleasure, whereas 'well-being' expressed the idea of a positive balance between pleasure and pain. Only this formulation could lead him to assert that most individuals live in a condition of well-being (Bentham [1814–1831] 1983: 130). Maupertuis's error consisted in a wrong definition of pleasure, according to which only the highest pleasures can be defined as such. Hence the conclusion that pain is the dominant sensation in human life (Baumgardt 1952: 557). Just like pains, pleasures can be graduated and cumulated. What is more important, the basic springs of action are not *present* pleasures and pains, but *expectations* of future pleasures. Expectations are not the causes of sufferings, but spurs inducing humans to improve their condition (Bentham [1814–1831] 1983: 133; see Guidi 1993).

The origins of Bentham's reformulation of sensationalist psychology can be traced back to Thomas Hobbes and Helvétius. But Bentham's systematic attempt functioned as a radical break in this tradition of thought. The description of a human world made up of dynamic individuals who anticipate future events and are engaged in a continuous effort of self-improvement was a real novelty.

In order to understand the relationship between Bentham's theory of expectations and his optimistic assessment of happiness, we must turn to his theory of motivation. The framework of this theory is provided in *IPML* (ch. 3) by the analysis of 'the four sanctions or sources of pain and pleasure', that is: (i) physical sources; (ii) popular opinions concerning the propriety of behaviour (the 'popular or moral sanction', a notion which shows some similarities with Adam Smith's 'impartial spectator'); (iii) legal and political regulations; and (iv) religious beliefs. In *Deontology*, applying the method of definition *per genus et differentiam*, Bentham ([1814–1831] 1983: 175–7) separates the 'political' sanction from the 'non-political'. The former is then differentiated into 'judicial' and 'administrative', while the non-political sanction is differentiated into 'collective' (the 'moral' or 'popular' sanction) and 'individual'. Finally, the 'individual sanction' is differentiated into 'retributive' (reciprocity in a narrow sense, that is, limited to single actions) and 'sympathetic' or 'antipathetic' (that is, sentiments of 'benevolence' and 'malevolence' towards others). Another chapter of *IPML* (ch. 6) examines the 'circumstances influencing sensibility'. These can be classified according to the 'sanctions', and range from health and strength to wealth, habitual occupation, moral opinions and moral biases. Among more complex circumstances, Bentham mentions sex, social class, education and the form of government.

This framework is necessary in order to introduce the analysis of the different 'qualities' of pleasures and pains (ch. 5 of *IPML*; *Table*). While the ultimate reason for action is the pursuit of happiness or well-being, the particular object of action depends on the combination of the external circumstances that influence sensibility. Bentham's classification of pleasures and pains in *IPML* is based on two characteristics: the persons involved (self-regarding and other-regarding feelings) and time. As shown in Table 4.1, time is the central feature of Bentham's approach, especially with regard to future (Bentham [1789] 1970: 42–6).

All pleasures are either of acquisition or of possession. The pleasure of novelty is the pleasure of acquisition belonging to the class of the pleasures of the senses. This class is in turn defined as the class of 'physical pleasures', in contrast to all other classes of 'mental pleasures' (Bentham [1789] 1970: 47). Pleasures of wealth, for instance, as far as they are distinct from the pleasures connected to the physical use of the 'matter of wealth', derive 'from the *consciousness* of possessing [or acquiring] any article or articles which stand in the list of instruments of enjoyment or security' (ibid.: 43,

Table 4.1   Species of pleasures in IPML

	Self-regarding	Extra-regarding
Enjoyment	Senses, novelty Wealth, skill, amity, reputation, power, religion (derivative pleasures) Memoir, imagination, association	Benevolence, malevolence
Expectation	Expectation of all the same pleasures mentioned above: 1. Particular of fixed expectations 2. Undetermined or floating expectations	
Relief from pain	'As many species as there are of pains'	

emphasis added). It can be observed that the structure of human sensibility is more composite with regard to 'mental pleasures' than to 'physical pleasures'. The former range from pleasures of possession, to pleasures of hope and altruistic feelings. Although from a merely quantitative viewpoint it may be true that 'pushpin is as good as poetry' (Bentham [1830] 1983: 139), the spiritual life is richer and more intense than the physical life.

The distinction between physical and mental pleasures is preliminary to that between pleasures of enjoyment and pleasures of expectation. The latter result from the anticipation of future events. Bentham underscores this intertemporal dimension by introducing a fundamental distinction between 'original pleasures', which are the object of perceptions, and 'derivative pleasures', which result from memory and imagination. Pleasures of memory derive from the recollection of past sensations 'exactly in the order and in the circumstances in which they were actually enjoyed or suffered' (Bentham [1789] 1970: 45; see [1815] 1983: 90); pleasures of imagination derive from memory, but sensations are incomplete and arranged in a different order: they may refer to past as well as to present and future events. Pleasures of expectation are a particular kind of those of imagination: they are 'the pleasures that result from the contemplation of any sort of pleasure, referred to time *future*, and accompanied with the sentiment of *belief*' (ibid., original italics).[11] There seems to be a difference of degree between imagination and expectations. Pleasures of imagination are the result of casual associations of ideas that affect the sphere of sensation and immediately influence the will, generating desires. Conversely, pleasures of expectation also involve the understanding, which anticipates future pleasures and performs a 'rational' analysis of the causal chains connecting past to present and upcoming events, thus producing a stronger

Table 4.2   Species of pain

		Self-regarding	Extra-regarding
Privation		'As many species as there are of pleasures' Desire, disappointment, regret	
Positive	Sufferance	Senses, awkwardness, enmity, 'ill-name', religion (derivative pains) Memory, imagination, association	Benevolence, malevolence
	Apprehension	Expectation of all the above species of pain, *including pains of privation*	

commitment of the will *sub specie* of persuasion and determination to act.[12] Crucial to this process is the Humean notion of 'belief', which implies that expectations are formulated according to the rules of causality (Hume [1739–1740] 1978: I, iii).

These remarks may explain why Bentham attributes to pleasures of expectation a key role as an inducement to action.[13] It is important to observe that pleasures of expectation are pleasures in themselves and are experienced during the whole interval between their conception and the ful-filment of expected events (and the 'pleasure of enjoyment' which eventu-ally they produce).

Turning to the classification of pains, its bidimensional structure largely corresponds to that concerning pleasures (Table 4.2, based on Bentham [1789] 1970: 46–9).

Bentham distinguishes between 'pains of privation' and 'positive pains'. Pains of privation are symmetric to pleasures of relief (ibid.: 46): as we shall see, they play an important role in human sensibility. Among positive pains, pains of sufferance correspond to pleasures of enjoyment, while pains of apprehension correspond to pleasures of expectation (ibid.: 45). However, pains of apprehension, like pains of memory and imagination, can refer both to positive pains and to pains of privation. Pains of priva-tion are of three types: pains of *desire*, *disappointment* and *regret*: signifi-cantly these pains, like the pains of apprehension, are also fundamentally grounded on expectations.[14] *Pains of desire* are felt 'when the enjoyment of any particular pleasure happens to be particularly desired, but without any expectation approaching to assurance' (ibid.: 46). *Pains of disappointment* are suffered when 'the enjoyment happens to have been looked for with a degree of expectation approaching to certainty, and that expectation is made suddenly to cease' (ibid.). Lastly, *pains of regret* concern past pleasures which are no longer felt, or pleasures which might have been enjoyed 'had such or such contingency happened, which, in fact, did not happen' (ibid.). Note that this classification makes no special room for Locke's 'uneasiness'. The 'pain of desire' is indeed a strong pain associated with a future pleasure, but the latter is not expected with a high degree of probability. Consequently, this pain is not considered as a primary inducement to action: only pains of apprehension seem to play this role.

The central argument that action is essentially determined by the expectation of future pleasures or relief from pains is developed in chapter 10 of *IPML* and in *Table*. 'By a motive states Bentham ([1789] 1970: 96) . . . is meant any thing that can contribute to give birth to, or even to prevent, any kind of action'. Bentham focuses on those motives which act on the will (that is, 'practical motives'), because 'it is only on account of their tendency to produce either pain or pleasure, that any acts can be material' (ibid.).

Motives can be either internal or external, either 'in *esse*' or 'in *prospect*'. The latter distinction is essential.

> Motive refers necessarily to action. It is pleasure, pain, or other event, that prompts to action. Motive then, in one sense of the word, must be previous to such event. But, for a man to be governed by any motive, he must in every case look beyond that event which is called his action; he must look to the consequences of it: and it is only in this way that the idea of pleasure, of pain, or of any other event, can give birth to it. He must look, therefore, in every case, to some event posterior to the act in contemplation: an event which as yet exists not, but stands only in prospect. (Ibid.: 98)

We are thus led to the core of the explanation of action (the example chosen is that of a fire):

> Of all these motives, that which stands nearest to the act, to the production of which they all contribute, is that internal motive in *esse* which consists in the expectation of the internal motive in prospect: the pain or uneasiness you feel at the thoughts of being burnt. (Ibid.: 98–9)

Ironically, the example chosen by Bentham – based on an expectation of pain – involves the feeling of 'uneasiness'. However, this motive is not the Lockean need of some pleasure which is not present, but the simple 'apprehension' of future pain.[15] Generally speaking, the role Bentham attributes to pleasures of expectation is predominant. As he states in 'The rationale of reward': 'what are all the other sources of enjoyment, when put in competition with hope?' (Bentham [1825] 1838–1843: 201).[16]

In *Table*, Bentham's theory of motivation is apparently more complex: an individual who is enjoying a pleasure, in order to conceive of a future pleasure must be under the influence of at least one of the following 'psychological phenomena': interest, desire, aversion (of the prospect of not having it); want; hope; fear (of not obtaining it). Desire, rather than expectation, is defined here as the 'efficient' cause of action (Bentham [1815] 1983: 94). However, the logical difference and independence between desires and expectations is not clearly stated: both refer to 'derivative' (future) pleasures and their 'expected causes' (ibid.: 92), and both require imagination. The only difference seems to be that fears and hopes are also accompanied by an intense persuasion of the future existence of a pleasure. Therefore, an individual may feel either a simple desire, which is a *pleasure of imagination* acting as a motive, or a hope (fear), which is a pleasure of imagination accompanied by a belief, that is, a *pleasure of expectation*. Hope seems to be a livelier state of mind than simple desire and, in so far as it exists, it replaces, as it were, the corresponding desire. Moreover, in another passage of *Table* Bentham still argues that 'nothing but the expectation of the eventual enjoyment of pleasure in some shape, or exemption from pain in some shape, can operate in the character of a motive' (ibid.: 105). The difference between desire and want (which is pain, in so far as it is unsatisfied) (ibid.: 90) clearly illustrates the central place of conscious expectations of pleasures in human motivation: a want is defined as something objectively, or better unconsciously needed, whereas a desire implies the consciousness of this need: 'Exposed to danger, a man has *need* of, and so far is in *want* of, all necessary means of safety, but so long as he is ignorant of the danger, he has no *desire* of or for any of them' (ibid.: 92, original italics).

These conclusions can be considered as the accomplishment of Bentham's critique of Locke and Maupertuis. Bentham's belief that wellbeing, that is, a positive balance between pleasures and pains, is the most probable condition of human life seems to be based on the role played by pleasures of imagination and pleasures of expectation in structuring motivation and action. Let us revert to the analysis of the value of pleasures and pains, 'axiomatically' calculated on the ground of the theory of dimensions. Since both desires and hopes are the fruit of imagination and are not 'original', that is, present pleasures, they are invested by the dimensions of remoteness and probability. Remoteness seems to be connected to imagination, hence to desires. Probability seems to be connected to the judgement of future fulfilment, and therefore to expectation as distinguished from pure imagination. According to Bentham's definitions, this implies that the value of pleasures of imagination and expectation is a fraction of that of the corresponding pleasure of enjoyment. However, a desire is a pleasure as a *means*, which 'promises to be contributory to the attainment of the *end* (that is, to the possession of the *pleasure* or the *exemption* which is the main object of the *desire*)'. It therefore 'operates in the character of an *incentive*, i.e. a *motive*: viz. by giving increase to the apparent *value* of the good in respect to *certainty*' (ibid.: 93, original italics). Hence a desire functions as an *incentive*, either reducing the remoteness or increasing the probability of the expected pleasure. Consequently, a desire (and still more a hope) is a state of mind that reduces the difference of value between a pleasure of enjoyment and a pleasure of imagination or expectation. This 'boosting' effect explains why desires and expectations, rather than needs and uneasiness, are so constant and universal springs of action.

But the constant presence in the human mind of these feelings is the main cause that makes happiness highly probable. Let us consider a single moment in the life of a person. The value of this moment is the result of a balance between different types of pleasures and pains felt at that moment: (a) pleasures of enjoyment; (b) pains of sufferance (including wants and pains of labour connected to action); (c) desires (pleasures of imagination); (d) aversions; (e) pleasures of hope; and (f) pains of fear. The possibility for the value of this moment to be positive is *ceteris paribus* connected to the intensity and duration of (a) to (f) and to the remoteness and probability of (c) to (f). But it is indirectly connected to the *constancy* and *duration* of pleasures of expectation and of desires, since these pleasures, which are means to action, are perceived during the whole period between the conception of a pleasure as an end, and its enjoyment (if any). In more detail: (i) 'original' pleasures (a) and pains (b) may exist or not at this moment; (ii) pains (b) may overbalance pleasures (a); and (iii) wants, aversions and fears may be felt or not according to circumstances. But it is fairly certain that at this very moment there are some pleasures of expectation and desires 'in action', and probably more than one. Their presence, therefore, may offset even an intense pain suffered at this moment. As Bentham puts it, '*Want* bears a common reference to pleasure and to pain; satisfied, it produces pleasure; unsatisfied, pain; though capable of being overbalanced by the pleasure of *hope*, i.e. of *expectation*' (ibid.: 90, original italics).

If we increase the time unit, the probability of meeting with pleasures and pains of type (a) and (b) is higher, and the balance between them depends on their comparative intensity, duration and other dimensions. But pleasures of expectations are still there, and (however intense) they are always *durable*, probably as long as the period considered, or they are replaced by other expectations in case of fulfilment or even of disappointment. As

Bentham clearly states in 'The rationale of reward' dealing with the award-ing of meritorious services:

> If there be the pain of disappointment after trial, there has been the pleasure of expectation before trial; and the latter, there is reason to believe, is upon an average much greater than the former. The pleasure is of longer continuance; it fills a larger space in the mind; and the larger, the longer it continues. The pain of disappointment comes on in a moment, and gives place to the first dawning of a new hope, or is driven out by other cares. If it be true, that the principal part of happiness consists in hope, and that but few of our hopes are completely real-ized, it would be necessary, that men might be saved from disappointment, to shut them out from joy. (Bentham [1825] 1838–1843: 226–7)

Lastly, hopes and desires are also endowed with a peculiar dimension of 'fecundity'. Two crucial economic variables like effort and invention, from which the growth of wealth and welfare depends, are stimulated by the expectation of future pleasures:

> It is the property of hope, one of the modifications of joy, to put a man, as the phrase is, into spirits; that is, to increase the rapidity with which the ideas he is conversant about succeed each other, and thus to strengthen his powers of com-bination and invention, by presenting to him a greater variety of objects. The stronger the hope, so that it have not the effect of drawing the thoughts out of the proper channel, the more rapid the succession of ideas; the more extensive and varied the trains formed by the principle of association, the better fed, as it were, and more vigorous, will be the powers of invention. In this state, the atten-tion is more steady, the imagination more alert, and the individual, elevated by his success, beholds the career of invention displayed before him, and discovers within himself resources of which he had hitherto been ignorant.
>   On the one hand, let fear be the only motive that prompts a man to exert himself, he will exert himself just so much as he thinks necessary to exempt him from that fear, and no more: but let hope be the motive, he will exert himself to the utmost. (Ibid.: 205)

This reconstruction explains the reasons why Bentham is so optimistic concerning the happiness balance of whole lives and of whole communities (Bentham [1814–1831] 1983: 131).

> To better his condition to acquire for the future some means of enjoyment more than at present he is in possession of, is the aim of every man. Not perhaps in the character of a universal proposition, true: but for argument sake, be it so. What then does it prove? – that in other particulars be the balance on the side of well-being or of ill-being, an element of well-being is in the possession of every man – a pleasure of expectation – a pleasure of hope. (Ibid.: 132)

4. Asymmetry restated: pain of loss and pleasure of gain

As mentioned above, some interesting peculiarities of Bentham's quantita-tive approach to pleasure and pain are expressed in the form of 'axioms of

mental pathology'. The origin of these axioms dates back to the manuscripts on civil and penal law of the 1770s and 1780s published by Dumont
in 1801, and references to them can be found in almost all Bentham's texts
on economics, politics and law. A systematic analysis of these 'axioms' was
attempted in 'Pannomial fragments', a text related to the composition of
the *Code* (Bentham [1830–1831], 1838–1843).

Some of the most significant are the following:

> The pleasure derivable by any person from the contemplation of pain suffered
> by another, is in no instance so great as the pain so suffered. (Ibid.: 225)

> So far as it depends upon wealth, – of two persons having unequal fortunes, he
> who has most wealth must by a legislator be regarded as having most happiness.
> (Ibid.: 228–9)

> The effect of wealth in the production of happiness goes on diminishing, as the
> quantity by which the wealth of one man exceeds that of another goes on
> increasing: in other words, the quantity of happiness produced by a particle of
> wealth (each particle being of the same magnitude) will be less and less at every
> particle. (Ibid.: 229)

These axioms are general propositions concerning quantitative relations
between types of pleasures and pains and between them and their sources.
Moreover, the first and the last highlight some general cases of *dispropor-
tion*: on the one hand, there is a difference in value between sympathetic and
antipathetic pleasures or pains and positive pleasures or pains; on the other
we have diminishing marginal utility. But perhaps the most intriguing of
these axioms goes as follows: 'It is worse to lose than simply not to gain'
(Bentham [1789] 1970: note 3). A passage of 'Institute of political
economy' more explicitly restates it as follows: 'by the nature and constitution of the human frame, sum for sum, enjoyment from gain is never equal
to suffering from loss' (Bentham [1800–1804] 1954: 348). Thus formulated,
this axiom implies that there exists a quantitative asymmetry between a
pleasure of acquisition and the correspondent pain of privation in the real-
location of a given good or benefit between two or more persons.[17]

A preliminary question concerns the epistemological nature of these
axioms. In the philosophical tradition, two opposed definitions of 'axiom'
stem, respectively, from Aristotle and from the Stoics. According to
Aristotle, axioms are self-evident and necessary statements that constitute
the ground of any theoretical reasoning. In the Stoical tradition, axioms
are 'what may be either true or false': their truth value can therefore be
'demonstrated' in some way.

Bentham explicitly discusses this question in the 'Preface' to *IPML*
(Bentham [1789] 1970: note 3), arguing that these statements 'have the same

claim to the appellation of axioms, as those given by mathematicians under that name; since, referring to universal experience as their immediate basis, they are incapable of demonstration, and require only to be developed and illustrated, in order to be recognised as incontestable'. The fact that axioms are based on 'universal experience' shows that Bentham attributes to them a truth value in terms of 'real entities' (that is, pleasure and pain). In *Constitutional Code*, the term 'axioms' is employed as a synonym of 'assumptions': 'These are expressive of certain supposed matters of fact: the existence of certain propensities in all human minds' (Bentham [1830] 1983: 118). Finally, in 'Pannomial fragments' the 'axioms of mental pathology' are defined as relationships between pleasures and pains on the one hand, and actions on the other. An axiom is:

> a proposition expressive of the consequences in respect of pleasure or pain, or both, found by experience to result from certain sorts of occurrences, and in particular from such in which human agency bears a part: in other words, expressive of the connexion between such occurrences as are continually taking place, or liable to take place, and the pleasures and pains which are respectively the result of them. (Bentham [1830–1831] 1838–1843: 224)

Therefore, since Bentham's definition of 'axioms' is proximate to the Stoical interpretation, which is in turn consistent with Newtonian empiricism, this implies that some kind of 'exposition' can be provided in order to justify them. The above quotation from *IPML* seems to suggest that such an explanation derives from their 'development' and 'illustration' in the logical contexts to which they are relevant. However, this does not necessarily mean *using* them as 'incontestable' assumptions: 'developing' them implies *exploring* the facts or 'real entities', that is, pleasures and pains, to which they are related. But since the formulation of these axioms already contains a 'real entity' as the subject of the propositions describing them, the appropriate method for their 'exposition' cannot be the 'method of paraphrasis' used for 'fictitious entities', that is, the method by which 'the name of the fictitious entity in question is made parcel of a *phrase*, which contains in it the correspondent and *expository* real entity' (Bentham [1815] 1983: 7, original italics).[18] It remains the classical method of analysis, whereby the pleasures and pains involved are reduced to their qualitative and quantitative component parts.

The case of the axiom stating that 'enjoyment from gain is never equal to suffering from loss' is particularly interesting. A first exposition of this axiom can be found in a passage of an early manuscript which had been translated into French by Camille Saint-Aubin[19] and published by Roederer in 1796 as an appendix to his edition of Cesare Beccaria's *Treatise on Crime and Punishment* translated by Morellet. In this text, published as

'Théorie des peines criminelles', the 'axiom' in question is defined as a set of 'principles' connected in a syllogistic chain:[20]

1. The more the hope is strong, the more the pain of disappointment is high.
2. The hope of keeping what a man has, is stronger than that of acquiring something more.
3. Hence, it is more unpleasant to lose, than simply not to gain.
4. Hence a reason for adjudicating a thing to a man who has a title to it, rather than to another who does not have it.
5. A title is a ground for hope. (Bentham 1796: 190–91)[21]

A minor difference between this formulation and the two quoted above is that here proposition (3) does not compare a pain of loss to a pleasure of acquisition, but a pain of loss to a pain of not acquiring something. In parallel, proposition (2) states that the pleasure of expectation of keeping something already possessed is in general stronger than the pleasure of expectation of *any* increase in possession. This point is in its turn explained by proposition (5), which asserts that the ground for such a difference in intensity may be given by an *entitlement*. So whereas, strictly speaking, the 'axiom' on asymmetry is presented in proposition (3), the syllogisms reveal that the essential quantitative difference is not primarily that between pains of loss and pleasures of acquisition (or pains of non-acquisition), but that between pleasures of expectation connected to pleasures of possession and pleasures of expectation connected to pleasures of acquisition. Note that proposition (2) states that pleasures of expectation associated with possession are *in every case* stronger than simple pleasures of expectation. Thus, this definition of the 'axiom on gain and loss' implies two typical elements of Bentham's philosophy: (i) his theory of value of pleasures and pains; and (ii) his classification of pleasures and pains of different kinds.

In a text connected with the composition of *Constitutional Code*, entitled *Official Aptitude Maximized; Expense Minimized*, Bentham introduces a distinction between 'fixed', and 'floating expectations' (Bentham [1830] 1993: 8–9), which helps us understand the role of disappointment in this connection. Fixed expectations must be considered as a 'technical' synonym of those expectations that, 'in ordinary language', are called 'vested interests' or 'vested rights' (ibid.: 36), and which result from established property rights (ibid.: 346). In contrast with them, 'floating' expectations correspond to all sorts of projects and desires concerning the improvement of future well-being.[22] Strictly speaking, as seen above, only fixed expectations are *expectations* in the strictest sense, since they are associated with a persuasion of their fulfilment. Floating expectations seem to be more similar to simple 'desires' as fruits of imagination. Hence, this distinction between 'fixed' and 'floating' expectations is central to the understanding of the nature of the 'axiom on loss and gain'. The reason why the disappointment of vested interests is so disruptive is that expectations result in this case from actual possession. Whereas the non-fulfilment of a pleasure of gain simply amounts to the disappointment of a typically floating expectation (and vice versa a pleasure of gain is simply the fulfilment of such an expectation), a pain of loss results from the disappointment of a fixed expectation, whose nature is that of a livelier sensation, and consequently whose value is higher than that of floating expectation.[23] To take a rather extreme example, the disappointment of my desire to buy a Ferrari is certainly less painful than that of my expectation to continue to possess the house in which I live. According to Bentham, the relation between a pleasure of gain and a corresponding pain of loss always presents a similar asymmetry.

A further reason that may explain the difference in intensity between a pleasure of fixed and a pleasure of floating expectation – which is implicit in the syllogisms of 'Théorie des peines criminelles' – relates to the dimension of 'probability': whereas a fixed expectation has a high probability of fulfilment, a floating expectation has a lower probability. So, the value of a given pleasure 'in prospect' being the same, its current (discounted) value is higher for those who are entitled to it.

These arguments can be strengthened by analysing the distinct pains and pleasures that compose, respectively, the pain of loss and the pleasure of gain. A loss consists at one and the same time in the loss of (i) a pleasure of enjoyment; (ii) a pleasure of possession (distinguished from the former since it is linked to the consciousness of possessing the object that produces such an enjoyment); and (iii) a pleasure of fixed expectation.[24] On the other hand, the acquisition of some thing, at the moment in which it is acquired, only consists in (i) a pleasure of enjoyment;[25] and (ii) a pleasure of floating expectation (the pleasure of acquisition). Of course, new pleasures of possession and expectation will ensue, but they are not relevant at the moment in which the gain takes place. Therefore, the weighting must always be made between two pleasures and the sum of three distinct and very strong 'pains of privation'.

Moving a step forward, the central role of disappointment in the pain of loss implicitly relates the loss–gain asymmetry to another important aspect of Bentham's analysis of pleasures and pains: the analysis of the consequences of actions, developed in *IPML* (ch. 12) and in other manuscripts from which Dumont drew the *Traités de législation civile et pénale* (Bentham [1801] 1829: II, 251–2). The issue of consequences is of primary importance in utilitarian ethics, since the latter belongs to the family of 'consequentialist' theories. However, significantly Bentham never deals with the problem in general terms: both the chapter of *IPML*, entitled 'Of the consequences of a mischievous act', and various passages of *Traités* develop this analysis only in negative terms, that is, in terms of 'evil' consequences.

Bentham distinguishes between consequences of the first order – or *primary* consequences – and of the second order – or *secondary* consequences. A primary consequence is the pleasure or pain enjoyed by a number of 'assignable' individuals, who are directly concerned by the action in question. A secondary consequence derives from the former, but it 'extends itself either over the whole community, or over some other multitude of unassignable individuals' (Bentham [1789] 1970: 143). As for the relation between secondary consequences and Bentham's theory of value of pleasures and pains, it is clear that the former appear when a pleasure or a pain of the first order is characterized by the two dimensions of 'fecundity' or 'purity'. As Bentham underlines, these dimensions are relevant 'when the value of any pleasure or pain is considered for the purpose of estimating the tendency of any *act* by which it is produced' (ibid.: 38–9, original italics). Moreover, the value of secondary consequences obviously depends on their 'extent', that is, on the 'multitude of unassignable individuals' who feel themselves affected by them, and finally – although Bentham is never explicit on this point – on the 'proximity' between the source of primary consequences and the persons involved.

But there are also some specificities on the qualitative side. Whereas primary consequences may result in every kind of pleasures and pains, secondary consequences are of two particular types only. On the one hand, they consist in a 'pain of apprehension': 'a pain grounded on the apprehension of suffering such mischiefs or inconveniences, whatever they may be, as it is the nature of the primary mischief to produce' (Bentham [1789] 1970: 144). Bentham defines this pain as 'alarm'. Note that the main cause of alarm is identified in pains of *disappointment* (Bentham [1830] 1993: 353).[26] On the other hand, any mischievous act produces an objective 'probability of pain', that is, the probability that the same pain may be suffered in the future 'in consequence of the primary mischief' (Bentham [1789] 1970: 144). This is the 'danger' of an act. The explanation of danger is connected to Bentham's theory of penal law, developed in *Traités* ([1801] 1829) and *Théories des peines légales* ([1811] 1830a), in particular to the relation between the probability of committing a crime and the measure and certainty of punishments. In 'Pannomial fragments', Bentham also introduces some effects 'of the third order' in turn generated by alarm, which bear a striking symmetrical resemblance to the advantageous effects of hope on productivity and inventiveness remarked above: these effects consist in the 'annihilation of existence by the certainty of the non-enjoyment of the fruit of labour, and thence the extinction of all inducement to labour' (Bentham [1830–1831] 1838–1843: 230).

Strictly speaking, the 'axiom on gain and loss' refers only to consequences of the first order. However, owing to the fact that a loss entails a strong feeling of disappointment, its social consequences may go well beyond it and generate those evils of the second and third order that diffuse insecurity and discourage labour and entrepreneurship. Therefore, taking the axiom in its broader social meaning, a pain of loss produces a supplement of pain of apprehension on a multitude of individuals.

All these specifications considered, it remains, however, that there may exist cases in which, from a purely quantitative viewpoint, a pleasure of acquisition proves to be *on the whole* (that is, all 'dimensions' and 'qualitative pleasures' included) greater than the correspondent pain of loss. At least, taking Bentham's theory of value, this case cannot a priori be excluded. Therefore, the 'axiom' cannot be rigorously deduced from Bentham's hedonistic psychology: it keeps that 'axiomatic' character that Bentham himself attributed to it.

The gain–loss asymmetry has an enormous importance in Bentham's ethical and political theory, since it shows that individuals evaluate their personal security and the security of their possessions more than any other pleasure.[27] More precisely, the existence of an asymmetry between pain and pleasure connected to pains of disappointment challenges Bentham's optimistic belief in the prevalence of happiness in human life. The legislator and the deontologist must know that their normative prescriptions must answer this fundamental need of the human frame.

5. Concluding remarks

A singular inner tension runs through Bentham's quantitative analysis of happiness. On the one hand, his definition of well-being as a balance between pleasures and pains and his critique of the pain-based versions of sensationalist philosophy make him conclude that happiness, relative happiness, is accessible to every individual and to humankind as a whole. On the other hand, the discovery of certain asymmetries between pain and pleasure, especially that between the pain of loss and the pleasure of gain, reveals that the existence of happiness is strictly subordinated to some institutional and social conditions, in the absence of which chaos and sufferings may prevail. Bentham's moral and political philosophy could be seen as an attempt to neutralize these potential evils that threaten human happiness.

As to Bentham's political and legal theory, in the work published by Dumont as *Principes du code civil*, the analysis of the 'axioms of mental pathology' is preliminary to a discussion on the relationships between equality and security as 'subordinate ends of government'. Bentham's conclusion is that: 'When security and equality are in opposition, there should be no hesitation: equality should give way. The first is the foundation of life – of subsistence – of abundance – of happiness, every thing depends on it. Equality only produces a certain portion of happiness' (Bentham [1801] 1838–1843: 311). In the writings connected to the composition of *Constitutional Code*, Bentham deduces from his distinction between 'fixed' and 'floating' expectations a normative rule denominated 'disappointment prevention principle' or 'non-disappointment principle'.[28] This principle is intended as a subordinate rule appended to the 'greatest-happiness principle'. Bentham ([1830] 1993: 342) considers it 'the chief and all-directing guide' in matters of retrenchment as well as 'of original distribution' (ibid.: 8, original italics). This central principle also functions as a check on the egalitarian implications of the principle of utility when associated with the 'axioms' concerning diminishing marginal utility.[29] Fixed expectations are connected to all activities of production and reproduction, and to the preservation of social order.[30] It is not an exaggeration to assert that expectations are the core of Bentham's political and economic theory.

Finally, moral education, a fruit of civilization, is equally important. The analysis of virtues developed in *Deontology* can be seen as an attempt to show how rational it is for individuals not only to adopt a prudential behaviour in self-regarding matters, but also to increase the scope of benevolence in their motivational framework. Bentham ([1814–1831] 1983: 184) regards beneficence motivated by benevolence as a contribution to a 'fund of general good-will', which is the ultimate guarantee of an increase of happiness.

Notes

1. In *Table* Bentham ([1815] 1983: 89) specifies that the fecundity of a pleasure, for an individual, 'is directly as the value of any pleasure or pleasures, *exemption* or exemptions, (viz. from pain), which, in case of his experiencing the pleasure, he will experience, otherwise not' (original italics).
2. In *Table* the purity of a pleasure is defined as 'inversely as the value of any *pain* or pains, *loss* or losses (viz. of *pleasure*), in such sort associated with it as that, in case of his experiencing the pleasure, a man will experience them, otherwise not' (Bentham [1815] 1983: 89, original italics).
3. The manuscripts transcribed by Halévy and Baumgardt are in University College, London, *Bentham Papers* (hereinafter UC) XXVII, 29–40. Douglas Long (1994) has demonstrated that they belong to an early unpublished work on 'Critical Jurisprudence' composed before *IPML*.
4. Bentham adds that also the value of non-marketable goods can be inferred by comparing the quantities of them that procure pleasures or pains that individuals consider equal to those procured by given quantities of marketable goods (Baumgardt 1952: 560).
5. 'There are it is true some men to whom the same sum would give more pleasure than to others: to the same man likewise the same sum would give more pleasure at one *time* than at another' (Baumgardt 1952: 559, original italics).
6. UC CLXX, 43–121. Halévy ([1901–1903] 1995: I, 314–21) published a fragment of this manuscript, entitled 'Représentation' (UC CLXX, 87–121).
7. Translations of passages from this manuscript are mine.
8. 'It may be known by the most impressive and infallible of all direct evidence, the evidence of a man's own senses' (Bentham [1814–1831] 1983, p. 130).

9. Bentham developed this theory in a manuscript partially published in Bowring's edition (Bentham 1838–1843, Vol. 8), and recently published in a bilingual edition (Bentham [1813–1814] 1997).
10. In some recent contributions, Lapidus and Sigot (2000) and Sigot (2001) have argued that this consciousness brought Bentham to discard the cardinalist approach. Their interpretation is based on two arguments. First, they enumerate some strictures of Bentham's quantitative analysis, especially those related to the mutual dependence between the 'dimensions' of pleasure and pain. They then argue that Bentham, conscious of these difficulties, was constrained to 'abandon the idea of a cardinal measure of utility in favour of their classification' (Sigot 2001: 20). The proof of this renunciation would be that in *IPML*, after a short chapter on the measure of utility, a series of more detailed chapters is devoted to the classification of the species of pleasure and pain, circumstances influencing sensibility, actions and so on. Second, they argue that the adoption of a taxonomic approach implied a drift towards an ordinal measure of utility. In order to achieve this result, Bentham had only to classify pleasures and pains by types, and then to assume that each individual orders these types according to their importance for the satisfaction of his/her needs. Sigot (2001) takes Bentham's statement that the value of different types of pleasures and pains varies from individual to individual according to circumstances as an attempt to go towards an ordering of pleasures and pains for each individual, and hence towards an 'ordinal' measure of utility. Both these arguments are questionable. First the inclusion in a published book of a chapter on the (cardinal) measure of utility proves that Bentham did not mean to abandon this part of his theory. Second, while it is evident that the existence of so many circumstances influencing sensibility makes the cardinal measure of utility actually complicated, the adoption of an 'ordinalist' approach would have required some explicit justification, which cannot be found either in *IPML* or in later works.
11. See Bentham ([1815] 1983: 90): Derived from imagination is expectation, 'if the conception formed of them be accompanied with a *judgement* more or less *decided* – a *persuasion* more or less *intense* – of the future realization of the pictures so composed' (original italics).
12. On the relationship between understanding and will in the process of motivation, see Bentham ([1789] 1970: 99; [1815] 1983: 92–3).
13. See Bentham ([1789] 1970: 99): 'Any objects, by tending to induce a belief concerning the existence, actual or probable, of a practical motive; that is, concerning the probability of a motive in prospect, or the existence of a motive *in esse*; may exercise an influence on the will . . .' (original italics).
14. The expression 'pleasures of hope' is synonymous with 'pleasures of expectation'. See Bentham ([1814–1831] 1983: 133).
15. Uneasiness is for Bentham almost a synonym of 'fear'. As a motive of action, it is of 'rougher' or inferior quality: it can be used by the legislator only in order to induce the respect of rules and the prohibition to perform certain actions, rather than a positive stimulus to improve one's well-being. This function of uneasiness is once again suggested in a passage of *Defence of Economy against the Right Honourable Edmund Burke*, a work first published in January 1817, and reprinted in 1830 as a part of *Official Aptitude Maximized; Expense Minimized*. This time, an explicit reference to Locke is made: 'In a certain sensation called *uneasiness*, Locke beheld, as his Essays tell us, the cause of everything that is done. Though on this occasion, with all his perspicuity, the philosopher saw but half his subject (for happily neither is pleasure altogether without her influence): sure it is that it is in the rougher spring of action that any ulterior operation, by which the constitution will be cleared of any on its morbific matter, will find its immediate cause' (Bentham [1830] 1993: 44–5, original italics).
16. In the French version edited by Dumont, the following nice comment is added to this statement: 'Elle donne la vie et le mouvement au monde moral; elle remplit les jours et les années, dont les plaisirs n'occupent que des instants fugitifs' (Bentham [1811] 1830b: 138).
17. The question is discussed in more detail in 'Principles of the civil code': Bentham ([1801] 1838–1843: 304–7).

18. 'Form of such a paraphrasis in the case of a right: "a man is said to have a right when, etc." ' (Bentham [1815] 1983: 7).
19. Saint-Aubin was a professor of public law and finance who taught in Germany and, after the Revolution, in France.
20. This text mentions 'the force of expectation, in matters of gain and loss', as one of the 22 'circumstances influencing sensibility' listed in it (Bentham 1796: 190). See also Bentham ([1789] 1970: 56).
21. Translations of passages from this text are mine.
22. Bentham ([1830] 1993: 8–9). Instead of a formal definition of 'floating expectations', Bentham proposes an example: 'Every solicitor, who sends a son of his to one of the Inns of Court, *expects* to see the same son on the Chancery Bench with the seals before him' (ibid., p. 8, original italics).
23. 'Under the circumstances under which a vested right is understood to have place, the expectation is regarded as being more intense than in the other case, so therefore the correspondent disappointment' (Bentham [1830] 1993: 357).
24. 'Possession or expectancy – in either of those two relative situations will be the subject-matter in question' (Bentham [1830] 1993: 342).
25. Note that the comparative value of this pleasure in the individual who loses and in the one who gains depends on the relative income of both, owing to decreasing marginal utility.
26. An important application of this theory of alarm is the analysis of general bankruptcy in the credit system, developed by Bentham in the manuscript 'Sur les prix' (1801). See Bentham [1801] 1954: 145–6; 161–4.
27. Probably for this reason, the classification of pains and pleasures provided in *Table* presents some interesting asymmetries. Bentham ([1815] 1983: 79–86) distinguishes here 14 classes of *pleasures and pains*, to which correspond an *interest*, and a series of *motives*. Differently from *IPML*, these classes are not grouped into more general categories. But the most interesting feature of this classification consists in the fact that some pains have no correspondent pleasure. While there are, for instance 'pleasures and pains of the taste' or 'pleasures and pains of sympathy', 'pains of labour' and 'pains of death' have no symmetric pleasure. Both are fundamental to human existence: while the former is related to the cost incurred in order to obtain other pleasures, the latter is related to the fundamental need of security.
28. As Bentham writes in his peculiar style: 'Correspondent to the import attached to the word *disappointment* is the import attached to the word *loss*. By the word loss is denoted the state of things which, with reference to the happiness of the individual in question, has place when, after having been the object of his expectation, anything considered in the light of [a] benefit fails to actually be, or about to be, in his possession' (Bentham [1830] 1993: 342–3).
29. On this point, see Parekh (1970).
30. Bentham considers the non-disappointment principle as the foundation of every 'prohibitory' law against offences.

References

Baumgardt, D. (1952), *Bentham and the Ethics of Today*, Princeton, NJ: Princeton University Press.
Bentham, J. ([1789] 1970), *An Introduction to the Principles of Morals and Legislation*, J.H. Burns and H.L.A. Hart (eds), London: Athlone Press.
Bentham, J. (1796), 'Théorie des peines criminelles', in C. Beccaria, *Traité des délits et des peines*, traduit de l'Italien par André Morellet, nouvelle édition corrigée précédée d'une correspondance de l'auteur avec le traducteur, accompagnée de notes de Diderot et suivie d'une *Théorie des lois pénales* par Jérémie Bentham, traduite de l'Anglais par Saint-Aubin, Paris: De l'imprimerie du Journal d'économie publique, de morale et politique.
Bentham, J. ([1800–1804] 1954), 'Institute of political economy', in Werner Stark (ed.), *Jeremy Bentham's Economic Writings*, Vol. 3, London: Allen & Unwin, 303–80.

Bentham, J. ([1801] 1829), *Traités de législation civile et pénale*, E. Dumont (ed.), 3 Vols, Paris: Bossange; reprinted in *Oeuvres de Jérémie Bentham*, Vol. 1, Brussels: Haumann; English translation of 'Principes du code civil' and 'Principes du code pénal', in Bentham (1838–1843), Vol. 1, 297–580.

Bentham, J. ([1801] 1954), 'The true alarm', in Werner Stark (ed.), *Jeremy Bentham's Economic Writings*, Vol. 3, London: Allen & Unwin, 61–216.

Bentham, J. ([1811] 1830a), *Théorie des peines et des récompenses*, Vol. 1, *Théorie des peines légales*, E. Dumont (ed.), Paris: Bossange; reprinted in *Oeuvres de Jérémie Bentham*, Vol. 2, Brussels: Haumann; English translation in Bentham (1838–1843), Vol. 2, 189–266.

Bentham, J. ([1811] 1830b), *Théorie des peines et des récompenses*, Vol. 2, *Des récompenses*, E. Dumont (ed.), Paris: Bossange; reprinted in *Oeuvres de Jérémie Bentham*, Vol. 2, Brussels: Haumann.

Bentham, J. ([1813–1814] 1997), *De l'ontologie et autres textes sur les fictions*, English edition by Ph. Schofield, translation and commentaries by J.-P. Cléro and Ch. Laval, Paris: Seuil.

Bentham, J. ([1814–1831] 1983), 'Deontology', in *Deontology, together with A Table of the Springs of Action and the Article on Utilitarianism*, A. Goldworth (ed.), Oxford: Clarendon Press, 117–281.

Bentham, J. ([1815] 1983), 'A Table of the Springs of Action', in *Deontology, together with A Table of the Springs of Action and the Article on Utilitarianism*, A. Goldworth (ed.), Oxford: Clarendon Press, 1–115.

Bentham, J. ([1825] 1838–1843), 'The rationale of reward', in *The Works of Jeremy Bentham*, J. Bowring (ed.), Vol. 2, Edinburgh: Tait, 189–266.

Bentham, J. ([1829] 1983), 'Article on utilitarianism', in *Deontology, Together with a Table of the Springs of Action and the Article on Utilitarianism*, A. Goldworth (ed.), Oxford: Clarendon Press, 283–328.

Bentham, J. ([1830] 1983), *Constitutional Code*, F. Rosen and J.L. Hume (eds), Oxford: Clarendon Press.

Bentham, J. ([1830] 1993), *Official Aptitude Maximized; Expense Minimized*, Ph. Schofield (ed.), Oxford: Clarendon Press.

Bentham, J. ([1830–1831], 'Pannomial fragments', in Bentham (1838–1843), Vol. 3, 211–230.

Bentham, J. (1838–1843), *The Works of Jeremy Bentham*, J. Bowring (ed.), 11 Vols, Edinburgh: Tait.

Dinwiddy, J.R. (1989), *Bentham*, Oxford and New York: Oxford University Press.

Goldworth, A. (1983), 'Editorial introduction', in Jeremy Bentham, *Deontology, together with A Table of the Springs of Action and the Article on Utilitarianism*, A. Goldworth (ed.), Oxford: Clarendon Press, xi–xxxvi.

Guidi, M.E.L. (1991), *Il sovrano e l'imprenditore, Utilitarismo ed economia politica in Jeremy Bentham*, Roma-Bari: Laterza.

Guidi, M.E.L. (1993), 'L'utilitarisme et les origines du savoir économique moderne: la thèse de la douleur, de Locke à Bentham', *Economies et sociétés*, Oeconomia. Histoire de la pensée économique, series, **18**, 33–65.

Guidi, M.E.L. (1995), *Pain and Human Action. Locke to Bentham*, Dipartimento di Studi Sociali, Università degli Studi di Brescia, DSS Papers STO 1-95, http://fausto.eco.unibs.it/~segdss/paper/guidi.pdf.

Halévy, E. ([1901–1903] 1995), *La formation du radicalisme philosophique*, 3 Vols, M. Canto-Sperber (ed.), Paris: PUF; English translation (not including the appendices), *The Growth of Philosophical Radicalism*, London: Faber & Faber, 1928.

Harrison, R. (1983), *Bentham*, London: Routledge & Kegan Paul.

Hume, D. ([1739–1740] 1978), *A Treatise of Human Nature*, L.A. Selby-Bigge and P.H. Nidditch (eds), Oxford: Oxford University Press.

Kelly, P.J. (1990), *Utilitarianism and Distributive Justice: Jeremy Bentham and the Civil Law*, Oxford: Oxford University Press.

Lapidus, A. and Sigot N. (2000), 'Individual utility in a context of asymmetric sensitivity to pleasure and pain: an interpretation of Bentham's *Felicific Calculus*', *European Journal of the History of Economic Thought*, **7**, 45–78.

Locke, J. ([1694] 1975), *Essay Concerning Human Understanding*, 1st edition, 1690, P.H. Nidditch (ed.), Oxford: Clarendon Press.
Long, D. (1994), 'A lost "magnum opus"? Bentham's *Elements of Critical Jurisprudence*', paper presented at the 4th ISUS (International Society for Utilitarian Studies) Conference, Tokyo, 27–29 August.
Marshall, A. ([1890] 1961), *Principles of Economics*, 9th (variorum) edn, C.W. Guillebaud (ed.), London: Macmillan.
Maupertuis, P. Moreau de ([1749] 1965), 'Essai de philosophie morale', in *Oeuvres*, Lyon, 1768, Vol. 1, reprinted with an introduction by G. Tonelli, Hildesheim: G. Olms.
Naudin, P. (1975), 'Une arithmétique des plaisirs? Esquisse d'une réflexion sur la morale de Maupertuis', in *Actes de la journée Maupertuis*, Paris: Vrin, 15–31.
Parekh, B. (1970), 'Bentham's theory of equality', *Political Studies*, **18**, 478–95.
Sigot, N. (2001), *Bentham et l'économie. Une histoire d'utilité*, Paris: Economica.
Verri, P. ([1781] 1964), 'Discorso sull'indole del piacere e del dolore', in *Del piacere e del dolore ed altri scritti di filosofia ed economia*, R. De Felice (ed.), Milan: Feltrinelli, 3–68.

5   Public happiness and civil society
Pier Luigi Porta and Roberto Scazzieri

1. Introduction

Happiness is a multifaceted concept whose roots may be traced back to philosophical anthropology. In particular, happiness has both an individual and a social dimension. The former is related to the sphere of feelings and moral sentiments. The latter is connected with moral sentiments and enabling conditions. The social dimension of happiness is linked with the individual dimension primarily through the existence of a sphere of interactions that is specifically associated with the social recognition of a certain class of individual feelings and achievements.

Public happiness may be associated with a constellation of *enabling conditions*, by which individuals (and social groups) find that their purposes are mutually recognized and their capabilities turned into actual 'functionings' (Sen 1985). The structure of public happiness calls attention to the role of social knowledge and institutions. The former translates private feelings into socially recognized codes of behaviour. The latter turns 'socially admissible' purposes into a set of feasible choices and actions.

The above perspective suggests that public happiness is associated with the interplay of cultural beliefs and social opportunities. Civil society is a sphere of possible outcomes resulting from the 'horizontal' interactions of individuals (or social groups). It may be considered as a virtual setting in which individuals (or groups) 'take up a position' relative to one another in virtue of a particular structure of admissible events.

The structure of the chapter is as follows. Section 1 introduces a conceptual framework in which public happiness is discussed from the point of view of the interaction between beliefs and social opportunities. Section 2 suggests that alternative ways to match beliefs and opportunities may be associated with radically different levels and 'compositions' of public happiness. Section 3 discusses the manifold ways in which the 'institutions' may reduce the distance between opportunities and beliefs in any given social (and historical) set-up. Here, Smith's and Kames's 'science of a legislator' is discussed in the light of Beccaria's and Verri's analyses of the linkage between moral feelings, legal structures and the 'balance' between cultural beliefs and economic (or social) opportunities. Section 4 introduces a 'mean distance' criterion, and calls attention to the fact that, under specific social and characterizing circumstances (close to the characterizing features of

Adam Ferguson's civil society, and of Adam Smith's commercial society), a synthetic measure of public happiness may be obtained. Section 5 discusses some implications of the social mean criterion for the ranking of social states and the formation of public choices. Section 6 brings the chapter to a close by considering the relationship between the social mean criterion and social diversity. In particular, this section calls attention to the fact that the social mean criterion may have a limited field of application. As we trespass the boundaries of civil society, the possibility of unambiguously ranking alternative social states characterized by social diversity could easily break down, unless diversity is associated with a multiplicity of rankings for any given individual (or group).

2. Beliefs, opportunities and public happiness

It may be argued that, once fundamental needs are satisfied, human happiness is a *cognitive state* associated with beliefs and opportunities. In general terms, the state of happiness in any given society is influenced by the way in which that society describes desirable goals and provides adequate means to their achievement. In Hume's view, a belief is considered to consist 'in a lively idea related to a present impression' (Hume 1739 [1989]). In other words, any given belief is associated with some degree of 'potency', or 'power . . . to influence decision' (Bacharach 2001, p. 5). This means that any given belief provides a focal point for the imagination, and makes certain traits salient at the expense of others. As argued above, beliefs are apt to influence decisions. However, the realization of any given decision presupposes adequate means. We may conjecture that individual happiness is often associated with the existence of a 'smooth' congruence structure relating beliefs to opportunities. On the other hand, a 'lumpy' congruence structure is likely to be associated with mental 'unevenness' not so different from the cognitive state that Adam Smith thought to be at the origin of theoretical systems and scientific discoveries (see 'The history of astronomy', in Smith 1980).

Happiness is a cognitive state primarily associated with the state of mind of individuals but also significantly related to a social dimension. This is because the 'settled' cognitive state associated with happiness often derives from social perceptions about the reasonableness of goals and the adequacy of means. The reflexive structure of any settled cognitive state is analysed in Smith's *Theory of Moral Sentiments* by means of the 'looking-glass' metaphor: '[w] e suppose ourselves the spectators of our own behaviour, and endeavour to imagine what effect it would, in this light, produce upon us. This the only looking-glass by which we can, in some measure, with the eyes of other people, scrutinize the propriety of our own conduct' (Smith 1759 [1976a, p. 112]). It may be argued that, in general, individual happiness presupposes the *expectation* of social approbation, and that the latter is more likely when goals and means are evenly distributed across the social spectrum.

The above argument suggests a linkage between private and public happiness that has often passed unnoticed. Private happiness reflects the expectation of social approval, and the latter is seldom forthcoming in the case of exceptional goals relative to means, or in the opposite case of excessive means relative to individual objectives. In short, a 'golden proportion' rule seems to be at work whenever individuals evaluate the likelihood of social approbation. Public happiness is a condition in which the expectation of social approval (the approbation of Smith's 'impartial spectator') is a relatively common state of shared beliefs.

The above state of social approbation is closely related to what Cesare Beccaria called the 'barbarity' and 'culture' of nations. In this connection Beccaria wrote: 'The barbarity of a nation, if that concept is to be taken in its precise and philosophical sense, is nothing but the ignorance of things useful to that nation, and of the means that are within reach in order to obtain it in a way conforming to the particular happiness of everyone' (Beccaria 1768 [1971, Vol. II, p. 802]).

In Beccaria's view, a nation cannot be considered to be a barbarous one as long as 'knowledge and beliefs are in equilibrium with needs and the maximum happiness conceivable by anyone' (ibid.). In this connection, Beccaria introduces a distinction between the barbarous and the savage state of a nation. The former is associated with the distance between knowledge and needs; the latter with the distance between the actual condition of society and the condition of 'maximum absolute happiness that is possible divided by the greatest possible number' (ibid.). The latter condition is one of 'maximum union', that is, of maximum sociability, as human beings most fully participate in the 'happiness' available to society.

Beccaria's conceptual framework suggests a twofold relationship among happiness, knowledge and needs. First, happiness is inversely related to the distance between knowledge and needs (that is, between knowledge and maximum subjective happiness). Second, happiness is directly related to maximum absolute happiness divided by the greatest possible number. In short, happiness lends itself to a two-dimension index, whose elements we may tentatively associate with subjective and objective happiness, respectively. Subjective happiness rises with knowledge and declines with needs; objective happiness is directly related to *both* subjective happiness and a measure of equality. It is worth noting that we are here dealing with two distinct concepts of distance. One is the distance between opportunities and desires for any given individual; the other is the distance of achievement levels *across* different individuals. The above argument suggests that happiness in society could be measured according to a hierarchical index. In symbols, H_i (or, the subjective happiness of individual i) is directly related to K_i (the state of knowledge of i) and inversely related to P_i (a proxy for the maximum aspiration level of that individual):

$$H_i = K / P.$$

Similarly, H_i^s (the objective happiness associated with social state s) is directly related to H^* (aggregate subjective happiness) and to E (the equality index):

$$H_i^s = H^*/ E.$$

The above conceptual structure implies that an increase in subjective happiness is not always conducive to greater objective happiness, and also that greater objective happiness may be compatible (within a certain range of variation) with lower happiness for certain individuals (or groups). In short, Beccaria associates the measurement of happiness with two concepts of distance: (i) the distance d between needs and means of satisfaction for each individual; (ii) the distance d^* between the actual distribution of happiness and the 'maximal' distribution of happiness (this is the case of maximum happiness 'divided by the greatest possible number'). The previous argument implies that d^* reflects the values of the different d_i's but also the overall criterion of 'maximum union' (which attaches higher weight to subjective happiness achieved under conditions of a moderately egalitarian distribution of individual satisfactions).

An economic theory of happiness is primarily a theory of the relationship among needs, means and beliefs. This is shown in Beccaria's analysis of the way in which needs come to be associated with the anthropological structure of human beings: according to Beccaria, needs arise as the means suitable for their satisfaction become generally available, and happiness is associated with the possibility of improvement. This may be identified with the possibility of reducing the distance between human needs and their reasonable satisfaction. In its turn, the possibility of improvement is associated with the existence of needs 'that should be varied and proportionately distributed amongst . . . capabilities' (Beccaria 1768 [1971, Vol. II, p. 807]). The variety of capabilities and a 'right proportion' among them is a condition enhancing learning and improvement, as it avoids a narrow-minded focus upon a single human faculty at the expense of the others:

[A]ssociations of ideas would thus be more reciprocal in human beings. These associations will be less strong in their initial combinations, and will thus be able to receive a greater number of elements in the most complex ones. As a result, associations of ideas would be more effective in human beings, and all their operations would be more varied. (Ibid.)

It is worth noting that Beccaria's theory of human improvement is at the same time a sophisticated account of human happiness, since happiness is associated with a balanced expansion of needs and human abilities. Division of labour derives from the variety of human strengths and abilities, but may lead to war, as the expansion of needs (which division of labour has made possible) could vastly exceed the expansion of resources and abilities (see ibid., p. 808).

Pietro Verri outlines a theory of public happiness quite close to that of Beccaria: 'The excess of wants over the ability to satisfy them is the measure of man's unhappiness; and no less so, of the wretchedness of a state' (Verri 1771 [1986, p. 4]). Once human beings have overcome a primitive state in which they 'are seldom unhappy, because their needs are few' (ibid.) a twofold path is open to humankind: 'need sometimes leads men to plunder, sometimes to trade' (ibid., p. 5). It is noteworthy that, differently from Beccaria, Verri does not seem to contemplate the possibility of improvement independent of trade. In his view, as needs exceed available means, a surplus produce should be generated that makes a country ready to participate in the reciprocal exchange of goods or services:

> Once a nation begins to move away from the savage state, recognising new wants and new comforts, it will be forced to increase its industry proportionately and multiply the annual output of its products; so that over and above its consumption, it will have a surplus which will correspond to the amount of foreign commodities it must seek from its neighbours. In this way, a country's annual production from the soil, and its national industry, tend naturally to increase along with increasing wants. (Ibid.)

In Beccaria, the variety of human abilities is associated with a flexible mindset that makes individuals ready to learn from a variety of sources and along multiple paths of discovery (see above). In Verri, the attention is focused on resources rather than abilities, and nations are supposed to come 'closer to happiness' as they seek 'a greater power to supply [themselves]' by means of trade (ibid., p. 4).

3. The political economy of public happiness

In the previous section, we examined public happiness from the point of view of cognitive states (cultural beliefs) and historical anthropology. The purpose of this section is to introduce a conceptual framework to be used in the assessment of public policy. In particular, this section discusses the manifold ways in which the 'science of the legislator' may investigate how effective government policy is in reducing the distance between opportunities and beliefs in any given social (and historical) set-up. A preliminary step of this analysis is to recognize that distance is a relative, not an absolute, concept (see also Keynes 1921, p. 7). This means that, in general, the distance between opportunities and beliefs cannot be assessed unless the personal distribution of opportunities and beliefs among the members of society is carefully identified. Apart from the special case of an egalitarian distribution of opportunities and homogeneous beliefs, the distance between opportunities and beliefs would generally be different from one individual (or social group) to another. In this case, the distribution of opportunities and beliefs may influence the level and structure of public happiness in a critical way. We may conjecture that different measures of public happiness may be obtained depending upon the system of weights used to identify the *social* distance between opportunities and beliefs. This is a third concept of distance with respect to the two concepts outlined above (see Section 2). For example, certain measures may privilege the 'peaks' by attaching special weight to the 'happiness distance' for the poorest individuals (or social groups). This approach is closely related to the Rawlsian conception of social justice, and leads to the conclusion that public happiness would be greatest in a social setting in which the above distance is smallest. Other measures may still privilege peaks but they may follow a different distance criterion, such as the happiness distance for the wealthiest individuals or social groups. This anti-Rawlsian approach would lead to the conclusion that maximum public happiness is achieved when the latter measure of distance is least.

Other measures of distance may privilege social averages, so that public happiness would be associated with the distance between *average* opportunities and beliefs. This approach leads to the evening out of peaks, so that 'extreme' conditions get a lower weight than conditions closer to a mean value. As a result, any smallest distance (greatest happiness) would in fact be a mean distance obtained through the elimination of extreme circumstances.

We may conjecture that policy affecting public happiness would be influenced by the distance criterion that has been adopted (see also above). In particular, any criterion attaching special weight to peaks (such as the Rawlsian criterion) calls attention to extreme circumstances. Legislation tends to be selective, and administration discretionary. In this case, governmental action is likely to consist of direct intervention aimed at the manipulation of events, rather than of incentives operating through free choices under uncertainty. A distance criterion based upon the elimination of peaks suggests a different approach to social policy. This is because the mean distance criterion averts attention away from extreme conditions, and suggests policies targeting average circumstances. In this case, legislation tends to be universal, and administration is often of a non-discretionary type. In particular, policy measures are often of the indirect type, as they operate through incentives and presuppose citizens or subjects capable of choosing from among a set of multiple options.

The above argument suggests the existence of a relationship between public happiness and measures of distance. Public happiness appears to reflect the system of weights used in mapping individual into social distances between opportunities and beliefs. A system biased towards the extremes attaches greatest weight to extreme conditions (see above). In this case, there is a significant chance that the extreme poverty of certain individuals or groups could bias the social distance towards the 'short side' of the happiness spectrum. On the other hand, an alternative (anti-Rawlsian) approach to peaks may lead to a bias towards the 'long side'. In either case, public happiness appears to reflect the greater weight of extreme conditions *vis-à-vis* social averages. Both the Rawlsian and the anti-Rawlsian criteria involve a bias towards a particular peak along the happiness spectrum. At the same time, 'peak criteria' attach lower weight to intermediate circumstances and social averages. A Rawlsian measure will rank social situations in terms of the 'worst-peak' criterion , while an anti-Rawlsian measure will rank them in terms of the 'best-peak' criterion. We may conjecture that, in social situations characterized by the concentration of individual distances around a mean value, the Rawlsian and anti-Rawlsian criteria would lead to distance measures not so different from the mean distance itself.

Social situations characterized by single-peak concentration around one or the other extreme suggest that public happiness may be evaluated very differently depending on whether the Rawlsian or the anti-Rawlsian criterion is followed. In the case of a single-peak distribution with concentration around the poverty extreme, the Rawlsian criterion would lead to a distance measure significantly close to that associated with the social mean criterion. Under the same conditions, the anti-Rawlsian criterion would lead to a measure of public happiness in sharp contrast with the social mean criterion. This difference would be reflected in different attitudes towards legislation and public policy. In the Rawlsian case, legislation (or policy) improving the happiness indices of the 'worst-off' social groups would also improve public happiness. In the anti-Rawlsian case, on the other hand, public happiness would seemingly be reduced if the worst-off social groups improve their situation at the expense of the most affluent social groups.

Multi-peak distributions suggest a more complex relationship of happiness to social distance, and point to the need for policy measures capable of 'targeting' different social groups in different ways. This is because multiple peaks are associated with more than one way in which a particular distribution may be associated with an aggregate measure of happiness. One way of dealing with this issue is to acknowledge that multiple peaks may be associated with a system of weights attaching special importance to one or the other extreme, or to a social average. A consequence is that one would be led to apparently paradoxical statements in the measurement of public happiness. A Rawlsian measure would lead to the view that public happiness is greatest when resources are as much as possible concentrated in the social groups in which the distance between opportunities and beliefs is least. An anti-Rawlsian measure, on the other hand, would lead to the opposite view that public happiness is greatest when resources are as much as possible concentrated in the most privileged social groups.

A possible way out of the paradoxes of public happiness is suggested by the social mean criterion considered above. This is because a social setting in which opportunities and beliefs are distributed across the whole population in such a way that most people are actually clustered around a social average, is one in which Rawlsian and anti-Rawlsian criteria give approximately the same measure of public happiness (see also above). In this case, extreme positions are quite close to the social mean. As a result, any Rawlsian or anti-Rawlsian bias *would not* be sufficient to shift collective happiness away from central values. In other words, there could be a range of social situations such that those mean positions are associated with a central interval in the actual distribution of opportunities and beliefs. In this case, public happiness would best be measured by the social mean (mean distance), as the latter would be an important focal point in the existing social structure.

Civil society may be identified with the range of social situations in which the above 'mean condition' is satisfied. The political economy of public happiness takes different forms depending on the distribution of opportunities and beliefs. In civil society, public happiness reflects a social mean (or 'mean range') of opportunities and beliefs. As a result, the political economy of public happiness comes to reflect the existence of 'central values' and their evolution over time.[1]

The paradigm of civil society suggests a specific approach to the economic analysis of public happiness, which makes it different both from the classical utilitarian approach to public choice and from the theory of enlightened despotism. This is because the consideration of civil society shifts attention away from individual choices, and highlights the *choice space* in which individuals (or groups) are likely to identify a pattern of mutually consistent actions. This choice space is the set of possible events that individuals (and groups) are likely to 'generate' by their interaction under the assumption of a 'mean' distribution of opportunities and beliefs (see also Scazzieri 2003).

4. The 'social mean' criterion

The above discussion has considered alternative foundations for the political economy of public happiness. In particular, we have highlighted that public happiness reflects measures of social distance, and that the political economy of public happiness may follow alternative courses depending on social weights. The civil society paradigm calls attention to a social setting in which the distribution of opportunities and beliefs is clustered around a social mean. This particular distribution is one in which individuals (or groups) are not radically different from each other in terms of the distance between opportunities and beliefs. In this situation, happiness is evenly distributed, and the political economy of happiness does not confront the Rawlsian or anti-Rawlsian paradoxes considered above. More specifically, shifts of resources from one extreme to the other (in the distribution of opportunities or in the distribution of beliefs) are likely to have little impact as far as the social mean is concerned. As a result, public happiness is more likely to be increased by a policy in which the two following targets are simultaneously sought: (i) the gradual concentration of opportunities and resources around a social mean; and (ii) the reduction of the mean distance between opportunities and beliefs.

The social mean criterion is not always relevant, as opportunities and beliefs are not always clustered around a social mean. However, the social mean is a relevant measure of distance (that is, a relevant measure of happiness) if the above concentration assumption is satisfied. In this case, greater opportunities are not necessarily associated with greater public happiness, as the mean distance between opportunities and beliefs may be increased. As noted by a number of writers, the civilization process may be associated with situations in which the emergence of new needs is not matched by the rise of adequate opportunities. In this case, knowledge and beliefs are no longer 'in equilibrium with needs' (Beccaria 1768 [1971]), and a situation of 'cultivated barbarity' (Broggia 1752) may arise. However, mean concentration suggests that, should any gap arise between opportunities and beliefs (needs), a policy targeting the mean would be immune from the biases associated with skewed distributions.

The civil society paradigm calls attention to a social setting in which measures of distance are not significantly biased by a Rawlsian or an anti-Rawlsian system of weights (see above). In other words, the distribution of opportunities and beliefs (needs) across individuals (or groups) makes *mean distance* a significant measure of public happiness. As a result, the political economy of happiness may be concerned primarily with the social mean, and public action could be seen as influencing public happiness primarily through its impact upon mean opportunities and beliefs.

The social mean criterion is closely associated with the theory of social happiness proposed in writings of the Scottish Enlightenment. The man 'of the happiest mould' considered by Smith is primarily a person capable of identifying the course of action most appropriate to any particular set of circumstances. He would be able to 'establish with exactness the point of propriety', but would differ from the impartial spectator in that 'he is a real man, however rarely to be found' (Vivenza 2001, p. 49). According to Smith, happiness is, in this case, closely related with congruence relatively to the impartial spectator. Indeed, the man of the happiest mould shares the impartial spectator's ability to identify a standard of property, but 'he also applies it to his own behaviour' (ibid.). This suggests a theory of individual happiness that is closely associated with cognitive frames and relational abilities. In Smith's account, the man of the happiest mould is primarily an individual able to identify a standard of 'practical virtue', and capable of following that standard in the actual course of his life. Similarly to the 'Stoical wise man', his happiness consists 'in the contemplation of the happiness and perfection of the great system of the universe' (Smith 1759 [1976, p. 277]). It also consists 'in discharging his duty, in acting properly in the affairs of this great republic whatever little part that wisdom had assigned to him' (ibid.). However, and differently from the Stoical wise man, Smith's man of practical virtue generally falls short of 'perfect virtue and happiness' (ibid., p. 291). He is primarily a man capable of practising 'imperfect, but attainable virtues', that is, virtues for which 'a plausible or probable reason could be assigned' (ibid.). In Smith's account, happiness is also, to a large extent, a social faculty, that is, a faculty by which the individual perception of propriety and congruence (between opportunities and beliefs) comes to be associated with a conjecture relative to the likelihood of social approbation. As a result, happiness is closely associated with the practice of imagination. Even satisfaction deriving from material wealth is often combined with admiration for 'the order, the regular and harmonious movement of the system, the machine or oeconomy by means of which it is produced' (ibid., p. 183).

Smith's theory of the impartial spectator suggests a general framework for his theory of happiness. This is because, in Smith's account, happiness is primarily a *cognitive state* associated with imagination and (expected) social approbation. A remarkable consequence of this point of view is that, on a *ceteris paribus* assumption, public happiness is likely to be greater in the case of congruence between individual standards and socially acceptable patterns of behaviour. We may conjecture that the above congruence would be maximum in a social setting characterized by concentration of opportunities and beliefs around a social mean (see above). The social mean criterion suggests that maximum public happiness could be achieved in a setting in which the measure of public happiness is not biased by the disproportionate weight of extreme positions.

5. Social choice, political choice and public happiness

The social mean criterion discussed above is closely associated with Smith's own view on the structure of commercial society as a social setting characterized by concentration around mean values for opportunities and beliefs. The above criterion suggests the possibility of stating the problem of social choice in a way that preserves the derivation of a social welfare function from individual rankings of alternatives but avoids some of the paradoxes associated with the method of majority decision. Kenneth Arrow proved that 'if we exclude the possibility of interpersonal comparisons of utility . . . the only methods of passing from individual tastes to social preferences which will be satisfactory and which will be defined for a wide range of sets of individual orderings are either imposed or dictatorial' (Arrow 1951 [1963, p. 59]). However, there are cases in which the derivation of social preferences from individual values can be satisfactory and preserve non-dictatorial characteristics. This is shown by the case of complete unanimity of individual preferences and by the case of single-peaked preferences. In both cases, the 'aggregate' ranking of social states may be derived from individual preferences on the assumption that certain features of similarity can be identified among the ways in which different individuals rank social states. This result led Arrow to note that 'like attitudes toward social alternatives . . . are needed for the formation of social judgements. Some values which might give rise to such similarity of social attitudes are the desires for freedom, for national power, and for equality' (ibid., p. 74). Indeed, Arrow was able to show that 'mathematically, at least, it is possible to construct suitable social welfare functions if we feel entitled to say in advance that the tastes of individuals fall within certain prescribed realms of similarity' (p. 81). Arrow also argues that features of similarity are often associated with a consensus on social ends, and that such a consensus may coexist with significant differences in the 'pragmatic imperatives' of different individuals (p. 83).

The social mean criterion calls attention to a particular (but theoretically important) case, which may be described as follows:

- opportunities and beliefs may vary significantly among individuals or social groups;
- individual (or group) *distances* between opportunities and beliefs are concentrated around a mean value (or, at least, around a central interval);

- partial similarity is associated with the 'closeness' of individual (or group) distances with respect to the social mean (and with respect to each other); and
- the partial similarity condition may be satisfied independently of any (partial) unanimity of pragmatic imperatives (in principle, it could even be satisfied in the absence of a consensus on social ends).

The above setting is compatible with social diversity. In principle, the concentration of distances around a mean value does not presuppose the 'closeness' of opportunity vectors, or the 'closeness' of individual preferences. Individuals (or social groups) may be significantly *distant* from one another in terms of resource endowments or pragmatic imperatives. Yet, they may be sufficiently *close* to one another if, for each individual (or group), the corresponding distance between opportunities and beliefs is considered. Happiness indices (as measured by the above distance) may be clustered together even if there are significant differences in the economic position of individuals, or in the way in which different individuals (or groups) rank pragmatic imperatives. In this particular case, public happiness results from the mean value criterion. This means that, in general, public happiness will go up or down depending on the happiness indices of individuals (or groups) close to the mean (or to the central interval), and independently of the happiness indices of individuals (or groups) close to the extremes. As a result, the political economy of public happiness could target the mean distance directly, and there would be no need to formally derive the 'aggregate' ranking of social states from the consideration of individual preferences.

The above conceptual framework suggests a pragmatic solution to certain social choice paradoxes. This is because, in this case, similarity is derived from measures of 'satisfaction distance' rather than from the immediate consideration of individual (or group) preferences. Indices of *public happiness* could thus be derived directly from the consideration of satisfaction distances (for individuals or groups), and the ranking of social states could reflect levels of public happiness in an immediate way. This approach to the problem of social choice suggests that political choice does not necessarily presuppose unanimity or a reduction of social diversity. Indeed, diversity would be consistent with social cohesion as long as the distribution of satisfaction distances is concentrated around the social mean. This is because, in this framework, social cohesion reflects the *proximity* of happiness indices, but does not presuppose the similarity of individual (or group) preferences. As a result, political choice could be based upon an extreme case of single-peak preference. Individuals may differ widely in terms of pragmatic goals and/or in terms of social ends, yet they could be significantly 'close' if the range of happiness indices is considered. In this case, it would always be possible to describe alternative social states by a one-dimensional 'mean value' variable, provided that the different individuals (or groups) are sufficiently close to one another. This is because proximity of individuals (or groups) entails a situation in which the social mean criterion may be applied. Alternative social states can be represented by mean-value happiness (a one-dimensional variable), and a single-peak ranking would be obtained. This means that, of two social states characterized by lower mean-value happiness than a reference state r^*, a rational politician would prefer the state characterized by the mean-value happiness closer to r^*. Similarly, of two social states characterized by higher mean-value happiness than r^*, a rational politician would prefer the state characterized by the mean-value happiness more distant from r^*. In formal terms, the representation of social states by mean-value happiness entails that there exists a strong ordering of social states such that, for each pair (x, y) of social states, the relation xRy and the assumption that state y is 'between' states x and z entails that state y is preferred to state z (see Arrow 1951 [1963, p. 77]).

A remarkable implication of the above argument is that multiple cleavages are possible without necessarily disrupting social cohesion. This is because cohesion reflects some degree of proximity, and the latter is compatible with multiple goals (or highly differentiated economic conditions) as long as 'satisfaction distances' are sufficiently close to one another. The above argument also suggests that cohesion may be disrupted if extreme positions along the happiness continuum are not clustered around the social mean. In this case, the social mean criterion described above cannot be applied in its pure form. A measure of public happiness presupposes a system of weights (often a social philosophy) suggesting a way in which extreme positions could be evaluated against one another, as well as against the social mean.

6. Conclusions: boundaries of civil society and public happiness
This chapter has examined the economic theory of public happiness by laying emphasis upon the relational dimension of happiness. We have done this by following a three-step strategy. First, we have taken up the eighteenth-century view of individual happiness as a measure of distance between opportunities and desires (Beccaria, Verri). Second, we have explored the implications of Beccaria's view that public happiness has an inherently social dimension. In particular, we have examined his propositions concerning relative and absolute happiness, and we have emphasized that, in either case, his approach entails a sophisticated analysis of what he calls the 'maximum union' among human beings. The concept of maximum

union suggests a link with the theory of 'civil society' developed by writers of the Scottish Enlightenment, and primarily by Adam Ferguson and Adam Smith. The third step of our analysis has consisted in the investigation of the social-mean criterion. This has led us to consider a measure of public happiness that is at the same time relational and 'local'. This is because the social-mean criterion suggests a useful measure of public happiness (and of its relation to the happiness of individuals and groups) as long as the *social structure* (described by the distribution of opportunities and beliefs) follows the clustering condition described above (clustering around the social mean). If the clustering condition is met, public happiness may be measured by an index that satisfies the following three properties. First, happiness is described as an individual or social distance (between opportunities and beliefs). Second, a cardinal measure of public happiness is possible. Third, alternative social states can be compared without assuming a significant reduction in social diversity (no similarity of pragmatic goals or social ends is assumed).

We have also noted that the social-mean criterion cannot be applied if the social structure is such that extreme positions cannot be overlooked. In this case, we seemingly fall outside the 'boundaries' of civil society. However, the role of extreme positions is less stringent if a society is fragmented along a multiplicity of cross-cutting divides. In this case, for example, economic cleavages may not coincide with ethnic, linguistic or religious cleavages, and a social equilibrium may emerge precisely because individuals (and groups) arrange social (and political preferences) along *different* scales existing side by side (see, for example, Axelrod 1970, pp. 162–4).

This suggests that there may still be a way to 'bundle together' individual measures of happiness without directly introducing a system of social weights. In this case, it may be impossible to achieve a single-peak ranking of social states, but social cohesion will be achieved through compensation and compromise across the different scales of individual (or collective) preference.

Note

1.   We may conjecture that a social situation in which most individual positions are clustered around the social mean is one in which the functionings of human capabilities are closer to full realization (see Sen 1985).

Bibliography

Arrow, K.J. (1951 [1963]), *Social Choice and Individual Values*, Cowles Foundation for Research in Economics at Yale University, New Haven, CT and London: Yale University Press.

Axelrod, A. (1970), *Conflict of Interest: A Theory of Divergent Goals with Applications to Politics*, Chicago: Markham.

Bacharach, M.O.L. (2001), 'Framing and cognition in economics: the bad news and the good', in *International School of Economic Research, XIV Workshop: Cognitive Processes and Rationality in Economics*, University of Siena, Certosa di Pontignano, 3–7 July, pp. 1–13.

Beccaria, C. (1768 [1971]), 'Pensieri sopra la barbarie e coltura delle nazioni e su lo stato selvaggio dell'uomo' (Thoughts on the barbarity and culture of nations, and on the savage state of man), in C. Beccaria, *Opere*, ed. S. Romagnoli, Vol. II, Florence: Sansoni, pp. 802–9.

Broggia, C.A. (1752), 'Lettere salutari politiche economiche e morali, di stato e di commercio, alla moda, gusto e bisogno, del secolo presente', ms. 354, Biblioteca Universitaria di Bologna.

Hume, D. (1739 [1989]), *A Treatise of Human Nature*, edited, with an Analytical Index, by L.A. Selby-Bigge; 2nd edn with text revised and variant readings by N.H. Nidditch, Oxford: Clarendon Press.

Kames, Lord (Henry Home, Lord Kames) (1774 [1796]), *Sketches of the History of Man, considerably enlarged by the last additions and corrections of the author*, Basel: J.J. Tourneisen.

Keynes, J.M. (1921), *A Treatise on Probability*, London: Macmillan.

Rawls, J. (1971), *A Theory of Justice*, Oxford: Oxford University Press.

Rothschild, E. (2002), *Economic Sentiments: Adam Smith, Condorcet, and the Enlightenment*, Cambridge, MA and London: Harvard University Press.

Scazzieri, R. (2003), 'An economic theory of civil society', Bologna: Institute of Advanced Study (IAS) and Department of Economics; Cambridge: Centre for Research in Arts, Social Sciences and Humanities (CRASSH), mimeo.

Sen, A. (1985), *Commodities and Capabilities*, Amsterdam: North-Holland.

Smith, A. (1759 [1976]), *The Theory of Moral Sentiments*, edited by D.D. Raphael and A.L.Macfie, Oxford: Clarendon Press.

Smith, A. (1776 [1976]), *An Inquiry into the Nature and Causes of the Wealth of Nations*, general eds R.H. Campbell and A.S. Skinner; textual ed. W.B. Todd, Oxford: Clarendon Press.

Smith, A. (1980), *Essays on Philosophical Subjects*, edited by W.P.D. Wightman and J.C. Bryce, Oxford: Clarendon Press.

Verri, P. (1771 [1986]), *Reflections on Political Economy*, edited by P. Groenewegen and translated by B. McGilvray. Reprints of Economic Classics, series 2, no. 4, Sydney, University of Sydney (English translation of *Meditazioni sulla economia politica*, Livorno: nella Stamperia dell' Enciclopedia, 1771).

Verri, P. (1781), 'Discorso sulla felicità' (A discourse on happiness), in Verri, *Discorsi sull'indole del piacere e del dolore, sulla felicità e sulla economia politica*, Milan: Giuseppe Marelli.

Vivenza, G. (2001), *Adam Smith and the Classics: The Classical Heritage in Adam Smith's Thought*, Oxford: Oxford University Press.

6 Kant on civilization, moralization and the paradox of happiness
Sergio Cremaschi

1. Kant on happiness

> Immanuel Kant is often thought to hold that happiness is not valuable, and even to have ignored it wholly in his ethics. This is a serious mistake. It is true that for Kant moral worth is the supreme good, but by itself it is not the perfect or complete good. To be virtuous, for Kant, is to be worthy of happiness, and the perfect good requires that happiness be distributed in accordance with virtue ... Happiness, or the sum of satisfaction of desires, is a conditional good. It is good only if it results from the satisfaction of morally permissible desires. But it is intrinsically valuable nonetheless: It is valued by a rational agent for itself, and not instrumentally.[1]

This assessment by a recent influential interpreter turns two centuries of misunderstanding upside down; in fact Kant was not the proponent of a 'grumpy' morality, which he thought indeed to be mistaken,[2] but only meant to avoid its opposite, an 'enticing' morality that would try to encourage virtuous conduct through promises of happiness as a reward to virtue, which he believed to be a corruption of genuine morality. Kant's polemics against eudemonism is well known, but also overstressed. In fact, he wanted to avoid doctrines corrupting the true principles of morality, or the simple reasons for acting that the conscience, or heart, of any plain man is able to perceive easily enough. But a desire to be happy was for him natural, and strong enough not to require any doctrine that would prompt us to pursue happiness as a duty. But he had it clear in his mind that, once we leave the point of view of the individual agent and adopt the point of view of God, the maximum amount of happiness in the world is the highest end, once the proviso is added that this should come with merit, or should be happiness with virtue.

Kant's definition of happiness is far from univocal. He talks of *Glückseichkeit* or *Glücksgaben* while indicating external goods, such as 'power, wealth, honour, and even health and the overall satisfaction and contentment with one's state'.[3] His highest good is presented as something different from happiness, indeed as a sum of happiness and virtue. Thus he tends to underrate the plausibility of the views proposed by ancient philosophers, although he is sometimes ambivalent: he is occasionally appreciative even of Epicurus whom he generally condemns as the proponent of a mistaken doctrine, and while he is closer to the Stoics, he nevertheless criticizes them for ignoring the sensuous side of human nature; finally, he is quite uncertain about Aristotle himself.[4]

2. Kant and political economy

The name of Kant hardly shows up in any history of economic thought, and yet Kant, who taught subjects as different as physical geography and military engineering and had a remarkable competence in chemistry, was not totally unaware of what had been going on in this field during the eighteenth century. In his lectures on physical geography he makes room for a mercantile geography which accounts for the ways in which different countries are naturally led to specializing in the production of different commodities, and then how commerce ties up different nations with the bounds of commerce, that is, bounds of friendship which pave the way towards a cosmopolitan society.[5]

In the 1770s he read Adam Smith's *The Theory of Moral Sentiments* (1759) in the German translation based on the second edition and Smithian concepts such as sympathy and the impartial spectator were not unfamiliar to him, even if he seems to have in mind more his contemporary German proponents of a doctrine of moral sentiments. By the time he published the 'Metaphysics of morals', he was also aware of the contents of the *Wealth of Nations* (1776) (which had been translated into German in the meanwhile) and referred approvingly to Smith's definition of money:

> Money is therefore (according to Adam Smith) 'that material thing the alienation of which is the means and at the same time the measure of the industry by which human beings and nations carry on trade with one another' – This definition brings the empirical concept of money to an intellectual concept by looking only to the form of what each party provides in return for the other.[6]

This provides a dogmatic a priori definition of money, 'which is appropriate to the metaphysics of right as a system'.[7] In addition, in his writings on the philosophy of history he shows the same keen awareness of the civilizing function of commerce as the Scottish philosophers, particularly Smith, and tries to locate it within the context of a complex dialectic between civilization and moralization.

And yet, a few decades afterwards, Kant had become a banner in the hands of German opponents of the 'English' greedy philosophy of 'Manchesterismus', also called 'Smithianismus' or finally 'Utilitarismus', all of the above-mentioned being identified with the selfish system of Bernard Mandeville, supposedly the spokesman of the capitalist spirit. All this would be of merely antiquarian interest, if it had not left some diehard traces in Continental philosophical culture. Instead, Kant the moral and political philosopher tried to deal with basically the same problem as Smith, namely how growth of wealth and civilization on the one hand, and of liberty and morality on the other may be made not only compatible, but also interdependent.

3.   Kant's impure practical reason

Kant's contribution to economic discourse has not been very popular. One reason for this is that his fragmentary contributions fit into a part of his work that fell into oblivion for a number of reasons, such as that of being published in the 1790s – when there was already a fierce debate raging about Kant's alleged ethical formalism as illustrated in his works of the 1780s – or not fitting the cliché created by the romantic critics of the Enlightenment. This part is the 'doctrine of prudence', or 'moral anthropology', or 'practical anthropology', or 'pragmatic anthropology' or 'empirical moral philosophy'[8] (and, at the very beginning of his intellectual career, 'moral geography').[9] The very plurality of names for the subject is telling: this part of Kant's philosophy is, more than a subdiscipline, a crossroads or a link, namely the discussion of the characteristics whereby human beings are members of both the kingdom of freedom and the kingdom of nature.[10] Indeed, it is one component of rational ethics, but also a part of 'cosmological knowledge' together with 'physical geography', and it discloses the sources of 'all the sciences, morals, technology, social customs, the method for educating and governing human beings, and accordingly of the practical sphere as a whole'.[11] The very variety of descriptions of the would-be discipline is telling: Kant had been struggling all is life with the status of this subdiscipline, a source of trouble but also, or precisely for the same reason, the unsuspected kernel of his philosophical work.

Pragmatic anthropology, if we agree to call it by its latest name, is a description of the ways in which moral sentiments and the faculty of moral judgement may develop in the individual as well as in humankind. It is in a sense the only 'practical' part of ethics *qua* ethical theory. If we adopt stricter criteria, practical ethics is ethics put into practice, not a doctrine, but instead a skill. If we adopt looser criteria, pure normative ethics cannot be applied to individual cases, where we are left with the faculty of judgement, and is limited to making explicit to us the reasons we have for acting according to the moral law, and only anthropology is 'practical', albeit in a limited sense, in so far as it provides strategies for education and policies for fostering the development of civilization.

Kant's real 'practical' ethics is not a discipline, but instead an activity, what Moses Mendelssohn in 1764 had called 'the practical [*Ausübende*] doctrine of morals'.[12] As Kant objected to Christian Garve in 1793, it is the faculty of judgement, not a set of abstract principles, that handles the individual case and solves moral dilemmas.[13]

It can be argued that there is also room for the empirical/theoretical social sciences, those that are based on causal explanations instead of 'observations', and which may explain social phenomena as if they were natural phenomena, governed by necessary laws. In fact, 'human actions', as phenomena corresponding to a noumenal entity that is free will, that is, when considered as if they were empirical, or causally determined, facts, are none the less 'determined in accordance with universal laws of nature, as is every other natural event'.[14] Thus, Kant's would-be empirical social sciences would be neither value free nor immediately subordinate to ethics, since the twofold teleology of ends allows for a system of 'pragmatic' ends, aiming at the subjective end of happiness as individuals are able to represent it to themselves, and to the objective end of the full development of humankind's potentialities, which is in turn connected with a moral end, the development of humankind's full moral powers.[15]

There are indeed, according to Kant, law-like connections among those ends that may be made the subject of study in themselves, not unlike Johannes Kepler who discovered the thread of natural phenomena, and Isaac Newton who discovered the hidden cause governing that thread, even if we are still waiting for a Newton of societal laws. Thus, the social sciences are not immediately moralized sciences (as German nineteenth-century alleged followers of Kant, and later on a number of Catholic social thinkers claimed), and yet they have some inherent link to the higher moral ends through the twofold teleology immanent in human action.[16]

4. Kant on the paradox of happiness

Let us come back to Kant and happiness, ruled out as a source of ethical standards on the one hand, and construed as an intrinsic value on the other, and let us try to make sense of what Kant says on the basis of the picture drawn in the two previous sections.

Kant was an avowed ethical rigorist, in the sense that he believed that moral reasons may only be presented in their purity, *qua* rational reasons, if they are to have any motivating force. But rigorism does not also logically entail asceticism, or hate for pleasure, for the passions or for sociability. This is rather the main content of Kantian mythology.

It is true that the reader of the *Foundations of the Metaphysics of Morals* may have the impression that morality be tantamount to reason, as contrasted with 'inclination' or self-love, and that the eventual source of moral evil is sensuousness. But, in spite of serious problems that may be detected in Kant's view of self-love and prudence,[17] it is fair to recall that Kant's main concern in this work was ruling out happiness as a possible ground for morality, indeed ruling out the current idea of happiness as a pseudo-concept in so far as happiness be understood as a pleasure that is constant through time, as 'the condition of a rational being in the world, to whom in his existence as a whole everything happens according to his wish and will'.[18]

But moral law contains no idea of any necessary connection between morality and happiness, since moral law is not a law of causal connections in the world, those connections whose control is the staple of any possible happiness, since 'the acting rational being in the world is not in the meantime the cause of the world and of nature itself'.[19] It is true that the quest for happiness is a duty, but in a special sense: as a kind of indirect duty, since a state of need as is carried by poverty may prompt us to violate the moral law.[20]

But there is some other state that cannot be identified with happiness as it is commonly understood, and which provides instead an example of an unconditionally desirable state. As early as the 1760s and 1770s, in the 'Reflexionen' Kant mentions '*Selbstzufriedenheit*' as an intermediate link between virtue and happiness, since it is at once an effect of virtue as well as an autonomous source of happiness; the quest for pleasure is an expression of dependence, while self-contentment (still understood in a Leibnitian mood as contemplation of one's own growth in perfection) is an expression of autonomy.[21] In the 1780s, putting the Leibnitian theme of perfection aside, Kant singles out the source of pleasure in the feeling of autonomy or freedom from causal determination. Self-contentment is 'a feeling of pleasure or of well-being in the accomplishment of duty that implies a causal power of reason in determining sensuousness in conformity to its own principles',[22] awareness of one's freedom in terms of independence from inclinations, and thus 'unshakable contentment that is of necessity linked with such awareness, that does not rest on any particular sentiment and deserves to be qualified as intellectual'.[23] Nature itself seems to have conceived as her own end for man a 'rational self-esteem' more than welfare, and even when man attains as much happiness as is possible in this world, Nature's design is apparently 'that he may reach it by his own efforts, and thus have an opportunity to be grateful to himself'.[24]

In so far as somebody who acts according to morality is not under the constraint of external causal powers, such as inclination or self-love, which is always an empirical cause, he is free: having 'goodwill', that is 'the indispensable condition for deserving to be happy'.[25] Only he who is master of virtue is 'free, healthy, wealthy, a king', since only he who is master of virtue 'is master of himself'.[26]

Kant had already been clear in his 'Lectures on moral philosophy' about two opposing mistakes into which ethics may fall: the former is that of becoming a kind of 'enticing ethics' that endeavours to persuade the audience of the eventual convergence between virtue and happiness; the other of becoming a kind of 'grumpy ethics' that opposes morality with the joys of life. It is true that 'if one had to allow for one mistake in ethics, it would be better to allow for the mistake of rough ethics', since it originates from concern with preserving the purity of moral principles, but it is none the less a mistake, since the source of evil does not lie in inclinations, but instead in the 'perversity of the heart'.[27] Kant always disapproved of ascetic kinds of morality. In the 'Lectures' he said that 'fanatical moralists' believe that mastery over the body is conquered by means of prohibiting everything that 'gives sensuous satisfaction to the body', but that practices of such a kind are 'monkish and fanatical virtues'.[28] Instead, the body should be cared for, avoiding any excess,[29] and pleasures may be recommended as far as they have a socializing function: drinking is not as bad as eating too much, and banquets bring, 'besides a purely physical pleasure, something which tends toward a moral end, namely bringing together several people and entertaining them for a while in mutual intercourse'.[30]

Happiness is still a problem, even if we cease looking at it in the mistaken light of a 'right to happiness' as most eighteenth-century thinkers did.[31] It becomes a problem once it is seen as the problem of the *summum bonum*, namely of the concomitance of virtue and happiness. The happiness of the just man is something that we desire for rational, not empirical reasons, and we may wish to be both happy and deserving of happiness (note that Adam Smith makes the same point).

The problem of theodicy, that is Gottfried Leibniz's and Pierre Bayle's question about the possibility of reconciling the existence of a benevolent Creator with lack of correspondence between virtue and happiness, admits of no answer, as Voltaire and Adam Smith had argued,[32] and Kant reaches the same conclusion.[33]

But for Kant, happiness with virtue is the key to a solution, and the Stoics were mistaken, in so far as, even if they 'were right in choosing virtue as a condition for the *Summum Bonum*', yet, 'not also including happiness had denied the sensuous aspect of human nature'.[34] Kant resolves the antinomies he had left open through a natural theology based on ethics as its starting-point and thus introduces the idea of God and an after-life.

5. Deception and unintended results
But it is desirable that truths about the final destination of man should be seen just as postulates, as consequences, not as preconditions of morality, since, had we been certain about the existence of an after-life, our actions

would have been as free as those of puppets; in a word, we have to be thankful to divine wisdom for 'what was left hidden to our eyes as much as for what was revealed'.[35]

Thus limits to knowledge and deception in knowledge are not only the tools by which self-love in drag manipulates human beings, but also a fundamental condition of human life, of action, of civilization, and finally of the process of moralization. Kant had learned from the sceptics and the Jansenists that transparency of consciousness is a delusion, that we may always detect, behind actions conforming to duty, disguised self-love or 'the dear self',[36] for 'the depth of man's heart is inscrutable'.[37] We cannot judge the actions we have carried out; what we can do is merely fix maxims for our prospective actions. The enemy virtue has to fight is not the passions, as the Stoics used to believe, since the passions are something natural, but rather an invisible enemy, the perversity of the human heart that 'through principles corrupting the soul, secretly undermines the original intention itself'.[38]

Deception plays a basic role in the history of humankind, in so far as it allows for a hidden twofold teleology of human action; in fact, human beings, while following the dictates of self-love, pursue such delusory ends as welfare, wealth and power or, in a word, happiness, and put to work and indeed improve their reason, both in its theoretical and in its technical aspects, as a means for attaining those ends. But human beings are systematically mistaken about the results they actually contribute in bringing about, first because happiness is a self-contradictory goal, second because individual human life is too short for men to enjoy the results of their efforts, and third because the unintended result of the interaction between the individuals' anti-social drives is a system of rights and regulations. The final result is a growth of enlightenment, learning, education and freedom, and this prepares the conditions for full development of the moral capacities with which humans are endowed. To sum up: human action is led by 'subjective' ends and, in the meanwhile, by ends pursued by nature through unintended results.

Deception is also an unavoidable requirement of virtue: civilization embodies politeness, and the latter carries the custom of feigning feelings of benevolence and respect for each other, even if there is no true sincere intention behind them. This does not amount to deceiving each other, since everybody knows that sincerity is never at home in worldly life, and politeness and civility at least provide a protective belt against instincts, which may yield an environment for the growth of true virtue.[39]

Note that the claim that limited knowledge is a precondition for morality is also central for Adam Smith in his critique of the Stoics and the Cambridge Platonists.[40] In addition, the idea of deception as a basic component of our knowledge of nature, of morality, and of social life is a central point of Smith's system of ideas and a point where Kant meets Smith's train of thought.[41]

6. Civilization or Moralization

There is a well-known passage in the 'Foundations of the metaphysics of morals' that has left commentators somehow puzzled. There Kant states:

> [In] the natural dispositions of an organised, i.e. teleologically adapted for life, being, we assume as an axiom that we will never find in it any tool for whatsoever goal that be not also the most effective and adequate for such goal. If Nature's only goal for a being that has reason and a will were its preservation, its welfare, in a word its happiness, then it would have ill-conceived its design by choosing the reason of such a creature as the executor of the mentioned plan. Since all actions that it has to carry out with a view to this goal and the overall pattern of its behaviour would be much more precisely indicated to it by instinct.[42]

As a consequence some (read: Jean Jacques Rousseau and his followers) are right in believing that civilization is useless as a means to happiness, and that if Nature's real goal had been the happiness of rational beings, it would have been much better leaving such an end to the care of something more reliable, such as instinct. It is because 'in so far as a cultivated reason dedicates itself to the perspective of enjoyment of life and happiness, to the same extent the human being departs himself from true contentment',[43] that misology, or hatred against reason, has arisen.

This passage starts making better sense when located within the framework of Kant's writings on the philosophy of history, where he contrasts civilization with moralization as two different phases in the growth of humankind. In this context, the growth of commerce and manufacture plays a distinctive role, namely that of the means of fostering civilization, even if all human efforts in this direction are prompted by the image of a deceptive goal, happiness.

Because of the opacity of consciousness, Kant believes that 'judgement' (a nearly-Aristotelian category that he believes to have the last word on individual prospective actions) is almost impossible on actions, committed by both ourselves and others, once they have been carried out, since 'real' intentions cannot be detected. Instead, some kind of reflective judgement, of the kind he depicts in the 'Critique of judgement', is quite practicable on the process of moral development. This means that we may look at the history of humankind as if it were a process of moral development not unlike the individual development described in Rousseau's *Émile*, and the good reason we have for believing that the agenda of human history is in fact a path to moralization is a moral necessity of believing in the possibility that morality may be fully realized.

Nature prompts men to undertake every kind of effort in order to obtain more comfort, wealth, safety – in a word, more happiness. Most of the time, individuals will not enjoy the results of their efforts, but will leave them instead to their offspring. Besides, self-love and unsociability bring people into mutual interaction, through war and conquest, and then through less-aggressive activities, such as commerce; commerce brings different people into mutual relationships and thus paves the way to a cosmopolitan society. Finally, the growth of the arts and sciences provides preconditions for the birth of learned institutions, a free press and public opinion, which are the basis for the use of reason in its critical capacities.

The process described, that is civilization, carrying Enlightenment, is a preliminary step to moralization, that is the rise of individuals from a state of minority to a state where they become their own master. Kant writes:

> Civil liberty cannot any more be really impaired unless every kind of activities, most of all commerce be seriously injured . . . If one hinders the citizen from looking after his own welfare in whatever manner he likes, provided that it may coexist with other people's freedom, he impairs vitality of industry as a whole . . . as a consequence limitations to the individual will be gradually reduced, universal religious freedom will be promoted; and, albeit mixed up with chimeras and extravagant fancies, Enlightenment will be gradually brought about.[44]

7.   The quest for happiness and the conquest of virtue

It may be fruitful to compare the misology passage with another in the writings on the philosophy of history where Kant states that, until the final goal of human history, namely a cosmopolitan federation of states, be attained, humankind shall suffer every kind of evil

> under the delusive cover of external welfare; and thus Rousseau was right in preferring the state of savages, if one does not consider the last stage to which our kind still has to raise itself. By means of art and science, we are cultured to a high degree. We are civilised, even too much, in every kind of courtesy and social decorum. But we are still far from being moralised.[45]

Both passages may be compared in turn with a well-known passage by Smith in *The Theory of Moral Sentiments*, where the same Rousseauvian theme is developed in order to show how wealth is useless for promoting happiness, and is pursued for the sake of imaginary ends, eventually prompted by the mechanism of sympathy by virtue of which we desire to be envied and honoured by our fellows. Smith adds that deception plays an unavoidable, and even useful, function in fostering the growth of commerce, the arts and sciences, and thus of civilization; indeed it is 'what first prompted him to cultivate the ground, to build houses, to found towns and republics, to invent and improve all the sciences and the arts'.[46] This eventually makes a free and peaceful society possible, one based, if not on 'perfect equality, perfect justice, and perfect liberty', at least on some second best.[47] The semi-sceptical and semi-pessimistic considerations by Smith in 1790 on the 'wise man' (to be contrasted with the prudent man) and his public spirit,[48] make sense when viewed within the framework of a dialectic between happiness, growth of opulence, moral losses as well as new opportunities for equality and dignity carried by this growth.[49]

Also Kant's philosophy of history is based on a similar dialectic: the quest for a delusory happiness is a spring of action, and it is self-love that prompts activity in order to dominate others, but the unintended results of the sum of such actions is a development of a system of civilized states under the rule of law and finally, we hope, of a cosmopolitan society. Such a path to be followed by human history is just a possibility; there is no science of the laws of historical development; we are left with a moral postulate that allows for a view of human history in terms of a route to moralization. The quest for happiness plays the role of a link between self-love and morality, and all the development of technique, geographical discoveries, and war first and commerce at a later stage, and then of manufacturing, and of the arts and sciences, is for Kant no less than for Smith a machine, one too complex and with too many side-effects to be considered as an efficient means to its 'subjective' end, that is, happiness.[50] But this combination of causes and effects is not too complex if viewed as a route to human improvement. And this makes morality (or the recovery of an original state of innocence) possible, while leaving human beings as disillusioned as ever about 'happiness',[51] unless the *summum bonum*, that is a state that includes both moral and non-moral elements, was ultimately to be taken by human beings as the true goal for action, instead of 'happiness'.

8. Conclusions: the quest for happiness, economics and morality
To sum up:

1. Kant was aware, following the heritage of hellenistic ethics and of its Renaissance revival, that wealth is a very poor means to happiness.
2. He added a more sophisticated claim, namely that the very idea of 'happiness', as understood in the eighteenth century, was contradictory; he was not fully aware of the comparative sophistication of Aristotle's idea of *eudaimonia*, and indeed he tended to mistake it for the eighteenth-century idea of happiness; his own idea of highest good

(a good where material well-being and moral worth are joined together) was closer to Aristotle's *eudaimonia* than to his own idea of *Glücklichkeit*.

3.   He had also learned the lesson of the sceptics and Jansenists, that men are led by deceptive ends.

4.   He was aware, more than any other man of the Enlightenment period, that human actions are also empirical phenomena that may be explained on the basis of laws like the universal laws of Nature of the new Galilean and Newtonian science.

5.   His 'real' idea of happiness is the idea of a state where man is both happy and deserving of happiness, that is the *summum bonum*; a state that includes both moral and non-moral elements, not unlike Aristotle's *eudaimonia*, which he probably never appreciated properly.

6.   A second best for the *summum bonum* is, on the one hand, 'content-ment', deriving from an awareness of not having purposely violated the moral law as well as from an awareness of having done one's best to develop the gifts of humanity in oneself.

7.   On the other hand, another second best is 'a morally valid happiness'; indeed the Stoics were mistaken in forgetting that man is both rational and sensible, and the second best that may be pursued on earth results from a sum of virtue with some amount of welfare, within the limits of civilization and sociability; *pace* the cynics and the anchorites, Kant's second-best number two is 'a good meal in good company';[52] this is an expression of a 'morally valid happiness' and rules of human refine-ment, as far as they help social intercourse, 'are a coating that helps virtue' and ascetic virtues are 'degenerate forms of virtue which do not encourage the practice thereof; once abandoned by the Graces, they cannot advance claims to humanity'.[53]

8.   The standard German nineteenth-century opposition notwithstand-ing, the kind of problems Kant faced were the same as those faced by Adam Smith; an important number of claims were shared, concerning civilization, the vanity of wealth, deception, and partly the nature of happiness; but, ironically, Kant, the alleged rigorist moral philosopher, had a more positive view of material satisfaction than Smith, the alleged founder of the greedy doctrine of self-interest.

Notes

In the notes, the page number of the English translation follows that of the original for those of Kant's works that are also available in English translation.

1.   Schneewind (1992, p. 333).
2.   Irwin (1996); Engstrom (1996); Pleines (1984).
3.   Kant (1785, p. 393 / 49).

4. See Engstrom (1996); Pleines (1984).
5. See Kant (1802, pp. 164–5).
6. Kant (1797, p. 289 / 436).
7. Ibid.
8. Kant (PPP, p. 99; MC, p. 245; MM, p. 1298; 1785, p. v; 1797, p. 217; MSV, p. 482 / 253; 1798, p. v).
9. Kant (1802, p. 164).
10. See Foucault (1964).
11. Kant (1773: 175 / 141); see also Manganaro (1983, ch. 1); Cremaschi (2003b).
12. Mendelssohn (1764, p. 315).
13. Kant (1793, pp. 278–89 / 281–90).
14. Kant (1784, p. 17 / 41).
15. Kant (1784, pp. 20–22 / 44–5).
16. See Manganaro (1983, ch. 1).
17. See, for example, Engstrom (1996).
18. Kant (1788, p. 124 / 239).
19. Ibid.
20. Kant (1785, p. 399 / 54; 1788, p. 93 / 214).
21. Kant (R 7202: 276–81 / 465–8).
22. Kant (1785, p. 460 / 160).
23. Kant (1788, p. 117 / 234).
24. Kant (1784, pp. 19–20 / 43–4).
25. Kant (1785, p. 393 / 49).
26. Kant (1798, p. 15).
27. Kant (1799, p. 37 / 83).
28. Kant (MC, p. 379; see also PPP, p. 213).
29. Kant (MC, p. 379).
30. Kant (1798, p. 428).
31. See Scuccimarra (1997).
32. See Cremaschi (2002b; Bruni 1987).
33. Kant (1791).
34. Kant (1788, pp. 11–13, 119 / 145–6, 235); see also Hill (1999); Manganaro (1983, ch. 5); De Luise and Farinetti (2001, ch. 26).
35. Kant (1788, p. 148 / 258); note that Adam Smith had made a similar point, using the same image of the 'veil of ignorance', and before him both Richard Cumberland and Leibniz had also done so.
36. Kant (1785, p. 407 / 62).
37. Kant (1797, p. 447 / 567).
38. Kant (1799, p. 58 / 101).
39. Kant (1798, p. 151).
40. See Cremaschi (2002b).
41. See Cremaschi (1989).
42. Kant (1785, p. 395 / 51).
43. Ibid.
44. Kant (1784, pp. 27–8 / 50–51).
45. Kant (1784, pp. 24–6 / 47–9).
46. Smith (1759, IV.i.10); see also Bruni (1987).
47. See Smith (1776, IV.ix.16–17).
48. See Smith (1759, VI.ii.ii–iii).
49. See Cremaschi (1984, ch. 4, 1989).
50. See Hirschman (1977); Bruni (1987).
51. See Manganaro (1983, ch. 2).
52. Kant (1798, p. 278).
53. Kant (1798, p. 282).

Bibliography

Bruni, F. (1987), 'La nozione di lavoro in Adam Smith', *Rivista di Filosofia Neoscolastica*, **79** (1), 67–95.

Cremaschi, S. (1984), *Il sistema della ricchezza. Economia politica e problema del metodo in Adam Smith*, Milan: Angeli.

Cremaschi, S. (1989), 'Adam Smith: sceptical Newtonianism, disenchanted republicanism, and the birth of social science', in M. Dascal and O. Gruengard (eds), *Knowledge and Politics: Case Studies on the Relationship between Epistemology and Political Philosophy*, Boulder, Co: Westview Press: pp. 83–110.

Cremaschi, S. (1998), '*Homo oeconomicus*', in H.D. Kurz and N. Salvadori (eds), *The Elgar Companion to Classical Economics*, Cheltenham, UK and Lyme, USA: Edward Elgar, pp. 377–81.

Cremaschi, S. (2002a), 'Two views of natural law and the shaping of political economy', *Croatian Journal of Philosophy*, **2** (5), 65–80.

Cremaschi, S. (2002b), 'Adam Smith's economic ethics and social theodicy', Paper presented at the 2002 ESHET (European Society for the History of Economic Thought) Annual Meeting, Rethymnon, March.

Cremaschi, S. (2003a), 'The absence of *homo oeconomicus* in Adam Smith', Paper presented at the 2003 ESHET (European Society for the History of Economic Thought) Annual Meeting, Paris, January.

Cremaschi, S. (2003b), 'Kant's empirical moral philosophy', in B. Berčić and N. Smokrović, *Proceedings of Rijeka Conference 'Knowledge, Existence and Action'*, Rijeka: Hrvatskvo društvo za analitičku filozofiju – Filozofski fakultet, 21–4.

De Luise, F. and G. Farinetti (2001), *Storia della felicità. Gli antichi e i moderni*, Turin: Einaudi.

Engstrom, S. (1996), 'Happiness and the highest good in Aristotle and Kant', in S. Engstrom and J. Whiting (eds), *Aristotle, Kant, and the Stoics*, Cambridge: Cambridge University Press, pp. 102–38.

Foucault, M. (1964 [1970]), 'Notice historique', in I. Kant, *Anthropologie du point de vue pragmatique*, Paris: Vrin.

Hill, T.E. Jr. (1999), 'Happiness and human flourishing in Kant's ethics', *Social Philosophy and Policy*, **16** (1), 143–75.

Hirschman, A.O. (1977), *The Passions and the Interests*, Princeton, NJ: Princeton University Press.

Irwin, T.H. (1996), 'Kant's criticism of *eudaimonism*', in S. Engstrom and J. Whiting (eds), *Aristotle, Kant, and the Stoics*, Cambridge: Cambridge University Press, pp. 63–101.

Kant, I., *(Ak) Kant's Schriften*, Ed. Berlin-Brandenburgischen Akademie der Wissenschaften, Berlin: Meiner-De Gruyter, 1902–.

Kant, I. (1773), 'An Marcus Herz', in *Ak*, X, pp. 143–6; Engl. transl. 'To Marcus Herz, late 1773', in Kant, *Correspondence*, ed. A. Zweig, Cambridge: Cambridge University Press, 1999, pp. 139–41.

Kant, I. (R) 'Reflexionen', in *Ak*, XV; Engl. transl. *Notes and Fragments*, ed. P. Guyer, Cambridge: Cambridge University Press, 2005.

Kant, I., (MC) 'Moralphilosophie Collins', in *Ak*, XXVII\1, pp. 237–473.

Kant, I., (PP) 'Praktische Philosophie Powalski', in *Ak*, XXVII\1, pp. 91–235.

Kant, I., (MSV) 'Metaphysik der Sitten Vigilantius', in *Ak*, XXVII\2,1, pp. 475–732, Engl. transl. 'Notes on the Lectures of Mr. Kant on the metaphysics of morals', in Kant, *Lectures on Ethics*, eds P. Heath and J.-B. Schneewind, Cambridge: Cambridge University Press, 1997, pp. 249–452.

Kant, I. (1784), 'Idee zu einer allgemeine Geschichte in weltbürgerlicher Absicht', in *Ak*, VIII, pp. 15–31; Engl. transl. 'Idea for a universal history with a cosmopolitan purpose', in Kant, *Political Writings*, ed. H. Reiss, Cambridge: Cambridge University Press, 1991 (2nd edn), pp. 41–53.

Kant, I. (1785), 'Grundlegung der Metaphysik der Sitten', in *Ak*, IV, pp. 384–463; Engl. transl. 'Groundwork of the Metaphysics of Morals', in Kant, *Practical Philosophy*, eds M. Gregor and Ch.M. Korsgaard, Cambridge: Cambridge University Press, 1996, pp. 37–108.

Kant, I. (1788), 'Kritik der praktischen Vernunft', in *Ak*, V, pp. 1–163; Engl. transl. 'Critique of practical reason', in Kant, *Practical Philosophy*, eds M. Gregor and Ch.M. Korsgaard, Cambridge: Cambridge University Press, 1996, pp. 133–271.

Kant, I. (1791), 'Über das Misslingen aller philosophischen Versuche in der Theodicee', in *Ak*, VIII, pp. 253–71; Engl. transl. 'On the miscarriage of all philosophical trials in theodicy', in Kant, *Religion and Rational theology*, eds A.W. Wood and G. Di Giovanni, Cambridge: Cambridge University Press, 1996, pp. 19–37.

Kant, I. (1793), 'Über den Gemeinspruch: Das Mag in der Theorie richtig sein, taugt aber nicht für die Praxis', in *Ak*, VIII, pp. 273–324; Engl. transl. 'On the Common Saying: "That may be correct in theory, but it is of no use in practice" ', in Kant, *Practical Philosophy*, eds M. Gregor and Ch.M. Korsgaard, Cambridge: Cambridge University Press, 1996, pp. 273–309.

Kant, I. (1797), 'Metaphysik der Sitten', in *Ak*, VI, pp. 203–493; Engl. transl. 'The Metaphysics of morals', in Kant, *Practical Philosophy*, eds M. Gregor and Ch.M. Korsgaard, Cambridge: Cambridge University Press, 1996, pp. 353–603.

Kant, I. (1798), 'Anthropologie in pragmatischer Sicht', in *Ak*, VI, pp. 117–353.

Kant, I. (1799), 'Die Religion innerhalb der grenzen der blossen Vernunft', in *Ak*, VI, pp. 1–202; Engl. transl. 'Religion within the boundaries of mere reason', in Kant, *Religion and Rational theology*, eds A.W. Wood and G. Di Giovanni, Cambridge: Cambridge University Press, 1996, pp. 39–215.

Kant, I. (1802), 'Physische Geographie', in *Ak*, IX, pp. 151–436.

Manganaro, P. (1983), *L'antropologia di Kant*, Naples: Guida.

Mendelssohn, M. (1764), *Abhandlung über die Evidenz in metaphysischen Wissenschaften, in Gesammelte Schriften*, Jubiläumsausgabe, 22 vols, Stuttgart: Bad Cannstatt, Fromann, 1971–95, Vol. II, 267–330.

Pleines, J.-E. (1984), *Eudaimonia zwischen Kant und Aristoteles. Glückseligkeit als höchstes Gut menschlichen Handelns*, Würzburg: Königshausen – Neumann.

Schneewind, J.B. (1992), 'Autonomy, obligation, and virtue: An overview of Kant's moral philosophy', in P. Guyer (ed.), *The Cambridge Companion to Kant*, Cambridge: Cambridge University Press, pp. 309–41.

Scuccimarra, L. (1997), *Kant e il diritto alla felicità*, Rome: Editori Riuniti.

Smith, A. (1759 [1976]), *The Theory of Moral Sentiments*, Oxford: Clarendon Press.

Smith, A. (1776 [1976]), *An Inquiry into the Nature and Causes of the Wealth of Nations*, Oxford: Clarendon Press.

PART II

UNDERSTANDING THE PARADOX OF HAPPINESS

7 If happiness is so important, why do we know so little about it?
Marina Bianchi

1. Introduction

The title of this chapter: 'If happiness is so important, why do we know so little about it?' requires some clarification. First of all, does it really indicate a paradox? In the economic theory of choice it is the maximization of own satisfaction, utility, or pleasure, that individuals pursue in their actions. Even in its modern axiomatic form and stripped of any characteristic that is not formal, subjects are still assumed to maximize a 'utility' function. But does this imply that we, as economists, should know much if anything about it? The answer that economists give is clear: 'No'. One reason is simple, and is based on the principle of consumer sovereignty. Individuals are the only real 'experts' as to their own actions and desires. What they decide to choose is what they know is best for them. Preferences can simply be inferred from choices with no plunge necessary into their possible nature, genesis or configuration. The assumption, then, that choices are preferences eliminates any element of paradox from the fact that such a fundamental dimension of economic choice as individual desires and motivations is so little studied and understood.

Yet this assumption is conditional on a second, more hidden one: that there is no tension or mismatch between choice and the maximization of preferences. Should conflict in any form exist, then choices would cease systematically to reveal individual preferences. In this case an analysis of preferences, how they form, what triggers them, and how they express themselves, would be not only justified but necessary. That is the line of reasoning followed by the economist Tibor Scitovsky.[1] In his *Joyless Economy* (1976 [1992]) and in a series of related papers published before and afterwards (see Scitovsky 1962 and 1986), he identified three likely sources of conflict that might lead to a divorce between choice and preferences: possible conflict between comfort and pleasure; conflict between standardized goods and individual needs and desires; and the gap between specialized knowledge and generalist skills. In discussing these themes, Scitovsky was able to shift the analysis directly to the different forms of satisfaction that may be linked to different consumption activities. Additionally, and with the aid of contemporary experimental neuro-psychology, he pioneered in uncovering the role that novelty, variety and complexity might play in both individual and social well-being.[2]

Since Scitovsky wrote *The Joyless Economy* (*JE*) much has been done to study the possible mismatches between choice and maximization. Consider, for example, in particular, the literature derived from, and inspired by, behavioural psychologists Kahneman and Tversky (1979). This literature has progressively identified, with the support of a strong body of experimental research, those situations in which individual decision making is prone to systematic error, and which thus violate simple maximization rules. These are primarily situations involving uncertainty, complexity, and intertemporal comparisons of utility, and they require a more refined concept of rationality in order to account for observed behaviour. What makes this approach especially relevant to economics is the fact that the study of paradigmatic violations of maximization does not imply an abandonment of the concept of rationality but rather a detailed specification of its procedural rules.[3]

In this chapter I shall concentrate on Scitovsky's analysis, and in particular on that part of his research that dealt with the role that joyful and stimulating activities can play in making life pleasant. Notwithstanding the passage of time, Scitovsky's approach both remains an important reference point in contemporary debates, and raises questions that still want for answers.

The chapter is organized as follows. I shall first analyse the distinction between defensive and creative consumption goods that is at the basis of Scitovsky's distinction between comfort-related activities and those that are pleasure related. The motivational theory that underpins this distinction will then be discussed. The aim is to clarify how creative consumption represents a 'technology' of consumption that can give rise to increasing returns. Problems arise when people privilege choices that lock them into technologies, the defensive ones, that have lower returns. It is no easy task to unlock these less rewarding patterns of behaviour since, as I shall show, both the costs of access to a superior technology and the costs of exiting from an inferior one are involved. I conclude with a section devoted to the problem of boredom and habituation.

2. Defensive and creative consumption

Of the various themes in *JE* undoubtedly the most relevant and innovative is Scitovsky's distinction between two different sources of human satisfaction, those linked to comfort-seeking activities, and those stemming from pleasurable but also stimulating activities.

In introducing this distinction, Scitovsky drew on a previous though neglected one made by the British economist Ralph Hawtrey. Hawtrey

(1926) distinguished between two types of goods and activities: those that mostly aim at relieving pain and discomfort, which he called 'defensive', and those that produce positive pleasure and which he called 'creative'. Satisfying our needs for rest, food and shelter are obvious examples of products and activities of the first type. Engaging in conversation or the arts, playing sports and games, solving difficult problems, are instead examples of the second, the creative ones. They are creative for Hawtrey not because they represent alternatives more intellectual than material, but because at their basis there is no specific need to be satisfied or to have harm removed. They require therefore, in order to be developed and used, an active effort on the part of the subject: an effort of imagination and knowledge, and a deployment of skills and time (ibid.: 189–90).[4]

Hawtrey's distinction among goods becomes in Scitovsky's hands a distinction between forms of satisfaction. The pleasure deriving from defensive consumption, or from all those commodities that maintain life and make it easier, Scitovsky called 'comfort'. The satisfactions deriving from creative consumption that, for him, provides most of life's pleasures, he called, simply, 'pleasure' (*JE*: 61).

But what makes these two forms of satisfaction so different from each other and why is it important to uncover this difference?

A first aspect of difference is easy to detect and is one already envisaged by Hawtrey. Framed by the specificity of the needs they have to satisfy and by the routines and codified rules of their consumption, defensive goods are more easy to learn and do not require special consumption skills. Not so creative products, whose more complex nature also requires more complex skills. Engaging in conversation and taking pleasure in it, reading a novel, listening to music, are all activities that require attention, concentration, memory, accumulated knowledge and intuition, all capabilities that have to be learned. In addition, they require time, and time that often, and contrary to the time needed for using comfort goods, cannot be compressed through productivity gains.[5] The first difference then is a difference in terms of costs of access, lower for defensive consumption and higher for creative consumption.

A second component of difference is more complex and bears on the returns associated with these two sources of satisfaction. When first formulating the law of decreasing marginal utility economists such as William Stanley Jevons and Alfred Marshall mentioned, even if with a certain ambivalence, the fact that some goods may represent an exception to the law. Jevons acknowledged this when he wrote that satiety applies, but only to 'the simple animal requirements, such as food, water, air, etc.', not to 'the desire for articles of taste, science or curiosity' which knows no limits (1871 [1970: 111–12]). Marshall for his part acknowledged the listener of music who, after repeated exposure, enjoys music more, not less, an example made much of by Stigler and Becker (1977).

But why is it the case that creative consumption can give rise to returns one does not tire of, or that, as in Marshall's example, seem to increase? Each of us knows the feeling of never wanting a holiday to end, or to be distracted from a line of research that is promising, or forced to interrupt a novel at its tensest moment. But why is it so? What are the ingredients that make a holiday, a line of research, or a novel so engaging? In other words, what is it that transforms all these activities into sources of sustained pleasure?

Two of Scitovsky's merits are that he recognized the relevance of this question and that he introduced to economists a body of psychological research that, at the time he was formulating his ideas, had just begun investigating the components of motivation in choice.[6] Central in those psychological studies was the concept of arousal, activated by the stimuli that the central nervous system receives from sense experiences and the brain itself, and the way arousal is connected with individual well- or ill-being (*JE*: 21).

To this body of literature I shall now turn, before taking up the question why creative activities may yield increasing pleasure.

3.   The role of novelty, complexity and variety

The neuro-physiological studies of the brain used by Scitovsky and that flourished in the 1960s and 1970s, are associated with the name of D.E. Berlyne. At their core was the older Wundt–Fechner curve of the experimental psychology of the mid-nineteenth century. According to Wundt, the functional relation between pleasure and arousal has an inverted-U shape. The pleasure of an experience increases with an increase of its level of stimulus, reaches a maximum and then decreases. Pleasure is maximal for intermediate levels of stimulus, neither too high nor too low. Berlyne, however, introduced an important modification to this model. As a consistent body of experimental research seemed to show, arousal is contrast or conflict related. The utility or pleasantness of a situation, in other words, appears to respond not to the levels of stimulus but to their changes relative to reference positions. On the horizontal axis of the basic Wundt diagram, Berlyne placed stimulus variables related to change: novelty, surprise, variety, uncertainty and complexity (Berlyne 1971, and Berlyne and Madsen 1973) (see Figure 7A.1 in the appendix).

In Berlyne's model two different sorts of changes in stimulus are pleasure inducing: arousal-boosting mechanisms, which cause us to go from situations felt to be boring to others felt to be less so, and arousal-reducing mechanisms, which can take us from situations felt to be threatening or painful to others more familiar and more comfortable.[7] Set against these findings, Scitovsky's distinction between two different sorts of satisfaction, one pain reducing and the other pleasure enhancing, also seemed to find some empirical support (Figure 7A.1 shows how Scitovsky's distinction may fit Berlyne's).

Yet neither arousal-boosting nor arousal-reducing strategies will ever be entirely successful in securing for us a position of rest, one of sustained maximum pleasure. Since, in Berlyne's modified version of the Wundt curve, pleasure results from changes, a situation of unchanging pleasure must also be one of diminishing pleasure (as in the dotted curves in Figure 7A.1).

It seems, then, that Berlyne's model simply restates the law of decreasing marginal utility in a different guise, repeated exposure causing decreasing pleasure, because of satiation and lack of stimulating change. In fact, this model of choice has more radical implications. By denying that maximum pleasure represents a position of rest, the equilibrium position so fundamental to economic modelling, it broadens agents' incentives and introduces a whole set of new variables to which people respond and that have to be taken into account.[8]

If one looks more closely at the mechanisms of satisfaction described in the Berlyne model, there are three variables on which change depends and that can increase or decrease welfare. The first is time.

Time is the immediate dimension along which relative variables such as novelty and variety can be measured. Depending on the time distance from the last exposure to a certain event, good or activity, its novelty may increase or decrease. The most exciting menu day after day becomes dull and conversely even a dull TV programme can be a pleasant change after a tense day. To alter the time interval or the duration of a determinate experience either actively or simply as an effect of changes in social conventions, has inevitable effects on its perceived utility. In terms of Scitovsky's framework, this means that the time factor can shift the boundaries between comfort and pleasure, a comfort activity, after a period of abstinence, becoming stimulating again and a stimulating activity becoming a familiar habit after continuous exposure.[9]

The second dimension of the variable of change is cognitive, and relates to knowledge in its broadest sense (including information, experience and skills). Novelty (though also perceptions of variety and complexity) represents any mismatch between past and present experience, between what we have known to be and what is now. Any increase or decrease in the gap between accumulated knowledge and new knowledge, in short, can affect the pleasantness of a given experience. Certain activities – solving a puzzle, familiarizing oneself with a new language – may at first seem threatening.

Initially, therefore, pleasure can be increased as the new becomes more familiar and one's comfort level rises. Later, however, comfort and early mastery turn to boredom, additional novelty, complexity and variety may need to be added to again increase stimulus. Think of adding irregular verbs to regular, more challenging dance steps to basics, sophisticated moves in a new sport.[10]

The third dimension is the context or space or dimension of an event (or activity, or good), where context is both the place an event occupies in relation to contiguous or distant events, and the social context within which it occurs. Here the same processes of familiarization and de-familiarization can be applied. The phenomenon of fashions – in sports, in literature, in art, and of course in dress – often stigmatized as a wasteful activity, will continue to be appealing and looked for. This is not only because pleasure can be increased by playing on the time interval between events, as when new trends are introduced or old ones rediscovered, as in revivals. It is also because fashions represent a subtle mixture between social competition and cooperation, between the novelty of distinction and the familiarity of belonging, that, even if only temporarily, captures change which is neither over- nor understimulating.[11]

We are now in a position to shed more light on our initial question: why is it that creative activities seem to be able to overcome the decreasing marginal utility that accompanies more comforting activities? The reason is that these activities, because of their internal complexity and variety, and because of their independence of mere need, can be a renewed source of novelty and change. Therefore, they can also be a source of sustained pleasure. They are open-ended. They endogenously produce change.

The reading of a novel, for example, can activate simultaneously all the three dimensions of novelty. The structure of the plot can play on the temporal dimension, arousing expectations and creating suspense through repetitions and delays and constantly postponing the desired climactic conclusion. It can play on the cognitive dimension, by challenging and contradicting our set of understandings and interpretations, or it can play on the space dimension, opening the reader to new, distant or imaginary worlds. Analogously, the feeling we often experience when on a holiday – we wish it would never end – is because it is an infrequent event in our lives; because its complexity and variety open us up to new experiences while displacing old ones, and because the contiguity with our familiar spatial and social environment is disrupted.[12] Repeating these activities, reading new novels – or re-reading old ones – listening to music repeatedly, enjoying new holidays, often amplifies instead of reducing the pleasure obtained from them, both their novelty and variety and our ability to appropriate them increasing with exposure.

Comfort activities, however, when they simply relieve our unease, easily lead to satiation, to the cessation of pain but also of pleasure.

This is what Scitovsky had in mind when, confusingly, he introduced a second definition of comfort. On the one hand, and more often, comfort is, as we have seen, the positive feeling that accompanies defensive consumption. It corresponds to those activities that increase well-being by reducing the discomfort associated with an excess of stimulus. On the other hand, and predominantly in *JE*, comfort is the feeling that corresponds to distinct levels of stimulus and depends on whether or not arousal is at its optimum (*JE*: 61). In this way the contrast between comfort and pleasure becomes a contrast between a position of status, comfort corresponding to the optimal level of arousal when utility is at, or close to, its optimum, and a position of change, pleasure being defined as the positive feeling that accompanies an alteration of status. (In terms of Figure 7A.1, the contrast is between point E of the curve and the movements along the curve).

These two definitions are clearly different, the first one belonging to the modalities of satisfaction, the second to the mechanisms that are supposed to underlie satisfaction (on this point, see also Bianchi 2003).[13] They overlap only if it can be said, as Scitovsky did though without introducing the necessary clarifications, that stimulating activities, contrary to the defensive ones, are also the ones that are most prone to endogenously produce change; they are those for which increasing complexity is matched by the formation of superior capabilities, and for which time can reveal new, as yet undetected, possibilities.[14] (Figure 7A.2 shows how creative activities in this dynamic setting tend to displace upwards the whole Wundt curve.)

This confusion led Scitovsky to overemphasize the dangers to individual well-being that might come from indulging in comfort-related activities. Pleasure seeking, being also identified with exploration and openness to change, is deemed superior to a self-contented status, one of comfort. In fact, as mechanisms for increasing pleasure through an increase or decrease of stimulus, neither of the two can be considered superior, both being pleasurable only relative to some reference point.

Although in the course of the chapter I shall continue to use the terms 'comfort' and 'pleasure', what they are meant to indicate is in fact a distinction between a form of consumption that is unskilled, easily rewarding and easily satiable and another that is skilled, creative and able to open up new opportunities. When so formulated, an imbalance against creative consumption can indeed be dangerous for individual and social well-being. As Sen (1996) has pointed out in the context of development strategies, it is the enlarged set of possibilities that skilled consumption creates that translates in addition into an enlarged individual freedom.

4. Comfort and pleasure: is there a conflict?

The preceding discussion has shown that activities and goods can differ in terms of their reward structures. However, they also differ in terms of their costs of access. The ability to exploit and enjoy all the dimensions of novelty that creative consumption can open up demands that the consumer be skilled. Being complex and varied, creative activities require an ability to draw on prior knowledge, to make connections and create new complementarities, to cross disciplinary boundaries. One can stop and enjoy a novel at the simple level of the plot, but pleasure increases, and in fact never ends, if one is able to discover and explore its connections with similar novels and to its surrounding history, and begins to appreciate its innovative qualities. Even an activity apparently as simple as conversing with friends requires, for it to be enjoyable, attention, memory, empathy, flexibility of interests, and an ability to engage and divert. Skills of this sort grow with exposure and they require time, both time to invest in developing and refining them and time to apply them. Compared with other activities that are need-orientated, that are part of daily routines, or which require few skills, creative pursuits are more costly. As Scitovsky put it, there is a trade-off here: pleasure is obtainable only at the cost of some discomfort and comfort at the cost of some pleasure.[15] This trade-off, however, does not pose any serious challenge to free and rational choice, since any choice involves such a trade-off between alternatives. Scitovsky, however, maintained that the case here is different (*JE*: 73).

One reason for this difference has to do with the fact that for these types of activity, costs and rewards are not simultaneous but belong to different points in time. The disadvantages of having invested in obtaining the easy and quick rewards of defensive and comfort-related activities will be felt only in the future when the accumulation of past choices turns out to be accompanied by less and less pleasure. Analogously, the increasing returns of creative activities will be available only after costly investments in the necessary skills and knowledge have been made.

None the less, the presence of delayed rewards is at the basis of any intertemporal decision process. The case of delayed consumption rewards is no different. As is well known, this is the approach taken by Gary Becker (1996) who has modelled the equilibrium effects that past consumption choices have on present ones. His model has also been extended to include those activities whose long-term outcomes can be harmful or less beneficial to the individual, but which are nevertheless engaged in (Becker and Murphy 1988).

Stigler and Becker (1977) addressed this problem initially by referring to the puzzling example offered by Marshall, that of the music lover whose love for music increases with consumption. This seemed to violate the assumption of decreasing returns associated with repeated exposure in consumption. The way Stigler and Becker solved the puzzle was to take into account in people's choices the internal economies of 'learning' that accompany the accumulation of 'music' consumption capital. As a result, the stock of individual music consumption capital becomes more efficient and decreases the shadow price of music consumption, providing an incentive for consuming still more music in the present.

Yet there are some activities, such as bad habits and negative addictions, for which past consumption depreciates the stock of consumption capital in the present either directly, through habituation and tolerance, and/or indirectly by causing ill health, job loss and loss of self-esteem. For these types of activity the shadow prices increase with consumption, yet people continue to indulge in them. Why is that so? The rational model of choice that Becker has developed over the years does not allow him really to answer the question, which requires an analysis of the motivation of choice, for the avoidance of which the original model with Stigler had been formulated. What the model says is simply that, given the intertemporal utility profile of individuals and their discount rate, addictive consumption, despite its harmful effects having been anticipated and afterwards regretted, is still the best response an individual can give (Becker and Murphy 1988, and Becker 1996: 77–138).[16]

Recent analyses and empirical investigations of decision mechanisms and in particular of problems of addiction have started to relax slightly the rationality assumption and to uncover inconsistencies of behaviour that appear to be systematic. Forms of behaviour associated with phenomena defined as endowment effects, loss aversion and, importantly, weakness of will and preference reversal can now be rationalized in a coherent interpretative structure that is slowly being admitted (or readmitted) into economic analysis. Scitovsky's approach is more in line with this enlarged type of analysis. For Scitovsky the internal diseconomies of habituation and tolerance that comfort goods impose on consumers are often undervalued because their distributed effects over time tend to render them unperceived and uncertain.[17] Yet, when these hidden non-monetary costs are revealed to consumers the pattern of past consumption cannot easily be undone. Once transformed into habits, the costs of exit from them have also become very high. The result is that a consumer may be trapped in a situation of overinvestment in comfort goods and underinvestment in welfare-enhancing creative skills.[18]

Scitovsky's account of how this occurs is one that sees choices as a succession of piecemeal decisions, taken routinely and with a limited horizon. This account has affinities with a more recent explanation of habit formation known as 'melioration'. According to the latter, in situations of distributed choices over time a person is unable to take into account all the 'internalities', the internal spillovers that past choices have on present ones and thus cannot calculate the overall utility function of the distribution of choices (Herrnstein and Prelec 1992: 241). What a person in fact does is to compare alternatives on the basis of their average utility, each time choosing the more rewarding. The equilibrium result, which corresponds to the point at which the average utilities of activities match, is not in general an optimum (which would obtain only if the marginal utilities were taken into account) (ibid.: 251). In this model then, as in Scitovsky's, people can find themselves in equilibrium, yet also, almost inadvertently, in a position that privileges just those activities that make them less happy. (Figure 7A.3 shows how equilibrium here differs from the optimum and coincides with overinvestments in less-rewarding consumption activities; on this point see also Metcalfe 2001, and Schelling 1978: 220.)

Recent developments in the literature on addiction have added another element to the story of distributed choices over time, one that also calls into question Becker's model. Even if agents were fully capable of calculating all the interactions of past and present behaviour, choices that involve delayed rewards often tend to display dynamic inconsistencies. The reason lies in the form of the discount function. In traditional models of expected utility the discount function is assumed to be exponential. This implies that individuals' intertemporal preferences are constant over time, and any given delayed reward, either one that delays from today to tomorrow or one that delays from next year to the day after, has the same discount rate. In fact, as Strotz noted in the 1950s, the individual discount function seems to vary depending on the time distance of the reward. An individual who prefers a larger delayed reward over a smaller, earlier reward when the moment of choice is distant, will reverse his/her preference order when the moment of choice draws near. The reward looms larger as it comes closer. This suggests a hyperbolic, rather than an exponential discount function (see Strotz 1955–56 and Thaler 1981: 127). Applied to the case of the contrast between comfort and stimulus this means that an individual who has a hyperbolic discount function may well prefer the higher advantages associated with creative consumption but, confronted with the immediately cashable rewards of defensive consumption, might opt for this second less-rewarding strategy. Again, individuals may fall into patterns of behaviour that according to their own preferences are less than optimal.

Recent literature, in short, tends to support the existence of some internal conflict in choices. Because of this conflict the actual choices taken may not be the best choices. The reason, we have discovered, is that because, once entrapped in an inferior consumption technology, the capability (and the freedom) of a person to revert to a superior one is impaired. Now, in fact, not only are the costs of access to the latter high, but also the costs of exit from the former have become high.

How these choices can be improved upon, and even what improvement means in this context, are questions that require us to analyse their underlying mechanisms, an analysis that, as we have seen, has only recently begun to gain a hearing among economists.

5. The culture of production versus the culture of consumption

There are two important factors in modern, western societies that for Scitovsky tend to reinforce these locked-in welfare-reducing choices and thus exacerbate the conflict between choices and preferences. The first is a cultural bias and has to do with the type of education consumers receive – here Scitovsky is referring chiefly to American consumers. Although access to education has long ceased to be restricted to an elite, its main focus is on providing the necessary professional training and specialized production skills rather than expanding the liberal arts education of the past (1972a: 39–40). Backed by a puritanical ethic that looks at consumption with suspicion (1972b: 49), in society at large it is a culture of production that prevails. As a consequence the investment of time, effort and money devoted to the acquisition of consumption skills falls far short of what is devoted to acquiring production skills. Paradoxically, then, the unprecedented increase in productivity that this culture of production has generated does not translate into ways of discovering how to enjoy time and occupy creatively the energies thus freed.

Nor can production skills be used in consumption. Production skills are specialized skills, the more so the greater the learning involved in acquiring them. Consumption instead is an activity that simultaneously involves many different aspects of our lives. For this reason it requires, to be enjoyable, all-encompassing, general skills (*JE*: 268).[19] The disquieting result for Scitovsky is that, as an effect of the division of knowledge, the more specialized production skills become the more costly it becomes to acquire general consumption skills, thus widening the gap between them (ibid.: 270).[20]

The second factor has to do with the negative side-effects of economies of scale and of mass production. The problem with mass-produced objects, Scitovsky urged, is not that they are of bad quality but that their monotonous sameness causes us to tire of them much more quickly (ibid.: 249).

This absence of stimulus in standardized goods also explains why we often replace or accumulate them much faster than is necessary for purely functional purposes (ibid.: 257, see also Scitovsky 1985: 200–201). On the one hand, the stimulus associated with mass-produced new varieties fades much more quickly than the initial pleasure they yield would lead us to anticipate. As in the case of the 'internalities' of past consumption, so too the externalities of the social context of consumption tend to be underestimated by consumers. In this case the diffusion of their numerous replicas increases the feelings of familiarity, of the already known, that conduce to habituation and to a rapid erosion of their original novelty. Moreover, since in mass-produced goods stimulus and comfort come in a single package over which individuals have no command (*JE*: 258, 256),[21] the comfort one buys with novelty can be much greater than expected or than one was intending to pay for.

The consequences for individual well-being of Scitovsky's approach are therefore clear. Because of their lower costs of access and higher costs of exit, comfort goods and comfort-seeking activities tend to crowd out stimulating activities, especially those more demanding in terms of time and human resources. Since, however, it is the latter activities that carry greater rewards in terms of individual well-being, the net effect on social welfare of this crowding out is negative. Society as a whole loses when people underinvest in more welfare-enhancing activities such as the creative ones. We compose a comfortable landscape for ourselves that may reduce rather than enhance the range of alternatives open to us.[22]

6.   Positional competition: is consumerism so bad?

Another source of possible mismatch between individual choice and maximization, and hence also between individual choice and social welfare, is what is called 'positional competition'. This occurs when consumers compete for status and relative position in the social hierarchy (Frank 1985). The problem in this case is that individual competitive advantages are measured by the access to and possession of goods that are scarce or become scarce as an effect of competition. The end result is that, when the sources of positional supply have dried up, nobody is better off for having participated in the race; as at a football match when everybody stands up to see better the process is self-defeating.

Unlike the conflict between comfort and pleasure addressed by Scitovsky, this source of conflict is a much older topic in economic literature, starting with the mercantilist complaint of the luxurious spending of the rich that, when focused on rarer foreign goods, represented a threat to the balance of payments. It also plays an important role in recent debates on the relation between happiness and income, where consuming for relative advantage is seen as a welfare-reducing practice.

Scitovsky dealt with this topic in *JE*, but also discussed it extensively in a review of Fred Hirsch's work, *The Social Limits to Growth*, published in 1976 (Scitovsky 1987 in 1995). Scitovsky began with a puzzle. If man's basic needs for material comforts are satiable, what feeds the unlimited demand that is implicitly assumed in our models of growth?[23] A possible answer is the existence of a second group of wants, already introduced by Marshall and his pupils, related to the social comforts of distinction and superiority. These are insatiable (ibid.: 98). However, there is an ambiguity in the concept of insatiable wants and insatiable demand, according to Scitovsky. Insatiable can mean both that demand is unlimited and that it is unfillable. Only when unlimited does the demand for status provide a stimulus to the economy; when unfillable, it does not. In Marshall's time, when status competition was more restricted to an elite and also involved goods produced in the material and reproducible economy, a self-feeding and limitless demand for status might be reproachable on moral grounds, but it still provided a positive stimulus to growth. Now, however, people compete not for the more but for the more exceptional and unique. As Hirsch argued, what makes a good positional is its scarcity value either in a physical sense – natural landscape, Old Masters, leisure space – or in a social sense, such as leadership in the jobs hierarchy (Hirsch 1976: 30). In this case, positional supply is given and demand becomes, as Scitovsky noted, unfillable.

In brief, then, status competition, being a competition for relative position, is a competition with no final winner.[24] The winner of today becomes the loser of tomorrow, when a new winner arrives. Additionally, when competition for status ends up nourishing a demand that is unfillable, its effects become even more vicious.[25] As Hirsch had already pointed out, a demand that competes for goods or services that are inherently scarce has the sole effect of causing an increase in their price. This inflationary effect, Scitovsky added, is also accompanied by a deflationary effect on employment since the resources freed by technological progress cannot be re-employed in the material sector, where demand remains limited because of satiability (Scitovsky 1995: 99).

The remedies for easing this form of competition for Scitovsky comprise a reduction of income inequality, which would increase the demand in the material sector and reduce it in the positional sector, and a reduction in the length of the working week, which would relieve unemployment pressures by reducing the supply of labour (ibid.:105).[26]

The argument just given for the ill effects of positional competition, however, whatever its formulation, is not convincing. Status competition is represented in terms of a contrast between the material, reproducible economy where the production of goods and services is open to technological innovation, and the positional economy where goods, services and work positions are scarce in some absolute or social sense (Hirsch 1976: 27). But why are these positional goods and activities scarce? All the examples provided, it is true, are examples of non-expandable supply, but this does not mean that positional competition, like any other form of competition, cannot find innovative ways to overcome scarcity. The history of collecting, where positional competition might be thought to be particularly active, offers innumerable examples of overcoming limited supply by discovering or rediscovering the as yet overlooked, and thus creating new sources of value. The same is true of urban change, as when for example, inner cities are rediscovered and revitalized and suburbs abandoned, often by less rich artistic or intellectual elites. Changes in fashion, too, are ways of coping with the progressive erosion of positional advantages that occur when fashions spread. In fact, competing for distinction is a stimulus to innovation in consumption, from the arts, where the crowding of one style provides the incentives to explore different ones,[27] to technological improvements that, starting with the imitation of the rare, bring about new discoveries.[28]

The case of 'crowding', however, another form that positional competition can take in Hirsch's analysis, is different. Here people compete for natural resources that are indeed scarce: think of clean air, uncongested roads, a noise-free environment. But the congestion and loss of quality that results from the overuse of these resources is less due to status – the quest for something because it is scarce – and more to the fact that standards of living have risen even as populations have increased. This, and not status competition, is another instance of the 'tragedy of the commons', of that multi-person prisoner dilemma game where unconcerted individual actions lead to suboptimal social outcomes (Schelling 1978: 225).

7.   Boredom, habituation and happiness

Not all stimulating activities require complex skills and difficult learning in order to be enjoyed. In fact, many activities can be highly exciting while not requiring any skill. This is the case with some drugs, with certain forms of gambling, and with many dangerous activities, such as extreme sports, violence, vandalism, and hatred acted out (see Scitovsky 1981: 131–2).

In the last years of his life, one of Scitovsky's concerns was the social problem of boredom. The lack of stimulating activities that relieve boredom was also at the basis of *JE*. Yet, as Scitovsky often remarked in an almost excessive self-reproach, *JE* was mostly focused on the boredom of the idle rich, who have easy access, through income and schooling, to numerous sources of stimulating and peaceful activities (see Scitovsky 1996). The case of modern unemployed youth is different; the idle, but poor young person who has had little or no exposure to skilled stimulation, and has more leisure than he/she can make use of, easily opts for the appeal of free excitement, despite the pernicious individual and social consequences. This, for Scitovsky, accounts for the gratuitous acts of violence among youngsters in American society.

Two otherwise felicitous developments have worsened the problem (see Scitovsky 2000). One is the women's liberation movement that, by easing women's entry into the labour force, has also reduced their presence in the family. Parenting, one of the most important and long-lasting factors in education, has become less vigilant and more hurried especially in those critical child years between the age of three and five that require a loving and encouraging parent. The second development, compulsory and free schooling, has left uncovered – at least in the United States – the pre-school years just at the time that most mothers' parenting was cut short (see also, 'Boredom, its causes and consequences', Undated typescript, p. 9).

Scitovsky looked at European solutions to the problem (in Scandinavian countries, but also in France and Italy): public pre-schooling, extended paid maternity leave, and the like. One of his recurrent policy recommendations, as in the case of positional competition, was the shortening of the work week, here as a means to facilitate parents' availability to their children.

This topic is strictly connected with the problem of the relation between happiness and income growth. Scitovsky was among the first to review and comment on Easterlin's studies of time series of self-reported well-being (see Easterlin 1974 and 1995).[29] As systematic studies since then have confirmed,[30] self-reported average happiness in each income cohort fails to rise with increases in income, while in the lower tail unhappiness actually increases. Collateral trends show crime, alcohol abuse and depression all increasing, after a period between the two wars in which they were stable, this despite income growth (see Layard 2003, Lecture 2: 19). The pattern holds for country after country.

Among the causes that might explain this apparent paradox, there has been found one that is particularly relevant, namely habituation. As far as income levels are concerned, habituation has been shown to be very strong. As one of the several empirical studies on the subject shows, when respondents are asked what after-tax family income they would deem just sufficient for a livable life, they reveal that the minimum acceptable income is strongly correlated with the level of actual income. A rise in actual income also causes an increase in acceptable minimum income (Van Praag and Frijters 1999: 422). As we have seen with Berlyne's modified Wundt curve, what once made an enjoyable difference – at the moment of change – is taken for granted afterwards. (On this point, see also Parducci's concept of relative happiness, 1995.)

Psychological studies on hedonic adaptation have also, and importantly, shown that some goods are more prone than others to habituation (see Frederick and Loewenstein 1999: 311). People do not seem to get habituated to the persistent stress of commuting, to noise and pollution, or to loneliness. On the other hand, what facilitates habituation and alleviates the pain of 'bads' and of undesirable events, such as the death of loved ones or ill health, is social support, as well as framing the event with a meaning.

Drawing on these studies Frank, in a fashion not unlike Scitovsky's, discusses how spending on some goods – on larger houses, bigger cars or TV sets – does produce pleasure, which, however, is not enduring, because of habituation. A different sort of spending, instead – devoting more hours to friends, to exercise, to vacations, and fewer to commuting – produces more-lasting pleasure (Frank 1999: 90). This illuminates the sense of frustration that seems to accompany our efforts to have access to higher consumption standards simply by spending more.

To apply this to the problem of boredom, habituation happens at every level of income, causing a constant upgrading in what is deemed to be an appropriate standard of living. Moreover, for the lower-income cohorts this translates into an even greater conflict between aspirations to a good and eventful life and the increasingly complex necessary skills. The gap between reach and grasp widens, and a sense grows of access denied. This lack of alternatives and emptiness of stimuli is what transforms boredom into a social malady that for Scitovsky is as bad as starvation.

The studies just mentioned confirm the importance of consumption skills, and the emancipatory and civilizing effects of education. They also confirm the importance of taking consumption seriously. Scholarship is moving then in directions Scitovsky would have desired, even if the study of the problem of boredom, of the effects that a lack of peaceful stimulating activities has on happiness, is still just in its early stages.

8.   Conclusions: are there such things as bad preferences?

In traditional economic analysis and in the Hayekian tradition of spontaneous order, the market process, with its system of abstract signals such as prices, is the most efficient process for diffusing dispersed knowledge and for correcting errors. Following Scitovsky, we have seen that there are some circumstances that possibly prevent people from knowing and realizing what is best for them, but where the corrective role of the market is also suspended. There are three sorts of such situations: those requiring the formation of consumption skills, those involving choice among activities with differing delayed returns, and habituation, which may generate lock-in outcomes.

We learn from Scitovsky that two alternative options often compete with each other in consumer choice. The first, which he associated with comfort-seeking activities, has low costs of access in terms of knowledge and skills, but also decreasing returns because of habituation. The second, by contrast, and represented by those activities that Scitovsky called creative, may have increasing returns in terms of stimulation and enjoyment, but also high costs of entry because of the more complex consumption skills required. As a result of their cost advantage, and despite their long-term lower returns, the comfort activities may crowd out the creative. Additionally, the trade-off between the two cannot be easily undone, because comfort consumption may also have high costs of exit. It may be easy to learn but also difficult to abandon.

For Scitovsky the principle of consumer sovereignty, which he accepted, does not exempt the economist from asking whether preferences do or even can express themselves in choices, and whether the working of the economy provides the right channels for their expression. This insight brought him to ask about the nature and meaning of preferences and desires, and the role that time, experience and contextual factors play in the shaping of them and vice versa.

Starting with Scitovsky we also begin to grasp a little more about these objects of rare attention in economics.

Notes

1. Tibor Scitovsky died on 1 June 2002. Born in Budapest in 1910, he left Hungary for England in 1935. He studied in Cambridge and at the London School of Economics. He reached the United States in 1939. There he taught at Stanford, Berkeley, and Yale. He continued to work and be active until his death.
2. In this chapter I shall use the terms 'welfare', 'well-being' and 'happiness', interchangeably. In Scitovsky's writings the term 'pleasure' also often overlaps with the others. For an analysis of their differences, for their relation to utilitarianism, and for a rediscovery of the relational element of well-being, see Bruni (2002).
3. For an overview of the wide range of economic problems to which this approach can be applied, see Thaler (1991).
4. The rich man, says Hawtrey, who has spent much of his income in securing the minimum discomfort and the maximum of leisure may still be at a zero point as far as his positive pleasure is concerned, as when somebody has weeded a garden but has not yet begun to plant (Hawtrey 1926: 190).
5. While a faster car may make the time of commuting shorter, it is impossible to compress the listening time of, say, a symphony. The importance of consumption time, a factor that is rarely taken into consideration when creative products are at stake, was recognized by Scitovsky as early as 1959, in an article that discussed the productivity lags that afflict the arts (see Scitovsky and Scitovsky 1959 and also Scitovsky 1983). He anticipated Baumol and Bowen's formulation of the cost disease phenomenon of the live arts (see Baumol and Bowen 1966, and, for an overview of the problem, Throsby 2001). These points are addressed in Bianchi (2003). See additionally Earl (2001) for a discussion of the consumption implications of enjoying an art product such as music.
6. In psychology too, a renewed interest in the determinants of well-being and in its underlying processes has reversed a pattern of substantial neglect that had long dominated in the discipline. As Kahneman stresses in the Preface to Kahneman et al. (1999), in psychology, whether behavioural or cognitive, the topics of enjoyment and suffering have attracted much less attention and systematic research than other psychological functions such as memory and attention. No entries at all are to be found, he notes, in introductory textbooks for happiness or well-being (ibid.: ix).

7. Recently some of Berlyne's findings, in particular those referring to the dimension of pleasure represented by complexity, have been challenged (see Martindale et al. 1990; see also Kubovy 1999).
8. Additionally, of course, it inevitably transforms the consumer from being a passive maximizer into an active and explorative agent. On this point, see Bianchi (1998b).
9. Repeatedly in *JE*, Scitovsky discussed how the use of time is a strategic variable in consumers' well-being. The traditions of feasts in poor countries, or the habit of spacing meals, are examples showing that intermittent complete satisfaction may be the best strategy when money constraints militate against full satiation of every need (*JE*: 67). Gossen (1854 [1983]) was the first economist to model the law of decreasing marginal utility and, significantly, he made it depend not on the quantity of the good consumed but on the time *frequency* of consumption. His innovative approach, however, though known to Léon Walras, was none the less neglected. For an analysis of these points, and the disruptive effects that the recognition of time can have on traditional choice theory, see Georgescu-Roegen (1983), Steedman (2001) and Nisticò' (2005).
10. An analysis of the various ways in which novelty can be used strategically in consumption choices is in Bianchi (1998a and 1999).
11. Nor should it come as a surprise that marketing devices try to enhance the appeal of goods by emphasizing and de-emphasizing their relationships of complementarity or non-substitutability with other goods, thereby exploiting or challenging consumers' familiarity with given goods (as discussed in Bianchi 2002).
12. In an interesting article commenting on Scitovsky's *JE*, Hirschman (1996: 540–41) describes the effect that participation in public life, and the company of others, has on well-being. In particular he discusses the civilizing effects of conviviality.
13. Benedikt (1996) in an article very appreciative of *JE*, none the less challenged Scitovsky by pointing out that striving to achieve maximum pleasure where novelty is at the 'right' level is at the basis of all those engaging and self-fulfilling activities that are the most satisfying, that is to say, Scitovsky's creative ones.
14. Csikszentmihalyi's analysis of the experience of flow has the same potential for inducing controlled change in human activities (Csikszentmihalyi 1975). Flow activities are arbitrary patterns that people use to give shape to their experience. They are arbitrary because they are independent of needs. Because of this freedom flow is potentially the most creative and fulfilling kind of experience and allows people to experiment with new actions and challenges. Examples of flow activities are chess, climbing, dancing and sports. I owe this link to the work of Csikszentmihalyi to the comments that my discussant Raj Raghunathan made at the conference on The Paradoxes of Happiness held in Milan in March 2003. He made a clear comparison stressing links and differences between Scitovsky's and Csikzentmihalyi's approach.
15. 'Most of us know that one must be tired to enjoy resting, cold to appreciate a warm fire, and hungry in order really to enjoy a good meal' (*JE*: 71). More, then, is not necessarily better. The more meals, rest and warmth we are able to obtain, the less enjoyable they will be.
16. See Elster and Skog (1999) and Skog (1999) for an analysis of addictive choices and a discussion of Becker's model.
17. In another instance, Scitovsky (1995: 203) calls these goods demerit goods, and opposes them to merit goods that enjoy internal economies which may also be undervalued.
18. Scitovsky also thought that the externalities that income increases create have their qualitative differences. An income increase that is used solely to add to comforts not only generates satisfactions that depreciate more quickly, it also contributes many more socially negative effects such as pollution (*JE*: 144, 209).
19. Conviviality (see note 12) is a perfect example of the complexity of consumption skills and of the fact that they are general, all-encompassing skills. The pleasures of conviviality require an ability to prepare food, to savour it, to converse, to entertain, to create a pleasing environment and so on.
20. See Morroni (2006) on the effects on specialization in the process of the division of knowledge.

21. This means, as Thaler (1991: 248) has noted, that the characteristics of goods cannot be stripped and traded separately. For a discussion of this point, see Bianchi (2002: 8).
22. For Sen, restricting access to alternatives also restricts individual freedom, even if these alternatives are not actually used (see Sen's 1996 comments on *JE*). On the contrary, through education and skills a person is enabled to extract more from what he/she has, and to make more-informed choices.
23. A similar question is asked in a recent paper by Loasby, who suggests that in order to understand demand creation one has also to understand the human capacity to create, modify and apply patterns (Loasby 2001). Much of the discussion in Witt (2001) is relevant to this topic.
24. Many authors, Scitovsky included, describe this as a zero-sum game. In fact, this is not the case since at the end of the game everybody is worse off.
25. Scitovsky, however, also stressed the positive forms that status competition can take. In *JE*, unlike other literature, he argued that status seeking also includes all those activities that are often not considered as such. Helping others – altruism or love – or stimulating others, can be seen as forms of status seeking or, more generally, expressions of a desire to belong (*JE*: 115). Scitovsky also showed how competition for status should be analysed as an effect of that quest for novelty that spurs innovation (see Scitovsky 1985: 201).
26. More interesting, though also more utopian, is Scitovsky's idea that a shorter work week would also provide a positive effect on welfare by reducing the demand for social status. In a leisure-orientated society, with a lower opportunity cost of leisure and greater attention to the quality of consumption time, people would be more prone to appreciate excellence irrespective of whether it yields income.
27. A striking example is fifteenth-century Florence.
28. The examples in this second case are many, but think of Bakelite, an early plastic that tried to imitate more precious materials such as ivory and amber and was then applied in multiple new ways (from radio cases to jewellery to electricity plugs) only to become, in recent years, a rarity itself. Or think of Wedgwood pottery, whose initial success and wide diffusion was largely due to the imitation of old Etruscan paintings and vases, in the pursuit of which it greatly contributed to technological developments and discoveries in glazing and firing.
29. Commenting on Easterlin's studies (see Easterlin 1974), Scitovsky listed four 'unmeasurable' measures of the quality of our lives (*JE*: 33) as possible causes of the low observed correlation between individual happiness and the secular rise of income: status, work satisfaction, novelty and habituation (ibid.: 139).
30. Many scholars have commented on and followed the track laid down by Easterlin: see Abramovitz (1979); Oswald (1997); Frank (1999); Diener (1999); and Frey and Stutzer (2002).

References

Abramovitz, M. (1979), 'Economic growth and its discontent', in M.J. Boskin (ed.), *Economics and Human Welfare. Essays in Honor of Tibor Scitovsky*, Academic Press, New York, pp. 3–21.

Baumol, W.J. and W.G. Bowen (1966), *Performing Arts: The Economic Dilemma*, Twentieth Century Fund, New York.

Becker, G.S. (1996), *Accounting for Tastes*, Harvard University Press, Cambridge, MA.

Becker, G.S. and K. Murphy (1988), 'A theory of rational addiction', *Journal of Political Economy*, **96**, 675–700.

Benedikt, M. (1996), 'Complexity, value, and the psychological postulates of economics', *Critical Review*, **10** (4), 551–94.

Berlyne, D.E. (1971), *Aesthetics and Psychobiology*, Appleton Century Crofts, New York.

Berlyne, D.E. and K.B. Madsen (eds) (1973), *Pleasure, Reward, Preference*, Academic Press, New York.

Bianchi, M. (1998a), 'Consuming novelty: strategies for producing novelty in consumption', *Journal of Medieval and Early Modern Studies*, **28** (1), 3–18.

Bianchi, M. (1998b), 'Taste for novelty and novel tastes. The role of human agency in consumption', in Bianchi (ed.), pp. 64–86.
Bianchi, M. (ed.) (1998c), *The Active Consumer. Novelty and Surprise in Consumer Choice*, Routledge, London and New York.
Bianchi, M. (1999), 'Design and efficiency. New capabilities embedded in new products', in P. Earl and S. Dow (ed.), *Knowledge and Economic Organization, Essays in Honour of Brian Loasby*, Vol 1, Edward Elgar, Cheltenham, UK and Northampton, MA, USA, pp. 119–38.
Bianchi, M. (2002), 'Novelty, preferences, and fashion: when goods are unsettling', *Journal of Economic Behavior and Organization*, **47**, 1–18.
Bianchi, M. (2003), 'A questioning economist: Tibor Scitovsky's attempt to bring joy into economics', *Journal of Economic Psychology*, **24**, 391–407.
Bruni, L. (2002), 'L'economia e i paradossi della felicità', in P.L. Sacco and S. Zamagni (eds), *Complessità relazionale e comportamento economico*, Il Mulino, Bologna, pp. 173–254.
Csikszentmihalyi, M. (1975), *Beyond Boredom and Anxiety*, Jossey-Bass, San Francisco, CA.
Diener, E. (1999), 'Subjective well-being: three decades of progress', *Psychological Bulletin*, **125** (2), 276–302.
Earl, P.E. (2001), 'Simon's travel theorem and the demand for live music', *Journal of Economic Psychology*, **22** (3), 335–58.
Easterlin, R. (1974), 'Does economic growth improve the human lot? Some empirical evidence', in P.A. David and M.W. Reder (eds), *Nations and Households in Economic Growth: Essays in Honor of Moses Abramovitz*, Academic Press, New York, pp. 89–125.
Easterlin, R. (1995), 'Will raising the incomes of all increase the happiness of all?', *Journal of Economic Behavior and Organization*, **27**, 35–48.
Elster, J. and O. Skog (1999), *Getting Hooked. Rationality and Addiction*, Cambridge University Press, Cambridge.
Frank, R.H. (1985), *Choosing the Right Pond. Human Behavior and the Quest for Status*, Oxford University Press, Oxford and New York.
Frank, R.H. (1999), *Luxury Fever. Why Money fails to Satisfy in an Era of Excess*, Free Press, New York.
Frederick, S. and G. Loewenstein (1999), 'Hedonic Adaptation', in Kahneman et al. (eds), pp. 302–29.
Frey, B. and A. Stutzer (2002), *Happiness and Economics. How the Economy and Institutions Affect Well-being*, Princeton University Press, Princeton, NJ.
Friedman, J. and A. McCabe (eds) (1996), *Critical Review*, Special Issue on Tibor Scitovsky's *The Joyless Economy* after Twenty Years, **10** (4).
Georgescu-Roegen, N. (1983), 'Herrmann Heinrich Gossen: his life and work in historical perspective', in Gossen (1854 [1983]), pp. xi–cxlix.
Gossen, H.H. (1854 [1983]), *The Laws of Human Relations and the Rules of Human Action Derived Therefrom*, MIT Press, Cambridge, MA.
Hawtrey, R.G. (1926), *The Economic Problem*, Longmans, Green & Co., London.
Herrnstein, R. and D. Prelec (1992), 'Melioration', in G. Loewenstein and J. Elster (eds) (1992), *Choice over Time*, New York: Russell Sage Foundation, pp. 235–64.
Hirsch, F. (1976), *The Social Limits of Growth*, Harvard University Press, Cambridge, MA.
Hirschman, A.O. (1996), 'Melding the public and private spheres: taking commensality seriously', in Friedman and McCabe (eds), pp. 533–50.
Jevons, W.S. (1871 [1970]), *The Theory of Political Economy*, Penguin Books, Harmondsworth.
Kahneman, D., E. Diener and N. Schwarz (eds) (1999), *Well-being: The Foundations of Hedonic Psychology*, Russell Sage Foundation, New York.
Kahneman, D. and A. Tversky (1979), '*Prospect theory. An analysis of choice under risk*', *Econometrica*, **47**, 263–91.
Kubovy, M. (1999), 'On the pleasures of the mind', in Kahneman et al. (eds), pp. 134–54.
Layard, R. (2003), 'Happiness: has social science a clue? Three Lectures', Lionel Robbins Memorial Lectures 2002–2003, mimeo.
Loasby, B. (2001), 'Cognition, imagination and institutions in demand creation', in Witt (ed.), pp. 13–28.

Martindale, C., K. Moore and J. Borkum (1990), 'Aesthetic preference: anomalous findings for Berlyne's psychobiological theory', *American Journal of Psychology*, **103** (1), 53–80.
Metcalfe, J.S. (2001), 'Consumption, preferences, and the evolutionary agenda', in Witt (ed.), pp. 43–64.
Morroni, M. (2006), *Knowledge, Scale and Transactions in the Theory of the Firm*, Cambridge: Cambridge University Press.
Nisticò, S. (2005), 'Consumption and time in economics: prices and quantities in a temporary equilibrium perspective', *Cambridge Journal of Economics*, **29** (6), 943–57.
Oswald, A.J. (1997), 'Happiness and economic performance', *Economic Journal*, **107**, 1815–31.
Parducci, A. (1995), *Happiness, Pleasure, and Judgment. The Contextual Theory and Its Applications*, Lawrence Erlbaum, Mahwah, NJ.
Schelling, T.C. (1978), *Micromotives and Macrobehavior*, Norton, New York.
Scitovsky, T. (1962), 'On the principle of consumer sovereignty', *American Economic Review, Papers and Proceedings*, **52** (2), 262–8.
Scitovsky, T. (1972a), 'What's wrong with the arts is what's wrong with society', in Scitovsky 1986, pp. 37–46.
Scitovsky, T. (1972b), 'Notes on the producer society', in Scitovsky 1986, pp. 47–69.
Scitovsky, T. (1976 [1992]), *The Joyless Economy: The Psychology of Human Satisfaction*, revised edition, Oxford University Press, Oxford.
Scitovsky, T. (1981), 'The desire for excitement in modern society', in Scitovsky 1986, pp. 128–35.
Scitovsky, T. (1983), 'Subsidies for the arts: the economic argument', in Scitovsky 1986, pp. 149–59.
Scitovsky, T. (1985), 'How to bring joy into economics', in Scitovsky 1986, pp. 183–203.
Scitovsky, T. (1986), *Human Desires and Economic Satisfaction. Essays on the Frontiers of Economics*, New York University Press, New York.
Scitovsky, T. (1987), 'Growth in the affluent society', in Scitovsky 1995, pp. 97–108.
Scitovsky, T. (1995), *Economic Theory and Reality. Selected Essays on their Disparities and Reconciliation*, Edward Elgar, Aldershot, UK and Brookfield, US.
Scitovsky, T. (1996), 'My own criticism of *The Joyless Economy*', *Critical Review*, **10** (4), 595–606.
Scitovsky, T. (2000), 'The wages of boredom', *New Perspectives Quarterly*, Spring, 45–51.
Scitovsky, T. (undated), 'Boredom – its causes and consequences', typescript, in Scitovsky papers, Rare Book, Manuscript, and Special Collections Library, Duke University, Durham, NC.
Scitovsky, T. and A. Scitovsky (1959), 'What price economic progress', *Yale Review*, **49**, 95–110.
Sen, A. (1996), 'Rationalism, joy and freedom', *Critical Review*, **10** (4), 481–94.
Skog, O. (1999), 'Rationality, irrationality, and addiction. Notes on Becker and Murphy's theory of addiction', in Elster and Skog, pp. 173–207.
Steedman, I. (2001), *Consumption Takes Time. Implications for Economic Theory*, Routledge, London.
Stigler, G.J. and G.S. Becker (1977), '*De Gustibus non est disputandum*', *American Economic Review*, **67** (2), 76–90.
Strotz, R. (1955–56), 'Myopia and inconsistency in dynamic utility maximization', *Review of Economic Studies*, **23**, 165–80.
Thaler, R.H. (1981), '*Some empirical evidence on dynamic inconsistency*', in Thaler 1991, pp. 127–33.
Thaler, R.H. (1991), *Quasi Rational Economics*, Russell Sage Foundation, New York.
Throsby, D. (2001), *Economics and Culture*, Cambridge University Press, Cambridge.
Van Praag, B.M.S. and P. Frijters (1999), 'The measurement of welfare and well being: the Leyden approach', in Kahneman et al. (eds), pp. 413–33.
Witt, U. (ed.) (2001), *Escaping Satiation. The Demand Side of Economic Growth*, Springer, Berlin.

Appendix 7A

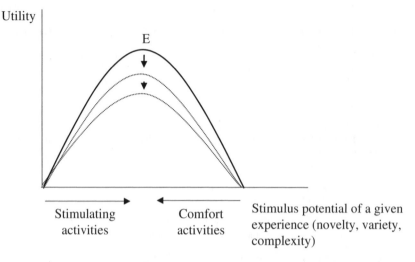

Note: The inverted-U shaped Wundt curve (solid curve) shows that the utility associated with a given experience can be increased in two ways: by increasing its novelty potential when this is felt to be too low (Scitovsky's stimulating activities), and by decreasing it when it is perceived as being too high or unsettling (Scitovsky's comfort activities). Since, however, for Berlyne, utility depends not on the levels of stimulus but on its changes, repeating the experience decreases its pleasure. The optimal position E is not dynamically stable, but shifts downwards with the repetition of the same experience.

Figure 7A.1   Wundt curve

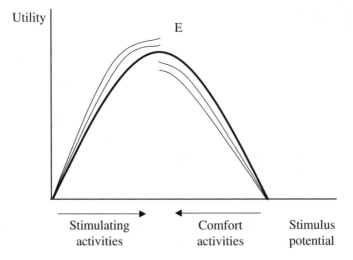

Note: In this figure the thin curves on the left are higher than the original heavier curve. They represent the potential increase in novelty and returns associated with repeated creative consumption. The lower curves on the right show instead the decrease in returns associated with the loss of novelty and habituation induced by repeated comfort activities.

Figure 7A.2   Increasing and decreasing returns

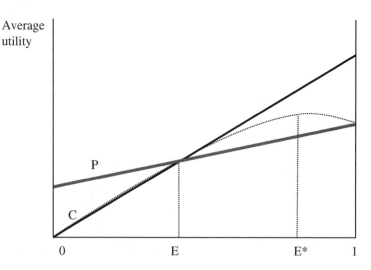

Note: The horizontal axis measures the amount of resources invested in pleasurable creative activities. The line P is the value function, measured in utility payoffs, associated with these activities. It increases as more resources are invested in creative activities. The line C is the value function associated with comfort activities, decreasing from the right to the left as investment in comfort increases. Point E is the equilibrium allocation. The dotted curve represents the total utility function resulting from the combined P and C utilities. Point E*, corresponding to maximum total utility, is the optimal choice. Equilibrium choice E thus corresponds to a too-low investment in creative activities.

Figure 7A.3   Overinvestment in comfort goods

8 Well-being and consumption: towards a theoretical approach based on human needs satisfaction
Monica Guillen Royo

1. Introduction

In the tradition of neoclassical economics, the study of consumption plays a central role. Yet its analysis has been based on rigid assumptions that limit its explanatory power. The assumptions, related to consumer sovereignty, exogeneity of preferences, rationality and insatiability, although challenged by several economists during the twentieth century, are still at the core of the conventional theory of consumer behaviour. Together they contribute theoretically to the commonly accepted view that consumption increases individual utility or well-being.

In the utilitarian tradition, utility has two main meanings: desire fulfilment and happiness (Sen 1985), both of which are thought to be related to individual well-being. Therefore, consumption is considered either to fulfil consumers' desires or to contribute to their happiness. Alternative approaches to well-being, such as the subjective well-being (SWB) and objective well-being (OWB) traditions, while rejecting most of the neoclassical assumptions, do not support the direct positive link between consumption and well-being.

SWB studies analyse the correlation between income and people's contentment, claiming that income is not satisfactorily correlated with subjective well-being measures. Consumption is hardly analysed as such, but results on income and SWB are taken as representing the effects of consumption. The best-known findings are related to the fact that although people in richer nations declare themselves to be on average happier than people in poorer nations (Diener and Biwas-Diener 2002), the causes appear not to be related to higher levels of income but to cultural transformations from collectivism to individualism (Ahuvia 2002), among other factors. Moreover, in developed countries, economic growth has not been associated with increases in SWB over the past decades (Easterlin 1995; Diener and Oishi 2000; Diener and Biswas-Diener 2002; Frey and Stutzer 2002). Thus, SWB studies provide the empirical evidence against the neoclassical tradition that relates consumption to well-being. However, SWB face some challenges in assessing the effect of consumption on well-being, the first related to the use of income as a proxy for consumption and the second due to the fact that people adapt to situations of deprivation.

Traditionally, OWB theories have not been utilized to analyse consumption but provide the framework for assessing patterns of consumption with regard to their success or failure in meeting certain predefined goals. Doyal and Gough (1991), Max-Neef (1991) and Nussbaum (2000), among others, have developed specific lists of human capabilities or human needs that have to be fulfilled for individuals to fully participate in their own form of life. Recently, OWB theories have been used as a framework for analysing patterns of consumption (Jackson and Marks 1999) thus opening the field for future research on consumption and well-being.

Drawing on the above discussion, this chapter approaches two main issues: first, the problems arising from the maintenance of the neoclassical approach to consumption regarding rationality, sovereignty, exogenous preferences and insatiability, which make the link between consumption and increased utility or happiness difficult to maintain. Second, the options opened by OWB theories with regard to analysing the impact of consumption on individual well-being.

The chapter begins with a description of the main assumptions of the neoclassical analysis of consumer behaviour. Thereafter, some of the main criticisms arising from mainstream and non-orthodox economists are presented, leading to a reconsideration of its adequacy in depicting the reality of consumption and its consequences on individual well-being. Finally, the SWB and OWB traditions are reviewed with regard to their potential to offer an alternative to the neoclassical economics approach to consumption and human well-being.

2.   The assumptions of neoclassical theory of consumption

The neoclassical theory of consumption undertakes a positivistic analysis of consumer choice as it attempts to depict how the individual goes through the process of choosing among bundles of goods when prices and income are given. In so doing they make several assumptions that simplify the individual's behaviour and allow for formalization and the later development of complex theories of consumption.

The assumptions supporting the theory of consumer choice as they are known today were established at the beginning of the twentieth century with the work of Samuelson (1938), who increased the formal rigour of the neoclassical analysis that had started with the marginalists[1] during the second half of the nineteenth century. Critiques and alternatives have arisen occasionally in the twentieth century but they 'have been too quickly fragmented and/or forgotten' (Ackerman 1997: 652) and will be examined later.

Drawing from the marginal utility theory, the neoclassical theory of consumer behaviour was developed considering:

1. A sovereign individual who acts in the market through given preferences and chooses what to purchase from the available information about goods and prices.
2. An individual who behaves rationally which implies that his/her aim is utility or welfare maximization and mostly in his/her own interest.[2]
3. Decreasing marginal utility for single goods is assumed, but the satisfaction achieved by increased consumption seems not to saturate.

Thus, the neoclassical theory of consumer choice makes strong behavioural assumptions: consumer sovereignty, exogeneity of preferences, utility-maximizing rational behaviour and insatiability. These assumptions conform with a theory that implies a direct positive relation between consumption and well-being. They provide the theoretical basis for the general widespread support to endless increases in economic growth. As the four fundamental assumptions mentioned are essential to justify the positive relation between consumption and well-being, it seems appropriate to describe them in a little more detail.

Consumer sovereignty
In the neoclassical analysis, the individual is considered to be sovereign in choosing among different consumption bundles. Consumers are autonomous in their choices and this implies that they play an active role in determining the amount and the characteristics of the goods offered in the market. As Penz (1986: 5) puts it 'consumer sovereignty implies that what is produced, how it is produced, and how it is distributed are to be determined by consumer preferences expressed through individual choices in a free market'. If consumer sovereignty prevails, production is understood as being subordinated to the requirements of the consumer expressed through his/her decisions in the market. This concept, although subject to a vast array of critiques, has become a central axiom to economic policy making in western countries and dominates the consumption sphere. Such a principle places economics far apart from value judgements as individuals are supposed to be the best judges of their acts.

Exogenous preferences
Neoclassical consumption theory studies the consumer process of generating demand as a process led by individual preferences, which are taken as given. Historically, individual preferences were taken as being generated in the environment in which the choice was taking place. Classical economists

considered that social norms and historical experience conditioned preferences. Thus, they took preferences as being shaped by the customs and the
society in which the individual lived (Nicolaides 1988). However, since the
marginalist revolution, in the second half of the nineteenth century, and
the beginning of the development of the theory of consumer demand, it
has been considered that individual tastes and preferences are given,
exogenous and stable, that is, they do not change over time.[3]

In neoclassical consumer theory, as preferences are exogenous the only
way to know them and maintain a coherent theoretical framework is to
extract them from the behaviour of the consumer in the market, following
Samuelson's (1938) revealed preference theory. To do that, neoclassical economics takes as granted convexity and stability of preferences during the
period when the behaviour of individuals is being observed (Varian 2003)
and to ascertain which bundle is preferred with regard to another one, consumers are observed in the situations in which they have to make the choice.
If they always choose X when they could choose Y, it will be asserted that
they prefer X to Y and thus that X is giving them more utility than Y. Thus,
neoclassical economics infers from the information provided by the market
demand, the structure of individual preferences.[4] This method is easy to
challenge as it only proves that observed choices, if they follow a certain
rule, are consistent with preferences defined in neoclassical terms (completeness, reflexivity and transitivity). But even in mainstream books of
economics it is acknowledged that this is only an abstract construct for the
purposes of a coherent economic model. As Varian (2003: 129) asks: 'Does
this prove that the constructed preferences actually generated the observed
choices? Of course not'. Therefore, in the theory of consumer choice, preferences are an abstract construct not related to the environment in which
they are generated and they are inferred in a way that cannot prove itself,
even to reflect actual consumer choices.[5] This in turn implies, not only
setting aside the problems associated with the identification of the variables
affecting choice but also ignoring the distinction among goods consumed
that had previously been analysed by classical political economists (Fine
and Leopold 1993).

Rationality
Rational behaviour is seen as that which is followed by individuals who assess
the alternative courses of action with regard to the benefits and costs they
may imply and choose the one with the best outcome for them. Rational
behaviour will imply, in neoclassical terms, that individuals seek to maximize their own utility or welfare, not necessarily accounting for the welfare
of others when having to decide upon different consumption bundles. If
individuals, for any reason, do not follow the maximizing behaviour,

neoclassical economics will regard them as being irrational. There are some commonly accepted exceptions to this definition, mainly when individuals do not have all the tools available to make an informed choice and information is too costly or is not generally available. Neoclassical economists refer to this situation as 'bounded rationality' instead of irrationality. Thus, the neoclassical individual is still purposive and rational but might not have all the necessary knowledge at his/her disposal.

Rationality in neoclassical economics remains linked to the maximization of utility. The concept of utility remains, since the marginalists, slightly related to the original utilitarian meaning given by Jeremy Bentham (1780), reworked and developed by John Stuart Mill (1863), which associated utility with happiness. Marginalists still considered that consumption generated welfare and that welfare or degrees of happiness could be measured and aggregated through cardinal utility functions to obtain specific values. Therefore, the level of utility achieved through consumption could be compared among different individuals and societies and through time.

Since the work of Vilfredo Pareto (1916), utility has been taken as an ordinal concept, implying the impossibility of making interpersonal and intertemporal comparisons – only the ordering of different goods or situations will count. The change from a cardinal view of utility to an ordinal one has several implications: as Sen (1985) states, the rank given by individuals to different goods or achievements as an ordering of a person's well-being is 'an heroic simplification' thus blurring the direct link between consumption and well-being through utility. Moreover, the shift from cardinal to ordinal utility also implies that the analysis of consumer behaviour abandons the concept of decreasing marginal utility of consumption. As Galbraith (1977) puts it, the analysis of consumption departs from the 'diminishing urgency of wants'.

Insatiability

In the neoclassical theory of consumption 'the only meaningful forms of individual satisfaction result from more consumption' (Ackerman 1997: 652). Ordinality and the revealed preferences principle justify not approaching satiation. Ordinality implies that consumption does not present diminishing marginal returns and the principle of revealed preferences interprets the fact that people buy more when they have more income as revealing the insatiability of their material desires (ibid.: 657). Also, sovereignty and rationality reinforce the concept of insatiability in neoclassical economics. People who know what gives them more utility or happiness and choose in order to maximize it cannot systematically overestimate the amount of goods needed to increase their utility. Individuals do not choose an excessive amount of goods, 'why should they' (Varian 1987: 48). Possibly there is no reason to think that anyone will choose to buy goods beyond the satiation point. However, it is a common experience in western households to face situations in which an excessive amount of the same good has been purchased (TV sets that are never used, spare shoes and dresses, perfumes, watches, mobile phone sets and so on) and this is not contemplated in the analysis due to the mentioned assumptions and to the fact that distinctions between categories of goods are not always taken into account.[6]

Until now, a broad picture of the neoclassical assumptions underlying the neoclassical theory of consumption has been depicted. The next section addresses some core criticisms of the foundations of the generally accepted framework.

3.   Discussing the neoclassical basic assumptions

The assumptions underlying the neoclassical theory of consumption have been criticized by mainstream and non-neoclassical economists.[7] However, as outlined in this section, most of the alternatives have relaxed some of the neoclassical assumptions, drawing on evidence from research in sociology, psychology and anthropology, while maintaining the others. This implies that besides the framework offered by institutionalists, there have been few successful attempts to provide a comprehensive alternative to the neoclassical paradigm. This section examines some of these attempts following the structure of the previous one.

Consumer sovereignty

The leading role of the consumer in the market has been widely criticized in the institutionalist[8] tradition mainly in the works of Galbraith (1977). He claimed that consumer sovereignty no longer stands as marketing, advertising and the prescriptive power of social norms subject individuals to supply pressure. Galbraith highlighted the creation of wants by the production system that influences consumer decisions not only by persuading them through advertising and marketing but also through the search for increased support from the state and related institutions. Wetherly (1996) expands on the effect of institutions other than markets, pointing out that they provide the requirements of the capitalist system to fulfil its basic need, that is, the pursuit of profit. Individual sovereignty seems to be constrained by the needs of capital not only through direct persuasive action but also indirectly through other institutions, such as, for instance, economic and social policies. By deciding the direction of policies such as transport, opening hours, working time and so forth, social policies guarantee production and the realization of profits, providing the necessary stable environment for the system to operate. Thus, consumer sovereignty is being challenged not just by the positive interference of the production system but by the socioeconomic systems that create the setting in which consumption takes place.

Exogenous preferences

Within mainstream economics some efforts have been made to recognize the endogeneity of preferences and incorporate them into the neoclassical formalization. Akerlof and Dickens (1990) consider that the analysis of consumer choice has to account for the behavioural assumptions behind psychological, anthropological and sociological research because they offer more plausible explanations of human behaviour. In their work, they apply the psychological theory of cognitive dissonance to the study of consumer choice. Cognitive dissonance theory introduces the fact that individuals manipulate their beliefs to confirm their desires. The inclusion of this assumption implies the need to incorporate into the formalization of consumer behaviour the process by which preferences are generated. This approach explains, for instance, the role of advertising as a mechanism that offers individuals the external justification they need to believe that they have acquired the goods that satisfy their needs. However, Akerlof and Dickens do not disregard the whole neoclassical paradigm, as they consider that the manipulation of beliefs is a conscious process.

Institutionalists have always accounted for the influences of social factors when approaching consumption. In particular, Duesenberry (1967), on the grounds of empirical evidence, rested his theory of the consumption function on the assumption that consumer preferences depend on relative social status. He based his assumptions on the fact that despite economic growth, savings were decreasing at all levels of income. He claimed that the reason for this happening was that individuals who were exposed to higher standards of living and better consumption goods longed to acquire them for themselves. Thus, in growing economies, as everyone's consumption rises, households will increase their consumption as well as decrease their savings.

Analytical Marxists such as Roemer (1986) have also addressed the issue of endogenous preferences. Roemer introduces in his formalization of consumer behaviour the productive forces and economic structure that determine preferences at a moment in time. When constructing his model he accounts for the effect of technology, institutions and ownership relations in the previous period and defines present preferences as being shaped by previous individual preferences. He still takes consumers as rational individuals but he sees them as being under pressure from institutions, technology, the position in the productive system and habituation when they choose among consumption bundles. As Philp and Young (2002: 327) point out, even 'those such as Roemer who have (sometimes) emphasised the social formation of preferences have often constructed models which rely on a broadly instrumental/calculating theory of human agency'.

Rational behaviour

Regarding the rational behaviour of consumers, Sen (1977) questions the adequacy of treating them as utility-maximizing egoistic individuals. He considers the neoclassical approach to be reductionist given that, for instance, choices driven by moral attachments to a group or collective are not taken as rational. Sen claims that there is no inconsistency in the behaviour of individuals acting because of compromise, therefore he proposes, within the neoclasical framework, to widen the concept of rationality to incorporate behaviours motivated by feelings other than egoism, such as compromise with a social, political or religious group.

Institutionalists also criticize neoclassical rationality, highlighting the function of habit as a guide to human behaviour. They do not see individuals as utility-maximizing agents but as human beings following habits and routines in their decision processes. The imitation and spreading of habits generate institutions,[9] which are seen at the same time as reinforcing and fostering particular behaviours and habits. Therefore, to focus the analysis of choice on homo economicus is also seen as a reductionist way of approaching individual behaviour because current social, personal and induced habits are shaping and constraining individual preferences and choices.

Some of the previous considerations have been recognized by several mainstream economists, and preferences previously seen as irrational such as the ones generated by commitment to a specific group or by addiction (Winston 1980), have been included in the neoclassical analysis. Habit, which for institutionalists explains rational choice, has also been addressed in orthodox writings. Habitual behaviour has been formalized in terms of earlier choices made by individuals, or as a choice in itself because lazy consumers do not have time to gather the necessary information to make a new choice every time they need to (Hodgson 1998).

Analytical Marxists also consider that if some patterns of human behaviour regarding choice can be traced, they are unlikely to be a consequence of the optimizing behaviour of homo economicus as the reasons for choosing a specific good might be of a completely different sort. Philp and Young (2002) give examples of the literature of internal conflict where people's choices are thought to be the result of their personal conflicts rather than the reaction to their true preferences. They also point out how some analytical Marxists, such as Hargreaves Heap, analyse action in the market as an expression of the beliefs of individuals rather than as an outcome of its maximizing process.

Insatiability

> When man has satisfied his physical needs, then psychologically grounded desires take over. These can never be satisfied or, in any case, no progress can be proven. The concept of satiation has very little standing in economics. It is held to be neither useful nor scientific to speculate on the comparative cravings of the stomach and the mind. (Galbraith 1977: 119)

Critics of the insatiability assumptions, unlike neoclassical economists, have always distinguished among drives motivating consumption. Distinct psychological–social–economic forces influence different categories of goods, therefore their satiability also varies. The requirement for food would easily be satiated, whereas the desire for status symbols, reinforced by marketing and social pressure might not present a foreseeable satiation point.

In the early twentieth century, Alfred Marshall (1920) already acknowledged the existence of higher and lower desires. In the 1930s, Keynes (1963) believed that absolute needs, those that are independent of social status, were satiable and therefore they showed a decreasing marginal utility. Keynes claimed that the need to accumulate would become another pathology to be treated by psychologists in one hundred years' time. Later, Scitovsky (1976) in his *Joyless Economy*, drawing from psychology studies, distinguished between the desire for comfort and pleasure, desires for the first being satiable whereas desires for the second might not be. As Ackerman (1997: 658) puts it, summarizing Scitovsky's argument 'as yesterday's novel pleasures become today's habits and tomorrow's socially defined necessities, maintaining the same level of pleasure requires new levels of consumption'. The distinction between higher and lower desires, absolute and relative needs and desires for comfort and pleasure show that satiation occurs for certain specific goods and should be incorporated into the theory of consumption.

The critics of these neoclassical assumptions have raised very important issues from which to rethink the theory of consumer choice. It is difficult to accept a theory of consumer choice that does not acknowledge the power of advertising, the framing power of socioeconomic institutions, the presence of habituation, commitment, beliefs and other factors affecting consumer choices. Moreover, not all goods have the same characteristics, and satiation plays an important role with regard to certain goods. Nevertheless, relaxing the neoclassical assumptions poses many problems with regard to formalization, making it difficult for neoclassical economics to build a completely new theory of consumption. Following Fine and Leopold (1993: 32): 'orthodox economics cannot be amended to incorporate a richer theory of consumption. It would have to be discarded altogether'. Institutionalists, who have offered a holistic approach incorporating the effect of institutions and culture in shaping individual behaviour, have been constantly accused of not being theoretically grounded and basing their analysis on the description of economic reality. Therefore, their approach has not been successfully supported as an option for replacing the neoclassical one.

4.   Consumption and well-being: challenging the neoclassical paradigm

The definition of well-being used in neoclassical economics is based on the concept of utility.[10] In order to elucidate the options that increase individual utility or well-being, neoclassical economists have referred to the behaviouristic revealed preferences theory of Samuelson (see Section 2) relating utility to choice. The revealed preferences axiom has been taken as a basis for economists to carry out macroeconomic empirical studies which implicitly attach higher levels of well-being to increases in consumption. Consequently, economists tend to assume that as economies grow their consumption increases, and so does aggregate utility or well-being.

The direct and positive relation between consumption and well-being has been widely discussed in the subjective and objective well-being literature. SWB has been investigated in medicine, sociology and psychology and traditionally defines well-being through the concepts of positive affect, negative affect and life satisfaction. In the SWB tradition, the impact of consumption on individual well-being is related to its effect on individuals' self-reported satisfaction. OWB studies have approached well-being 'as the attainment of certain values which can be specified independently of the individual concerned' (Gasper 2004: 9) and under this approach, consumption is seen as having a positive impact if it facilitates the achievement of these values, for instance, enhancing individual's capabilities (Nussbaum 2000) or increasing the satisfaction of basic needs (Doyal and Gough 1991).

Subjective well-being and consumption: saturation and adaptation

Scholars supporting the SWB approach have openly criticized the utilitarian approach in neoclassical economics and the revealed preferences principle. In their review of happiness studies, Frey and Stutzer (2002) claim that observed behaviour, used to infer the utility of outcomes in neoclassical economics, does not give a good insight into individual well-being. They see it as a very narrow concept that does not account for individuals' experienced utility; therefore they suggest complementing it with a subjective approach.

> The subjective approach to utility offers a fruitful *complementary* path to study the world. Firstly, subjective well-being is a much broader concept than decision utility: it includes experienced utility as well as procedural utility, and is for many people an ultimate goal. That is not the case for other things we may want, such

as job security, status power, and especially money (income). We do not want them for themselves but rather to give us the possibility of making ourselves happier. Secondly, the concept of subjective happiness allows us to capture human well-being directly. This creates a basis for explicitly testing fundamental assumptions and propositions in economic theory. (Ibid.: 405, original italics.)

However, it is not clear to what extent SWB can provide evidence of the impact of consumption on well-being. First, consumption has not been studied as such, and research in SWB has not normally distinguished between the type of goods acquired and those consumed. Second, different levels of consumption have generally been approached through investigating the correlation between income and well-being which has been shown to be low and not significant beyond certain levels of income.

In the SWB tradition, income has been the proxy for consumption. Researchers have argued that income accounts for less than 8 per cent of the explanation of well-being and that other life domains such as family (Rojas 2004), relatedness (Argyle 1987), individualist values (Ahuvia 2002) or rivalry (Fafchamps and Shilpi 2004) are most influential. Moreover, although people in richer nations are on average happier than people in poorer nations, differences in wealth within nations show only a small positive correlation with happiness (they explain only 2–3 per cent of the variance in SWB between individuals[11]). Furthermore, economic growth in developed countries has not been associated with increases in SWB beyond a middle-income level over the past decades (Easterlin 1995). These paradoxical results have been the basis for several studies enquiring into the reason for the slow increase or stabilization of SWB measures when income rises. For instance, Ahuvia (2002), in his search for a reason for the low correlation between income and happiness in cultures where consumption levels are above those required to lift people out of poverty, finds that when basic needs are met, other factors play a more important role in increasing well-being. He claims that 'Once one has a roof over one's head, a job, and food on the table, increases in income generally explain less than 1% of the variance in SWB' (ibid.: 24). He argues that the factors playing a key role are related to the fact that economic development fosters cultural transformations 'away from obligation and toward the pursuit of happiness' which 'is part of a broader transition away from collectivism and toward individualist cultural values and forms of social organisation' (p. 25). Frey and Stutzer (2002) reinforce this view, maintaining that 'additional material goods and services initially provide extra pleasure, but it is usually only transitory. Higher happiness with material things wears off. Satisfaction depends on change and disappears with continued consumption' (ibid.: 414).

Thus, SWB studies anticipate a weak relationship between consumption and well-being, which becomes even weaker above a certain level of income, thus supporting the criticisms of the insatiability axiom. However, low-income individuals in developing countries have not always been reported to experience higher levels of satisfaction as income increases. Other factors seem again to override income in their importance in raising satisfaction. Theories of adaptation have long studied this phenomenon.

Martha Nussbaum in her 2000 book *Women and Human Development* tackled adaptive preferences in the way they were defined by Elster (1983).[12] Nussbaum argued that adaptation is a generalized phenomenon in developing countries as women get used to deprivation or constrained liberties. She exemplifies adaptation, drawing on evidence from Indian women experiencing abusive marriage, discriminatory wage structure, discriminatory system of family income sharing and unhealthy or unsanitary conditions. She found that women under those circumstances internalize their situation and live their life and make their choices in adverse surroundings without seeing them as oppressive – which they would look to alien eyes and even to their eyes if they had the opportunities to experience extended liberties or options. Thus, 'oppressed women' would declare themselves to be more satisfied with their life than an initial account of their situation through objective socioeconomic measures would indicate.

Nussbaum's work shows that individuals might report relatively high levels of well-being even if they are objectively deprived. Theories of adaptive preferences have been complemented with evidence from SWB studies in developing countries or among poor social groups. Biswas-Diener and Diener (2001) and Fafchamps and Shilpi (2004) claim that poor people do not report low levels of SWB as would be expected from their 'objective' situation, since other factors such as rivalry and strong social relationships play a major role even when income rises.

Hence, it is not clear how SWB studies can provide an alternative assessment to the neoclassical approach in terms of the relationship between consumption and well-being. First, because the correlation has been tested mainly through income, which is weakly correlated to SWB, and other factors seem generally more significant even at low levels of income. Second, because if people adapt to objective poverty, the relationship between consumption and well-being might not be best approached through subjective indicators. The final subsection presents the alternative offered by the OWB approaches.

OWB and consumption: towards a research agenda
OWB theories maintain that there are universal characteristics from which individual well-being can be assessed. The OWB tradition has been developed in different disciplines from philosophy to psychology generally, arguing for the need of minimum standards for an individual to lead a

'good life'. Under this approach, consumption is seen as an activity that provides individuals with goods and services that have an effect on their well-being through the satisfaction of its characteristic elements. The neo-classical axioms are not assumed, and most of the OWB theories include thorough criticism of some of them, mainly sovereignty (Doyal and Gough 1991: 23–4, 53) endogenous preferences (Nussbaum 2000: 119–28) and rationality (Doyal and Gough 1991: 120–26).

Although the need for objective measures of well-being has been widely supported, the risks associated with universalism have left the academic world with few successful attempts to build a specific list.[13] Only three of them are examined here, namely the works of Nussbaum (2000), Doyal and Gough (1991) and Max-Neef (1991). Their works share the common aim of depicting a list of universal requirements to achieve a certain level of well-being and differ in the type of analysis that can be derived from them (Gasper 1996). OWB approaches have usually been criticized for being against differences in culture, not allowing for individual diversity and being paternalistic. All these criticisms have been opposed by the authors mentioned above, who have generally acknowledged that universalistic lists of central capabilities or needs require the information that a bottom-up approach can provide to enrich or even adapt these lists to different values or societies.[14]

Nussbaum (2000) proposes a normative approach to evaluate the desir-ability of a given societal situation based on a list of 10 central human func-tional capabilities[15] related to what people are able to do and to be. Defining capabilities and thresholds for each capability, Nussbaum is specifying a space to compare societies in terms of their success in meeting them. Her framework does not assume any of the neoclassical assumptions about individual behaviour and stresses that adaptive preferences are leading most of the choices in developing countries. She undertakes a thorough criticism of subjective welfarism in chapter 2 of her book, claiming that a preferences-based approach is unable to account for the many ways in which unjust background, low expectations, fear and habit affect people's choices. However, Nussbaum's 'thick vague theory of the good' does not explicitly tackle consumption and its effectiveness in enhancing human functional characteristics. Her framework could be used to analyse the impact of different consumer goods on the elements of the list but this has not been attempted so far. Moreover, the criticisms that arise regarding the contents of the list, such as assigning the same weight to 'bodily integrity' and 'play' and its lack of empirical validation (Clark 2002), makes it a con-tested task.

The theory of human need (THN) of Doyal and Gough (1991) defines a list of needs ranked from universal goals through basic to intermediate needs. As universal goals they identify avoidance of serious harm, social participation and critical participation. Physical health and autonomy are considered the basic needs. Intermediate needs represent the characteristics that human needs satisfiers have to comply with (1991: ch. 10) and are grouped into 11 categories: adequate nutritional food and water; adequate protective housing; non-hazardous work and physical environments; appropriate health care; security in childhood; significant primary relationships; physical and economic security; safe birth control and child-bearing; and appropriated basic and cross-cultural education (ibid.: 202). Whereas needs are considered universal, satisfiers depend on the culture and the society in which the individual is living and they are directly related to consumer goods and services.

Satisfiers are represented mainly by consumer goods and services. The THN, like Nussbaum's approach, is not preference based and does not adopt the rigid neoclassical axioms. It explicitly criticizes consumer sovereignty and endogenous preferences but also tackles rationality and insatiability. With regard to consumer sovereignty, Doyal and Gough draw on the work of Penz (1986), who supports the use of normative judgements in order to avoid the inconsistencies derived from considering individuals as the leading force behind the production and distribution of consumer goods. They justify the development of a universalist theory of human need as an alternative to the assumption of sovereignty, which has proved to be theoretically and empirically unsustainable. In relation to endogeneity of preferences, the THN recognizes the impact of customs, society and markets on choices, shaping them and affecting their evolution. Rationality is also accounted for as a component of the definition of the basic need for autonomy but it is not bounded by what is socially or legally accepted or by a maximizing behaviour of any kind. Finally, satiation is also addressed although mainly from the side of the production system. Doyal and Gough argue that increased production will not always increase well-being as not all kinds of goods are directed to satisfying basic needs. As they put it, 'an economy which prioritises the production of needs satisfiers will, all things being equal, enhance overall opportunities for successful participation to a greater extent than another economy with the same aggregate output but with a higher share of luxury production' (1991: 237).

To sum up, the THN offers a potential alternative framework to analyse the impact of consumption on well-being. The operationalization of the theory using macro aggregates in Part III of the book shows its capacity to incorporate the analysis of consumption. Nevertheless, to clarify the relationship between satisfiers and commodities and to classify consumer goods and services with regard to the needs they satisfy is a challenging task, which has not yet been undertaken.

An explicit attempt to relate consumption to human needs satisfaction was developed by Max-Neef (1991) in his book *Human-Scale Development*. He proposed a taxonomy of human needs based on axiological categories (subsistence, protection, affection, understanding, participation, idleness, creation, identity and freedom) in order to have an instrument for development policy and action. He developed a matrix where the above categories are crossed with the essential categories of being, having, doing and interacting, resulting in different satisfiers. Max-Neef stressed the distinction between needs and satisfiers and the fact that not all societies are equally successful in their attempts to realize human needs. His definition of satisfiers is different from the one used in the THN, as satisfiers are not identified with economic goods, they are social practices, forms of organization, political models and values. In the Max-Neef model, economic goods as well as economic systems are affecting the efficiency of a satisfier in realizing needs. As Max-Neef (1991: 25) puts it 'while a satisfier is in an ultimate sense the way in which a need is expressed, goods are in a strict sense the means by which individuals will empower the satisfiers to meet their needs'.

Max-Neef takes needs as motives for consumption. He conceived of needs as deprivation and potential, the latter related to the 'degree that needs engage, motivate and mobilize people' (ibid.: 24). However, consumer goods do not always satisfy needs as their effect on satisfiers varies among societies and across time. Max-Neef identified five types of satisfiers: violators or destroyers; pseudo-satisfiers; inhibiting satisfiers; singular satisfiers; and synergic satisfiers.[16] The first three are the most potentially dangerous because if they are increasingly consumed they might impede development and jeopardize what has been achieved in terms of well-being in a given society. In the Max-Neef framework, the effect of consumer goods on well-being can be analysed relating them to the five types of satisfiers. A very interesting exercise utilizing the Max-Neef theory has been undertaken by Jackson and Marks (1999) using data of consumer expenditure in the UK between 1954 and 1994. They do not use the Max-Neef classification of satisfiers but relate consumer goods to his taxonomy of human needs. The analysis focused on the mismatch between material goods and non-material needs as the latter are poorly satisfied through consumption but generate an increasing amount of purchases. They concluded that UK patterns of consumption presented a threat to human well-being defined in terms of human needs.

In general, OWB theories offer an appealing framework from which to study the impact of consumption on well-being. However, there have not been many attempts to undertake an analysis of consumption through these theories as the linkages between consumer goods and capabilities or human needs are not always linear. The work of Jackson and Marks analysing consumption in the UK with regard to the Max-Neef taxonomy of human needs offers a promising reference point for further developments.

5.   Concluding remarks

Common views about the positive causal relationship between consumption and well-being are theoretically supported by the assumptions of the neoclassical theory of consumption. These assumptions have proved to be controversial, sparking many criticisms from economists. Nevertheless, they are still at the core of the neoclassical consumer theory since none of the proposed alternatives has been accepted as providing a comprehensive framework from which to study consumer behaviour.

Sovereignty has been challenged by the purposeful action of marketers and other institutions supporting market activities. Exogeneity of preferences is difficult to maintain if it is acknowledged that habituation, psychological states and social relations play a major role in shaping preferences. Rationality related to a self-interested maximizing individual is too narrow as the reality of everyday choices is mainly led by habit, customs, commitments and beliefs. Finally, satiation seems at odds with the reality of consumption since not only are goods heterogeneous, but also the drives to consume them.

The fact that the assumptions that support the neoclassical theory of consumption are so contested justifies searching for an alternative approach to consumption and well-being. Under the SWB and OWB traditions there have been interesting contributions to the study of consumption and consumption patterns. The SWB has generally approximated consumption through income, investigating its correlation with subjective accounts of individual satisfaction. Conclusions show that a rise in income is not always translated into an increase in well-being – not even in developing countries – since other psycho-sociological factors play a major role. However, the richness of consumption is not always well accounted for by approximating it through income. Goods and services differ in their cultural meaning, in their use, in their availability and in their social characteristics, and all these attributes have different effects on individual well-being. SWB studies will better contribute to the understanding of consumption if, when investigating their relation to well-being, they take into account the different characteristics of goods consumed and the variables affecting their attributes. Furthermore, SWB research on consumption could be enriched by considering the results of OWB studies. OWB research on the effect of consumer goods on a specific list of components of well-being will help to identify the potential dangers of certain patterns of consumption. Once identified, researchers will face the challenging tasks of discovering why 'objectively' harmful goods are consumed and if the reason has something to do with their impact on people's contentment.

Notes

1. The marginal utility revolution started with Stanley Jevons's *Theory of Political Economy* (1871), Carl Menger's (1871) *Economics* and Léon Walras's *Elements of Pure Economics* (1874–1877). Utility appears as the source for the derivation of demand curves for consumer goods.
2. 'The first principle of Economics is that every agent is actuated only by self-interest' (Edgeworth 1881 in Sen 1977: 317).
3. This is a general assumption based on the works of Samuelson (1938), where he claims that the preference scale which is the basis of individual action 'does not vary in the course of his action over time' (Rothband 1956: 230).
4. To infer the structure of individual preference, the observations undertaken have to follow the strong axiom of revealed preference which would imply transitivity in the preferences that lead to the choices observed. The strong axiom of revealed preference asserts (Varian 2003: 128) that if consumers reveal directly or indirectly that they prefer $X = (x_1, x_2)$ to $Y = (y_1, y_2)$ and X is different from Y then they cannot reveal directly or indirectly that they prefer Y to X.
5. Hollander (2001: 28) discusses the revealed preference theory and considers that the 'behavioristic utility concept with utility defined as preference fulfilment is not actually operationally meaningful' and that 'at least some circumstances of choice are necessarily endogenous to the measurement process'.
6. In neoclassical consumer theory, some categories of goods are acknowledged such as Giffen goods, luxuries and public goods, but those are supposed to be exceptions to the standard goods acquired by consumers.
7. For a comprehensive insight into the works of economists who have provided alternatives to the main assumptions of the neoclassical consumer theory, see Ackerman (1997). He identifies the contributions that might serve as foundations of a new economic theory of consumption.
8. Institutionalism arose at the end of the nineteenth century with Thorstein Veblen, John R. Commons and Wesley Mitchell. These early institutionalists are to be distinguished from new institutionalists such as Douglass North, Richard Posner, Andrew Schotter and Oliver Williamson. The first institutionalists take institutions as being created by the evolution of previous existing institutions instead of from a 'hypothetical, institution-free state of nature' (Hodgson 1998: 184). This is the approach considered here as it emphasizes institutional and cultural factors when explaining individual behaviour, thus, offering an alternative to the neoclassical assumptions.
9. Institutions 'encompass not simply organisations – such as corporations, banks and universities – but also integrated and systematic social entities such as money, language and law' (Hodgson 1998: 179).
10. For a thorough description of the different concepts of well-being, see Des Gasper (2004).
11. Ahuvia (2002: 24) surveys the works of Andrews and Whitney (1976); Campbell et al. (1976); Larson (1978); Diener et al. (1985, 1993); Clark and Oswald (1994); Ahuvia and Friedman, (1998); and Schyns (2000).
12. Jon Elster (1983: 25) defines adaptive preference formation as 'the adjustment of wants to possibilities – not the deliberate adaptation favoured by character planners, but a causal process occurring non-consciously. Behind this adaptation there is the drive to reduce the tension or frustration that one feels in having wants that one cannot possibly satisfy'.
13. Several lists have been advanced in the development studies, economics and philosophy literature. For a comparison of the most relevant ones, see Gasper (1996) and Clark (2002: 81–92).

14. See Doyal and Gough (1991: 35–45), Nussbaum (2000: 41–50) and Gough (2002: 3).
15. The headings under which Nussbaum gathers the central human functional capabilities are: life; bodily health; bodily integrity; sense imagination and thought; emotions; practical reason; affiliation; other species; play and control over one's environment. She sees all capabilities as being of equal rank and therefore they cannot be prioritized.
16. Violators or destroyers annihilate the satisfaction over time of the need they aim at and they impair the satisfaction of other needs. Pseudo-satisfiers give a false sense of satisfaction of a given need and are induced through propaganda, advertising and other means of persuasion. Inhibiting satisfiers oversatisfy a given need, curtailing the possibility of satisfying other needs, and originate in customs and habits. Singular satisfiers satisfy the need they are meant to satisfy and synergic satisfiers satisfy simultaneously different kinds of needs.

References

Ackerman, F. (1997), 'Consumed in theory: alternative perspectives on the economics of consumption', *Journal of Economic Issues*, **31** (3), 651–64.
Ahuvia, A. (2002), 'Individualism/collectivism and cultures of happiness: a theoretical conjecture on the relationship between consumption, culture and subjective well-being at the national level', *Journal of Happiness Studies*, **3** (1), 1–21.
Ahuvia, A. and D. Friedman (1998), 'Income, consumption, and subjective well-being: toward a composite macromarketing model' *Journal of Macromarketing*, **18**, 153–68.
Akerlof, A.G. and W.T. Dickens (1990), 'The economic consequences of cognitive dissonance', in G.A. Akerlof (ed.), *An Economist Theorist's Book of Tales*, Cambridge: Cambridge University Press, **5**, 123–45.
Argyle, M. (1987), *The Psychology of Happiness*, New York: Methune.
Bentham, J. (1780), 'An introduction to the Principles of Morals and Legislation', in J.H. Burns and H.L.A. Hart (eds), *Collected Works of Jeremy Bentham* (1970), London: Athlone Press.
Biswas-Diener, R. and E. Diener (2001), 'Making the best of a bad situation: satisfaction in the slums of Calcutta, *Social Indicators Research*, **55**, 329–52.
Clark, A.E and A.J. Oswald (1994), 'Unhappiness and unemployment', *Economic Journal*, **104**, 648–59.
Clark, D.A. (2002), *Visions of Development: A Study of Human Value*, Cheltenham, UK and Northampton, MA, USA: Edward Elgar.
Diener, E. and R. Biswas-Diener (2002), 'Will money increase subjective well-being?', *Social Indicators Research*, **57**, 119–69.
Diener, E. and S. Oishi (2000), 'Money and happiness: income and subjective well-being across nations', in E. Diener and E.M. Suh (eds), *Subjective Well-being across Cultures*, Cambridge, MA: MIT Press, Chapter 8.
Doyal, L. and I. Gough (1991), *A Theory of Human Need*, London: Macmillan.
Duesenberry, J.S. (1967), *La renta el ahorro y la teoria del comportamiento de los consumidores*, Madrid: Alianza editorial.
Easterlin, R. (1995), 'Will raising the incomes of all increase the happiness of all?', *Journal of Economic Behavior and Organization*, **27**, 35–47.
Elster, J. (1983), *Sour Grapes: Studies in the Subversion of Rationality*, Cambridge: Cambridge University Press.
Fafchamps, M. and F. Shilpi (2004), 'Subjective well-being, isolation, and rivalry', unpublished manuscript.
Fine, B.and E. Leopold (1993), *The World of Consumption*, London: Routledge.
Frey, B.S. and A. Stutzer (2002), 'What can economists learn from happiness research?', *Journal of Economic Literature*, **50**, June, 402–35.
Galbraith, J.K. (1977), *The Affluent Society*, 3rd edition, London: André Deutsch.
Gasper, Des (1996), 'Needs and basic needs', in Gore Kohler, C. Gore, U.-P. Reich and T. Reich (eds), *Questioning Development*, Marhung: Metropolis-Verlag, pp.. 71–101.
Gasper, Des (2004), 'Subjective and objective well-being in relation to economic inputs: puzzles and responses', Paper for the International Workshop on Researching Well-being in Developing Countries, Delmenhorst, Germany, 2–4 July.

Gough, I. (2002), 'Lists and thresholds: comparing theory of human need with Nussbaum's capabilities approach', Draft paper for Conference on Promoting Women's Capabilities: Examining Nussbaum's Capabilities Approach, Cambridge, 9–10 September.

Hodgson, G.M. (1986), 'Behind methodological individualism', *Cambridge Journal of Economics*, **10**, 211–24.

Hodgson, G.M. (ed.), (1998), *The Foundations of Evolutionary Economics: 1890–1973*, Vol. 2, Cheltenham, UK and Lyme, USA: Edward Elgar.

Hollander, H. (2001), 'On the validity of utility statements: standard theory versus Duesenberry's', *Journal of Economic Behaviour and Organization*, **45** (3), 227–49.

Jackson, T. and N. Marks (1999), 'Consumption, sustainable welfare and human needs – with reference to UK expenditure patterns between 1954 and 1994', *Ecological Economics*, **28**, 421–41.

Keynes, J.M. (1963), *Essays in Persuasion*, New York: WW. Norton & Co.

Marshall, A. (1920), *Principles of Economics*, London: Macmillan.

Max-Neef, M. (1991), *Human-Scale Development: Conception, Application and Further Reflection*, London: Apex.

Mill, J.S. (1863), 'Utilitarianism', in R. Crisp (ed.), *Utilitarianism: John Stuart Mill* (1998 reprint), Oxford: Oxford University Press.

Nicolaides, P. (1988), 'Limits to the expansion of neoclassical economics', *Cambridge Journal of Economics*, **12**, 313–28.

Nussbaum, M. (2000), *Women and Human Development*, Cambridge and New York: Cambridge University Press.

Pareto, W. (1916 [1963]), *Mind and Society*, New York: Dover.

Penz, P. (1986), *Consumer Sovereignty and Human Interests*, Cambridge: Cambridge University Press.

Philp, B. and D. Young (2002), 'Preferences, reductionism and the microfoundations of analytical Marxism', *Cambridge Journal of Economics*, **26**, 313–29.

Roemer, J.E. (1986), *Analytical Marxism*, Cambridge: Cambridge University Press.

Rojas, M. (2004), 'The complexity of well-being. A life satisfaction conception and a domains-of-life approach', Paper for the *International Workshop on Researching Well-being in Developing Countries*, Delmenhorst, Germany, 2–4 July.

Rothbard, M.N. (1956), 'Toward a reconstruction of utility and welfare economics', in M. Sennholz (ed.), *On Freedom and Free Enterprise: Essays in Honor of Ludwig von Mises*, Princeton, NJ: D. Van Nostrand Co., pp. 224–62.

Sannuelson, P. (1938), 'A note of the pure theory of consumers' behaviour', *Economica*, **5** (17): 61–71.

Scitovsky, T. (1976), *The Joyless Economy: An Inquiry into Human Satisfaction and Dissatisfaction*, Oxford: Oxford University Press.

Sen, A. (1977), 'Rational fools: a critique of the behavioral foundations of economic theory', *Philosophy and Public Affairs*, **4** (6), 317–45.

Sen, A. (1985), Commodities and Capabilities, Amsterdam: North-Holland.

Varian, H.R. (1987), *Microeconomia Intermedia*, Barcelona: Antoni Bosch.

Varian, H.R. (2003), *Intermediate Microeconomics: A modern approach*, London: W.W. Norton & Co.

Wetherly, P. (1996), 'Basic needs and social policies', *Critical Social Policy*, **16** (1), 45–65.

Winston, C.G. (1980), 'Addiction and backsliding. A theory of compulsive consumption', *Journal of Economic Behaviour and Organization*, **1**, 295–324.

9 Enjoyment of life, the structure of time and economic dynamics
Mario Cogoy

1. Introduction: happiness and enjoyment

This chapter will examine enjoyment of life[1] as a contribution to happiness. Enjoyment and happiness are difficult goals to attain, and require a considerable amount of effort. Although enjoyment and happiness are closely related, there are also important differences between the two. Enjoyment is firmly rooted in the process of action: an activity can be enjoyed while it is taking place and enjoyment will fade away when the activity is coming to an end. Enjoyment is therefore intimately related to, and inseparable from, time. It is also unstable by nature, since it can easily turn into its opposite at the slightest disturbance. Happiness is more robust and more comprehensive than enjoyment and reflects a general feeling of a person about the overall quality of his/her life. Happiness is a less action-orientated and a more self-reflexive state of the mind. It summarizes past experience in a non-trivial way and for this reason it may also be plausibly argued that a person is unlikely to be happy if he/she has not experienced sadness and depression in previous periods of his/her life.

Although happiness and enjoyment are different things, I shall adopt an activity-orientated view of happiness in this chapter. A 'good life' is an active life and enjoyment in action is therefore one of the main constituent materials out of which happiness is made. All kinds of activities require time, and therefore enjoyment also requires time, since no pleasure or 'welfare' or 'utility' can be attained without making use of a portion of the permanent flow of time. I shall call the time allocated to enjoyment 'enjoyment time'.

Since enjoyment is unstable, the task of preserving the enjoyable qualities of time requires a continuous effort.[2] There are many inputs necessary to this effort: consumption goods, consumption capital, infrastructure, social networks, environment, services, information, knowledge, skills and so on. Enjoyment is therefore a complex activity, rather than just an effortless absorption of consumption goods, as is sometimes assumed in the economic theory of consumption. I shall not discuss the full complexity of enjoyment activities, but focus on only two important inputs: knowledge (including skills) and consumption goods.

Skills and knowledge are inputs as necessary to enjoyable activities as are consumption goods, and significantly determine the outcome of such activities. I am aware that there may be good reasons to dispute that knowledge can make humans happier. I shall nevertheless adopt a moderate version of the Enlightenment's view and recognize that some positive role can be played by knowledge and skills in enhancing enjoyment of life.

Knowledge and skills directly affect life enjoyment in two ways. An enjoyable activity can be positively influenced by personal individual skills: a car trip will be more pleasant if the driver is a skilled driver; a match of tennis is more interesting, if it is played by skilful players; and so on. In complex modern societies, however, knowledge plays a more pervasive role, since in advanced industrial societies welfare is less and less dependent on the direct use of individual commodities, and becomes increasingly rooted in socio-technical systems, that is, in networks of commodities, infrastructures and services.

For example, cars alone do not provide any transportation service, but only as components of a network including roads, parking lots, repair shops, gasoline stations, insurance, traffic rules and legislation, traffic police, and the like. In a similar way, energy services depend on distribution networks, end-use technologies, the quality of buildings and so on. Residential comfort depends on neighbourhoods, urban planning, commuting time, and the aesthetic and energetic quality of buildings. The performance of socio-technical systems significantly depends therefore on the quality of the interactions between system parts, and on the social knowledge which is embodied in the design, and applied to the control, the operation and the evolutionary adaptation of such systems. For this reason, with increasing complexity of enjoyment activities, the relative weight of knowledge rises, as compared to consumption goods. This implies that a new space opens up for the use of knowledge: knowledge contributes not only to the design of more efficient processes in the production of commodities, but also to the efficient design and the operation of socio-technical systems. The same endowment with time and commodities can lead to a higher level of enjoyment, if it is supported by a higher level of knowledge and technology, since knowledge and technology serve to make a better use of resources, not only in production, but also in enjoyable activities. This is a direct consequence of assuming that technical progress pertains not only to the realm of production, but also to the realm of enjoyment. In other words, knowledge and technology affect welfare not only indirectly, as they improve the efficiency of production activities, but also directly, as they make possible a more efficient use of given consumptive resources (Michael and Becker 1973; Becker 1976). Human capital therefore influences the efficiency of efforts in the production of enjoyment in a similar way, as it increases the efficiency of factors in production.

The flow of enjoyment time is also serviced by a flow of commodities, and the intensity of enjoyment also depends therefore on the flow of consumption goods supporting each unit of time. Individuals can choose higher levels of commodity intensity for their activities, if they feel that more elaborate material lifestyles yield a better quality of enjoyment.

I shall assume a constant population of N identical individuals involved in the same kinds of activity. The time available to each individual is normalized to 1. E (enjoyment time) is the portion of time which each individual allocates to enjoyable actions ($0 \leq E \leq 1$). C is total social consumption. Consumption intensity of action or material lifestyle can then be defined as:

$$\varphi = \frac{C}{NE}, \tag{9.1}$$

where C/N is per capita consumption and φ is per capita consumption per unit of enjoyment time.

In an activity-orientated approach, commodities, time and knowledge are functionally related and their interaction defines the 'enjoyment technology' individuals are adopting. Consider first the effects on enjoyable activities of a marginal increase in E. An increase in enjoyment time with constant φ implies a temporal extension of activities of the same type, whereas an increase, or a decrease in φ reflects a switch to activities of higher, or lower, commodity intensity. For this reason, a marginal increase in E will influence enjoyment activities in a contradictory way. On the one hand enjoyment time will increase, but on the other hand commodity intensity φ will decrease because of (9.1). The per capita flow of commodities C/N will have to be 'diluted' over an increased flow of time. Each unit of time will be serviced by a reduced commodity flow, and this in turn means that the type of consumptive activity has changed to an activity of lower commodity intensity. A marginal increase in E will therefore have only a positive influence on enjoyment, if the effect of an increase in time prevails over the negative effect of a lower commodity intensity of action. Consider next a marginal increase in commodity intensity φ. It is by no means evident that such an increase must lead to an increase in enjoyment for all values of φ, ranging from zero to infinity. If there is an upper bound on the quantity of commodities servicing a unit of enjoyment time, the marginal effect of an increase in φ may be negative beyond that upper bound.

The functional relationship between time, commodity intensity and knowledge makes the difference between the 'doing' and the 'having' approach in welfare economics. In the having approach, a portion of time called leisure can be directly enjoyed by simply abstaining from labour (Chase 1967; Oulton 1993; Baldassarri et al. 1994; Ladrón-de-Guevara et al. 1999). In the leisure approach, commodities and time are not related to each other by the functionality of action, and no question arises of what consumers will do with an additional quantity of time. Strictly speaking, therefore, leisure does not exist in this chapter, since disposable time can be enjoyed only if it is embedded in activities transforming consumption goods and knowledge into time-dimensional enjoyment of life. Enjoyment time is therefore not just a different word for leisure, but rather denotes the difference between a leisure approach and an activity-orientated approach to enjoyment.

Under the above premises the welfare of each individual can be defined as:

$$U = U(E, \varphi, H_C), \quad U_E > 0; \ U_{H_C} > 0; \ U_\varphi > 0 \text{ for some range of } \varphi, \quad (9.2)$$

where H_C is human consumption capital improving the design of socio-technical systems in which enjoyable activities are embedded. (U_x is the partial derivative of U with respect to argument x.) $U = U(E, \varphi, H_C)$ can be interpreted as an enjoyment technology, describing how time, commodity services to time units, and the quality of consumptive designs are combined into activities generating welfare. Knowledge plays the role of a public good in enjoyment activities, since the quality of socio-technical designs, as expressed in the level of human consumption capital, improves the quality of enjoyment time of all of society's members.

It is important to note that the level of commodity intensity φ and the level of consumption knowledge H_C are independent from each other. It may be historically true that the progress of knowledge and technology has been accompanied by an increase in the commodity intensity of enjoyable actions. No necessary causality between the two should be assumed, however. The level of commodity intensity is a free choice of individuals, and different types of material lifestyles are compatible with the same level of knowledge in consumption.

Of course, consumers may also have preferences on items other than E, φ and H_C. They may like other types of time expenditure, such as, for example, research time spent in accumulating human capital, or even production time. They may also appreciate 'conspicuous' commodities independently of their use in actions. The enjoyment technology function may be extended therefore to contain other arguments, but I shall use (9.2), in order to stress the main point of this chapter: enjoyment activities have a time-dimensional output, and the production of qualified enjoyment time is the primary final result of the economic process.

Because of (9.1), it is feasible for individuals to increase φ to infinity by setting $E = 0$, and choosing in this way an infinite commodity intensity of action, without allocating any time to enjoyable activities. I shall call this kind of behaviour 'commodity hoarding', since welfare is derived in this case from 'having' commodities, instead of 'doing' something with them. Commodity hoarding is a rather uninteresting oddity, and the enjoyment technology has to be specified therefore in such a way as to rule out commodity hoarding and deliver interior solutions for E and φ. I shall investigate two (out of many possible) specifications.

One possible specification is bad substitutability. If enjoyment time, commodity intensity and consumptive knowledge are bad substitutes, consumers will not be interested in an unlimited expansion of commodity intensity at the expense of enjoyment time.

Formally, if we specify the consumption technology as:

$$U = \frac{1}{\lambda}(E^{\lambda} + \varphi^{\lambda} + H_C^{\lambda}), \quad \lambda < 1, \qquad (9.2a)$$

it is easy to check that commodity hoarding will not occur. I shall therefore study enjoyment dynamics in Section 3 under the assumption of bad substitutability. $\lambda < 0$ is quite reasonable an assumption, since it means, that consumers are only moderately disposed to trade enjoyment time against commodity intensity and that they are not willing to adopt enjoyment technologies based on commodity hoarding.

An additional possible specification is given by a bound on commodity intensity, for example, by congestion. It may be argued that the dimension of the commodity flow sustaining one unit of enjoyment time has an upper bound, and if commodity intensity of consumption were to go beyond that limit, congestion would be the consequence, that is, a decrease in welfare due to an excess of commodity intensity.[3]

In the congestion case (9.2) can be written, for example, as:

$$U = \frac{1}{\lambda}\{E^{\lambda} + [\varphi(K - \varphi)]^{\lambda} + H_C^{\lambda}\}, \quad \lambda < 1. \qquad (9.2b)$$

$\frac{1}{2}K$ is the maximum level of consumption intensity, beyond which the negative influence of congestion on enjoyment begins to develop.

This approach has some points in common with Becker's theory of 'time allocation' and with household economics (Becker 1965, 1976; Michael and Becker 1973; Stigler and Becker 1977; Gronau 1977, 1986; Juster and

Stafford 1991). Following Becker, utility is not defined on commodities, but on the outputs of activities. Moreover, if enjoyment production is an effort requiring activity, and if technical progress is considered to be a means of reducing effort to obtain a given result, there is no reason to confine the effects of technical progress to the realm of production. The accumulation of knowledge can improve the efficiency of enjoyment activities similar to the way it fosters production (Michael and Becker 1973; Becker 1976; Stigler and Becker 1977). This chapter focuses, however, on the fact that the output of enjoyment activities is time-dimensional, so that it is necessary to allocate time not only to production, but also to enjoyment. Enjoyment time is vital and cannot be rationalized away by 'improvements' in the enjoyment technology.

Section 2 describes a general model of enjoyment activities and human capital accumulation. Sections 3 and 4 discuss bad substitutability and congestion as possible specifications for (9.2). Section 5 concludes.

2. The model

I shall model production and research along lines that are familiar from human capital models of endogenous growth, with only a few minor changes. Since I am not interested in the difference between physical and human capital, but rather in the effects of the expansion of knowledge and technology on enjoyment and on the structure of time, I shall assume that commodities are produced with the aid of production labour and human capital only. As the growth properties of an economy do not depend on the existence of two factors that can be accumulated (physical capital and human capital), but only on the dynamic equation describing the growth of such a factor (Rebelo 1991), a human-capital-only economy is endowed with all necessary features that are required for discussing the effects of technical progress on the structure of time.

Commodity production is described by:

$$C = NPH_p,$$ (9.3)

where P is the share of disposable time which each individual allocates to production and H_p is human capital used in production. NPH_p is therefore total assisted production labour.

I assume that non-depreciating human capital is increased by assisted research labour. Research labour is assisted by the overall knowledge accumulated in production and consumption. Production and consumption knowledge act therefore as externalities to assist labour in research. Production and consumption are therefore rival uses of human capital, whereas its use in research is non-rival.

$$\dot{H} = \delta NRH, \quad \delta > 0, \tag{9.4}$$

where δ is a fixed coefficient, R is the share of disposable time each individual allocates to research, and H is total human capital, that is, the sum of consumption human capital and production human capital:

$$H_C + H_p = H. \tag{9.5}$$

Since the rate of growth of human capital depends on research time, it also depends on the size of the population. Clearly:

$$P + R + E = 1. \tag{9.6}$$

Equation (9.6) is the time-budget constraint of each individual.

Time is divided into three parts in the above described economy: production time, research time and enjoyment time.[4] It is assumed, that only enjoyment time delivers pleasure, whereas production and research time are justified only if they contribute to the task of increasing the quality of enjoyment time. For this reason, the economy can be described as a process of production of time by means of time. In this process, production and research time contribute to the generation of time of higher quality (enjoyment time), which is the final outcome of the economic process.

Human capital is divided into two parts: production capital and consumption capital. Both parts together assist research labour as externalities in the production of new human capital.

Equation (9.4) acts analogous to Lucas (1988) and Rebelo (1991) as a potential engine of growth in the economy. The planner in charge of searching for the social optimum can in principle turn off this engine by allocating no labour time to research and waiving in this way the external benefits of human capital accumulation. Whether this is optimal or not depends on how individuals evaluate enjoyment time, lifestyles and the design quality of enjoyable activities. I shall discuss different possible outcomes in Sections 3 and 4, where I discuss the solutions of the model.

The planner solves:

$$\max \int_0^\infty e^{-\rho t} U(E, \varphi, H_C) dt, \quad \rho \geq 0 \tag{9.7}$$

subject to (9.1), and (9.3) to (9.6). ρ is the rate of discount.

The first-order conditions and the transversality condition are:

$$\mu \delta NHP = \varphi U_{\varphi} \qquad (9.8)$$

$$EU_E - \varphi U_{\varphi} = H_p U_{\varphi} \qquad (9.9)$$

$$EU_{H_C} = PU_{\varphi} \qquad (9.10)$$

$$\frac{\dot{\mu}}{\mu} = \rho - \delta N(1 - E) - \delta NP \frac{H_C}{H_p} \qquad (9.11)$$

$$\lim_{t \to \infty} e^{-\rho t} \mu H = 0, \qquad (9.12)$$

where μ is the shadow price of human capital.

Equations (9.9) and (9.10) state optimal static conditions of time and human capital allocation. It has already been noted that a marginal increase in enjoyment time has contradictory effects on enjoyable activities, since an expansion of time, all other things remaining equal, leads to activities of lesser material intensity. The left-hand side of (9.9) summarizes the net effect of a marginal increase of enjoyment time, while the right-hand side measures the effect on enjoyment of a marginal increase in time invested in commodity production. In a similar way, equation (9.10) equates the marginal gain of human capital in the design of enjoyment processes with the marginal effect of an increase of human capital in commodity production.

Equations (9.8) to (9.12), together with the constraints, describe the optimal path. This path depends on the choice of the consumption technology. Two possible specifications are studied in the next section.

3. Bad substituibility
If we assume consumption technology (9.2a), equations (9.8) to (9.10) become:

$$\mu \delta NHP = \varphi^{\lambda} \qquad (9.8a)$$

$$E^{\lambda} - \varphi^{\lambda} = H_p \varphi^{\lambda - 1} \qquad (9.9a)$$

$$EH_C^{\lambda - 1} = P \varphi^{\lambda - 1}. \qquad (9.10a)$$

It is easy to see that an optimal stationary state can be calculated by inserting $\dot{\mu}/\mu = \dot{H}/H = 0$ into equations (9.1), (9.3) to (9.6), (9.9a), (9.10a) and (9.11).

It is not possible to solve explicitly for all variables as functions of $\rho/\delta N$, but it is possible to solve for $\rho/\delta N$ and all other variables as functions of E:

$$\frac{\rho}{\delta N} = (1 - E) + (1 - E)^{\frac{1-2\lambda}{1-\lambda}} E^{\frac{\lambda}{1-\lambda}} \tag{9.13}$$

$$P = 1 - E \tag{9.14}$$

$$C = N(1 - E)^{\frac{1}{\lambda}} E^2 \tag{9.15}$$

$$H = (1 - E)^{\frac{1-\lambda}{\lambda}} E^2 + (1 - E)^{\frac{1-2\lambda}{\lambda(1-\lambda)}} E^{\frac{2-\lambda}{1-\lambda}} \tag{9.16}$$

$$H_C = (1 - E)^{\frac{1-2\lambda}{\lambda(1-\lambda)}} E^{\frac{2-\lambda}{1-\lambda}} \tag{9.17}$$

$$H_p = (1 - E)^{\frac{1-\lambda}{\lambda}} E^2 \tag{9.18}$$

$$\varphi = (1 - E)^{\frac{1}{\lambda}} E. \tag{9.19}$$

The stationary values of the variables depend on $\rho/\delta N$, that is, on the relative values of the rate of discount and the technical coefficient of human capital accumulation multiplied by the size of the population. In particular, lower rates of discount yield higher stationary values of enjoyment time, consumption, commodity intensity, and all types of human capital, and to a lower stationary value of P. E tends to 1 and P tends to zero, as discounting tends to zero. This is because human capital substitutes labour in production. Time is made available in this way for enjoyment. The degree of development of economic forces depends on the rate of discount: the lower the rate of discount, the higher the level of human capital to be accumulated before reaching the stationary point, and the closer the stationary value of enjoyment time to its upper bound of 1.

The stationary values of the variables also depend on the elasticity of substitution. In order to better understand the relationship between λ and the stationary value of enjoyment time, it is convenient to take logarithms, and rewrite (9.13) as:

$$\lambda = \frac{\log\left[\dfrac{\rho}{\delta N(1 - E)} - 1\right]}{\log\left[\dfrac{\rho}{\delta N(1 - E)} - 1\right] + \log\left[\dfrac{E}{1 - E}\right]}. \tag{9.20}$$

For $\delta N > \rho$ the graph of (9.20) is shown in Figure 9A.1 in the appendix.

Inverting the relationship, we can conclude that the stationary value of E ranges from $\delta N/(\delta N + \rho)$ to $(2\delta N - \rho)/2\delta N$, as λ varies from $-\infty$ to 0.

The transitional dynamics for this model can be numerically studied for given values of the parameters. I use GAMS-CONOPT software for calculating the transitional paths. For parameter values: $\delta = 1$; $\rho = 0.2$; $\lambda = -0.5$; $N = 1$, the transitional paths are shown in Figure 9A.2.

With bad substitutability the physical bound on E limits the growth of the economy, since material lifestyles and a good design of consumptive systems can only to a limited extent compensate consumers for a fundamental shortage of time (Linder 1970). Unbounded growth would be therefore nonoptimal. With a low rate of discount, however, the system can develop consumption and the qualitative design of enjoyable activities to high levels, and drive enjoyment time close to its upper physical bound of one.

4. A bound on consumption intensity

In this section I shall assume a bound on commodity intensity φ.

Adopting (9.2b) as the enjoyment technology, (9.8) to (9.10) become:

$$\mu\delta NHP = \varphi^\lambda (K - \varphi)^\lambda \frac{K - 2\varphi}{K - \varphi} \tag{9.8b}$$

$$E^\lambda = (\varphi + H_p)\varphi^{\lambda-1}(K - \varphi)^\lambda \frac{K - 2\varphi}{K - \varphi} \tag{9.9b}$$

$$EH_C^{\lambda-1} = P\varphi^{\lambda-1}(K - \varphi)^\lambda \frac{K - 2\varphi}{K - \varphi}, \tag{9.10b}$$

The values of the variables in the stationary state can be determined by setting: $\dot{\mu}/\mu = \dot{H}/H = 0$. Eliminating all other variables we get:

$$\varphi = (1 - E)^2 \left[\frac{\rho - \delta N(1 - E)}{\delta N} \right]^{\frac{1-\lambda}{\lambda}} \tag{9.21}$$

$$(1 - E)E^\lambda = \varphi^\lambda (K - \varphi)^\lambda \frac{K - 2\varphi}{K - \varphi}. \tag{9.22}$$

For parameter values: $\delta = 1$; $\rho = 0.2$; $\lambda = -0.5$; $N = 1$; $K = 10$ the solution can be represented as in Figure 9A.3. The graph of (9.21) has a discontinuity at $E = (\delta N - \rho)/\delta N$. The discontinuity point shifts to the right, as the rate of discount decreases.

The graph of (9.22) has an initial point $\varphi = 0$; $E = 0$ and a final point $\varphi = \frac{1}{2} K$; $E = 1$. Figure 9A.3 shows that the stationary values of enjoyment time and commodity intensity tend to $\varphi = \frac{1}{2} K$ and $E = 1$ as the rate of discount tends to zero. Again, time is substituted by human capital in production and is thus made available for enjoyment. The rate of discount decides how far this substitution will go.

The transitional dynamics for parameter values: $\delta = 1$; $\rho = 0.2$; $\lambda = -0.5$; $N = 1$; $K = 10$ is represented in Figure 9A.4. In the congestion case the pattern of development of the variables is the same as with bad substitutability, but the order between consumption and production human capital is reversed. This is because commodity intensity is bounded and less human capital and labour are used in production. The structure of enjoyment activities is therefore more time intensive and makes more use of improvements in the design quality of actions.

5.   Conclusions

In the preceding sections, I have argued that considering enjoyment as an activity significantly affects the dynamic behaviour of the economy. In an activity framework not only consumption goods, but also other ingredients of consumptive actions, as enjoyment time and the design quality of consumptive activities, become important in the production of welfare. The long-run dynamics of the system depends therefore on the behaviour of all components of consumptive activities over time. The degree of substitutability and possible bounds on system variables are factors determining the long-run behaviour of the system. In the bad substitutability case, the economic system has a stationary state that depends on the rate of discount, the size of the population and the elasticity of substitution. In the congestion case, physical output is limited. With low rates of discount the dynamic forces of the system concentrate on increasing the design quality of consumption and driving enjoyment time to its upper bound of one.

It is important to underline that the two examples studied in Sections 3 and 4 are only two out of many possible specifications, and that there is ample scope therefore for studying other aspects of enjoyable activities, which are not addressed in this chapter. Once it is admitted that enjoyment is an activity, which is more complex than can be described by the simple consumptive absorption of commodities, it is quite understandable that the number of aspects under which enjoyable actions can be viewed increases, and that a multiplicity of approaches can develop.

'Leisure' is not a credible candidate for modelling the complexity of consumption in modern societies, since the notion of leisure admits a third use of time besides production and research, but ignores the functional relation between time, commodities and knowledge in enjoyable actions.

Know-how in consumption is as important as know-how in production. Insisting on skills, knowledge and technical progress in enjoyable activities[5] serves to move a step towards a more realistic view of technical progress in the process of growth. It may be argued that one of the outstanding features of technical progress is the opening up of alternative possible choices in lifestyles. At a high level of knowledge and technology, extending enjoyable time or improving the design quality of consumptive systems should be considered to be a valid alternative to the target of increasing per capita consumption. Economic theory should provide an analytical framework to investigate such possibilities. With a low elasticity of substitution between commodities and time, exponential growth becomes obsolete in view of the basic scarcity of time (Linder 1970).

The approach presented here also has implications for environmental policies (Cogoy 2004), since the absolute mass of commodity production is, with all necessary qualifications, a major source of environmental damage (Daly 1992). For this reason, it is important that models adopted to investigate dynamics and change allow for more alternative sources of welfare than just material consumption. The study of the endogenous structure of time and of the role of knowledge in consumption is therefore not only a realistic tool for the analysis of the effects of technical progress in modern societies, but also an important analytical element for the study of sustainable paths of economic development.

Notes

1. 'Enjoyment of life' is, according to Georgescu-Roegen (1966, p. 97), the final result of the economic process.
2. I shall ignore the survival sector of the economy, and assume therefore, that economic activities are mainly directed at delivering amenities of life, after the fundamental needs of society have been satisfied.
3. Another possible bound on consumption could arise from environmental constraints, since unbounded consumption is likely to produce environmental degradation, even if abatement technologies are available. In this case a limit exists on C, rather than on φ, as in the congestion case, since it is the absolute quantity of consumption, and not the intensity of consumption per hour, which is a potential limit to growth. I shall examine congestion as a bound on φ. Environmental constraints, as a bound on C, could also be analysed along similar lines.
4. Notice that the conceptualization introduced above has nothing in common with the conceptualization (paid work and leisure) commonly used in time-budget analysis (Gershuny 1993). Production labour refers to the output of the process (commodities) and not to the forms of payment. Enjoyment time can be paid if people manage to get payments for doing what they like. The distinction between production and enjoyment activities does not necessarily coincide with the distinction between the market and the non-market sectors of the economy. Since I do not address the question of how production and consumption processes are socially organized (market versus non-market social organization), the question of payments is here irrelevant. (On market versus non-market organization and the social embeddedness of consumption, see Cogoy 1999.)
5. Although 'consumption skills' and 'consumption knowledge' are rarely recognized in models of economic dynamics, they are widely accepted as important analytical tools in

time-use studies (Gershuny 1993) and in consumer research (Park et al. 1994). 'Consumption capital' and learning in consumption ('beneficial addiction') are central ideas in Stigler and Becker (1977). On 'consumption knowledge' and 'consumption skills' see also Witt (1998) and Cogoy (1999).

References

Baldassarri, M., P. De Santis and G. Moscarini (1994), 'Allocation of time, human capital and endogenous growth', in Baldassarri, L. Paganetto and E. Phelps (eds), *International Differences in Growth Rates: Market Globalisation and Economic Areas*, London: Macmillan, pp. 95–110.

Becker, G.S. (1965), 'A theory of the allocation of time', *Economic Journal*, **75**, 493–517 (reprinted in Becker 1976).

Becker, G.S. (1976), *The Economic Approach to Human Behavior*, Chicago and London: University of Chicago Press.

Chase, E.S. (1967), 'Leisure and consumption', in K. Shell (ed.), *Essays on the Theory of Optimal Economic Growth*, Cambridge, MA: MIT Press, pp. 175–80.

Cogoy, M. (1999), 'The consumer as a social and environmental actor', *Ecological Economics*, **28**, 385–98.

Cogoy, M. (2004), 'Dematerialisation, time allocation, and the service economy', *Structural Change and Economic Dynamics*, **15**, 165–81.

Daly, H.E. (1992), 'Allocation, distribution and scale: towards an economics that is efficient, just and sustainable', *Ecological Economics*, **6**, 185–93.

Georgescu-Roegen, N. (1966), *Analytical Economics. Issues and Problems*, Cambridge, MA: Harvard University Press.

Gershuny, J. (1993), 'Post-industrial convergence in time-allocation', *Futures*, June, 578–86.

Gronau, R. (1977), 'Leisure, home production and work. The theory of the allocation of time revisited', *Journal of Political Economy*, **85**, 1099–123.

Gronau, R. (1986), 'Home-production, a survey', in O. Ashenfelter and R. Layard (eds), *Handbook of Labour Economics*, Vol. 1, Amsterdam: North-Holland, pp. 273–304.

Juster, F.T. and F.P. Stafford (1991), 'The allocation of time: empirical findings, behavioural models, and problems of measurement', *Journal of Economic Literature*, **29**, 471–522.

Ladrón de Guevara, A., S. Ortigueira and M.S. Santos (1999), 'A two-sector model of endogenous growth with leisure', *Review of Economic Studies*, **66**, 609–31.

Linder, S. (1970), *The Harried Leisure Class*, New York: Columbia University Press.

Lucas, R.E. Jr. (1988), 'On the mechanics of economic development', *Journal of Monetary Economics*, **22**, 3–42.

Michael, R.T. and G.S. Becker (1973), 'On the new theory of consumer behaviour', *Swedish Journal of Economics*, **75**, 378–96 (reprinted in Becker 1976).

Oulton, N. (1993), 'Widening the human stomach: the effect of new consumer goods on economic growth and leisure', *Oxford Economic Papers*, **45**, 364–86.

Park, C.V., D.L. Mothersbaugh and L. Feick (1994), 'Consumer knowledge assessment', *Journal of Consumer Research*, **21**, 71–82.

Rebelo, S. (1991), 'Long-run policy analysis and long-run growth', *Journal of Political Economy*, **99**, 500–521.

Stigler, G.J. and G.S. Becker (1977), '*De gustibus non est disputandum*', *American Economic Review*, **67**, 76–90.

Witt, U. (1998), 'Learning to consume. A theory of wants and the growth of demand', Working Paper 9806, Max-Planck Institute for Research into Economic Systems, Jena.

Appendix 9A

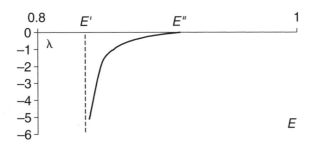

Note: Parameter values $\delta = 1; \rho = 0.2; N = 1$;
$E' = \delta N/(\delta N + \rho)$, $E'' = (2\delta N - \rho)/2\delta N$.

Figure 9A.1   Bad substitutability: the stationary value of enjoyment time

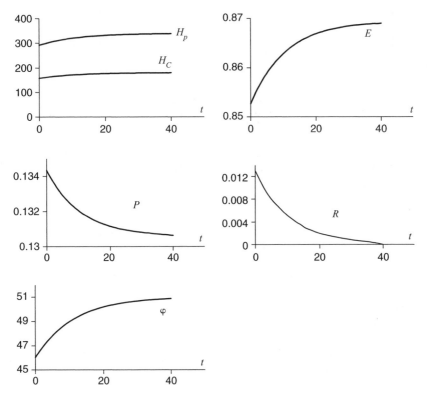

Note: Parameter values: $\delta = 1; \rho = 0.2; \lambda = -0.5; N = 1$.

Figure 9A.2   Bad substitutability

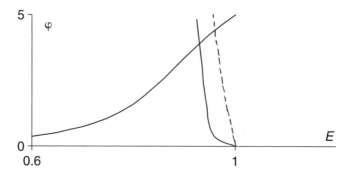

Note: Parameter values: $\delta = 1$; $\rho = 0.2$; $\lambda = -0.5$; $N = 1$; $K = 10$.

Figure 9A.3   The stationary point with congestion

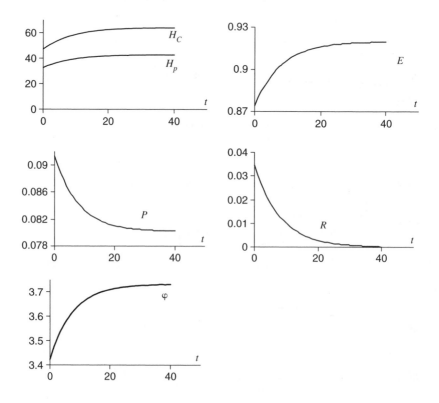

Note: Parameter values: $\delta = 1$; $\rho = 0.2$; $\lambda = -0.5$; $N = 1$; $K = 10$.

Figure 9A.4   Congestion

10 Experienced versus decision utility of income: relative or absolute happiness

Maarten Vendrik and Johannes Hirata*

1. Introduction

A central finding in happiness research is low correlations between income and happiness. This is remarkable since most people seem to attach a high value to a rise in their income, as indicated by their behaviour (for example, labour supply) and stated preferences (see, for example, Frank 1999 and Easterlin 2001). This 'classical' paradox manifests itself on at least three levels. First, in most developed nations, average happiness has not or only slightly increased in the last half-century despite economic growth. Second, cross-sections of average happiness levels across developed countries reveal weak or zero income effects on happiness (for example, Frey and Stutzer 2002). Finally, in cross-sections of individual happiness levels within a given developed country, income–happiness correlations and effects turn out to be small in comparison with those for other determinants of happiness, especially over the top 75 per cent of a country's income distribution (see, for example, Diener et al. 1993; Frey and Stutzer 2002).

The first (time-series) version of the paradox has been explained by Easterlin (1974, 2001) and Frank (1997) in terms of rising aspirations and positional externalities. The second version of the paradox, the absence of a substantial income effect on happiness for cross-sections of developed countries, can be explained in a similar way, but the third version for cross-sections of individuals has received little systematic attention in the literature (see Frey and Stutzer (2002) for a discussion of the role of relative income and treadmills) and requires a more subtle approach. Although these explanations sound convincing, econometric or statistical studies which test these explanations on the level of individual cross-sections are rare and have produced mixed results. For American, German and Swiss data, McBride (2001), Ferrer-i-Carbonell (2005) and Stutzer (2004), respectively, find econometric support for the influence of relative-income variables (see also Schyns (2001) for Russia), but Diener et al. (1993) find no evidence. In the view of Diener et al. and Veenhoven (1991), happiness is absolute rather than relative, reflects satisfaction of universal needs rather than social comparison, and represents an emotional feeling rather than a cognitive judgement.

The first purpose of this chapter is to investigate the plausibility of these claims versus those of Easterlin and Frank by a careful analysis of the results of the econometric/statistical studies mentioned above. Our general conclusion from this analysis is that Stutzer's (2004) estimation results in favour of Easterlin's (2001) aspiration-level theory look especially convincing, and that the absence of any evidence for an influence of relative-income variables in Diener et al.'s study may be due to misspecifications of such influence. On the other hand, Stutzer's results also suggest that the explanations of the income–happiness paradox in terms of rising aspirations and positional externalities may only be partial. Moreover, there is some evidence that, contrary to what is assumed in the aspiration-level theory, causality is not so much running from aspiration levels towards happiness, but rather from happiness towards aspiration levels (Headey et al. 1991). More specifically, people who have a predisposition to feel unhappy tend to have higher aspiration levels than those with a disposition to feel happy. This suggests that the hedonic-level-of-affect component of happiness may be more fundamental than its cognitive-evaluation component in the sense of the former influencing the latter rather than the other way around.

This calls for a perhaps more fundamental explanation of the income–happiness paradox in terms of the affective component of happiness. A possible candidate for such an explanation is offered by the findings of Kasser and Ryan (1993, 1996; see also Kasser and Ahuvia 2002). They make a distinction between intrinsic goals (like self-acceptance and affiliation) and extrinsic goals (like financial success and social recognition) and find that persons who focus strongly on extrinsic goals tend to be relatively less happy. This points to a second kind of discrepancy between (*ex ante*) decision utility and (*ex post*) experienced utility of income[1] on top of that brought about by unanticipated rises of the aspiration level as suggested by Easterlin. Thus, a second purpose of this chapter is to investigate the extent to which this approach may offer an alternative explanation of the income–happiness paradox. We conclude that it has some potential, but that, in its present stage, it yields less-specific predictions with respect to the paradox than the aspiration-level approach. Furthermore, there seem to be some intriguing interrelations between both approaches.

The organization of this chapter is as follows. First, Section 2 gives a short review of the main empirical findings with respect to the income–happiness paradox. Section 3 analyses the explanations of the paradox in terms of rising aspirations and positional externalities as well as the mixed evidence from individual cross-section studies. Section 4 discusses the alternative explanation suggested by the intrinsic/extrinsic goals approach of

Kasser and Ryan. Finally, Section 5 makes some concluding remarks on the interrelations between the two approaches.

2. Main empirical findings

Most people seem to attach a high value to their level of income. This is evidenced by their economic behaviour as well as by their stated preferences. Examples of the former revealed preferences are the dominant role of the wage rate in individual labour supply decisions (Pencavel 1986; Killingsworth and Heckman 1986) and the recurrence of strikes of labour unions for a higher wage. Another example is the 'luxury fever' in consumption as documented in Frank (1999) for the USA. Stated preferences can, for instance, be inferred from the results of the well-known survey of Cantril (1965) about the concerns of people in 14 countries (as mentioned in Easterlin 2001). In answers to open-ended questions about what people want out of life, material circumstances, especially standard of living, were, in every country, mentioned most often.

Against this background, it is surprising that happiness research usually yields low or at best moderate correlations between income and life satisfaction in developed countries. To bring some order into the data, we classify the empirical results by two criteria. The first criterion is the level of aggregation, where a distinction is made between an individual focus and a national focus. The second criterion is the comparison perspective, which can be either a cross-section or a time-series perspective. This classification gives rise to a two by two matrix as in Table 10.1.

The most striking result is that the correlations between average life satisfaction and average income in developed countries over time (category 2b) are not significantly different from zero for many countries and for most periods (see, for example, Frey and Stutzer 2002, sec. 4.3). This is consistent with Easterlin's (2001) finding from a synthetic cohort analysis that life satisfaction is practically constant over any given cohort's life cycle. This finding suggests that correlations between individual life satisfaction and income over time (category 1b) are zero or low. Even major changes in income like winning a lottery may have positive effects on life satisfaction

Table 10.1   A classification of life-satisfaction research

Level of aggregation / Comparison perspective	Cross-section	Time series
Individual	1a	1b
National	2a	2b

only in the short run (Gardner and Oswald 2001), but zero or even negative effects in a longer run (Argyle 1999). For cross-sections of average life satisfaction and average income in developed countries (category 2a), it is found that income effects and correlations are weak or zero across countries with an average annual income level above US$10,000 (for example, Diener and Suh 1999; Kenny 1999; Frey and Stutzer 2002). Moreover, for particular datasets of developed as well as developing countries, the correlations are even insignificant when variables for individualism (as defined by Hofstede 1991) or equality are controlled for (Diener et al. 1995).

Finally, cross-sectional correlations between individual life satisfaction and income within developed countries (category 1a) tend to be higher, but are still low in comparison with those for other determinants of life satisfaction (see, for example, Frey and Stutzer 2002, sec. 4.4.1). For example, for data for the USA, Diener et al. (1993) found correlations of 0.13 and 0.12 (implying that less than 2 per cent of the variance in life satisfaction is explained by variations in income) and Easterlin (2001) found a correlation of 0.20. Moreover, they established a curvilinear pattern in the relation between income and life satisfaction.[2] For income levels above US$10,000, Easterlin's data are easily calculated to imply an average 'elasticity' of life satisfaction with respect to income of roughly 0.2, which seems small. A similar pattern can be observed in other industrialized countries (see, for example, Inglehart 1990, table 7–10). For West Germany, Glatzer (1991) found no clear income effect on life satisfaction between the second and fifth income quintiles. For Switzerland, Frey and Stutzer (2002: 83–5) even found a somewhat lower life satisfaction for the highest-income group than for the second highest.

A problem in judging the size of non-zero (positive) income effects is that it seems very hard to assess whether these effects are smaller than the size one may expect on the basis of income-related behaviour and preferences. In the case of labour supply behaviour one should then also know the effects on life satisfaction of leisure and working time. Therefore, at this stage of research, we can only say that positive income effects on life satisfaction seem small in comparison with what one could expect on the basis of income-related behaviour and stated preferences. Just like the zero-income effects reported above, this suggests a difference between, on the one hand, the (*ex ante*) decision utility which is supposed to govern income-related behaviour and, on the other, the (*ex post*) life satisfaction as a result of that behaviour. In the context of this chapter we assume that the decision utility of alternative income levels is given by the expected contributions of income levels to life satisfaction.[3] On the other hand, the *ex post* experienced contribution of the chosen income level to life satisfaction is referred to as experienced utility.[4]

3. Dynamics of aspiration levels and positional externalities

General analysis

Economists like Easterlin (1974, 2001) and Frank (1997) consider as one of the important explanations for the empirical findings reported above the dynamics of rising aspiration levels and positional externalities. The working of these dynamics in the four cases of the paradox described above can be explained as follows.

There are two main effects involved, namely hedonic adaptation and positional externalities. In general terms, hedonic adaptation is the reduction of the hedonic, that is, happiness-relevant, response to a constant or repeated stimulus (Frederick and Loewenstein 1999: 302). It can take the form of a shift of the baseline stimulus level, that is, the stimulus experienced as neutral (baseline shift), or that of a reduction of the intensity of any given response without a shift of the zero point (desensitization; ibid.). In this context, two kinds of adaptation process can be distinguished: psychophysical and cognitive. The distinguishing feature of psychophysical adaptation is that the sensory response to a constant or repeated stimulus itself is reduced (for example, pupil contraction). Cognitive adaptation, on the other hand, involves a reassessment of an invariant perception (for example, getting used to the conveniences of one's new car). This kind of adaptation is the most relevant one for the case of life satisfaction, in which cognitive evaluation and judgement play an important role. It implies that people get used to a higher or lower income level and accordingly adjust their level of life satisfaction. This involves a baseline shift rather than desensitization and renders a person's life satisfaction negatively dependent on his/her income in the past.

The second main effect can be summarized under the heading of 'positional externalities'. These can be divided into two kinds of effect. The first effect we will call 'secondary inflation' (Hirata 2001: 36; see also Figure 10.1). Analogous to the expansion of the monetary mass that

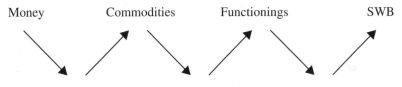

| Money | Commodities | Functionings | SWB |

Primary inflation   Secondary inflation   Frame-of-reference effect

Source: Hirata (2001: 37).

Figure 10.1   The utility chain linking money and subjective well-being (SWB)

reduces the value of money with respect to commodities, the expansion of the average income in 'real terms' or in terms of 'commodity purchasing power' (that is, corrected for what we will call 'primary inflation') may lead to a reduction of the value of income with respect to what Sen (1985) calls 'functionings'.[5] This effect is at work in its purest form where positional goods are involved. A positional good (Hirsch 1976: 27) is characterized by some absolute limitation on its availability to society, either because it is a rival good in fixed supply (for example, Van Gogh's masterpieces) or because an increase in consumption will lead to congestion (for example, an isolated beach). Positional goods are therefore valued for their relative superiority, which, because of their absolute scarcity, does not erode as society becomes richer. In all cases the payoff of one's effort or expenditure to obtain a positional good depends to a large extent on the effort and expenditure of others because one's payoff is a function of one's position in some kind of competition. A given functioning, for example, having a holiday in a lonely cottage, will then become ever more expensive because it requires finding ever more remote places as the newly rich settle on the formerly quiet spots.

Apart from positional goods, the cost of a given functioning in terms of commodities also depends on the lifestyle of others as far as social interactions link individuals together. For example, as people become richer and own more cars, and society becomes richer to build additional roads, public transport may deteriorate (as has arguably been the case in Los Angeles, for example). As a consequence, some people will be forced to buy a car in order to get to places where they formerly could go by bus. The additional expenditures involved do not, however, enter into the calculation of the official (primary) inflation rate, because in terms of goods and services consumption does indeed increase. Yet, in order to express the 'functioning purchasing power' of money, prices have to be corrected for secondary inflation as well.

The second kind of positional externality could be called the 'frame-of-reference effect' (see Frank 1997). This effect is at work to the extent that the increase of our reference group's consumption reduces the life satisfaction we derive from a given activity, increasing our aspirations and evaluation standards. For example, when all families in our neighbourhood increase their holiday spending, our own desire to go on similarly adventurous holidays is likely to increase, and our capacity to enjoy any given holiday trip to decrease. The frame-of-reference effect is closely linked to what in the psychological literature is called 'relative deprivation' (Stouffer et al. 1949) and social comparison (Festinger 1954; Olson et al. 1986).

The distinction between secondary inflation and the frame-of-reference effect can best be formulated in terms of functionings. Secondary inflation is the rate of real income growth required to maintain our level of functionings, whereas the frame-of-reference effect alters the set of functionings that will maintain an individual's level of life satisfaction (see Figure 10.1). The former is a primarily external allocative effect, while the latter is rather internal or psychological (also called 'practical' and 'social–psychological' effects, respectively; for example, Vendrik 1993: 112). Since functionings reflect objective living conditions (not to be confused with material living standards), we have here an important distinction between indirect income effects on life satisfaction via living conditions and direct income effects on life satisfaction. To be sure, the two effects will often be hard to separate in practice. For example, expensive clothes may serve partly to maintain our level of the functioning of social recognition and partly to raise this level of functioning so as to maintain our level of life satisfaction (or perhaps to effectively raise life satisfaction). Nevertheless, the distinction between the secondary inflation and the frame-of-reference effect will be useful as a conceptual distinction which we shall use below.

In both cases of positional externalities, a person's life satisfaction (LS) will negatively depend on the income of other people (for example, in a person's social reference group in the case of frame-of-reference effects). Identifying which 'other people' are involved is a very thorny problem, which has prompted researchers to make simplifying approximations. A useful approximation is to assume that a person's LS depends negatively on the average income in his/her social group Y_s, which is the group of people in the person's categories of age, sex, education, income, region of residence and so on (Ferrer-i-Carbonell 2005). In addition, there will be an influence from wider groups, which can be captured by the average income in a person's community or region of residence Y_r (Diener et al. 1993; Stutzer 2004) and/or the average income in a person's cohort (McBride 2001) or country, Y_c. These variables as well as past income Y_{-1} we call 'relative income standard' (RIS) variables.

Several studies have shown the impact of RIS variables on satisfaction with income (for example, Kapteyn and Wansbeek 1985; Clark and Oswald 1996; Van Praag and Frijters 1999), but there are only a few studies that have tried to estimate the effect of RIS variables on overall LS. For our purposes, the most useful ones are statistical/econometric studies of cross-sections of individual inhabitants of developed countries (category 1a in Table 10.1). In fact, we know of only three, namely McBride (2001) for US data, Ferrer-i-Carbonell (2002) for German data and Stutzer (2004) for Swiss data.[6] The last one is particularly interesting since it uses data for aspiration level as an intermediate variable between RIS variables and LS. The aspiration level of 4,554 respondents to a Swiss survey between 1992 and 1994 was measured in two ways: (i) as the income level that people consider to be sufficient for their entire household according to answers to a standard income evaluation question (see Van Praag 1993); and (ii) as the household income that people consider to be an absolute minimum. Both measures have the advantage that they capture not only adaptation and frame-of-reference effects, but also secondary (together with primary) inflation. Therefore, and since Stutzer's study yields important additional insights in comparison with the other studies, we use Stutzer's model with some different RIS variables as our framework.

Specific analysis
Stutzer assumes that a person's LS is related to his/her income Y and income aspiration level Y^* as:

$$LS = \alpha + \beta \ln Y - \gamma \ln Y^* + \delta \ln \mathbf{X} + \varepsilon, \quad (10.1)$$

where $\mathbf{X}$ is a vector of control variables and ε is an error term. The parameters β and γ are supposed to be non-negative and δ is a vector of parameters. Equation (10.1) can be rewritten as:

$$LS = \alpha + (\beta - \gamma) \ln Y + \gamma (\ln Y - \ln Y^*) + \delta \ln \mathbf{X} + \varepsilon, \quad (10.2)$$

which separates the effect of the discrepancy between log income and log aspiration level from the pure effect of the log income level. The discrepancy variable can also be written as $\ln(Y/Y^*)$. Stutzer finds that this variable has a sizeable and significantly positive effect on LS ($\gamma > 0$), whereas $\ln Y$ 'as such' has only a slight and insignificantly positive effect ($\beta \approx \gamma$). Thus, an equal relative rise of income and aspiration level will produce two completely offsetting effects on LS for these Swiss data (as assumed by Easterlin (2001: 473) in his model).

However, the question is: do income and aspiration levels rise at the same pace? (This is a crucial assumption in Easterlin's model.) To answer this question, we assume, in line with Stutzer, that the aspiration level Y^* depends on the RIS variables introduced above as

$$\ln Y^* = \varphi_0 + \varphi_{-1} \ln Y_{-1} + \varphi_s \ln Y_s + \varphi_r \ln Y_r$$
$$+ \varphi_c \ln Y_c + \chi \ln \mathbf{Z} + \varepsilon^*, \quad (10.3)$$

where $\mathbf{Z}$ is a vector of control variables and ε^* is an error term. The parameters φ_{-1}, φ_s, φ_r and φ_c are supposed to be non-negative parameters and χ is a vector of parameters. Since the social influence from closer groups can be expected to be stronger than that from wider groups, we expect $\varphi_s > \varphi_r > \varphi_c$ with φ_c referring to country.[7] Stutzer approximates people's previous income Y_{-1} with their reported household income and models social influence by the effect of average income in a person's community of residence Y_r, but excludes the other social-influence variables in equation (10.3).[8] He then finds significant estimates for φ_{-1} and φ_r of 0.40 and 0.19, respectively. He notes that the latter estimate may also include the positive effect on income aspirations of higher costs of living in communities with a higher average income. Interestingly, in terms of Figure 10.1, these higher costs of living can be explained as both an effect of higher consumer prices due to a higher aggregate demand (primary inflation) and an effect of higher expenditures on positional goods to reach given levels of functionings (secondary inflation). In order to disentangle the effects of costs of living and of social comparison, Stutzer includes an indicator for social interactions with neighbours in his regressions and finds that at least 0.11 of the estimate 0.19 of φ_r can be attributed to social comparison. Together, Stutzer's estimates for φ_{-1} and φ_r suggest that when a rise in income is accompanied by proportional rises in average income Y_r as well as previous income Y_{-1}, the aspiration level Y^* also rises, but at a slower pace than Y. More specifically, a 10 per cent increase in income then leads to a 6 per cent increase in aspiration level. Thus, Easterlin's assumption that income and aspiration levels rise at the same pace over the life cycle is not confirmed by Stutzer's results.

For a much smaller American dataset (324 usable observations) for 1994 McBride (2001) finds less significant, but possibly stronger effects of RIS variables on life satisfaction. As a proxy for the effect of Y_{-1} he uses four dummy variables which indicate the degree to which a person thinks his/her standard of living is better or worse than his/her parents' standard of living when they were that age. As a social-influence variable he adopts the average income in a person's cohort Y_c, where the cohort consists of everyone from 5 years younger than the person to 5 years older. In careful ordered-probit regressions, McBride then estimates the direct effect of these variables, Y and control variables on LS without an intermediate variable for aspirations. To assess the implications of his results in the context of our framework, we substitute equation (10.3) for the aspiration level Y^* into equation (10.1) for LS, yielding:

$$LS = \alpha - \gamma\varphi_0 + \beta\ln Y - \gamma\varphi_{-1}\ln Y_{-1} - \gamma\varphi_s \ln Y_s - \gamma\varphi_r$$
$$\ln Y_r - \gamma\varphi_c \ln Y_c + \delta\ln X - \Gamma\gamma\chi\ln Z + \varepsilon - \gamma\varepsilon^*. \qquad (10.4)$$

From his regressions McBride finds estimated coefficients for $\ln Y$ and $\ln Y^c$ with the expected signs. However, these coefficients are not separately significant, but only jointly significant in combination with the other coefficients. Although these estimates cannot be considered as direct estimates of β and $\gamma\varphi_c$, their difference in size strongly suggests that $\gamma\varphi_c$ is substantially larger than β. McBride uses his cross-section estimates to simulate the development of the average *LS* of synthetic cohorts over the life cycle (as considered by Easterlin 2001; category 1b in Table 10.1). In this case a considerable part of the positive effect of a rise in average income *Y* on average *LS* seems to run via the four dummy variables for the effect of Y_{-1} since the parents' standard of living when they were of the same age is likely to be more or less fixed. As a result, the simulations reveal a downward or zero trend in average *LS* over time, where the downward trend is attributed by McBride to problems in the measurement of the dummies for Y_{-1}. Thus, McBride can replicate the approximate constancy of average *LS* in American cohorts over the life cycle as found by Easterlin (2001), and thus lend support to both this finding and Easterlin's explanation. McBride also aggregates the cohort simulations to simulations of average *LS* in the whole American population over time (category 2b in Table 10.1) and replicates the zero trend which is found empirically. However, McBride does not consider these results conclusive because of separate insignificance of the coefficients of the income and some of the RIS variables and because of structural differences of the income and RIS parameters between high- and low-income groups (see the end of the next subsection).

For a much larger dataset for West and East Germany (about 16,000 individuals) for 1992–1997, Ferrer-i-Carbonell (2005) finds significant negative effects of ln average income in a person's social group Y_s (similar education and age, and same region, that is, West or East Germany) on *LS*. These effects have approximately the same size as the effects of ln income *Y* on *LS*, implying that the coefficients β and φ_s in equation (10.4) are similar in magnitude. This predicts zero trends of average *LS* in German social groups and cohorts over time (see Glatzer 1991, Table 13.9). Moreover, it does so without including a proxy for Y_{-1}.

In general, a full explanation of zero trends in average LS in developed countries over time requires that the sum of coefficients $\gamma\varphi_{-1} + \gamma\varphi_s + \gamma\varphi_r + \gamma\varphi_c$ in equation (10.4) approximately equals β. For Stutzer's estimation results, where $\beta \approx \gamma$, this implies that the sum of RIS coefficients $\varphi_{-1} + \varphi_s + \varphi_r + \varphi_c$ in equation (10.3) should be approximately equal to one. In this national time-series case a rise in average income is accompanied by a proportional rise in all average RIS variables, and this would then lead to a proportional rise in the aspiration level Y^* by virtue of equation (10.3), implying no change in *LS* according to equation (10.2) with $\beta \approx \gamma$. Stutzer does not estimate effects of the RIS variables Y_s and Y_c in equation (10.3), but since Y_s (the average income in a person's social group of people with similar income) is probably strongly positively correlated with Y_{-1} the effect of Y_s is likely to be included for the greater part into the estimated

$\varphi_{-1} = 0.40$. Moreover, an additional effect of Y_c (in cohort or country) can be expected to be smaller than the estimated effect $\varphi_r = 0.19$ of Y_r. So, even if Stutzer had been able to estimate the effects of Y_s and Y_c (which is of course impossible for a country's Y_c in a national cross-section), the total estimated sum of RIS coefficients in equation (10.3) would probably be substantially lower than one. Still, Stutzer's estimation results can account for a large part of an explanation of the zero trends in average *LS* in developed countries over time.

By the same token, the weak or zero income effects on average *LS* in cross-sections of developed countries (category 2a in Table 10.1), in which all RIS variables vary along with average income, can be explained by the results of McBride and Ferrer-i-Carbonell and, at least partially, by those of Stutzer. The zero trends in average *LS* of cohorts in developed countries over time (category 1b) are explained for a smaller part by Stutzer's results since then the RIS variables Y_r and Y_c for community or region of residence and country will not fully follow variations in average Y in the cohort over time. This as well as the previous analysis is summarized in Table 10.2. Here the '+ +' signs in the second column indicate the relatively strong positive effects of a rise in Y on *LS* or decision utility (*DU*); '–' indicates that a rise in Y is counteracted in its effect on *LS* by a proportional rise in the respective RIS variable; '0' indicates no rise in the respective RIS variable or *LS*; and '0/–' indicates an in-between case of a less-than-proportional rise in the respective RIS variable. Finally, the signs in the last column indicate the overall reaction of *LS* or *DU* to a rise in Y.

Finally, the aspiration-level approach can give an explanation of the empirical finding that the income effects on *LS* are higher in cross-sections of individuals in a developed country (category 1a) than in the other cases. In that case past income Y_{-1} and average income in a person's social group (with similar income) Y_s will be proportionately higher for rich persons than for poor persons, but the average income in the country Y_c is the same for rich as for poor persons and the average income in the community or

Table 10.2 Effects of rises in income and relative income standards on life satisfaction and decision utility

	Y	Y_{-1}	Y_s	Y_r	Y_c	*LS* or *DU*
National *LS* over time	+ +	–	–	–	–	0
Cross-sect. of national *LS*	+ +	–	–	–	–	0
Cohort *LS* over time	+ +	–	–	0/–	0/–	0
Cross-sect. of individual *LS*	+ +	–	–	0/–	0	+
Decision utility *DU*	+ +	0	0	0	0	+ +

region of residence Y_r may not differ very much between rich and poor people. As a result, the positive effect of a higher income Y on LS is counteracted only (or primarily) and less than completely by the negative effects of higher Y_{-1} and Y_s on LS.

At the same time, this result can also form the basis for an explanation why the income effects on LS in individual cross-sections in a developed country are lower than what one may expect on the basis of the high value that people seem to attach to their level of income, as indicated by their behaviour and stated preferences (see Section 2). Following Easterlin (2001), we assume that in decisions related to income individuals maximize their expected LS as given by equation (10.1). However, they are assumed not to anticipate that when they get a higher income Y, their past income Y_{-1} and some of the other three relative income standards will rise as well over time. Hence, a doubling of their income will raise their decision utility by 0.74 β points,[9] so 0.32 points for Stutzer's estimated β of 0.43. However, the life satisfaction that individuals experience after an income-raising decision has been made (that is, their experienced utility) will be lower than expected since some or all of the RIS variables will have risen along with their income. In the context of the individual cross-sections, the RIS variables that have higher values for higher Y are primarily Y_{-1} and Y_s. This raises the aspiration level of a rich as compared to a poor person, and hence suppresses the difference in LS between the rich and the poor. A doubling of Y, and hence of Y_{-1} and Y_s (at constant Y_r), will now imply a difference in LS of $0.74 \times (\beta - \gamma\varphi_{-1} - \gamma\varphi_s) = 0.21$ points for Stutzer's estimates ($\beta = 0.43$, $\gamma = 0.38$, $\varphi_{-1} = 0.40$, assuming that the effect of φ_s is included in the estimate of φ_{-1}). Thus, according to Stutzer's estimates, the income effect on LS in a Swiss individual cross-section is about two-thirds (0.21/0.32) of the supposed income effect in people's average decision utility. For a German dataset, Ferrer-i-Carbonell's estimated $\gamma\varphi_s \approx \beta$ even implies an approximately zero-income effect, which is consistent with the absence of a clear income effect on LS between the second and fifth income quintiles of a West German cross-section as found by Glatzer (1991). Hence, we can say that the impression of a lower-income effect on LS in individual cross-sections as compared to the income effect on decision utility is consistent with what the aspiration-level approach predicts. Nevertheless, the former impression has still to be underpinned by quantitative estimates.

An important point to note is that even when people fully anticipate rises in their past income Y_{-1} and in the average income in their social environment, there is a prisoner's dilemma effect of positional externalities on their decision utility. In that case, people anticipate that a rise in their income Y will only lead to a moderate or zero rise in their LS, but also that no rise in Y will imply a fall in their LS when the income in their social environment rises. This gives them an incentive to take income-raising decisions, but if everybody does so, nobody will gain much in *LS*. This represents an explanation of the above paradoxes in terms of collective irrationality, which does not require the individual irrationality of a discrepancy between decision and experienced utility.

Critical studies

Thus, the aspiration-level (and positional-externalities) approach seems quite successful in explaining at least partially the empirical findings of zero or low correlations between income and life satisfaction on different levels of analysis. However, individual and national cross-section studies by Diener et al. (1993 and 1995) raise doubts about the empirical relevance of the aspiration-level approach. The former study analyses 10-year longitudinal data for SWB and many determining variables in a probability sample of 4,942 American adults. This comprises one cross-section of individuals surveyed between 1971 and 1975 and another one for the same individuals between 1981 and 1984. The correlations between family income and SWB were 0.13 and 0.12, respectively, and curvilinear relations between income and SWB were established. However, no evidence for the influence of RIS variables on SWB was found. Possible adaptation effects were examined by exploring the effect that income changes from the first to the second period had on SWB, controlling for the level of income. This did not yield significant results. Furthermore, the SWB levels of people with comparable incomes living in poorer versus richer geographical areas (a county or contiguous counties) were compared with each other. This did not yield significant differences either. Similarly insignificant effects of RIS variables were found in cross-national studies by Diener et al. (1993, 1995). The 1995 study is the more extensive one and comprises SWB data for 55 countries as reported in probability surveys and a large college student sample. Possible adaptation effects were examined by correlating the growth of per capita real GDP of nations with SWB. This produced insignificant or inconsistent correlations with the main correlation being insignificantly negative when absolute levels of income were controlled for. Social comparison was taken into account by investigating its effects on SWB in three ways. One of the correlations had the 'wrong' sign and was significant, the other two correlations were insignificant.

These results of Diener et al. are striking when we compare them with the results of Stutzer, McBride and Ferrer-i-Carbonell as discussed above. However, the following points on Diener et al.'s results can be made. First, in the individual cross-section study (Diener et al. 1993), SWB was measured as a hedonic-level-of-affect balance (the preponderance of pleasant over unpleasant affect). Although such hedonic measures of SWB tend to be strongly positively correlated with life satisfaction measures, hedonic affect seems to be less sensitive to adaptation and social comparison than the more cognitive evaluation measure of life satisfaction (see Frey and Stutzer 2002, sec. 1.2, for a discussion; see also Peiró 2003).

Second, Diener et al. (1993) themselves raise the point that the 10-year period over which the income change was measured in their cross-section study might be too long since complete adaptation is likely to occur within a shorter time period. Still, they had expected some correlation with SWB from recent changes in the income of some individuals in the cross-section. On the other hand, in the national cross-section study (Diener et al. 1995), correlations of SWB with growth of per capita GDP, which represents income changes over one year, were insignificant or inconsistent as well. Stutzer's result that approximating people's previous income Y_{-1} with their current income yields a significant estimated coefficient φ_{-1} in equation (10.3) for the aspiration level Y^* suggests that the insignificant results (Diener et al. 1993, 1995) may be due to an adaptation of Y^* to Y within much less than a year. In that case a large part of the effects of adaptation in the analyses of Diener et al. would be included as a negative effect of Y on SWB within the net positive effect of Y. Diener et al.'s insignificant or inconsistent correlations may also be due to an 'overshooting' of aspiration levels over fast-rising income levels in countries with rapid economic growth (as mentioned by Diener et al. 1995: 852). This may be modelled by assuming that the coefficient φ_{-1} in equation (10.3) for the aspiration level is an increasing function of relative income growth $\Delta \ln Y$. The important thing to note here is that Diener et al.'s insignificant adaptation results are not necessarily inconsistent with the aspiration-level approach.

Diener et al.'s (1993, 1995) insignificant or negative results for social comparison can have different possible reasons, as extensively discussed by Diener et al. (1993: 217–21). Going into that is beyond the scope of this chapter, but we would like to suggest here one other possible reason. Living as a rich person in a poor country might not only have the benefits of a higher relative income (in terms of SWB), but also have costs due to worse general living conditions such as less security and worse public facilities. Conversely, living as a poor person in a rich area may not only have the costs of a lower relative income, but also benefits due to better general living conditions. These benefits and costs may more or less counterbalance each other, leading to no significant net effect of the economic prosperity in one's living area on SWB.[10] Such possible differences in living conditions are not likely to affect aspiration levels such as modelled in Stutzer's equation (10.3) or to play a role in the impact of average cohort or social-group incomes in the models of McBride and Ferrer-i-Carbonell.

Another paper which is critical about the aspiration-level approach and the implied happiness-is-relative view is Veenhoven (1991). In a general analysis he argues that extreme claims on the basis of that view are unwarranted. Again, it is beyond the scope of this chapter to discuss all his arguments, but one criticism is particularly important and interesting in the present context. He finds that the higher the GDP of a country, the lower the correlation between individual happiness and income. This is inconsistent with the assumption that relative-income effects are just as strong (or weak) at low-income levels as they are at high-income levels. Indeed, McBride (2001) finds that RIS variables appear to have much stronger effects on life satisfaction for those in higher-income groups than for those in lower-income groups, while the effect of an increase in income is much smaller. This can explain Veenhoven's finding, but it raises the question where these differences in reactions to relative (and absolute) income come from. Yet, an important point to note is that this explanation does not require abandoning the relative-income approach. More in general, the negative results of Veenhoven (1991) and Diener et al. (1993, 1995) with respect to this approach seem to apply to particular specifications of the relative-income hypothesis, and hence are not able to reject more general and flexible versions of the relative-income hypothesis, which allow some impact of absolute income on *LS* as well.

Our conclusion from this short survey is that a lot more empirical research is needed to test the aspiration-level approach, but that first econometric results, in particular those of Stutzer (2004), look promising. Together with empirical analyses like those of Easterlin (2001), they suggest that the aspiration-level (and positional-externalities) approach can explain a large part of the stylized facts with respect to the correlations of income and life satisfaction. However, the suggestion from Stutzer's estimates that this explanation may only be partial leaves room for other possible explanations. Moreover, there are indications (Headey et al. 1991) that causality is not so much running from aspiration levels towards happiness, but rather from happiness towards aspiration levels (see also Richins and Dawson 1992: 313). This possibility is analysed in the context of an alternative explanation of a discrepancy between decision utility and experienced utility of income in the next section.

4. Intrinsic versus extrinsic goals

Motivational SWB theory

Veenhoven (1991) emphasizes that even in affluent societies overall life satisfaction does not entirely depend on cognitive comparison, but also on how one feels affectively. In his view, overall life satisfaction not only has a cognitive component which indicates the 'degree to which an individual perceives her aspirations to be met' (contentment), but it also has an affective component representing the 'degree to which the various affects a person experiences are pleasant' (hedonic level), prior to any cognitive evaluation. This hedonic level of affect draws on the gratification of basic bio-psychological needs. To the extent that life satisfaction depends on this need gratification, it hinges, in Veenhoven's view, on absolute levels of income rather than relative levels. This view finds support in the empirical results of Diener et al. (1993, 1995) as discussed at the end of the previous section.

Diener et al. (1993: 220–21) also discuss some reasons why income may make a difference in (hedonic) happiness even beyond the level of meeting one's elementary biological needs. Two reasons they mention are remarkable and important in the present context. First, status may accrue to people with relatively greater wealth, even at high levels of income. Second, society may generate needs in people which can be better met with an increasing income. For example, the structure of richer societies may make it difficult to do one's grocery shopping by bus (see above). Interestingly, both reasons imply that the hedonic level of affect emphasized by Veenhoven depends on relative income, the former via a frame-of-reference effect, the latter via secondary inflation (see the explanations in Section 3). This suggests that a needs approach to happiness has some overlap with the relative-income-standard approach. It also suggests that we should make a distinction between a category of needs the satisfaction of which primarily depends on absolute income, and a category of needs the satisfaction of which primarily depends on relative income.

An approach which implies such a distinction and which moreover implies a second source of difference between decision utility and experienced utility of income can be based on the research results of Kasser and Ryan (1993, 1996; see also Kasser and Ahuvia 2002) about intrinsic and extrinsic goals. Their data show first of all that a distinction between intrinsic goals – self-acceptance, affiliation, community feeling and physical fitness – and extrinsic goals – financial success, social recognition and appealing appearance – actually does reflect a consistent pattern in people's preferences: the mutual correlation of the importance scores given to each goal is substantial within each group of goals, but negligible across the two groups. That is, someone who declares financial success to be a relatively important goal will in general place more importance on other extrinsic goals than on intrinsic goals.

As a second result, it turned out that subjects giving relative centrality to extrinsic goals tended to score lower on subjective well-being measures than subjects for whom intrinsic goals were more central,[11] and this result appeared not to be influenced by the actual income of respondents. For brevity, we will call this the *motivational SWB theory*. On the whole it seems safe to conclude (i) that it makes sense to distinguish between intrinsic and extrinsic goals and (ii) that giving priority to extrinsic goals over intrinsic ones is generally associated with reduced well-being.

To relate the motivational SWB theory back to the distinction between decision and experienced utility, these findings can be interpreted as follows. It seems reasonable to assume that the relative importance an individual attaches to a particular goal will determine with how large a weight this dimension will impact on decision utility. *Experienced* utility, however, appears to be more or less independent from the goal priorities an individual holds. In other words, the fact that a person finds financial success particularly important does not mean that he/she will actually derive more satisfaction from achieving financial success than anybody else. As a consequence, a person who overemphasizes extrinsic goals will be characterized by a discrepancy between decision and experienced utility: his/her decisions will not effectively maximize experienced utility. Decision and experienced utility will only coincide when there is some optimal assignment of relative weights to extrinsic and intrinsic goals in decision utility.

There is a conspicuous parallel between the extrinsic/intrinsic distinction and the respective roles of relative and absolute income. It seems that the satisfaction of extrinsic desires – in particular, social recognition and financial success – is to a large extent relative, while the satisfaction of intrinsic desires – especially affiliation and community feeling – is much less dependent on social comparison. Strong evidence supporting this view comes from studies of pay satisfaction, which regularly find a strong correlation between (experienced) satisfaction with income and relative-income variables (Kapteyn and Wansbeek 1985; Clark and Oswald 1996). Hence, for a person who gives high priority to extrinsic goals, decision utility may be expected to be strongly influenced by relative-income considerations and adapting aspiration levels. On the other hand, the experienced utility of such a person depends more strongly on the satisfaction of intrinsic needs, which is much less sensitive to relative income. Although the results of Diener et al. (1993) suggest that, even in higher-income brackets, experienced utility is still somewhat sensitive to absolute income, overall it will depend less on income than the decision utility of people focusing on extrinsic goals. If in developed countries the overemphasis on extrinsic goals is pervasive (as argued by Lane 2000, for example), we can expect a substantial effect from the discrepancy between decision and experienced utility of these people that will be felt on all levels of aggregation.

A recent study by Nickerson et al. (2003) further investigated the relation between the extrinsic goal of financial success and happiness, and produced interesting results. As a main result they found that actual income moderates and even neutralizes the negative effect of an extrinsic focus on happiness.

In contrast to the Kasser and Ryan (1996) results, the richer the group you look at, the less will be the 'happiness bonus' of less financially focused people. Eventually, as you move up the income ladder, the happiness difference between the most and the least financially motivated groups fades to less than 0.1 on a 5-point scale (for 1995 incomes above US$100,000).[12] Hence, if the results can be interpreted temporally (and not only cross-sectionally),[13] it is true that a financially focused individual will derive more happiness from becoming rich than a person placing less value on financial success. On the other hand, however, the fact that financial success is a person's top priority does not mean that, once he/she has achieved wealth, he/she will be happier than someone who achieved financial success without really caring that much about it. The crucial point is that the latter person will start out with higher happiness to begin with, allowing him/her to end up on the same happiness level. It should be noted that a comparison is made between one group of people who actually attained the extrinsic goal to which they aspired (financial success) and another who cherish more intrinsic priorities that they may or may not have achieved (even though they also happen to be rich). In other words, this comparison does not tell us how the happiness derived from achieving an extrinsic goal relates to that derived from achieving an intrinsic goal. The fact that financial success does not make extrinsically focused people happier than intrinsically focused individuals, however, suggests that the attainment of intrinsic goals may actually bring a higher happiness payoff.

Top-down interpretation
The motivational SWB theory can now be related to the aspiration-level theory discussed in the previous section as follows. There is some evidence (Diener 1984; Headey et al. 1991; Schyns 2001) that causality may be running not only from domain satisfactions/aspiration levels towards life satisfaction ('bottom up', as assumed in the aspiration-level theory), but also from life satisfaction towards domain satisfactions/aspiration levels ('top down'). In particular, for Australian data (1981–87) Headey et al. found top-down causation for satisfaction with material living standard, which comes close to financial situation. This raises the question how then is life satisfaction determined? One possible explanation starts from the observation that, according to the motivational SWB theory, the degree of life satisfaction depends strongly on the satisfaction of intrinsic needs and this tends to be lower for persons who give higher priority to extrinsic goals. These persons will then declare themselves to be less satisfied with more or less all domains (due to top-down causation), including financial situation. However, the hedonic and the cognitive levels of satisfaction of such people may be inconsistent: while from their general mood they will claim to be

unhappy with their financial situation (hedonic level), their cognitive evaluation of matters will give them little reason to complain about their finances (cognitive level). To reduce this cognitive dissonance, they may revise their aspiration level upwards, much as if they thought, 'my financial situation doesn't seem to be that bad at first sight, but I would certainly be a happier person if I had more money'. In the context of equation (10.3) for the aspiration level Y^*, this could be modelled by assuming that the φ coefficients are higher the more unhappy a person is. At the same time, his/her focus on financial success (and, more generally, extrinsic goals) will be reinforced, which further suppresses his/her hedonic level of life satisfaction. Thus, we would have a loop of reinforcing negative feedbacks between focus on extrinsic goals and hedonic level of life satisfaction, with the cognitive levels of life and domain satisfactions and aspiration levels only being derivatives. Exogenous determinants of this feedback loop would primarily be culture on a collective level and personality traits on an individual level.

What is still missing in this tentative theory is an explanation of the bias towards financial success or extrinsic goals in general. It is not obvious why cognitive dissonance between (lower) hedonic level of affect and (higher) cognitive satisfaction should be reduced by revising extrinsic aspiration levels only, and not also by revising aspirations of intrinsic goals as well. The mechanism described above, one might think, could as well lead an unhappy nature to place priority on the pursuit of intrinsic goals such as friendship and community feeling. The reason why an unhappy character is more likely to focus on extrinsic than intrinsic values might be the perceived control over the respective domain satisfactions. Such people may (perhaps correctly) believe that they have more control over their earning power than over the number and quality of friendships. People indeed appear to spend much more time and effort on education aimed at improving their value on the labour market than on enhancing the ability to make friends. While this explanation seems to be a plausible one, we concede that further research is needed to substantiate this argument.

Failure to learn and wanting versus liking
Apart from the question 'through which mechanism exactly does the bias towards extrinsic goals operate?', it should be noted that the mere existence of a systematic bias against (experienced) utility maximization, which is also posited by the aspiration-level theory, would clearly be an embarrassment to the rational-behaviour hypothesis that is central to much of economic theory. While this hypothesis does not claim that people will always succeed in maximizing utility in an absolute sense, it does claim that people learn from past mistakes and will not commit a particular type of error

systematically. Rationality in this sense would require that a financially well-endowed individual who has for some while sought happiness in ever-more material affluence, realizes that aspiring more wealth does not pay off as expected. As a consequence the individual would revise his/her value priorities in favour of intrinsic goals and discover that this is the more efficient strategy.

So, do people really fail to learn? Are they irrational after all? Psychologists who have examined human decision processes more closely indeed tend to subscribe to such a view.[14] Loewenstein and Schkade (1999), for example, conclude:

> Learning from experience does not seem to offer a broad cure for prediction errors because intuitive theories are often resistant to change, memories of experience are often themselves biased or incomplete, and experiences rarely repeat themselves often enough to make diagnostic patterns noticeable. (p. 85)

They even doubt that expected hedonic payoff is a conscious deliberation in everyday decision making in the first place:

> In fact, as Langer (1989) and others have pointed out, many decisions involve little conscious deliberation. People decide based on rules . . . habits . . . and gut feelings, none of which involve explicit predictions of future feelings. The most common source of experimental surprise could therefore be the absence of an explicit prediction in the first place.[15] (p. 100)

This interpretation is also strengthened by neurophysiological evidence. As Berridge (1999) reports, wanting and liking (corresponding to decision and experienced utility, respectively) emerge from two separate neural substrates (p. 541). In experiments involving the manipulation of particular brain regions of rats, it is possible to demonstrate states of 'wanting without liking' (eating unswallowable food) and 'liking without wanting' (refusing tasty food). Such states have also been observed in human drug addicts. Even though it is difficult to demonstrate the existence of this dissociation between wanting and liking in healthy individuals, the physiological separation of wanting and liking suggests that they will not, as assumed in most of economic decision theory, naturally coincide, but that some – possibly complex and perhaps fallible – intermediary process is at work in human decision making. Observed choice might therefore not accurately reflect where people derive satisfaction from.

The evidence reviewed in this section has been merged to a theory in which there is a mutual interaction between focus on extrinsic goals and hedonic level of life satisfaction. On the one hand, people who overemphasize extrinsic goals will end up less happy than those who place higher priority on intrinsic goals because their decisions will be based on systematically biased predictions of experienced utility. The failure to draw the appropriate lessons from the consistent failure to realize the hoped-for happiness payoff will perpetuate such a pattern. On the other hand, it can be argued that a predisposition to be unhappy will make a person prioritize extrinsic goals, probably because people believe they have more control over the satisfaction of extrinsic than of intrinsic desires and because they do not realize that the adaptation of aspiration levels renders the pursuit of extrinsic goals partly self-defeating.

By means of the motivational SWB theory we are able to account for the finding that the observed behaviour and the stated preference for income overstate the contribution of income to actual life satisfaction. People who overemphasize extrinsic over intrinsic goals will neglect those needs whose fulfilment would durably enhance well-being while excessively focusing on those needs whose pursuit will not bring lasting increases of happiness.

5. Conclusions

Let us take stock of the relative merits of the two approaches discussed in Sections 3 and 4. Both the aspiration-level and the extrinsic/intrinsic-needs approach point to sources of discrepancies between decision utility and experienced utility of income. In addition, the theory of positional externalities supplements these explanations in terms of individual irrationality with the implications of collective irrationality. Both the aspiration-level theory and the theory of positional externalities yield much more specific explanations of zero or low correlations between income and life satisfaction at different levels of analysis (see Table 10.2) than the intrinsic/ extrinsic-goals approach so far.

On the other hand, the aspiration-level approach presupposes that the relations between aspiration levels/domain satisfactions and life satisfaction are purely bottom up, while there is considerable evidence to the contrary.[16] When aspiration levels and domain satisfactions are endogenously determined by life satisfaction (top down), the intrinsic/extrinsic-goals approach explains why focusing on financial success in decision utility yields little gain in experienced utility.

There is now some evidence (for example, Schyns 2001) that top-down and bottom-up relations may work at the same time, resulting in feedback loops. The bottom-up relations may then imply that the low sensitivity of life satisfaction to fulfilment of extrinsic goals may be partly due to the dynamics of aspiration levels and positional externalities. What, at the very least, becomes clear from these results, is that a black-and-white dichotomy between, on the one hand, aspiration-level approaches in terms of relative happiness and, on the other hand, needs approaches in terms of absolute happiness does not appear to be appropriate.

Notes

*   We thank Bart Golsteyn, Amado Peiró, Alois Stutzer, Ruut Veenhoven, Geert Woltjer and other conference participants for helpful comments and Peggy Schyns for sending us some of her papers.
1. The distinction between decision utility and experienced utility has been introduced by Kahneman and Tversky (1984).
2. Regressing life satisfaction on log income, Easterlin (2001: 468) finds a linear relation.
3. For the sake of simplicity, we assume that decision utility is cardinal and that expected and actual life satisfaction are separable in income and other variables (for example, leisure).
4. As usual in happiness research (see, for example, Frey and Stutzer 2002, sec. 1.2), we consider (overall) life satisfaction as a specific concept of subjective happiness or well-being. Life satisfaction is strongly influenced by cognitive processes, and should be distinguished from more hedonic measures of subjective or objective happiness (see Peiró 2003, for an empirical application of this distinction).
5. 'A functioning is an achievement of a person: what he or she manages to do or to be. . . . It has to be distinguished from the commodities which are used to achieve those functionings. . . . It has to be distinguished also from the happiness generated by the functioning, for example, actually cycling around must not be identified with the pleasure obtained from that' (Sen 1985: 10).
6. Diener et al.'s cross-section study (1993) uses subjective well-being data for hedonic level of affect (see below).
7. An interesting hypothesis of Easterlin (2001) is that younger people have wider social reference groups than older people and that past personal experience becomes more important over the life cycle. In the context of equation (10.3), this suggests that φ_s and φ_{-1} grow and φ_f and φ_e decrease over the life cycle.
8. Stutzer also estimates the effects of some other RIS variables in his regressions, which yields interesting results. However, these results are less important in the context of this chapter.
9. It is easily shown that the decision utility will rise by $2/\varepsilon$ times β points, where $\varepsilon = 2.718$.
10. Schyns's (2002) results even suggest dominant living-condition effects of national wealth on SWB.
11. Sagiv and Schwartz (2000) argue that this effect depends on whether the environment encourages or discourages such values, but Kasser and Ahuvia (2002) produce evidence to the contrary (examining a sample of Singaporean business students) and claim that Sagiv and Schwartz's study refers to different concepts ('power' instead of 'extrinsic values') and suffers from small sample sizes ($n = 42$).
12. Unfortunately the authors do not report significance levels, but it seems safe to assume that the positive difference of $+0.03$ for the highest income group (above US$200,000) is not significant. It certainly is not substantial when compared to -0.84 for the lowest income group (up to US$1,000).
13. Even though the authors claim – with some justification – to be doing a longitudinal study, the results presented here are to be interpreted cross-sectionally since no change of wealth and happiness over time is analysed (even though the parents' household income in 1975 is controlled for in some settings).
14. In fact not only psychologists do. Easterlin (2001) is an economist who also breaks with the identity of decision and experienced utility in the context of his aspiration-level theory.
15. The rational behaviour hypothesis can of course be saved – once more – by claiming that, at the end of the day, following imperfect rules of the day and 'gut feelings' is more efficient than spending much effort looking for the perfect decision. Whether this argument is valid in this context will depend on how bad these rules and habits really are.
16. This evidence as well as the contribution of intrinsic domain satisfactions to life satisfaction are neglected in economic approaches like that of Van Praag et al. (2002).

References

Argyle, M. (1999), 'Causes and correlates of happiness', in D. Kahneman, E. Diener and N. Schwarz (eds), *Well-Being: The Foundations of Hedonic Psychology*, New York: Russell Sage Foundation: 353–73.

Berridge, K.C. (1999), 'Pleasure, pain, desire, and dread: hidden core processes of emotion', in D. Kahneman, E. Diener and N. Schwarz (eds), *Well-Being: The Foundations of Hedonic Psychology*, New York: Russell Sage Foundation: 525–57.

Cantril, H. (1965), *The Pattern of Human Concerns*, New Brunswick, NJ: Rutgers University Press.

Clark, A.E. and A.J. Oswald (1996), 'Satisfaction and comparison income', *Journal of Public Economics*, **61**, 359–81.

Diener, E. (1984), 'Subjective well-being', *Psychological Bulletin*, **95** (3), 542–75.

Diener, E., M. Diener and C. Diener (1995), 'Factors predicting the subjective well-being of nations', *Journal of Personality and Social Psychology*, **69**, 851–64.

Diener, E., E. Sandvik, L. Seidlitz and M. Diener (1993), 'The relationship between income and subjective well-being: relative or absolute?', *Social Indicators Research*, **28**, 195–223.

Diener, E. and E.M. Suh (1999), 'National differences in subjective well-being', in D. Kahneman, E. Diener and N. Schwarz (eds), *Well-Being: The Foundations of Hedonic Psychology*, New York: Russell Sage Foundation: 434–50.

Easterlin, R.A. (1974), 'Does economic growth improve the human lot? Some empirical evidence', in P.A. David and M.W. Reder (eds), *Nations and Households in Economic Growth: Essays in Honor of Moses Abramowitz*, New York and London: Academic Press, 89–125.

Easterlin, R.A. (2001), 'Income and happiness: towards a unified theory', *Economic Journal*, **111** (473), 465–84.

Ferrer-i-Carbonell, A. (2005), 'Income and well-being: an empirical analysis of the comparison income effect', *Journal of Public Economics*, **89**, 997–1019.

Festinger, L. (1954), 'A theory of social comparison', *Human Relations*, **7**, 117–40.

Frank, R.H. (1997), 'The frame of reference as a public good', *Economic Journal*, **107**, November, 1832–47.

Frank, R.H. (1999), *Luxury Fever: Why Money Fails to Satisfy in an Era of Excess*, New York: Free Press.

Frederick, S. and G. Loewenstein (1999), 'Hedonic adaptation', in D. Kahneman, E. Diener and N. Schwarz (eds), *Well-Being: The Foundations of Hedonic Psychology*, New York: Russell Sage Foundation: 302–29.

Frey, B.S. and A. Stutzer (2002), *Happiness and Economics: How the Economy and Institutions Affect Well-Being*, Princeton, NJ and Oxford: Princeton University Press.

Gardner, J. and A.J. Oswald (2001), 'Does money buy happiness? A longitudinal study using data on windfalls', unpublished manuscript, Warwick University.

Glatzer, W. (1991), 'Quality of life in advanced industrialized countries: the case of West Germany', in F. Strack, M. Argyle and N. Schwarz (eds), *Subjective Well-Being: An Interdisciplinary Perspective*, Oxford: Pergamon: 261–79.

Headey, B., R. Veenhoven and A. Wearing (1991), 'Top-down versus bottom-up theories of subjective well-being', *Social Indicators Research*, **24**, 81–100.

Hirata, J. (2001), 'Happiness and economics: enriching economic theory with empirical psychology', Masters thesis, Maastricht University, http://johanneshirata.gmxhome.de.

Hirsch, F. (1976), *The Social Limits to Growth*, Cambridge, MA: Harvard University Press.

Hofstede, G. (1991), *Cultures and Organizations*, Boston, MA: McGraw-Hill.

Inglehart, R. (1990), *Culture Shift in Advanced Industrial Society*, Princeton, NJ: Princeton University Press.

Kahneman, D. and A. Tversky (1984), 'Choices, values and frames', *American Psychologist*, **39**, 341–50.

Kapteyn, A. and T. Wansbeek (1985), 'The individual welfare function: a review', *Journal of Economic Psychology*, **6**, 333–63.

Kasser, T. and A. Ahuvia (2002), 'Materialistic values and well-being in business students', *European Journal of Social Psychology*, **32** (1), 137–46.

Kasser, T. and R.M. Ryan (1993), 'A dark side of the American dream: correlates and financial success as a central life aspiration', *Journal of Personality and Social Psychology*, **65**, 410–22.
Kasser, T. and R.M. Ryan (1996), 'Further examining the American dream: differential correlates of intrinsic and extrinsic goals', *Personality and Social Psychology Bulletin*, **22**, 280–87.
Kenny, C. (1999), 'Does growth cause happiness, or does happiness cause growth?', *Kyklos*, **52** (1), 3–26.
Killingsworth, M. and J. Heckman (1986), 'Female labour supply: a survey', in O. Ashenfelter and P.R.G. Layard (eds), *Handbook of Labor Economics*, Vol. 1, Amsterdam: North-Holland, 103–204.
Lane, R.E. (2000), *The Loss of Happiness in Market Democracies*, New Haven, CT: Yale University Press.
Langer, E. (1989), *Mindfulness*, Reading, MA: Addison-Wesley.
Loewenstein, G. and D. Schkade (1999), 'Wouldn't it be nice? Predicting future feelings', in D. Kahneman, E. Diener and N. Schwarz (eds), *Well-Being: The Foundations of Hedonic Psychology*, New York: Russell Sage Foundation: 85–105.
McBride, M. (2001), 'Relative-income effects on subjective well-being in the cross-section', *Journal of Economic Behavior and Organization*, **45**, 251–78.
Nickerson, C., N. Schwarz, E. Diener and D. Kahneman (2003), 'Zeroing in on the dark side of the American dream: a closer look at the negative consequences of the goal for financial success', *Psychological Science*, **14** (6), 531–6.
Olson, J.M., C.P. Herman and M.P. Zanna (eds) (1986), *Relative Deprivation and Social Comparison: The Ontario Symposium*, Vol. 4. Hillsdale, NJ, and London: Lawrence Erlbaum.
Peiró, A. (2003), 'Happiness, satisfaction and socioeconomic conditions: some international evidence', paper presented at the Conference on The Paradoxes of Happiness in Economics, Milan, 21–23 March.
Pencavel, J. (1986), 'Labour supply of men: a survey', in O. Ashenfelter and P.R.G. Layard (eds), *Handbook of Labor Economics*, Vol. 1, Amsterdam: North-Holland, 1–102.
Richins, M.L. and S. Dawson (1992), 'A consumer values orientation for materialism and its measurement: scale development and validation', *Journal of Consumer Research*, **19** (3), 303–16.
Sagiv, L. and S.H. Schwartz (2000), 'Value priorities and subjective well-being: direct relations and congruity effects', *European Journal of Social Psychology*, **30** (2), 177–98.
Schyns, P. (2001), 'Income and satisfaction in Russia', *Journal of Happiness Studies*, **2**, 173–204.
Schyns, P. (2002), 'Wealth of nations, individual income and life satisfaction in 42 countries: a multilevel approach', *Social Indicators Research*, **60**, 5–40.
Sen, A.K. (1985), *Commodities and Capabilities*, Amsterdam: North-Holland.
Stouffer, S.A., E.A. Suchman, L.C. DeVinney, S.A. Star and R.M. Williams (1949), *The American Soldier: Adjustment During Army Life*, Vol. 1, Princeton, NJ: Princeton University Press.
Stutzer, A. (2004), 'The role of income aspirations in individual happiness', *Journal of Economic Behavior and Organization*, **54** (1), 89–109.
Van Praag, B.M.S. (1993), 'The relativity of the welfare concept', in M.C. Nussbaum and A.K. Sen (eds), *The Quality of Life*, Oxford: Oxford University Press: 362–85.
Van Praag, B.M.S. and P. Frijters (1999), 'The measurement of welfare and well-being: the Leyden approach', in D. Kahneman, E. Diener and N. Schwarz (eds), *Well-Being: The Foundations of Hedonic Psychology*, New York: Russell Sage Foundation: 413–33.
Van Praag, B.M.S., P. Frijters and A. Ferrer-i-Carbonell (2002), 'The anatomy of subjective well-being', Tinbergen Institute Discussion Paper TI 2002-022/3, www.tinbergen.nl.
Veenhoven, R. (1991), 'Is happiness relative?', *Social Indicators Research*, **24**, 1–34.
Vendrik, M.C.M. (1993), 'Collective habits and social norms in labour supply: from micro-motives to macrobehavior', Doctoral thesis, Maastricht University.

11 Past product experiences as determinants of happiness with target product experiences: implications for subjective well-being
Rajagopal Raghunathan and Julie R. Irwin

1. Introduction

What makes us happy? This is a question philosophers (for example, Aristotle 1934), psychologists (for example, James 1890 [1948]) and economists (for example, Bentham 1789 [1948]) have pondered over, in one fashion or another, for well over two centuries. In the course of attempting to address this question, several paradoxes have arisen. For example, it is unclear that amassing material wealth necessarily translates into greater happiness, either at the individual level (for example, Brickman et al. 1978) or at the societal or national level (for example, Easterlin 1974). A second, somewhat disturbing – if not paradoxical – finding, is that current happiness with one's experiences in a particular domain (say, at work) is likely to be negatively correlated with one's future happiness in the same domain (for example, Parducci 1984). The research we report in this chapter is related to the second issue.

Within the field of marketing, it is well established that consumers often seek products for their hedonic potential (for example, Holbrook and Hirschman 1982). For example, we visit museums, take vacations, watch movies, or play video games with the intent of deriving enjoyment, and would not continue to do so if they stopped providing enjoyment. A question that naturally follows, then, is: what features of a product determine the enjoyment from it? Intuitively, it is clear that the hedonic quality of a product experience – its overall pleasantness or unpleasantness – is an important determinant of enjoyment. For example, *ceteris paribus*, we are likely to enjoy a vacation to Bali more than we are likely to enjoy a vacation to, say, Des Moines, Iowa. Further, it is reasonable to assume that previous experiences will impact the enjoyment we derive from a future, 'target' experience. Thus, for example, if we had recently visited spectacular locations (for example, Bali, Greece and so on), the enjoyment we derive from a visit to an average vacation spot (say, Washington, DC) will likely be lower than if we had recently visited mediocre locations (for example, Des Moines, Iowa or Kansas City, Kansas).

It follows from the above discussion that the happiness from past experiences in a context is likely to be negatively correlated with the happiness from future experiences in the same context. In this sense, consumers are constantly on a hedonic product treadmill; increased pleasure from a set of hedonic goods means the next good must be that much better to induce the same level of happiness.

We set out to establish the veracity of this simple and seemingly intuitive prediction across several experiments. Interestingly, as discussed in the next section, past research relevant to this issue reveals contradictory findings. On the one hand, findings from research on assimilation-contrast effects (for example, Martin 1986; Schwarz and Bless 1992) suggest a pattern of results opposite to what we have envisaged in our discussion above. On the other hand, findings from research on range-frequency effects (for example, Parducci 1984) predict results consistent with our intuition.

The rest of this chapter is structured as follows. First, we briefly discuss the assimilation-contrast and range-frequency theories, and then build our model of predictions. Then, we review findings from two studies, and end with a discussion of the insights our findings provide to addressing the question with which we began this chapter: what makes us happy?

2.   Assimilation-contrast versus range-frequency predictions
Assimilation-contrast theories
Assimilation-contrast theories (for example, see Martin 1986; Schwarz and Bless 1992) are a subset of a broader set of theories on what are known as 'context effects'. In essence, these theories are about how we judge or evaluate stimuli, and suggest that one's judgment of a target stimulus (for example, product, person and so on) depends on contextual factors, such as, what else is around the target at the time of judgment, and what preceded the judgment of the target stimulus. Findings indicate, for example, that people provide more favorable judgments for a music system when listening to a good (versus bad) song that is being played on it (for example, Gorn et al. 1993). In this instance, music is a contextual influence on judgments of the music system (target). Findings on assimilation-contrast effects (for example, Martin 1986; Schwarz and Bless 1992) indicate that a target from a certain category will elicit more favorable evaluations following exposure to favorable stimuli from the same category. Thus, for example, our impression of a democratic candidate is likely to be more favorable when we have just been exposed to other democratic candidates about whom we think favorably; in contrast, our judgments of this target would be less favorable following exposure to democratic candidates about whom we think unfavorably.

Extending the assimilation-contrast theories' predictions to the context of judging happiness from consumption experiences suggests that exposure to more hedonically pleasing products from a certain category (for example, vacation spots) should lead to more favorable judgments of a target from the same category. Thus, according to the assimilation-contrast theories, our impressions of a particular target vacation spot, say, Bangkok, Thailand, is likely to be more favorable when we have been exposed to exemplary vacation spots, such as Bali, Rome and so on, and less favorable when we have been exposed to mediocre vacation spots, such as Des Moines, Iowa or Kansas City, Kansas.

These predictions appear counter to our intuitions about how contexts should affect our enjoyment of product experiences. Below, we turn to the predictions of the range-frequency theory, whose predictions are more consistent with our intuitions.

Range-frequency theory

Parducci's (1984) range-frequency theory suggests, in essence, that people's happiness with a target experience in a certain category is a function of the range of hedonic quality of past experiences in the same category, as well as the frequency of past experiences that are above (and below) the hedonic quality of the target experience. Specifically, the theory predicts that the happiness with a target experience will be directly proportional to: (i) the range of past experiences below the target experience, and (ii) the frequency of past experiences below the target experience, and inversely proportional to: (i) the range of past experiences above the target experience, and (ii) the frequency of past experiences above the target experience. Thus, for example, a person earning a wage of $500 in a week is likely to be more happy with this wage: (i) the lower the wages he/she has earned in the past, and (ii) the higher the frequency with which he/she has earned wages lower than $500 in the past, and the lower the frequency with which he/she has earned wages higher than $500 in the past.

Extending the range-frequency theory's predictions to the context of judging happiness from consumption experiences suggests that exposure to superior (inferior) products from a certain product category (for example, vacation spots) should lead to less (more) favorable judgments of a target product from the same category. Thus, according to the range-frequency model, our impressions of a particular target vacation spot, say, Bangkok, Thailand, is likely to be less favorable when we have just been exposed to exemplary vacation spots, such as Bali, Rome and so on, and more favorable when we have just been exposed to mediocre vacation spots, such as Des Moines, Iowa or Kansas City, Kansas.

3. Proposed model

As should be clear from the above discussion, the assimilation-contrast theory's predictions are the exact opposite of the predictions of the range-frequency theory. Whereas the former predicts that happiness with a target experience will be directly proportional to enjoyment derived from previous experiences in the same context, the latter predicts that enjoyment derived from a target experience will be inversely proportional to enjoyment derived from previous experiences in the same context.

Although the assimilation-contrast theory's predictions have been found to be robust across a variety of contexts (for example, see Schwarz and Bless 1992), we believe that the results obtained in a product context will be compatible with the predictions of the range-frequency model. Our belief is based on the intuition that consumers evaluate products differently from how they evaluate other stimuli. Specifically, we believe that, rather than transferring the enjoyment derived from past experiences in a product category to a target experience in the same category – resulting, as predicted by the assimilation-contrast theory, in a direct relationship between the two variables – consumers will compare the hedonic quality of the target experience with that of the past experiences – resulting in an inverse relationship between the two variables. Such a comparison, we believe, occurs relatively spontaneously in a product-evaluation context for the following reason. In consumerist societies, people have a plethora of products from which to choose and are continually bombarded with persuasive messages that urge them to favor one product over another. In such settings, consumers with a well-developed product comparison schema (that allows them to evaluate products by comparing them to competitive offerings in a relatively automatic fashion) may be especially well equipped to maneuver through the clutter of products. We thus predict that exposure to superior (inferior) products from a certain product category (for example, vacation spots) should lead to less (more) favorable judgments of a target product from the same category. In summary, we expect that:

> H1 Under conditions of category match, exposure to a more (less) pleasant context will result in lower (higher) target product evaluations.

Note that, thus far, our discussion has been focused on the circumstances where there is a match between the product categories of the context and target. What may we expect of enjoyment from a target experience when it follows other experiences from a different category? Should we expect that exposure to superior (inferior) products from a certain product category (for example, vacation spots) should lead to less (more) favorable judgments of a target product from a different category? Or should we expect the opposite pattern of results – such that, the greater the happiness from the context, the more will the enjoyment be from a target product belonging to another category?

We expect the latter pattern of results under conditions of mismatch between target and context categories. This is because viewing hedonically pleasant (unpleasant) stimuli may induce a good (bad) mood and, under conditions where the target is not from the same category as the context, this mood may be transferred to the target (for example, Isen et al. 1978; Schwarz and Clore 1983). This is similar to the operation of music as a contextual influence, referred to earlier. Thus:

> H2   Under conditions of category mismatch, exposure to a more (less) pleasant context will result in higher (lower) target product evaluations.

Five studies were conducted, in all, to test for these hypotheses.[1] We report results from two of these studies in some detail. Results obtained in the other studies were, overall, consistent with the results obtained in the two studies reported in this chapter.

Study 1: vacation spots
The objective in this study was to show that people's happiness with a target experience is: (i) inversely proportional to happiness with the context when target and contextual stimuli are from the same category (category-match condition), and (ii) directly proportional to happiness with the context when target and contextual stimuli are from different product categories (category-mismatch condition).

We selected the category of vacation spots and cars to test these predictions. Informal talks with undergraduate students revealed that going on vacation can be a distinctly pleasurable activity or a particularly boring one; thinking of vacations in affective terms thus appeared easy and natural for our subjects. Based on results of a pretest, in which subjects were asked to indicate the amount pleasure they would derive from going on vacation to several different vacation spots on a five-point scale (1 = 'Going to this vacation spot would not give me any pleasure', 5 = 'Going to this vacation spot would give me great pleasure'), a total of 42 different vacation spots were used in the main study.

The Golden Pagoda of Thailand, with an average rating of 3.0 and a standard deviation of 0.95 served as the 'target' spot in the category-match condition. In the category-mismatch condition, the target product was an automobile (Toyota Camry). A pretest, in which subjects were asked to rate 62 different automobiles on a five-point scale (1 = 'Driving this automobile would give me no pleasure', 5 = 'Driving this automobile would give me great pleasure') revealed that the Toyota Camry had an average rating of 3.0 (standard deviation = 0.33).

One hundred and thirty-four subjects participated in this study, which consisted of two stages. In the first stage, they were exposed to 26 different pictures of vacation spots. Roughly half the participants were exposed to good-quality vacation spots, and roughly half were exposed to bad-quality ones. Then, in the second stage, the subjects in each of these groups were asked to judge the target vacation spot. Again, roughly half the participants within each of the two groups were asked to judge a target from the same category as that of the context (namely Golden Pagoda, Thailand) using an 11-point scale (1 = 'Going on vacation to this spot will not give me any pleasure', 11 = 'Going on vacation to this spot will give me great pleasure'), while the other half were asked to judge a target from a different product category (namely, the Toyota Camry), on an 11-point scale (1 = 'Taking this car for a test-drive will not give me any pleasure', 11 = 'Taking this car for a test-drive will give me great pleasure'). After rating the target product, subjects provided overall happiness ratings for the contextual stimuli.

Our results indicated, first, that the overall happiness with the context was higher when participants had been exposed to the good (versus bad) set of vacation spots (M = 8.57 and M = 6.43, respectively), $F(1, 127) = 8.01, p < 0.001$. The focus of this study, however, was on ratings of happiness with the target product. The hypothesized effects (see hypotheses 1 and 2) implied an interaction. Consistent with this expectation, the 2-way pleasantness-of-context X category match interaction was significant, $F(1, 127) = 15.11, p < 0.001$, indicating that happiness with the target product depended on whether the category of target product matched the category or contextual stimuli or not. Indeed, confirming both hypotheses 1 and 2 (see Figure 11.1), follow-up analyses revealed that: (i) exposure to the more pleasant context lowered happiness with target product (M = 5.76), compared to exposure to the less pleasant context (M = 7.41), $F(1, 127) = 23.14, p < 0.001$, under conditions of category match, and (ii) exposure to the more pleasant context increased happiness with target product (M = 7.89), compared to exposure to the less pleasant context (M = 6.12), $F(1, 127) = 32.50, p < 0.001$, under conditions of category mismatch.

Study 2: category-match framing
Results from study 1 indicate, consistent with hypotheses 1 and 2, that more favorable past experiences in a product context produce lower happiness ratings of a target under conditions of category match, and higher happiness ratings of a target under conditions of category mismatch. However, often, the degree of category match (between target and

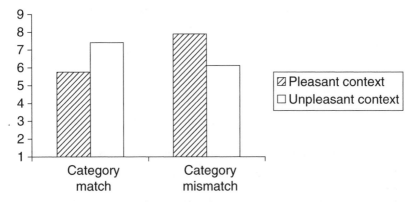

Figure 11.1 *Happiness from target product as a function and pleasantness of context set, and match versus mismatch between target and context product categories*

context) may be subjectively determined. That is, perceptions of category match may depend on how they are framed relative to each other. Consider, for example, a variety show in which a mimic follows a comedian. Are the mimic and the comedian part of the same (variety entertainment) category or are they from different and noncomparable categories? Similarly, consider the experience of staying in a hotel during a vacation. Will the experience of staying in the hotel be bundled with other experiences of the vacation, even if the other experiences take place out of the hotel? Or will the vacation experiences be perceived as belonging to separate (for example, hotel versus out-of-hotel) categories?

The objective in study 2 was to test whether the same target product could elicit different happiness ratings, depending on how it is framed. In other words, we aimed to replicate the results of study 1 using a framing manipulation to create perceptions of match versus mismatch between target and context.

Two hundred and twenty undergraduates participated in this study. As in study 1, pictures of more (or less) pleasant vacation spots were used in the context set. After viewing each spot in the context, subjects rated the amount of happiness they were likely to derive from going on vacation to that spot on a five-point scale (1 = 'Going on vacation to this spot would give me no pleasure', 5 = 'Going on vacation to this spot would give me great pleasure'). Subjects then rated the target product, which was the picture of a living room. For roughly half the subjects (category-match condition), this picture was titled 'Vacation Rental' and for the other half (category-mismatch condition), the picture of the room was titled 'Apartment Rental'. These titles served to frame the target as part of the same abstract-level category as the vacation spots (both belong to the category of vacations) or to two different categories (vacations and apartments), respectively. The framing manipulation was strengthened by the words used in the five-point rating scale subjects used to rate the target: 1 = 'Staying in this Vacation Rental [Apartment Rental] would be give me no pleasure', 5 = 'Staying in this Vacation Rental [Apartment Rental] would give me great pleasure'.

Successful replication of results from study 1 depends on whether the 'vacation rental' and 'apartment rental' target-frame manipulations lead, respectively, to the pattern of results predicted by hypotheses 1 and 2, respectively. First, consistent with our expectations, a 2-way, pleasantness-of-context X framing interaction emerged, $F(1, 206) = 25.81$, $p < 0.001$, suggesting that happiness with the target depended on perceptions of category match between context and target. Follow-up analyses revealed (see Figure 11.2), consistent with our predictions, that: (i) exposure to the more pleasant context resulted in lower target product ratings ($M = 3.27$), compared to exposure to the less pleasant context ($M = 4.22$), $F(1, 206) = 27.54$, $p < 0.001$, when the target was framed as a 'vacation rental', and (ii) exposure to the more pleasant context resulted in higher target product ratings ($M = 3.86$), compared to exposure to the less pleasant context ($M = 3.47$), $F(1, 206) = 4.12$, $p < 0.05$, when the target was framed as an 'apartment rental'.

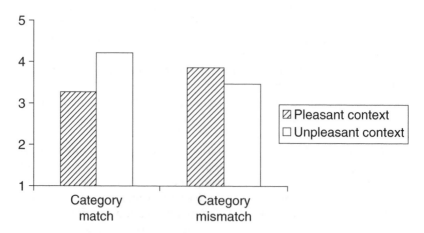

Figure 11.2   Happiness from target product as a function and pleasantness of context set, and framing of match versus mismatch between target and context product categories

4. General discussion

Results from study 1 indicate that consumers will derive greater happiness from a consumption experience when it follows: (i) less (versus more) pleasant experiences from the same category, and (ii) more (versus less) pleasant experiences from other product categories. These results conceptually replicate and extend a number of findings from studies on happiness, which show that the pleasure from an event is inversely proportional to pleasure from previous events in the same domain (for example, Brickman et al. 1978; Parducci 1984). In other words, consumers are continually walking a hedonic treadmill (Brickman and Campbell 1971). If previous product experiences are pleasurable, the next product experience (in the same category) needs to be even better in order to induce the same level of satisfaction. The adaptation-level principle (see Helson 1964), which underlies the classic finding that winning a lottery does not guarantee a lifetime of happiness, just as becoming a paraplegic does not imply a lifetime of sadness (Brickman et al. 1978), thus appears to extend to product evaluation contexts as well.

Study 1 dealt with situations involving unambiguous category match versus mismatch. However, in many situations, it may be difficult to ascertain clearly whether there is a match versus mismatch between context and target. For example, do people generally think of the taxi ride back from a Broadway play as part of the play-watching episode? Or will they treat the ride as a separate entity and evaluate it as such? Our findings suggest that perceived match between target and context can determine whether contrast or assimilation effects occur. Specifically, when there is ambiguity with respect to the extent of product match/mismatch between target and context, happiness from the target experience is determined by whether the target category is perceived to match or mismatch that of the contextual stimuli. When the target is perceived to match contextual stimuli, less (versus more) pleasant contextual experiences produce higher (lower) happiness from the target. In contrast, when the target is perceived to mismatch contextual stimuli, less (versus more) pleasant contextual experiences produce lower (higher) happiness from the target.

Implications for subjective well-being

The answer to the question, 'what makes people happy?' is complicated, as revealed by several apparent paradoxes that emerge from past research (for example, see Easterlin 1974; Brickman et al. 1978). In the present research, our focus was narrow: we wished to determine whether people's happiness with a product experience increases or decreases as a function of their happiness with past experiences in the same versus other product contexts.

Our findings have straightforward implications for agents interested in the welfare of consumers: they suggest that consumption experiences should be arranged in an improving sequence over the lifespan of consumers. This is because the subjective happiness with a target experience, as we have seen, is inversely proportional to the pleasantness of past experiences in that context. It appears that consumers spontaneously compare a specific product experience with other experiences in the same category, and a worsening sequence is therefore likely to hurt the overall happiness derived from the sequence, while an improving sequence is likely to have a beneficial impact on the overall utility from the experience stream. While this proposition follows logically from our findings – and people appear to intuitively understand this rule (for example, see Loewenstein and Prelec 1992) – it contradicts the positive time discounting assumed by economists, according to which 'rational' agents should prefer a worsening (versus improving) sequence.

The present socioeconomic context, in which technological advancements appear to be showing a positive slope, then, augurs well: products currently available are generally better than the ones that came before, and are likely to be inferior to the ones that will follow. Natural forces thus appear aligned to increase the chance that the sequence of product experiences over current consumers' lifetimes will lead to beneficial impact on hedonic utility from product consumption. However, such a conclusion should be drawn with caution. First, it is not entirely clear if the pleasure derived from consumption is of a type that can be sustained in the long run. Scitovsky (1976) has suggested that, while creative goods (for example, those associated with learning new skills) offer the potential to provide consumers with utility on a continual basis, comfort goods (for example, normal TV programs such as sitcoms or soap operas) do not. So, depending on the overall mix of goods available for consumption, aggregate consumer utility may show either a positive or a negative trend.

Second, even if consumers stand to benefit from improvements in technology on the aggregate, our findings suggest that individual consumers (or agents acting on their behalf) should actively seek to control their product experiences to correct for any deviations from the prescribed (improving sequences) path. For example, one may deliberately choose to postpone a 'once-in-a-lifetime' type of experience (for example, going on vacation to the most desirable vacation spot), until a later point in one's life.

Consumers may also take advantage of the findings obtained under conditions of category mismatch in our studies. These findings indicate that the beneficial and detrimental emotional impact of product experiences in one context overflow to the next. These results point to value in strategically managing affective consequences of consumption through seeking pleasurable experiences in one context when an unpleasant experience in another context is likely to follow. For example, one may seek to alternate a hedonically pleasing experience in one context (for example, through a sumptuous dinner at a fancy restaurant), with a not-so-good, but perhaps necessary experience in another context (such as, for example, meeting with a client). This will increase the chances that hedonic utility derived from the combined event is maximized. However, it should be noted that such a conscious strategy may be doomed to failure, since an important precondition to the effectiveness of such a strategy, perhaps, is not being aware of the processes underlying it (for example, Suls and Fletcher 1985). That is, being aware of one's intentions (namely, maximizing consumption utility) may actually frustrate attempts to do so. For instance, in the above example, one's awareness of the impending unpleasant experience may erode into the utility from the dinner itself. To some extent then, the ability to not think of future or past unpleasant events may be an important skill to acquire.

Finally, under conditions of ambiguity about the category membership of either contextual stimuli or the target stimulus, consumers (or the agents acting on their behalf) may strategically frame the target as belonging to the same or a different category as that of the contextual stimuli, so as to maximize hedonic benefits. For example, in traveling to a desirable vacation spot in a less-than-desirable means of transportation, consumers may encode the travel experience as part of the whole vacation experience, thereby bringing up the enjoyment of the travel itself. Likewise, consumers may do well to segregate a hedonically unpleasant experience (for example, a bad ballet performance) from one that follows it (for example, dinner at a restaurant). Once again, however, the success of such a strategy would appear to depend on lack of awareness of the processes underlying the effects; in this instance, an ability to convince oneself into believing the framing one has deliberately adopted with the specific aim of maximizing hedonic utility may be important in achieving this goal.

Note

1. Three of these studies were reported in Raghunathan and Irwin (2001), and test the hypotheses proposed in this chapter, as well as other related hypotheses.

References

Aristotle (1934), *Nicomachean Ethics*, Translated by H. Rackham, Cambridge, MA: Harvard University Press.

Bentham, J. (1789 [1948]), *An Introduction to the Principle of Morals and Legislation*, Oxford: Blackwell.

Brickman, P. and D.T. Campbell (1971), 'Hedonic relativism and planning the good society', in M.H. Apley (ed.), *Adaptation-level Theory: A Symposium*, New York: Academic Press, pp. 287–302.

Brickman, P., D. Coates and R. Janoff-Bulman (1978), 'Lottery winners and accident victims: is happiness relative?', *Journal of Personality and Social Psychology*, **36**, 917–28.

Easterlin, R.A. (1974), 'Does economic growth improve the human lot? Some empirical evidence', in P.A. David and M.W. Reder (eds), *Nations and Households in Economic Growth: Essays in Honor of Moses Abramowitz*, New York: Academic Press, pp. 89–125.

Gorn, G.J., M.E. Goldberg and K. Basu (1993), 'Mood, awareness and product evaluation', *Journal of Consumer Psychology*, **2** (3), 237–56.

Helson, H. (1964), *Adaptation-level Theory*, New York: Harper & Row.

Holbrook, M.B. and E.C. Hirschman (1982), 'The experiential aspects of consumption: consumer fantasies, feelings and fun', *Journal of Consumer Research*, **9**, 132–40.

Isen, A.M., T.E. Shalker, M.S. Clark and L. Karp (1978), 'Affect, accessibility of material in memory, and behavior: a cognitive loop', *Journal of Personality and Social Psychology*, **36**, 1–12.

James, W. (1890 [1948]), *Psychology*, New York: World Publishing Company.

Loewenstein, G. and D. Prelec (1992), 'Preferences for sequences of outcomes', *Psychological Review*, **100**, 91–108.

Martin, L.L. (1986), 'Set/reset: use and disuse of concepts in impression formation', *Journal of Personality and Social Psychology*, **51**, 493–504.

Parducci, A. (1984), *A Relational Theory of Happiness*, Hillsdale, NJ: Lawrence Erlbaum.

Raghunathan, R. and J.R. Irwin (2001), 'Walking the hedonic product treadmill: default contrast and mood-based assimilation effects in judgments of predicted happiness with target product', *Journal of Consumer Research*, **28** (3), 355–68.

Schwarz, N. and H. Bless (1992), 'Constructing reality and its alternatives: an inclusion/exclusion model of assimilation and contrast effects in social judgment', in L.L. Martin and A. Tesser (eds), *The Construction of Social Judgments*, Hillsdale, NJ: Erlbaum, pp. 217–45.

Schwarz, N. and G.L. Clore (1983), 'Mood, misattribution and judgments of well-being: informative and directive functions of affective states', *Journal of Personality and Social Psychology*, **45**, 513–23.

Scitovsky, Tibor (1976), *The Joyless Economy*, Oxford and New York: Oxford University Press.

Suls, J. and B. Fletcher (1985), 'The relative efficacy of avoidant and nonavoidant coping strategies: a meta-analysis', *Health Psychology*, **4** (3), 249–88.

12 The life plan view of happiness and the paradoxes of happiness

Mark Chekola

1. Introduction

'The Paradoxes of Happiness in Economics', the topic of the conference held in Milan, 21–23 March 2003, arises because empirical studies of happiness and well-being have produced some results that are counterintuitive and paradoxical. For instance, after achieving a basic level of income, increases in income do not seem to lead to greater happiness; and while people see work as a burden, work seems important to happiness and unemployment detrimental to happiness.

In order to deal with these paradoxes I believe it is important to be clear about the concept of happiness. As a philosopher, I find some of the references to happiness in discussing these issues disappointingly unclear, limited and barren. In the end what we are concerned with here is our lives. We need a concept of happiness that is rich and full enough to capture what it is that we really seek when we want our lives to be happy. In addition, we need to focus on the nature of happiness (what it is) rather than the conditions of happiness (its causes, conditions and determinants). Social scientists are concerned to be as objective as possible and, in seeking data to use in their studies, want the data to be acceptable, valid and objective, and to be relatively easily collected. Those concerns are understandable. But we must be careful not to let them lead to employing an unacceptably shallow or simple concept of happiness or well-being. I believe the tools of philosophy can be of help with regard to these issues.

I shall offer a view of the nature of the happiness of a life that I believe captures what it is we think of as a happy life, when we think clearly about it, and which fits in with some of the important discussions of happiness in the history of human thought, such as by Aristotle, John Stuart Mill and others. I shall refer to it as the 'life plan view of happiness'.[1]

The view I argue for is that happiness (of a life) is:

1. the realizing of a life plan (one's higher order desires) *along with*
2. the absence of *both* (a) serious felt dissatisfaction and (b) an attitude of being displeased with or disliking one's life *and*

3. a disposition to experience favorable feelings and attitudes associated
    with the realizing of one's life plan.

This view of happiness sees a happy life as one in which a person's higher-order desires, the relatively more comprehensive, permanent and important desires the person has, are in the process of being realized. (For many people these desires will include career goals, relationships, important traits or virtues that one wants to have and so on.) That is the main claim of the view. However, I add two further conditions. There can be serious felt dissatisfaction even where one's life is, objectively, going well, if someone suffers from depression. In addition, there is a disposition to experience favorable feelings and attitudes associated with the realizing of this set of higher-order desires. These positive feelings and attitudes are common or typical, but not necessary, not always present, in a happy life. They (particularly favorable feelings and attitudes) are what some empirical studies of happiness focus on because of a trust of self-reports and a sense that people's reports of their feeling satisfied or experiencing positive moods will be easier to quantify and compare. Before we focus on happiness when applied to a life, we must take note of different senses or uses of 'happiness'.

2.   Uses of 'happiness'

The word 'happiness' has a number of different uses, and it will be important to distinguish the life use, which we are concerned with here, from the others. First, sometimes it is used to refer to a feeling or emotion, such as with regard to a notable success or good fortune ('He was quite happy when he found out he had got the job'). Second, it is sometimes used to refer to a mood, such as when we say 'John was in a happy mood today'. This use indicates the presence of a disposition to have happy feelings and to see things as being favorable. Third, there is a behavior use, exemplified by the adverb 'happily', such as in 'The children played happily'. This use applies to situations where someone is doing something enthusiastically, with vigor, or cheerfully. The fourth use, the attitude use, such as in 'John is happy with his job', and 'John is happy with his children's school work', indicates that one is content, satisfied or pleased with something; one likes it the way it is and does not want a change in it.

These four uses are different from the life use, the use I believe to be the most important. When we say 'John is a happy person', or when Aristotle claims 'Happiness is virtuous activity of the soul', (Aristotle 1915: Book I, Chapter 7: 1098 a 16) happiness is attributed to a life or a portion of a life. It is clearly different from a feeling, a mood, or happy behavior. And while people who are happy often have an attitude of being happy with their lives, I shall later argue that we should not identify the life use with an attitude.

It may be that the other uses of the word 'happiness' can be seen as being derived from the life use (for instance, perhaps the feeling use is derived from the life use in terms of a feeling of happiness being a state of the person indicative of a happy life). It is the life use on which we must focus to be clear about the nature of happiness. To summarize, the five uses or senses of the word 'happiness' are:

- feeling – 'I feel so happy';
- mood – 'She's in a happy mood';
- behavioral – 'The children played happily';
- attitude – 'I'm happy with how it worked out'; and
- life – 'He lived a happy life'.

3. Happiness of a life

The question 'What is happiness?' is ambiguous: sometimes the question is about what its *nature* is; sometimes the question is about what its *conditions*, antecedents or determinants are, or how it might be brought about (adequate income, satisfying personal relationships, meaningful work and so on). It is the *nature* of happiness with which we shall be concerned.

The view of happiness I hold bears some resemblance to classical Greek theories, such as Aristotle's. The Greeks saw the key ethical question as 'What is the good life?'. For Aristotle, it consists of 'virtuous activity', using our reason in the development of our characters, our actions and thinking, over a relatively long period; it is not a feeling, or a state. It is, he claims, *final* – the ultimate aim of our desires; and *self-sufficient* – when we have it we lack nothing significant (Aristotle 1915: Book I).

The utilitarians held a view of happiness that sees it as either pleasure or as a collection of pleasures. Jeremy Bentham claimed: 'By utility is meant that property of any object whereby it tends to produce benefit, advantage, pleasure, good or happiness, (all this in the present case comes to the same thing)'. (Bentham 1780 [1967: 368]).

Bentham believed we could determine right actions by carrying out a calculus, a hedonic calculus. John Stuart Mill's view sees happiness as a collection of pleasures, but is complicated by the fact that 'qualities' of pleasures may make a difference. He claims, about happiness, that

> [It is] not a life of rapture, but moments of such, in an existence made up of few and transitory pains, many and various pleasures, with a decided predominance of the active over the passive and having, as the foundation of the whole, not to expect more from life than it is capable of bestowing. (Mill 1963: 255)

The utilitarians, of course, had significant influence on the development of economics. Conceiving happiness in this way suggests a relatively more straightforward way of collecting empirical information about happiness that is an inviting part of the view for many. However, if there are problems with this way of conceiving happiness, this may be undermined.

A problem with the collection view, the view that happiness of a life consists of pleasures, is that it is unclear how large the collection would have to be to constitute happiness of a life. If we note what Mill has to say, we might also ask what *kind* of collection it must be. In addition, it seems committed to a thesis of proportionality: the larger the collection, the happier the person would be, at least for single individuals and perhaps also for comparing individuals.   But there are counterexamples, problem cases. First, there are happy persons with relatively few pleasures, such as people living simple lives, and ascetics. Some of the Hellenistic philosophers emphasized control of and limiting our desires as key to happiness. Second, there seem to be cases of people with a great many pleasures who are unhappy. The Don Juan/Don Giovanni story may be an example. Third, there seem to be cases where people have roughly the same number of pleasures and yet they vary in happiness. Fourth, one individual may find a period of his/her life when he/she has a smaller collection of pleasures happier than a period during which he/she has a larger collection of pleasures.

I believe a view of happiness such as this fails to take seriously the complexity of the structure of our lives and the ends and desires we have. The view I call the 'life plan view' is, I believe, much better at doing this.

The main condition of my analysis of happiness is that it is the realizing of a life plan. The notion of a life plan[2] is founded on an understanding of human behavior according to which there is a stratification of desires into higher- and lower-order desires. The life plan is understood to be the set of higher-order desires (ends) of a person. Typically these will include desires about the kind of person one wants to be, life goals (which may include a career), desires concerning relationships with others. This could be called an *inclusive* end, for it has as its object the harmonious and orderly satisfaction of a number of desires. There are some people who have *dominant* ends, whose object is a single prime desire (to be a successful artist, to win the Olympics). My view can allow for that.

But first, let me indicate that my use of 'plan' does not involve the implication that people have an elaborate blueprint of their lives. Some uses of the term 'plan' focus on a design or scheme for realizing a particular end, but others focus on aims, intentions or goals (for example, 'He went to the university with the plan of studying law'). The focus of 'plan' in this sense is on the ends or goals a person has, and not on designs for achieving them.

Persons have desires which go well beyond the moment. They have desires, plans, intentions for the future. Some see this as part of the nature of what it is to be a person. When we examine the major desires people have

I think we find that they can be seen to form what I call a life plan. Some life plans are very sketchy, some are very detailed.

To understand what this life plan is we must first have a clear understanding of the orders of desires and ends in persons. Orders of desires can be distinguished in terms of the complexity of the object of desire.[3] The distinction is a relative one, because it is impossible to isolate and name separate orders or levels very neatly. A first-order desire will be one whose object is a single or small group of things, state of affairs and so on. A higher-order desire is one whose object is not a single or small group of things or state of affairs. For example, a desire to write a book has as its object a complex set of activities that would occur over a relatively long period of time. In addition, there are some higher-order desires whose objects form an open-ended series, such as a desire for knowledge.

As I use 'life plan', it is made up of the higher-order desires of the person. The criteria we can use to pick out higher-order desires which make up elements of the life plan are permanence, comprehensiveness and importance. They are relatively more permanent: though they can change they do not change rapidly or frequently. These desires are relatively more comprehensive, affecting many of the lower-order desires and ends of the person. Finally we have the third criterion, importance: elements of the life plan are important desires whose frustration brings serious dissatisfaction. Typically these higher-order desires concern occupational goals, desires to have certain personal relationships, desires to be a certain kind of person, important avocational goals and so on. To illustrate the distinction of higher- and lower-order desires, here are some examples:

- Desiring to help improve the conditions of human beings would be higher order.
- Desiring to help in establishing a program to give food aid to starving people would be a lower order than the first, but still relatively higher in order.
- Desiring to get to the support of donors to establish the program would be still lower in order.
- Desiring to meet with a potential donor would be lower – a relatively 'first-order' desire.

The two other conditions of my analysis of happiness, which are subordinate, are: (i) the absence of serious felt dissatisfaction and the absence of an attitude of being displeased with or disliking one's life; and (ii) a disposition to experience favorable feelings and attitudes associated with the realizing of one's higher-order desires. These conditions are what the feeling and attitude views of happiness overstress. With regard to the first, serious felt dissatisfaction normally accompanies a failure in realizing the life plan. However, there are cases where there is felt dissatisfaction, such as serious depression, where it is not the case that, objectively, one's higher-order desires are not being realized. Similarly, an attitude of disliking or being displeased with one's life can also rule out happiness even where a life plan is being realized. For example, John Stuart Mill, in his famed 'mental crisis' felt he no longer had a strong desire for his goal of social reform, feeling that these goals were not his own autonomous goals, but, rather, his father's.[4] If this sort of negative attitude were to be unresolved, and continue, it would seem to rule out happiness. So these are things that can get in the way and rule out happiness.

The positive condition, a disposition to experience favorable feelings and attitudes, is true of happiness, but only in the sense of having the disposition. This is a typical concomitant or 'byproduct' of happiness, not its nature. So my view emphasizes happiness as an objective state of affairs (the realizing of one's higher-order desires, life plan). Subjective states of the individual, such as feelings and attitudes, come up in terms of negative conditions, which can rule out happiness, and a disposition to have positive feelings and attitudes.

There is one remaining view of the nature of a happy life that we are ready to consider now: the attitude view of happiness. This view analyses happiness as being pleased with one's life or liking one's life. There is some intuitive plausibility to this view: it just seems to be the case that happy people like their lives. In addition there are the following two phenomena that seem to lend plausibility to the view: (i) there are people who are unhappy even though their important desires are satisfied and (ii) there are some people who are happy and others who are unhappy living the same sort of lives. These phenomena suggest that the attitude one takes toward one's life is particularly important with regard to happiness.

From a philosophical point of view, there are several things about the concept of attitude that we should note: first, an attitude is a complicated set of dispositions to have certain thoughts, feelings, emotions and so on; and second, unlike emotions and feelings, attitudes are to some extent under our control. Thus, when the attitude view claims that happiness is being pleased with or liking one's life that means roughly that happy people have a complicated set of dispositions to think about their lives fondly, to have feelings of pleasure with regard to important features of their lives, to have no feelings of strong regret about their lives and so on.

If we ask what 'being pleased with one's life' means, there seem to be two possibilities: a strong sense of 'pleased with' and a weak sense. I believe neither will work for an analysis of the nature of happiness of a life. First, the strong version involves being positively pleased with one's life. This seems to exclude some lives where we might claim a person is happy but yet 'pleased with' in the strong sense is too strong. For example, there are cases of people not being positively pleased with their lives while going through trying difficulties or working for some future goal or some difficult cause. Rather than being 'pleased with' life in the strong sense, here something like one's being in a state where one would have been displeased with one's life if it were not lived in this way seems closer to the truth.

If we try a weak sense of 'pleased with' it will mean, roughly, 'not being displeased'. This will handle the problem case for the strong sense we discussed, but it seems to allow cases that should be excluded. First, consider the case of a severely developmentally disabled person. Let us assume that as long as basic needs (food, shelter and so on) are taken care of, this person is pleased with life (in the weak sense). I think we may be inclined to say that this would not count as a happy life, but the attitude view in the weak sense would not rule it out. The life plan view can account for this. If one is incapable of higher-order desires and thus incapable of having a life plan (and this seems to be what is so unfortunate about this condition), the question of happiness or unhappiness does not arise. Another sort of case is that of a person who is pleased with his/her life, but the attitude is the result of taking some drug over a long period of time.

I think what is true but overstressed by the attitude view is that a negative attitude of being displeased with one's life rules out happiness. But that people are typically pleased with the realizing of a life plan is something that is contingently true; it is neither a necessary nor a sufficient condition of happiness. But it is so regularly true that it has come to be identified as happiness by some.

4. Criticisms of the life plan view and responses

I shall discuss some criticisms of the life plan view of happiness, primarily those of Michael Pendlebury (2000) and Margaret Urban Walker (1998). Both see a life plan view of happiness or well-being as 'careerist'. Walker claims that it is part of an overemphasis on autonomy, failing to see people's lives as 'situated' and connected integrally with others (1998: 131). Both claim that this sort of view does not describe the lives of many people. It is normative and *ascriptive*, rather than *descriptive*, valuing and recommending a life lived as something like a career. Walker claims that the view embodies middle-class values about life, and leaves out the lives of people who are less well off and often forced to make decisions by circumstance, unable to be guided as much by the future (ibid.: 134–5). Pendlebury sketches the life of a person who is easygoing and lives with little deliberation and planning, and finds it satisfying. As boring as some may find it, 'it would clearly be a life that is well worth living . . . other things being equal, if a life feels good to the liver, then it is good. And I would add (adapting a phrase of Tweedledee's), if it doesn't, it ain't' (2000: 4).

First let me note that the life plan view as I have developed and argued for it is not intended to emphasize life as a career, or even that one's career must necessarily be a key part of one's happiness. Instead, I have argued that people do have important higher-order desires that structure their lives, and that the realizing, the ongoing process of satisfying these desires can be understood to be the happiness of a life. I have to admit that my use of the word 'plan' in the name of the view does invite the sort of interpretation and criticism that Pendlebury and Walker give against it. However, as I argued earlier, I am using 'plan' in a sense that does not imply a design or scheme.

I believe that the view I have argued for is open enough to allow for many kinds of lives. Some will be more structured than others. Some will be planned in the sense of having a kind of design developed in the light of the future; some will be spontaneous. It seems to me that Pendlebury's easy-going person who wants to live a fairly simple, comfortable, go-with-the-flow kind of life has a life plan consisting, at least in part, of those broad goals. The major desires and goals of some people are deliberately and thoughtfully chosen, perhaps inviting the description of being relatively autonomous. Some people simply adopt the general values and goals of those around them. In many western societies this will include for many seeing a career as an important higher-order desire in one's life. Those are different sorts of life plans, different sets of higher-order desires. We may judge one as being better in certain ways (from perhaps a moral point of view, or the point of view of likelihood of success), but those are value judgments about the life plans, and not judgments about whether they are life plans.

I see these critiques of the life plan view as being critiques of certain kinds of life plans, not the life plan view as such. Whatever view of happiness we hold, it should allow for a wide range of lives as being happy lives. People differ and have different interests. We could see Pendlebury's and Walker's critiques as being a critique of social pressures in rich, developed countries asking people to put great emphasis on a career, and living one's life as a career.

Let me turn to Pendlebury's claim, in defense of the easygoing, carefree person, that 'if a life feels good, it is good'. I would suggest adding, right away, 'prima facie'. Prima facie, if a life feels good, it is good. But *prima facie*, and not always. There is the case of the drugged life that feels good but which we would claim is not itself good. I have argued that feeling good is a typical accompaniment or byproduct of realizing one's life plan. Nevertheless, I put emphasis on the state of realizing the life plan, and not the feelings. And sometimes (though perhaps not often) one could be mistaken about one's higher-order desires being realized. Because one believes (albeit mistakenly) that one's higher-order desires are being realized one feels good about one's life. I would argue that in this case one feels good about one's life, but it is a life that is not really a happy life. (We could call this the 'fool's paradise' case.) So while it may be that generally if it feels good it is good, it is not a definitional truth, as Pendlebury seems to see it. Let us now move on to some applications of the concept of happiness in economics.

5. Economics and the social sciences and happiness

Earlier I noted Jeremy Bentham's claim that 'utility is . . . that property of any object whereby it tends to produce benefit, advantage, pleasure, good or happiness, (all this in the present case comes to the same thing)' (Bentham 1789 [1967: 368]). Bentham seemed confident that ethics could be made more objective, scientific, by using a 'hedonic calculus'. This seems to be the hope of many who seek a way of empirically collecting data about happiness or well-being.

Before looking at several of the attempts I want to say something about the terms 'objective' and 'subjective' and how they are used, sometimes confusingly, in different senses. Sometimes they are used to refer to the source of information of a judgment in a way that is something akin to 'external' versus 'internal'. If I tell you that I feel warm, tired and unfocused in my thoughts I am referring to 'internal', subjective states, and reporting them to you. If you take my temperature and find it to be 102 degrees Fahrenheit, that is 'external', just as is feeling my forehead and finding it very warm to the touch. I shall call this sense of the pair objective/subjective the 'judgment sense'. Sometimes 'objective' and 'subjective' are used to make a claim about whether a judgment can be true or false. For instance, if someone claims that the statement that a painting is beautiful is subjective, they mean that it is a particular judgment made by someone, and it is not true or false. It is, basically, their 'opinion'. Objective judgments are true or false, not 'subjective', not 'just a matter of opinion'. For instance, the painting is rectangular in shape would be an 'objective' judgment. It is either true or false, not just a matter of opinion, and someone could be wrong about it. I shall call this the 'truth value sense' of objective/subjective.

A clear goal of empirical studies of happiness has been to find a way of collecting data about happiness or well-being that has credibility, 'validity', is somehow confirmable as true. How do you collect such data? If it has to do with people's lives, it would appear that there is no clear 'external' way to collect such data by having researchers observe people. One has to ask people, ask for their own reports, hence reports of 'subjective' well-being, a judgment referring to internal states of the individual – feelings, moods, attitudes and so on. For our data to be reliable we have to believe it to be objective (truth value sense), while it consists of subjective (judgment sense) reports of individuals.

I am not an economist, but it is my impression from some of my readings in economics that at some point in the twentieth century economics abandoned the idea of attempting to measure utility, or to use the concept in any way reflecting on subjective things such as states of mind of persons. Instead, the concept of utility was understood in terms of preference and choice (for example, 'decision utility'), both seen as being observable without any knowledge of the goings on in people's minds (Frey and Stutzer 2002a: 19–20). Frey and Stutzer suggest that the positivist commitments of standard economic theory held that 'Subjectivist experience (for example, captured by surveys) is rejected as being "unscientific," because it is not objectively observable' (Frey and Stutzer 2002b: 404). The return to happiness, or subjective well-being, seems to be based on two things. First, it is based on a sense that without attention to this something is being missed. The title of Richard Easterlin's pathbreaking paper, 'Does economic growth improve the human lot?' raises this concern. In a footnote he quotes with seeming approval the claim 'What is the economic system supposed to do? The answer that it should contribute to human happiness is as good a start as any' (Easterlin 1974: 90). Easterlin's claim that increases in income (after a certain level of basic income has been achieved) do not result in an increase in happiness is one of the key paradoxes leading to the Milan conference. Second, it is based on a belief that some empirical studies of subjective well-being or happiness meet sufficient criteria of objectivity to feel confidence in using them.

I would like to look at several of the ways 'happiness' or 'subjective well-being' has been defined in relatively recent literature in economics, and raise some questions about those definitions. Let me first examine a very recent discussion, that of Frey and Stutzer in *Happiness and Economics*. On the very first page of the book they claim: 'But there has certainly not been any consensus as to what happiness is. It means different things to different people. It is open for everyone to define for themselves what happiness is' (2002a: 3). Now they certainly could not really mean this. If they did it is hard to see how they would write a whole book on happiness and economics. And indeed they do use the term in much of the rest of the book as if it were not as subjective (truth sense) and relativistic as this. Just after this, in a section entitled 'Concepts of happiness', they look at two 'polar concepts of happiness'. One is 'subjective happiness' which is what surveys seek to capture in terms of 'global self-reports' by individuals (ibid.: 4). The other is 'objective happiness', which they claim 'refers to physiological approaches, which endeavor to capture subjective well-being, especially by measuring brain waves', perhaps by something like a 'hedonometer' (ibid.: 5). Here they seem to be claiming that happiness judgments are subjective in the sense of being internal to individuals and if we want to collect objective (truth sense) data we have to determine some way of finding an objective (judgment sense) correlate to the reported subjective (judgment sense) states. It seems to me this is a confused and far too stringent demand of objectivity. In addition, I have already argued that interpreting the life use of the term 'happiness' in terms of feeling states that might be reported or detected by physiological measuring of brain waves is a gross distortion. It suggests something like the soma pills in Aldous Huxley's novel *Brave New World*.

Now they do go on to offer a kind of analysis of happiness (in terms of subjective well-being) themselves:

> Subjective well-being is an attitude consisting of the two basic aspects of cognition and affect. 'Affect' is the label attached to moods and emotions. Affect reflects people's instant evaluation of the events that occur in their lives. The cognitive component refers to the rational or intellectual aspects of subjective well-being. It is usually assessed with measures of satisfaction. It has been shown that pleasant affect, unpleasant affect, and life satisfaction are separable constructs. (Frey and Stutzer 2002a: 11)

This seems to be a version of what I have called the attitude view of happiness, claiming happiness consists of an attitude of being pleased with and liking one's life. Here they are using 'objective' and 'subjective' in the sense that the attitude is subjective ('I like my life') and the cognitive judgments which might be made ('I'm achieving my goals', 'I have a loving family' and so on) are objective.

This seems to me to be a confusing way to characterize things, though the confusion is perhaps understandable given the way that 'subjective' and 'objective' are used in different senses. If I judge my life to be happy, it seems to me that I am (whether rightly or wrongly) making a claim about my life that I believe is objectively true. I see it to be a happy life. My attitude of liking it arises because of the sort of life it is. Now, if you challenge me, and ask me why I believe it is happy, I might say 'Because I like it', but I think that is shorthand for my believing it is the kind of life to be liked by me. By saying that the attitude has a 'cognitive component' they are bringing into consideration the features of the person's life. But why see that as a component of the attitude? It seems to me that the attitude is an attitude about one's life, and it is the features of that life that we should focus on. The positive attitude may be an indication that we should pay attention to that, but, as I have argued earlier, I think there are problems with identifying the happiness of a life with the attitude.

Now let us turn to an earlier discussion of defining subjective well-being and happiness, that by psychologist Ed Diener in his pathbreaking 1984 article 'Subjective well-being'. Early in the article he indicates 'Definitions of well-being and happiness can be grouped into three categories': (i) definitions in terms of external criteria – something like a life's meeting a normative standard (he puts Aristotle's definition in this category); (ii) life satisfaction – the sort of thing that social scientists focus on, 'what leads people to evaluate their lives in positive terms'; and (iii) the everyday sense, 'a preponderance of positive affect over negative affect' (Diener 1984: 543). I have a number of disagreements with this way of categorizing theories of happiness and well-being. It is too limited and rigid and mischaracterizes some views. But I want to focus on where he goes from there, for this article seems to be a pathbreaking, early attempt to make happiness and well-being, and specifically *subjective* well-being, a focus of research in empirical psychology. He goes on to claim 'The area of subjective well-being has three hallmarks': (i) 'it is subjective'; (ii) 'subjective well-being includes positive measures' (avoiding mental health's focus on just negative factors); and (iii) measures of subjective well-being include 'a global assessment of all aspects of a person's life' (ibid.: 543–4).

The purpose here is clear: to find a way of seeing the concepts of happiness and well-being as respectable for empirical psychology (and, perhaps, sociology, economics and so on). In doing this we must be careful, however, not to pare down and straitjacket the concept of happiness to make it empirically respectable and measurable in a manageable way so as to produce interesting and useful data. With this we end up with a kind of reductionism that does not do justice to what we think about when we think about happiness. I think we can have it both ways. I think we can have a philosophically richer concept of happiness but at the same time satisfy concerns for respectable, manageable and useful ways of collecting data. It seems that use of the term 'subjective well-being' is an attempt to talk about happiness of a life but keep it manageable from an empirical point of view.

I would like to make a couple of observations about the quest for reliable, valid data. If we want data about whether people are living happy lives we do want, first of all, to be as clear as we can about what we understand to be the nature of a happy life. I have argued that it is not simply being pleased or satisfied with one's life (though generally this sort of attitude is true of happy people), nor is it simply having positive feelings and moods. So we cannot simply look for those things.

In his 1974 article, when discussing the measurement of happiness, Easterlin refers to two types of data (Easterlin 1974: 91). The first type consists of surveys with Gallup poll-type questions, such as 'In general, how happy would you say that you are – very happy, fairly happy, or not very happy?'. The second set of data involves a more complicated procedure devised by Albert Hadley Cantril in which people are asked to devise a continuum based on their own goals, values and so on and then this is used as a measuring device in questioning the person ('the Self-Anchoring Striving Scale' technique). Questions include 'All of us want certain things out of life. When you think about what really matters in your own life, what are your wishes and hopes for the future?'.

Easterlin claims that 'in the Gallup poll and Cantril approaches the concept of happiness underlying them is essentially the same. Reliance is placed on the subjective evaluation of the respondent – in effect, each individual is considered to be the best judge of his own feelings' (Easterlin 1974: 92). I think he is likely wrong in claiming that they imply the same concept of happiness. An approach like the Cantril approach could well be used by someone understanding the concept of happiness in the way that I have recommended. Not so with the Gallup poll approach. If we want to be more accurate in collecting reliable data about happiness I think we need to use the more sensitive, nuanced surveys, though they are more difficult.

In addition, if we think about my claim about how happiness can be ruled out by the negative condition of disliking or being displeased with one's life, I think we will want to pay attention to the role that depression plays in the lives of some people and in societies with regard to happiness. Andrew Oswald has suggested studying psychiatric data regarding mental distress and data related to suicide and attempted suicide, as evidence of extreme unhappiness (Oswald 1997: 1820–25). I think collecting this sort of data will be very important, too, if we want reliable, helpful data about happiness.

So, it seems to me that if we want helpful and reliable data about happiness we need to forgo the simple surveys, because they easily mislead us about happiness, though they are tempting because of their ease. We will want to use methods of collecting data that are compatible with a richer, more accurate conception of the happiness of people's lives.

6. Paradoxes of happiness

I would like to conclude by sketching some of the implications my view of the happiness of a life has on some of what are called 'the paradoxes of happiness'.

A paradox is something that is contrary to expectation or belief. In logic, to resolve paradoxes, we look for either false principles of reasoning or false assumptions on which they are based.

Let us take first a famous paradox of happiness from the history of philosophy. It is sometimes referred to as the 'paradox of hedonism', when it is stated in terms of pleasure: while we desire pleasure (happiness), directly seeking it is doomed to failure. How would I set about seeking pleasure or happiness directly? The view of happiness I have argued for claims that it consists in the realizing of our higher-order desires. We have desires with various general or particular objects. Happiness comes while we are in the process of realizing, achieving those desires. It is not something one can seek directly. The paradox is due to a false assumption about the nature of happiness (or pleasure) and desire.

What about the paradox that in developed countries increased income does not result in any significant increase in happiness? If happiness is generally an inclusive end consisting of a set of higher-order desires structuring one's life, then, of course, it would be unlikely that money alone would have a significant effect on it. Now it is true that people are often preoccupied with money, and think 'if only I had lots of money'. However, we do not need to think long to realize that this is an easy misconception. (It may also show a need for caution in surveys, since we and others may sometimes not be thinking very clearly about our own happiness when we answer the questions.) In addition, data about income are relatively easy to collect. That, combined with a kind of intuition that if people are better off economically they ought to be better off (happier) in their lives, makes it easy to assume that we should expect data collected to show a correlation between increased happiness and increased income. Here the paradox seems to be based on a combination of false assumptions and false reasoning.

Finally, let us consider a paradox about work: people often regard work as a burden, but 'empirical research on happiness strongly suggests that being unemployed, even when receiving the same income as when employed, depresses people's well-being markedly' (Frey and Stutzer 2002b: 403). This is another case where when we think more clearly we can see that we ourselves may have some misconceptions about our own happiness. Work may function in a number of ways with regard to our higher-order desires: it may be related to career goals; it may be related to the kind of person we want to be (competent, needed, productive); it may figure in a desire to have a sense of the structure of our time. With regard to these various things, unemployment may involve at least an interruption to the realizing of important desires we have. And if it does this even where there is no loss of income, it further shows complications in using income as an assessment of well-being.

In sum, I believe we can develop a clearer conception of happiness when it is applied to lives. I have argued for the life plan or higher-order desires view as a plausible understanding of the nature of happiness. This has implications on how the concept of happiness has been used in economics, and on studies attempting to collect data on happiness or well-being. In addition, I believe it can give some helpful insights about some of the 'paradoxes of happiness'.

The questions posed in the organizing of The Paradoxes of Happiness in Economics conference provided an excellent opportunity to bring together people from different disciplines to use the tools and literature of their disciplines to cooperate in developing solutions. The separation of disciplines in the academic world, while useful in many ways, has limited us. How could we deal with the 'paradoxes of happiness in economics' without involving, along with economics, psychology, sociology and philosophy?

Notes

1. I have argued for this view more fully in Chekola (1975).
2. Josiah Royce (1908) seems to be the first person to use the term 'life plan'. He discusses it in *The Philosophy of Loyalty*, particularly in Lecture IV. John Rawls (1971) also uses it in *A Theory of Justice*. Neither of these give the notion of the life plan the kind of underpinnings in terms of the stratification of orders of desires for which I have argued.
3. This is different from Harry G. Frankfurt's (1971) use of levels of desire in his analysis of freedom of the will in 'Freedom of the will and the concept of a person'. In this treatment a first-order desire is a desire to do or not do something, a second-order desire is a desire to have or not have a certain desire. For him, a criterion of being a person and having freedom of will is to have second-order volitions (desires) that are effective, leading to action (p. 10). I am emphasizing a system of desires where higher-order desires are desires with more complex objects (which may also be desires, but may also be other things).
4. Mill's description of his 'mental crisis' is contained in his *Autobiography* (1923: 113): 'it occurred to me to put the question directly to myself: "Suppose that all your objects in life were realized; that all the changes in institutions and opinions which you are looking forward to, could be completely effected at this very instant: would this be a great joy and happiness to you?". And an irrepressible self-consciousness distinctly answered, "No!". At this my heart sank within me; the whole foundation on which my life was constructed fell down. All my happiness was to have been found on the continual pursuit of this end. The end had ceased to charm, and how could there ever again be any interest in the means? I seemed to have nothing to live for'.

References

Aristotle (1915), W.D. Ross (trans.), *Nicomachean Ethics*, Oxford: Oxford University Press.

Bentham, J., (1789 [1967]), 'The principles of morals and legislation', in A.I. Melden (ed.), *Ethical Theories*, Englewood Cliffs, NJ: Prentice-Hall, 367–90.

Chekola, M. (1975), 'The concept of happiness', Doctoral dissertation, University of Michigan 1974, *Dissertation Abstracts International*, **35**, 4609A, University Microfilms, 75–655. Available in PDF form at www.mnstate.edu/chekola.

Diener, E. (1984), 'Subjective well-being', *Psychological Bulletin*, **95**, 542–75.

Easterlin, R. (1974), 'Does economic growth improve the human lot? Some empirical evidence', in Paul A. David and Melvin W. Reder (eds), *Nations and Households in Economic Growth: Essays in Honor of Moses Abramovitz*, New York: Academic Press, 89–125.

Frankfurt, H.G. (1971), 'Freedom of the will and the concept of a person', *Journal of Philosophy*, **68**, 5–20.

Frey, R. and A. Stutzer (2002a), *Happiness and Economics*, Princeton, NJ: Princeton University Press.

Frey, R. and A. Stutzer (2002b), 'What can economists learn from happiness research?', *Journal of Economic Literature*, **40**, 402–35.

Mill, J.S. (1923), *Autobiography*, London: Oxford University Press.

Mill, J.S. (1963), 'Utilitarianism', in Albert Levi (ed.), *The Six Great Humanistic Essays of John Stuart Mill*, New York: Washington Square Press.

Oswald, A. (1997), 'Happiness and economic performance', *The Economic Journal*, **107**, 1815–31.

Pendlebury, M. (2000), 'Against the careerist conception of well-being', *Philosophical Forum*, **31**, 1–10.

Rawls, J. (1971), *A Theory of Justice*, Cambridge, MA: Harvard University Press.

Royce, J. (1908), *The Philosophy of Loyalty*, London and New York: Macmillan.

Walker, M.U. (1998), 'Career selves: plans, projects and plots in "whole" life ethics', in Margaret Urban Walker (ed.), *Moral Understandings: A Feminist Study in Ethics*, New York: Routledge, 131–52.

PART III

RELATIONAL GOODS

13 The income–unhappiness paradox: a relational goods/Baumol disease explanation

*Leonardo Becchetti and Marika Santoro**

1. Introduction

The lives of our generation have definitely been enriched by a much wider range of consumption goods and living opportunities than those of any other generation in the past. Standard economic theory tells us that a wider range of consumption opportunities, accompanied by rising per capita income, should satisfy our taste for variety, ease our budget constraint and allow us to attain higher indifference curves, thereby increasing our happiness.

In spite of this, however, recent econometric studies show that: (i) there is no positive relationship between economic growth and happiness; (ii) the marginal contribution of additional wealth on happiness for rich individuals is negligible (Oswald 1997); and (iii) the reduction of social life and social capital may reduce individuals' happiness (Putnam 2000; Lane 2000;[1] Bruni 2002). A purely descriptive but interesting example of this comes from the 'very happy' index of the US National Survey questionnaire, decreasing from 7.5 to 7 per cent in the 1946–90 period, while per capita GDP has risen in the same period from US$6,000 to US$20,000 (Bruni 2002). A similar absence of correlation between per capita income and happiness may be found in Great Britain, Ireland, and East and West Germany.[2]

One way to understand and explain this paradox is to look at the effects of two driving forces of economic and social change: technological progress and the information and communication technology revolution.[3] These forces have dramatically improved some aspects of our lives while leaving others substantially unchanged. Easier and cheaper transportation, together with faster computers and internet connection, have appreciably increased both our productivity and the quality of our leisure. This means that technological progress enables us to produce far more goods and to enjoy much higher quality of leisure in the same unit of time than past generations could do.

At the same time, though, other parts of our leisure activities still require the same time. Activities such as raising and educating children,[4] creating good relationships with friends, building up communities (defined as 'relational leisure' in this chapter, but also partially identifiable with what is usually defined as 'social capital' in the economic literature) require gratuitous and non-instrumental effort and, in most cases, almost the same time as they did hundreds of years ago. This is because such activities are only partially supported by new technologies since virtual communication (Gaspar and Glaeser 1988) is only a complement and not a substitute for crucial face-to-face communication.

An economist soon understands that these two facts (rising productivity of labour and of the quality of non-relational leisure, and stagnating productivity of relational leisure) are not unrelated since the opportunity cost of one hour spent in relational leisure is exactly the same as the forgone enjoyment of one hour of non-relational leisure or the forgone income of one hour spent at work.[5]

Since production of relational leisure generally requires a minimum fixed amount of, say, $\delta > 1$ hours everyday, the opportunity cost of relational leisure grows δ times the increase in labour productivity. We therefore face a kind of 'Baumol disease' (Baumol 1967; Baumol et al. 1989) between the productivity of hours worked, on the one hand, and the productivity of relational leisure, on the other. Just as in the well-known comparison between manufacturing and some kind of services (such as performing arts), technological progress dramatically increases the opportunity cost of the activity (relational leisure) whose productivity is stagnating, or in other words, of the activity which requires the same time and dedication it required before the technological revolution.[6]

This Baumol effect is not enough, though, to generate the inverse income–happiness relationship. To obtain theoretical results which mimic the above-mentioned empirical findings we need to consider that relational leisure is a public good whose production is a decentralized process depending on a transformation function with additive and superadditive components. Our assumption on the importance of superadditive components has philosophical grounds in the Nussbaum (1986) concept of 'fragility of goodness', where such fragility depends, consistently with Aristotle's concept of *eudaimonia*, on his relational component. As Nussbaum argues, happiness is not entirely in our hands, as it depends on the quality of our relationship and therefore on the behaviour of others.

Under this assumption, when technological process raises labour productivity, the opportunity costs of relational leisure may be so high as to generate a prisoner's dilemma in which the dominant strategy is that of providing the individually optimal and not the socially optimal effort in the production of relational leisure.[7] This decentralized decision may generate a coordination failure and a reduction of happiness.

The idea of a relational failure in industrialized societies due to the public good characteristics of relational goods has already been discussed in the literature (Antoci et al. 2001; Bartolini 2004). Moreover, the literature already presents some crowding-out mechanisms which also illustrate the negative relationship between wealth and relational goods.

According to Hirsch (1976), in affluent societies, as the quantity of consumption goods increases, the time needed to consume them becomes more scarce and more expensive. In addition, the relevance of negative consumer–consumer externalities generates pressures for high levels of consumption in order to keep one's own relative social position. These two forces lead to substitution of time-intensive activities (such as investment in relational goods) with time-saving activities in consumption.

A second illustration of the trade-off is proposed by Antoci et al. (2001), who identify a vicious circle of 'socially immiserizing' growth. According to the authors, people react to the deterioration of relational goods by raising consumption levels and, in order to reach this goal, by increasing time spent in current or future income-generating activities (hours worked or human capital investment). The consequent output growth generates further increase in the opportunity cost of relational goods and then reinforces the mechanism.

Our contribution within this framework is that of illustrating a different simple channel which directly relates the income–unhappiness dilemma to technological progress which raises the opportunity cost of time spent in relational goods and creates a dramatic divergence in relative prices between the relational good and other goods typical of the Baumol disease.

The model is very simple because its purpose is to illustrate that it is possible to obtain the income–unhappiness dilemma even with a very simple game-theoretical approach and with comparative statics.

The chapter is divided into five sections (including introduction and conclusions). In Section 2 we formally define a 'static income–unhappiness dilemma' (the prisoner's dilemma triggered by the rising labour productivity and determined by the impossibility of achieving a Pareto-superior pair of strategies) and a 'sequential income–unhappiness dilemma' (a situation in which the past cooperative equilibrium in the production of relational leisure is preferred to the present non-cooperative, Pareto-inferior, equilibrium even though labour productivity is higher than before).

In Sections 3 and 4 we illustrate a model in which the two dilemmas arise. In our theoretical framework, individuals maximize utility under a time/money constraint and under the technological constraints on the production of consumption goods and on the production of relational leisure. We therefore analyse what happens when technological progress increases labour productivity and wages, thereby raising more than proportionally the opportunity cost of relational leisure. We illustrate here how the higher costs of relational leisure may generate a problem of coordination failure when the game is non-cooperative, causing the production of the relational leisure to fall. This reduces consumption opportunities and, consequently, makes people worse off than before.

In these sections of the chapter we outline parametric conditions under which the static and the sequential dilemmas apply showing their relationship with: (i) separability/non-separability of arguments in the utility function; (ii) relative cost of effort spent in the production of the physical and of the relational good; (iii) dichotomic/non-dichotomic choice of production of the relational good; and (iv) asymmetries in players' productivities.

2.   The definition of the static and sequential income–unhappiness paradoxes and the game

Let us consider a simple repeated 2-player, 2-action game. Each player $i \in I = \{1, 2\}$ has actions a_{ij}, $j \in J = \{1, 2\}$ and decides whether to spend a certain amount $m \in \Re_+$ of the disposable time, T, to produce a particular kind of leisure, which we define as a relational good or relational leisure, lr.

The disposable actions are simply defined as a_{i1} = produce (P) and a_{i2} = not produce (NP), or spend or not spend time for production of relational leisure.

The individuals' technology for the production of the relational leisure is given by the transformation function h:[8]

$$h(l^r, t_i^{lr}; \kappa), \tag{13.1}$$

where t_i^{lr} is the time that the individual $i = 1, 2$ spends on the production of the relational leisure lr and κ is an initial endowment vector of human capital input to production.[9]

Each person divides his/her time between production of relational leisure, t_i^{lr} and market labour supply, n_i. We set pure leisure to be equal to zero, for simplicity. The time constraint is:

$$t_i^{lr} + n_i = T, \quad t_i^{lr}, n_i \geq 0; \quad i = 1, \ldots, n. \tag{13.2}$$

Therefore, the cost of producing relational leisure is given by the reduced time available for working.

Players' preferences over strategies are represented by a payoff-utility function, $U_i(x_i, lr)$, that depends on x_i, a composite market good which each agent consumes directly, and on lr, the relational leisure. Therefore, it also depends on the actions of each individual, P (produce) and NP (not produce), so that

$$U_i(x_i(a_{ij}), \; lr(a_{ij})). \tag{13.3}$$

The following payoff matrix is defined on the disposable actions (that is on the fact that the two players may decide to produce or not produce the relational good).

Player 2		
Player 1	Produce	Not produce
Produce	$U_{1,t}(P, P/w_1), U_{2,t}(P, P/w_2)$	$U_{1,t}(P, NP/w_1), U_{2,t}(P, NP/w_2)$
Not produce	$U_{1,t}(NP, P/w_1), U_{2,t}(NP, P/w_2)$	$U_{1,t}(NP, NP/w_1), U_{2,t}(NP, NP/w_2)$

Both players maximize the payoff function subject to the usual time/budget constraint:

$$px_i = w_i(T - t_i^{lr}), \quad i = 1, \ldots, n, \tag{13.4}$$

where x_i is the amount of consumption goods consumed, p is the price of the consumption good, w is the wage rate and T is total daily hours which can be devoted to work.

The maximization problem is also subject to the technology constraint implicit in the production function (13.1) of the relational good. Within this setting we provide the following two definitions.

Definition 1 A static income–unhappiness dilemma is a situation in which technological progress generates a γ-fold increase in labour productivity and in the wage rate,[10] w_i, such that, for player 1, and, symmetrically, for player 2:

$$U_{1,t}(P_1, P_2/w_{1,t}) > U_{1,t}(.,./w_{1,t}),$$

but:

$$U_{1,t+1}(NP_1, P_2/\gamma w_{1,t}) > U_{1,t+1}(P_1, P_2/\gamma w_{1,t}) >$$

$$U_{1,t+1}(NP_1, NP_2/\gamma w_{1,t}) > U_{1,t+1}(NP_1, P_2/\gamma w_{1,t})$$

and

$$w_{1,t}(T - t^{lr}_{1,t}{}^*) < \gamma w_{1,t}(T - t^{lr}_{1,t+1}{}^*),^{11}$$

where $t^{lr}_{1,t}{}^*$, $t^{lr}_{1,t+1}{}^*$ are the optimal response functions for player 1, at time t and $t+1$, respectively.

Definition 2   A sequential income–unhappiness dilemma is a situation in which we can add the $U_{1,t+1}(NP_1, P_2/\gamma w_{1,t}) < U_{1,t}(P_1, P_2/w_{1,t})$ condition to the previous ones.

The static dilemma simply consists of a wage rise which creates a classical prisoner's dilemma. At time t the wage is low enough to make the joint cooperative behaviour $(P_1, P_2/w)$ a Nash equilibrium of the game. At time $t+1$ the γ-fold increase in labour productivity and wages is such that: (i) the cooperative payoff becomes inferior to the free-riding payoff for player 2 when player 1 decides to cooperate and to produce the relational good; (ii) the cooperative payoff becomes inferior to the free-riding payoff for player 2 when player 1 decides not to cooperate; and (iii) the payoff when both players free ride becomes inferior to the cooperative payoff. In this case the joint non-cooperative pair of strategies $(NP_1, NP_2/\gamma w)$ is the unique Nash equilibrium of the game even though it is Pareto dominated by the joint cooperative pair of strategies $(P_1, P_2/\gamma w)$.

In addition, as a direct consequence of the prisoner's dilemma, labour income in $t+1$ is higher than in t. Therefore we have that, *ceteris paribus*, people are richer but unhappy because there is a Pareto-superior equilibrium that cannot be attained.

In the sequential dilemma we more directly relate current to past happiness and also require that the joint cooperative payoff at time t be strictly preferred to the payoff at time $t+1$, in addition to all the static dilemma conditions.

It is intuitively clear that the static dilemma arises only within a limited range of wage increases. The increase must be neither 'too' small (to avoid the cooperative solution remaining the dominant strategy) nor 'too' high (to avoid the joint non-cooperative solution dominating the cooperative solution). The range for obtaining the sequential dilemma must be smaller and contained in the previous one. If, in fact, the wage rise is too high, there may be a static dilemma, but the current non-cooperative equilibrium may still be preferred to the past cooperative equilibrium. This is what we try to show in the next sections, considering two specifications of the production function of the relational good.

3. Income–unhappiness dilemmas under different functional assumptions
Static and sequential income–unhappiness dilemmas under separable utility function and quadratic relational effort in the production of the relational good

We start with a trivial case in which a labour productivity rise leads from the cooperative to the free-riding solution thereby generating a prisoner's dilemma. We demonstrate this simple proposition:

Proposition 1 When players with a separable utility function, a partially separable production functi of the relational good with a superadditive term, and quadratic relational effort choose between investing or not in relational goods, technological progress may increase wages so that they fall in a range in which the two players of the relational game are subject to a prisoner's dilemma. To obtain this result the increased real wage must enter a range between one and two times the marginal rate of substitution between the utility of relational leisure and consumption.

Consider a game with two individuals in which both individuals maximize the following separable utility function:

$$\max U_i = \alpha x_i + \beta lr, \tag{13.5}$$

where x_i represents a consumption good which each agent consumes directly and lr a good which we call 'relational leisure'.

The 'technology' constraint on the production of the relational good presents the following specification:

$$h = t_i^{lr} + t_{-i}^{lr} + t_i^{lr} t_{-i}^{lr}, \quad \text{for } t_i^{lr}, t_{-i}^{lr} \leq k \tag{13.6}$$

and

$$h = 2k + k^2, \quad \text{for } t_i^{lr}, t_{-i}^{lr} > k. \tag{13.7}$$

The relational good is therefore a public good since it is clearly non-rivalrous and non-excludable.

Note that the production function of the relational good has both an additive and a superadditive component and reaches its bound at $t_i^{lr} = k$. After that level the productivity of additional hours spent in the relational goods is zero.

The amount of relational good produced is consumed by both players, once they have subtracted the cost of the effort spent in the production.[12] Hence, the net consumption/constraint for relational leisure is:

$$lr \leq h - (t_i^{lr})^2 = t_i^{lr} + t_{-i}^{lr} + t_i^{lr} t_{-i}^{lr} - (t_i^{lr})^2, \quad \text{for } t_i^{lr}, t_{-i}^{lr} \leq k. \tag{13.8}$$

By replacing the constraints in the utility function the problem for player one becomes:

$$\max U_1 = \alpha \frac{w_1}{p}(T - t_1^{lr}) + \beta[t_1^{lr} + t_2^{lr} + t_1^{lr}t_2^{lr} - (t_1^{lr})^2]$$ (13.9)

and, symmetrically, for player 2.

The first-order condition for an internal solution is:

$$-\alpha \frac{w_1}{p} + \beta[1 + t_2^{lr} - 2(t_1^{lr})] = 0,$$ (13.10)

so that:

$$t_1^{lr*} = -\frac{\alpha}{2\beta} \frac{w_1}{p} + \frac{1}{2}(1 + t_2^{lr}).$$ (13.10')

In the case of a symmetric equilibrium ($t_1^{lr} = t_2^{lr}$) we have:

$$t_1^{lr*} = -\frac{\alpha}{\beta} \frac{w_1}{p} + 1.$$ (13.11)

This conclusion shows that the utility function is always decreasing in t_1^{lr} if the absolute value of the marginal cost of relational leisure, (w_1/P), times the marginal rate of substitution between consumption and relational leisure (β/α in this case or 1 if $\alpha = \beta = 1$), is higher than one. Therefore, if such a condition holds, under the dichotomic choice of all or no effort in the production of the relational good, the optimal individual solution is the decision of not investing any time in relational leisure. The payoff associated with the non-cooperative symmetric solution, $t_1^{lr} = t_2^{lr} = 0$ (which is possible if $w_1/p = w_2/p = \beta/\alpha$) is given by:

$$U_1^*(NP, NP) = \alpha \frac{w_1}{p}T.$$ (13.12)

Consider now the socially optimal number of hours spent in producing the relational good:

$$\max U = U_1 + U_2 = \alpha \frac{w_1}{p}(T - t_1^{lr}) + \alpha \frac{w_2}{p}(T - t_2^{lr})$$

$$+ 2\beta(t_1^{lr} + t_2^{lr} + t_1^{lr}t_2^{lr}) - (t_1^{lr})^2 - (t_2^{lr})^2.$$ (13.13)

The first derivative with respect to t_1^{lr} yields:

$$\frac{\partial U}{\partial t_1^{lr}} = -\alpha \frac{w_1}{p} + 2\beta(1 + t_2^{lr} - t_1^{lr}).$$ (13.14)

In the case of a symmetric equilibrium ($t_1^{lr} = t_2^{lr}$) this derivative is positive (the utility is increasing) if $w_1/p = w_2/p < 2\,\beta/\alpha$ when the marginal cost of one hour spent in relational leisure is less than twice his/her marginal rate of substitution with respect to the marginal utility of consumption.

In this case the utility maximization requires that each individual chooses to dedicate the maximum amount of time to the relational leisure, so that $t_1^{lr} = t_2^{lr} = k$ is the symmetric cooperative equilibrium. In the same circumstance the associated payoff is:

$$U_1^*(P, P) = \alpha \frac{w_1}{p}(T - k) + 2\beta k. \tag{13.15}$$

Consider now a situation in which technological progress raises real wages from a level in which $w_1/p = w_2/p < \beta/\alpha$ to a level in which they are $\beta/\alpha < \gamma(w_1/p) = \gamma(w_2/p) < 2(\beta/\alpha)$.

It is clear that, if before we were in a situation in which investing the maximum number of hours was the optimal individual and social solution, we now fall into a situation in which it is individually optimal not to invest at all in relational goods, while it is socially optimal to invest in them the maximum number of hours.

To define the payoff matrix of the game, consider what happens when one of the two players chooses the individual optimum and the other the social optimum. In that case we would fall into the following intermediate non-cooperative equilibria: first,

$$t_1^{lr} = k, \quad t_2^{lr} = 0 \tag{13.16}$$

with the associated payoff:

$$U_1^*(P, NP) = \alpha\gamma\frac{w_1}{p}(T - k) + \beta(k - k^2); \tag{13.17}$$

and second,

$$t_1^{lr} = 0, \quad t_2^{lr} = k \tag{13.18}$$

with the associated payoff:

$$U_1^*(NP, P) = \alpha\frac{w_1}{p}T + \beta k. \tag{13.19}$$

Therefore, taking into account all payoffs considered in (13.12), (13.13), (13.17) and (13.19), we have a prisoner's dilemma if:

$$U_1^*(P, NP) < U_1^*(NP, NP) < U_1^*(P, P) < U_1^*(NP, P),^{13} \tag{13.20}$$

or

$$\alpha\frac{w_1}{p}(T-k)+\beta(k-k^2)<\alpha\gamma\frac{w_1}{p}T<\alpha\gamma\frac{w_1}{p}(T-k)$$
$$+2\beta k<\alpha\gamma\frac{w_1}{p}T+\beta k. \tag{13.20'}$$

We therefore need that $\gamma\,w_1/p>\beta/\alpha$ (if $\alpha=\beta=1$, $\gamma\,w_1/p>1$) in order to respect the inequality between the third and the fourth terms. Taking into account the condition for the derivative to be positive, the sufficient condition becomes $\beta/\alpha<\gamma(w_1/p)<2(\beta/\alpha)$ (if $\alpha=\beta=1$, $1<\gamma\,(w_1/p)<2$). The two players of the relational game fall into a prisoner's dilemma when the increased real wage enters a range between one and two times the marginal rate of substitution between the utility of relational leisure and consumption.

Conditions for a sequential dilemma require the *ex ante* (before the increase in productivity) joint cooperative solution to be preferred to the current non-cooperative solution after the productivity change, or:

$$\alpha\frac{w_1}{p}(T-k)+2\beta k>\alpha\gamma\frac{w_1}{p}T.$$

This condition may be simplified in:

$$\gamma<1+\left(2\beta k-\alpha\frac{w_1}{p}k\right)\bigg/\alpha\frac{w_1}{p}T,$$

where the second term in the right-hand side of the inequality is clearly smaller than 1. Therefore, if:

$$1<\gamma<1+\left(2\beta k-\alpha\frac{w_1}{p}k\right)\bigg/\alpha\frac{w_1}{p}T,$$

we have both the static and the sequential dilemma, while if:

$$1+\left(2\beta k-\alpha\frac{w_1}{p}k\right)\bigg/\alpha\frac{w_1}{p}T<\gamma<2,$$

only the static dilemma applies.

Static and sequential income–unhappiness dilemmas under separable utility function and no relational effort
In this subsection we shall show that our results do not depend crucially on the assumption of quadratic effort in the production of relational good even though, if we remove this assumption, the parametric bounds of the region in which the prisoner's dilemma arises change.

Proposition 2 When players with a separable utility function, a partially separable production function of the relational good with a superadditive term, choose between investing or not in relational goods, technological progress may increase wages so that they fall in a range in which the two players of the relational game are subject to a prisoner's dilemma. The range is crucially affected by the number of hours spent investing in the relational good.

Consider again a game with two individuals where both individuals maximize the utility function in (13.1) under the transformation function (13.2).

Each person divides his/her time between production of the relational good t_i^{lr} and market labour supply. Thus the time constraint is still:

$$t_i^{lr} + n_i = T, \quad t_i^{lr}, n_i \geq 0; \quad i = 1, \ldots, n, \tag{13.21}$$

and the utility maximization is subject to the usual time/budget constraint:

$$px_i = w_i(T - t_i^{lr}), \quad i = 1, \ldots, n, \tag{13.22}$$

where x_i is the amount of consumption goods consumed, p is the price of the consumption good, w is hourly wage, T is total daily hours which can be devoted to work.

The 'technology' constraint on the production of the relational good presents the same specification as in the previous subsection:

$$h(t_{-i}^{lr}, t_i^{lr}; 1) = t_i^{lr} + t_{-i}^{lr} + t_i^{lr}t_{-i}^{lr}, \quad \text{for } t_i^{lr}, t_{-i}^{lr} \leq k \tag{13.23}$$

and

$$h = 2k + k^2, \quad \text{for } t_i^{lr}, t_{-i}^{lr} > k. \tag{13.24}$$

Exactly as before the production function of the relational good has both an additive and a superadditive component and reaches a bound at $t_i^{lr} = k$.

The amount of relational good produced is entirely consumed by players so that the net consumption/constraint for the relational leisure is:

$$lr \leq h = t_i^{lr} + t_{-i}^{lr} + t_i^{lr}t_{-i}^{lr}, \quad \text{for } t_i^{lr}, t_{-i}^{lr} \leq k. \tag{13.25}$$

By replacing the constraints in the utility function the problem for player 1 becomes:

$$\max U_1 = \alpha \frac{w_1}{p}(T - t_1^{lr}) + \beta(t_1^{lr} + t_2^{lr} + t_1^{lr}t_2^{lr}) \qquad (13.26)$$

and, symmetrically, for player 2.

The first derivative with respect to t_1^{lr} yields:[14]

$$\frac{\partial U}{\partial t_1^{lr}} = -\alpha \frac{w_1}{p} + \beta(1 + t_2^{lr}), \qquad (13.27)$$

which is negative if $w_1/p < \beta/\alpha(1 + t_2^{lr})$ (or, if $(w_1/p) < (1 + t_2^{lr})$, when $\alpha = \beta = 1$).

If this inequality holds, under the dichotomic choice of investing or not in the relational good, the optimal individual solution is the decision of not investing in relational leisure and the payoff associated with the non-cooperative symmetric solution, $t_1^{lr} = t_2^{lr} = 0$, is given by:

$$U_1^*(NP, NP) = \alpha \frac{w_1}{p}T. \qquad (13.28)$$

Consider now the socially optimal hours spent in producing the relational good:

$$\max U = U_1 + U_2 = \alpha \frac{w_1}{p}(T - t_1^{lr}) + \alpha \frac{w_2}{p}(T - t_2^{lr}) + 2\beta(t_1^{lr} + t_2^{lr} + t_1^{lr}t_2^{lr}).$$

The first derivative with respect to t_1^{lr} yields:

$$\frac{\partial U}{\partial t_1^{lr}} = -\alpha \frac{w_1}{p} + 2\beta(1 + t_2^{lr}). \qquad (13.29)$$

So this derivative is positive (the utility is increasing) if $w_1/p < 2(\beta/\alpha)/(1 + t_2^{lr})$ (or, if $\alpha = \beta = 1$, when $w_1/p < 2(1 + t_2^{lr})$.

In this case, the utility maximization requires that each individual chooses to dedicate the maximum level of time to the relational leisure, so $t_1^{lr} = t_2^{lr} = k$ is the symmetric cooperative equilibrium. The associated payoff is:

$$U_1^*(P, P) = \alpha \frac{w_1}{p}(T - k) + 2\beta k + \beta k^2. \qquad (13.30)$$

Consider now a situation in which technological progress raises real wages from a level in which $w_2/p = w_1/p < (\beta/\alpha)/(1 + t_2^{lr})$ to a level in which they are $w_2/p = w_1/p < 2(\beta/\alpha)/(1 + t_2^{lr})$. It is clear that, if before we were in a situation in which investing the maximum number of hours was the optimal solution, we now fall into one in which it is individually optimal not to invest at all in relational goods, while it is socially optimal to invest the maximum number of hours.

To define the payoff matrix of the game, consider what happens when one of the two players chooses the individual optimum and the other the social optimum. The intermediate non-cooperative equilibria in this game are, first,

$$t_1^{lr} = k, \ t_2^{lr} = 0, \tag{13.31}$$

with the associated payoff:

$$U_1^*(P,NP) = \alpha\gamma\frac{w_1}{p}(T - k) + \beta(k), \tag{13.32}$$

and second,

$$t_1^{lr} = 0, \ t_2^{lr} = k, \tag{13.33}$$

with the associated payoff:

$$U_1^*(NP, P) = \alpha\gamma\frac{w_1}{p}T + \beta k. \tag{13.34}$$

Taking into account these payoffs, we have a prisoner's dilemma if:

$$U_1^*(P, NP) < U_1^*(NP, NP) < U_1^*(P, P) < U_1^*(NP, P) \tag{13.35}$$

or:

$$\alpha\gamma\frac{w_1}{p}(T - k) + \beta(k) < \alpha\gamma\frac{w_1}{p}T < \alpha\gamma\frac{w_1}{p}(T - k)$$
$$+ 2\beta k + \beta k^2 < \alpha\gamma\frac{w_1}{p}T + \beta k.^{15} \tag{13.36}$$

In order to respect the inequality between the first and the second terms, we need that $\gamma(w_1/p) > \beta/\alpha$ (if $\alpha = \beta = 1, \gamma(w_1/p) > 1$) while, in order to respect the inequality between the second and the third, we need that $\gamma(w_1/p) < (\beta/\alpha)(2 + k)$ (if $\alpha = \beta = 1, \gamma(w_1/p) < (2 + k)$) and, finally, that $\gamma(w_1/p) < (\beta/\alpha)(1 + k)$ (if $\alpha = \beta = 1, \ \gamma(w_1/p) < (1 + k)$). Therefore, taking into account the three inequalities, the sufficient condition for the dilemma becomes $\beta/\alpha(1 + k) < \gamma(w_1/p) < \beta/\alpha(2 + k)$ (if $\alpha = \beta = 1, 1 + k < \gamma(w_1/p) < 2 + k$). When the technologically induced wage rise is such that the wage enters the above described range, the two players fall into a prisoner's dilemma. The range is crucially affected by the number of hours spent in the investment in the relational good.

To have a sequential dilemma together with the static one we require that the joint cooperative solution before the increase in productivity be preferred to the current non-cooperative solution after the productivity change or:

$$\alpha(w_1/p)(T-k) + 2\beta k + \beta k^2 > \alpha\gamma(w_1/p)T, \text{ which may be simplified in:}$$

$$\gamma < 1 + \left[2\beta k(1+k) - \alpha\frac{w_1}{p}k\right]\Big/\alpha\frac{w_1}{p}T.$$

Therefore, if:

$$1 < \gamma < 1 + \left[2\beta k(1+k) - \alpha\frac{w_1}{p}k\right]\Big/\alpha\frac{w_1}{p}T,$$

we have both the static and the sequential dilemma, while, if:

$$1 + \left[2\beta k(1+k) - \alpha\frac{w_1}{p}k\right]\Big/\alpha\frac{w_1}{p}T < \gamma < 2,$$

only the static dilemma applies.

4.   Income–happiness dilemmas under changes in relative preferences
Changes in relative preferences and static and sequential income–unhappiness dilemmas under separable utility function

All previous examples assume that players give equal weights to consumption and to the relational good. In this subsection and in those that follow we analyse how the likelihood of the occurrence of the static and sequential income–unhappiness dilemma is affected by the relative preferences for consumption and the relational good.

The analysis of the case in which preferences are separable leads us to formulate the following proposition:

Proposition 3   With (i) a separable utility function in which consumption and the relational good are given different weights; and (ii) a partially separable production function of the relational good with a superadditive term, a threshold value of wage increasing technological progress exists such that the two players of the relational game fall into a prisoner's dilemma. The prisoner's dilemma arises only for those players giving relatively higher weight to consumption with respect to the relational good.

Consider the problem of the individual player having the following separable utility function

$$\max U_i = x_i^\alpha + lr^\beta, \tag{13.37}$$

subject to the usual time/budget constraint (13.3) and 'technology' constraint (13.1) on the production of the relational good.

To find the social optimum we must solve:

$$
\begin{aligned}
\max U_1 + U_2 = {} & \left[\frac{w_1}{p}(T - t_1^{lr}) \right]^\alpha + (t_1^{lr} + t_2^{lr} + t_1^{lr} t_2^{lr})^\beta \\
& + \left[\frac{w_2}{p}(T - t_2^{lr}) \right]^\alpha + (t_1^{lr} + t_2^{lr} + t_1^{lr} t_2^{lr})^\beta.
\end{aligned}
$$

The first-order condition with respect to agent 1 yields:

$$-\frac{\alpha w_1}{p} \left[\frac{w_1}{p}(T - t_1^{lr}) \right]^{\alpha - 1} + 2(1 + t_2^{lr})\beta(t_1^{lr} + t_2^{lr} + t_1^{lr} t_2^{lr})^{\beta - 1} = 0. \tag{13.38}$$

The solution to this equation gives $t_1^{lr**} = t_2^{lr**}$ or the socially optimal level of relational effort.

To find individual optimum we must solve:

$$\max U_1 = \left[\frac{w_1}{p}(T - t_1^{lr}) \right]^\alpha + (t_1^{lr} + t_2^{lr} + t_1^{lr} t_2^{lr})^\beta. \tag{13.39}$$

The first-order condition yields:

$$-\frac{\alpha w_1}{p} \left[\frac{w_1}{p}(T - t_1^{lr}) \right]^{\alpha - 1} + (1 + t_2^{lr})\beta(t_1^{lr} + t_2^{lr} + t_1^{lr} t_2^{lr})^{\beta - 1} = 0. \tag{13.40}$$

The solution of this equation gives $t_1^{lr*}(t_2^{lr})$, that is, the individually optimal level of time spent in producing the relational good as a function of the time spent by the other player.

To define the payoff of the game, consider that the joint cooperative solution yields:

$$U_1^*(P_1, P_2) = \left[\frac{w_1}{p}(T - t_1^{lr**})\right]^\alpha + [t_1^{lr**} + t_2^{lr**} + (t_1^{lr**})^2]^\beta. \quad (13.41)$$

The payoff when player 1 cooperates and 2 does not cooperate is:

$$U_1^*(P_1, NP_2) = \left[\frac{w_1}{p}(T - t_1^{lr**})\right]^\alpha + (t_1^{lr**} + t_2^{lr*} + t_1^{lr**}t_2^{lr*})^\beta, \quad (13.42)$$

the payoff when 1 does not cooperate and 2 cooperates is:

$$U_1^*(NP_1, P_2) = \left[\frac{w_1}{p}(T - t_1^{lr*})\right]^\alpha + (t_1^{lr*} + t_2^{lr**} + t_1^{lr*}t_2^{lr**})^\beta, \quad (13.43)$$

and, finally, the payoff when neither 1 nor 2 cooperates is:

$$U_1^*(NP_1, NP_2) = \left[\frac{w_1}{p}(T - t_1^{lr*})\right]^\alpha + (t_1^{lr*} + t_2^{lr*} + t_1^{lr*}t_2^{lr*})^\beta, \quad (13.44)$$

The prisoner's dilemma again arises if:

$$U_1^*(P, NP) < U_1^*(NP, NP) < U_1^*(P, P) < U_1^*(NP, P) \quad (13.45)$$

and symmetrically for player 2.

Numerical solutions to different specifications of utility and transformation functions

We solve this problem numerically for a reasonable range of parameter values. We consider the game in which both players choose between the cooperative strategy (the socially optimal number of hours invested in the relational good under the cooperative maximization) and a 'temptation strategy' (the individually optimal number of hours invested in the relational good when the opponent cooperates). Without loss of generality we normalize w/p to 1 and assume $\alpha + \beta = 1$ since we are mainly interested in relative weights to consumption and relational goods. We consider discrete decimal changes in α and β and discrete choices in hours of relational effort. Table 13.1 gives a synthesis of results obtained.

With $w/p = 1$ a divergence between individual and social optimum arises only when the consumption weight is ≥ 0.7, while the prisoner's dilemma arises only when there is a sufficient gap between private and socially optimal number of hours spent investing in the relationship. This occurs only when the relative weight given to consumption (α) is 70 per cent (the relative weight given to the relational good is 30 per cent).

With a three-fold rise in wages the divergence between individual and social optimum arises when $0.6 \geq \alpha \geq 0.9$. We have the prisoner's dilemma extended to situations in which α is 60 and 80 per cent, while, in the situation in which the same parameter is 70 per cent we fall into an equilibrium in which one of the two players is worse off and the other is better off.

If we remove the assumption of equal productivity among players we find another clear case for the static wage–unhappiness dilemma with the same features shown in Table 13.1 (see Table 13.2).

Parametric examples in Tables 13.1 and 13.2 clearly show that, when we remove the assumption of equal weights to the two arguments of the utility function, we find that the prisoner's dilemma applies only for a given range of relative preferences. When the relative weight given to consumption is too high or too low the dilemma does not arise.

From the comparison of Tables 13.2 and 13.1 it emerges that technological progress generating an asymmetry in real wages between players also generates a (static) income–unhappiness dilemma exactly in the same way it does in the symmetric case.

Changes in relative preferences, static and sequential income–unhappiness dilemmas under non-separable constant returns to scale (CRS) utility function

The rationale for extending our exploration to the adoption of a non-separable utility function is that the two goods may be complementary in consumption and that the enyojment in consuming goods may be enhanced by the production of relational goods.

If we take a non-separable utility function the individual player maximizes:

$$\max_{(lr)} U_i = x_i^\alpha lr^\beta \qquad (13.46)$$

subject to the time/budget constraint (13.1) and to the constraint on the 'technology' of production of the relational good (13.8).

Table 13.1   Parameter ranges for the prisoner's dilemma under a separable CRS Cobb–Douglas utility function (symmetric players' productivity)

α (relative weight of consumption)	β (relative weight of relational good)	Optimal number of hours spent investing in the relational good in the cooperative solution	Optimal number of hours spent investing in the relational good in the non-cooperative 'temptation strategy'	Prisoner's dilemma?
		$w/p = 1$		
0.1	0.9	8	8	No
0.2	0.8	8	8	No
0.3	0.7	8	8	No
0.4	0.6	8	8	No
0.5	0.5	8	8	No
0.6	0.4	8	8	No
0.7	0.3	4	1	Yes
0.8	0.2	1	0	No
0.9	0.1	1	0	No*
		$w/p = 3$		
0.1	0.9	8	8	No
0.2	0.8	8	8	No
0.3	0.7	8	8	No
0.4	0.6	8	8	No
0.5	0.5	8	8	No
0.6	0.4	8	3	Yes
0.7	0.3	1	0	No*
0.8	0.2	1	0	Yes
0.9	0.1	0	0	No

Note: * There is no prisoner's dilemma but the game has two Nash Equilibria (NE) in which one players cooperates and the other does not. As a consequence, even in this case one of the two players is worse off with respect to the joint cooperative solution.

To find the social optimum we must solve:

$$\max U_1 + U_2 = \left[\frac{w_1}{p}(T - t_1^{lr}) \right]^\alpha (t_1^{lr} + t_2^{lr} + t_1^{lr} t_2^{lr})^\beta$$

$$+ \left[\frac{w_2}{p}(T - t_2^{lr}) \right]^\alpha + (t_1^{lr} + t_2^{lr} + t_1^{lr} t_2^{lr})^\beta. \tag{13.47}$$

Table 13.2 *Parameter ranges for the prisoner's dilemma under a separable CRS Cobb–Douglas utility function (asymmetric players' productivity)*

α (relative weight of consumption)	β (relative weight of relational good)	Optimal number of hours spent investing in the relational good in the cooperative solution	Optimal number of hours spent investing in the relational good in the non-cooperative solution	Prisoner's dilemma?
		$w/p = 1$, $w/p = 2$		
0.1	0.9	8	8	No
0.2	0.8	8	8	No
0.3	0.7	8	8	No
0.4	0.6	8	8	No
0.5	0.5	8	8	No
0.6	0.4	8	8	No
0.7	0.3	4	1	No
0.8	0.2	1	0	Yes
0.9	0.1	1	0	No*
		$w/p = 1$, $w/p = 3$		
0.1	0.9	8	8	No
0.2	0.8	8	8	No
0.3	0.7	8	8	No
0.4	0.6	8	8	No
0.5	0.5	8	8	No
0.6	0.4	8	3	Yes
0.7	0.3	1	0	No*
0.8	0.2	1	0	Yes
0.9	0.1	0	0	No

The first-order condition with respect to agent 1 yields:

$$\frac{-\alpha w_1}{p}\left[\frac{w_1}{p}(T - t_1^{lr})\right]^{\alpha-1}(t_1^{lr} + t_2^{lr} + t_1^{lr}t_2^{lr})^{\beta}$$

$$+ 2(1 + t_2^{lr})\beta(t_1^{lr} + t_2^{lr} + t_1^{lr}t_2^{lr})^{\beta-1}\left[\frac{w_1}{p}(T - t_1^{lr})\right]^{\alpha} = 0. \quad (13.48)$$

The solution to this equation gives $t_1^{lr**} = t_2^{lr**}$ or the socially optimal level of relational effort.

To find individual optimum we must solve:

$$\max U_1 = \left[\frac{w_1}{p}(T - t_1^{lr})\right]^{\alpha}(t_1^{lr} + t_2^{lr} + t_1^{lr}t_2^{lr})^{\beta}, \tag{13.49}$$

and the first-order condition yields:

$$\frac{-\alpha w_1}{p}\left[\frac{w_1}{p}(T - t_1^{lr})\right]^{\alpha - 1}(t_1^{lr} + t_2^{lr} + t_1^{lr}t_2^{lr})^{\beta}$$

$$+ (1 + t_2^{lr})\beta(t_1^{lr} + t_2^{lr} + t_1^{lr}t_2^{lr})^{\beta - 1}\left[\frac{w_1}{p}(T - t_1^{lr})\right]^{\alpha} = 0. \tag{13.50}$$

The solution of this equation gives $t_1^{lr*}(t_2^{lr})$, that is, the individually optimal level of time spent in producing the relational good as a function of the time spent by the other player.

To define the payoff of the game consider that the joint cooperative solution yields:

$$U_1^*(P_1, P_2) = \left[\frac{w_1}{p}(T - t_1^{lr**})\right]^{\alpha} + [t_1^{lr**} + t_2^{lr**} + (t_1^{lr**})^2]^{\beta}. \tag{13.51}$$

The payoff when player 1 cooperates and 2 does not cooperate is:

$$U_1^*(P_1, NP_2) = \left[\frac{w_1}{p}(T - t_1^{lr**})\right]^{\alpha} + (t_1^{lr**} + t_2^{lr*} + t_1^{lr**}t_2^{lr*})^{\beta} \tag{13.52}$$

and the payoff when 1 does not cooperate and 2 cooperates is:

$$U_1^*(NP_1, P_2) = \left[\frac{w_1}{p}(T - t_1^{lr*})\right]^{\alpha} + (t_1^{lr*} + t_2^{lr**} + t_1^{lr*}t_2^{lr**})^{\beta}. \tag{13.53}$$

Finally the payoff when neither 1 nor 2 cooperates is:

$$U_1^*(NP_1, NP_2) = \left[\frac{w_1}{p}(T - t_1^{lr*})\right]^{\alpha} + (t_1^{lr*} + t_2^{lr*} + t_1^{lr*}t_2^{lr*})^{\beta}. \tag{13.54}$$

The prisoner's dilemma again arises if:

$$U_1^*(P, NP) < U_1^*(NP, NP) < U_1^*(P, P) < U_1^*(NP, P), \tag{13.55}$$

and symmetrically for player 2.

Numerical solutions of the game under the assumptions already described in the previous subsection (normalization of w/p to 1, $\alpha + \beta = 1$ and comparison between the cooperative strategy and a 'temptation strategy') are presented in Table 13.3.

From the analysis presented in Table 13.3 it is clear that non-separability of consumption and relational leisure under the CRS assumption enlarges the area of the prisoner's dilemma but gives no role to the technological progress.[16] The prisoner's dilemma does not depend on changes in real wages. Results presented in Table 13.3 do not change substantially when we consider asymmetric changes in real wages.[17]

Table 13.3   *Parameter ranges for the prisoner's dilemma under a non-separable CRS Cobb–Douglas utility function (symmetric players' productivity)*

α (relative weight of consumption)	β (relative weight of relational good)	Optimal number of hours spent investing in the relational good in the cooperative solution	Optimal number of hours spent investing in the relational good in the non-cooperative solution	Prisoner's dilemma?
		$w/p = 1$		
0.1	0.9	8	8	No
0.2	0.8	8	8	No
0.3	0.7	8	8	No
0.4	0.6	8	8	No
0.5	0.5	8	8	No
0.6	0.4	8	6	Yes
0.7	0.3	7	4	Yes
0.8	0.2	5	3	Yes
0.9	0.1	2	1	Yes
		$w/p = 3$		
0.1	0.9	8	8	No
0.2	0.8	8	8	No
0.3	0.7	8	8	No
0.4	0.6	8	8	No
0.5	0.5	8	8	No
0.6	0.4	8	6	Yes
0.7	0.3	7	4	Yes
0.8	0.2	5	3	Yes
0.9	0.1	2	1	Yes

5.   Conclusions

In this chapter we have explored the feasibility and the limit of a paradox by which the intermediate goal of economic growth and the higher goal of happiness are in conflict.

We have shown that, under a plausible representation of individual preferences, it is possible to outline situations in which income grows but happiness stagnates or is reduced.

We examined potential factors which may generate the dilemma (players' relative productivity, dichotomic or continuous discrete choice of time invested in relational goods, separability/non-separability of preferences, specific assumptions on the relative cost of effort spent in the production of the physical and of the relational good).

We found formal solutions for simpler cases and numerical solutions in more complex cases showing that the occurrence of the dilemma crucially depends on the assumption of separability/non-separability of preferences and on the understanding of the specific features of the production of relational goods (additivity and superadditivity plus public good features).

We believe that these results are particularly interesting since they show that the 'relational Baumol disease' alone may generate income–unhappiness paradoxes under reasonable parametric conditions. The limited range in which the dilemma occurs necessarily implies that other important factors of the contemporary socioeconomic environment must enter the picture to reinforce the paradox. A first candidate is obviously a law of decay of investment in relational activities which depends on the stock of past investment.

If we add other important factors of contemporary socioeconomic environment, such as the increased risk in financial and job markets and induced changes in the relative preferences towards consumption, this paradox might be reinforced. However, these extensions are behind the scope of the simple exercise presented in this chapter.

Notes

*   The authors would like to thank two anonymous referees, L. Bruni, B. Gui, M. Pugno, R. Sugden, S. Zamagni and all other participants in the 2005 Milan conference on 'happiness and capability' for their useful comments and suggestions. The usual disclaimer applies.

1.   In his empirical work, Lane (2000) also shows that individuals' happiness is positively related to the number of hours spent in social activities.

2.   For updated information on empirical analyses on wealth and happiness, see www.eur.nl/fsw/research/happiness. Information contained here must be evaluated with care. It is well known that in the field of panel surveys, time comparisons on the same panel in a single country are much more reliable than cross-country comparisons among heterogeneous panels. Therefore, if it is hard to say whether Americans are more or less happy than Europeans, it is easier to track the dynamic relationship between happiness and income in each country.

3. These two forces are responsible for what Cairncross (1997) calls the 'death of distance' or for the sudden acceleration of economic integration between different areas in the last thirty years (Robertson 1992; Giddens 2000).

4. We believe that a relational public good (that is, parental agreement) is an important, although not the only, input of children's education, if we consider a typical definition of relational goods: 'Relational goods are local public goods that can only be produced and consumed through the joint action of several individuals, whose identities become relevant' (Antoci et al. 2001).

5. Putnam (2000) quotes two pieces of evidence which support this hypothesis. First, labour market participation reduces investment in social capital by working women. Second, investment in social capital appears to be reduced by the availability of television sets (representing an example of non-relational leisure). The problem is that, from the empirical point of view, the negative relationship between investment in social (relational) capital and the opportunity cost of time is difficult to disentangle from the role of human capital which is, on the one hand, a complement of social capital (that is, college education) and, on the other, raises productivity and the opportunity cost of time.

6. The rising opportunity cost of leisure is a well-known phenomenon evidenced by several authors (for example, Biswanger 2001; Pugno 2003).

7. Are these features of the model consistent with stylized facts of hours worked and leisure? The correspondence is difficult to evaluate because of the lack of adequate statistics distinguishing between relational and non-relational leisure. Consider, however, that: (i) the amount of time allocated to market work in the US by married households has increased markedly (31.2 per cent) over the post-war period. This is mainly due to a rise in labour-force participation by married females (Greenwood and Guner 2004). As a result, weekly hours worked per person have risen by 7.2 per cent from 1950 to 1990 as a combination of a reduction of 14 per cent of males and an increase of 74 per cent of females (McGrattan and Rogerson 1998); (ii) indirect evidence on depletion of relational goods is provided, for instance, by Schiff (1992) who argues that the US evinces a striking phenomenon of a 'higher level of wealth for a huge number of people, on the one hand, and a weaker social support structure, on the other hand (including a higher crime rate, weaker interpersonal relations and more isolation)'. Indirect evidence of this phenomenon is provided, according to the author, by the creation of alternative institutions where people who are less closely connected can interact (for example, singles bars, dating services, nursing homes and so on).

8. The h function is assumed continuous and twice differentiable.

9. We normalize k to one in the following.

10. We assume a competitive equilibrium in the production of consumption goods, with a constant return to scale, homogeneous of degree one, production function.

11. This last inequality is always true if the previous condition is respected.

12. Note that this is equivalent to account for disutility of the effort spent in the production of the relational good in the payoff function.

13. This condition is a sufficient condition for the prisoner's dilemma under the assumption that players' payoffs are symmetric in the two equilibria in which they choose different strategies ($U_1^*(P, NP) = U_2^*(NP, P)$). Under this assumption, (13.20') necessarily implies that $U_2^*(NP, P) < U_2^*(NP, NP) < U_2^*(P, P) < U_2^*(P, NP)$ which is the sequence of player 2's payoffs needed to have the dilemma.

14. From inspection of the maximand it is clear that this problem has no internal solution.

15. Symmetry assumptions under which (13.36) is a sufficient condition for the prisoner's dilemma are described in note 8.

16. In this case the determinant of the wealth/unhappiness effect may only be a factor which associates the technological progress induced wage rise to a shift of preferences towards a relatively higher weight on consumption (that is, positive relationship between technological progress and advertising expenditure which generates the shift of tastes towards consumption).

17. Results on asymmetric changes in real wages under non-separable CRS preferences and results in the quadratic effort case with separable and non-separable CRS preferences

demonstrate that our main findings are determined by the separability/non-separability assumption (the area of the dilemma widens when real wages rise under separable preferences, is larger but remains the same when real wages rise under non-separable preferences). These results are omitted for reasons of space and are available from the authors on request.

References

Antoci, A., P.L. Sacco and P. Vanin (2001), 'Economic growth and social poverty: the evolution of social participation', Bonn Economics Discussion Papers, 13.

Bartolini, S. (2004), 'Una spiegazione della fretta e della infelicità contemporanee', in L. Bruni and P.L. Porta (eds), *Felicità ed economia*, Milan: Guerini e Associati.

Baumol, W.J. (1967), 'Macroeconomics of unbalanced growth', *American Economic Review*, **57**, 415–26.

Baumol, W.J., S.A.B. Blackmann and E.N. Wolff (1989), *Productivity and American Leadership*, Cambridge, MA: MIT Press.

Biswanger, M. (2001), 'Technological progress and sustainable development. What about the rebound effect?', *Ecological Economics*, **36**, 119–32.

Bruni L. (2002), 'L'economia e i paradossi della felicità', in P.L. Sacco and S. Zamagni (eds), *Complessità relazionale e comportamento economico, materiali per un nuovo paradigma della relazionalità*, Bologna: Il Mulino.

Cairncross, F. (1997), *The Death of Distance*, London: Orion.

Gaspar, J. and E.L. Glaeser (1998), 'Information technology and the future of cities', *Journal of Urban Economics*, **43** (1), January, 136–56.

Giddens, A. (2000), *Runaway World: How Globalisation is Reshaping Our Lives*, London: Routledge.

Greenwood, J. and N. Guner (2004), 'Marriage and divorce since World War II: analyzing the role of technological progress on the formation of households', Économie d'avant garde, Research Report No. 8, University of Rochester, Rochester, NY.

Hirsch, F. (1976), *Social Limits to Growth*, Cambridge: Harvard University Press.

Lane, R. (2000), *The Loss of Happiness in the Market Democracies*, New Haven, CT: Yale University Press.

McGrattan, E.R. and R. Rogerson (1998), 'Changes in hours worked since 1950', *Quarterly Review*, Federal Reserve Bank of Minneapolis, Winter, pp. 2–19.

Nussbaum, M. (1986), *The Fragility of Goodness: Luck and Ethics in Greek Tragedy and Philosophy*, Cambridge: Cambridge University Press.

Oswald, Andrew J. (1997), 'Happiness and economic performance', *Economic Journal*, Royal Economic Society, **107** (445), 1815–31.

Pugno M. (2003), 'The subjective well-being paradox. A suggested resolution based on relational goods', Paper presented at the Conference on The Paradoxes of Happines in Economics, Milan, 21–23 March.

Putnam, R. (2000), *Bowling Alone*, New York: Simon & Schuster.

Robertson, R. (1992), *Globalisation*, London: Sage.

Schiff, M. (1992), 'Social capital, labor mobility, and welfare', *Rationality and Society*, **4**, 157–75.

14 The subjective well-being paradox: a suggested solution based on relational goods
Maurizio Pugno*

1. Introduction

'Subjective well-being', often called happiness, is arousing increasing interest among economists and economic psychologists through resumed study of the Benthamite approach to utility (Ng 1978; Kahneman et al. 1999; Easterlin 2001; Frey and Stutzer 2002; Layard 2003; and symposia in the *Economic Journal* 1997, and in the *Journal of Economic Behavior and Organization* 2001).[1] An underlying reason for this interest is that per capita income has increasingly become an overoptimistic proxy for well-being, especially in the affluent economies. The most systematic evidence on this problem is provided by survey research on self-reported happiness (Veenhoven 1994). Further significant and more dramatic evidence emerges from the proliferation of specific forms of malaise such as mental depression and suicides.

A 'subjective well-being paradox' can be more precisely identified in the richest countries during recent decades. Let us first define 'subjective well-being' (SWB) as including both a cognitive judgement on satisfaction with one's current life, and one's prevalent affective state. A paradox arises because the various indices of SWB exhibit little improvement or even deterioration, while per capita income, which is the main proxy for material well-being, displays a definite rising trend. The paradox is heightened by the fact that the inability of income to yield SWB has not substantially discouraged individuals from supplying their labour. In other words, technical progress is, by and large, not used to achieve more leisure and thus decelerate income growth. By contrast, effort, if not working time, is supplied to a greater amount, and with consequent greater stress.

The main explanation for the paradox offered by the economic literature is based on the Duesenberry (1949) type of comparative effect. Easterlin provides the prime example of the use of this approach. He first assumes that SWB positively depends on current income and negatively depends on aspirations about future income, and that aspirations are based on past income. He then conjectures, and supports with some evidence, that 'material aspirations change over the life cycle roughly in proportion to income'

(Easterlin 2001: 473). As a result, SWB may remain constant while income increases, and work effort is not discouraged.

Although this explanation is interesting, it is lacking in a major respect which has a discouraging effect on active policies. It fails to explain why the recent deterioration of SWB is such a major phenomenon (see Section 2). This failure entirely changes the problem of inadequacy of per capita income as a proxy for SWB. The suspicion that self-reported SWB is downwardly biased because of measurement and other problems turns into the intuition that SWB is affected by some significant factor which is not captured by income and which is deteriorating. Easterlin's explanation of constant SWB evinces the drawback to analysis which considers only income. It ignores the fact that a constant gap between aspirations and realizations implies that individuals do not learn, and that they commit systematic errors, with the further uncomfortable consequence that deteriorating SWB entails a tendency to commit more serious errors. Moreover, the failure to recognize that SWB deteriorates in some important instances changes the requisite policy from less inaction to urgent intervention. Ethical reasons would suffice, but the economic effects of deteriorated SWB should be also considered.[2]

This chapter attempts to extend Easterlin's explanation of the paradox by showing that SWB may diminish even with no increase in the aspirations/realizations gap. Moreover, it provides several justifications for an incomplete adjustment of aspirations whereby individuals fail to maximize SWB. In order to obtain these results, the chapter not only recognizes that SWB is not of purely material concern; it also extends the analysis of well-being in a largely unexplored direction by acknowledging that individuals pursue close personal relationships as a specific and important life-goal. There is broad consensus in the psychological literature on the importance of personal relationships for SWB, especially those with a partner, friends and relatives. Psychologists recognize that close personal relationships not only determine SWB but also affect mental and physical health, and even life expectancy.

The economic literature has traditionally studied only the material component of SWB. Authoritative exceptions have been Ng (1978, 2003) and Scitovsky (1976), who suggest that the study of happiness must include psychology, and that many pleasures are not purchased in the market. More precisely, Scitovsky argues that individuals tend to overconsume in comforts and to underconsume and underinvest in pleasures, which implies that they are generally unable to solve the problem of maximizing SWB.

Some economists have recently recognized that both the exchange of economic goods and the underlying personal relationships matter in economic interaction among individuals. The production and consumption of other distinctive goods, namely 'relational goods' (RGs), are thus identified in the literature. The idea is an interesting one, but the analysis is still in its infancy. This chapter applies it to solving a macroeconomic problem, so that assumptions that greatly simplify the analysis become particularly attractive.

There are principally two of these simplifying assumptions. The first is that the production/consumption of RGs is due to a final intentional behaviour which is specific and different from all the other more usual economic behaviours. In reality, this difference is not so clear-cut. For example, the exchange of labour hours for a wage is in fact not a purely material transaction as is assumed here. This is because close personal relationships are far more important during leisure time than they are during working time. The second simplifying assumption is intended to capture a neglected aspect of human nature in personal relationships: emotions and feelings. It is assumed that individuals are unable to predict accurately – not even on the basis of past experience – how much SWB will be yielded by the time spent on closely relating to others. Emotions and feelings render encounters invariably somewhat surprising. By contrast, it is assumed that individuals can predict the utility deriving from traditional economic goods with accuracy.

In spite of these simplifying assumptions the analysis is still complex, not least because psychology apparently lacks a formally rigorous and widely accepted theory of SWB. Moreover, many studies in psychology, psychiatry, neurobiology and sociology highlight aspects of interest to the present analysis on the basis of survey and experimental data, as well as of clinical-based research and informal explanations. In order to resolve the paradox, therefore, this chapter integrates the diverse contributions of these various disciplines into a single framework, attempting to provide an analysis which is rigorous but still exploratory and informal.

The analysis will be organized into a set of assumptions and functional relationships, with brief discussion of their empirical bases in the psychological literature, and explanation of how the model works. The model is built around the interaction between the consumption of standard economic goods and of RGs as representative of close personal relationships. The theoretical framework is the simple economic analysis of the consumption/leisure choice usually adopted to explain the labour supply curve. No notion of altruism or social norms is used. However, a crucial extension in the analysis is the application of the concepts of experienced utility, decision utility and aspirations proposed by Kahneman and collaborators. This extension will entail analysis of the dynamics of the model when a gap between aspirations and realizations occurs. As will be shown, the model is also able to endogenize individuals' preferences.

The organization of the chapter is as follows: Section 2 sets out the motivations of the research; Section 3 presents and discusses the model in some detail and with numerous references to the literature, given that the analysis is interdisciplinary; Section 4 draws the conclusions.

2.   Motivations

This section first briefly surveys the empirical relevance of the SWB paradox, then critically surveys how it has been explained by the psychology and economic literature, evidences the importance of close personal relationships for SWB, shows how they have deteriorated, and finally outlines the results of the literature on increasing 'materialism' in the affluent economies.

Evidence underlying the paradox

The evidence on self-reported happiness usually considers the proportion of persons who consider themselves to be 'very happy' on a three-point scale. In the US, this index declined from 2.4 to 2.2 between 1946 and 1991, while real per capita income rose by a factor of 2.5 over the same period. In Japan real per capita income rose sixfold between 1958 and 1991, but the proportion of 'very happy' respondents remained largely unchanged over the same period (Frey and Stutzer 2002: 9 and 77). A time-series study of 10 advanced countries shows that none of them exhibits a significant (at 5 per cent) positive correlation between self-reported happiness and per capita income, while the US and Belgium report a significant negative correlation (Kenny 1999; see also Diener and Suh 1997).[3] Nor does cross-country analysis yield much more comforting evidence if the advanced countries are considered: the correlation changes from weak in Easterlin's (1974) famous article to insignificant in the more recent studies (Kenny 1999; Diener and Biswas-Diener 2002).

Far more dramatic, even if partial, are the indicators of SWB like suicides and depression. Between 1970–87 and 1990 the suicide rate among adolescents and young adults rose from 8.0 to 13.2 in the US, and from an unweighted average of 6.9 to 9.8 in the four major European countries (Lane 2000: 23). Oswald (1997: 1825) observes that suicide rates among men have been rising in almost all western countries since the early 1970s. Lester and Yang's (1997) survey of several studies shows that the correlation between per capita income and suicide rates has been positively significant for the US since the Second World War, and for a cross-section of the European countries (see also Jungeilges and Kirchgaessner 2002; and Huang 1996).[4] The picture appears less bleak in the most recent period, since 'only' Ireland and Spain among the western countries exhibit rising suicide rates (Chishti et al. 2003; Levi et al. 2003).

Mental depression is a good indicator of SWB, since it has been tested as strictly inversely correlated with SWB (van Hemert et al. 2002). Unfortunately, depression is very widespread, as is well known, but it is impossible to make exact estimates of its incidence. Some experts maintain that depression has increased tenfold in the US since the Second World War, and that the rate is similar in Canada, Sweden, Germany and New Zealand (Myers 1993: 43; Lane 2000: 347–8). The future prospects are also very alarming (WHO 2001).[5]

Given this evidence that 'money does not buy happiness', one would expect people to substantially reduce their work effort devoted to making money. However, in the US both average annual and average weekly hours for men but especially for women have risen in the past two decades (Schor 1992; Bluestone and Rose 2000). Since the late 1970s, overtime has increased as well (Golden 1998). In the EU, working time per employee has declined, mainly due to the introduction of regulations on the standard workday. However, the dynamics have decelerated in the last decades, and women's participation especially has greatly increased, so that the average rate of the working-age population has increased (Lehndorff 2000).

The main explanations for the paradox in the literature
The evidence of constant SWB while per capita income has increased finds straightforward explanation in the psychology literature, but this is an explanation which is still unsatisfactory. 'Personality theory' predicts SWB on the basis of personal traits, whether they are dispositions towards happiness or unhappiness. In so far as these traits are genetic, as some evidence suggests that they are (Lykken and Tellegen 1996), SWB remains stable over time (Goldsmith and Campos 1986; Costa et al. 1987; Costa 1994). However, this extreme version of the 'personality theory' has been contradicted by the finding that SWB is variable for single individuals (Headey and Wearing 1989), and personality traits seem statistically to explain only a portion of the variance of SWB indices (Diener 1996; Diener et al. 1999: 279–80).[6]

'Adaptation-level theory' is complementary to personality theory, since it predicts that external shocks, like unforeseen rises in income, will have only temporary effects on SWB because of habituation (Helson 1964; Brickman et al. 1978). Hence, personality traits set the baseline level towards which SWB reverts after the shocks (Headey and Wearing 1989). However, this theory too is unsatisfactory, because adaptation seems to occur only slowly and even incompletely (Diener et al. 1999: 280; Lucas et al. 2003; Easterlin 2005). Moreover, adaptation appears instead to conceal a strategy to substitute the goals to be pursued (Diener et al. 1999: 284–5), while measurement problems seem serious (Frederick and Loewenstein 1999).

'Livibility theory' argues that the correlation between SWB and per capita income is no longer significant when one moves from the developing to the developed economies, because income is able to satisfy primary needs but not higher-order ones like self-actualization (Veenhoven 1995). However, if income exhibits this decreasing marginal utility, why do people not unambiguously decrease their commitment to work?

The 'discrepancy theory' argues that SWB depends on the aspirations/ realizations gap. The standards for comparison may be the experience of other people, past conditions, or ideal aspirations (Michalos 1985; Inglehart 1990). This theory is flexible, and economists, who concentrate on material SWB, have found it easy to adapt. Easterlin's attempt to resolve the paradox was mentioned in the Introduction. Another important strand in the economic literature focuses on the aspiration for positional goods, which are inherently scarce because of congestion or exclusion (Hirsch 1976; Layard 1980; Frank 1985; Cooper et al. 2001; Corneo and Jeanne 2001). However, as Ng (1978) simply shows, in this case a reduction in SWB when income typically rises can only be explained if aspirations for positional goods increasingly go unrealized, which is implausible.

The importance and the deterioration of close personal relationships

The importance of close personal relationships for SWB has been documented not only by several subfields of psychology but also by psychiatry, sociology and anthropology. The research methods employed for this purpose include surveys, experiments, cross-cultural comparisons, and case studies (Myers 1993; Argyle 1999; Diener et al. 1999).

On surveying a wide spectrum of the literature on almost 300 items, Baumeister and Leary (1995) conclude that the desire for interpersonal attachments is a fundamental human motivation. They do so on the following grounds. First, it is spontaneous, and it does not need material advantage; rather, people appear to devote much time and effort to fostering supportive relations with others. Second, interpersonal attachments exhibit diminishing returns. Third, 'people strongly and generally resist the dissolution of relationships . . . [T]his resistance appears to go well beyond rational considerations of practical or material advantage' (p. 503). Fourth, deprivation of stable, good relations has been linked to a wide array of pathological and aversive consequences, from physical and mental illness to traffic accidents and suicides. Fifth, the attachment is essential because of its character of companionship and intimacy, so that the qualities of both relatedness and interaction are required. Simple affiliation and generic social support appear of less consequence, while mere social contacts may be important for selecting closer ties (see also Lane 2000: 27).

Sixth, 'the evidence for brain mechanisms is supportive but inadequate to prove innateness' (Baumeister and Leary 1995: 518).

These conclusions are important from an economic point of view, that is, *vis-à-vis* economic goods and material well-being. In fact, individuals appear intentionally to pursue personal relationships, and they devote time to this purpose. Personal relationships seem to be essential and to function as imperfect substitutes for economic goods, and similarly have diminishing returns. The quality of relationships appears crucial, though it is not pursued simply according to rational principles, or simply according to an innate drive.

In spite of the importance of personal relationships, several psychological and sociological studies show on the basis of certain indices that they have deteriorated in recent years. In the US between the beginning of the 1970s and 1994, the proportion of those 'very happy' with their marriages declined from 67.5 to 61.5 (Lane 2000: 24). Over the same period, the proportion of persons who frequently visited relatives and neighbours dropped by several points (pp. 104–5), while the proportion of those who did not think that 'most people could be trusted' rose from 52 to 58.5 (p. 27). Other evidence shows a fourfold rise in the divorce rate, a rise from 25 per cent to 39 per cent of adult singles between 1960 and 1995, and the reduction to one half of remarried women between the 1960s and the 1980s (Myers 1999). Dramatic data on infanticides in the US show that in almost all cases they are perpetrated by intrafamily assailants. The homicide rate of babies aged one year or less rose from 51 per million-population in 1974–78 to 84 in 1995–99 (Pritchard and Butler 2003). Finally, the evidence on suicide and depression can be considered in an analogous manner, since loneliness crucially correlates with suicide (Baumeister and Leary 1995), as well as with depression (Peplau and Perlman 1982).

'Materialism'

As a complement to the deterioration of close personal relationships, 'materialism' appears to be increasing in the most affluent economies – as discussed by a large body of literature (Lane 2000: ch. 8). Richins and Dawson (1992: 308) define 'materialism' as 'a set of centrally held beliefs about the importance of possession in one's life and measures the three belief-domains: acquisition centrality, the role of acquisition in happiness, and the role of possession in defining success'.

This literature draws two main conclusions, which are particularly interesting for this chapter: the possession of material goods may substitute for close personal relationships when these are unsatisfactory (Richins 1994; Rindfleisch et al. 1997; Kasser and Ryan 2001); those who pursue materialism report lower SWB than others (Belk 1985; Kasser 2000; Lane

2000: 143 and ch. 8).[7] Lane (p. 145) also observes that the great importance attached to money makes people more depressed and anxious.

3.   The model

In order to explain the SWB paradox a model is proposed which includes both economic goods and RGs as representative of close personal relationships. After the model has been closed with a simple production side, it can be described as an extension in some crucial directions of the standard labour/leisure model explaining labour supply. The model will be built step by step in the following subsections.

The simple economic framework of the model
Let us assume that the economy is characterized as follows:

A1   Many identical firms compete to produce one good only, called 'economic good'.

A2   A single production technique is available, and it employs only labour with constant returns.

A3   The population comprises workers and a fixed proportion of younger individuals who have not yet entered the labour market; births, new workers and deaths are the same in number for each given period.

A4   The working population atomistically competes to supply homogeneous units of labour for a wage.

A5   The utility function is the same for both workers and young individuals, it is concave in two complementary arguments: an economic good, and a 'relational good', both of them fixed baskets of goods.

A6   Each worker is endowed with a fixed amount of time, which can be devoted either to work and producing the economic good, or to consuming/producing the 'relational good'.

A7   Workers provide the economic goods to young individuals for free, as demanded by the latter.

The results deriving from these assumptions are that the productive technique fixes labour productivity per time unit, which is equal to the (real) wage rate per time unit, and that utility maximization yields the individual and aggregate participation rate in production of the economic good, and the amount of income earned, which is totally spent on the economic good. Thus determined is the economic/'relational' goods composition.

This closely resembles the standard model of labour supply, if leisure replaces the 'relational good'. Note, however, the effects on the labour supply due to the assumption of complementarity in both the consumption/leisure case and the economic/'relational' goods case. An innovation in the production technique, and thus an increase in the wage rate per time unit, reduces the labour supply or the participation rate, while it increases both consumption and leisure, that is, both kinds of goods.[8] To obtain an outcome consistent with the SWB paradox, further assumptions will be added in the next subsections.

'Relational goods': definition and restrictions

The first crucial change proposed to the standard model is the replacement of leisure with RGs. This concept is new in the literature, although the importance of human relationships in economic life and well-being has been emphasized since Adam Smith (Bruni 2000; Sugden 2002). The recent endeavour has been to treat personal relationships in a way which is directly comparable to economic goods (see Gui 2000 for a brief survey).

RGs are defined as 'a subset of local public goods, as they enter two or more persons' utility functions' (Uhlaner 1989: 254). In fact, they 'can only be enjoyed with some others', because 'with RGs the jointness of consumption itself provides a benefit' (pp. 254–5). This benefit can be measured, and it may be highly asymmetric between the partners (Gui 2000). The production and consumption of RGs coincide, so that they are not an exchange of pre-existing economic goods (Donati 1991; Gui 1994; Zamagni 1999). Finally, 'RGs are to some extent noncontractible, as favourable reciprocal dispositions cannot be effectively secured throughout monetary incentives' (Gui 2001: 8). Therefore, they can be defined as not marketable (Ng 1975).

In this chapter the definition of RGs is restricted in three ways. First, RGs are considered to be pure goods, that is, they are excluded from and unrelated to the production and exchange of economic goods.[9] Second, they are considered to be flow goods which cannot be accumulated. This restriction makes the analysis simpler, but it does not appear crucial.[10] Third, RGs are a matter of intentional choice in the same way as economic goods are, because they can be evaluated when they take place. However, unlike economic goods, they yield a benefit which the individual cannot predict with any accuracy; nor is past experience a reliable basis for prediction. This restriction, which is discussed below (p. 275), is rather stringent, but it captures and emphasizes a neglected though essential aspect of human relationships: the unintentional onset of emotions and feelings.

Experienced well-being, and aspirations for future well-being
The second crucial change proposed to the standard labour/leisure model is application of the comparison approach as developed by several economists and psychologists. The idea that individuals compare their spendings against some prior standard was introduced by Duesenberry (1949) with his relative income hypothesis. Psychologists, for instance Michalos (1985), find evidence that the hypothesis on satisfaction as a function of the gap between aspirations and realizations has been successful. This approach has been made more rigorous by Kahneman and colleagues, who put forward the following concepts: experienced and predicted utility as distinct from the standard decision utility, and the aspiration level.

According to Kahneman and Snell (1992: 188), 'the experienced utility of an outcome is defined by the quality and intensity of the hedonic experience associated with that outcome . . . [and] . . . the predicted utility of an outcome is defined by the individual's beliefs about the experienced utility of that outcome some time in the future'. By contrast, 'decision utility of an outcome is the weight assigned to that outcome in a decision' (Kahneman 2000a: 761). Finally, the aspiration level is 'a value on a scale of attainment that lies somewhere between realistic expectation and reasonable hope' (Kahneman 2000b: 687).

In this chapter, SWB will be simply used for 'utility', so that aspirations refer to SWB derived from consuming the various goods. Namely:

A8   Decisions for maximizing future SWB are based on aspirations, rather than on mechanistic predictions extrapolated from past SWB obtained from similar goods, or from the observation of the SWB of other people. Aspirations emphasize the role of affects.

Several psychologists and neurobiologists have studied the importance of affects in an individual's motivation and behaviour (for a survey, see Pugno 2004). An interesting finding is that depression or happiness, and personal affective traits like extroversion and neuroticism, significantly influence individuals' selection and evaluation of the information relevant to their aspirations (see the surveys by Diener et al. 1999: 282–5; and Morris 1999). In particular, social comparison proves to be subjective and upwardly biased (Lane 2000: 305–6). A specific study shows that this bias is due to the materialistic orientation (Sirgy 1998) (see below, pp. 276–7). More radically, Damasio (1994) argues that decisions are supported by emotions. In particular, an individual's experiences – according to Damasio – are characterized by 'somatic markers', which are specific reactions in the neurophysiological system attached to representations of the experiences in the mind, often on an unconscious basis.[11]

It might be said that a higher content of affect in the aspirations for RGs than for economic goods (Zajonc 1980; Clark and Brissette 2003) implies that also prediction of future SWB is more uncertain in the former case. Learning the consumption of economic goods is usually highly effective, not only directly but also from experiences of others. The same conclusion cannot be easily sustained with regard to the consumption of RGs. The following assumption is thus made:

A9   Realized SWB and aspirations for future SWB coincide for economic goods, while the possible gap between them is maintained for RGs.

Unfortunately, there is not a great deal of empirical evidence specifically obtained from testing this assumption. However, van Dijk and Zeelenberg (2002) find that individuals react to person-related disappointment very differently from the way in which they react to outcome-related disappointment.[12] In the former case individuals tend to avoid experiences with others, in the latter case they persist in their behaviour. Hence, what matters is not the extent of uncertainty in the prediction of RGs versus economic goods, but the kind and the effects of uncertainty (see below, pp. 276–9).

The 'subjective well-being function'
The idea that SWB is determined by the gap between aspirations and realizations, and A9 which limits the existence of the gap to RGs suggest specification of the following 'SWB function', which complements the specification in A5:

A10   (Experienced) SWB depends positively and multiplicatively on economic goods and on realized RGs, and negatively on the gap between aspirations and realization of RGs.

This function is clearly inspired by Kahneman and Tversky's 'prospect theory',[13] and by the literature on 'disappointment' (Bell 1985; Looms and Sugden 1986; Inman et al. 1997; Zeelenberg et al. 2000). Note that SWB maximization is pursued on the basis of the expected levels of the variables. In particular, the expected gap may by extrapolated from experience of past gaps. When SWB is actually experienced, the gap is realized. More precisely, it can be defined a 'disappointment' when aspirations are not completely realized (overprediction), and an 'elation' when aspirations prove to be too conservative (underprediction). Therefore, a disappointment affects the SWB negatively, and an elation affects it positively.

However, to the extent that aspirations for RGs are not realized as they have been in the past, SWB is not maximized. In the case of overprediction,

SWB is lower than it would be if aspirations were completely realized. To maximize SWB, the allocation of time would have to be more favourable for the production of the economic good, since well-being from RGs would have been experienced as smaller. By contrast, if underprediction is the case, elation arises, and hence SWB is greater but not optimal. One may expect an allocation of time more favourable to RGs to yield even greater SWB.

In the SWB function, the two kinds of goods are complementary (A5), that is, greater consumption of economic goods increases aspirations for additional RGs. This means that economic goods embody an instrumental value. Examples are transport and communications goods and services, which can be bought for the purpose of enjoying close personal relationships.

However, complementarity would also imply that the supply of individual labour is decreasing for rising wages, contrary to the SWB paradox. We are now able to state that it is more correct to refer to complementarity between economic goods and aspirations (rather than realizations) for RGs, and that the disappointment of aspirations may induce an individual to turn complementarity between the two goods into their substitutability (see below pp. 277–8 and 281).

Inputs and production of relational goods
Time is not the only obvious input for RGs. As Cauley and Sandler (1980) and Gui (2000) noted, individual characteristics and economic goods can also be included among such inputs. Their treatment here is original, however.

The consumption of economic goods affects the production of RGs both as a level, through A10 on the multiplicative specification of the SWB function, and as a change, through the complementarity assumption (A5).

Individual characteristics are clearly involved in the production of RGs, in so far as they can be evaluated along the dimension of disposition towards RGs. This is a positive, prosocial affect, inclusive of feeling, disclosure and responsiveness, that can be seen as a mood or as a personality trait sometimes synthesized by the terms extroversion and neuroticism (Kelley 1986).

Moreover, a distinctive technique linking the inputs and the output of RGs can be identified in the interaction among persons. This is the main source of emotions and feelings.

Let us therefore assume:

A11   RGs per time unit for an individual positively depend on the level of and changes in the economic goods used, on the individual's and his/her partner's dispositions towards RGs, and on the interaction among all the individuals involved.

Uncertainty in the prediction of future well-being from relational goods

Economists usually consider the information set to be the necessary and crucial condition for decisions to be taken. In his study of personal relationships, Becker (1996) assumes that individuals are sufficiently informed to maximize SWB.[14] Cauley and Sandler (1980) treat personal relationships as the conscious management of reciprocal externalities in certainty conditions.

This chapter follows a different line of inquiry by starting from the observation that the prediction of future well-being from RGs is uncertain: more specifically, it is uncertain in an endogenous way and to an unknown and variable extent. In fact, RGs depend, among other things (A11), on an individual's disposition towards RGs and on his/her interaction with others. However, the strength of these determinants is partially unknown to the individual in advance, because the disposition and the reaction to others are imbued with emotions and feelings, which essentially arise unconsciously.

There is a large amount of literature supporting this claim. On the one hand, numerous neurobiological studies show that personal identity, that is, the self that decides and behaves, is built day by day on both conscious and unconscious bases (Damasio 1994, 1999; LeDoux 1996, 2002; Lane 2000: 285; Boncinelli 2002; see also Lane 1991: chs 5–6). On the other hand, the psychology, psychiatry and psychotherapy literature maintains that an individual's ability to establish good close personal relationships depends on the formation of an unconscious mental dimension from his/her birth onwards (Fagioli 1971), or on the type of attachment formed in relationships during infancy, when cognitive functions are still incomplete (Siegel 1999).

The role of emotions has only recently attracted attention in the economic literature. Some economists consider 'excessive' emotional arousal to be a constraint on rational thought (Kaufman 1999 and the literature cited therein), but this view has been criticized as obsolete by psychologists (Hanoch 2002 and the literature cited therein).

Past experience of consumption of RGs provides only shaky foundations for prediction. In fact, emotions affect memory recall (Diener et al. 1999: 282–5; Morris 1999), and past events appear to be remembered with a systematic bias (Kahneman et al. 1997). Moreover, past experiences vary greatly, and homogeneous information is scarce.

Therefore, the available information with which the individual can build the subjective probability distribution of the expected level of RGs produced/consumed per time unit will yield a fat tails distribution.[15] Nor will information updating greatly reduce errors in prediction. The following assumption may thus be stated:

A12   The probability that an individual realizes aspirations for RGs remains low over his/her life cycle.

The 'excessive' aspirations of young individuals
The affective component of aspirations is not constant over the life cycle but decreases with age. Infants do not make cold predictions based on past experience; they simply 'hope to find a breast' and depend entirely on other people for satisfaction of both their physiological needs and their psychic desires.[16] Unfortunately, since physiological needs are more tangible, they are usually more completely satisfied. Disappointments from personal relationships therefore ensue.

Young people typically have high aspirations, while adults report a closer gap between aspirations and realizations. This is confirmed not only by common knowledge but also by specific studies (Campbell et al. 1976; Argyle 1987: ch. 9; Diener et al. 1999: 291–2).

The following assumption can thus be stated:

A13   The younger age group of the population exhibits the greatest positive gap between aspirations and realizations of RGs.

Therefore, the prediction of future well-being from RGs is not simply wrong with a high probability but tends to be biased upwards. This implies that updating the probability distribution of the expected level of RGs per time unit through their realizations means a leftward correction of the distribution, where RGs are lower.

Reduction in the time devoted to personal relationships and the push to materialism
When people are disappointed by close personal relationships, they usually react in some way.[17] Three reactions can be identified:

A14   Reducing the time devoted to RGs.

A15   Reducing the disposition towards RGs.

A16   Reducing aspirations for RGs.

This subsection discusses the first reaction; the other two are dealt with in the following subsections.

Reducing the time devoted to RGs is a reaction typical of adults, who are able to change the time allocation previously chosen in an attempt to reduce disappointment in the future. This is a reaction due to a dynamic maximization which induces adults to seek greater consumption of economic goods. Also young individuals may consume more economic goods as a consequence of disappointment from close personal relationships: they demand more economic goods from adults, who will in turn work harder. Infants often simultaneously experience both disappointment and over-attention by adults to their physiological needs. This change is greatly stimulated by advertising and fashion (Belk and Pollay 1985).

These facts are studied by the literature on the push to materialism in affluent economies. But this literature also concludes that individuals who emphasize materialism yield less SWB than the others (see above, pp. 269–70). This is a cross-individual version of the SWB paradox, which can be explained by the model starting from A10, A13 and A14). It in fact follows that the greater the disappointment from RGs experienced by an individual, the less his/her SWB and the greater his/her push to materialism.[18]

However, there is also much evidence to show that SWB decreases with age, although its dynamics after the age of 40 needs further scrutiny. Studies in clinical psychology, psychiatry and psychotherapy agree that infancy and youth are critical ages, because disappointments and other problems particularly depress the well-being of individuals (Stern 1985; Lane 2000: 84). Several econometric studies find that SWB decreases from the age of around 20 to the age of around 40, and then moderately increases. However, these studies also show that the individual's marital status has by far the most important effect on SWB. Divorce, separation and widowhood dramatically reduce SWB (Helliwell 2003; see also Frey and Stutzer 2002; Blanchflower and Oswald 2004).[19] Moreover, the finding that SWB is U-shaped with age has been criticized because it is not based on panel data, and it may be due to a composition effect across different generations (Easterlin 2001: 470; see also Santos 2004). If SWB is followed along the same cohorts, a constant or even a declining trend emerges from 21–30 to 85–90 (Easterlin 2005). Finally, studies on suicide report the highest rates in the group of oldest people. In particular, in the US this suicide rate increased from 24.9 to 42.0 per 100,000 residents during the 1990–98 period, while among the white widowed men the rate reached 84.0 (Institute of Medicine 2002).

This evidence is thus consistent with the SWB paradox on time basis, but its explanation requires further analysis.[20]

Reducing the disposition towards relational goods, and the vicious circle of depression

The second reaction to disappointment is a reduction in the disposition towards RGs, although this generally takes place unconsciously.[21] This reaction makes the uncertainty in predicting future RGs special: in fact, an unconscious reduction in dispositions towards RGs means that the realized

RGs update the subjective probability distribution of RGs only partially. If the reduction in the disposition were fully known, the probability distribution would be further corrected to the left. Unconscious information on RGs thus explains the tendency to overpredict SWB from RGs, and the difficulty of learning from past errors.[22]

The reduction in the disposition toward RGs is not only a one-step effect; it triggers a vicious circle through A11: from disappointment to less disposition, from less disposition to less well-being from realized RGs, and hence to further disappointment. This I shall call the 'vicious circle of depression'.

Numerous studies provide evidence for the vicious circle of depression. The link between disappointment and a reduction in the disposition towards RGs is supported by the same studies on the reduction of well-being in infancy mentioned in the previous subsection. Other evidence is provided by Berenbaum et al. (1999), who report that depression and anxiety are linked not only to parental loss and maltreatment, especially during childhood (see also Lane 2000: 84), but also to particular dramatic or everyday stressful events (Argyle 1987: ch. 6; Headey and Wearing 1989). The link that feeds back from a reduction in disposition toward RGs to a reduction in the realization of RGs is supported by Morris (1999), who observes that depression promotes self-focus and discourages active involvement in the pursuit of environment goals. Segrin and Dillard (1992) find, on the basis of a large body of literature, that depression induces rejection by others.[23] Moreover, depressed individuals show systematic disappointments with their experiences, and they regard themselves as systematically inadequate because they tend to fix their aspirations at such high levels with respect to their own disposition that disappointment inevitably ensues (Legrenzi 1998). Abbey and Andrews (1986) confirm that depression is the main (negative) cause of SWB (see also Pavot et al. 1990). Finally, the vicious circle of depression also emerges from Lane (2000: 157) and from (Argyle 1987: ch. 2).[24]

The reduction of the aspirations for relational goods
The third reaction to disappointment from RGs is a reduction in aspirations for RGs. This reaction both reduces the negative effect on SWB (A10), and decelerates the vicious circle of depression. It can be represented as a reduction in the preferences for RGs, thus changing the SWB function (see above, pp. 273–4).

This reaction seems in fact successful to some extent, in so far as the evidence of the recovery of SWB from around the age of 40 onwards is reliable. More precisely, the phenomenon has been explained as a change of reaction with age, that is, as 'a gradual shift from assimilative [that is, changing life circumstances to personal preferences] to accommodative [that is, adjusting preferences to given situational constraints] mode of coping with increasing age' (Diener et al. 1999: 291; see also Diener and Fujita 1995).

However, some individuals may be particularly able to reduce aspirations and thereby completely prevent depression. They succeed if they are able to cancel any aspiration for RGs and thus prevent disappointment itself. However, this means that they must desensitize themselves to any outcome deriving from personal relationships.[25] Desensitization is known in 'adaptation theory' (see above, p. 267) as a structural form of adaptation (Frederick and Loewenstein 1999), while it has been called 'anaffectivity' in psychopathology when it deals with personal relationships (Fagioli 1971).

In this case, the reduction in the preferences for RGs is substantial, eventually changing the relationship between RGs and economic goods from complementarity to substitutability. As a consequence, materialism has greatly increased, and economic goods become more final, and eventually cease being instrumental in raising RGs.

Therefore, the individuals who deliberately attempt to reduce their aspirations for RGs eventually appear to be more materialist, and thus with lower SWB than others (see above, pp. 269–70).[26] Moreover, radical desensitization to RGs may bring the individual to the dangerous point of losing touch with human values, attempting physical (Frederick and Loewenstein 1999) as well as mental (Fagioli 1971) violence against others and him/herself. However, even if the individual is able to prevent depression and enjoy great SWB from economic goods by substantially reducing his/her aspirations for RGs, s/he cannot avoid, as a product of desensitization, causing more severe disappointments for his/her children than s/he originally experienced.

The full dynamics of the model

In this subsection the model will be completely assembled and recapitulated by means of the flow-chart in Figure 14.1, and its dynamics will be studied. The causal links are represented in the figure by arrows, and the signs of the links appear in the label on the arrow line (see Figure 14.1).

The SWB depends on (1) the consumption of economic goods, on (2) the realization of RGs, and on (3) the aspirations/realization gap of RGs. Economic goods are produced by (4) adopting a technique, and by (5) employing labour time in a proportion L of the individual's fixed (unitary) endowment. RGs are produced/consumed by using the proportion of time left $(1 - L)$. The realization of RGs depends on (8) the consumption of economic goods, and on the disposition towards RGs, both that of the individual (9 and 10) and that of the partners (11 and 12). Note that links (10) and (12) negatively enter determination of the gap.

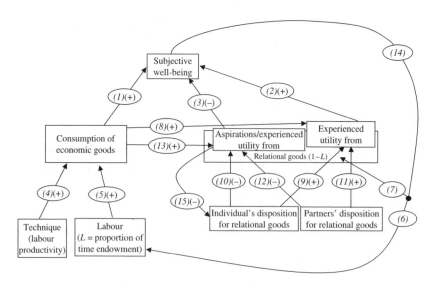

Figure 14.1   Flow chart of the model

The static solution of the model is obtained by temporarily assuming that aspirations for RGs are completely realized, and that productive techniques and all the dispositions towards RGs are given. SWB can thus be maximized, and the time allocation for the individual can be determined (14).

Let us then shock the model with A12 on the excess of aspirations by young individuals. The three reactions (A13–15) thus follow the disappointment. First, the negative effect on SWB (through (3)) induces the individual to reduce the time devoted to RGs $(1 - L)$ (through (7)), and, conversely, to increase working time (L) (through (6)), and hence consumption of economic goods (through (5)). Second, disappointment induces the individual unintentionally to reduce his/her disposition towards RGs (through (15)), which feeds back to the realization of RGs, and to disappointment (through (10)), thus triggering the vicious circle of depression. Third, aspirations for RGs will be slowly reduced until the gap with respect to realizations has been closed, and the vicious circle will be halted. As a result, income and the consumption of economic goods increase, whereas SWB increases less, or even decreases if the reduction of the realization of RGs is sufficiently great.

Finally, explaining the SWB paradox requires the aggregation of individual dynamics both within and across generations. The fact that an individual's aspirations are generally 'excessive' in the first part of the life cycle (see above, p. 276) can explain why average income within generations increases over time, and why SWB on average increases less or decreases.

These dynamics also take place across generations because depressed and anaffective individuals pass on to their children the cumulated effects of their disappointments, that is, they induce greater disappointments.

Technical progress and strengthening effects
Introducing technical progress as an increase in labour productivity strengthens the main result of the model. In fact, the consequent increase in the wage rate enables individuals to consume more economic goods (through (4)), thus widening the gap with the more sluggish dynamic of SWB.

However, the tendency of working time to increase is damped by technical progress. Yet this is consistent with the evidence, which does not always indicate that individual working time is increasing, as witness the European countries (see above, p. 267). When working time is determined by collective agreements, which thus restrict individuals' choice, they will work with greater effort for higher wages and, possibly, with greater stress (Lane 1991: 482–3; 2000: 163–4; Cross 1993). The conclusion of the model should be modified only slightly.

The dynamics of the model are further strengthened by an assumption on the complementarity between the two kinds of goods:

A17 An increase in the consumption of economic goods induces a greater positive effect on aspirations than on realizations of RGs (through (8) and (13)).

This assumption may be justified on the same basis as A12 on excessive aspirations by young individuals. High aspirations for RGs probably imply the prediction of the marked instrumentality of economic goods for improved personal relationships. In this possible case, disappointments are strengthened, which fuels the overall dynamics of the model even further. A new vicious circle is added through (13)–(3)–(14)–(6)–(5).

4. Conclusions

Per capita income has tended to grow in the advanced countries even in the most recent decades, and it still remains the final objective of economic policy. When income rises, in fact, numerous problems disappear or are alleviated. The objective indices of well-being, like equality of income distribution or the number of ecological treaties, appear to be positively and significantly correlated with per capita income (Diener and Suh 1997; Heylighen and Bernheim 2000). However, self-reported SWB and per capita income in the advanced countries are not correlated over time (or across countries). Sociologists and psychologists report increasing signs of serious malaise in the affluent societies. The main examples are increasing rates of mental depression and high suicide rates. The paradox therefore arises that further increases in material wealth do not make people happier, and yet this does not dissuade them from working harder. Economists have also now turned their attention to this problem.

This chapter takes the implications of SWB data seriously and has accordingly sought an explanation for them. Psychological studies, both social and clinical, show that the main determinant of SWB is close personal relationships. This is confirmed by econometric studies, with the consequence that this chapter has moved in this direction rather than towards those more usual for economists, like the effects of unemployment and inflation on SWB (Clark and Oswald 1994; Di Tella et al. 2003). The sluggish or deteriorating SWB over recent decades highlighted by various indices of personal relationships suggests that structural rather than cyclical factors are at work.

A model has therefore been proposed which, although exploratory in character, elaborates the standard labour/leisure model by replacing leisure with time spent on close personal relationships. The latter have been analysed as relational goods which spring from an individual's particular disposition towards others, and they are consumed through human interaction, thus developing emotions and feelings. Unlike economic goods, the well-being obtained from RGs is very difficult to predict. Nor is past experience of much help, because persistent originality within close personal relationships is due to the unconscious component of both dispositions and emotive interactions among people.

The dynamics of the model are triggered by the reactions of individuals to the disappointment caused by overpredicting RGs. The various aspects of this phenomenon have been described by the psychology and other literature. Children and young people are more prone to disappointment, and adjusting to it may take their entire lives. The first reaction, which is mainly intentional, is to substitute RGs with economic goods, being encouraged to do so by parents when young, and then to increase working time and effort. The second reaction, which is mainly emotional, is to reduce one's disposition towards RGs, thus fuelling further disappointment and generating a vicious circle of depression. The third reaction is to reduce aspirations for personal relationships. This enables the person to decelerate and halt the vicious circle of depression – or even avoid it, but at the cost of radical desensitization (that is, a great reduction in the preference for RGs) and a switch from complementarity between economic goods and RGs to their substitutability. Therefore, the SWB resulting from RGs generally deteriorates over the life cycle of individuals, although economic SWB increases.

The SWB paradox can thus be resolved. Unintentional mechanisms play an important role at the individual level, while the transmission of greater disappointments to subsequent generations is the crucial mechanism at the aggregate intergenerational level.

Policy implications can only be outlined here in the form of two general observations. Many resources should be devoted to education and, in particular, to the development of personal relationships among children (see, for example, Blau 1991), whose disposition towards RGs is generally greater. Second, formal knowledge about personal relationships should be increased by interdisciplinary research within and between the social and human sciences, and with special attention paid to the contribution of the arts.

Notes

* I wish to thank the participants at the Milan conference on The Paradoxes of Happiness in Economics, 21–23 March 2003, and in particular Johannes Hirata. My special thanks go to Stefano Bartolini for our intense discussions on the main issues of the chapter.
1. For a discussion of the shortcomings of the various approaches to utility, see Sen (1984, 1985).
2. As an example, Lane (2000: 329) reports, commenting on the data of several studies: 'the mildly depressed have one and a half times the number of disability days as normal people, and the severely depressed have five times as many lost days as the mildly depressed, an escalating curve. For a variety of reasons, including early death from heart attack and especially from suicide, the depressed and the unhappy are likely to have shorter lives than others'.
3. Di Tella et al. (2003) find a positive correlation between self-reported happiness and per capita income for a panel of advanced countries in the short run; however this result is more uncertain for the long run, where, moreover, a negative time trend emerges.
4. Moreover, according to Lester and Yang, if suicide rates are regressed against the unemployment rate and per capita income for European countries, only the latter variable emerges as positively significant.
5. 'Fifteen years ago international bodies would not have even included depression on the list of things to study. . . . Major depression already ranks fourth in the leading causes of the global burden of disease. If projections are correct, within the next 20 years it will have risen to second place' (WHO 2001: 5).
6. Even personal traits are found to be variable from the age of 20 to the age of 60 (Srivastava and John 2003).
7. Diener and Biswas-Diener (2002) show that this result is confirmed even if controlled for income.
8. The maximization of the utility function

$$U = \left(\alpha C^{\frac{\sigma-1}{\sigma}} + \beta H^{\frac{\sigma-1}{\sigma}} \right)^{\frac{\sigma}{\sigma-1}}$$

subject to the time constraint $1 \le L + H$ and income constraint $C \le wL$, where C is consumption, H leisure, L labour, w the wage rate, σ the elasticity of substitution, and productivity (π) is equalized to wages, yields the (starred) solution

$$L^* = \frac{1}{1 + \left(\frac{\beta}{\alpha} \right)^{\sigma} (\pi)^{1-\sigma}}.$$

If $\sigma < 1$, then $(\partial L^*/\partial \pi) < 0$.

9.   The role of the RGs in exchange has been examined by Gui (2000).
10. It will be shown below that the experience of RGs displays cumulative effects. For RGs as durable assets, see Gui (1996).
11. Zajonc (1980: 155) also observes that 'Most of the time, information collected about alternatives serves us less for making a decision than for justifying it afterwards'.
12. The outcome-related case also includes the outcome due to individuals' performance, for example, ability at work.
13. 'Value should be treated as a function in two arguments: the asset position that serves as reference point, and the magnitude of the change (positive or negative) from that reference point' (Kahneman and Tversky 2000: 32).
14. For criticisms of this approach, see Frank (1988: ch. 10), Cowen (1989) and Caplan (2003).
15. A unimodal distribution is implicitly assumed, but if it were multimodal, uncertainty would be even greater.
16. According to Fagioli (1971), at birth the infant reacts to the striking contrast between previous foetal homeostasis and the new stimuli of material reality by making this reality non-existent in his/her mind, and, at the same time, by creating an internal image of his/her previous condition. From this image derives the 'hope to find a breast' and the search for satisfaction in close personal relationships.
17. Easterlin (2001, 2004), as seen above, does not specifically consider any reaction to disappointment – or more precisely any change in the previous behaviour. Instead, the psychology literature offers interesting insights, rather than conclusions, on the effects of disappointments on decision making (Zeelenberg et al. 2000; van Dijk et al. 2003).
18. Sirgy (1998) proposes a theoretical explanation of why materialistic individuals are less happy, but our model in addition explains why some individuals are more materialistic than others. The mechanism of substitution between RGs and economic goods, together with the idea of negative externalities in the production of material goods on non-market goods, like environmental goods and RGs, has been proposed as an alternative explanation for the SWB paradox (Bartolini and Bonatti 2002, 2003).
19. Blanchflower and Oswald (2004) tentatively estimate that, in the US, approximately 100,000 of 1990$ extra per annum would be necessary to 'compensate' an individual for a marital separation, while the corresponding figure for an unemployed man is $60,000. Moreover, it seems that the neutral long-run effect of marriage in the aggregate, after the adaptation has taken place, is an average between a positive effect for some individuals and a *negative* effect for others (Lucas et al. 2003).
20. In fact, according to the analysis thus far, it would predict that more economic goods and less RGs *increase* the level of the after-disappointment SWB, although the level of the before-disappointment level will not usually be reached.
21. This feedback enters the realization of RGs but not the decision on RGs. These properties of endogeneous but unaware information in the decision process are also considered by Benabou and Tirole (2006), although applied to the material world, rather than to RGs. They propose a similar but different solution of the SWB paradox, by arguing that disappointment on optimistic beliefs vanishes because individuals unconsciously repress unfavourable information. However, besides the curious conclusion that stagnant well-being is due to optimistic individuals, it is not clear why these individuals repeatedly repress information on the material world without shifting their attention to the domain of personal relationships.
22. Systematic insufficient learning is also explained by a typical human bias called 'projection bias in predicting future utility' (Kahneman and Snell 1992; Rabin 1998; Loewenstein and Schkade 1999; Loewenstein et al. 2003). In this case, however, the bias lies in the human disposition to be conservative, and not in accessibility of information.
23. By contrast, a happy disposition seems to increase investment in vigorous, outwardly directed action. Happy people are more disposed to relate with others, and more generous (Argyle 1987: ch. 7). Moreover, the ability of individuals to organize experiences congruent with their aspirations appears to be particularly influenced by happiness (Diener et al. 1999: 285).

24. A virtuous circle may also arise for those individuals who mainly experience elations from relational goods. This condition may explain the apparent increasing returns from relational goods, as conjectured by Frank (1997) and Lane (2000: ch. 5).
25. Argyle (1987: 186–7), in arguing for the 'levelling off of emotions' with age, reports some data on the reduction of emotions, and in particular the reduction of *positive* emotions.
26. A cross-country econometric study by Helliwell (2003) shows that the lack of trust in others is negatively and significantly correlated with SWB.

References

Abbey, A. and F.M. Andrews (1986), 'Modeling the psychological determinants of quality of life', in F.M. Andrews (ed.), *Research on the Quality of Life*, Ann Arbor, MI: University of Michigan Press, 85–115.
Argyle, M. (1987), *The Psychology of Happiness*, London: Routledge.
Argyle, M. (1999), 'Causes and correlates of happiness', in D. Kahneman, E. Diener and N. Schwarz (eds), *Well-being: The Foundations of Hedonic Psychology*, New York: Russell Sage Foundation, 353–73.
Bartolini, L. and L. Bonatti (2002), 'Environmental and social degradation as the engine of economic growth', *Ecological Economics*, **41**, 1–16.
Bartolini, L. and L. Bonatti (2003), 'Endogenous growth and negative externalities', *Journal of Economics*, **79**, 123–44.
Baumeister, R.F. and M.R. Leary (1995), 'The need to belong: desire for interpersonal attachments as a fundamental human motivation', *Psychological Bulletin*, **117** (3), 497–529.
Becker, G.S. (1996), *Accounting for Tastes*, Cambridge, MA and London: Harvard University Press.
Belk, R.W. (1985), 'Materialism: trait aspects of living in the material world', *Journal of Consumer Research*, **12**, 265–80.
Belk, R.W. and R. Pollay (1985), 'Images of ourselves: the good life in twentieth century advertising', *Journal of Consumer Research*, **11**, 887–97.
Bell, D.E. (1985), 'Disappointment in decision making under uncertainty', *Operations Research*, **33** (1), 1–27.
Benabou, R. and J. Tirole (2006), 'Belief in a just world and redistributive politics', *The Quarterly Journal of Economics*, **121** (2), May.
Berenbaum, H., C. Raghavan, H.-N. Le, L. Vernon and J. Gomez (1999), 'Disturbances in emotions', in Kahneman et al. (eds), 267–87.
Blanchflower, D.G. and A.J. Oswald (2004), 'Well-being over time in Britain and the US', *Journal of Public Economics*, **88** (7–8), 1359–86.
Blau, D.M. (1991) (ed.), *The Economics of Child Care*, New York: Russell Sage Foundation.
Bluestone, B. and S. Rose (2000), 'The enigma of working time trend', in L. Golden and D.M. Figart (eds), *Working Time: International Trends, Theory and Policy Perspectives*, London and New York: Routledge, 21–37.
Boncinelli, E. (2002), *Io sono, tu sei: l'identità e la differenza negli uomini e in natura*, Milan: Mondadori.
Brickman, P., D. Coates and R. Janoff-Bulman (1978), 'Lottery winners and accident victims: is happiness relative?', *Journal of Personality and Social Psychology*, **36**, 917–27.
Bruni, L. (2000), 'Ego facing alter: how economists have depicted human interaction', *Annals of Public and Cooperative Economics*, **71** (2), 285–313.
Campbell, A., P.E. Converse and W.L. Rodgers (1976), *The Quality of American Life*, New York: Russell Sage Foundation.
Caplan, B. (2003), 'Stigler–Becker versus Myers–Briggs?', *Journal of Economic Behavior and Organization*, **50**, 391–405.
Cauley, J. and T. Sandler (1980), 'A general theory of interpersonal exchange', *Public Choice*, **37**, 587–606.
Chishti, P., D.H. Stone, P. Corcoran, E. Williamson and E. Petridou (2003), 'Suicide mortality in the European Union', *European Journal of Public Health*, **13**, 108–14.

Clark, A.E. and A.J. Oswald (1994), 'Unhappiness and unemployment', *Economic Journal*, **104** (424), 648–59.

Clark, M.S. and I. Brissette (2003), 'Two types of relationship closeness and their influence on people's emotional lives', in R.J. Davidson, K.R. Scherer and H.H. Goldsmith (eds), *Handbook of Affective Sciences*, Oxford: Oxford University Press, 824–35.

Cooper, B., C. Garcia-Penalosa and P. Funk (2001), 'Status effects and negative utility growth', *Economic Journal*, **111** (473), 642–65.

Corneo, G and O. Jeanne (2001), 'On relative-wealth effects and long-run growth', *Research in Economics*, **55** (4), 349–58.

Costa, P.T. (1994), 'Traits through time, or the stability of personality', Paper presented at the meeting of the American Psychological Association, Los Angeles, 12–16 August.

Costa, P.T., R.R. McRae and A.B. Zonderman (1987), 'Environmental and dispositional influences on well-being', *British Journal of Psychology*, **78**, 299–306.

Cowen, T. (1989), 'Are all tastes constant and identical?', *Journal of Economic Behavior and Organization*, **11** (1), 127–35.

Cross, G. (1993), *Time and Money: The Making Of Consumer Culture*, London: Routledge.

Damasio, A.R. (1994), *Descartes' Error: Emotion, Reason and the Human Brain*, New York: Avon Books.

Damasio, A.R. (1999), *The Feeling of What Happens: Body and Emotion in the Making of Consciousness*, New York: Harcourt, Brace & Jovanovich.

Di Tella, R., R.J. MacCulloch and A.J. Oswald (2003), 'The measurement of happiness', *Review of Economics and Statistics*, **85** (4), 809–27.

Diener, E. (1996), 'Traits can be powerful, but are not enough: lessons from subjective well-being', *Journal of Research in Personality*, **30** (3), 389–99.

Diener, E. and R. Biswas-Diener (2002), 'Will money increase subjective well-being?', *Social Indicators Research*, **57** (2), 119–69.

Diener, E. and F. Fujita (1995), 'Resources, personal strivings, and subjective well-being', *Journal of Personality and Social Psychology*, **68** (5), 926–35.

Diener, E. and E.M. Suh (1997), 'Measuring quality of life: economic, social and subjective indicators', *Social Indicators Research*, **40**, 187–216.

Diener, E., E.M. Suh, R.E. Lucas and H.I. Smith (1999), 'Subjective well-being: three decades of progress', *Psychological Bulletin*, **125** (2), 276–302.

Donati, P. (1991), 'Il ruolo delle iniziative di "terzo sistema" nelle politiche sociali', in C. Borzaga (ed.), *Il terzo sistema: una nuova dimensione della complessità sociale*, Padua: F. Zancan, 67–82.

Duesenberry, J. (1949), *Income, Saving, and the Theory of Consumer Behavior*, Cambridge, MA: Harvard University Press.

Easterlin, R.A. (1974), 'Does economic growth improve the human lot? Some empirical evidence', in P.A. David and W. Reder (eds), *Nations and Households in Economic Growth: Essays in Honor of Moses Abramovitz*, New York: Academic Press, 89–125.

Easterlin, R.A. (2001), 'Income and happiness: towards a unified theory', *Economic Journal*, **111**, 465–84.

Easterlin, R.A. (2005), 'Building a better theory of wellbeing', in L. Bruni and P.L. Porta (eds) (2005), *Economics and Happiness*, Oxford: Oxford University Press.

Fagioli, M. (1971), *Istinto di morte e conoscenza*, 10th edn 2002, Rome: Nuove Edizioni Romane (partially translated in www.nuoveedizioniromane.it/catalogo/libri_mf1.html).

Frank, R. (1985), 'The demand for unobservable and other nonpositional goods', *American Economic Journal*, **75**, 101–16.

Frank, R. (1988), *Passions within Reasons: The Strategic Role of the Emotions*, New York: Norton.

Frank, R. (1997), 'The frame of reference as a public good', *Economic Journal*, **107**, 1832–47.

Frederick, S. and G. Loewenstein (1999), 'Hedonic adaptation', in Kahneman et al. (eds), 302–29.

Frey, B.S. and A. Stutzer (2002), *Happiness and Economics: How the Economy and Institutions Affect Well-being*, Princeton, NJ: Princeton University Press.

Golden, L. (1998), 'Working-time policy, hours determination, and regulatory reforms in the US and other industrialized countries', *International Review of Comparative Public Policy*, **10**, 51–75.

Goldsmith, H.H. and J.J. Campos (1986), 'Fundamental issues in the study of early temperament', in M.E. Lamb, A.L. Brown and B. Rogoff (eds), *Advances in Developmental Psychology*, Hillsdale, NJ: Erlbaum, 231–83.

Gui, B. (1994), 'Interpersonal relations: a disregarded theme in the debate on ethics and economics', in A. Lewis and K.E. Warneryd (eds), *Ethics and Economic Affairs*, London: Routledge, 251–63.

Gui, B. (1996), 'On "relational goods": strategic implications of investment in relationships', *International Journal of Social Economics*, **23** (10/11), 260–78.

Gui, B. (2000), 'Beyond transaction: on the interpersonal dimension of economic reality', *Annals of Public and Cooperative Economics*, **71** (2), 139–68.

Gui, B. (2001), 'Economic interactions as encounters', Dipartimento di Scienze Economiche, Padua, Italy, mimeo.

Hanoch, Y. (2002), 'The effects of emotions on bounded rationality: a comment on Kaufman', *Journal of Economic Behavior and Organization*, **49**, 131–5.

Headey, B. and A. Wearing (1989), 'Personality, life events, and subjective well-being', *Journal of Personality and Social Psychology*, **57** (4), 731–9.

Helliwell, J.F. (2003), 'How's life? Combining individual and national variables to explain subjective well-being', *Economic Modelling*, **20** (2), 331–60.

Helson, H. (1964), *Adaptation-level Theory*, New York: Harper.

Heylighen, F. and J. Bernheim (2000), 'Global progress I: empirical evidence for ongoing increase in quality-of-life', *Journal of Happiness Studies*, **1** (3), 323–49.

Hirsch, F. (1976), *Social Limits to Growth*, Cambridge, MA: Harvard University Press.

Huang W.-C. (1996), 'Religion, culture, economic and sociological correlates of suicide rates', *Applied Economics Letters*, **3**, 779–82.

Inglehart, R. (1990), *Cultural Shift in Advanced Industrial Society*, Princeton, NJ: Princeton University Press.

Inman J.J., J.S. Dyer and J. Jia (1997), 'A generalised utility model of disappointment and regret effects on post-choice evaluation', *Marketing Science*, **16** (2), 97–111.

Institute of Medicine (2002), *Reducing Suicide: A National Imperative*, Washington, DC: National Academic Press.

Jungeilges, J. and G. Kirchgaessner (2002), 'Economic welfare, civil liberty, and suicide', *Journal of Socio-economics*, **31**, 215–31.

Kahneman, D. (2000a), 'New challenges to the rationality assumption', in D. Kahneman and A. Tversky (eds), *Choices, Values, and Frames*, Cambridge, New York and Melbourne: Cambridge University Press; New York: Russell Sage Foundation, 758–74.

Kahneman, D. (2000b), 'Expected utility and objective happiness', in D. Kahneman and A. Tversky (eds), *Choices, Values, and Frames*, Cambridge, New York and Melbourne: Cambridge University Press; New York: Russell Sage Foundation, 673–92.

Kahneman, D., E. Diener and N. Schwarz (1999) (eds), *Well-being: The Foundations of Hedonic Psychology*, New York: Russell Sage Foundation.

Kahneman, D. and J. Snell (1992), 'Predicting a changing taste: do people know what they will like?', *Journal of Behavioral Decision Making*, **5**, 187–200.

Kahneman, D. and A. Tversky (2000), 'Prospect theory: an analysis of decision under risk', in D. Kahneman and A. Tversky (eds), *Choices, Values, and Frames*, Cambridge, New York and Melbourne: Cambridge University Press; New York: Russell Sage Foundation, 17–43.

Kahneman, D., P.P. Wakker and R. Sarin (1997), 'Back to Bentham? Explorations of Experienced Utility', *Quarterly Journal of Economics*, **112**, 375–405.

Kasser, T. (2000), 'Two versions of the American dream: which goals and values make for a high quality of life?', in E. Diener and D.R. Rahtz (eds), *Advances in Quality of Life Theory and Research*, Kluwer: Dordrecht, 3–12.

Kasser, T. and R.M. Ryan (2001), 'Be careful what you wish for: optimal functioning and the relative attainment of intrinsic and extrinsic goals', *Personality and Social Psychology Bulletin*, **22**, 280–87.

Kaufman, B.E. (1999), 'Emotional arousal as a source of bounded rationality', *Journal of Economic Behavior and Organization*, **38**, 135–44.

Kelley, H.H. (1986), 'Personal relationships', in R. Gilmour and S. Duck (eds), *The Emerging Field of Personal Relationships*, Hillsdale, NJ: Lawrence Erlbaum, 3–13.

Kenny, C. (1999), 'Does growth cause happiness, or does happiness cause growth?', *Kyklos*, **52** (1), 3–25.

Lane, R.E. (1991), *The Market Experience*, Cambridge and New York: Cambridge University Press.

Lane, R.E. (2000), *The Loss of Happiness in Market Democracies*, New Haven, CT and London: Yale University Press.

Layard, P.R.G. (1980), 'Human satisfaction and public policy', *Economic Journal*, **90**, 737–50.

Layard, P.R.G. (2003), 'Happiness has social clue?', Lionel Robbins Memorial Lectures, 3–5 March, London School of Economics.

LeDoux, J. (1996), *The Emotional Brain. The Mysterious Underpinnings of Emotional Life*, New York: Simon & Schuster.

LeDoux, J. (2002), *Il sé sinaptico: come il nostro cervello ci fa diventare quelli che siamo*, Milan: Cortina.

Legrenzi, P. (1998), *La felicità*, Bologna: Mulino.

Lehndorff, S. (2000), 'Working time reduction in the EU', in L. Golden and D.M. Figart (eds), *Working Time: International Trends, Theory and Policy Perspectives*, London and New York: Routledge, 38–56.

Lester, D. and B. Yang (1997), *The Economy and Suicide: Economic Perspectives on Suicide*, Commack, NY: Nova Science.

Levi, F., C. La Vecchia and B. Saraceno (2003), 'Global suicide rates', *European Journal of Public Health*, **13**, 97–8.

Loewenstein, G., T. O'Donoghue and M. Rabin (2003), 'Projection bias in predicting future utility', *Quarterly Journal of Economics*, **118** (4), 1209–48.

Loewenstein, G. and D. Schkade (1999), 'Wouldn't it be nice? Predicting future feelings', in Kahneman et al. (eds), 85–105.

Looms, G. and R. Sugden (1986), 'Disappointment and dynamic consistency in choice under uncertainty', *Review of Economic Studies*, **53**, 271–82.

Lucas, R.E., A.E. Clark, Y. Georgellis and E. Diener (2003), 'Reexamining adaptation and the set point model of happiness: reactions to changes in marital status', *Journal of Personality and Social Psychology*, **84** (3), 527–39.

Lykken, D. and A. Tellegen (1996), 'Happiness is a stochastic phenomenon', *Psychological Science*, **7**, 186–9.

Michalos, A.C. (1985), 'Multiple discrepancies theory', *Social Indicators Research*, **16**, 347–413.

Morris, W.M. (1999), 'The mood system', in Kahneman et al. (eds), 169–89.

Myers, D.G. (1993), *The Pursuit of Happiness*, New York: Avon.

Myers, D.G. (1999), 'Close relationships and quality of life', in Kahneman et al. (eds), 374–91.

Ng, Y.K. (1975), 'Non-economic activities, indirect externalities, and third-best policies', *Kyklos*, **28** (3), 507–25.

Ng, Y.K. (1978), 'Economic growth and social welfare: the need for a complete study of happiness', *Kyklos*, **31**, 575–87.

Ng, Y.K. (2003), 'From preference to happiness: toward a more complete welfare economics', *Social Choice and Welfare*, **20** (2), 307–50.

Oswald, A.J. (1997), 'Happiness and economic performance', *Economic Journal*, **107**, 1815–31.

Pavot, W., E. Diener and F. Fujita (1990), 'Extroversion and happiness', *Personality and Individual Differences*, **11**, 1299–306.

Peplau, L.A. and D. Perlman (1982) (eds), *Loneliness*, New York: Wiley.

Pritchard, C. and A. Butler (2003), 'A comparative study of children and adult homicide rates in the US and the major western countries 1974–1999', *Journal of Family Violence*, **18** (6), 341–50.

Pugno, M. (2004), 'Razionalità e motivazioni affettive: nuove idee dalla neurobiologia e psichiatria per la teoria economica?' (Rationality and affective motivation: new ideas from neurobiology and psychiatry for economic theory?), Discussion Paper, no. 1, Department of Economics, University of Trento.

Rabin, M. (1998), 'Psychology and economics', *Journal of Economic Literature*, **36** (1), 11–46.
Richins, M.L. (1994), 'Special possession and expression of material values', *Journal of Consumer Research*, **21**, 522–33.
Richins, M.L. and S. Dawson (1992), 'A consumer values orientation for materialism and its measurements: scale development and validation', *Journal of Consumer Research*, **19**, 303–16.
Rindfleisch, A., J.E. Burroughs and F. Denton (1997), 'Family structure, materialism, and compulsive consumption', *Journal of Consumer Research*, **23** (4), 312–25.
Santos, C. (2004), 'Understanding well-being: a new look at the impact of adaptive hedonic responses', University College London, mimeo.
Schor, J. (1992), *The Overworked American: The Unexpected Decline of Leisure*, New York: Basic Books.
Scitovsky, T. (1976), *The Joyless Economy*, Oxford and New York: Oxford University Press.
Segrin, C., and J.P. Dillard (1992), 'The interactional theory of depression: a meta-analysis of the research literature', *Journal of Social and Clinical Psychology*, **11** (1), 43–70.
Sen, A. (1984), 'The living standard', *Oxford Economic Papers*, **36** Supplement, 74–90.
Sen, A. (1985), *Commodities and Capabilities*, Amsterdam: North-Holland.
Siegel, D.J. (1999), *The Developing Mind: toward a Neurobiology of Interpersonal Experience*, New York: Guilford.
Sirgy, M.J. (1998), 'Materialism and quality of life', *Social Indicators Research*, **43**, 227–60.
Srivastava, S. and O.P. John (2003), 'Development of personality in early and middle adulthood: set like plaster or persistent change?', *Journal of Personality and Social Psychology*, **84** (5), 1041–53.
Stern, D. (1985), *The Interpersonal World of the Infant*, New York: Basic Books.
Sugden, R. (2002), 'Beyond sympathy and empathy: Adam Smith's concept of fellow-feeling', *Economics and Philosophy*, **18** (1) 63–87.
Uhlaner, C.J. (1989), 'Relational goods and participation: incorporating sociability into theory of rational action', *Public Choice*, **62**, 253–85.
van Dijk, W.W. and M. Zeelenberg (2002), 'What do we talk about when we talk about disappointment?', *Cognition and Emotion*, **16** (6), 787–807.
van Dijk, W.W., M. Zeelenberg and J. Van der Pligt (2003), 'Blessed are those who expect nothing: lowering expectations as a way of avoiding disappointment', *Journal of Economic Psychology*, **24**, 506–16.
van Hemert, D.A., F.J.R. van de Vijver and Y.H. Poortinga (2002), 'The Beck Depression Inventory as a measure of subjective well-being: a cross national study', *Journal of Happiness Studies*, **3**, 257–86.
Veenhoven, R. (1994), 'World databases of happiness: correlates of happiness', Erasmus University, Rotterdam.
Veenhoven, R. (1995), 'The cross-national pattern of happiness', *Social Indicators Research*, **43**, 33–86.
World Health Organization (WHO) (2001), *The WHO Report 2001: Mental Health, New Understanding, New Hope*, Geneva: WHO.
Zajonc, R.B. (1980), 'Feeling and thinking', *American Psychologist*, February, 151–75.
Zamagni, S. (1999), 'Social paradoxes of growth and civil economy', in G. Gandolfo and F. Marzano (eds), *Economic Theory and Social Justice*, London: Macmillan, 212–36.
Zeelenberg M., W.W van Dijk, A.S.R. Manstead and J. Van der Pligt (2000), 'On bad decisions and disconfirmed expectancies: the psychology of regret and disappointment', *Cognition and Emotion*, **14** (4), 521–41.

15 The not-so-fragile fragility of goodness: the responsive quality of fiduciary relationships

*Vittorio Pelligra**

This word 'fides', means 'rope' which binds and links us together. (A. Genovesi 1770 [1924: 148])

The advantage of humankind of being able to trust one another, penetrates into every crevice and cranny of human life: the economical is perhaps the smallest part of it, yet even this is incalculable. (J.S. Mill 1848: 131)

1. Introduction

In 1986, Martha Nussbaum developed her well-known argument of the so-called 'fragility of goodness' (Nussbaum 1986). According to her reading of Aristotle's theory of *eudaimonia* (meaning 'human flourishing', an enlarged view of 'happiness'), the pursuit of the good life, which ultimately leads to happiness, is doomed to be subject to the will of fate. Since, in fact, one of the constitutive elements of such an enterprise is the possibility of building meaningful interpersonal relationships, and the quality of such relationships is necessarily a function of others' behaviour and such a behaviour is, in turn, out of the control of the subject itself, our own happiness is ultimately in others' hands. That is one of the reasons why our own happiness has always been so strongly perceived as related to luck.

However, a critical point in Nussbaum's argument is that, while *ego* can only decide to open his/her life to the influence of *alter* before knowing whether such an influence will be positive or negative, that is to expose him/herself to the risk of opportunism, at the same time, it is implicitly assumed that such trustful behaviour does not change in any respect the quality of the relationship, that is that *alter's* preferences are stable over time and unresponsive to *ego's* own actions.

In this chapter I shall challenge such an assumption by arguing that most of the time real people are indeed responsive to others' behaviour and that is particularly evident in the domain of fiduciary relationships. The basic idea is that trustful actions tend to elicit trustworthy responses. That mechanism finds its roots in what Smith (1759 [1976]) defined as an innate desire for the good opinion of other, which produces a certain tendency to fulfil certain expectations that a given class of behaviours (that is, trustfulness) may credibly signal. I shall call such a mechanism 'trust responsiveness', and this chapter will examine the results of an experiment designed to test its empirical relevance.

Section 2 discusses the relationship between trust and happiness in relation to the problem of the agent's responsiveness. The 'phenomenon of trust' and the relevant empirical evidence is, then, framed in game-theoretical terms in Section 3. From that discussion it will emerge how such evidence may in principle be accounted for by many different theories, besides trust responsiveness: altruism, inequity aversion, team thinking and reciprocity (Section 4). The experimental design described in Sections 5–8 has been conceived to discriminate between the observational implications of the various theories. The data are reported and discussed in Sections 9 and 10, and Section 11 concludes.

2. Happiness and Trust

The relation that binds happiness and trust is very well expressed by Bernard Williams: 'What is great is fragile and what is necessary may well be destructive' (1981: 202). If we have to trust Aristotle, happiness springs from a 'good life' and such a good life has among its most important ingredients others' friendship. A happy person is a person with friends, because a genuine friendship (*philia*) is the cradle of our own virtues. But, as we know, a meaningful interpersonal relationship includes freedom of action and the impossibility of controlling others' actions, some of which could, therefore, turn out to be harmful for the individual, thus thwarting the person's aspiration to happiness.

Thus arises the central paradox of happiness: happiness is a social product but by living a social life the individual is exposed to the, not always beneficial, will of others.[1]

This paradox represents the essence of the Greek tragedy tradition. Consider, for example, Sophocles' *Antigone*. In the darkest hour of the story, near the end, when the action (read: the human condition) seems to be paralysed, a feeble ray of hope comes from an old blind man, Tiresia, and his young friend. They are the only moving actors on the scene, even though their moving appears to be contrary to any logic because the youth does not know where to go and the old man does not know how. The latter needs the youth's eyes and the former needs the old man's experience. They can only survive because of their mutual trust. Therein lies an intimation of the understanding of the paradox of happiness if we try to unfold the dynamics of such an interaction.

But how can reciprocal trust constitute the way out of the paradox when it is well known that the trust may be painfully betrayed? And in fact, this is why Nussbaum (1986) considers that a good and happy life is within reach, but ultimately, extremely fragile. Her argument rests on an implicit assumption of agents' preferences, namely that agents' preferences are stable and unresponsive. Behind such an assumption there is the (implicit, I think) acceptance that the mechanism that generates people's behaviour is the same in both parametric and strategic choice problems, which is, on closer scrutiny, the same core assumption of classical game theory.

However, such an assumption is empirically ungrounded and I shall challenge it by considering the implications of the possibility that agents' preferences are responsive, that is, endogenously generated in an interpersonal relationship. This implies that choices in a parametric or a strategic environment are guided by different motivational mechanisms.

Before expanding that idea further I shall first consider in more formal terms the relationship between Tiresia and his young friend, which I take as an icon of the problem of trust.

3.   The semantics of trust

A brief glance at the recent literature on the topic of trust, shows that there is a heterogeneity of meanings and usages of the terms 'trust', 'trustful' and 'trustworthy'. My particular treatment of the term 'trust' will essentially be a concept that implies the following elements characterizing the behaviours open to agents involved in a fiduciary interaction:

1.   potential negative consequences;
2.   risk of opportunism; and
3.   lack of control.

Consider the relationship between the old blind man, Tiresia, and the young boy in *Antigone*. That situation possesses all three elements mentioned above. The relationship is symmetric and by entering into it, each of the agents exposes himself to the risk of opportunistic behaviour which emerges because of the imperfect control that can be exerted on each other's actions. The potential negative consequences refers to the fact that entering a trustful action may lead to outcomes both better and worse than those attainable in isolation. All these elements are summarized in the 'trust game' (TG) depicted in Figure 15.1:

- point 1 is described by $b < a$;
- point 2 depends on $e > f$; and
- point 3 is obtained by modelling the game as a non-cooperative, two-stage sequential game.

Player A chooses first either L or R; in choosing L, players get a payoff pair equal to (a, d). But if A chooses R, the choice passes to B, who, in turn,

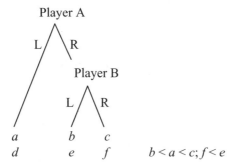

Figure 15.1   The trust game: the basic elements of a trusting interaction

can choose either L or R. In the first case B gets e and A, b; in the second case B gets f and A gets c.

Given such a payoff matrix and the relations between its elements, the game-theoretical advice for a rational course of action will be for A to choose L and stop the game there. A's reasoning goes backward as follows: 'If I play R, B will play L (because by doing so, B gets $e>f$) and I would get b which is the worst of all possible outcomes [from A's perspective]; therefore in playing L, if not c, at least I can get a, which is better than b'.

Although A's preferred outcome in this game would be that described by (c, f), such a situation is not an equilibrium outcome and, in fact, it is achievable only when both player A deviates from his/her individually rational course of action L choosing R, and player B renounces his/her rational strategy L, by opting for R. On the contrary, the rational strategy that emerges by backward induction is described by the concept of subgame perfect Nash equilibrium[2] which yields the outcome (a, d).

If an out-of-equilibrium pair of strategies like (R, R) is selected, we would say that A trusts B (not to be opportunistic) and that, on the other side, B repays such a trust by behaving in a non-opportunistic way.

The definitional problem at this stage can be confronted only at a behavioural level. It is important to give a clear characterization of trustful and trustworthy behaviours and that is only possible by referring to observational considerations.

Formally, subject A's behaviour is *trustful* when: (i) in a situation that can be modelled as a TG; and (ii) player A plays R. Correspondingly B's behaviour is *trustworthy* when: (i) and (ii) apply, and (iii) player B plays R.

The strategies described in (ii) and (iii) can be interpreted, respectively, as trustful and trustworthy because the former implies that player A exposes him/herself to the risk of B's opportunistic behaviour, and the latter implies that player B's choice attributes to A, a payoff greater than he/she would have got by playing an equilibrium strategy.

4.   Theory and evidence

In situations like that described by the trust game, standard game theory suggests a course of action that leads to suboptimal outcomes. Nevertheless, in a number of experimental situations[3] a different pattern of behaviour emerges. A significant number of As, in fact, prefer to give the move to the Bs by playing R, and a significant number of Bs resist the temptation of the opportunistic choice (L) by playing R. Such a combination of behaviours (A chooses R and B chooses R) may be described as trustful and trustworthy (T&T). These 'anomalous' behaviours cannot be satisfactorily accounted for by traditional theories[4] based on self-interest, the role of reputation, bounded rationality, or on the re-description (cognitive or revealed preferences type) of the payoffs in the game.

In what follows I shall focus on models that assume that players are motivated not only by their self-interest but also by some form of other-regarding considerations. In some of the models such additional elements are introduced into an extended utility function that the players aim at maximizing in the usual way. Such models may be defined as 'consequentialist', since in fact, players' choices are orientated only by their consequences. On the other hand, other models develop new solution concepts that formalize an agent actuated not only by the outcomes of his/her choices but also by the way such consequences are attained. These models can thus be defined as 'procedural'. In the former class are models based on the idea of altruism and inequity aversion, while the latter are built around the ideas of reciprocity, team thinking and trust responsiveness. These models are relevant for the present discussion because, in one way or another, they are all able to rationalize a sequence of T&T behaviours.

Tiresia's and his young friend's cooperative behaviour may arise for a number of reasons: for instance, from their both being altruists and each concerned about the other's welfare. But they may also be bound together by their sense of reciprocity: because one is being kind to the other, the latter reciprocates and is kind in turn. A third explanation may be based on the agents' taste for equality. They are both in need and aim at improving their condition but this is done without, contextually, increasing the 'distance' between them. A fourth possibility may be that the two agents tend to identify themselves as a team and to act according to a plan that the team wants to pursue. A fifth and final explanation for the two agents' behaviour relies on the effect that a manifest reliance may exert in motivating trustworthiness. Indeed, it is likely that many more alternative explanations can be developed to rationalize Tiresia's and his friend's conduct, but I shall confine my discussion to the fifth, because this has already been formalized in well-known game-theoretical models.

My manifest preference is for the principle of trust responsiveness, which I think provides the most satisfactory picture of what is going on between the two characters *in Antigone* and in general in any trusting relationship. A first reason lies in the fact that, as empirically established (Falk and Fischbacher 1999), people are interested not only in the outcome of their choices, but also in the process chosen to produce certain consequences. This consideration leads us to favour the procedural theories over the consequentialist ones. Second, I suspect that Tiresia's and his friend's behaviour is motivated by something more pristine and unconditional, rather than mere reciprocity or team membership. While these reasons may be somehow plausible, it is ultimately an empirical issue. All five theories are, in fact, empirically equivalent: they are all consistent with observing both A and B playing R in a trust game.

My next step will be to develop a test capable of discriminating between all the alternative behavioural principles, and to do that I shall first briefly sketch the arguments underlying each of the models.

Altruism

In the first model I consider here, the agent is motivated by altruistic concerns. An altruistic subject can be defined as one whose utility increases as others' welfare[5] increases, and decreases as others' welfare decreases. Since altruistic agents are self-centred agents, such variations are usually weighted in a way that *ego* attributes more importance to his/her own utility relative to that of *alter*.

In formalizing that principle I follow Margolis (1982), who simply introduces an other-regarding factor into the traditional utility function. This allows me to draw observable and testable predictions.[6]

In a TG, if B is motivated strongly enough by altruism, then it could be rational for him/her to resist the opportunistic choice of L and play R. In so doing, in fact, B will benefit from an indirect increase in utility deriving from the increase of A's utility. With such an altruistic attitude, it becomes rational for A to be trustful by playing R.

It is worth noting that such a class of models is based on a purely forward-looking logic, as players are motivated exclusively by the consequences their actions would produce and not by others' choice.

Inequity aversion

Another class of theories that can be used to explain the evidence at issue is based on the idea of inequity aversion (Fehr and Schmidt 1999; Bolton and Ockenfels 2000). Agents are inequity averse when they are endowed with a taste for distributional fairness in such a way that they aim both at maximizing their payoff and minimizing the difference between their own payoff and those of the other agents. The underlying idea is that people dislike being part of an unequal distribution of wealth but, in such an unequal distribution, they dislike even more being in a disadvantageous position rather than in an advantageous one.

This kind of theory can explain the choice of (R, R) in games like the TG, provided that the weight attached to inequity considerations is strong enough, because player B is motivated to play R in order to determine a situation (c, f) which is less unequal than the alternative one (b, e).

As for theories of altruism, in inequity aversion-based theories, agents are forward looking, that is, they are motivated exclusively by the features of the outcomes that their action could determine.

Team thinking

While the two classes of theories based on altruism and inequity aversion described above represent a sophistication of the traditional theory of games, but ultimately are based on minor departures from its basic structure, the following theories discharge some of the core assumptions of traditional game theory. While the two former principles affect subjects' preference orderings, but the agents continue to be instrumentally rational and choose actions that bring about their most preferred outcome, switching to team thinking implies for the subjects a kind of preference and reasoning that cannot be described within the traditional framework of instrumental rationality. In particular, what is radically different is the connection existing between preferences and actions, that is, the way the former determine the latter.

This theory embodies a model of agents that perceive themselves as members of a team.[7] Such membership implies the existence of particular kinds of preferences, namely 'team preferences' (Sugden 2000). While altruism and other theories affect the preference formation process, the theories of team thinking postulate a different, non-instrumentally rational, way of satisfying team preferences.

In these theories (Sugden 1993; Bacharach 1999), agents choose a course of action that, although it may appear as non-instrumentally rational, constitutes, nevertheless, 'their part' in satisfying the preferences of the group they identify with. In these theories the agent, in fact, undertakes a course of action that despite not being individually optimal, represents his/her part in the combination of actions that is best for the team, provided that all the other members follow the same reasoning style.

The most crucial and distinctive feature of team-thinking reasoning is how utility determines individual action. While agents are instrumentally rational when they pursue actions that lead to the maximization of their individual utility, team thinkers are considered rational when they choose actions that are part of the team plan, despite their property of leading to individually optimal outcomes. This is somehow puzzling, but for a team thinker, collective good outcomes are reasons for actions by the team, but not reasons for actions by individual agents; for individual agents, they are contingent consequences of good plans.

Given such a criterion of rationality we may expect that if in the TG the two players A and B perceive themselves as belonging to the same group, what will become crucial therefore, is no longer the maximization of the individual utility of each subject but choosing the actions that are perceived as a part of the team plan to achieve the team objective. If the team objective is to gain as much as it can,[8] in a 2-player game like the TG, the goal of the team could be operationalized as the maximization of an increasing and symmetric function of the payoffs of the two players.[9] For the members of a team the strategies (R, R) are the best choice because the B player also contributes to the team objective, in the same way as an out-of-condition football player would choose to relinquish his/her place in the final match to a team-mate who is in better shape.

Reciprocity

Another well-known class of theories that can be used as an explanation of the phenomenon of trust is that based on the idea of reciprocity. Such theories incorporate the idea that agents are willing to sacrifice part of their material wealth in order to be kind to those who have shown kindness to them and to punish those who have been mean.

Reciprocity has been formalized in different ways. We shall focus here on the pioneering work of Matthew Rabin (1993). In Rabin's model, payoffs depend not only on players' actions, as in the classical theory, but also on players' intentions, beliefs and emotions. The games where such factors affect players' behaviour are defined as psychological games.

Consider two players, A and B. In a psychological game, A's *ex ante* utility depends not only on what A does and what A believes B will do, but also on A's belief about B's belief about what A will do. Rabin uses such a framework to introduce the idea of 'reciprocating fairness' in such a way that players evaluate other players' choices not only on the basis of the payoffs they lead to, but also on the basis of the 'degree of kindness' incorporated in, or manifested by, certain choices. Such a degree of kindness is measured using as a benchmark a particular value called an 'equitable payoff'. When the payoff A actually gets by playing his/her equilibrium strategy is higher (lower) than the equitable payoff, B has been kind (mean) towards A.

In this framework players' responses depend, via the reciprocating kindness assumption, on the intentions incorporated in each choice, in the sense that the same choice can be assessed (eliciting different responses) depending on the motives or intentions that underlie it. According to Rabin, 'motives can be inferred from a player's choice of strategy from among those choices he has, so which strategy a player could have chosen (but did not) can be as important as which strategy he actually chooses' (1993: 1289).

Players aim to maximize a utility function that is made up of a material part and a psychological part. The latter is given by the product between one's own kindness and the belief about the other's kindness. Thus A's being kind (mean) to B, when he/she expects A to be kind (mean), positively contributes to both A's and B's utility, while mixed situations are a source of disutility. One obtains a fairness equilibrium when both players maximize their own utility, given that their first- and second-order expectations about the other's first- and second-order expectations are confirmed in equilibrium.

It is reasonable to think that with respect to the problem of trust, the expectation of a reciprocating behaviour could well be the rationale for behaviours like (R, R) in the TG. And in fact, that is intuitively plausible. But when we consider such a situation more deeply, we see that things are more complicated.

First, Rabin builds a model which is intended only for strategic form, 2-person, complete information games, that is, it is not directly applicable to sequential games like the trust game. In order to do so, some amendments are needed. But there is a second and more substantial flaw that affects the model. Although a pair of strategies (R, R) seems coherent with the logic of reciprocating fairness, it is not a formal implication of the model: it does not constitute a fairness equilibrium.

Therefore to apply Rabin's model to my discussion of trust, the model has to be amended in different respects. Some of these amendments have recently been suggested by Daniel Hausman (1998), who suggests, in order to overcome the original model's limitations, substituting, as a reference point for the measurement of kindness, the value of the Nash payoff for Rabin's equitable payoff.[10] The intuition behind such an amendment is: 'If you provide a benefit to me in playing your materially self-interested equilibrium strategy, then you are not being kind to me, and there is nothing unfair if I pursue my own material self-interest' (p. 10).

Given such an amendment, A's trustful choice is now perceived by B as incorporating a positive degree of kindness. That would justifies B's trustworthy response.

Trust responsiveness

The last theory I shall examine is based on the idea of 'trust responsiveness', which implies that, given the subject's prior preference structures, the mere fact of being the object of someone's trust, may alter the prior preferences and provide an additional reason to behave trustworthily.

Elsewhere (Pelligra 2005) I have explored at some length the genesis and the functioning of such a mechanism. What is worth noting here, is that the root of such an idea can be traced, through the path of the Scottish Enlightenment, back to Aristotle. At the core of the trust responsiveness mechanism we find two basic elements: first, Aristotle's theory of *philia*, which considers self-knowledge as a product of a friendly relationship, and second, what Smith considers, in his *Theory of Moral Sentiments* (1759 [1976]), as the most basic motive of social action, that is, the need for recognition, namely, the desire to be loved and approved of. In Smith's own words:

> Nature, when she formed man for society, endowed him with an original desire to please, and an original aversion to offend his brethren. She taught him to feel pleasure in their favourable, and pain in their unfavourable regard. She rendered their approbation most flattering and most agreeable to him for its own sake; and their disapprobation most mortifying and most offensive. (III, 2.1)

The desire to be praised but also, praiseworthy along with the aversion to being the object of others' resentment, constitutes the ground from which a trustworthy attitude may spring. Consider an interaction like the TG. If we reason forward, assuming our fellow player is rational, and we observe him/her playing trustfully, we may infer that he/she expects, at the end of the day, to get a payoff no worse than he/she would have got playing Nash. The player's actions therefore, may be taken as a signal of his/her expectations. Moreover such a signal is credible because it is costly. The cost being represented, in fact, by the risk of a potential opportunistic and detrimental choice. The player knows that, and he/she knows I know. And I know that he/she knows that I know, and so on.

At this point, assuming that I am endowed with the Smithian social desires, although an opportunistic choice may lead to a higher material payoff, such a choice is necessarily associated with a conscious frustration of the other player's expectations which, in turn, generates psychological disutility. The opposite is true for a trustworthy choice, from which one gets material loss and psychological gain. Therefore, the actual decision will be the epiphenomenon of such an internal struggle between material (wealth generated) and psychological (socially generated) concerns.

Summing up it may be said that:

1. the principle of trust responsiveness assumes that players are sensitive to others' expectations;

2.   such expectations are revealed by choices; and
3.   that kind of mechanism implies a model of forward-looking reasoning.

In Pelligra (2003) I have presented a formal model of trust responsiveness based on forward induction and strategies as credible signals of players' expectations. Observationally this model is consistent with a pair of strategies (R, R) being chosen in a TG.

So far I have described a set of theories all consistent with a pattern of T&T behaviours. The coexistence of such overlapping explanatory principles need to be somehow disentangled if we have to investigate the empirical relevance of the trust responsiveness hypothesis. To this end it is necessary to design an experiment that allows us to find patterns of behaviour that are both consistent with the trust responsiveness hypothesis and inconsistent with all the other principles.

In what follows, first I describe the different goals of the experimental design, second, the different predictions of each model are formally discussed and tested. The experimental procedure as well as the hypothesis are discussed. Finally the results are presented. The data obtained from the experiment provide support, though not conclusive, for the hypothesis that the trust responsiveness is one motivating factor affecting players' choices in all the classes of games considered.

5.   The experiment: aims

The experimental design has two main features: first, it allows testing for general predictions that, in a given class of games, distinguish trust responsiveness from the other, observationally equivalent theories (discriminative task), and second, it produces highly controlled tests of specific predictions of the trust-responsiveness mechanism (exposure and regret).

Discriminative task

In order to distinguish the functioning of trust responsiveness from the other alternative explanations, I have designed different classes of interactions that imply choices which, if selected, would be inconsistent with each of the alternative models' predictions; that is, to isolate trust responsiveness by blocking explanations based on all the other explanatory principles.

First, the experiment aims to distinguish between reciprocity and trust responsiveness. In order to do so, we compare players' behaviour in two different games (Figures 15.2 and 15.3). The game depicted in Figure 15.2 is a usual 'trust game' (TG). While in this game B's non-opportunistic behaviour could be described in terms of reciprocity, aiming to benefit A for his/her beneficial choice of R, in the game depicted in Figure 15.3,

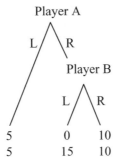

Figure 15.2   The trust game

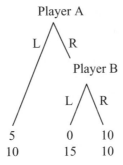

Figure 15.3   The gratuitous trust game

which I call 'the gratuitous trust game' (GTG), B's move cannot be explained in terms of reciprocity: A's choice, in fact, cannot influence B's payoff. If one observes the (R, R) outcome in a GTG game, then the pattern of behaviour cannot be explained in terms of reciprocity. However, this pair of strategies is still consistent with altruism, team thinking, inequity aversion and trust responsiveness.

In order to further discriminate between such alternative explanations, it is possible to devise another situation, which can be described using the game form depicted in Figure 15.4. In this game, the 'symmetrical trust game' (STG), it can be shown that a B player motivated by inequity aversion or altruism would play L, whereas a B player motivated by team thinking would be indifferent between the two alternatives L or R. Only a B player motivated by trust responsiveness would be consistent in playing R.

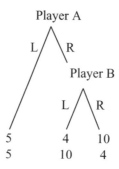

Player A

L / \ R

Player B

L / \ R

5	4	10
5	10	4

Figure 15.4   The symmetrical trust game

Consider in fact, the payoff matrix in the subgame, which is symmetrical with respect to the outcomes of the two players.

This means that a player who attaches the same weight to his/her payoff as to the other's payoff would be indifferent between the two outcomes and therefore to the two strategies L and R. While that is true for a team thinker, by definition we know that both altruism and inequity aversion assumes that *ego's* payoffs are weighted more than *alter's* payoffs, which implies that, given the symmetry in the subgame payoff matrix, both altruistic and inequity- averse players would opt for the L-strategy. Therefore, if we observe B players playing R, such behaviour could be considered consistent only with trust responsiveness, while inconsistent with all the other principles.

Exposure and regret
The discriminative task is only the first dimension of this experiment which aims to investigate behaviours that all the models, apart from trust responsiveness, would predict would not to occur. To qualify and strengthen that first aspect, the present design allows us to explore two additional factors that may complete the picture of a trust-responsive agent: 'exposure' and 'regret'. In Pelligra (2003) I have formalized the hypothesis of trust responsiveness with particular attention to B's behaviour. The model implies that B's willingness to behave trustworthily is affected by an element of 'regret', the result of what B has been excluded from by A's choice of R. Such a measure is given by the difference $(d - f)$ (see Figure 15.5). The model does not consider explicitly the trustor's (A's) motivational structure, apart from his/her knowledge of B's decision function. However, in the experiment I investigate an additional aspect of the trustor's behaviour, by assuming that the trustor's willingness to behave trustfully is affected by his/her degree of

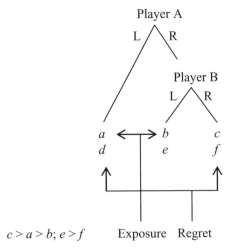

Player A

L / \ R

Player B

L / \ R

a ← → b c
d e f

$c > a > b; e > f$ Exposure   Regret

Figure 15.5   *Exposure and regret*

'exposure'. Exposure describes the magnitude of the risk that A is undertaking by playing R, that is, by being trustful. Such a concept can be operationalized and measured as the difference $(a - b)$ (see Figure 15.5).

Thus, exposure and regret refer to elements that are supposed to affect the trustor's willingness to be trustful and the trustee's willingness to be trustworthy.

Summarizing, the hypotheses are that:

H1   A's willingness to be trustful is negatively correlated with exposure;

H2   B's willingness to be trustworthy is positively correlated with exposure;

H3   B's willingness to be trustworthy is negatively correlated with regret.

It is important to note that while H1 and H2 are merely plausible intuitive hypotheses,[11] H3 is a formal implication of the model of trust responsiveness (Pelligra 2003).

H1 suggests that the higher the risk of a material loss from being trustful, the lower the trustor's willingness to behave so. H3 suggests that the higher the risk the trustor is undertaking by being trustful, the higher the trustee's willingness not to let him/her down. In order to explore such hypotheses I have designed the experiment around two basic games defined as 'asymmetrical' (Figure 15.6) and 'symmetrical' (Figure 15.7), which are different with respect to the payoff structures in the subgame.

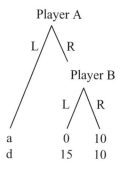

Figure 15.6   An asymmetrical game

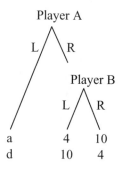

Figure 15.7   A symmetrical game

I let the two parameters *a* and *d* vary in a given range, in order to observe players' behaviour for different values of exposure and regret. In particular, For $a = (5, 9)$ in both games and for $d = (5, 9, 10, 11)$ in the asymmetrical games and $d = (0, 3, 4, 5)$ in the symmetrical games.

Figure 15.8 provides a synthetic summary of all the 16 games that can be derived from the two basic structures (asymmetric and symmetric) and the various combinations of *a* and *d*. The symmetrical and asymmetrical forms are denoted by 'S' or 'A' and the two numbers that follow are the values that parameters *a* and *d* assume in that particular game.

The games can be distinguished along three different dimensions:

1. asymmetric or symmetric (upper and lower part of Figure 15.8);
2. the value of 'regret' (increasing as we move from left to right); and

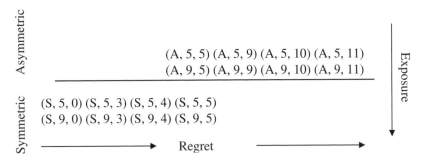

Figure 15.8   All the 16 versions of the trust game

3.   the value of 'exposure' (increasing as we move top-down in each sub-
     section).

This allows us to control for three different features:

1.   the subgame perfect Nash equilibrium is in all games 'A plays L';
2.   the payoff matrix in the subgame remains fixed while varying the other
     payoffs (a and d); and
3. a and d assume particular values.

The reasons for point 1 are trivial: I want to study 'anomalous' patterns of
behaviour. Point 2 allows us to control for all the effects consistent with theories that assume some form of backward-looking reasoning. I am interested in observing subjects' choices when confronted with the same
outcomes but different bygones (outside options), that is, B's reaction to A's
playing R when A's choice prevents B from evaluating different sets of outcomes. In so doing I am limiting the scope of possible explanations for the
effects I may find.

The reason why I have chosen particular ranges of variations for a and d
(point 3) is as follows. Given the two game structures and points 1 and 2,
the ranges $d = (5, 9, 10, 11)$ for A-games and $d = (0, 3, 4, 5)$ in S-games, allow
the representation of a wide variety of different situations: cases in which
T&T behaviour is mutually beneficial ($d = (5, 9)$ in A-games and $d = (0, 3)$
in S-games); cases in which A benefits while B is not affected ($d = (10)$ in
A-games and $d = (4)$ in S-games); and cases in which A benefits while B is
slightly harmed ($d = (11)$ in A-games and $d = (5)$ in S-games). The last cases
consider only slight harm because I want 'A plays R' to represent a trustful
move, not a presumptuous one. With regard to the range for $a = (5, 9)$, those
values represent situations in all the games where for A to be trustful

implies increasing risk or exposure; this variation may affect both A's and B's behaviour.

6.   Predictions

In the following subsections, I shall discuss the pattern of behaviour that each of the explanatory principles I have been examining predicts for each of the 16 games that I consider in the experiment.

Material self-interest

First we shall consider the hypothesis of materially self-interested behaviour. If the subjects are motivated solely by material self-interest and they believe that the others are being motivated by material self-interest, then the solution for each game can be inferred by standard game-theoretic reasoning: the subgame perfect Nash equilibrium, computed by backward induction, which in each of the 16 games corresponds to A choosing L.

Altruism

If agents are motivated by altruistic concerns (and assuming that they give more weight to their own wealth than to other people's) they prefer strategies that assign their opponent more, compared to strategies that give them less. Therefore we should observe B players choosing R in A-games but L in S-games.

Team thinking

In A-games such a theory is consistent with the observation of T&T behaviour, but in S-games we should observe an equal distribution of choices among B's two options, 'play R' and 'play L'. On the contrary, a systematic prevalence of one of the two of B's options would be inconsistent with team thinking.

Inequity aversion

As in the case of altruism, here the other's preferences are taken into account, but to a degree that is lower with respect to *ego's* preferences; therefore, inequity aversion-based theories predict that in S-games, B players, when called on to play, prefer to play L rather than R.

Reciprocity

Strictly speaking, reciprocity, as formalized in Rabin's model, cannot explain (R, R) in any of the A-games. A is kind to B in (R, R) if $10 < a$ and $d < 10$. Since what B gets by playing R is always equal or lower than the equitable payoff, A's degree of kindness is always ≤ 0. This is true for each A-game. However, the conclusion is not very different in the case of S-games. In these games, B's equitable payoff (when he/she expects A to play R) is given by $(4+4)/2$, except when $d=5$ in the (S, 5, 5) and (S, 9, 5) games (for those last games therefore the conclusion is valid *a fortiori*). A's kindness is calculated as the difference between 4 and the equitable payoff which is always 0 (or negative in the two games cited above).

Following Hausman (1998), I shall introduce a minor modification to Rabin's model. This amendment refers to the substitution of the equitable payoff, as a benchmark for kind behaviour, simply with the usual Nash outcome. B's (expected) move has to be considered kind when it contributes to letting A get a payoff higher than that he/she would have got, had B played his/her Nash strategy.

Such a modification allows Rabin's model to be tested using the present experimental design. T&T behaviours are consistent with the prediction of the amended Rabin model as long as $f > d$, that is as long as the payoff B gets from the trustworthy strategy is greater than that from playing the Nash equilibrium strategy. In this case in fact, when A plays R, his/her kindness to B is nil. Therefore B is motivated to act only by material considerations, and the comparison among payoffs ($e > f$ in this case) would push him/her towards the opportunistic choice.

When $f \leq d$, Rabin's model is no longer consistent with the observation of trustworthy choices. When we consider the S-games, we can see that the predictions are similar. The model, in fact, can predict B's trustworthy behaviour only when $d < 4$, that is, when B's payoff from playing R is greater than that from playing Nash, otherwise the opportunistic choice is the suggested one. Given all these specifications it is important to bear in mind that I am not testing Rabin's model; what I am actually testing is the principle of reciprocating fairness, as introduced by Rabin but using a slightly different formalization. Such a hybrid model makes precise and unambiguous predictions about subjects' behaviour in all the games we consider in the experiment, which are in the spirit of Rabin's idea of reciprocity .

According to Rabin's concept of reciprocity, we should expect B players to be trustworthy in S- and A-games, as long as the difference between what they get from being trustworthy and what they get from playing Nash, in equilibrium, is positive. The number of trustworthy choices should increase as this difference increases.

Trust responsiveness
Considering the 16 A- and S-games of the experimental design, it is possible to show that the model of trust responsiveness presented in Pelligra (2003), is consistent with a pattern of (R, R) strategies in all the A- and S-games.

A further implication of the model is that B's willingness to behave trustworthily should increase as *a* increases, which is what we shall discover by testing for the exposure effect.

Null hypotheses
The experiment has been devised as a formal test for the idea of trust responsiveness. Such a test refers to general hypotheses about the expected behaviour for each of the alternative principles and specific hypotheses about the functioning of trust responsiveness. The general hypotheses imply a differentiation between trust responsiveness and the other explanatory principles, self-interest, altruism, reciprocity, inequity aversion and team thinking, regarding what may be defined as the field of application or degree of generality of each of them.

The general hypotheses refer to a number of situations (games) where a certain kind of behaviour is consistent with trust responsiveness and not with the other principles. The specific hypotheses, on the contrary, refer to specific qualitative predictions of trust responsiveness that may be observed in all the games under consideration. The theories being tested here, provide (a) unconditional and (b) qualitative predictions.

Unconditional predictions
We know that the theory of *self-interest* predicts that B chooses L and (if it is also part of the theory that A believes B to be self-interested) that A chooses L. Given the assumption that each agent weights his/her own payoffs higher than those of others, *altruism* predicts that B plays L in S-games; *inequity aversion* predicts that B plays L in S-games; given some extra assumptions about the nature of team preferences, *team thinking* predicts that B plays L and R with equal probability in S-games. *Reciprocity theory* makes unconditional predictions for some games but not for others; it predicts that A plays L if $f \leq d$, but makes no firm prediction if $f > d$.

Qualitative predictions
This class of predictions refers to how behaviour will vary across games as the value of some parameter changes. More specifically: all the theories except for self-interest, which does not permit A to play R, predict that 'A plays R' is less frequent as *a* increases (that is, as A's exposure increases); *trust responsiveness* predicts that 'B plays R' is more frequent as *a* increases (that is, as A's exposure increases); I shall also explore the hypothesis that 'B plays R' is less frequent as *d* increases (that is as B's regret increases).

8. Experimental procedure

The data were gathered during six sessions involving 134 first-year economics students. The sessions were held in the information technology lab of the School of Economics at the University of Cagliari (Italy) in the period from April to June 2001. The subjects were recruited on a voluntary basis, and were all inexperienced. Given this pool of subjects, while preserving anonymity, the computer program randomly chose pairs of subjects, assigning them a role (A or B) and letting them play one of the 16 games until one of the final nodes was reached. After this, each of the two players of each pair was paired with another player, and they were assigned a new role and a new game to be played.

This process continued until all the possible combinations of players, roles and games were exhausted. The number of combinations was subject to two constraints: players do not play with the same player in the same role twice, and they do not play the same game in the same role twice. We introduced such a rule to avoid any sort of reputation or social pressure effect.

The number of observations of B players' choices was conditional on A players' choices. To maximize the number of observations we used an alternative treatment in which each player played in the B role facing the A players' hypothetical trustful choices.[12]

From these two procedures, characterized by one-off situations, anonymity and complete randomization, we extracted from a total of 134 subjects, 95 observations for each of the 16 games considered. In each session each player produced a sequence of choices of variable length (depending on the total number of subjects signed in to each session). One of those choices was selected by the software to be played for real. This is a form of a random-lottery incentive system commonly used in these types of experiment (Cubitt et al. 1998). No show-up fees were paid for attending the experiment.

Each subject received an average reward of 15,000 old Italian lire (about €7.5, or £5 Sterling). The actual payoffs are represented by the numbers shown at each end-node in the games multiplied by 2000.

9. Results

The results are numerically and graphically reported in Table 15.1 and Figures 15.9–10. The data are inconsistent with the general hypotheses based on self-interest, altruism, inequity aversion, team thinking and reciprocity and consistent with the general hypotheses of trust responsiveness.

Consider *self-interest* (and mutual belief of self-interested behaviour) as embodied by traditional game theory. An inspection of Table 15.1 and in particular of the values of AR and BR in both A- and S-games, suggests that a non-negligible proportion of both A and B players do not play their self-interested strategies.

Table 15.1   Data summary

Asymmetric games					Per cent			
a = 5, d =	5	9	10	11	a = 5, d =	5	9	10	11

	5	9	10	11		5	9	10	11
AL	65	39	49	52	AL	68.4	41.1	51.6	54.7
AR	30	56	46	43	AR	31.6	58.9	48.4	45.3
BL	43	50	42	44	BL	74.1	64.1	62.7	67.7
BR	15	28	25	21	BR	25.9	35.9	37.3	32.3

a = 9, d =	5	9	10	11	a = 9, d =	5	9	10	11
AL	74	82	70	68	AL	77.9	86.3	73.7	71.6
AR	21	13	25	27	AR	22.1	13.7	26.3	28.4
BL	36	35	38	46	BL	69.2	76.1	69.1	79.3
BR	16	11	17	12	BR	30.8	23.9	30.9	20.7

Symmetrical games					Per cent				
a = 5, d =	1	3	4	5	a = 5, d =	1	3	4	5
AL	62	50	50	58	AL	65.3	52.6	52.6	61.1
AR	33	45	45	37	AR	34.7	47.4	47.4	38.9
BL	51	48	51	55	BL	87.9	80.0	85.0	87.3
BR	7	12	9	8	BR	12.1	20.0	15.0	12.7

a = 9, d =	1	3	4	5	a = 9, d =	5	9	10	11
AL	81	79	84	71	AL	85.3	83.2	88.4	74.7
AR	14	16	11	24	AR	14.7	16.8	11.6	25.3
BL	36	43	41	38	BL	76.6	84.3	85.4	76.0
BR	11	8	7	12	BR	23.4	15.7	14.6	24.0

Note: Number of subjects: 134; Number of observations per game: 95.

At the same time, the same dataset is inconsistent with the theory of *altruism*. According to this theory, we should observe in S-games all the B players choosing L; which is clearly not the case here. The same prediction is implied by the *inequity-aversion* theory.

For the principle of *team thinking* to be consistent with the data, we should have observed an equal proportion of Bs opting for both L and R, in S-games, which did not happen as formally emerges from an 'equality of proportion test',[13] which leads us to reject the null hypothesis.

A slightly more complicated prediction arises in the case of *reciprocity*. Such a principle, as we have seen, allows B players to play R as long as $f \leq d$, and play L for $f > d$; since we still observe Bs playing R when $f > d$ (as in the case of games (A, 5, 11) and (A, 9, 11)), we cannot consider such a theory to be consistent with our dataset; the reciprocity-based theory does not account for all kinds of behaviour which seem to embody some form of trust.

Consider now *trust responsiveness*. Consider in particular its unconditional (*a*-type) and qualitative (*b*-type) predictions. According to the *a*-type predictions, we should observe B playing R as a consequence of A having chosen to play R in all 16 games. Moreover, the *b*-type, qualitative predictions imply that as *a* increases, the exposure increases, and the number of Bs playing R increases as well.

We also consider the hypothesis (H1) that relates an increase in exposure to a decrease in the number of As who play R.

The effect of exposure on the As' and the Bs' choices is graphically described in Figure 15.9, for A- and S-games, respectively, as the value of *a* changes, for given values of *d*. The Figure shows graphically a strong effect of exposure on As' choices, in the expected direction. As *a* goes from 5 to 9, the number of As choosing R decreases in both A- and S-games.

Unfortunately the effect of exposure and regret on the Bs' choices is ambiguous. This clearly appears from Figure 15.10, and is confirmed by statistical analysis.[14]

10. Discussion

The first aim of the experiment was to test for the existence and relevance of trust responsiveness. This was done by testing theoretical predictions not implied by the other theories. The fact that 12–32 per cent of B subjects choose R even when $d = 11$ (that is, when regret is positive) gives support for trust responsiveness since the null hypothesis is that the predicted effect does not occur. This result is consistent with the findings reported by Dufwemberg and Gneezy (2000) and Bacharach et al. (2001) who strongly support the self-fulfilling quality of trust, namely, trust responsiveness.

However, the second aspect of the experiment, that is, the test for the effect of changes in exposure, and changes in regret, on the frequency of (B plays R), produces ambiguous results. Indeed, we cannot confidently reject the null.

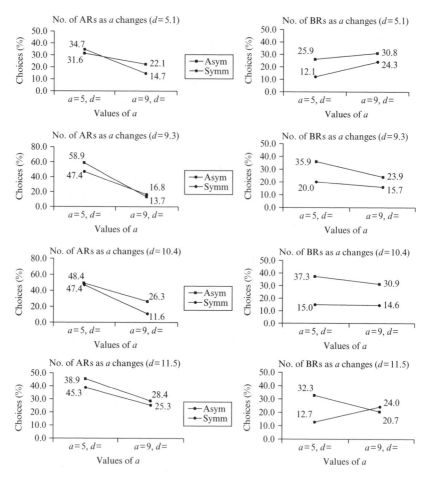

Figure 15.9   Exposure effect on As and Bs choices

11.   Conclusions

In this chapter I have discussed the relationship between trust and happiness. Happiness needs trust but trust may lead to betrayal and unhappiness. That is the paradox that led Nussbaum (1986) to argue for the fragility of goodness. In this chapter I suggest that although 'goodness' may be fragile in some respects, it is not as fragile as Nussbaum thinks. If we assume that agents' preferences may be modified during a particular kind of interaction (that is, trustworthiness may be 'activated' by trustfulness), then we should treat those preferences as endogenous.

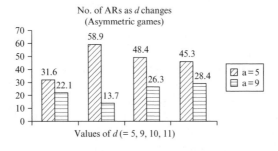

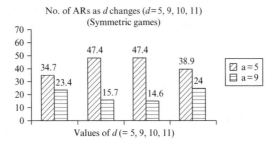

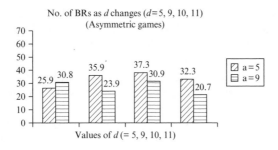

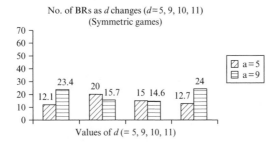

Figure 15.10   A and B player's choices in A- and S-games

I tested the empirical relevance of the principle of trust responsiveness that accounts for an agent's desire to fulfil, given certain conditions, others' expectations. Since a trustful action can be 'read' as a signal of an expectation of trustworthiness, the hypothesis of trust responsiveness implies that being the object of others' trust is in itself an additional reason for a trustworthy response. The mechanism reduces the risk of opportunism and the fragility of goodness, as Nussbaum intends.

I have provided a definition for trustful and trustworthy behaviours in a particular class of games, the trust games. Several alternative explanatory principles that can account for the empirical evidence have been critically discussed, including the idea of trust responsiveness. The existing evidence was not refined enough to discriminate among all the theories, so to solve this problem I developed a test able to distinguish, in pair-wise comparisons, a field of applicability for each theory.

The results of the experiment are presented and discussed. From the data I have obtained, the principle of trust responsiveness emerges as the one showing the greatest consistency with all the classes of strategic interactions considered. Such a positive result is partially mitigated by the fact that other implications of the model, namely those related to 'exposure' and 'regret' are inconclusive.

To conclude, let us borrow from Smith again: 'there is a satisfaction in the consciousness of being beloved, which, to a person of delicacy and sensibility, is of more importance to happiness, than all the advantage which he can expect to derive from it' (1759 [1976], III, 2.1).

Thus we have come full circle with my general argument, which aims to understand how trust and happiness are so strongly intertwined. Trust is perceived to be crucial for happiness because one cannot be happy in isolation. Second, trust, at least in the narrow sense of trustworthiness that we considered here, seems to be based on the desire to be praised and praiseworthy. Finally, such a desire to be loved, as Smith emphasizes, contributes to happiness both indirectly, by providing reasons for trustworthiness, and directly, by providing fulfilment of one of our most basic needs.

Notes

*   I owe a great debt to Michael Bacharach, Luigino Bruni, Mark Chekola, Robert Frank, Benedetto Gui, Shaun Hargreaves-Heap, Robert Sugden and Stefano Zamagni, whose comments and critical remarks, have, on several occasions, helped shape this chapter. I have also benefited from discussions after presentations to audiences in Bologna, Cagliari, Milan, Norwich, Oxford and Padua. The usual disclaimer applies. Financial support from the Regione Autonoma della Sardegna, Fondazione Veritatis Splendor, Bologna and from MURST-University of Padua is gratefully acknowledged.
1.   The Greeks before Aristotle saw the struggle for a happy life as the struggle for independence and self-sufficiency, not only with respect to other agents but also because of

'fate'. They considered the quest for happiness as both a strategic and a parametric problem. I shall focus here on only the strategic issue.

2. For brevity I shall sometimes refer to the 'subgame perfect Nash equilibrium' as the 'Nash equilibrium'. But it is obvious that when considering a sequential game, the former concept applies.

3. See, for example, the experiment based on the gift-exchange game (Fehr et al. 1997 and Fehr and Gächter 1997), the best-shot game (Fehr et al. 2000), the simultaneous and sequential prisoner's dilemma (Bolle and Ockenfels 1990) and the investment game (Berg et al. 1995).

4. See Pelligra (2002) for a critical review of the traditional alternative explanations.

5. I shall use the two terms 'utility' and 'welfare' because it is necessary to distinguish between two different concepts of utility, $U_i(.\,,.)$ and $x_i(.\,,.)$. In game-theoretical terms, the latter represents players' objective payoffs (that is, money) while the former represent players' extended or overall utility (that is, a function of those payoffs).

6. The correspondent utility function can be formalized as follows: $U_A(s, t) = x_A(s, t) + \alpha_A x_B(s, t)$. Where $x_A(s, t)$ is player A's material payoff associated with the pair of strategies (s, t), and $x_B(s, t)$ is B's material payoff associated with the same pair of strategies. The parameter α_A ($0 < \alpha < 1$) represents A's sensitivity to altruistic concerns. For the sake of simplicity I am considering here just one among many different specifications of altruism. See in this respect Andreoni (1990), Andreoni and Miller (2002) as well as Charness and Rabin (2002).

7. The economic theories of team thinking do not consider how a team comes about but they take the existence of the team as a given. Answering this question, however, is extremely important for building a coherent theory of team agency. If we assume that subjects sometimes consider themselves as an individual, sometimes as a member of a team, and that affects their way of reasoning, we must find a principle that justifies such a 'switch' between different styles of reasoning. Such a principle would emerge from an analysis of the ontology of the team, and attempts to develop such an ontology have been made by Gilbert (1989), Tuomela (1995) and Pettit (1996 [2000]).

8. See Sugden (2000) for a discussion of the 'objectives problem', that is, how to identify for a given team, what their objectives are.

9. Given that Sugden does not provide us with a formal model of team thinking, I had to speculate in order to find a suitable operationalization that preserves the 'spirit' of his theory. I have been guided by the consideration that each member of the team takes it for granted that the others are doing their part to accomplish the team objective and that this coincides with the maximization of the team's overall material wealth. If we assume that A and B perceive themselves as members of a team and that interpersonal comparisons of utility are allowed, we may operationalize players' behaviour as being aimed at the maximization of an increasing and symmetric function of the payoffs of the two players. That the function is increasing in wealth is trivial, that it is symmetric, represents the (egalitarian) way each player perceives him/herself within the team. Despite the fact that each member may have a different task to accomplish, in order to pursue the team plan, their preferences are team preferences where what really matters is not the individual task but its being functional to the team objective.

10. Hausman (1998) makes the rather restrictive assumption that the equilibrium is unique.

11. Although I am applying these hypotheses only to trust responsiveness, H1 applies to all the theories I have been considering here. This is not true for H2 and H3 since these assume the existence of some form of backward-looking form of reasoning, which is excluded by theories of altruism and inequity aversion.

12. We tested for treatment effects and found that the two procedures do not present significant differences in the choices they elicited. The presence of a second treatment involving hypothetical choices emerges from the fact reported in Table 15.1, that the total number of Bs' choices is greater that the number of As' R choices.

13. Where the proportions of BL and BR are compared statistically.

14. To test for the effect of *exposure* and *regret* on the As' and the Bs' willingness to behave trustfully and trustworthily I have estimated the following model running four logit regressions: $xR = \beta_0 + \beta_1(\text{Regret}) + \beta_2(\text{Exposure}) + \varepsilon, \qquad x = [A, B]$.

The model assumes that an individual's propensity to behave trustworthily comprises a deterministic term, reflecting the effects of the explanatory variables, regret and exposure, and a random error term which includes an individual-specific component. This allows for the possibility that some subjects will be more likely to be trustworthy than others even after controlling for the explanatory variables. In particular, this logit model estimates the probability of observing A or B playing R as a function of the values assumed by regret and exposure.

First, let us consider exposure. We expected β_2 to be negative and the data confirmed such an expectation: the effect of an increase in the value of exposure strongly affects the As' willingness to behave trustfully (that is, to choose R) in both A- and S-games.

Relatively to the Bs' behaviour one should expect β_2 to display a positive sign. The logit shows us that exposure affects the Bs' behaviour only in A-games and that the coefficient's sign is negative, opposite to that expected. At the same time, there seems to be no significant *regret effect* on the Bs' behaviour.

References

Andreoni, J. (1990), 'Impure altruism and donations to public goods: a theory of warm glow giving', *Economic Journal*, **100**, 464–77.

Andreoni, J. and J.H. Miller (2002), 'Giving according to GARP: an experimental test of the consistency of preferences for altruism', *Econometrica*, **70**, 737–53.

Bacharach, M. (1999), 'Interactive team reasoning: a contribution to the theory of cooperation', *Research in Economics*, **53**, 117–47.

Bacharach, M., G. Guerra and D. Zizzo (2001), 'Is trust self-fulfilling? An experimental study', mimeo, Bounded Rationality in Economic Behaviour, University of Oxford.

Berg, J., J. Dickhaut and K. McCabe (1995), 'Trust, reciprocity and social history', *Games and Economic Behaviour*, **10**, 122–42.

Bolle, F. and A. Ockenfels (1990), 'Prisoner's dilemma as a game of incomplete information', *Journal of Economic Psychology*, **11**, 69–84.

Bolton, G. and A. Ockenfels (2000), 'ERC: a theory of equity, reciprocity and competition', *American Economic Review*, **90**, 166–93.

Charness, G. and M. Rabin (2002), 'Understanding social preferences with simple tests', *Quarterly Journal of Economics*, **117**, 817–69.

Cubitt, R., C. Starmer and R. Sugden (1998), 'On the validity of the random lottery incentive system', *Experimental Economics*, **1**, 115–31.

Dufwemberg, M. and U. Gneezy (2000), 'Measuring beliefs in an experimental lost wallet game', *Games and Economic Behaviour*, **30**, 163–82.

Falk, A. and U. Fischbacher (1999), 'A theory of reciprocity', mimeo, University of Zurich.

Falk, A., E. Fehr and U. Fischbacher (2000), 'Testing theories of fairness: intentions matter', Working Paper No. 63, Institute for Empirical Research in Economics, University of Zurich.

Fehr, E. and S. Gächter (1997), 'How effective are trust- and reciprocity-based incentives?', in A. Ben-Ner and L. Putternam (eds), *Economics, Values and Organisation*, Cambridge: Cambridge University Press, 337–63.

Fehr, E., S. Gächter and G. Kirchsteiger (1997), 'Reciprocity as a contract enforcement device: experimental evidence', *Econometrica*, **65**, 833–60.

Fehr, E. and K.M. Schmidt (1999), 'A theory of fairness, competition and cooperation', *Quarterly Journal of Economics*, **114**, 817–68.

Genovesi, A. (1770 [1924]), *Lezioni e Commercio o di Economia Civile*, Rome: Società Tipografica dei Classici Italiani.

Gilbert, M. (1989), *On Social Facts*, London: Routledge.

Hausman, D. (1998), 'Fairness and trust in game theory', mimeo, London School of Economics, London.

Margolis, H. (1982), *Selfishness, Altruism, and Rationality. A Theory of Social Choice*, Chicago: Chicago University Press.

Mill, J.S. (1848), *Principles of Political Economy*, London: John W. Parker.

Nussbaum, M. (1986), *The Fragility of Goodness: Luck and Ethics in Greek Tragedy and Philosophy*, Cambridge and New York: Cambridge University Press.

Pelligra, V. (2002), 'Fiducia R(el)azionale', in P.L. Sacco and S. Zamagni (eds), *Complessità Relazionale e Comportamento Economico*, Bologna: Il Mulino, 291–335.

Pelligra, V. (2003), 'Trust and economics: theoretical and experimental investigations', Unpublished PhD thesis, School of Economic and Social Studies, University of East Anglia, Norwich.

Pelligra, V. (2005), 'Under trusting eyes: the responsive quality of trust', in B. Gui and R. Sugden (eds), *Economics and Social Interactions*, Cambridge: Cambridge University Press, 105–24.

Pettit, P. (1996 [2000]), *The Common Mind: An Essay on Psychology, Society and Politics*, 2nd edn, Oxford: Oxford University Press.

Rabin, M. (1993), 'Incorporating fairness in game theory', *American Economic Review*, **83**, 1281–301.

Smith, A. (1759 [1976]), *The Theory of Moral Sentiments*, Indianapolis, IN: Liberty Classics.

Sugden, R. (1993), 'Thinking as a team: towards an explanation on non-selfish behaviour', *Social Philosophy and Policy*, **10**, 69–89.

Sugden, R. (2000), 'Team preferences', *Economics and Philosophy*, **16**, 175–204.

Tuomela, R. (1995), *The Importance of Us: A Philosophical Study of Basic Social Notions*, Stanford, CA: Stanford University Press.

Williams, B. (1981), 'Philosophy', in M.I. Finley (ed.), *The Legacy of Greece: a New Appraisal*, Oxford: Oxford University Press, 121–36.

16 Happiness, morality and game theory
*Luca Zarri**

1. Introduction

As far as contemporary economically advanced societies are concerned, it would be hardly deniable that people's search for happiness is significantly affected not only by the satisfaction of material needs, but also by several non-material sources such as psychological and social factors, as well as by the pursuit of complex, morally-charged goals, as a growing body of experimental and empirical contributions tends to confirm (see, for example, Easterlin 2001; Fehr and Gächter 2002; Rabin 2002). Recent evidence suggests that money is less and less able to buy happiness and, in this light, Rabin (1993: 1283) correctly remarks: 'Welfare economics should be concerned not only with the efficient allocation of material goods, but also with designing institutions such that people are happy about the way they interact with others'. These two types of objectives (that is, material and non-material ones) seem to interplay in complex ways; for instance, it is often the case that the pursuit of non-material ends such as the search for social prestige or freedom of choice crucially passes through the attainment of monetary gains. As an example of this, we may think of a status-seeking agent deciding to buy a luxury car or an expensive yacht in order to more effectively signal a given status level (regardless of its reflecting his/her actual social position or not): in the agent's view, status acts as a source of (positional) utility directly provided by the (instrumental) relationship established with other subjects belonging to his/her 'reference group'. It seems clear, then, that, in so far as we aim at getting significant insights over the often paradoxical meanings of a multifaceted notion such as 'happiness' within advanced economic systems, the above recalled interplays need to be seriously taken into account.

Within such a complex framework, the specific aim of this chapter is to provide a contribution to the understanding of the aforementioned relationship (between material and non-material determinants of individual happiness) in the context of non-cooperative game theory. The point is that while both theoretical and empirical studies on happiness have been growing rapidly in the last years, we still lack researches focusing on the attempt to reconcile happiness with game theory, that is, to analyse happiness within strategic interaction scenarios. As Section 2 will show, exploring the connection between happiness and non-cooperative game theory is crucial as, in strategic interaction situations, players' subjective conception of happiness alters their evaluation of each possible outcome. One of the major purposes of this methodological work is to shed light on the primitive concepts constituting two-player, simultaneous-move non-cooperative games in order to properly account for the crucial interplays taking place between (suitably defined) 'preferences' and *moral principles*. In order to do so, the following issues will be specifically addressed: what kind of difficulties arise when a relevant, non-material source of individual happiness such as morality is included in the *payoffs* of the game? Can we incorporate *any* moral principles within individual payoffs?

The structure of the remainder of the chapter is the following. In Section 2 we briefly recall some of the main stages in the history of utility and happiness in economics, with a special focus on the relevance of the so-called 'Pareto turn' and on the most significant features of the 'revealed preference' approach. Section 3 shows that non-cooperative game theory can deal with *some* moral principles (the ones we label as 'preferential' moral principles) through a proper respecification of individual payoffs (shifting from standard to 'extended' payoffs). In Section 4, however, we make clear that 'non-preferential' moral principles, such as Kantian principle of universalizability, cannot be satisfactorily modeled by simply respecifying players' payoffs: with regard to this set of moral principles, we suggest taking a step forward, as the very nature of principles of morality other than utility maximization calls for non-utilitarian solution concepts. In Section 5, we shed light on what we term the 'as if paradoxes of happiness in economics', that is, on the paradoxical implication according to which, in some social settings, even utility maximizers get better results by acting 'as if' they were driven by a non-utilitarian moral principle. Section 6 concludes.

2. Rational choices and revealed preferences in non-cooperative games

Before directly entering into the major theoretical issues addressed in this work, a preliminary methodological clarification is in order. In dealing with the themes specified above, we will often have recourse to what is probably the best known among two-person, non-cooperative games: the prisoner's dilemma (PD).[1] However, we maintain that most of the considerations developed in Sections 2, 3, 4 and 5 also hold in so far as we refer to other relevant strategic interaction scenarios that lend themselves to be modeled in game-theoretic terms. The main reason for choosing the PD as the reference social structure is twofold. First, many of the game theorists, economists and philosophers quoted and critically reviewed here with regard to the methodological issues at stake (such as Ken Binmore, Amartya Sen, Elizabeth Anderson and Robert Sugden) have often clarified their positions by directly referring to this game. In this light, shifting from one author to another by always considering the same game structure should help in expositional terms. Second, the PD can be seen as the metaphor *par excellence* of social situations where (a) individualistic rationality fails and (b) even utility-maximizing agents would reach better results by acting on principles of action other than Nash behavior (or, at least, by acting as if they were driven by 'proper' non-utilitarian principles; on this, see Section 5). Therefore, such a game structure will play a critical role in making clear the main implications drawn in the present contribution with regard to a characterization of happiness within strategic interaction scenarios.[2]

According to the 'revealed preference' approach, individual preferences are to be interpreted in terms of choice, as choices 'reflect' preferences. As Sen (1982: 1–2) observes:

> Preference here is simply *defined* as the binary relation underlying consistent choice. In this case 'counter-preferential' choice is not empirically different, but simply impossible. *Non*-preferential choice is, of course, possible, since the choices may lack the consistency needed for identifying a binary relation of preference, but obviously it cannot be the case that such an identified preference relation exists and the choices are 'counter' to it.

In this light, we are already able to draw a simple, direct implication from this characterization of preferences: choice, not preference, ends up being the basic, 'salient' concept of any theory grounded on such definition of preferences. Leonard Savage's formal theory seems to prove this as 'although Savage's axioms are formulated in terms of the concept of preference, it seems that he regards *choice* as *the more fundamental concept*: the idea is to construct a theory of rational choice, not of rational preferences' (Sugden 1991: 758; italics added).

However, it is important to point out that the reasons behind the greater salience of 'choice' with respect to 'preference' are not purely theoretical, but also historical. In this regard, the decisive moment in the history of economic thought coincides with the so-called 'Pareto turn' (or 'indifference curve' or 'ordinalism revolution'), the event that starts driving a wedge between neoclassical thinkers and contemporary scholars as to the interpretation of 'utility'. The early neoclassical economists tended to explain preferences by postulating a *one-dimensional* scale of inner psychological experience (referred to in terms of 'happiness' or 'pleasure'), but the difficulties arising from the search for such a measure pushed economists to gradually adopt a revealed preference approach to utility, where 'preferences are whatever dispositions lie behind observed choices, and the formal properties of preference which guarantee an ordering – completeness, reflexivity and transitivity – are postulated *as properties of rationality*' (Sugden 2001: F221–2). Sugden (2002) maintains that, after the Paretian turn, the concept of the utility function has been retained, but has been reinterpreted as a representation of individual preferences, which in turn are seen as whatever the agent takes to be choice-relevant reasons. Ng (1997) correctly observes that the main motives justifying such a method-ological revolution – related to the attempt to make economic analysis based on more objective grounds – are quite clear and sound, but he also adds that all this has been carried to an excess, preventing economics from successfully dealing with several important issues. He further interestingly asserts that psychology went through a similar process, due to the Watson–Skinner behaviorist revolution, recently resulting in the well-known cognitive turn.

The above argument clearly indicates that the historical process briefly described, while making choice the central concept of economic theory, has started assigning a less and less relevant role to the classical notion of 'utility',[3] certainly the conceptual category which turned out to be more closely related to the idea of 'happiness'. As a consequence, happiness itself has never played thereafter a significant role in economics: therefore, if today we wish to re-discover the importance of such a concept and to incorporate it into the formal structure of economic theory – in the light of a rather stimulating wave of empirical and experimental studies cen-tered either directly on happiness or on specific components of it – we need to understand whether (re)introducing happiness in our theory is compat-ible with the maintenance of a 'revealed preference' approach. In this regard, from the point of view of the historical evolution of ideas on the theme, it seems to be the case that bringing happiness back into econom-ics will take the form of a sort of theoretical counterrevolution, with respect to the Pareto turn recalled above.

According to Sen and Williams (1982), however, the whole picture is even more complex and blurred, as the two different interpretations of preference (that is, the pre-Paretian, Benthamite perspective and the post-Paretian, choice-centered view previously mentioned) still ambiguously coexist within contemporary economic theory. Further, they observe that 'The ambiguity of the term "preference" facilitates this dual picture of utility, since linguistic convention seems to permit the treatment of "pre-ferring" as choosing as well as taking what a person (really) "prefers" as what would make him better off' (p. 12). Sen (1994) expresses a similar view by claiming that both a *choice-salience* interpretation and a *well-being* interpretation of preference are present in contemporary econom-ics. In this regard, we may add that Kahneman et al.'s (1997) well-known distinction between *decision utility* and *experienced utility* seems to con-ceptually parallel the same dichotomy. In the same vein, Rabin (1997: 4) asserts:

For positive analysis, the usefulness of the utility-maximization framework depends on whether choice data can be usefully organized by positing that people maximize stable utility functions. A more controversial and rarer question about this framework is whether the preferences which people seem to maximize correspond to the well-being they actually experience. Many economists consider such a question off limits, feeling that 'by definition' the actions of informed people reflect what makes them happy. But there is a coherent sense in which even outcomes intentionally chosen may not maximize a decision maker's experienced well-being.

As far as game theory is specifically concerned, it is important to note that this discipline was born *after* the crucial Pareto turn occurred in economics: as a consequence, in its intense development during the last decades, the process of progressive construction of its formal structure has been deeply rooted within a behavioristic, revealed preference approach. As Sugden (1991: 757) points out: 'When economists and game theorists feel obliged to justify their use of these concepts, they still turn to Savage'. However, while recognizing that such a close connection between behaviorism and game theory is not a difficult task, justifications of it on methodological grounds are not so easy to find. A rather relevant (and probably the most significant) exception is Binmore's massive work (1994, 1998), which contains *inter alia* a systematic attempt to explain in which sense the methodological foundations of non-cooperative game theory necessarily lie in a strong version of the revealed preferences perspective. More specifically, it is the case that, in so far as one mechanically transfers this approach to game theory, Binmore's position automatically follows: formally, there are no reasons why we should not incorporate 'whatever affects choice' into players' preferences, that is, into game payoffs.

3.   'Extended payoffs' and 'preferential' moral principles
Binmore (1994: 97–98) affirms:

It is a common source of misunderstanding for it to be thought that game theorists intend a payoff to be some naïve measure of a player's individual welfare, like a sum of money. However, game theory is based on the principle that the players act as though seeking to maximize the payoff they receive at the end of the game. A naïve view of the nature of a payoff will therefore sometimes not suffice. For example, it is easy to quote situations, especially in a moral context, where almost nobody would regard the amount of money that he gets as being the major determinant in deciding what to do. Game theorists therefore understand the notion of a payoff in a sophisticated way that makes it tautologous that players act as though maximizing their payoffs. Such a sophisticated view makes it hard to measure payoffs in real-life games, but its advantage in keeping the logic straight is overwhelming.

Our judgments are often biased by the belief that well-known categories such as, say, 'goods' or 'externalities' represent objective features of economic interactions. By claiming this, we tend to forget that, by contrast, characterizing a certain 'object' as a good or a bad, as a private or public good, as a relational or positional good or as a positive or negative externality always critically depends on the subjective value-system of the agents we are referring to in our analysis. The point is that while in a homogeneous and relatively simple society it will be quite easy for its members to agree one with the other at this level, in a heterogeneous and relatively complex one differences in this regard are likely to be rather important and non-negligible. Such a subject dependence clearly holds also as far as the concept of 'game' is concerned: the ranking of all possible outcomes of a non-cooperative game crucially depends on each agent's value-system. For example, the same 'material payoff' can yield completely different consequences in terms of overall 'subjective payoffs' depending on players' 'motivations', that is, attitudes towards others. Properly speaking, each cell of a normal form game contains 'utilities', which can or cannot be a (more or less complex) function of some material payoffs that the game theorist considers significant for a proper description of the game. In this light, as far as individual goals are concerned, utilities can incorporate both an objective dimension (that is, material rewards such as a sum of money) and a subjective one (critically dependent on each player's values): therefore, via utilities, both dimensions can be simultaneously accounted for by the game theorist.

In other words, it is the case that the same monetary payoffs may translate into individuals' 'utilities' in different ways, according to each agent's 'happiness technology' (for this expression, see Menicucci and Sacco 1996), in a world of motivationally heterogeneous players. We may add that the more a society is motivationally heterogeneous, the greater the difference between monetary payoffs and utilities and the more the description of the game in terms of 'objective' payoffs is lacking and unsatisfactory. So far, our reasoning is perfectly compatible with Binmore's revealed preference view: game payoffs need not coincide with some naïve measure of individual welfare like a sum of money. If this has often been the case, the reason has basically to do with the well-known, strong historical salience of the self-interest assumption in both economics and game theory. It is only when material net benefits perfectly coincide with the underlying 'utilities' that it is totally legitimate to describe a game by identifying individual payoffs with the physical consequences faced by each player in correspondence with each possible outcome.[4]

In recent years, with the development of behavioral and experimental economics, more and more studies have started focusing on 'extended payoffs' incorporating not only material benefits but also psychological factors, social rewards and moral principles: let us think of the literature on psychological games (Geanakoplos et al. 1989; Rabin 1993) as well as of the related experimental works on positive and negative reciprocity (see, for example, Fehr and Gächter 1999, 2002; Fehr and Fischbacher 2002). Inserting such non-material benefits into the payoffs of the game is a fully legitimate operation right because of the above reasoning: in so far as these non-monetary goals are assumed to be a component of players' 'objective function', there are no formal reasons preventing the model builder from taking them into account. In other words, we may assert that the relevance of the self-interest assumption in the history of economic thought has tended to make us forget that, on purely formal grounds, game theory is well equipped to deal with other, more complex and sophisticated objective functions as well. As Hollis (1994: 118) observes, 'strictly, the standard first principle assumes only that agents are guided by their own preferences. In this sense saints are as "self-interested" as sinners and the theory of Rational Choice is not committed to any view about how saintly or sinful we are'.[5]

We ought to proceed even farther along this path, in order to lay stress on the following point: not only the model builder has access to formal tools which, in principle, are capable of properly taking such non-material rewards into account; in so far as such factors are considered important by the players themselves, he/she has to incorporate them into their 'extended payoffs' (or 'utilities'). When they are deemed important by the players, but, for some reason, the game theorist expresses the payoffs in purely material terms, then the resulting game will necessarily turn out to be improperly specified, as what matters in a game are players' preferences, not the modeler's ones. This observation seems to be in line with Ng's (1997: 1848–9) view, according to which happiness is far more important than more objective concepts such as choice, preference and income as 'happiness is the ultimate objective of most, if not all people . . . We want money (or anything else) only as a means to increase our happiness. If having more money does not substantially increase our happiness, then money is not very important, but happiness is'.

With reference to Binmore's objections to Sen's (and also, implicitly, to Sugden's) position, the major thesis defended here can be summarized as follows: on the one hand, in so far as we adopt a purely utility-maximizing, instrumental view of rationality (where preferences – and, consequently, payoffs – are broadly defined as 'whatever agents maximize' when strategically interacting with each other), we may easily agree with Binmore that *any* preferences (including 'moral preferences') ought to be already embedded in the extended payoffs of the game *before* the game starts. Hausman and

McPherson (1994: 260) seem to adopt a similar (though more prudent) view as they argue:

> The standard theory of rationality says that A's choices are determined by A's preferences. This sounds a bit like the claim that A is self-interested, but the impression is misleading. To say that A is self-interested is to make a claim about *what* A prefers. Utility theory does not rule out preferences for acting on moral principles or preferences for serving the interests of others. We are not claiming here that all moral theories are compatible with the standard theory of rationality. Our point is only that utility theory does *not* imply self-interest.

We agree with Binmore as well as with Hausman and McPherson that some moral principles are compatible with a maximizing framework, in both strategic and non-strategic interaction scenarios.

In this light, if, say, a pre-play, material game takes the form of a PD but players are *altruists*, then, depending on their degree of altruism, the 'proper' or 'right' game (that is, the one that takes account of all the relevant dimensions and not only of the material one) may well take the form of either an assurance game (AG) where, both (cooperate, cooperate) and (defect, defect) are Nash equilibria in pure strategies, or an other-regarding game (OR), where cooperation is the dominant strategy for both agents. Sen (1973: 251) himself agrees on this point, as he has no difficulties in admitting:

> the entire problem under discussion can be easily translated into the case in which each person does worry about the other's welfare as well and is not concerned only with his own welfare. The numbers in the pay-off matrix can be interpreted simply as welfare indices of the two persons and each person's welfare index can incorporate concern for the other.

What Sen is clarifying here is that in so far as we deal with a moral motivation such as altruism, defined as 'concern about the other's welfare' (elsewhere, he qualifies this motivation as 'sympathy'; see, for example, Sen 1974), we can easily account for such a moral category through a simple respecification of individual payoffs, without altering any other element of the game as a whole. Selfish, altruistic or other types of preferences can be easily accommodated in the formal framework of non-cooperative game theory, as game payoffs are to be interpreted as 'welfare indices', reflecting players' (possibly heterogeneous) motivational systems.

4. 'Non-preferential' moral principles, solution concepts and happiness

The considerations developed in Section 3 show that not only selfish preferences but also pro-social (like altruism) or anti-social ones (like envy) can be easily modeled in game-theoretic terms, through a proper specification of individual payoffs. However, it is worth asking the following question: do people systematically act on the basis of their *preferences*? Are all possible principles of action based on the attempt to maximally satisfy one's preferences? Our point is that, in so far as we properly define individual preferences, we need to provide a negative answer to such questions. In particular, we claim that, for agent A, acting on his/her preferences may entail deciding *not* to act *morally* (and vice versa): in other words, it is intuitive to consider 'preferential behavior' as a form of action that may not be in line with a person's moral system, but that, by contrast, is directly linked to his/her non-rational impulses and inclinations, so that, as we all know, serious inner conflicts may arise between personal preferences and moral prescriptions. In this light, the qualitative difference between the two types of action is well captured by the well-known Kantian distinction between autonomous and heteronomous behavior: as Van Hees (2003: 338) observes, in such a perspective 'an individual can either act morally, or be under the sway of her inclinations, desires etc. If she acts morally, i.e. if she acts "from the moral law", she is said to act autonomously. On the other hand, if she acts on the basis of her impulses, inclinations, etc., she is acting heteronomously'.

In such an interpretation, a person's autonomy is closely related to the frequency of his/her morally justified actions, whereas forces such as desires and inclinations (that is, in our interpretation, 'preferences') would tend to make his/her behavior heteronomous. For example, with regard to Sen's (1977) distinction between sympathy and commitment, we may argue that while sympathy can be considered as a 'preferential' moral principle, commitment appears as a non-preferential one, as committing to a given behavior implies, by definition, acting against one's (properly defined) preferences. At this stage, we maintain then that a meta-principle through which both forms of 'preferential' and 'non-preferential' behavior can be incorporated within a unifying framework is provided by Anderson's (2001: 30) priority claim: 'The Priority of Identity to Rational Principle: what principle of choice it is rational to act on depends on a prior determination of personal identity, of who one is'.[6] Anderson's claim highlights that there is something prior to behavioral choice: the choice of which principle of choice to act on. It is at this meta-choice level that agents have to decide whether to be, say, Kantian players, team thinkers (see Sugden 2000) or utility maximizers. She is not arguing that only one principle of choice is rational, but simply asserting that the outcome of such a meta-choice crucially depends on the agent's self-conception.

Can we account for Anderson's priority claim in game-theoretic terms? Let us assume that, with respect to a given strategic interaction scenario, some players' identity is affected by preferential moral principles only but also that, say, other players' identity depends on acting on non-preferential moral principles: are we allowed to model such a situation through the language of game-theory? Sugden (2001: F222) criticizes Binmore's (1994) interpretation of utility indices in games on the grounds that he has recourse to

> a particularly strong form of revealed preference theory, in which it is a matter of definition that an individual's choices *always* reveal her preferences. Thus, once a game has been specified, with utility indices for the various possible outcomes, certain propositions about what a player will do (for example, that she will not choose a dominated strategy) are *necessary truths*, and not merely the implications of particular solution concepts which game theorists are free to dispute (I: 104–110). I am not convinced that this is the most useful – or indeed the conventional – way of interpreting utility in games.

In the light of the above reasoning on Anderson's priority claim and of Sen's and other scholars' defense of non-utilitarian moral concepts such as commitment or duty, Sugden's critique to (strong forms of) the revealed preference approach sounds rather plausible: is it necessarily part of the definition of 'payoffs' that players choose the strategy yielding the highest payoff value, given the opponent's strategy? Is such a definition implied by the formal structure of the game? In our view, we are allowed to provide a negative answer to this question, as, in principle, we may have recourse to different solution concepts with regard to the same game structure, that is, we can assume that players choose by relying on principles of action other than a criterion based on a purely instrumental account of rationality such as utility maximization.

Sen (1994) is very clear in stating that (a) there are deep reasons inducing us not to systematically respecify the payoffs in so far as we want to incorporate in our formal structure concepts such as commitment and also that (b) these reasons, far from being exclusively formal, have a mainly substantive nature. In other words, matters like 'what is the game' correctly describing a given situation and 'how should agents play it' ought to be treated separately, as, with respect to a given game, different moral principles may be captured by distinct solution concepts. While knowing players' (extended) payoffs is crucial in order to correctly specify what game is going to be played, such information in itself is not sufficient to tell us how rational agents will play that game: in so far as we interpret extended payoffs as reflecting agents' preferences, their choices need not be mechanically driven by (extended) payoffs only.[7] We believe that Anderson's priority claim allows us to draw such important implications for game theory: in so far as *identity* – and not preferences – is seen as the *primum movens* of individuals' choice process, we cannot rule out, *ex ante*, that a certain game's payoffs are common knowledge among the players but that such players, without behaving inconsistently, decide to act on a principle of action other than utility maximization. This is equivalent to asserting that agents' principle of action is not part of the definition of game payoffs and that, therefore, the maximizing format need not universally apply.

In particular, it seems to us to be misleading to have recourse to such a format when the players' decision process is significantly affected by non-preferential moral criteria. Further, in our view the above reasoning also entails that, other things being equal, a given game structure (say, a PD) keeps on being the same even if players' identity induces them to adopt a non-utilitarian mode of rationality: the point is that the departure from a logic of play such as utility maximization occurs at a level which is different from the (pre-play) level of (suitably defined) individual preferences (captured by properly specified game payoffs).[8] According to the interpretation suggested in this chapter, it would be unsatisfactory to avoid such depart-ure in terms of logic of play by accommodating the moral principle under study through a simple respecification of the game's payoffs: the problem is that – unlike situations where morally charged preferences such as altruism (or sympathy) are involved – by so doing we would simultaneously alter the very nature of such non-preferential moral criteria and, therefore, we would not do justice to them.

By (a) introducing a rationality concept other than utility maximization and (b) preserving the original game structure, we are allowed to make such a non-utilitarian principle of action choice-relevant while at the same time making clear the distinction between preferential and non-preferential factors. Further, this approach is useful in order to comparatively analyse what actually happens (when a non-preferential solution concept is involved) and what would happen if the players were driven by their prefer-ences only (that is, if they decided by simply choosing the strategy yielding the highest payoff): this clearly entails that counterpreferential choices may well occur within this scenario. As anticipated above, a further advantage of interpreting (a) payoffs as reflecting individual preferences and (b) solution concepts in the light of the principles of action adopted by the players, without establishing any mechanical and necessary connection between (a) and (b), is the following: such a framework allows us to incorporate potential inner conflicts between preferences and non-preferential moral principles in the formal structure of a non-cooperative game, that is, to explicitly consider the complex interplays taking place between different ver-sions of rationality. This implies that, with reference to a given game struc-ture, fruitful links between solution concepts and moral principles might be established, while at the same time making clear that both preferences and non-preferential moral criteria affect, to some degree, players' choices.

5. The paradoxes of happiness in strategic interaction scenarios

Amartya Sen, in one of his classic contributions (Sen 1985), focuses on three notions of 'privateness': (i) self-centered welfare, (ii) self-welfare goal, and (iii) self-goal choice, claiming that such concepts are quite independent of one another: (i) a choice is not necessarily driven by the pursuit of a given goal; (ii) a goal is not necessarily aimed at increasing the person's own welfare and, further, (iii) aiming at increasing one's welfare does not always entail increasing one's consumption levels. Kahneman et al.'s (1997) more recent and well-known distinction between decision utility (basically the choice-based characterization of utility Sen refers to) and experienced utility (conveying a Benthamite, content-based characterization of utility) seems to be partly related to Sen's considerations: as far as individual 'welfare' or 'happiness' is concerned, choice may well happen to be 'externally inconsistent' (Hsee 2003), that is, it may reveal itself unable to increase the chooser's happiness level.[9] As Rabin (1997: 43) observes, 'Not knowing your own "experienced utility function" is obviously important for the welfare implications of choice, and the main lesson of this material is that economists ought recognize that people may not correctly predict what makes them happy'.

The point we would like to make here is that the above recalled wedge between choice and happiness is quite a general phenomenon, observable in both strategic and non-strategic interaction scenarios. As far as social environments where choice occurs under parametric conditions, several explanations can be simultaneously considered, like evolving aspirations (see Rabin 1997; Easterlin 2001) and hedonic adaptation (see Frederic and Loewenstein 1999). A further and not necessarily alternative explanation of the choice–happiness wedge is the one suggested by Hsee (2003), referring to this possibility as to a form of 'choice-consumption inconsistency':

> In situations where people choose between hedonic consumption options, the external consistency question becomes whether the option people choose delivers the best consumption experience. . . . If people choose an option that delivers worse consumption experience over one that delivers better consumption experience, holding costs constant, we say that they exhibit a choice-consumption inconsistency.

Hsee's (2003) explanation lies in the so-called JE–SE mode distinction. He maintains that an important, though largely neglected, contributor to choice-consumption inconsistency is *evaluation mode*, in the sense that choice is usually made in the joint evaluation (JE) mode, with several goods to be compared, whereas consumption occurs in the separate evaluation (SE) mode, where one good only (the one previously bought by the agent in the JE) is present. Once we take this distinction into account, we are not entitled to conclude that choice reveals the underlying preference structure of the agent. The simultaneous presence of multiple options to be compared *ex ante* generates a bias (Hsee and Zhang (2004) call it *distinction bias*) and may lead to choices which turn out to be unpleasant (or less pleasant than expected) *ex post*: the evaluation mode may then drive a wedge between decision utility and experienced utility.

The choice–happiness wedge illustrated above is even more likely to occur in strategic interaction scenarios, that is, in social contexts where agents interact strategically, constantly aiming at correctly predicting others' preferences and behaviors. Interestingly, Sen (1973) seems to note that the gap between individual preferences and welfare is greater the more social interaction is complex, that is, we could say, the more it takes place in a sophisticated, strategic interaction situation – the subject matter of game theory. As we observed above, it is frequently the case that the actual degree of happiness people experience *ex post* (experienced utility) significantly differs from the one expected *ex ante* (predicted utility). In social contexts where agents interact strategically, that general proposition holds because 'disappointing' equilibria can occur even though every player would have preferred to end up in a different outcome (like inefficient, mutual defection equilibria in the PD). In such scenarios, it is worth specifying that, unlike what happens in non-strategic contexts, there is nothing inherently paradoxical in the fact that we cannot choose what we would prefer (for example, an 'I defect–You cooperate' outcome in a PD for a selfish player) when our actions are interdependent the one with the other. This point is expressed very clearly by Binmore (1994: 103):

> Personally, I see no paradox at all in the fact that independent choice behavior by rational agents should sometimes lead to Pareto-inefficient outcomes. The rules of the Prisoners' Dilemma create an environment that is inimical for rational cooperation and, just as one cannot reasonably expect someone to juggle successfully with his hands tied behind his back, so one cannot expect rational agents to succeed in cooperating when constrained by the rules of the Prisoners' Dilemma.

In social dilemmas and other strategic interaction environments, it is of interest to remark that selfish players could obtain better results if they behaved *as if* they had a preference for cooperation or through a principle of action other than utility maximization. In other words, in such contexts it is the case that if agents act on a non-maximizing principle of action, they may receive an individual benefit which is greater than the one they would obtain via explicit utility maximization. In the PD, for example, if we assume that players' principle of action is, say, (pseudo)'Kantian rationality', then the equilibrium they reach is the best possible outcome this interaction scenario may yield from two different points of view, that is, from both (a) a Kantian and (b) a utility-maximizing perspective. As to the former perspective, it is easy to see that the equilibrium outcome of mutual cooperation is consistent with the moral prescription that each agent Kantianly decides to comply with, that is, with the universalizable law prescribed by the categorical imperative illustrated in Kant's *Groundwork*: 'Act only on that maxim whereby thou canst at the same time will that it should become a universal law'. As Sugden (1991: 756) observes, 'reasons may override desires: it may be rational to do what one does not desire to do. As the example of the Prisoner's Dilemma suggests, this line of thought threatens to undermine game theory'. A very similar point was lucidly made by Rapoport (1987: 975), arguing that developments of game theory 'provide a rigorous rationale for Kant's Categorical Imperative; act in the way you wish others to act. Acting on this principle reflects more than altruism. It reflects a *form of rationality*' (italics added).

However, an even more interesting point is that such an equilibrium constitutes the best possible outcome even if agents were genuinely utility-maximizing players and only 'as if' Kantians, that is, had adopted a Kantian principle of action for purely instrumental reasons. In other words, in social dilemma scenarios, being 'englightened utility maximizers' who consciously decide to opt for a Kantian moral law but, at the same time, keep on evaluating their own welfare in purely preferential terms, may turn out to pay off, that is, to be a better comprehensive strategy with respect to actual utility maximization. In this regard, Sen (1973: 258) affirms: 'Even in the absence of a contract, the parties involved will be better off following rules of behaviour that require abstention from the rational calculus which is precisely the basis of the revealed preference theory. People may be induced by social codes of behaviour to act *as if* they have different preferences from what they really have'. Similarly, with regard to the PD, Sen (1985) observes that if agents acted on the basis of some 'as if' ordering, they may achieve better results than by choosing individualistically. See Menicucci and Sacco (1996) for interesting insights on this.

In our view, this appears as one of the most interesting 'paradoxes of happiness in strategic interaction scenarios', that is, a paradox arising in game-theoretic settings, where, by definition, rationality has a strategic and not a parametric nature. Anderson (2001: 27), commenting on Sen's (1977) famous essay, observes that what is foolish in a PD is not the lack of a preference for cooperation:

> [I]t is hardly foolish to not prefer the act of cooperating in itself, apart from its consequences. What is foolish about non-cooperators is not their preferences, which are perfectly understandable, but their principle of rational choice. And

what makes that principle foolish is its act-consequentialist structure. Any principle of rational choice that evaluates an individual's act solely according to its marginal causal impact on valued outcomes will meet the same difficulties. This is one powerful reason why many people are drawn away from act-consequentialism toward rule-consequentialism, or toward non-consequentialist frameworks.

On methodological grounds, such considerations suggest that introducing a softer link between preference and choice (that is, a departure from the pure version of the revealed preferences approach) may allow for the achievement of important substantive results even within an ultimately utility-maximizing framework, as far as PD-like social interactions are concerned. In other words, what happens in social dilemmas (which are relatively special but rather frequent and relevant interaction scenarios) is somehow the opposite with respect to what is predicted by the 'as though' thesis defended by revealed preferences theorists. Their position is that any non-maximizing principle can, in fact, be conceptualized in maximizing terms, even when agents are not aware of this; by contrast, we claim here that, in social dilemmas, not only do Kantian players preserve their identity at a behavioral level and are neither actual nor 'as though' utility maximizers, but also that even utility maximizers would better adopt an enlightened reasoning and, without altering their actual, ultimately preference-centered rationality, act as though they were Kantian players.[10]

6.   Concluding remarks

In the light of the analysis developed in the previous sections, we can identify the following advantages in adopting the approach suggested here. In the first place, such an analytical framework allows us to discriminate the causal role of (suitably defined) 'preferences' and non-preferential moral principles – seen as distinct determinants of 'expected happiness' – on individual behavior within strategic interaction settings. As a consequence, it can account for the complex interplays taking place between two such dimensions, so that, in principle, even potential conflicts between them (occurring at intra-individual level) may be explored. Recognizing that the search for happiness in advanced societies increasingly depends on such interaction between preferential and non-preferential factors seems to be a significant reason for proceeding along the path indicated above.

Second, as we have seen, several important social scenarios exist where, in so far as we have recourse to non-utilitarian solution concepts such as, say, the Kantian principle of universalizability or team reasoning (on this, see Sugden 2000), individual players are capable of obtaining results which are Pareto superior to the ones they would get within a classic, maximizing framework. In the light of the considerations developed in the last section, social dilemmas can be seen as one of the most interesting settings where, as far as the link between happiness, morality and game-theoretic solution concepts is concerned, paradoxical implications arise. The main thesis defended in Section 4 can be summarized as follows: in several social situations where agents interact strategically, even for utility maximizers the achievement of the maximum degree of happiness may occur as a byproduct of non-preferential principles of action, that is of principles of action not aimed at generating such an effect. Symmetrically, within such strategic interaction environments, purposely utility-maximizing patterns of behavior lead to disappointing results: with regard to the PD, Aumann (1987: 468) points out: 'The universal fascination with this game is due to its representing, in very stark and transparent form, the bitter fact that when individuals act for their own benefit, the result may well be disaster for all'. A further and related paradox within such settings has to do with the fact that, provided that they decide to behave as if they were driven by the pursuit of ends other than preference satisfaction, utility maximizers can become happier than by acting individualistically. Happiness can then arise, in the contexts under study, either as the predictable consequence of enlightened utility-maximizing agents or as an unintended effect of non-preferential behavior, but not as the predictable consequence of choices made by standard utility-maximizing agents.

Notes

*   I would like to thank Luigino Bruni, Pier Luigi Porta and participants in the International Conference on The Paradoxes of Happiness in Economics, University of Milano-Bicocca, where an earlier version of this chapter was presented. I am also indebted to Robert Sugden for his invaluable and constant suggestions throughout this work as well as to Shaun Hargreaves Heap, Piergiovanna Natale, Paolo Vanin, Stefano Zamagni, the seminar audience at UEA and participants in the Workshop on Social Preferences and Happiness, University of Verona, for helpful comments and insights. The usual disclaimers apply.

1. Strictly speaking, several real-life situations where collective action problems are likely to arise would call for the generalized version of the PD, that is, the *n-person prisoner's dilemma* (or *social dilemma*). However, for simplicity, we will continue to refer exclusively to the classic one-shot PD setting, though we believe that most of the qualitative considerations developed here extend naturally to larger and more complex social environments.

2. At this stage, though this will appear to many as an obvious remark, it is worth pointing out that, while hereafter and throughout the chapter we will take for granted that in a PD the Pareto-efficient outcome of mutual cooperation is individually and socially desirable, we are not claiming that, with regard to real-life situations having the PD structure, the same proposition holds from the point of view of society as a whole. Such a broader conclusion would hold only if either (i) the set of players coincided with the set of all citizens or (ii) interaction within this setting brought about beneficial effects for society as a whole (as is the case when, say, the voluntary provision of a public good such as education, environment preservation or health is concerned). On this, see Sacco and Zarri (2002).

3. In his pioneering contribution to the theory of 'revealed preferences', Samuelson (1938) argued that his aim was 'to develop the theory of consumer's behaviour freed from any

vestigial traces of the utility concept' (quoted in Sen 1973: 242). With reference to this approach, Little (1949) asserted that 'the new formulation is scientifically more respectable [since] if an individual's behaviour is consistent, then it must be possible to explain that behaviour without reference to anything other than behaviour' (quoted in Sen 1973: 242).

4. Even in this respect, the PD provides a clear example of such a coincidence: here, in so far as players are assumed to exclusively care about their material payoffs, it makes sense to specify the game by inserting in each cell the 'years of prison' each of them would get as a consequence of the combination of the player's and his/her opponent's strategic choices.

5. In the same vein, Camerer (2003: 26) claims: 'The payoffs are *utilities* for consequences. That is, in the original game the consequences may be money, pride, reproduction by genes, territory in wars, company profits, pleasure, or pain. A key assumption is that players can express their satisfaction with these outcomes on a numerical utility scale. The scale must at least be ordinal – i.e. they would rather have an outcome with utility 2 than with utility 1 – and when expected utility calculations are made the scale must be cardinal (i.e., getting 2 is as good as a coin flip between 3 and 1)'(original italics).

6. In the same vein, Zamagni (2003) asks the following question: 'How can the idea of an agent who chooses autonomously and rationally be reconciled with the idea that happiness has to do not only with the satisfaction of preferences (utility) and thus of interests, but also with affections, emotions, moral dispositions – in a word, with personal identity?'.

7. Camerer (2003) defines a game as consisting 'of the "strategies" each of several "players" have, with precise rules for the order in which players choose strategies, the information they have when they choose, and how they rate the desirability (or "utility") of resulting outcomes' (p. 2). As we can see, how to play is *not* part of the definition of the game. He further adds: 'It is important to distinguish *games* from game *theory*. Games are a taxonomy of strategic situations, a rough equivalent for social science of the periodic table of elements in chemistry. Analytical game *theory* is a mathematical derivation of what players with different cognitive capabilities are likely to do in games' (p. 3). That he believes, as we do, that action may derive from decision criteria other than utility-maximization, can be inferred from the following statement: 'Dominance is important because, if utility payoffs are correctly specified . . . and *players care only about their own utility*, there is no good reason to violate strict dominance' (p. 26, italics added).

8. In the light of these considerations, we do not agree with Binmore's (1994: 27) critique of Sen: according to Binmore, Sen is confusing 'what has to be analyzed with how the analysis is conducted. When a game comes to be analyzed, intelligibility demands that matters like those raised by Sen should *already have been incorporated* into the structure of the game. If the players have the power to *alter their preferences* to commit themselves to behaving in certain ways *before* the play of the Prisoners' Dilemma, then it is *not the Prisoners' Dilemma* that they are playing, but some more complicated game. . . . Players cannot alter the game they are playing. If it seems like they can, it is because the game has been improperly specified'(italics added).

9. It is interesting to remark that such a risk of external inconsistency of choice, with respect to a purpose such as happiness, had been anticipated by Kant.

10. It should be clear, at this stage, that while for expositional ease we are constantly referring to (pseudo) Kantian rationality, the line of reasoning developed here has a far wider reach and applies to any non-preferential principle of action which, in social dilemmas, is capable of making mutual cooperation a feasible equilibrium outcome.

References

Anderson, E. (2001), 'Symposium on Amartya Sen's Philosophy: 2. Unstrapping the straitjacket of "preference": a comment on Amartya Sen's contributions to economics and philosophy', *Economics and Philosophy*, **17** (1), 21–38.

Aumann, R. (1987), 'Game theory', in J. Eatwell, M. Milgate and P. Newman (eds), *The New Palgrave: A Dictionary of Economics*, Vol. 2, London: Macmillan.

Binmore, K. (1994), *Game Theory and the Social Contract. Volume I: Playing Fair*, Cambridge, MA: MIT Press.

Binmore, K. (1998), *Game Theory and the Social Contract. Volume II: Just Playing*, Cambridge, MA: MIT Press.

Camerer, C. (2003), *Behavioral Game Theory*, Princeton, NJ: Princeton University Press.

Easterlin, R.A. (2001), 'Income and happiness: towards a unified theory', *Economic Journal*, **111**, 465–84.

Fehr, E. and U. Fischbacher (2002), 'Why social preferences matter – the impact of non-selfish motives on competition, cooperation and incentives', *Economic Journal*, **112**, 1–33.

Fehr, E. and S. Gächter (1999), 'Reciprocal fairness, heterogeneity, and institutions', Paper presented at the American Economic Association (AEA) Meeting in New York, 3–5 January.

Fehr, E. and S. Gächter (2002), 'Altruistic punishment in humans', *Nature*, **415**, 137–40.

Frederic, S. and G. Loewenstein (1999), 'Hedonic adaptation', in D. Kahneman, E. Diener and N. Schwarz (eds), *Well-being: The Foundations of Hedonic Psychology*, New York: Russell Sage Foundation, 302–29.

Geanakoplos, J., D. Pearce, and E. Stacchetti (1989), 'Psychological games and sequential rationality', *Games and Economic Behaviour*, **1**, 60–79.

Hausman, D. and M. McPherson (1994), 'Economics, rationality, and ethics', in D. Hausman (ed.), *The Philosophy of Economics*, Cambridge: Cambridge University Press, 252–77.

Hollis, M. (1994), *The Philosophy of Social Science*, Cambridge: Cambridge University Press.

Hsee, C.K. (2003), 'Inconsistency between choice and experience', Paper presented at the International Conference on The Paradoxes of Happiness in Economics, University of Milan-Bicocca, 21–23 March.

Hsee, C.K. and J. Zhang (2004), 'Distinction bias: misprediction and mischoice due to joint evaluation', *Journal of Personality and Social Psychology*, **86** (5), 680–95.

Kahneman, D., P. Wakker and R. Sarin (1997), 'Back to Bentham? Explorations of experienced utility', *Quarterly Journal of Economics*, **112** (2), 375–406.

Menicucci, D. and P.L. Sacco (1996), 'Rawlsian altruism and efficiency', *Studi e Discussioni*, **102**, Department of Economics, University of Florence.

Ng, Y. (1997), 'A case for happiness, cardinalism, and interpersonal comparability', *Economic Journal*, **107**, 1848–58.

Rabin, M. (1993), 'Incorporating fairness into game theory and economics', *American Economic Review*, **83**, 1281–302.

Rabin, M. (1997), 'Psychology and economics', Berkeley Department of Economics, Working Paper no. 97-251, University of California at Berkeley.

Rabin, M. (2002), 'A perspective on psychology and economics', *European Economic Review*, **46**, 657–85.

Rapoport, A. (1987), 'Prisoner's dilemma', in J. Eatwell, M. Milgate and P. Newman (eds), *The New Palgrave: A Dictionary of Economics*, Vol. 3, London: Macmillan.

Sacco, P.L. and L. Zarri (2002), 'Collective action dilemmas and norms of social reasonableness', *Ars Interpretandi. Yearbook of Legal Hermeneutics*, **7**, 401–25.

Sen, A. (1973), 'Behaviour and the concept of preference', *Economica*, **40**, 241–59.

Sen, A. (1974), 'Choice, ordering and morality', in S. Körner (ed.), *Practical Reason*, Oxford: Blackwell, 54–67.

Sen, A. (1977), 'Rational fools: a critique of the behavioral foundations of economic theory', *Philosophy and Public Affairs*, **6**, 317–44.

Sen, A. (1982), *Choice, Welfare and Measurement*, Oxford: Basil Blackwell.

Sen, A. (1985), 'Goals, commitment, and identity', *Journal of Law, Economics and Organization*, **1** (2), 341–55.

Sen, A. (1994), 'The formulation of rational choice', *American Economic Review*, **84** (2), 385–90.

Sen, A. and B. Williams (1982), *Utilitarianism and Beyond*, Cambridge: Cambridge University Press.

Sugden, R. (1991), 'Rational choice: a survey of contributions from economics and philosophy', *Economic Journal*, **101** (407), 751–85.

Sugden, R. (2000), 'Team preferences', *Economics and Philosophy*, **16**, 175–204.

Sugden, R. (2001), 'Ken Binmore's evolutionary social theory', *Economic Journal*, **111**, F213–43.
Sugden, R. (2002), 'Beyond sympathy and empathy: Adam Smith's concept of fellow feeling', *Economics and Philosophy*, **18**, 63–88.
Van Hees, M. (2003), 'Acting autonomously versus not acting heteronomously', *Theory and Decision*, **54** (4), 337–55.
Zamagni, S. (2003), 'Happiness and individualism: an impossible marriage', Paper presented at the International Conference on The Paradoxes of Happiness in Economics, University of Milan-Bicocca, 21–23 March.

17 Why are people so unhappy? Why do they strive so hard for money? Competing explanations of the broken promises of economic growth

Stefano Bartolini

1. Introduction

For millennia, human history has been dominated by the substantial stability of per capita income, the reason being that any rare and slow increase in output generated – *à la* Malthus – population growth.

Approximately two centuries ago, the onset of economic growth triggered by the Industrial Revolution heralded the advent of a new era, replete with promises of improvements in the human condition. From the outset, however, it was evident to many that matters were not simple: the new road forward was paved with dramatic social and environmental costs. Nevertheless, during the subsequent two centuries it generally seemed that the game was worth the candle. After all, the prospect of a progressive increase in purchasing power held out at least two seductive promises: first, the reduction of the conditioning that the need to have money imposes on individual choices; and second, the increase in the degree of satisfaction that people feel in their own lives. The two promises were obviously connected. It seemed reasonable to expect, after all, that human beings freed from mass poverty would feel better.

The ample availability of data regarding the relevant variables allows one to try to give an answer to the question: has growth lived up to its promises?

Section 2 very briefly surveys the evidence, which shows that economic growth has largely betrayed its promises. Rich countries seem peopled by a dissatisfied humanity, largely absorbed in a feverish hunt for money. This evidence, removed over a long period, gives rise to disquieting questions: should growth be abandoned as a prospect of improvement of the human condition? Is it truly inevitable that money cannot buy happiness? Is material well-being incapable of contributing to the satisfaction that humans feel about their lives? Should we stop recommending growth as a prospect of progress to both rich and poor countries? Should we abandon economic prosperity as a way to human progress or does the problem lie elsewhere? What, however, could be an alternative way?

The answers to these questions depend on the explanation that is given for the betrayal of growth's promises. The answers are, in fact, very different if the broken promises derive from our biology, our culture, our technology or the economic and social organization.

Section 3 analyses the main explanations for this evidence furnished by economists, sociologists and psychologists. In Section 4, I argue that all of them except one encounter serious empirical difficulties. The exception is the explanation based on the idea that relative position is important in agents' preferences.

Section 5 discusses another explanation; the one provided by GASP (growth as substitution process) models, which show how social and environmental degradation can be the engine for both growth as well as the dissatisfaction that it generates. These models emphasize the role of negative externalities as an engine of growth and their predictions seem consistent with the empirical evidence. Even though the GASP approach organizes various bodies of literature into a single discourse on money, time and happiness, its overall results are surprising for each of the literatures involved. Not only, obviously, for the theory of endogenous growth – given its insistence on the role of positive externalities as the engine of growth – but also for all the other literatures involved: development, social capital, happiness, environmental and labor economics, economic history, economic sociology and psychology.

Section 6 concludes and the appendix provides an outline of the GASP models.

2.   The broken promises of growth
Surprisingly unhappy

A man or woman of the nineteenth century would probably have been astonished to learn that a world freed from mass poverty would have remained marked by mass dissatisfaction. And it is likely that this would be equally surprising to those billions of human beings who still languish in poverty.

None the less, this seems to be exactly what has happened. The ample availability of data regarding plausible indicators of the degree of satisfaction that individuals feel in their own lives, demonstrates beyond question that individuals populating rich countries feel that the promise of greater happiness held out by growth has not been fulfilled. The most relevant data probably concern 'subjective well-being', that is to say the self-evaluation of individuals with regard to their well-being. Whether one considers the time-series or the cross-country data, the correlation between subjective well-being and income is generally nonexistent or negative (see the 'classics' by Easterlin 1974 and 1995, and Oswald 1997). Also the analyses of objective data on well-being, such as those concerning the diffusion of mental illnesses, suicides, alcoholism, drugs, psychopharmaca and so on, converge with the data on subjective well-being in pointing out a disappointing trend in the well-being of rich countries.

Why are people so unhappy? Why has the enormous growth of per capita income recorded in the western countries since the Second World War not increased happiness? How can we explain Lane's paradox that 'the economic . . . institutions of our time are products of the utilitarian philosophy of happiness but seem to have guided us to a period of greater unhappiness' (Lane 2000, p. 13)?

The issue of unhappiness and explanations of the malaise afflicting the advanced societies have recently provoked an animated debate which, besides giving rise to a new branch of economics ('happiness economics'), has involved sociologists (Veenhoven 1993; Baumann 2002), psychologists, political scientists (Lane 2000), and demographers.

Surprisingly striving for money

Old expectations   For a great part of the modern history of the western world, it seemed reasonable to expect that long-run growth would increase leisure. For instance, John Maynard Keynes predicted that by 2030 the average working week in Britain would amount to only 15 hours. Keynes's forecast reflected the prevailing cultural climate of his time. This climate was pervasive up to the 1970s, when the debate on the prospects of the imminent 'leisure society' was still lively. The increase in purchasing power was expected to reduce the pressure that economic necessities exert on individual choices and the importance of money in determining the course of our lives would diminish as a consequence. In a society freed from mass poverty, individuals' decisions regarding the use of their time would be emancipated from the slavery imposed by the need for money.

Moreover, the growth in wealth was expected to release people from the obligation to accumulate in order to defend themselves against economic fluctuations, uncertainty, the hardships of old age and to safeguard the future of their descendants.

In short, it seemed legitimate to believe that the diminution of the difficulty in ensuring present and future consumption would have reduced individuals' interest in money. As a consequence, they would make fewer sacrifices in terms of time and present consumption aimed at acquiring income and wealth. The day would come when money would no longer be a central concern.

To what extent has growth fulfilled this promise? One of the various paradoxes to be found in the literature considered in this chapter is that the

disappearance of mass poverty has not substantially reduced the importance of money in our lives, at least not according to the main indicators of
money's importance: the efforts that people make to acquire income and
wealth. Or in other words, the extent to which they work and the extent to
which they save. A brief outline of the evidence follows.

Saving trends   The beginning of the growth process of an economic
system – that is, the transition from an agricultural economy to an industrial one – is associated with a dramatic rise in the saving rate: this, indeed,
is a feature shared by all industrial revolutions (Krugman 1995). In practice, industrial transition also marks the shift of the saving rate to a more
stable and higher level. This level, in fact, remains surprisingly high even
in rich countries where people make greater sacrifices (in terms of present
consumption) than one might expect in economies that have accumulated
an enormous quantity of wealth. All in all, therefore, the evidence indicates that industrialism is associated with a strong propensity to accumulate. The transition to a post-industrial economy does not modify this
feature. [1]

Labor trends   Economic growth is associated with the intensive use of
human labor. In fact, three stylized facts seem to be evident:

1.   Industrial revolutions are associated with an explosion in the labor
      supply – as well as in accumulation rates – taking the form of dramatic
      increases in the participation rate, in working time and so on
      (Krugman 1995; Bartolini and Bonatti 2002; Antoci and Bartolini
      2004). England was the first country to experience the 10-, 12-, 14-hour
      workday of the Industrial Revolution, and a century would pass before
      the pre-industrial eight-hour workday once again became the rule.
      Since then, the mobilization of human resources has been an empiri-
      cal regularity shared by all industrial revolutions until the second-
      generation Asian Tigers. This mobilization of human resources during
      industrial revolutions is accompanied by a massive redistribution of
      the population between countryside and city and between agriculture
      and industry. In practice, this process involves the rapid urbanization
      of the vast masses of underemployed peasants, who swell the ranks of
      the cheap industrial labor force indispensable for the take-off.
2.   The time evolution of work effort subsequent to the industrial trans-
      ition seems disappointing. In fact, the overwhelming majority of the
      increase of work productivity in the past century was allocated to
      increasing output and not leisure time. [2] Why is 'industrialism biased
      toward producing goods rather than leisure'? (Cross 1993, p. vii).

3. The prospects of the post-industrial economy are equally discouraging. The figures on the work hours in the largest post-industrial economy of the world – the United States – mostly indicate that they are increasing (Schor 1993; Bluestone and Rose 2000).[3]

Summing up, growth begins with an explosion of the labor supply, continues with a weak and unstable reduction in the work effort and concludes its performance, for now, with an increase in working time and a rapid expansion of time-impoverished social groups in the largest example of a post-industrial economy.

There is, therefore, good reason to be disappointed. The three stages of economic growth – the industrial take-off, the industrial stage, and the post-industrial one, as we historically know them – do not give rise to any optimism with regard to the capacity of economic growth to represent a decisive progress towards humanity's mastery of its own time. The expectations of a substantial increase in leisure time, which have pervaded a great part of modern history, have not been fulfilled. Work still absorbs most of people's vital energies and money is still the greatest of their desires, at least to judge from what they are willing to put up with to acquire it.

Why is the acquisition of money still the overriding life-goal of people living in rich and productive economies? Why is time pressure a problem typical of the contemporary age? Why does every study on the matter document that people feel oppressed by a 'time squeeze'? What induces people to work so hard in economies that grow constantly more productive?

3. Explanations

The evidence just discussed depicts a greedy and unhappy humanity despite a dramatic increase in purchasing power. The responsiveness of well-being, the labor support and the saving rate to long-term variations in income and wealth, is very low or null. Why has the mass freeing from the imperatives of subsistence not emancipated people from their enslavement to money and brought them greater happiness?

Why people are so unhappy
At least four explanations have been proposed for the disappointing long-run trend of happiness in the psychological, sociological and economic literature on the topic.

1. *The set point theory*   According to this theory, the individual propensity to happiness is a personal trait of largely genetic origin and influenced by personality (Lykken and Tellegen 1996). The explanation for

the stagnation of happiness is that happiness is a stochastic phenomenon. Chance distributes unequal amounts of happiness among people's genetic codes, leaving the average level unchanged.

2. *The decreasing marginal utility of money*   This idea – that of a progressive saturation of needs, or at least of those needs that can be satisfied by marketable goods – is very general and is consistent with a variety of approaches, including mainstream growth theory. It may evoke an image of societies that are affluent and sated with regard to material needs, but in which individuals cannot purchase what they truly need. This idea is compatible with a broad variety of critiques of materialism and consumerism and also with a large body of studies, mainly psychological, which emphasize the primary importance of the quality of the relational world in which individuals live in determining their happiness. And it is furthermore consistent with several other explanations furnished by psychologists and sociologists.[4]

3. *Adaptation*   An increase in income has only temporary effects on people's happiness because they progressively adapt to the new circumstances (Helson 1964; Brickman and Campbell 1971). This theory is often presented as the flip side of the coin of one of the keys of human evolutionary success, the elevated capacity to adapt. That which saves us from sinking into despair in the face of adversity also prevents us from elevating ourselves to a more stable, higher plane of experience under favorable circumstances. Adaptation theory is sometimes presented in conjunction with set point theory: the effects of external circumstances on happiness are temporary and its long-term level is determined by biology and personality. However, these two theories are compatible but nevertheless distinct. It is in fact possible that the effects of an increase in income on happiness are temporary, but that the long-run level of happiness is determined by factors other than genes and personality.

4. *The importance of relative position*   There is a proliferation of terms in economic theory (status concern, relative income or wealth effects, Veblen effects, competition for positional goods, rivalry, quest for rank, social comparisons) that refer to the same idea: namely that relative position matters in individual preferences. If it is a person's relative position that counts, then a general increase in income cannot increase the happiness of everyone because his or her relative position remains unchanged.

Note that explanations 3 and 4 can be expressed, and often are, in terms of aspirations. Indeed the lack of correlation between income and happiness is explained in both cases by the fact that aspirations increase with income. The difference between the two theories is the answer to the question: what determines the dynamic of aspirations? In the former case, the answer is 'experience'; in the latter, it is 'the others'. As we shall see, this difference gives rise to very different predictions.

The first three explanations are different versions of the idea that 'money cannot buy happiness'. This idea is common to all three theories, although it is based on completely different considerations in each of them. In the set point theory, the contention is that no external factor is able to exert a permanent influence on happiness because the latter is a invariant trait. In the second case (decreasing marginal utility of money), growth cannot increase happiness beyond a certain level because needs become saturated – or at least those needs whose satisfaction can be bought. In the third case, it is the constant adaptation of aspirations to the growth of income that renders money unable to purchase anything but temporary happiness.

Any money-can't-buy-happiness theory, therefore, is consistent with the lack of correlation between income and happiness, but it has a problem: such consistency is obtained at the price of counterfactual predictions regarding the trend in work and saving. In fact, these theories tend to predict that people's interest in money will diminish through time because of the disappointing impact of income on happiness. If people perceive this disappointment, they will tend to revise their choices and reduce their efforts to acquire money. In other words, if people realize that their happiness depends on, say, personal traits, or that adaptation will sooner or later annul the advantages of an increase in income, or that money cannot satisfy needs that are essential, they will react by reducing their efforts aimed at making money. In short, if money cannot buy happiness, the labor supply and the saving rate will be highly responsive to variations in labor productivity and wealth.

As we have seen, this prediction is counterfactual. Of course, money-can't-buy-happiness theories may provide a different prediction if they included a theory of the failure of rationality, which shows that individuals systematically overestimate the impact of consumption on their happiness. But, as we shall discuss below, these theories generally do not include such a theory. Thus, these explanations of the trend of happiness are obtained at the price of counterfactual predictions, as far as people's interest in money is concerned.

The explanation based on the importance of relative position does not suffer from this problem because it is not grounded on the idea that money cannot buy happiness. The former buys the latter, but it does so *ceteris paribus*: that is, as long as other individuals do not increase their wealth. Hence, the disappointing trend of happiness with respect to income does not depend on the fact that each individual's money does not buy his or her happiness, but rather on the fact that the money of other individuals buys his or her unhappiness. This characteristic is crucial because, as we shall see in the next subsection, it allows relative-position-matters theory to predict the persistence of a high priority of money in individual choices in economies experiencing long-run growth, differently from the money-can't-buy-happiness theories.

Why people strive so much for money

Why has almost all the increase in labor productivity been devoted to increasing output and not leisure? This subsection examines two possible explanations of the evidence suggesting that the importance given to money in individual choices displays a marked persistence in the presence of a long-term increase in income and wealth: the explanation offered by growth theory and the one based on the importance of relative position.

Endogenous growth   Growth theory should be naturally suited to explaining the trend in leisure time. After all, the allocation of increments in labor productivity between increased output and increased leisure is a matter of crucial importance to a theory of growth. Indeed, an economy that devoted increased productivity entirely to increasing leisure would not achieve any growth of output. It should be noted that this carries the important implication that an increase in productivity is not a sufficient condition for growth to be generated.

Generally speaking, growth theory has concentrated on identifying mechanisms – accumulation and technical progress – that plausibly explain the long-term increase in the productivity of labor. This exclusive attention seemingly alludes to the fact that an increase in labor productivity is a sufficient condition for growth to come about. But, as said, explaining why an economy grows should also involve explaining why people do not choose to use their increased labor productivity to increase leisure rather than output. What is it, therefore, that induces individuals to work long hours in economies that grow ever-more wealthy and productive?

Unfortunately, the majority of growth models cannot be used to provide an answer to this question because they assume that the labor supply is given. This implies the initial assumption of the result which is to be obtained: namely that the increase in labor productivity is allocated to increasing output rather than leisure. It is, therefore, necessary to build models that include the labor supply among the endogenous variables, if the above question is to be answered.

But a problem arises when the labor/leisure choice is included in models of endogenous growth. In fact, perpetual growth tends to disappear in these models, if the labor supply is endogenous. This is because individuals tend to react to increased productivity by reducing their labor supply. In other words, once the labor/leisure choice is included, endogenous growth models tend to predict that individuals will use the long-term increase in labor productivity to augment their leisure, not their output.[5]

The prediction that the labor supply will be highly responsive to technological advances has two unpleasant implications for the endogenous growth theory: one empirical and the other theoretical. The empirical implication is that this prediction is counterfactual. The theoretical one is that accumulation and technical progress, that is those factors that are indicated as the engines of growth, its primum and secundum movens, are not sufficient to generate perpetual growth.

Likewise, the fact that the marginal productivity of capital does not decrease (as in models of endogenous growth) is not a sufficient condition for the saving rate to be sufficiently sustained over time to ensure perpetual growth. In economies that grow ever richer, in fact, individuals may choose to reduce their efforts to accumulate. Indeed, it is precisely this prediction that endogenous growth models tend to make when the labor supply is endogenized. Perpetual growth also flags because individuals reduce their saving rate: agents tend to respond to increased wealth by reducing their work effort devoted to accumulation (Duranton 2001; Bartolini and Bonatti 2003b).

Summing up, the fragility of endogenous growth models with respect to the endogenization of the labor supply, implies that they fail to explain why an economy follows a perpetual growth path. Consequently, growth theory seems to lack a tertium movens of growth, besides accumulation and technical progress. Growth theory seems to fail to identify the tertium movens able to motivate people not to reduce their efforts aimed at income and wealth in economies that grow ever richer and ever-more productive. In fact, according to endogenous growth models, agents will tend to respond to increasing labor productivity and wealth by enjoying life more (that is, reducing labor effort and accumulation) than is necessary for ensuring perpetual growth.

However, some peculiarity of preferences may support the endogenous growth theory. Models with an endogenous labor supply that generate perpetual growth can certainly be obtained by assuming that the income effect does not dominate, or only weakly dominates, the substitution effect, that is if a relatively low preference for output with respect to leisure is assumed. Hence, the only explanation for the persistently high importance of money in advanced economies that seems consistent with mainstream growth theory, is that this importance depends on the fact that people want money much more than they want time. This explanation predicts a strong correlation between income and well-being. In fact, an explanation of the time squeeze, based on the fact that income variations have a greater impact than time variations on individual well-being, carries the implication that individual well-being is highly responsive to variations in income. If it is not time that truly makes people happy, then it must be money.

But the problem with this prediction is, as we have seen, that it is counterfactual. In other words, mainstream growth theory can provide predictions that are consistent with the trends of the labor effort and the saving rate only by paying the price of counterfactual predictions with respect to the trend of happiness.

Relative position matters   The second explanation for the lack of correlation between income and happiness, is the one based on the importance of relative position – an explanation that we have already found to be consistent with the trend exhibited by happiness in economies that experienced long-run growth. If it is relative position that matters, agents are induced by competition for status to work hard and to save much. In a world where relative position counts, and the well-being of those with constant real incomes is bound to worsen if other people increase their income, there are strong incentives for agents to strive for money.[6] Consequently, the explanation based on the importance of relative position is compatible – unlike explanations of the money-can't-buy-happiness type – with the persistence of a high degree of interest in money in affluent economies.

4.   The happiness paradox

Note that the literatures on working time, saving rate and happiness have, to date, conducted the debates on each trend in an entirely separate manner and with no awareness of the linkages among them.

Note also that, with the exception of the explanation based on the importance of relative position, every explanation of each of the two trends (importance of money and happiness) implies counterfactual predictions as far as the other trend is concerned. The explanation of the persistence of the importance of money, based on the low preference for leisure, tends to predict that happiness will be highly responsive to an increase in income, while the money-can't-buy-happiness explanations of the happiness trend predict that people will progressively lose interest in money.

It is not surprising that these theories should find it difficult to provide a joint explanation of the two trends. After all, the question that must be answered is a highly puzzling one: why do people strive so much for money if money cannot buy happiness? In the literature on the topic, this question is known as a 'happiness paradox'. Any joint explanation of the evidence should be able to account for this paradox.

Relative position and the paradox of happiness

Thus far, we have encountered only one promising explanation for the various trends considered: the relative-position-matters explanation, which too is put forward disjointedly to explain each of the two trends. According to this explanation, the trends in saving, work and happiness depend on a coordination failure. Individuals are induced to overwork and to overaccumulate by positional competition. The incentives to work effort and accumulation, produced by competition for relative position, generate growth. But growth is a general improvement in the absolute position. Consequently, it cannot generate a general increase in well-being, because what matters is the relative position. In an economy of this kind, the well-being of everyone cannot improve. Hence the desire to 'keep up with the Joneses' is at the root of the happiness paradox.

In other words, the relative-position-matters explanation can provide the growth theory with that tertium movens of growth, which is able to render it compatible with the happiness paradox. The quest for rank is, in fact, able to motivate individuals to dedicate high efforts to work and to accumulation even in the presence of long-run growth, so as to assure perpetual growth and to explain why it does not increase happiness.[7]

Policy if relative position matters

The literature that deals with the importance of relative position in preferences has emphasized various policy implications:

1. *Fiscal* In economies in which relative income is the relevant positional variable, an income tax is Pareto improving because it reduces the incentives to overwork generated by competition for relative position (Layard 2003). In models where the positional variable is, instead, wealth, agents tend to overaccumulate and efficiency is ensured by the taxation of wealth (Corneo and Jeanne 2001).
2. *Redistributive* Inequality tends to boost the incentives provided by positional competition. This justifies recommendations for a policy aimed at reducing inequality.
3. *Social* In order to reduce opportunities for positional competition: 'we should avoid those games against other people, which are intrinsically zero sum' (Layard 2003, p. 13). Any academic is probably able to think of examples of the organization of university studies, which promote competition for status among students.

The feature shared by all these prescriptions is that they respond to the need to impede the waste of resources resulting from a general endeavor for a goal that cannot be achieved by everybody. These recommendations show that ways exist to reduce or eliminate this waste. But they do not indicate how happiness can be progressively increased. A long-run improvement in the human condition is not possible if desires are essentially relative: at least, not until those desires change.

Two positions have been taken up on whether a change of this kind is possible. According to the first – which is also put forward by authoritative evolutionary psychologists (Pinker 1997) – the human interest in relative position is unalterable, because its origin is biological: it originates, in fact, in the cognitive processes that depict the horizon of the possible in the human species. Aspirations are modeled on what is considered reasonably obtainable, and the main source of information on the 'reasonably obtainable' is what other people have obtained.

The second position considers change in preferences to be possible, because they are largely shaped by certain institutions. Hence, the formation of preferences can be orientated by means of institutional change. Educational policy and the regulation of mass media are two ways in which public policy can influence the formation of preferences.

It is claimed that our system of child rearing should foster the pursuit of absolute, not relative goals. Serious claims can be raised that the present system does exactly the opposite (Layard 2003).

Television is accused of playing a pernicious role in the formation of our relative aspirations: 'TV creates discontent by bombarding us with images of body shapes, riches and goods we do not have' (ibid., p. 16). These criticisms have major implications for the regulation of the television system. For example: 'why should advertising not be limited to the provision of information?' (ibid. p. 17).

A way to increase general happiness exists, therefore, but it requires the long and uncertain time-scale of a policy intended to reduce the importance of rank in preferences.

A more radical version of these ideas maintains that a society based on competition tends to generate a system of values – success, power and so on – which are relative by their very nature. Hence, the preferences generated by a market society, prevent exploitation of the opportunities to increase well-being associated with the economic prosperity that it generates.

5.   Explanation based on social and environmental degradation

A further explanation of the happiness paradox was recently presented, based on the idea that social and environmental degradation fuel both growth as well as the dissatisfaction that it generates (Bartolini and Bonatti 2002, 2003a, 2003b, 2004a, 2004b, 2006; Antoci and Bartolini 2004). An outline of these models is provided in the appendix.

This approach starts from the consideration that well-being and productive capacity depend largely on goods that are not purchased in the market but are freely provided by the social and natural environment. The growth process generates extensive negative externalities, which reduce such social and environmental assets. These negative externalities may be an engine of growth, given the capacity of the market to supply costly substitutes for the diminishing free goods. Indeed, if agents can purchase substitutes for free resources, they will react to the decline in their well-being or in their productive capacity by increasing their use of marketable goods. In other words, negative externalities force individuals to increasingly rely on private goods in order to prevent a decline in their well-being or productive capacity. In this way, social and environmental degradation contributes to an increase in output. This increase feeds back into the negative externalities, giving rise to a further diminution in common assets to which agents react by increasing output, and so on. A self-reinforcing mechanism thus operates, whereby growth generates social and environmental depletion and such depletion generates growth. Hence, growth takes the form of a process of substitution, whereby free final (or intermediate) goods are progressively replaced with costly goods in the consumption (or production) patterns of individuals.

According to these GASP models, the importance that individuals attribute to money remains high in the presence of a long-term increase in income and wealth, because they have to defend themselves against negative externalities. The need to escape environmental and social degradation is the motivation to strive for money, the tertium movens of growth, which growth theory has failed to identify.

In fact, alongside the trend of the labor supply, the trend of the saving rate also depends on social and environmental cleavages because in this framework, social wealth also includes social and environmental capital as well as private capital, but agents can accumulate only the latter. Hence, agents react to the progressive depletion of commons by keeping their saving rate high. The growing social and environmental poverty produces a negative wealth effect, which boosts accumulation despite the increasing private wealth.

In this view, industrial revolutions are the paradigmatic example of this mechanism: they are the most striking processes of labor supply and accumulation mobilization because they are the most striking processes of social and environmental cleavages recorded by economic history.

According to GASP models, however, the two broken promises of growth are two sides of the same coin. People strive so much for money because money is their private way out from the decay of what they have in common; and this decay is what explains why money does not buy happiness. Negative externalities explain why people work and save so much, but also explain why people's efforts are not rewarded with increased well-being. Indeed, in this framework, economic prosperity does not increase happiness because negative externalities force individuals into overwork and overaccumulation, which results in an excessive depletion of social and environmental assets. Growth appears, thus, to be a coordination failure.

The dark side of growth

The idea behind GASP models is that one way to motivate people to accumulate money is to create a society in which increasingly less can be obtained for free; that is, a society in which opportunities to acquire well-being in ways which do not pass through the market, become increasingly scarce and in which well-being can, therefore, only be purchased.

According to this approach, mainstream theory of growth is unable to explain the happiness paradox because it tells only part of the growth story – that part of the story, that is, in which goods are luxury goods for one generation, standard goods for the next, and absolute necessities for the one after that. The history of economic growth is, obviously, full of examples of this process. But the other side of this story is that of free goods that become scarce and costly ones for the next generation and luxury goods for the one after that.

Urbanization is widely associated with phenomena of this kind. A world in which silence, clean air, swimming in clean seas or rivers or pleasant strolls become the privilege of uncontaminated places and tropical resorts, is a world which tends to spend considerable resources on evading the unlivable environments that it has constructed. The periodic mass migrations known as summer holidays, which one observes in rich countries, or the fact that tourism from rich countries has become an important resource for many poor ones, may not be indicative of higher living standards, but rather a response to deterioration in the quality of life.

Of special importance in explaining growth's betrayal of its promises of well-being, is the interpretation of social capital as 'relational goods', a term that denotes the contribution to well-being made by human relations (see Ulhaner 1989; Gui 1987). That the quality of relations is of crucial importance for happiness is an assertion supported by both a number of studies in the social sciences as well as by evolutionary principles (Lane 2000). From this point of view, rich societies are experiencing a gigantic relational failure. Loneliness is regarded as a great social and personal problem, and so, too, is the poor quality of relations (ibid. p. 85). The progressive spread of market relations, based exclusively on personal advantage, seems to be associated with relational desertification (Polanyi 1968; Hirsch 1976; Bartolini and Palma 2002). The evidence of a decline in social capital in the USA (Putnam 2000), echoes the theme of the destructive impact of the market society on social relationships and cohesion developed by a large and multidisciplinary literature, which probably began with the conservative and socialist critiques of the Industrial Revolution.

Urbanization, too, plays a role in determining the availability of relational goods. Market societies tend to shape the urban space according to a range of relational activities, which is very selective with respect to the original sense of the city, that of a center of aggregation. Western cities are, in fact, built for work and trading, but not to facilitate encounters between its inhabitants. The poverty of relational occasions and of low-cost meeting places and, in parallel, the abundance of costly opportunities for leisure activities typical of urban life, seem a paradigmatic example of the GASP substitution mechanism. The urban distress of social groups with the most amount of free time, the most relational needs and the least money – namely young people and the elderly – testify to this situation. It may be for these reasons that 'the city is the engine of growth' (according to the World Bank) and also the crux of the mass dissatisfaction in rich societies.

However, independently of the variety and complexity of the causes of the relational failure of the market societies, the point is that relational poverty may induce numerous forms of compensation with material goods. Some examples concern the dramatic development of the home entertainment and security sectors, which may be boosted by various aspects of the social climate degradation. Moreover, the substitution mechanism emphasized here, may help explain some changes in lifestyle. The enormous accumulation of produced goods and the worship of everything that is private, which characterizes market societies, may be reactions to the erosion of everything that is common to people.

In conclusion, the relational and environmental failure of market societies may be at the core of the explanation of both the capacity of those societies to generate growth and of the latter's betrayal of its promise of happiness.

Policy in a GASP world

GASP models suggest that the market economies may have constructed a world unsuited to the exploitation of the enormous potential for increased happiness, generated by accumulation and technical progress.

Policies intended to correct these distortions may assume different forms. The GASP approach may support the view that rich economies are overworked and the demand for legislation to reduce working time. It may also support the view that a pure market economy is characterized by an excessive depletion of environmental assets, and then support demand for extensive environmental policy.

Given the emphasis on the importance of relations for human happiness, this approach further suggests that social policies intended to improve relations should be introduced. Urban policy seems one example of the possibility of implementing relational policy. This policy should be aimed at contrasting the tendency to organize urban space to the benefit of production and consumption well beyond the point in which this excessively harms people's relational interests – that is, their interests in making cities also places for living.

In short, the GASP models suggest that collective action is important for the control of the inefficiencies generated by the economies described.

Note that the policy implications of the GASP explanation differ greatly from those of the explanation based on relative position. Current experience and the future risk of diminished well-being derive from an institutional problem, not from a biological or cultural one. The problem lies in the price system, which does not receive signals about the importance of fundamental needs. It is, therefore, the economic organization that must be changed. A more ample role must be destined to the collective action aimed at the allocation of common resources that are crucial for happiness.

In this view, the happiness paradox does not carry the implications that there is no prospect of improving the human condition nor that we should stop thinking to economic prosperity as important for making people happier. The problem is not growth but its social and environmental costs. The fact that money does not buy happiness stems neither from biology nor from culture; money is unable to buy happiness amid a pattern of growth burdened by excessively high social and environmental costs. However, the social and environmental degradation experienced by developed countries is not an ineluctable fate. It is probable that many of the problems to which GASP models allude, could be greatly alleviated by focusing social policies on the humanization of relations among peoples and between people and the environment.

6.   Concluding remarks and future research

Systematic errors

The happiness paradox has often been interpreted as evidence indicating a failure of individual rationality or, in any case, a certain distance between the economic paradigm of rationality and real individuals (Scitovsky 1976; Sen 1996).

In reality, the preceding discussion shows that the paradox does not implicate *per se* the evidence that individuals commit systematic errors. In fact, two of the approaches to the happiness paradox that I have discussed – the relative-position-matters and the GASP approaches – are in terms of failure of coordination and not of rationality. What is common to the two explanations is that the position of an individual with a constant purchasing power worsens when others increase their purchasing power. Within this context, whether the motivation is to keep up with the Joneses or to defend oneself from environmental and social degradation, it is perfectly rational to increase one's own purchasing power if others do so. In this sense, the happiness paradox is explained in both cases as a coordination failure and not as a rationality failure.

Therefore the existence of failures of rationality is crucial only for the capacity to explain the paradox of the third approach, that of money-can't-buy-happiness theories.

For this motive, these theories should include a theory of the failure of rationality, which is lacking for now. The lack of such a theory is a serious weakness of the money-can't-buy-happiness theories, because the type of systematic errors implied is very strong. If money cannot buy happiness why do people not realize it, sooner or later? How can one explain the persistence over many generations of the 'consumer societies'? Furthermore, why do the people that have created these societies not give clear signs of possessing other priorities than just making money?

The present lack of a theory answering these questions, implies neither that it cannot be created nor that there exists no evidence of systematic errors. Even if the happiness paradox does not necessarily demonstrate the existence of a failure of rationality, it can still be deduced by other evidence – at least for what concerns the systematic underestimation of the importance of relational needs compared to material ones.[8]

At least two roads can be followed in furnishing a theory of rationality failure able to explain this evidence. The first consists in founding rationality failure on the cognitive processes on which individual decisions are based. A large body of literature offers fertile terrain for this idea, beginning with neurobiological and psychological studies.[9] The second possible research strategy may try to explain systematic errors by focusing on the impact of institutions on the cognitive tools that individuals dispose of. This approach rests on the idea – widespread in the social sciences – that the social context plays a role in shaping the cognitive tools employed by individuals. For example, systematic errors in selecting the priorities between relational and material needs may be influenced by advertising.

Appendix 17A   The impossible commercial

Advertising tends to persuade people of the following message: 'If you feel insecure and inadequate, you'll feel better if you consume more. If you're afraid of being excluded and seek confirmation that you belong to this society, go out and spend'. A simple clarification of why the tendency to produce messages of this sort is intrinsic to advertising is provided by the following storyboard for a commercial that we shall never see:

Scene One   A small car is parked outside a block of flats, close to a set of traffic lights. Sitting in the car is a middle-aged man of nondescript appearance and with a pleasant face. He is calmly waiting for someone.
Scene Two   A luxury car draws up to the traffic lights, pulling up next to the car described in Scene 1. Sitting up front is the chauffeur; beside him is an attractive secretary with an expression of feigned interest on her face. In the rear, three distinguished businessmen are talking animatedly. The atmosphere in the car is charged with tension and veiled threats. Seated in the middle of the rear seat is a middle-aged man. He is the owner of the car and the boss of the chauffeur and the secretary. He typifies success: a handsome face, a Hollywood tan, thick silver hair. But these clash with his strained and jittery demeanor. The secretary thinks, 'Now the jerk's probably going to get angry because he's making less than he thought on the deal, so he'll forget to buy me that jewelry he promised'. The businessman's mobile phone rings. He answers, 'Ah, Mickey, how many times have I told you not to call me when . . . Right . . . Of course, I hadn't forgotten your football game . . . But, look, something's come up and I really can't take you . . . But, don't worry, I'll get you one of those super play stations, so you'll be happy just the same . . . But now I've got things to do . . . Speak to you later . . . bye'. (To the other businessmen) 'Sorry, but you know what kids are like'. Then (to the chauffeur) 'Get on with it' (the traffic light is still red) . . . can't you see we're late'. Then (to the other businessmen) 'So if you don't agree . . . I'll be forced to . . .'. The car runs the red light.
Scene Three   The front door of the block of flats opens. Out pops a blithe little girl aged about 10. She jumps into the car: 'Come on, daddy, let's go. I'm so excited . . . my first dance show . . .'. They drive away laughing. The voice-over to the commercial – wise, calm, deep, paternal – intones: 'Your time, your love . . . your life'.

Why will we never see a commercial of this kind? Because, of course, nobody sells the products being advertised. Nobody sells time and affection; indeed, having more of them may entail buying less. Yet there are plenty of bad and costly alternatives that can be purchased. Hence the advertised remedy for dissatisfaction is: 'Buy more not less. All you need is more money'.

Appendix 17B   The GASP models
General features
All GASP models share three characteristics:

1. Production or utility functions of N identical individuals depend, beyond the usual variables, on the endowment of a non-excludable and non-rival renewable resource, which can be interpreted as social or environmental capital.
2. Production and/or consumption of the output generate negative externalities affecting the level of the open-access resource.
3. Time is a control variable (except in Bartolini and Bonatti 2004b).

The above structural characteristics have been included in three types of dynamical models:

1. without accumulation or endogenous technical progress (Bartolini and Bonatti 2002, 2006; Antoci and Bartolini 2004);
2. with accumulation and without endogenous technical progress (Bartolini and Bonatti 2003a, 2004a; Wagner 2004); and
3. with both accumulation and endogenous technical progress (Bartolini and Bonatti 2003b, 2004b).

The three types of models show that negative externalities feed growth through the impact that they have on, respectively, the labor supply, accumulation and technical progress. A synthesis of the results follows.

Type 1 models show that negative externalities feed the labor supply. Agents progressively increase the labor supply in order to finance the increase in output aimed at compensating the reduction of the free resource.

The possibility of generating a dynamic of output also in models without accumulation and technical progress, is a relevant result for the growth theory. In fact, the technical problem in building growth models lies in generating an output dynamics. What all growth models have in common, is that this dynamic is generated by accumulation and/or technical progress, the primum and secundum movens of growth. I have argued above that the presence of accumulation and/or technical progress may not be a sufficient condition for generating growth. These three models imply that they are not even necessary for generating Solowian growth. Antoci and Bartolini (2004) obtain this result in an evolutionary context, while in Bartolini and Bonatti (2002, 2006) the result is obtained through optimizing agents. Bartolini and Bonatti (2002) focus on the determinants of multiple equilibria.

These three models show the action of negative externalities as the tertium movens of growth at the pure state, that is to say without interacting with the other two movens of growth. Type 2 and Type 3 models focus instead on the way negative externalities interact with accumulation and technical progress. Indeed, *Type 2 models show that negative externalities feed accumulation*. This result is obtained by augmenting three Solow–Ramsey growth models with GASP explanatory variables. In Bartolini and Bonatti (2003a) the common resource enters only the utility functions while in Bartolini and Bonatti (2004a) it enters only the production functions. Wagner (2004) expands Bartolini and Bonatti (2003a) by including exogenous technical progress and population growth.

Type 3 models show that endogenous technical progress feeds growth because of negative externalities. In fact, negative externalities can influence both the type of technical progress that the economic system tends to produce (Bartolini and Bonatti 2004b) as well as the use it makes of this progress (Bartolini and Bonatti 2003b). In both cases, such influence is beneficial to growth.

- Bartolini and Bonatti (2004b) show that negative externalities generate the type of technical progress that feeds growth, if technical progress is intentional. In fact, this model assumes that individuals can develop two different kinds of technologies, namely technologies which increase the productivity of labor or those which decrease the negative impact of economic activity on social and environmental resources. The allocation of R&D between these two types of technical progress responds to price incentives. Consequently, there is no incentive to develop technologies that economize resources whose price is zero, such as social and environmental ones, and technical progress concentrates on technologies that economize costly factors, such as labor. This model shows that if negative externalities are internalized, the technological trajectory of the economy is more protective of the social and natural environment, the pace of labor productivity increase is slower and the steady-state growth rate is lower. In other words, the incompleteness of markets, that is, missing markets for social and environmental resources, distort technical progress which concentrates on technologies that boost growth.
- Bartolini and Bonatti (2003b) show why technical progress generates perpetual growth, that is, why individuals do not allocate the long-run increment in labor productivity to increasing leisure time and why they do not substantially reduce accumulation with the rise in wealth. The reasons are provided by negative externalities. In fact, if technical progress is unintentional, that is, if it is the result of

positive externalities, it generates perpetual growth only in the presence of negative externalities. In their absence, individuals tend to reduce their work effort and their saving rate as the economy becomes richer and more productive. This slows the growth rate and, in the long run, brings it to a complete halt.

In both models the steady-state welfare of the representative individual is constant in a *laissez-faire* economy. Therefore, they suggest that there are two explanations for why a stable and rapid long-term technical progress has not increased happiness: the wrong type of technical progress has been produced and that which has been produced, has been employed in a wrong way. Both cases are due to a coordination failure.

However, all GASP models can easily generate growth dynamics in which the steady-state welfare of the representative individual declines or remains stable. Growth tends to 'go too far', beyond that point in which the increase in private goods is more than offset by the decline in common resources. More details are provided in the following.

Models without accumulation or technical progress
In the evolutionary game presented by Antoci and Bartolini (2004), an *N* number of identical individuals can choose between a consumption structure based mainly on private goods or derive their well-being principally from a common asset (an open-access renewable resource). In fact, they have two strategies: work little or hard. If the choice is the first one, their payoff depends largely on the common resource (in addition to the produced good and leisure); with the second choice, they dispose of less leisure but have greater access to private goods, which are substitutes of the open-access resource, thus reducing the impact that negative externalities have on their well-being. Indeed, the availability of the environmental good depends negatively on the level of activity. Essentially, therefore, individuals can choose between having little time or little money. The first option, unlike the second one, allows one to escape in part from negative externalities. As usual in evolutionary games, the dynamic of the strategies chosen by agents depends on a replicator dynamics that is, on the pay-offs differential, which is to say from the relative advantage of the two strategies. This depends on the availability of the resource, which in turn depends on the level of activity. In fact, the higher the level of activity, the greater the worsening of the payoff of the 'work little' strategy because it depends also on the endowment of the common good. The game shows that an economy of this type can be trapped in dynamics in which the attempt of some agents to escape from negative externalities by passing from the 'work little' to the 'work hard' strategy, increases these negative externalities and

triggers a self-reinforcing mechanism, which progressively induces all agents to work hard. These dynamics can be Pareto worsening, in the sense that if all agents were to coordinate themselves by all choosing to work little, the increase of the social and environmental quality (and of leisure time) would more than offset the reduction in output.

In Bartolini and Bonatti (2002), well-being depends on leisure time and on two perfect substitutes: the open-access good and the produced one, whose efficiency in substituting the common depends on a technological parameter. N optimizing agents act in perfectly competitive goods and labor markets and the households receive as dividends the profits of the firms. The time evolution of the common asset depends on the difference between its spontaneous renewal flow and the damage caused by economic activity. Two different laws of motion of the open-access asset are analysed. According to the first, economic activity has an impact only on the future quality of the environment, with no effect on present well-being. In the second, production also affects the resource of the current period. If production also affects present well-being, then multiple equilibria (with rational expectations) are possible, because each individual might find it convenient to dedicate more (less) time to work and to consume more (less) of the produced good if convinced that the dominating social values will induce the rest of society to do the same. In this case, the diffusion of a more (less) 'conservative' attitude towards the environment and a less (more) 'consumption-orientated' lifestyle can induce less (more) growth. Hence this model stresses the role of collective beliefs and cultural attitudes in selecting the growth path. However, long-run equilibria characterized by a higher level of activity are Pareto dominated. As a consequence, we may have a coordination failure leading the economy to be locked in a long-run equilibria, which are Pareto dominated by some other possible steady states characterized by a lower level of activity.

The model with optimizing agents presented in Bartolini and Bonatti (2006) assumes that the produced good could also be destined to the satisfaction of needs different from those satisfied by the environmental good. It is shown that this does not alter the results obtained in Bartolini and Bonatti (2002). Furthermore, the impact of (exogenous) technical progress on labor supply and on well-being is analysed. Surprisingly, technical progress decreases the steady-state welfare of the representative individual. The reason lies in an inefficient allocation of technical progress. In fact, the model predicts that technical progress will tend to be allocated to increasing the production of substitutes for diminishing resources, instead of increasing leisure time. But this high labor supply in the presence of technical progress depends on a coordination failure. Individuals would prefer lower levels of activity in exchange for greater leisure time and free resource. Agents, however, are induced by the presence of negative externalities to allocate the increase in productivity to increasing the production of substitutes for the declining common asset (up to the point of increasing the labor supply), because their uncoordinated efforts do not take into account the social cost of the growth in output. The result is an excessive use of environmental and labor resources.

It should be noted that the result that negative externalities can generate an output dynamics has been obtained both in evolutionary models as well as with optimizing agents. This gives robustness to the proposition that negative externalities can generate growth, showing that it does not depend on assumptions about the bounded, or otherwise, rationality of agents.

The models that I present in the following two subsections incorporate the GASP mechanism into the main paradigms of growth theory – exogenous and endogenous growth – in order to show how negative externalities interact with accumulation and technical progress.

Models with accumulation and without endogenous technical progress
Bartolini and Bonatti (2003a, 2004a) and Wagner (2004) include negative externalities in an exogenous growth context *à la* Solow–Ramsey.

Bartolini and Bonatti (2003a) show that negative externalities boost accumulation and, therefore, the steady-state level of activity when the open-access resource enters the utility functions. Furthermore, contrary to standard results in the presence of a renewable resource, the steady-state welfare of the representative individual improves if individuals discount the future more heavily. The reason is that, in this case, individuals will accumulate relatively less, leaving a larger supply of common goods for future generations. This result reverses the traditional environmental explanation for the problems of the sustainability of growth (intended in this paper as sustainability of well-being) based on the selfishness of the current generations, that is to say on the too high level of the discount rate. Note that the possibility of posing the sustainability question in terms of (intertemporal) ethics, that is, intergenerational equity (as is traditionally posed), is entirely based on the presumption that the discount rates are too high. The propensity of present generations to exploit resources crucial for the future exceeds their right to do so defined on the basis of some plausible criterion of intergenerational equity. According to Bartolini and Bonatti (ibid.), the problem of sustainability does not lie in the intergenerational conflict but in the coordination failure among individuals belonging to the same generation. The sustainability question is, therefore, a problem of efficiency and not of equity, since it is a coordination problem. In fact, the economic system may not reflect the discount rate of individuals and this gap could increase with the reduction of the discount rate. The problem stems from the fact that an asset that can be privately accumulated is a perfect substitute for one that cannot be privately accumulated. In this context, rational individuals are spurred to defend themselves from decumulation of what they have in common by accumulating that which can be privately accumulated. The greater their interest in the future, the more they will act this way. The result is that the more individuals are benevolent towards the future, the worse they leave the future for their descendents, due to a coordination failure amongst themselves, caused by the missing market for the open-access resource. The normative problem, thus, is the creation of institutions, which allow the individuals belonging to the same generation to coordinate their preference for the future and not that of establishing lower discount rates. There does not, therefore, necessarily exist conflict in human nature between individual or generational interest and that of the species.

Wagner (2004) extends Bartolini and Bonatti (2003a) by including exogenous technical progress and population growth. He finds that both amplify the substitution mechanism, causing growth to increase and welfare to decrease.

Bartolini and Bonatti (2004a) show that the substitution mechanism may also operate in production. Indeed, in this model, social and environmental assets enter only the production functions and not the utility ones, which depend only on output and leisure. They show that, under certain conditions, the erosion of social and environmental capital may enhance growth, that is, increase the steady-state level of activity. The reason is that individuals may also undertake expenditures to defend themselves against negative externalities when these affect their productive capacities. In the case of social capital, for instance, agents may react to its decline by shifting to transactional modes that employ private goods rather than public ones. Many transaction costs, in fact, are intrinsically a defense against opportunism. But the increased output produces a further decrease in social (or environmental) assets, which feeds back into the mechanism. Hence, also when the substitution mechanism operates in production, individuals may react to the erosion of social capital by expanding the production of private goods. The unintended result will be a further erosion of social (or environmental) capital, and this may trigger a process of self-fueling growth.

Models with both accumulation and endogenous technical progress
In Bartolini and Bonatti (2003b), it is shown that negative externalities may be a necessary condition for generating perpetual growth. It is shown, in fact, that in a Ramsay–Rebelo AK model of endogenous growth, if time is considered as a control variable, the model is no longer able to generate

endogenous growth. A known difficulty of the endogenous growth models is involved, in which the increase in labor productivity tends to generate, in the long run, an increase in leisure time that depresses growth. Furthermore, the increase in wealth due to accumulation tends, in the long run, to depress the saving rate. It is shown that if in this model output is a substitute for a renewable free resource, which is deteriorated by consumption processes, the model returns to generating endogenous growth. This is due to the fact that the presence of negative externalities induces individuals to safeguard their well-being by increasing their consumption of the output. In order to finance this consumption, agents keep their labor supply and their saving rate high along the growth path, thus feeding perpetual growth.

Bartolini and Bonatti (2004b) focus on the allocation of R&D efforts between technologies that improve the social and environmental quality and technologies that enhance input efficiency in the production of private goods. It is assumed that the direction of technical progress is induced by the relative price of resources, as suggested by the theory of 'induced technical progress'. The core of the theory is the hypothesis that the higher the relative price of a resource, the stronger will be the incentive to allocate R&D in technologies which save on the use of that resource, because application of the innovation will be more profitable. In this model, under *laissez faire*, given the incompleteness of markets (markets for open-access resources are absent), price signals distort the direction of technical progress, which wholly concentrates on technologies that economize on priced resources (such as labor). As a consequence, the resource is asymptotically depleted and perpetual growth is generated but households' welfare remains stagnant in the long run. By contrast, under an authority imposing the internalization of the negative externalities, R&D is also invested in resource-saving technical progress; the steady-state growth rate is lower but the resource tends to be preserved and the welfare of households grows forever.

Notes

1. There is a controversy about saving rate trends, concerning the variables that most accurately express the economic concept of saving. If we include capital gains in savings, the US rate in the 1995–98 period was the highest since the 1960s (Gale and Sablehouse 1999).
2. For example, Maddison's data (1995) on working hours covering more than 120 years exhibit a stable tendency to decline in western countries (with the exception of the USA), which is very weak if compared to the increase in labor productivity and output. However, per capita labor input displays a much weaker tendency to diminish, with major and prolonged reversals of tendency, compared to working time. See Bartolini and Bonatti 2002. The reason for this is that per capita labor input (annual average working hours × total employment/total population) is influenced by the historical trend for the participation rate to increase.

3. In the case of the savings rate trends the controversy concerns which are the data that must be considered as conceptually correct, while in the case of the working time the debate focused on which data are the most reliable. However, according to the type of data considered, the results can vary considerably (Bluestone and Rose 2000; see also Figart and Golden 2000 for a critical survey of the controversy on the subject).
4. For example, the pioneering work by Maslow (1943 [1970]) predicted the disappointing trend of happiness in affluent societies on the basis that there exists a hierarchy of needs. When material needs have been satisfied, the increase in happiness depends on the satisfaction of needs that occupy a higher position in the hierarchy, such as the need for love and belonging or that for self-realization. Economic growth, however, is able to satisfy only material needs. Scitovsky's (1976) distinction between comfort and stimulation is also compatible with the idea of the decreasing marginal utility of money. Growth produces an increase in comfort, but it is the stimulating activities that are able to render life happier and money has a limited purchasing power with regard to these latter.
5. Bartolini and Bonatti (2003b) show that if a Ramsey–Rebelo AK model is augmented by treating the units of time devoted to work, h, ('capital operating time') as a choice variable, the resulting AKh model does not generate endogenous growth in the absence of negative externalities. Duranton (2001) shows in an endogenous, growth model with overlapping generations, that when the labour supply is made endogenous, production remains bounded if leisure and consumption are (gross) substitutes.
6. Bowles and Park (2005) show the importance of relative position effects in determining manufacturing work hours in ten countries over the 1963–98 period. Schor (1998), using a US sample, shows that the impact of these effects on saving decision is significant.
7. The role of relative wealth effects as an engine of growth is shown in Corneo and Jeanne (2001). Among the growth models including the concern of individuals for their relative position, see, for instance, Fershtman et al. (1996) and Corneo and Jeanne (1999), who focus on the impact of the initial distribution of wealth on the growth rate.
8. Kasser (2000) shows that individuals with a greater propensity to pursue relational goals systematically achieve higher levels of well-being. This finding is consistent with those of recent econometric, sociological and psychological studies, which highlight the priority impact of personal relations on well-being.
9. However, these ideas have penetrated the economic literature: see, for example, behavioral and experimental economics or theories of bounded rationality. An interesting analysis has been conducted by Pugno (2004), who addresses the need for a theory of rationality failure capable of explaining systematic errors by individuals in identifying what is most important for their happiness. Drawing on the psychological and neurobiological literature, Pugno seeks to show the existence of other systematic motives ('emotional' or 'intrinsic'), which flank rational ones in determining choices.

References

Antoci, A. and S. Bartolini (2004), 'Negative externalities, and labor input in an evolutionary game', *Environment and Development Economics*, 9: 1–22.

Bartolini, S. and L. Bonatti (2002), 'Environmental and social degradation as the engine of economic growth', *Ecological Economics*, 41: 1–16.

Bartolini, S. and L. Bonatti (2003a), 'Undesirable growth in a model with capital accumulation and environmental assets', *Environment and Development Economics*, 8: 11–30.

Bartolini, S. and L. Bonatti (2003b), 'Endogenous growth and negative externalities', *Journal of Economics*, 79: 123–44.

Bartolini, S. and L. Bonatti (2004a), 'Social capital and its role in production: does the depletion of social capital depress economic growth?', *Quaderni del Dipartimento di Economia Politica*, Università degli Studi di Siena, no. 421.

Bartolini, S. and L. Bonatti (2004b), 'Does technical progress increase long-run welfare?', *Quaderni del Dipartimento di Economia Politica*, University of Siena working paper no. 435.

Bartolini, S. and L. Bonatti (2006), 'The mobilization of human resources as an effect of the depletion of environmental and social assets', *Metroeconomica*, 57: 193–213.

Bartolini, S. and R. Palma (2002), 'Economia e felicità: una proposta di accordo', in L. Bruni and V. Pelligra (eds), *Economia come impegno civile*, Rome, Città Nuova, pp. 121–58.

Baumann, Z. (2002), *La solitudine del cittadino globale*, Milan: Feltrinelli.

Bluestone, B. and S. Rose (2000), 'The enigma of working time trend', in L. Golden and D.M. Figart (eds), *Working Time: International Trends, Theory and Policy Perspectives*, London and New York: Routledge, pp. 21–37.

Bowles, S. and Y. Park (2002), 'Emulation, inequality, and work hours: was Thorstein Veblen right?', mimeo, Santa Fe.

Brickman, P. and D.T. Campbell (1971), 'Hedonic relativism and planning the good society', in M.H. Apley (ed.), *Adaptation-level Theory: A Symposium*, New York: Academic Press, pp. 287–302.

Corneo, G. and O. Jeanne (1999), 'Pecuniary emulation, inequality and growth', *European Economic Review*, **43**: 1665–78.

Corneo, G. and O. Jeanne (2001), 'On relative wealth effects and long-run growth', *Research in Economics*, **55**: 349–58.

Cross, G. (1993), *Time and Money: The Making of Consumer Culture*, London: Routledge.

Duranton, G. (2001), 'Endogenous labor supply, growth and overlapping generations', *Journal of Economic Behaviour and Organization*, **44**: 295–314.

Easterlin R. (1974), 'Does economic growth improve the human lot? Some empirical evidence', in P.A. David and M.W. Reder (eds), *Nations and Households in Economic Growth: Essays in Honor of Moses Abramovitz*, New York and London: Academic Press. pp. 89–125.

Easterlin R. (1995), 'Will raising the income of all increase the happiness of all?', *Journal of Economic Bahaviour and Organization*, **27**: 35–48.

Fershtman, C., K.M. Murphy and Y. Weiss (1996), 'Social status education and growth', *Journal of Political Economy*, **104**: 108–32.

Figart, D.M. and L. Golden (2000), 'Introduction and overview: understanding working time around the world', in Golden and Figart (eds), *Working Time: International Trends, Theory and Policy Perspectives*, London and New York: Routledge, 1–17.

Gale, W.G. and J. Sablehouse (1999), 'Perspectives on the household saving rate', *Brookings Papers on Economic Activity*, **1**: 181–224.

Gui, B. (1987), 'Eléments pour une définition d'économie communautaire', *Notes et Documents*, **19–20**: 32–42.

Helson, H. (1964), *Adaptation Level Theory: An Experimental and Systematic Approach*, New York: Harper & Row.

Hirsch, F. (1976), *Social Limits to Growth*, Cambridge, MA: Harvard University Press.

Kasser, T. (2000), 'Two versions of the American dream: which goals and values make for a high quality of life?', in E. Diener and D.R. Rahtz (eds), *Advances in the Quality of Life*, Dordrecht: Kluwer, pp. 3–12.

Krugman, F. (1995), *Pop Internationalism*, Cambridge, MA: MIT Press.

Lane, R. (2000), *The Loss of Happiness in Market Democracies*, New Haven, CT and London: Yale University Press.

Layard, R. (2003), 'Has social science a clue? Three lectures', Lionel Robbins Lectures 2002–03, mimeo.

Lykken, I. and A. Tellegen (1996), 'Happiness is a stochastic phenomenon', *Psychological Science*, **7**: 180–89.

Maddison, A. (1995), *Monitoring the World Economy 1820–1992*, Paris: OECD.

Maslow, A.H. (1943 [1970]), *Motivation and Personality*, New York: Harper & Row.

Oswald, A.J. (1997), 'Happiness and economic perfomance', *Economic Journal*, **107**: 1815–31.

Pinker, S. (1997), *How the Mind Works*, New York: W.W. Norton.

Polanyi, K. (1968), *The Great Transformation*, Boston, MA: Beacon.

Pugno, M. (2004), 'Rationality, emotions and interpersonal relations', Discussion Paper no. 1, Department of Economics, University of Trento.

Putnam, R.D. (2000), *Bowling Alone: The Collapse and Revival of American Community*, New York: Simon & Schuster.

Schor, J. (1998), *The Overspent American: Upscaling, Downshifting and the New Consumer*, New York: Oxford University Press.

Schor, J. (1993), *The Overworked American: The Unexpected Decline of Leisure in America*, New York: Basic Books.

Scitovsky, T. (1976), *The Joyless Economy*, Oxford and New York: Oxford University Press.

Sen, A. (1996), 'Rationality, joy and freedom', *Critical Review*, **10**: 481–94.

Ulhaner, C.J. (1989), 'Relational goods and participation: incorporating sociability into a theory of rational action', *Public Choice*, **62**: 253–85.

Veenhoven, R. (1993), *Happiness in Nations: Subjective Appreciation of Life in 56 Nations 1946–1992*, Rotterdam: Erasmus University Press.

Wagner, G. (2004), 'Undesirable growth fuelled by environmental degradation', mimeo, Harvard University.

18 On the demand for grandchildren: tied transfers and the demonstration effect*
Donald Cox and Oded Stark†

1. Introduction
A fifth of all first-time homebuyers in the United States receive help with their housing purchases from relatives, mainly parents. This help is substantial, averaging over half the required downpayment (Engelhardt and Mayer 1994). Parental assistance with housing downpayment is an example of a private transfer earmarked for the purchase of a particular good, that is, it is a 'tied transfer'. Such transfers, though common, pose a difficulty for theories of private transfers. Theories of altruistic giving predict that a parent can do no better to enhance the well-being of the recipient child than to give cash with no strings attached. Any other monetary transfer could impose on the child a utility-depressing constraint. Theories of exchange-related giving, where the transfer is payment for future child services, similarly predict that the child would prefer cash. It is an efficient means of remuneration, leaving the child free to acquire his most preferred consumption bundle.

Several ideas have been advanced to explain tied transfers. One idea is that preferences are 'paternalistic', in the sense that donors care about the composition of the recipient's consumption. Another idea is that although tied transfers need not be paternalistic, altruistic parents give their children illiquid assets, such as education and housing, to prevent the children from overconsuming and being in perpetual need of parental assistance. A third idea is based on liquidity constraints. Adult children are likely to face severe borrowing constraints when trying to purchase a home. If private transfers were designed to overcome acute liquidity constraints, we would expect them to occur upon the purchase of a home when the constraints are likely to be particularly severe.

In a related work,[1] we point out that each of these explanations of tied transfers has considerable shortcomings and that a deeper analysis of the underlying motives for these transfers can shed new light on how parents and their adult children interact. In this chapter we study such a motive. We argue that parents provide help to their children with housing because housing is complementary with the production of grandchildren. Drawing on our idea of the 'demonstration effect' in intergenerational transfers

(Cox and Stark 1996) we suggest a reason as to why parents would want to subsidize the production of grandchildren. We focus on the possibility that a child's conduct is conditioned by the parents' example. Parents may want to take advantage of the child's learning potential by engaging in care provision for their *own* parents when children are present and can observe their parents' behavior. Parents who expect to require attention, care, and old-age support have an incentive to behave in a distinct exemplary manner. Such behavior gives rise to a derived demand for *grandchildren*, because potential grandparents know that they will be treated better by their own children if conditioning of grandchildren is at work.

We empirically explore the interaction between tied transfers, liquidity constraints, and the demonstration effect by studying newly available data from the National Survey of Families and Households (NSFH) in the United States. This survey contains a variety of measures of private transfers between parents and their adult children as well as considerable information concerning intergenerational relations. We find that tied transfers appear to be driven in part by the transfer recipient's fertility plans and concerns about the adequacy of the housing situation for the bearing and raising of children. In addition, we find gender differences in the intensity with which unmarried adult children are subsidized for the production of grandchildren: the plans and concerns of single male respondents have an especially large impact on housing transfers. Further, among grandparents and potential grandparents there are gender differences in the propensity to give housing transfers. We show that these patterns are consistent with predictions of the demonstration-effect approach. Thus, our analysis provides a rationale for the demand for grandchildren, a relationship that has largely been ignored both in economics and in demography.

In Section 2, we outline the demonstration-effect argument and briefly present and discuss several empirical implications pertaining to the argument. In Section 3, we present preliminary considerations concerning tied transfer behavior and baseline results. In Section 4, we draw on the argument of Section 2 to explore, test, and provide a novel explanation for the incidence and the patterns associated with intergenerational housing down-payment transfers. We obtain considerable support for the demonstration-effect hypothesis. In Section 5, we provide concluding remarks.

2.   The demonstration effect

Analytical considerations

The demonstration-effect approach seeks to explain the provision of care, companionship, and other forms of assistance and attention that adult children provide to their parents. This is achieved by expanding the domain of analysis of intergenerational interaction from two generations to three: we focus on the possibility that the child's conduct is conditioned by parental example, and that parents take advantage of their children's learning potential by providing attention and care to their *own* parents when children are present to observe and are amenable to be impressed. We refer to this parental behavior as the 'demonstration effect'. The idea that attention and care of parents is aimed at instilling appropriate conduct in children generates an array of insights and hypotheses concerning inter-generational relationships. One such prediction is that would-be grandparents have an incentive to subsidize the 'supply' of grandchildren.

Consider a family comprising members of three generations: a child (K), a parent (P), and a grandparent (G). Each person lives for three periods, first as a K, then as a P, and finally as a G. P wants K to help in the next period when P becomes a G and K becomes a P. To demonstrate to K the appropriate way to behave in the next period, P provides visible help to G when K is around to watch and be conditioned. It follows that aid from P to G depends positively on the presence of K.[2]

Our theory predicts assistance from young to old even if the young are selfish. Thus, we can explain such assistance without relying on altruism, which may well be tenuous in light of biological considerations[3] and existing evidence. Note that if informal care-giving by family members living outside the recipient's household is motivated by altruism, expansion of formal care-giving should reduce informal care-giving. Not so, however, if the motive is demonstration. Pezzin et al. (1996: 671) report that in a test of a generously expanded public financing of home care for disabled elderly recipients conducted in the United States from 1982 to 1985 (sample size of 2,955 care givers), the public home-care provision resulted 'in only small reductions in the overall amount of care provided by informal care-givers to unmarried persons and no reductions for married persons'. This evidence of limited or no substitution of formal care for informal care is inconsistent with the altruistic motive for transfers.

Nor does our argument rely on 'strategic bequests' to prompt transfers from adult children to their parents (Bernheim et al. 1985). Although strategic considerations may play a role in some families, they cannot account for instances in which care is given to parents who did not accumulate appreciable quantities of bequeathable wealth, or where such care occurs when testamentary discretion is prohibited by law.

To see how imitative behavior of children induces transfers from parents to grandparents and how the demonstration effect gives rise to a derived demand for grandchildren, consider a setup based on Bergstrom and Stark (1993) and on Cox and Stark (1996).

Assume, for simplicity's sake, and to begin with, a single-parent, single-child family. The parent, P, seeks to maximize the expected value of her utility, $U(x, y)$ where x is what the maximizer does for her mother, G, and y is what the maximizer's daughter, K, does for the maximizer, P. Suppose that with probability $0 \le \pi \le 1$ a daughter will simply imitate her mother's action, while with probability $1 - \pi$ the daughter will choose an action to maximize her expected utility, aware though that her own daughter may be an imitator. Thus, a mother, P, chooses to maximize:

$$EU(x, y, \pi) = \pi U(x, x) + (1 - \pi)U(x, y) \qquad (18.1)$$

where U is a twice-differentiable utility function with negative marginal utility from the first argument ($U_1 < 0$, because caring for G requires exertion of effort) and positive marginal utility from the second argument, ($U_2 > 0$, because receiving care from K is beneficial). To derive P's choice of x we differentiate equation (18.1) with respect to x to obtain:

$$EU_1 = \pi(U_1^I + U_2^I) + (1 - \pi)U_1^s, \qquad (18.2)$$

where subscripts denote partial derivatives, superscript I denotes utility if K is an imitator, that is, $U^I \equiv U(x, x)$, and superscript S denotes utility if K is a selfish maximizer, that is, $U^S \equiv U(x, y)$. From the first-order condition for maximization,

$$- [\pi U_1^I + (1 - \pi)U_1^s] = \pi U_2^I. \qquad (18.3)$$

The left-hand side of equation (18.3) is the marginal cost of transferring to one's parent, while the right-hand side is the marginal benefit from receiving, which, in turn, is equal to π times the marginal utility of receiving from one's child. Thus, the likelihood of *not* being imitated ($\pi < 1$) taxes one's transfer to one's parent. Let us denote the solution to the maximization problem as x^*. We can express the solution as a function of the exogenous variables, so that $x^* = x^*(y, \pi)$.

In the context of the present inquiry, the following two implications of this framework are of particular interest. First, the mother's equilibrium choice of care for G is increasing in her daughter's probability of imitation π ($\partial x^*/\partial \pi > 0$). Intuitively, a higher probability that care to G will be imitated raises the marginal benefit of providing such care. To see this formally, note that from equation (18.2) it follows that:

$$EU_{13} = U_1^I + U_2^I - U_1^s \qquad (18.4)$$

and from equation (18.3) it follows that:

$$-\left(U_1^I + \frac{U_1^s}{\pi} - U_1^s\right) = U_2^I,$$

and

$$-\frac{U_1^s}{\pi} = U_2^I + U_1^I - U_1^s. \qquad (18.5)$$

From equation (18.2) we have $EU_{11}dx^* + EU_{12}dy + EU_{13}d\pi = 0$. For $dy = 0$ and using equations (18.4) and (18.5),

$$\frac{\partial x^*}{\partial \pi} = \frac{-EU_{13}}{EU_{11}} = -\frac{U_1^I + U_2^I - U_1^s}{EU_{11}} = -\frac{-U_1^s}{\pi EU_{11}} = \frac{U_1^s}{\pi EU_{11}} > 0, \qquad (18.6)$$

recalling that $U_1^s < 0$ and that the sufficiency condition implies $EU_{11} < 0$.

Clearly, the prevalence of imitative behavior benefits G. This prevalence requires not only that with some strictly positive probability K will imitate, but also, and of course, that K exists. Let us then drop the assumption of a single-child family. If there is no child around who could imitate, $\pi = 0$. In this case equation (18.1) becomes:

$$EU(x, y) = U(x, 0), \qquad (18.1')$$

which, because $U_1 < 0$, is maximized with $x = 0$. Since the demonstration effect is inoperative, no transfers from P take place. *We infer that G will prefer P to have a child than to be childless.* Alternatively, let us examine the case of a family with n children. If $n > 1$, a given act of transfer will be imitated by each of these observing children. If each child behaves in the same manner, we have:

$$EU(x, y, \pi, n) = \pi U(x, nx) + (1 - \pi)U(x, ny), \qquad (18.1'')$$

$$EU_1 = \pi U_1^I + \pi U_2^I n + (1 - \pi)U_1^s. \qquad (18.2')$$

Then, P's choice of x, x^{**}, is x that solves:

$$-[\pi U_1^I + (1 - \pi)U_1^s] = \pi U_2^I n. \qquad (18.3')$$

Comparing equation (18.3') with equation (18.3) – the case of only one child, since the marginal benefit is now higher (the marginal benefit curve shifts up by n to intersect the marginal cost curve at a higher x), $x^{**} > x^*$. Demonstration is more 'productive' in the presence of several children than in the presence of only one child, and hence more is being transferred by P to G.[4] *We infer that G will prefer P to have several children.*[5] Assuming that G controls resources that can be used to induce the production of children by P, it follows that G would want to subsidize P's production of K. One way to subsidize the production of grandchildren is to give help in the form of housing, which is likely to be complementary with fertility. While our analysis does not yield bounds on this subsidy, it points to its existence: an expected gain should be accompanied by willingness to incur a cost.

Our approach rationalizes, then, a derived demand for grandchildren that heretofore has been disregarded or treated in an ad hoc manner. Standard theories of fertility begin with a specification of the parent's preferences and constraints, while the preferences and choices of grandparents are apparently ignored.[6]

Evidence concerning the demonstration effect
A necessary condition for the demonstration effect to work is for early life-cycle events to affect behavior later on. Imitative behavior must be prevalent. Thus, the first issue to consider is whether early childhood experience affects behavior in adulthood. In particular, if a child observes his or her parents making transfers to his or her grandparents, will this observation affect the child's future transfer behavior?

In our working paper (Cox and Stark 1996), we have explored this issue using household micro-data, retrospective case studies, and controlled experiments. What follows is a brief summary of this preliminary work. Illuminating evidence comes from the first wave of the NSFH, conducted in the United States between March 1987 and May 1988. The survey contains information on 13,008 households (Sweet et al. 1988). The NSFH was suitable for our initial exploration of imitative behavior because it contains information about in-kind transfers provided by children to their parents, as well as retrospective information on early life-cycle experiences. We found that early transfer experience did indeed affect subsequent transfer behavior. Survey respondents were asked if a grandparent had ever moved in with the family when the respondent was a child (below 19 years old). They were also asked if their *own* parents had ever moved in with them when the respondents headed their own households. The incidence of sharing housing with parents was 27 per cent higher for the respondents whose grandparents had moved in when the respondents were children.

Of course, these unconditional means may have captured much more than the intergenerational transmission of preferences. They could well reflect a correlation in budget constraints. But a statistically significant, positive effect of grandparent coresidence held up even when we controlled for the earnings and net worth of the respondents, and for the parents' permanent income. Early grandparent coresidence increased the probability that the respondent's parent(s) had moved in by an amount similar to the unconditional figures above. Still, these findings are open to criticism because of the omission of a potentially important variable – the income of the grandparents. Suppose the grandparent moved in with the parent because the former was quite poor. With positive intergenerational correlation in incomes, the coresidence of the grandparent could be picking up the effects of unobservables in parental income. Yet the NSFH contains information that further helps to mitigate the problem of intergenerational correlation of incomes. Since our approach is concerned with the formation of *preferences*, we looked at a variable that measured the willingness of respondents to make transfers to their parents. Respondents were asked if they agreed or disagreed with the following statement: 'Children should let aging parents move in with them when the parents are too old to live on their own'. The five possible responses ranged from 'agree strongly' to 'strongly disagree'. We recognize that there can be considerable differences between what people say and what they do, but the respondents were not likely to have overstated their generosity for the sake of impressing the interviewer because the respondents filled out a questionnaire in private. Further, as long as any response error is uncorrelated with the grandparent coresidence variable, the orthogonality condition will be satisfied. Ordered probit, controlling for respondent and parental characteristics, revealed the same results as those discussed above: having a grandparent move in when the respondent was young positively and significantly affects attitudes concerning house sharing with parents.

While these results must be interpreted cautiously, we note that there are forces that could have affected attitudinal responses in an opposite direction. Having a grandparent move in likely diverts family resources from the child, exerting a negative influence on the willingness to have parents move in. Yet despite possible influences such as this, we found a positive effect. Our findings are consistent with evidence that habit plays an important role in consumer behavior (see Heien and Durham 1991; Becker 1992). Exposure to repeated, especially regular attention and care by parents to grandparents could implant a 'habit' of care-giving in adulthood.

We have extensively reviewed findings from the psychology, demography, and sociology literature and found considerable evidence consistent with our micro-data-based evidence reported above. We found demographic evidence that events experienced during childhood impinge strongly on conduct in adult life and that the family context in which children grow up is important. Teenage fertility and divorce are two examples.[7] Daughters of teenage mothers have been found to face significantly higher risks of teenage childbearing than daughters of older mothers. Patterns of marriage and childbearing behavior tend to be repeated intergenerationally (Kahn and Anderson 1992). Children of divorced parents appear more prone to divorce than those whose parents stay married.

Even if researchers using household micro-data could control perfectly for budget-constraint variables, there are reasons why intergenerational congruence in behavior and attitudes might not necessarily imply parental influence as a *causal* mechanism. Parent–child attitude similarity could be generated, for example, by the media, genetics or even child influences on parents (Glass et al. 1986). While household micro-data studies are not informative about the causal nature of attitude transmission, our review of controlled, laboratory experiments of social psychologists did point to a causal mechanism between parental role models and child imitators. Bandura (1986) cites several laboratory studies showing that children mimic punishment techniques inflicted on them when given an opportunity to punish others. And numerous controlled experiments cited by Eisenberg and Mussen (1989) indicate that children's pro-social behavior – giving gifts to others, for example – is enhanced when role models increase their own pro-social behavior.[8]

We started our analysis of the demonstration effect by posing the following question: assuming that by setting an example parents can influence the preferences of their children, is there evidence that parents use this leverage to enhance their own well-being? We addressed this issue by investigating the effects that children of respondents have on the 'services' that respondents provide to their own parents. The hypothesis is that, in line with the results of our theoretical work, the *presence* of children will increase the quantity of services that respondents provide to their parents.

We measured services by respondent–parent contact (visits and telephone calls) as, for example, did Bernheim et al., and we employed a long list of controls (both respondent characteristics and parental characteristics) in our estimating equation. In addition to these regressors we added a dummy indicating whether the respondent's household was childless, and the number of children by broad age categories (4 and under, 5 to 18, and older than 18). Having a child increased parent–child contact by 7 per cent. Further, we found that contact was sensitive to the age of children. For example, having a child older than 18 increased contact by 14 per cent. But we also found that having several younger children reduced contact (mostly visits), presumably because of increased costs. Yet another possible reason is that having several children lessens the need for parents to use the demonstration effect. Suppose parents want a child to provide attention and care when the parents reach old age. If the likelihood that *a* child will give care is independent, or largely independent, of the presence of other children, and if there is some random, independent probability of a child being of a 'caring type', then a larger number of children translates into a higher such likelihood.

Presumably, visits are more effective as a means of setting an example than telephone calls. If this is so, and the demonstration effect is important, then the *composition* of contact should be affected by the presence of children. We found some evidence in support of this prediction. The fraction of contact comprising visits was higher for households with a child than for childless households. Further, the fraction of contact is not linear in the number of children. Presumably because of cost considerations, for example, having more than three children aged 5–17 was associated with a lower fraction of visits.

We found that respondent contact with parents was responsive to income and prices. As could be expected with regard to a time-intensive activity, higher earnings reduced contact. We considered distance as a proxy for the price of contact. As expected, distance exerted a negative effect on respondent–parent contact. But the elasticity of contact with respect to distance was quite low in absolute value, which is in line with findings from other data sources (for example, Klatzky 1971). This suggests that there are few substitutes for parent–respondent contact. (Supplementary evidence on this issue is provided by Hill (1970), who interviewed three generations of 85 families about financial and in-kind transfers exchanged between generations. He found that survey respondents accorded to non-familial sources of in-kind aid and contact, such as clergy or social workers, quite a low preference ranking compared to familial sources.)

The evidence appears to be consistent with the idea that parents cannot buy attention (or attention of the right type) in the marketplace. Presumably, with regard to a service as special as filial attention, the market can provide only poor substitutes. Moreover, by its very nature, attention is personal and intimate, and as such is difficult to define. Therefore, the transaction costs associated with an arrangement to have attention supplied from outside the family are bound to be quite high.

Parental income was inversely related to contact, contrary to the findings of Bernheim et al. This finding is intriguing because it suggests that the promise of a bequest conditional on desirable behavior as measured by contact may not be an important determinant of parent–child contact. Indeed, the parental income effect is consistent instead with the idea that contact may in part be motivated by altruism. However, part of the parental income effect may have to do with the demonstration effect as well. If market consumption and attention received are substitutes, richer parents have a smaller incentive to instill filial loyalty. This reasoning could also *explain* the finding of Bernheim et al., that parental pension wealth was inversely related to child–parent contact.

While the NSFH data cannot be brought to bear directly on the demonstration effect, a recent special module of a different household survey, the Health and Retirement Study (HRS), can.[9] A large component of the HRS was designed for learning about family behavior, and in this regard it is akin to the NSFH. Further, since the HRS is concerned with aging issues it includes information pertaining to the care of elderly parents by their adult children. The fifth wave of the HRS, conducted in the year 2000, featured a special module that asked a random subsample of respondents directly about their motivation to provide for their parents. Specifically, respondents were given the following instructions:

> These next statements are about your parents. If your parents are deceased, please think back to when they were alive. Please tell me if you agree, disagree or are neutral about how well each statement applies to you.

In response to the statement 'I (do/did) for my parents what they did for their parents', the most frequent category was 'agree': 46 per cent of the 1,086 households. The least frequent was 'disagree' (25 per cent), and the remaining respondents' answers were categorized 'neutral'. This is direct evidence that patterns of transfers to the elderly tend to be repeated intergenerationally by a significant proportion of households.

While missing from the question above is any element of demonstration, another question in the module was phrased in such a way as to ask respondents about what they *saw* their parents do for their own parents. Again, the response categories were 'agree', 'neutral', or 'disagree', but this time the statement was cast in the negative: 'I (won't/didn't) do for my parents what I saw my parents do for their parents'. There was a higher concordance here between the generations: 52 per cent of the respondents disagreed with this statement, and only 11 per cent agreed. (As before, the response of the remainder was categorized 'neutral'.) Only a small minority report willfully doing something different than what they observed their own parents do. While these responses deserve further scrutiny, the simple percentages reported appear to provide compelling, direct evidence that the demonstration effect is at work in the provision of care by adult children to their parents.

3.   Preliminary considerations and baseline findings
Prior to empirically exploring, in Section 4, the demonstration-effect rationale for housing downpayment transfers, we consider several conventional explanations that pertain to tied transfers and to housing downpayments.

Tied transfers
Perhaps the earliest mention of tied transfers in modern-day economic theory is a section in Becker's (1974) seminal paper on altruism and social

interaction. Becker posits that tied transfers stem from the donor's desire to encourage consumption by the recipient of 'merit' goods, such as education and housing. Becker emphasizes a result that parallels simple textbook analyses of vouchers – that earmarked giving is not immune to problems of fungibility. On the one hand, if the recipient is contributing to the purchase of the targeted good, the donor might as well give a general cash transfer; tied transfers and cash transfers are equivalent. On the other hand, if tied transfers force the recipient to choose a different consumption bundle than he or she would have chosen upon receipt of a cash transfer, then the transfers are worth less to the recipient than their cash value. In this case, the donor must be motivated by more than unvarnished altruism, since he could have improved the recipient's well-being by removing the strings attached to the transfer. Pollak (1988) argues that 'paternalistic' preferences, that is, concerns over the composition of the recipient's consumption, are a self-evident fact of family life. For example, most parents would not be pleased to learn that their contributions toward their child's college tuition were spent at a luxury car dealership rather than at the bursar's office. While the fact of paternalistic preferences is unassailable, however, we think that it is worth probing more deeply into the *origins* of such preferences. Pollak offers several explanations including parental concerns about status and about the child's long-run interests, but in our view his list of underlying motivations for paternalistic preferences is far from complete.

Becker and Murphy (1988), and Bruce and Waldman (1991) advance still another explanation for tied transfers. They call attention to the Samaritan's dilemma, a problem that confronts altruists who interact repeatedly with their beneficiaries. Parental safety nets can lead to moral hazard, whereby children, knowing that they can be bailed out, work too little or spend too much.[10] Parents might seek to counter such behavior by making educational transfers, or transfers of illiquid assets such as housing in an attempt to determine the child's saving.

While we agree that giving transfers for educational purposes might be an effective strategy for dealing with the Samaritan's dilemma, we are skeptical about a similar explanation with regard to housing. Bruce and Waldman's model contains only one asset, but in reality the fungibility across several assets could thwart parental attempts to control their children's saving. For example, transfers for housing downpayments might simply 'crowd out' the child's own financial saving. There is some evidence that is consistent with this effect. Engelhardt and Mayer (1998) use data from a random sample of recent home buyers in 18 major US cities and find that households who received help with housing downpayments had savings rates that were 40–50 per cent lower than those who did not. Guiso and Jappelli (2002) examine an Italian survey of income and wealth and find that receiving help with housing downpayments is associated with a 1- to 2-year reduction in the time spent saving for home ownership. And while it is possible, as Engelhardt and Mayer point out, to partially explain some of this relationship as transfers being targeted to inherently low savers, there is an additional problem with the argument that housing transfers represent an attempt by paternalistic parents to lower their children's consumption. The purchase of a house is likely to be associated with increases in other forms of spending, such as purchases of consumer durables, and a larger living space is likely to lead to increased ongoing expenses on heat, other utilities, and upkeep.

A third explanation for tied transfers in the form of housing downpayment is that the transfers are a response to liquidity constraints faced by recipients. Artle and Varaiya (1978) and Engelhardt (1996) call attention to the fact that downpayment requirements can create liquidity constraints for households. Lending institutions require that homebuyers pay a percentage of the value of the house as a downpayment, and the minimal percentage typically ranges from 5 per cent to 20 per cent.[11] In addition, homebuyers are usually required to pay brokerage fees, legal fees, loan origination fees, title search fees, and so on. Engelhardt, and Artle and Varaiya show that if a household's user cost of owning is less than that of renting, but the household does not yet have the necessary downpayment funds, it will be liquidity-constrained until it saves the amount of the downpayment. Engelhardt finds that household consumption is depressed prior to the purchase of a house, supporting the idea that downpayment requirements cause households to be liquidity-constrained.

If the required downpayment truly creates a liquidity constraint, then perhaps the 'tied' nature of housing transfers is more apparent than real. The fact that transfers take the form of help with the downpayment is in a sense coincidental. They might just as well be viewed as cash transfers. What matters though is timing; liquidity constraints become particularly severe when the household is striving to amass enough cash to qualify for a mortgage. The earmarking of parental transfers for housing might have more to do with parental concerns about children's liquidity constraints than with housing *per se*.

Data

As already mentioned, the 13,008 NSFH households were initially interviewed between March 1987 and May 1988.[12] A follow-up to this first wave of the NSFH was conducted between July 1992 and May 1994. The NSFH is aptly suited for studying the determinants of tied transfers because it contains information on help with housing downpayments as well as cash transfers in general. We use information from both waves of the survey, but focus on intergenerational transfers that took place during the second wave (NSFH-II). The main reason for this attention is that in the next section of the chapter we are interested in finding out how *subsequent* help with housing downpayments is related to the housing concerns cum fertility plans reported in the self-enumerated questionnaire in the *first* wave of the survey. In addition to questions about *inter vivos* transfers, the NSFH contains extensive information about family structure and parental characteristics, which we use to construct measures of parental permanent income. A telephone interview with one randomly selected parent of the respondent was conducted in NSFH-II. This interview was similar to but shorter than the main respondent interview and resulted in 3,348 completed parental questionnaires.

There was significant attrition (3,000 households) between the first and second waves of the survey. A third of these attriters had either died or were too ill to answer the survey. Most of the remaining two-thirds were either refusals or households that could not be traced. (See Appendix 18A, 'Criteria used to determine the final sample'.)

Since our focus is on interhousehold transfers between parents and children, we deleted respondents who were coresiding with a parent or with an in-law or who had no living parents or in-laws. We also eliminated cases with inconsistent or incomplete information about the spouse, missing or inconsistent housing information, missing information on respondent's age or education, missing information about private transfers, or missing information about fertility plans. We also deleted respondents aged 65 or older and any households who had insufficient information for calculating permanent income. These sample selection criteria leave us with a sample of 5,461 households.

Variables

Dependent variables

General transfers   We estimate probit equations for the incidence of both 'general' transfers and help with housing downpayments. So-called general transfers include both cash and miscellaneous transfers in-kind. Survey respondents were asked to report on gifts and loans received from friends and relatives. After being reminded that they were being asked about transfers originating from outside the household, each respondent was asked:

> In the last 12 months have you (or your wife/or your husband) received a gift worth more than $200 at any one time from anyone not living with you at the time? Include gifts of items such as a car, furniture, jewelry, or stocks, as well as gifts of money.

The respondent was then asked to identify the donor (for example, a parent, a brother) and report the amount received. Next, he or she was asked a similar set of questions regarding loans, and a final set of questions was asked about transfers received for 'day-to-day expenses or educational expenses'.[13] We aggregated across these categories and netted out any corresponding transfers given to parents or in-laws, so that we can deal with net inflows.

Housing transfers   Survey respondents were asked a series of questions about home purchases made since they were interviewed in the first wave of the NSFH. They were asked if they purchased a home. Homebuyers were asked what were the total purchase price and the amount of their downpayment. They were then asked about help with downpayments: 'Did you receive any financial gifts or loans from relatives or friends to help you buy or build this home?'. Respondents were asked to name up to three sources of help (for example, parents, in-laws, siblings), and report separately the amounts of gifts and loans received toward the purchase of the house.

Descriptive statistics for private transfer receipts, fertility plans, and housing concerns are provided in Table 18.1. *Inter alia*, the table shows that housing transfers are quite large, especially when compared to general transfers. The latter occur for a little over a fifth of the 5,461 households in our sample (Table 18.1, part I). About a fifth of the 1,819 households purchasing a house between survey waves received a housing-related transfer (Table 18.1, part II). Among recipients, however, the average housing transfer was five-and-a-half times larger than the average general transfer ($23,506 versus $4,289.) Not surprisingly, both forms of transfer are highly skewed, but the disparity in their magnitude holds for median values ($9,000 versus $1,300) as well (Table 18.1, parts I and II).

An additional way to put the value of the housing transfers in perspective is to compare them to the value of the required downpayment. Both the mean and median of housing transfers exceeded, respectively, the mean and median of required downpayments (Table 18.1, part II). More than half of the recipients of housing transfers – 183 out of 345 – received financial help greater than the required downpayment.

Explanatory variables
Respondent permanent income   Permanent income, that is, age-standardized earnings purged of transitory error components, is estimated using earnings data from both waves of the NSFH. Standard Mincerian earnings functions are estimated where individual log-earnings are regressed on education, a cubic in age, occupational dummies, region, race, and

Table 18.1   Some descriptive statistics

I. General transfers

	Number	Per cent
Households in the sample	5,461	100.00
Households who received general transfers	1,178	21.57
	Mean	Median
Value of general transfer among recipients	$4,289	$1,300

II. Housing transfers

	Number	Per cent	(Per cent of subsample)
Households in the sample	5,461	100.00	–
Households who purchased a house between survey waves	1,819	33.31	(100.00)
Households who received help with house purchase	345	6.32	(18.97)
Households whose help exceeded the required downpayment	183	3.35	(10.06)
	Mean	Median	
Value of housing transfer among recipients	$23,506	$9,000	
Required downpayments	$17,120	$8,000	

III. Fertility plans and housing concerns

	Recipients of housing transfer		Nonrecipients of housing transfer	
	Number	Per cent	Number	Per cent
Households who purchased a house between survey waves	345	100.00	1,474	100.00
Households who are sure that they want a(nother) child	129	37.39	327	22.18
Households who want a(nother) child and have housing concerns	71	20.58	144	9.77

Source: Authors' tabulations from the NSFH.

marital status. Most individuals have two earnings observations, so we can identify fixed effects for them. For others, we use the technique of King and Dicks-Mireaux (1982), which relies on outside information about earnings error components, to construct permanent income measures.[14]

Parental permanent income   The first wave of the NSFH contains information on parental schooling, occupation, and age. We use this information to impute parental income from earnings functions estimated within the NSFH sample. We also use parental earnings information obtained from the respondent's parent interviews.

General transfers, housing transfers, and liquidity constraints
An appealing explanation of *inter vivos* transfers is that they are used to help recipients overcome borrowing constraints (Ishikawa 1974; Cox 1990; Engelhardt 1996). Do private transfers appear to respond to liquidity constraints? How do housing-related transfers compare to the more general-purpose transfers?

To draw inferences about the connection between liquidity constraints and private transfers, we use an empirical specification proposed in Cox (1990), which makes a distinction between the private-transfer effects of current and of permanent incomes of potential recipients. These alternative measures of income are predicted to have opposite effects on private transfer receipt, with the effect of current income being negative, and the effect of permanent income being positive. The intuition for the first result is that a rise in current income alleviates the liquidity constraint and lessens the need for a private transfer. The intuition for the second result is that with current income constant, a rise in permanent income increases desired consumption; since private transfers help close the gap between desired consumption and current income, transfers rise.

In addition to current income and permanent income, our empirical model includes age interactions with the current earnings and permanent incomes of respondent households and parental households. The idea is that liquidity constraints are more likely to be binding for younger households so that the divergent transfer effects of current income versus permanent income would be more pronounced for them as opposed to their older counterparts. Further, following Zeldes (1989), we enter an additional indicator of liquidity constraints – whether the household's financial assets fell short of 2 months' worth of earnings, which we also interact with age. We also include demographic attributes of the household: whether it is headed by a single female, the marital status of the respondent, and race.[15] Finally, we include the number of living parents and in-laws.

General transfers We estimated and present in Table 18.2 a probit equation for incidence of general transfers received. The pattern of coefficients in Table 18.2 conforms to the liquidity-constraint hypotheses: the probability of transfer receipt is inversely related to current earnings and positively related to the measure of permanent income, and these effects attenuate with age. For a household headed by a 25-year-old, an increase in earnings from the 25th to the 75th percentile is associated with nearly a 3 percentage-point reduction in the probability of receiving a transfer. The equivalent increase in the household's permanent income is associated with a 2 percentage-point increase in the probability of receipt (although this effect is only on the margin of statistical significance). Being liquidity-constrained according to Zeldes's (1989) criterion, that is, holding financial assets

Table 18.2   The incidence of general transfers. Dependent variable: transfer receipt (1 = Yes, 0 = No)

	Marginal effect	Asymptotic t-value	Variable mean
Respondent characteristics			
Current earnings	-0.020×10^{-4}	-2.16	45,483
Permanent income	0.014×10^{-4}	1.29	41,426
Current earnings $\times$ age[a]	0.050×10^{-6}	2.17	1,830,111
Permanent income $\times$ age	-0.028×10^{-6}	-1.00	1,639,971
Financial assets $< 1/6$th earnings	0.167	3.39	0.39
Financial assets $< 1/6$th earnings $\times$ age	-0.003	-2.62	14.59
Per-capita parental income[b]	0.107×10^{-4}	11.09	14,170
Number of living parents + in-laws	0.044	5.96	2.36
Married, spouse present	0.043	1.99	0.65
Female-headed household	0.049	2.13	0.25
Black	-0.096	-5.43	0.13
Constant	0.024	-20.55	1.00
Number of observations		5,461	
Recipients		1,178	
Non-recipients		4,283	
Log-likelihood		$-2,615.19$	
χ^2		464.64	
Dependent variable mean		0.22	

Notes:
a. '$\times$ age' denotes variable interacted with age of household head.
b. Income of parents plus in-laws divided by the number of living parents plus in-laws.

Source: Authors' tabulations using the NSFH.

amounting to less than one-sixth of current yearly earnings, is associated with an increase in the probability of transfer receipt of over 8 percentage points. Like the effects of earnings and permanent income, the effects of having low financial assets on the probability of transfer receipt diminishes with age, and each of these effects becomes negligible as the household reaches its forties. The measure of parental permanent income enters positively and its value is quite large. An increase in per-capita parental income from the 25th to the 75th percentile is associated with more than a 9 percentage-point increase in the probability of receiving a transfer.[16] Having an additional living parent increases the probability of transfer receipt by 4 percentage points, as does being married. Consistent with many other studies of *inter vivos* transfers, households headed by single females are more likely to receive a transfer (+ 5 percentage points) while black households are less likely to receive a transfer (−10 percentage points).

Housing transfers   A similar probit, now applied to the receipt of housing transfers, is presented in Table 18.3. Gauging the responsiveness of housing transfers to liquidity constraints is somewhat more complicated than gauging the responsiveness of general transfers because the former are given only to home-purchasers, a select subsample whose income and other attributes could be expected to differ from those of the overall population. In particular, by virtue of being able to purchase a house, they are apt to be less likely to face liquidity constraints than those who did not purchase a house.[17] Estimates of the responsiveness of housing transfers to liquidity constraints must take into account the fact that such transfers take place only for the subsample of households who have purchased a home. Accordingly, we focus on housing transfers among the subsample of home-purchasers.

The estimation results for housing transfers are presented in Table 18.3 (which parallels the framework used in Table 18.2). The first column of Table 18.3 contains a simple probit estimation for housing transfers, conducted for the sample of home-purchasers. The second column of Table 18.3 contains estimates that take account of possible selection bias associated with the decision to purchase a home.[18]

We find little evidence of liquidity-constraint effects for housing transfers. For example, having low financial assets relative to earnings appears to matter little for the receipt of housing transfers. None of the terms associated with low financial assets or permanent income is even marginally significant in Table 18.3.[19] Further, these results do not appear to be the artifact of possible attenuation bias from measurement error in income or assets.[20]

Thus, we conclude that the conventional approach to explaining private transfers, which relies on considerations of liquidity constraints, does not perform well.[21] Does the raw tabulation in Table 18.1, part III, that suggests

Table 18.3 The incidence of housing transfers: households who purchased a house between survey waves. Dependent variable: transfer receipt (1 = Yes, 0 = No)

	Probit		Nested probit		Variable mean
	Marginal effect	Asymptotic *t*-value	Marginal effect	Asymptotic *t*-value	
Respondent characteristics					
Current earnings (000s)	0.002	0.98	0.001	0.87	54.51
Permanent income (000s)	0.002	0.85	0.001	0.62	48.58
Current earnings (000s) × age/100	−0.006	−1.14	−0.004	−1.09	20.68
Permanent income (000s) × age/100	−0.003	−0.55	−0.002	−0.40	18.15
Financial assets < 1/6th earnings	−0.025	−0.29	−0.025	−0.29	0.37
Financial assets < 1/6th earnings × age	0.002	0.86	0.002	0.92	13.37
Per-capita parental income (000s)	0.008	4.63	0.006	4.44	15.61
Number of living parents/in-laws	0.044	3.46	0.036	3.07	2.70
Married, spouse present	0.007	0.18	0.007	−0.10	0.75
Female-headed household	0.045	1.00	0.041	0.94	0.17
Black	−0.110	−2.89	−0.092	−2.52	0.06
Constant	0.020	−10.36	0.021	−5.83	1.00
Number of observations	1,819		1,819		
Recipients	345		345		
Non-recipients	1,474		1,474		
Log-likelihood	−813.57		−3,777.93		
χ^2	139.97		77.92		
Dependent variable mean	0.19		0.19		

Note: The nested probit adjusts for the sample-selection bias associated with restriction of the sample to homebuyers. Purchasing a house and receiving a housing-related transfer are estimated jointly. Variables entered in the house-purchase equation are earnings, permanent income, financial assets, dummies for financial assets missing and for low financial assets, a quadratic in the age of the household head, per-capita parental income, number of living parents/in-laws, family size, the amount of housing equity in wave 1, marital status (married, divorced, married since wave 1), female headship status, race (Black), dummy indicating missing value for wave 1 home equity, a dummy for inter-city migration since wave 1, dummies for job change (respondent and spouse) since wave 1, and dummies for attaining a job (respondent and spouse) since wave 1. Estimated correlation between unobservables in the house-purchase equation and housing-transfer equation: −0.245, std. err. = 0.125. The probit equation for house purchase is given in Appendix ('Additional results'), available upon request.

Source: Authors' tabulations using the NSFH.

that housing concerns intersected with fertility plans are associated with receipt of housing transfers, point to a different explanation? Can the demonstration-effect approach better explain the patterns of intergenerational transfers in the form of housing downpayments?

4.   Transfers for housing downpayments and the demonstration effect

We weave together our demonstration-effect approach to intergenerational transfers with our interest in explaining tied transfers in the form of help with house purchases. Our key idea is that tied transfers for housing constitute an encouragement or an inducement by would-be grandparents, or grandparents, to their adult children for the production of grandchildren. The demand of would-be grandparents for grandchildren is derived from the interaction among members of three generations that we have delineated in Section 1.

When children express both a desire to have children and a concern that their existing housing facilities constitute a barrier to having children, a tied transfer in the form of downpayment assistance, as compared to a pure cash transfer, neither compels the recipients to revise their consumption bundle nor raises their utility by less. Unlike a housing downpayment transfer made prior to the children having children, a promise of a cash transfer subsequent to having children suffers from two drawbacks. First, the promise of an *ex post* cash transfer cannot mitigate a present-day binding housing liquidity constraint. Second, there is a natural desire to acquire or install the prerequisites for bearing and rearing children prior to having children. Especially because having children is irreversible, would-be parents can reasonably be expected to be averse to the risk of producing children only to find out thereafter that they are unable to adequately house them. The intersection of the importance attached to a 'correct' sequence and the binding liquidity constraint render an arrangement of children first and cash rewarded thereafter largely untenable.

Basic results

We augment our estimating equation for housing help by using a series of variables related to fertility plans and to housing concerns. In the main interview of the first wave of the NSFH, survey respondents were asked to report their intentions for having children. The questions about fertility plans were asked of female respondents aged 39 or younger, single male respondents aged 44 or younger, and any married male respondents whose spouse or partner was aged 39 or younger. Respondents were asked 'Do you intend to have (a/another) child sometime?'. Respondents were also asked how sure they were of their intention.

The same age groups of respondents filled out a self-enumerated questionnaire that dealt with considerations in the decision to have another child. The module began with the statement:

> Below is a list of things that some people consider when having a child or having another child. Please circle how important you feel each is to you at the present time.

Respondents were given a Likert scale ranging from one (not at all important) to seven (very important) for a variety of factors presumed to influence fertility decisions. Among these was housing, or more precisely, 'Being able to buy a home or a better home'. We chose the top two numerical responses to signify that the respondent was concerned about housing in the fertility decision. We then created a series of dummy variables related to fertility plans, the certainty with which those plans were held, and concerns about housing. Specifically, we created the following eight dummies:

> want child (sure), concerned about housing;
> want child (unsure), concerned about housing;
> want child (sure), unconcerned about housing;
> want child (unsure), unconcerned about housing;
> don't want child (unsure), concerned about housing;
> don't want child (sure), concerned about housing;
> don't want child (unsure), unconcerned about housing; and
> don't want child (sure), unconcerned about housing.

The reference category comprises those respondents who were not asked the questions, and presumably the probability of having a child is quite low for this group, so that, for all intents and purposes, we will refer to this category as the infertile group. We entered the dummies in the probit analysis for housing transfers received.

Our underlying idea here is that parents who are keen to set in motion or to amplify demonstration-effect behavior will be more willing to provide housing downpayment assistance when they know that the fertility outcome is relatively certain as opposed to when it is not. Note that the 'want child (sure), concerned about housing' category is not one of a decisive want. Had the want been absolute, would housing have constituted a binding concern? The thought that parents would better assist the unsure, tilting them in the desired direction while leaving the sure to themselves since they will end up producing children regardless, is not all that appealing; the former may still not be prompted to produce children, and the latter's binding constraint is unearthed.

Our basic results are presented in Table 18.4. In line with a key prediction of the demonstration-effect approach – that parents are more inclined

Table 18.4   The incidence of housing transfers: households who purchased a house between survey waves. Dependent variable: transfer receipt (1 = Yes, 0 = No)

	Probit		Nested probit		Variable mean
	Marginal effect	Asymptotic *t*-value	Marginal effect	Asymptotic *t*-value	
Respondent characteristics					
Current earnings (000s)	0.002	0.90	0.001	0.81	54.51
Permanent income (000s)	−0.0002	−0.09	−0.0003	−0.24	48.58
Current earnings (000s) × age/100	−0.005	−1.07	−0.004	−1.03	20.68
Permanent income (000s) × age/100	0.002	0.32	0.002	0.42	18.15
Financial assets < 1/6th earnings	−0.080	−0.96	−0.066	−0.94	0.37
Financial assets < 1/6th earnings × age	0.004	1.62	0.003	1.66	13.37
Per-capita parental income (000s)	0.007	4.23	0.005	4.09	15.61
Number of living parents/in-laws	0.039	3.10	0.032	2.79	2.70
Married, spouse present	0.031	0.74	0.025	0.47	0.75
Female-headed household	0.071	1.51	0.059	1.43	0.17
Black	−0.107	−2.89	−0.089	−2.57	0.06
No children	0.110	1.84	0.091	1.89	0.30
Number of children	0.103	2.09	0.085	2.15	1.44
Number of children squared	−0.025	−2.42	−0.021	−2.46	3.67
Fertility-plan and housing-concern variables					
Want child (sure), concerned	0.164	3.92	0.136	3.77	0.12
Want child (unsure), concerned	0.114	2.97	0.092	2.85	0.12
Want child (sure), unconcerned	0.081	2.24	0.065	2.15	0.13
Want child (unsure), unconcerned	0.070	1.90	0.056	1.84	0.12
Don't want child (unsure), concerned	0.079	1.58	0.061	1.49	0.05
Don't want child (sure), concerned	0.045	0.76	0.036	0.74	0.03
Don't want child (unsure), unconcerned	0.092	1.90	0.077	1.90	0.05
Don't want child (sure), unconcerned	0.032	0.67	0.025	0.64	0.05
Constant	0.004	−8.79	0.023	−6.29	1.00

Table 18.4   (continued)

	Probit		Nested probit		Variable mean
	Marginal effect	Asymptotic *t*-value	Marginal effect	Asymptotic *t*-value	
Number of observations		1,819		1,819	
Recipients		345		345	
Nonrecipients		1,474		1,474	
Log-likelihood		−799.21		−3,764.04	
χ^2		168.69		98.57	
Dependent variable mean		0.19		0.19	

Note: The nested probit adjusts for the sample-selection bias associated with restriction of the sample to homebuyers. Purchasing a house and receiving a housing-related transfer are estimated jointly. Variables entered in the house-purchase equation are earnings, permanent income, financial assets, dummies for financial assets missing and for low financial assets, a quadratic in the age of the household head, per-capita parental income, number of living parents/in-laws, family size, the amount of housing equity in wave 1, marital status (married, divorced, married since wave 1), female headship status, race (Black), dummy indicating missing value for wave 1 home equity, a dummy for inter-city migration since wave 1, dummies for job change (respondent and spouse) since wave 1, and dummies for attaining a job (respondent and spouse) since wave 1. Estimated correlation between unobservables in the house-purchase equation and housing transfer equation: −0.214, std. err. = 0.126. The probit equation for house purchase is given in Appendix ('Additional results'), available upon request.

Source: Authors' tabulations using the NSFH.

to offer assistance to their children when the assistance is more likely to entail the production of grandchildren, we find that the fertility-plan/housing-concern variables have a large impact on the probability of receiving a housing transfer. Those respondents who report that they are sure that they want a child, and for whom housing looms large in the fertility decision, are nearly twice as likely to receive a housing transfer as those who are sure that they do not want a child and are less concerned about housing. The estimates from the probit analysis in the first column of Table 18.4 indicate that the predicted probability of receiving a housing transfer for a household whose respondent is sure that he/she wants a child and is concerned about housing (and whose other variables are set at sample means) is 25 per cent, compared to 13.6 per cent for a respondent who is sure that he/she does not want a child and is unconcerned about housing. The predicted probability for the reference category, that is, those who presumably are not likely to be able to have children, is 11.1 per cent. The corresponding pattern from the nested probit in the second column of Table 18.4 is nearly identical.[22]

The dummies for responses concerning fertility plans and housing concerns can be approximated by a linear pattern. We re-estimated the probits in Table 18.4 substituting a linear summary measure of fertility plans and housing concerns. We recoded the dummies so that the one reflecting the highest 'needs' (want child for certain, concerned about housing) was given a value of eight, the lowest (don't want a child for certain, unconcerned about housing) was coded as one, and the reference category was coded as zero. These results imply predicted probabilities that are similar to those alluded to above.[23]

We also added information about the number of children in the household as regressors in Table 18.4. We included a dummy indicating if there were no children in the household, as well as a quadratic in the number of children. The probability of receiving housing transfers responds to the number of children in a nonlinear way. With other variables set at sample means, the probability of transfer receipt is higher when the household has two children than if it has one child, but it is highest when the household has no children. For example, homebuyers with two children are two and one-half percentage points more likely to receive than those with one, and one-half a percentage point less likely to receive than those with no children. We note though that the said responses are small relative to the fertility-plan/housing-concern variables discussed above.[24]

Differences by sex
Our approach leads us to expect gender differences in the incentive to undertake demonstration-effect actions because men and women have substantially different life expectancies: in the United States, the difference between the life expectancies of females and males is nearly 7 years. Moreover, since wives are usually younger than husbands, husbands are much more likely than their wives to have a spouse present to take care of them when they become aged and infirm; compared to men, women are more likely to have to rely on children rather than on spouses for attention and care in old age. Since women have a longer expected horizon than men over which to reap the benefits from inculcating children, they have more to gain from exercising demonstration, and therefore a stronger incentive than men to engage in demonstration. There is abundant existing evidence consistent with this idea. Women provide much more help to elderly parents than men. For example, Stoller (1983) finds that daughters provide twice as much help to parents as sons do. Further, these differences are not fully explained by differential time valuation, because they are obtained even after controlling for wages (for example, Kotlikoff and Morris 1989).

These considerations imply that women would need less subsidization than men for the production of children, since they have a considerably stronger incentive to use the demonstration effect. Hence, we expect that would-be grandparents or grandparents would be more responsive to the fertility plans and concerns of sons than of daughters.

Another reason for expecting differential subsidization by gender has to do with the custody of children in the event of a marital breakup.[25] Consider the case of a *G* with an unmarried *P*-daughter and an unmarried *P*-son. Suppose that parents are not interested in the quality of the marriage of their son or their daughter *per se*, but that a higher quality marriage will be associated with a lower likelihood of marital breakup, and that resources bundled with *P* positively affect the quality of *P*'s marriage. Thus, giving more resources to a daughter, thereby enhancing the quality of her marriage, brings no returns in terms of retaining children upon a marital breakup, assuming that in the case of a marital breakup it is the mother rather than the father who retains the children. However, giving more resources to a son, thereby enhancing the quality of his marriage *will* bring returns in terms of retaining children because the likelihood of marital breakup will be lower. A *P* who retains the children is more likely to engage in demonstration-effect activities than a *P* who does not.

We investigated separately the effects of the summarized plans/concerns variable on the probability of receiving housing help for married couples versus single females and versus single males (Table 18.5). In line with the predictions of the demonstration-effect approach, we found that fertility plans/housing concerns had a much larger impact for single males than for single females, for whom the estimated impact of the variable is almost negligible.

The transfer behavior of husbands' parents and wives' parents
One possible criticism of the results presented so far is that the estimated effects of fertility plans and housing concerns on parental help with housing could in large part be due to parental altruism. Such plans and concerns may reflect the needs of children to which altruistic parents respond by making the appropriate transfers. Yet parental altruism as a motive for housing transfers to children should not be expected to differ by children's fertility plans, only by children's housing needs. Since differentiation by fertility plans is in evidence, altruism may not be the underlying motive for housing transfers. One possible way to test for the presence of altruistic motives for transfers is to focus on married couples and look at the separate effects of the income of husbands' parents versus the income of wives' parents. The altruism hypothesis predicts that the parents of a person whose spouse's parents are rich are likely to give less – a standard case of the 'crowding out' of private transfers predicted by the altruism model.[26] We investigated the receipt of help with housing for

Table 18.5   *The incidence of housing transfers: households who purchased a house between survey waves. Fertility-plan cum housing-concern variable entered interactively. Dependent variable: transfer receipt (1 = Yes, 0 = No)*

	Probit		Nested probit		Variable mean
	Marginal effect	Asymptotic *t*-value	Marginal effect	Asymptotic *t*-value	
Respondent characteristics					
Current earnings (000s)	0.002	1.07	0.001	0.97	54.54
Permanent income (000s)	−0.0003	−0.15	−0.0004	−0.35	48.59
Current earnings (000s) × age/100	−0.006	−1.21	−0.004	−1.16	20.69
Permanent income (000s) × age/100	0.002	0.30	0.002	0.43	18.15
Financial assets < 1/6th earnings	−0.059	−0.72	−0.050	−0.70	0.37
Financial assets < 1/6th earnings × age	0.003	1.39	0.003	1.43	13.33
Per-capita parental income (000s)	0.007	4.26	0.005	4.16	15.62
Number of living parents/in-laws	0.036	2.86	0.029	2.52	2.70
Married, spouse present	0.195	2.28	0.176	2.14	0.75
Female-headed household	0.400	2.57	0.340	2.57	0.17
Black	−0.092	−2.41	−0.075	−2.04	0.06
Distance	−0.150	−2.07	−0.130	−2.25	−0.08
Number of siblings	−0.013	−2.46	−0.010	−2.36	5.87
Childless	0.125	1.89	0.104	1.97	0.30
Number of children	0.101	2.12	0.083	2.19	1.44
Number of children squared	−0.024	−2.35	−0.019	−2.41	3.67
Fertility-plan and housing-concern variables					
Plans and Concerns (P&C)	0.012	1.55	0.009	1.51	3.68
P&C × single female	−0.013	−1.48	−0.011	−1.62	0.53
P&C × single male	0.037	1.99	0.030	1.99	0.31
P&C × distance	0.023	1.33	0.017	1.23	−0.27
P&C × siblings	0.001	0.99	0.001	0.98	21.66
P&C × childless	−0.005	−0.71	−0.004	−0.78	1.06
Constant	0.000	−6.07	0.019	−4.99	1.00
Number of observations	1,817		1,817		
Recipients	344		344		
Nonrecipients	1,473		1,473		

Table 18.5   (continued)

	Probit		Nested probit		Variable mean
	Marginal effect	Asymptotic *t*-value	Marginal effect	Asymptotic *t*-value	
Log-likelihood		−786.16		−3,745.35	
χ²		191.05		107.79	

Note: The nested probit adjusts for the sample-selection bias associated with restriction of the sample to homebuyers. Purchasing a house and receiving a housing-related transfer are estimated jointly. Variables entered in the house-purchase equation are earnings, permanent income, financial assets, dummies for financial assets missing and for low financial assets, a quadratic in the age of the household head, per-capita parental income, number of living parents/in-laws, family size, the amount of housing equity in wave 1, marital status (married, divorced, married since wave 1), female headship status, race (Black), dummy indicating missing value for wave 1 home equity, a dummy for inter-city migration since wave 1, dummies for job change (respondent and spouse) since wave 1, and dummies for attaining a job (respondent and spouse) since wave 1. Estimated correlation between unobservables in the house-purchase equation and housing transfer equation: −0.268, std. err. = 0.130. The probit equation for house purchase is given in Appendix ('Additional results'), available upon request.

Source: Authors' tabulations using the NSFH.

husbands and wives separately in Table 18.6.[27] For husbands, we find that the income of in-laws is inversely related to the probability of receiving help from own parents with housing, as the altruism model predicts, but the estimated impact is not statistically significant. But for wives, we find that the income of in-laws is *positively* and significantly related to the probability of receiving help from own parents with housing, a result that is in contrast to the altruism model. We conclude that the results we find for the connection between fertility-plans-cum-stated-housing-concerns and transfers are not simply an artifact of altruistic preferences.[28]

Additional results reported in Table 18.6 lend support to the demonstration-effect idea. Recalling the argument that since women have a longer life expectancy than men, they have more to gain from an operative demonstration effect, we entered as separate regressors dummy variables that capture the living situation of the parents: whether the parents are together or whether the father or mother is alone. (The reference category is that the parents are both alive but are separated.) We find that, consistent with the prediction of the demonstration-effect approach, having a mother living alone raises the probability of receiving help with housing, compared to the other categories. For example, for husbands, having a mother living alone rather than a father living alone raises the probability

Table 18.6   The incidence of housing transfers: households who purchased
a house between survey waves. Bivariate probit analysis:
transfers to husbands and wives estimated separately.
Dependent variable: transfer receipt (1= Yes, 0=No)

	Husbands			Wives		
	Marginal effect	Asymptotic *t*-value	Variable mean	Marginal effect	Asymptotic *t*-value	Variable mean
Respondent characteristics						
Current earnings (000s)	−0.004	−1.32	61.51	−0.002	−0.55	61.51
Permanent income (000s)	0.004	1.13	55.61	0.003	0.85	55.61
Current earnings (000s)×age/100	0.009	1.03	23.12	0.005	0.52	23.12
Permanent income (000s)×age/100	−0.009	−0.94	20.53	−0.012	−1.02	20.53
Financial assets <1/6 earnings	−0.112	−1.04	0.39	−0.084	−0.72	0.39
(Financial assets <1/6 earnings) × age	0.005	1.49	13.51	0.003	0.84	13.51
Black	0.023	0.38	0.04	−0.079	−1.36	0.04
Distance from parents	0.008	0.17	−0.13	−0.019	−0.39	−0.11
Number of own siblings	−0.015	−2.74	3.38	−0.012	−2.25	3.24
Have no children	0.164	1.70	0.15	0.082	1.02	0.15
Number of children	0.093	1.52	1.81	0.049	0.89	1.81
Number of children squared	−0.021	−1.60	4.59	−0.012	−1.08	4.59
Fertility plans – housing concerns	0.016	3.33	3.93	0.011	2.34	3.93
Parental variables						
Per-capita parental income (0000s)	0.068	3.25	1.588	0.053	2.25	1.598
Father alone	−0.051	−1.14	0.084	−0.048	−0.88	0.066
Mother alone	0.038	0.78	0.267	0.202	3.30	0.217
Parents together	0.025	0.70	0.520	0.059	1.67	0.571
Parent in bad health	−0.061	−2.16	0.182	0.021	0.70	0.182
In-law variables						
Total in-law income (0000s)	−0.007	−0.99	2.365	0.016	2.44	2.319
Distance from in-laws	0.004	0.07	−0.112	0.165	2.70	−0.127
Constant	0.010	−4.66	1.000	0.015	−4.34	1.000
Estimated correlation of unobservables			0.41			
Estimated standard error of correlation			0.10			
Observations			806			
Recipients		111			107	
Nonrecipients		695			699	
Log-likelihood			−562.27			
χ^2			104.64			
Dependent variable mean		0.138				0.133

of receiving help with housing by 7.1 percentage points (significant at the 0.1 level). For wives, the impact is qualitatively similar, but larger: 22.8 percentage points (significant at the 0.01 level). These demographic effects are consistent with the idea that it is women, and even more so women who experience vulnerability, who are more interested in cultivating the familial bonds that lead to future transfers. Again, these results would not be generated by the standard altruism model, which makes no prediction one way or the other concerning the differential altruism of mothers versus fathers.

Complementary results

We have investigated several additional empirical issues.[29] First, we looked at transfer *amounts* in addition to transfer *incidence*. As is often the case with private transfers, the estimations of amounts are less precise than the estimations of incidence. Further, we investigated the connection between fertility plans and housing concerns, and general transfers. Following the hint of Table 18.1, part III, we estimated an analogue of Table 18.4 for general transfers and found that wanting a child and being concerned about housing were positively related to the probability of receiving a general transfer, though the estimated effects are less pronounced and less precisely estimated than those for housing transfers. We also estimated an analogue of Table 18.5 for general transfers and found that fertility plans and housing concerns did not interact with gender in the same way as housing transfers. A key feature of our argument concerning housing transfers is that they represent a transfer targeted to assets that could improve the quality of the marriage and the likelihood of the presence of children. We did not find the same pronounced differences in the interaction of fertility plans/concerns and gender for general transfers, indicating that these transfers do not behave in the same way as housing transfers.

5.   Complementary reflections and concluding remarks

By expanding the domain of analysis from two generations to three, we cast the issue of tied transfers in a new light. We achieve this by pursuing the idea that transfers for housing constitute a means for inducing the production of grandchildren which grandparents deem desirable in light of the demonstration effect. In addition to a new perspective of tied transfers, our approach provides a novel way of looking at the involvement of grandparents in the fertility decisions of their children.

Most fertility models either ignore would-be grandparents or grandparents, or relegate them to the shadows. For example, Easterlin's (1973) approach to fertility, whereby parental expectations and preferences are shaped by grandparents' wealth, does not assign an active role to grandparents. It is the grandparents' *wealth*, rather than their actions, which influences fertility. Becker (1991) accords a similarly tangential role to grandparents in fertility decisions: 'One would expect the number of children to depend, *perhaps only indirectly*, on the income of grandparents' (p. 199, emphasis added). In Becker's treatment of desired fertility, grandparent's income serves only as a proxy of unobserved parental earning abilities. As in Easterlin's model, grandparents play no active role in the determination of the number of grandchildren.

An approach to fertility which could predict an active role for grandparents is that of evolutionary biology, but this approach suffers from a number of shortcomings. Evolutionary theory posits that an individual's motivation is to maximize 'extended fitness', that is, one's own expected number of surviving offspring plus the relatedness-weighted sum of the fitness of one's relatives. The probability of a given gene being shared between a grandparent and a grandchild is one-fourth, certainly close enough to impel grandparents to be 'helpers at the nest'. But the low levels of fertility in industrialized countries suggest that extended fitness is a dubious maximand. To a first approximation, the progeny-maximizing birth strategy would be to have as many children as possible, the effects of this strategy on child quality notwithstanding (Kaplan 1994; Bergstrom 1996). In Kaplan's words (p. 784), 'it is likely that the low fertility behavior and high adult consumption levels characteristic of modern industrial society will not be explained by models of current fitness maximization'.

Our demonstration-effect approach attributes an active role to the would-be grandparents or grandparents. There is an ever-growing body of evidence that in traditional societies as in modern societies, grandparents make substantial contributions to the production and the rearing of grandchildren. Kaplan (1994) studied three traditional societies and found that the increased demands for food generated by the arrival of children were not met solely by members of the parent generation – grandparents provided as well. Cardia and Ng (1997), using recently available evidence from the Health and Retirement Survey in the United States, report substantial contributions of time-related transfers from grandparents in the form of childcare. Such behavior parallels the tied transfers to which we have referred.

We are not dismissive of the argument that individuals want to have grandchildren because they like grandchildren, just as we will not be dismissive of the argument that people marry out of love. But while there is a rich literature on the economics of marriage, there is no literature on the 'economics of grandchildren'. We seek to contribute to the development of such a literature by alluding to a vector of attractions, each capable of inducing a demand for grandchildren, even though we single out for close scrutiny a particular element in this vector. (Elements that could be included in this vector are: having grandchildren serves as a catalyst of bringing families closer together; having grandchildren induces 'demonstration-effect' behavior; having grandchildren is joyous.) The admission of several attractions renders it necessary to devise discriminating tests. Such tests are not difficult to come by. Consider, for example, the joy-of-having-grandchildren attraction versus the demonstration-effect attraction. If grandchildren are demanded regardless of demonstration-effect considerations, then we would not expect would-be grandparents to be more attentive to the constraining factors for having grandchildren that sons face as opposed to daughters. Or, if would-be grandparents were motivated by purely altruistic considerations, there would have been no reason for them to be more forthcoming in providing help with a downpayment when the child chooses to live closer (which is a good predictor of the child's intention or inclination to engage in 'demonstration-effect' behavior). Yet we see from Table 18.5 that living closer to the parent does indeed increase the probability of receiving a housing transfer.

Demonstration-type behavior is not the only possible means of conditioning future conduct. An alternative would be for parents to rely on schools or churches as a means of inculcating child loyalty. Yet indeed, demographic patterns for religious participation appear to be *explained* by the demonstration effect.[30] In addition, anecdotal evidence from Israel pertaining to adults with no living parents (the generation whose parents were lost in the Holocaust) indicates that these adults disproportionately participated in parent–teacher committees, and attended religious services together with their children more frequently and regularly than adults with living parents.

Can transfers from children tomorrow be prompted by transfers to children today? The prospect or process of 'direct reciprocity' may not work out as intended, for several reasons. If transfers are costly and if the children's move is the second and last in a sequence of (two) moves, the children may have no incentive to reciprocate. The notion that, since the children obviously observe their parents transferring to them they will surely be inclined to transfer to their parents because observation translates into inclination, can be problematic. If the act of the parents is replicated (as stipulated, for example, by the demonstration-effect approach), then giving to the children today can be followed and mimicked by the children, upon becoming adults, giving to their children tomorrow. The combination of inculcation and replication can well result in transfers down rather than back. Transfers can be decomposed into two constituent parts: the act of the transfer and the direction of the transfer. Children who are exposed to their parents transferring to them can 'reciprocate' by engaging in the act without replicating the direction. The possibility that transferring to children today results in the children, upon becoming adults, transferring to their children tomorrow, could best be eliminated if the children will not have children themselves. Yet the evidence presented in this chapter suggests that the transfer to children is aimed at supporting them producing children rather than at discouraging them from doing so.

Our approach can help resolve a controversy between two schools of thought in demography: one which advocates the idea that fertility demands are determined by the desire for old-age security that children provide (Caldwell 1976), and another which argues that the demand for children is driven by evolutionary forces (for example, Turke 1989). These two strands of thought make conflicting predictions regarding the direction of flows of resources and aid between generations: the first predicts a resource flow from young to old; the second predicts a resource flow from old to young. The debate has become somewhat stymied because of the preponderance of evidence indicating that resources flow in *both* directions. Such two-way flows of transfers are precisely what is predicted by our demonstration-effect approach. Resources flow downward, in the form of tied transfers, to encourage the production of grandchildren, and flow upward, in the form of help and assistance, as parents attempt to inculcate the appropriate values in their children. Moreover, when adult children provide their parents with attention and care they simultaneously provide their children with exemplary conduct. By expanding the domain of analysis from the standard two-generation format to three generations, we can explain disparate phenomena such as the connection between tied transfers and the production of grandchildren, and shed additional light on the multigenerational family as an arena in which the transfer of resources, the provision of services, and the formation of preferences are causally interlinked.

Notes

*   Previously published in *Journal of Public Economics*, **89** (9–10), September 2005, pp. 1165–97. © 2005 Elsevier. Reprinted with kind permission.

†   We are indebted to two anonymous referees for thoughtful advice and constructive comments. We thank Geoff Somes for excellent research assistance. Financial support from the National Institute on Aging (grant R01-AG13037), the Humboldt Foundation, and the Sohmen Foundation is gratefully acknowledged. The dataset used in this chapter, the National Survey of Families and Households, was generated with the help of a grant form the Center for Population Research of the National Institute of Child Health and Human Development. The survey was designed and carried out by the Center for Demography and Ecology, University of Wisconsin-Madison under the direction of Larry Bumpass and James Sweet. The fieldwork was undertaken by the Institute for Survey Research at Temple University.

1.   An appendix to this chapter ('Liquidity constraints and private transfers') is available from the authors upon request.

2. Note that conventional theories of the allocation of time and money within the family could well predict the opposite effect, since young children place demands on the parent's time and income, so that the competing presence of young children would *reduce* the assistance that P gives to G. For additional discussion of the demonstration effect and empirical evidence, see Cox and Stark (1996), Wolff (2001) and Ribar and Wilhelm (2002).

3. Hamilton's (1964) theory of inclusive fitness predicts that parental altruism toward children contributes more to inclusive fitness than altruism that works the other way around. In the words of Dawkins (1976: 115). 'In a species in which children have a longer average life expectancy than parents, any gene for child altruism would be labouring under a disadvantage'.

4. In the words of Hogan et al. (1993, p. 1432) 'parent–child exchanges of support are most common when dependent grandchildren are present . . . Thus, the most appropriate focus for research on intergenerational support is on lineages that contain grandchildren'.

5. We interpret x loosely, that is, as a 'system of values', a composite commodity – the caring and giving of attention to parents. Children who are *inculcated* to provide care and attention will find it hard not to do so. With the giving and caring trait in place, the likelihood of free-riding when $n > 1$ (reliance on other children providing) is low. Indeed, P may reason that whereas her children, as non-inculcated maximizing adults, may resort to free-riding behavior, grown-up children will not be so inclined if instilled with the caring trait when young. The possibility of free riding is further mitigated by the concern that a free-riding behavior by K upon becoming P will be imitated (having been so demonstrated) by P's own children.

6. Grandparents are not anywhere mentioned, for example, in the recent survey of fertility behavior by Hotz et al. (1997).

7. Further examples of imitative behavior that we reviewed in our preliminary search of the extant literature include: parenting techniques (Sears et al. 1957); child abuse (Bandura 1986, p. 265); affectional closeness (Rossi and Rossi 1990), and early family relationships and assistance (Whitbeck et al. 1991). These findings are consistent with Becker's (1992) prediction that through habit formation, early life events can have a significant impact on behavior later in life.

8. For example, in a typical study (Rosenhan and White 1967), fourth- and fifth-graders face a situation in which they must decide whether to donate some of their winnings from a game to charity. The treatment group is shown the example of a 'model', (that is, an adult who demonstrates, solely by example, the norm of giving). These children were more likely to contribute than those in the control group, which had no such model. Rosenhan and White also found that repeated examples reinforce the impact of the model on imitative behavior.

9. The HRS was first conducted in 1991, with interviews of 12,652 respondents from 7,702 US households. Because it was designed for analysing issues related to retirement and aging, at least one respondent per household was within the 50–60 age bracket. The HRS has been conducted every 2 years since 1991 and it contains special modules of questions on specific issues for subsamples (usually around 10 per cent) of respondents. The information discussed below is drawn from a special submodule in the fifth wave of the survey, which dealt with respondent motivation for the provision of care to parents.

10. For detailed analyses of the inefficiencies that can arise from altruistic preferences, see Bernheim and Stark (1988), and Bergstrom (1989).

11. Engelhardt (1996) summarizes the general reasons for the downpayment requirement: it makes homeowners share the risk associated with a fall in the value of the house; and it gives homeowners a stake in the property, thus mitigating moral hazard problems associated with maintenance of the house. Furthermore, lenders confronted with imperfect information about the borrowers' probability of default and by adverse-selection problems might use the downpayment requirement as a device for screening out borrowers who are less likely to repay.

12. The original release of the first wave of the NSFH contained 13,017 households, but subsequently 9 observations were found to be invalid and were deleted from the file.

13. The transfer modules in NSFH-II are unusual in that both the respondent and his or her spouse are given exactly the same questionnaire with identical wording (that is, each is asked about transfers that he (she) or his (her) spouse received). The wording of the questionnaire therefore implies that having either respondent or spousal information is sufficient for measuring transfers. In practice, however, there were several instances in which one spouse reported a transfer and the other did not. In these cases, it was assumed that the household received the positive transfer that was reported.

14. Although a long panel would be desirable for measuring permanent income, even a 2-year panel, such as ours, can significantly mitigate measurement error from transitory earnings. Details pertaining to the construction of the respondents' permanent income, the estimation of the earnings functions, and to the imputations of parental permanent income are provided in Appendix ('The construction of permanent income'), available upon request.

15. Cox (1987) discusses the importance of demographic characteristics of households and their role in underlying transfer motives.

16. An alternative specification reinforced these results. Rather than estimating permanent income, we included its determinants, such as years of schooling, and permanent income indicators such as the average earnings associated with the occupations of the respondent and spouse, and age. As in Table 18.2, the probability of transfer receipt fell with earnings, and the effect attenuated with age. Average occupational earnings, an indicator of permanent income, was positively associated with the probability of transfer receipt, again attenuating with age. Years of education of the household head together with the age interaction term are jointly highly significant and positive. And, consistent with the liquidity constraint hypotheses, transfers are targeted to younger households. These results are contained in Appendix ('Additional results'), available upon request.

17. For example, the average current earnings of home purchasers is substantially higher than that of non-purchasers – $54,510 versus $40,924.

18. The second-column estimates in Table 18.3 are from a nested probit model in which the decision to purchase a house is modeled jointly with the receipt of housing transfers. The specification of the purchase decision is guided by considerations discussed in Henderson and Ioannides (1986) and Ioannides and Kan (1996). See Table 18.3 for a list of the covariates in the housing decision equation. Estimates of the first-stage probit are contained in Appendix ('Additional results'), available upon request. The direction of the selection bias is negative, which accords with our priors. (For example, unobservables, such as having a good credit rating, would likely be positively related to home purchases but inversely related to help with downpayments.) But the estimated selection effect is only on the margin of statistical significance, and there is little difference between the coefficients in the adjusted and non-adjusted estimations.

19. When we base our liquidity-constraint variable on Wave 1 values rather than on Wave 2 values so as to measure constraints prior to home purchase, we find that receipt of housing transfers is insignificantly related to liquidity constraints for the younger two-thirds of the households in the sample. For the remaining and older one-third of the households, receipt of housing transfers is positively and significantly related to being financially strapped. This finding is not in line with conventional views that attribute liquidity constraints particularly to younger households who presumably had a lesser opportunity to establish reputation in credit markets (see, for example, Hayashi 1985; Jappelli 1990). In addition, disaggregation by region – a measure of exogenous variation in housing prices – did not uncover any systematic evidence of a liquidity-constraint effect on housing transfers. This result may not be all that surprising. It could have been argued that (especially when it comes to purchasing a house) liquidity constraints exhibit geographical variation since house prices exhibit considerable locational variation. However, the incidence of a liquidity constraint that households wishing to buy a house face may not be systematically and positively related to the price of a house since households in, say, rural areas where house prices are low, also have low incomes.

20. The NSFH data contain extensive information reported by interviewers concerning the quality of the interview, which allows us to investigate directly the issue of measurement

problems. Interviewers were asked a battery of questions concerning the comprehension, cooperation, and interest among respondents, the rapport between interviewer and respondent, and the extent of interruptions during the interview. Each component of interview quality was gauged on a Likert scale from 1 to 7. We focused on the subsample of interviews rated in the two best Likert classifications for all criteria associated with interview quality ($n = 1,224$). The estimation results for this subsample are similar to those reported in Table 18.3 and are provided in Appendix ('Additional results'), available upon request.

21. An alternative specification of transfer behavior reinforces the findings in Tables 18.2 and 18.3. We estimated a bivariate model describing the transfer/no transfer decision, and, conditional on a transfer, whether it was housing-related or not. Conditional on a transfer taking place, the probability that it takes the form of a housing transfer is increasing in recipient household income, consistent with the idea that it is general transfers that tend to be targeted to liquidity-constrained households. These results are contained in Appendix ('Additional results'), available upon request.

22. Could our estimated relationship between fertility plans cum housing concerns and housing transfers be spuriously generated by a plausibly heritable, and omitted, preference characteristic, namely, altruisim? Could it be that our findings emanate from us encountering altruistic parents – who are readily available to provide housing transfers – having children whose altruistic inclination renders them more likely to want to parent children? The first wave of the NSFH contains useful information on subjective feelings of closeness toward parents. Respondents were asked to rate the quality of their relationships with their parents and with their in-laws on a Likert-type scale of 1 ('very poor') to 7 ('excellent'). Assuming that these measures reasonably capture the extent of intrafamilial altruism, we replicated Table 18.4, including this time these measures. Our results remained unchanged. Furthermore, the measures themselves, while positive, were not statistically significant.

23. The linear restriction generated a $\hat{\chi}^2$ of 2.85 (ordinary probit) and a $\hat{\chi}^2$ of 2.80 (nested probit), versus $\chi^2_{0.5}$ of 14.07. The marginal impact on the probability of transfer receipt of this summarized measure is 1.4 percentage points (asymptotic t-value = 3.59).

24. One possible objection to our single-equation specification is the simultaneity between fertility plans/housing concerns and housing transfers. Indeed, our framework implies causality in both directions: would-be grandparents respond to the plans and concerns of the parental generation, but such plans and concerns themselves can be influenced by housing transfers. In our data, however, the reporting of plans and concerns, which is given in the first wave of the NSFH, substantially predates the purchase of a house, which occurs subsequent to the wave 1 interview. The time elapsing between these two events averages a little under 3 years, with a maximum of 7 years. Because of the sequencing we treat the plans/concerns variable as predetermined – that is, we assume that the measure is independent of subsequent disturbances in the probit. We conducted a test for weak exogeneity following the procedure derived by Smith and Blundell (1986), and found evidence strongly supportive of this assumption. We included a residual vector obtained from an auxiliary regression of summarized plans/concerns on a vector of wave 1 measures including respondent age, male and female labour force status and earnings, home ownership and housing equity, number of children, female headship, marital status, male and female education levels and financial assets. It was not possible to reject the hypothesis of weak exogeneity of the plans/concerns variable for the parameters of the equation for receipt of housing transfers even at the 0.25 level.

25. A recent study using data from a survey conducted in 1995 indicates that one-third of all first marriages in the United States end within 10 years (Bramlett and Mosher 2001).

26. See also, for example, Andreoni (1989).

27. We employ a bivariate probit technique to account for the correlation in unobservables between husbands and wives, which turns out to be large and precisely estimated. Such a specification precludes us from controlling for the selection bias associated with home ownership, because the resulting multivariate probit model would present practical difficulties from the computational problems associated with trivariate integration.

Note, however, that in the nested models in Tables 18.3–6, estimated selection bias from the home ownership decision is never significant at conventional levels.

28. If what motivates parents to furnish their children with housing assistance is a desire to have the children engage in demonstration-effect activities, then we would expect the assistance not only to activate such an engagement but also to render it more likely. Specifically, does house purchasing associated with the receipt of downpayment assistance, as compared to house purchasing not associated with the receipt of downpayment assistance, result in children locating themselves closer to their parents? It turns out that home purchasers tended to move further away from the parents: about 110 miles further away from the husband's parents and about 60 miles further away from the wife's parents, on average. But those receiving help with housing did not move that far: those helped by the husband's parents moved only 50 miles away from their parents; those helped by the wife's parents moved 30 miles away. These reduced distances are not statistically significant at conventional levels, however.

29. The results are contained in Appendix ('Additional results'), available upon request.

30. In fact, in light of the arguments about sex differences in life expectancy noted above, we would expect women to be disproportionately engaged in the moral training of children. Empirical studies of religious participation (Azzi and Ehrenberg 1975; Ehrenberg 1977) are consistent with this expectation; women are disproportionately involved even after controlling for intervening determinants such as wage differences. These studies also indicate that participation increases with the number of school-aged children.

References

Andreoni, J. (1989), 'Giving with impure altruism: applications to charity and Ricardian equivalence', *Journal of Political Economy* **97**, 1447–58.

Artle, R. and P. Varaiya (1978), 'Life cycle consumption and homeownership', *Journal of Economic Theory* **18**, 38–58.

Azzi, C. and R. Ehrenberg (1975), 'Household allocation of time and church attendance', *Journal of Political Economy* **83**, 27–56.

Bandura, A. (1986), *Social Foundations of Thought and Action*, Prentice-Hall, Englewood Cliffs, NJ.

Becker, G.S. (1974), 'A theory of social interactions', *Journal of Political Economy* **82**, 1063–93.

Becker, G.S. (1991), *A Treatise on the Family*, Harvard University Press, Cambridge, MA.

Becker, G.S. (1992), 'Habits, addictions and traditions', *Kyklos* **45**, 327–46.

Becker, G.S. and K.M. Murphy (1988), 'The family and the state', *Journal of Law and Economics* **31**, 1–18.

Bergstrom, T.C. (1989), 'A fresh look at the rotten-kid theorem – and other household mysteries', *Journal of Political Economy* **97**, 1138–59.

Bergstrom, T.C. (1996), 'Economics in a family way', *Journal of Economic Literature* **34**, 1903–34.

Bergstrom, T.C. and O. Stark (1993), 'How altruism can prevail in an evolutionary environment', *American Economic Review* **83**, 149–55.

Bernheim, B.D., A. Shleifer and L.H. Summers (1985), 'The strategic bequest motive', *Journal of Political Economy* **93**, 1045–76.

Bernheim, B.D. and O. Stark (1988), 'Altruism within the family reconsidered: do nice guys finish last?', *American Economic Review* **78**, 1034–45.

Bramlett, M.D. and W.D. Mosher (2001), 'First marriage dissolution, divorce and remarriage: United States', *Advance Data from Vital and Health Statistics*, vol. 323, National Center for Health Statistics, Hyattsville, MD.

Bruce, N. and M. Waldman (1991), 'Transfers in kind: why they can be efficient and non-paternalistic', *American Economic Review* **81**, 1345–51.

Caldwell, J.C. (1976), 'Toward a restatement of demographic transition theory', *Population and Development Review* **2**, 321–66.

Cardia, E. and S. Ng (1997), 'An analysis of intergenerational linkages via transfers in kind', mimeo, Boston College, Chestnut Hill, MA.

Cox, D. (1987), 'Motives for private income transfers', *Journal of Political Economy* **95**, 508–46.

Cox, D. (1990), 'Intergenerational transfers and liquidity constraints', *Quarterly Journal of Economics* **105**, 187–217.

Cox, D. and O. Stark (1996), 'Intergenerational transfers and the "demonstration effect"', mimeo, Boston College, Chestnut Hill, MA.

Dawkins, R. (1976), *The Selfish Gene*, Oxford University Press, Oxford and New York.

Easterlin, R.A. (1973), 'Relative economic status and the American fertility swing', in E.B. Sheldon (ed.), *Family Economic Behavior*, Lippincott, Philadelphia, pp. 166–223.

Ehrenberg, R. (1977), 'Household allocation of time and religiosity: replication and extension', *Journal of Political Economy* **85**, 415–23.

Eisenberg, N. and P.H. Mussen (1989), *The Roots of Prosocial Behavior in Children*, Cambridge University Press, Cambridge and New York.

Engelhardt, G.V. (1996), 'Consumption, down-payments and liquidity constraints', *Journal of Money, Credit and Banking* **28**, 255–71.

Engelhardt, G.V. and C.J. Mayer (1994), 'Gifts for home purchase and housing market behavior', *New England Economic Review*, 47–58.

Engelhardt, G.V. and C.J. Mayer (1998), 'Intergenerational transfers, borrowing constraints, and saving behavior: evidence from the housing market', *Journal of Urban Economics* **44**, 135–57.

Glass, J., V.L. Bengston and C.C. Dunham (1986), 'Attitude similarity in three-generation families: socialization, status inheritance, or reciprocal influence?', *American Sociological Review* **51**, 685–98.

Guiso, L. and T. Jappelli (2002), 'Private transfers, liquidity constraints and the timing of homeownership', *Journal of Money, Credit and Banking* **34**, 315–39.

Hamilton, W.D. (1964), 'The genetical evolution of social behavior (I and II)', *Journal of Theoretical Biology* **7**, 1–32.

Hayashi, F. (1985), 'The effect of liquidity constraints on consumption: a cross-sectional analysis', *Quarterly Journal of Economics* **100**, 183–206.

Heien, D. and C. Durham (1991), 'A test of the habit formation hypothesis using household data', *Review of Economics and Statistics* **73**, 189–99.

Henderson, J.V. and Y.M. Ioannides (1986), 'Tenure choice and the demand for housing', *Economica* **53**, 231–46.

Hill, R. (1970), *Family Development in Three Generations: A Longitudinal Study of Changing Family Patterns of Planning and Achievement*, Schenkman, Cambridge, MA.

Hogan, D.P., D.J. Eggebean and C.C. Clogg (1993), 'The structure of intergenerational exchanges in American families', *American Journal of Sociology* **98**, 1428–58.

Hotz, V.J., J.A. Klerman and R.J. Willis (1997), 'The economics of fertility in developed countries', in M.R. Rosenzweig and O. Stark (eds), *Handbook of Population and Family Economics*, Elsevier, New York, pp. 275–347.

Ioannides, Y.M. and K. Kan (1996), 'Structural estimation of residential mobility and housing tenure choice', *Journal of Regional Science* **36**, 335–63.

Ishikawa, T. (1974), 'Imperfection in the capital market and the institutional arrangement of inheritance', *Review of Economic Studies* **41**, 383–404.

Jappelli, T. (1990), 'Who is credit-constrained in the U.S. economy?', *Quarterly Journal of Economics* **105**, 219–34.

Kahn, J.R. and K.E. Anderson (1992), 'Intergenerational patterns of teenage fertility', *Demography* **29**, 39–57.

Kaplan, H. (1994), 'Evolutionary and wealth flows theories of fertility: empirical tests and new models', *Population and Development Review* **20**, 753–91.

King, M.A. and L. Dicks-Mireaux (1982), 'Asset holdings and the life cycle', *Economic Journal* **92**, 247–67.

Klatzky, S.R. (1971), *Patterns of Contact with Relatives*, American Sociological Association, Washington, DC.

Kotlikoff, L.J. and J.N. Morris (1989), 'How much care do the aged receive from their children? A bimodal picture of contact and assistance', in D.A. Wise (ed.), *The Economics of Aging*, University of Chicago Press, Chicago, pp. 149–72.

Pezzin, L.E., P. Kemper and J. Reschovsky (1996), 'Does publicly provided home care substitute for family care? Experimental evidence with endogenous living arrangements', *Journal of Human Resources* **31**, 650–75.

Pollak, R. (1988), 'Tied transfers and paternalistic preferences', *American Economic Review* **78**, 240–44.

Ribar, D.C. and M.O. Wilhelm (2002), 'Transfers and the formation of children's preferences: evidence from three generations of Mexican-Americans', mimeo, George Washington University, Washington, DC.

Rosenhan, D. and G.M. White (1967), 'Observation and rehearsal as determinants of prosocial behavior', *Journal of Personality and Social Psychology* **5**, 424–31.

Rossi, A.S. and P.H. Rossi (1990), *Of Human Bonding*, Aldine & Gruyter, New York.

Sears, R.R., E.E. Maccoby and H. Levin (1957), *Patterns of Child Rearing*, Row, Peterson, Evanston, IL.

Smith, R.J. and R.W. Blundell (1986), 'An exogeneity test for a simultaneous equation Tobit model with an application to labor supply', *Econometrica* **54**, 679–85.

Stoller, E.P. (1983), 'Parental caregiving by adult children', *Journal of Marriage and the Family* **45**, 851–8.

Sweet, J., L. Bumpass and V. Call (1988), 'The design and content of the National Survey of Families and Households', Working Paper NSFH-1, Center for Demography and Ecology, University of Wisconsin-Madison.

Turke, P. (1989), 'Evolution and the demand for children', *Population and Development Review* **15**, 61–90.

Whitbeck, L.B., R.L. Simons and R.D. Conger (1991), 'The effects of early family relationships on contemporary relationships and assistance patterns between adult children and their parents', *Journal of Gerontology* **46**, S330–S337.

Wolff, F.C. (2001), 'Private intergenerational contact and the demonstration effect', *Applied Economics* **33**, 143–53.

Zeldes, S.P. (1989), 'Consumption and liquidity constraints: an empirical investigation', *Journal of Political Economy* **97**, 305–46.

Appendix 18.A

Table 18A.1 Criteria used to determine the final sample

Original NSFH wave 1 sample size	13,008
Attrition from wave 1 to wave 2	3,000
Reasons for attrition:	
Too ill	276
Deceased	763
No way to retrieve data	5
Nonusable partial	48
Not complete by end of study	174
Final household refusal	5
Final language barrier	7
All tracing exhausted	733
Clean-up tracing dead-end	13
Final refusal	972
Not completed	4
Inconsistent or incomplete information about spouse	156
Spouse's wage missing	1
Missing amounts for value of house purchase, capital gain, or downpayment	3
Housing downpayment inconsistent with purchase price	10
Residing with parent	544
Respondent's age missing	6
Discrepancies in respondent information on age or gender between surveys	48
Inadequate information for calculation of permanent income	14
All parents and in-laws are deceased	3,444
Head's education missing	16
Respondent aged 65 or older	132
Missing information on private transfers	105
Missing information about ability to have, or desire for more children	68
Final sample size	5,461

PART IV

DATA AND POLICIES

19 Values and happiness in Mexico: the case of the metropolitan city of Monterrey

Jose de Jesus Garcia, Nicole Christa Fuentes, Salvador A. Borrego, Monica D. Gutierrez and Alejandro Tapia

1. Introduction

The relationship between happiness and its determinants has been the theme of many studies. Relevant advances on the study of happiness have been made in developed countries like the United States, the UK and Australia; however, research on happiness in Latin American countries is incipient. Although theories and results from industrialized countries constitute an important reference, happiness determinants may differ between developed and developing countries, especially if societal and personal values are different.

Happiness determinants such as money income, health and personality have been thoroughly explored, while research analysing the effect on certain personal values on happiness is limited.

Conventional wisdom tells us that Latin American countries are characterized as countries of strong traditional values. Thus, an understanding of the role personal values play in the construction of happiness in Latin American societies becomes relevant, because values may be one of the key determinants for happiness in these countries. Moreover, as there is no 'definitive' or 'bullet-proof' model available that perfectly accounts for happiness, a further search of models and specifications is recommended.

This chapter explores the relationship between happiness and its determinants in the northern Mexican city of Monterrey. Data from a survey conducted during the late part of 2002 were used to run different models and specifications in order to confirm or reject previous findings and, especially, to try to assess whether personal values influence happiness. Special emphasis was placed on a multiplicative function aiming at exploring whether determinants of happiness are imperfect substitutes.

The structure of this chapter is as follows. A review of relevant literature regarding the study of happiness is presented in Section 2. Section 3 describes the data and Section 4 presents a description of the model development. A description of the main findings and results are presented in

Section 5. Finally, a discussion of the results and some conclusions are included in Sections 6 and 7, respectively.

2.   Relevant literature

Definition and measurement of happiness

In order to study happiness it is necessary to define the concept. One of the most conventional definitions refers to happiness as an attitude towards one's own life, the degree to which an individual judges the overall quality of his/her life as a whole in a favorable way (Veenhoven 1984). The word 'happiness' is often used interchangeably with the term 'subjective well-being'.[1] This suggests a subjective appreciation of life; it is the subject who makes the appraisal even though it is not clear how the subject appraises it (Veenhoven 1997).

Having defined the concept of happiness the next relevant issue is whether it can be measured. Research on subjective well-being (SWB) has increased considerably, and so has the number of available measures. The study of happiness relies largely on evidence from surveys. Data are collected through direct questioning via interviews or self-administered questionnaires in which individuals self-rate their happiness on a single item or on a multi-item scale. The increase in the research on happiness has been accompanied by an intense evaluation of SWB measures (Diener 1984; Larson et al. 1985); a significant body of knowledge has been developed and fairly dependable measures are now available.

Researchers need to gather information on different life domains to understand what makes for happiness. Quality of life surveys often include measures of social background, personality, satisfaction with domains of life, social networks and economic affluence. The use of indices rather than isolated variables to account for differences in SWB is a common practice. Indices, which are more comprehensive measures, allegedly account for more differences in a measure of subjective well-being. Headey et al. (1985) incorporate into their models of well-being four sets of variables: social background, personality, social support networks and satisfaction with particular domains of life. Socioeconomic status, for instance, is then operationalized by an index that comprises information on gross family income, occupational status of the main breadwinner and the respondent's level of educational attainment. Mullis (1992) created a measure of economic well-being based on permanent income, annualized net worth and poverty level income. Headey et al. (1985) measure well-being with the life-as-a-whole, self-fulfillment and positive affect indices, which are often used as measures of happiness, while Mullis (1992) constructed an index based on the respondent's levels of happiness in the life domains of standard of living, housing, health, area of residence and leisure-time activities, and a dimension of life in general. Tepperman and Curtis (1995) built a life satisfaction scale for use with national adult samples from the USA, Canada and Mexico. Their satisfaction factor is an index that includes six variables from the World Values Survey.[2] Diener (1995) created two measures of national quality of life: the basic QOL index, for developing countries[3] and the advanced QOL index, for highly industrialized nations.[4]

With information on happiness and different life domains it becomes necessary to build a model that explains the relationship between happiness and the independent variables. Several attempts have been made to create a model that would help understand what makes for happiness (Stones and Kozma 1991; Mullis 1992; and Headey 1993). The relationship between happiness and other variables has been estimated by simple and multiple regression analysis, for instance. Many studies maintain that SWB can be modeled with the use of a linear function in which happiness is considered the dependent variable and known variables like demographic, social and economical aspects are taken as explanatory (Frey and Stutzer 2002). Subjective data are treated ordinarily so that higher reported SWB reflects higher well-being of a person (ibid.). An additive specification allows for complete substitution as one can compensate a considerable health loss, for instance, with a large amount of money to maintain happiness levels unchanged. In a multiplicative specification, happiness determinants are taken as imperfect substitutes; one element, for instance money, can partially compensate for a reduction in other elements but no element may equal zero as SWB would be driven to zero as well. The multiplicative specification is reasonable as it establishes limits to the substitutability among the factors involved in the explanation of happiness behavior. Hence, individuals can substitute money for health but only up to a point where individuals who are ill can still enjoy the benefits of money. Once a person becomes very ill, no amount of money can substitute for the physical health needed to enjoy life. Similarly, a certain amount of money is necessary as not even the highest level of physical health can substitute for the complete absence of money. Based on the arguments mentioned, a model is proposed to try to account for the variance in happiness of people living in the metropolitan area of Monterrey.

How values could explain the income paradox
Several attempts have been made to explain the weak relationship between income and happiness and to solve for the income paradox.[5] One reason why income might not strongly predict higher SWB, explains Diener, is that 'most people must earn their money, and wealthier people thus might be required to spend more time in work, and have less time available for leisure and social relationships' (Diener 2002: 121). He additionally suggests that

'wealthy people might adapt to their conditions and have rising expect-ations and desires that counteract the effects of the desirable circumstances of their lives' (p. 121). Mullis (1992) theorizes that the weak relationship between income and happiness could be the result of using reported income as a measure of economic well-being and recommends the construction of a comprehensive measure of economic well-being to account for SWB. Perhaps the lack of a strong relationship between money and happiness could also be explained by the role culture and values play in people's lives. Mallard states that 'in some cultures, success may be defined by the amount of money one has, the type of house and car one can afford, how happy one's family is, the extent to which one travels the world, and the extent to which one is educated' (Mallard et al. 1997: 265). So, depending on intrin-sic values, a person might define happiness in terms of money and thus be unhappy if he/she considers the amount of money available to him/her as insufficient. It is possible that the effect of income on happiness depends on an individual's beliefs and on the importance a person assigns to economic affluence.

Perhaps culture and values can help explain the income paradox. The answer to the question of what the 'good life' is could strongly depend on the values a person or a society has. Schwartz (1994) defines human values as desirable goals, varying in importance, that serve as guiding principles in people's lives. Diener and Suh (2000: 3) state that 'if societies have different sets of values, people in them are likely to consider different criteria rele-vant when judging the success of their society'. Following this reasoning, it is possible that people with different sets of values consider different aspects as important when evaluating their satisfaction with life. For one person humility may be most important, whereas for another more weight might be placed on being economically affluent. Hence, people who cannot attain their values and goals, or live according to their values, might be less satisfied and happy (Diener and Suh 2000). It was mentioned above that a possible explanation for the lack of association between income and hap-piness could derive from differences in people's beliefs and values. Partial explanation to the paradoxes of happiness may also draw from the influ-ence that moral and ethical values have on individuals. Kasser and Ryan (1996) argue that in spite of growing up in a much more affluent society, today's young adults are slightly less happy compared to their grandparents and have a greater risk of depression. They call the 'conjunction of mater-ial prosperity and social recession the American Paradox', and explain that the more people strive for goals such as money, the more likely they are to be less happy.

On the issue of values, for instance religiosity, interesting studies have revealed a correlation between faith and happiness. In order to solve the income paradox, we ought to look at the relationship between faith and SWB as these have been proved to be positively associated. It is possible that some people are happy regardless of their income level due to their religiosity, as being religious helps us through difficult times. Perhaps the phenomenon of getting richer but not happier can be explained by the fact that the increase in money and consumption has been accompanied by a loss of spirituality and religiosity and this loss negatively compensates for the rise in income. The values approach could also help explain why even the poorest individuals report high SWB (Diener and Oishi 2000). If an individual assigns limited importance to income then it should not have a strong influence on his/her happiness level.

One of the goals of this research is to explore whether values are an important determinant of individual happiness in a country like Mexico, where religion and other values play a key role in education, both within and outside the home. Perhaps SWB can represent the degree to which people are accomplishing the values they hold dear. Diener and Suh maintain:

> SWB includes components that are dependent on pleasure and the fulfillment of basic human needs, but also includes people's ethical and evaluative judgments based on particular norms and values of each culture. Thus SWB reflects to some degree how much people are living in accord with evolutionary imperatives an individual needs, but also represents judgments based on the particular norms and values of each culture. (2000: 4)

3.   The data

The empirical analysis was performed using the results of a survey[6] conducted in the metropolitan area of Monterrey, Mexico. Data collection took place during November and December of 2002 following a one-stage cluster sampling design. A questionnaire was devised to collect information concerning the following groups of variables: (i) subjective well-being; (ii) life satisfaction; (iii) values; (iv) positive and negative affect; (v) health; (vi) religion; (vii) economic; and (viii) social and demographical variables. The target population was individuals aged 15 years and above living in the metropolitan area of Monterrey. The sample size was 80 street blocks and a total of 574 individuals were interviewed. See Appendix 19A for a summary of the descriptive statistics of the most relevant variables.

4.   Model specification

The model here proposed rests on the assumption that people want to be happy and want to increase their happiness level during their lifetime. The model is used to test an additive specification and a multiplicative relationship specified as a Cobb–Douglas type function, which aims at accounting for the substitution that could be imposed on the explanatory variables (Ormel et al. 1999). Also, this model allows for the use of indices created with several variables that were previously tried independently.

The model considers a happiness index as the dependent variable and includes three independent variables: an economic index, a health-related index and an index related to personal values, under the assumption that an individual's personal values may constitute another substitute for factors such as monetary income, or physical health. Although several indices have been suggested in the literature, for instance, the Subjective Happiness scale, the Satisfaction with Life scale and the Bradburn scale, new indices were constructed in this study after carrying out a factorial analysis. A description of the indices used is as follows (all the questions and the weighting used to construct these indices are available on request):

Happiness index

a.   How happy are you?
b.   How happy were you yesterday?
c.   How intensely happy have you felt in recent days?
d.   How satisfied are you with your state of happiness?
e.   How happy have you felt compared to those around you?

Economic index

a.   How satisfied do you feel with your material possessions?
b.   How satisfied are you with your income?
c.   Compared with those around you, how do you compare your material possessions?
d.   Compared with those around you, how do you compare your income?

Health-related index

a.   How do you rate your personal health?
b.   How many times have you visited the doctor in the last three months?
c.   How satisfied are you with your health nowadays?
d.   How important for you is taking care of your health?

Index related to personal values   What importance do you give to the following:

a.   justice;
b.   service to others;

c. respect;
d. honesty;
e. work;
f. sincerity;
g. freedom;
h. family;
i. time.

A general model considering a happiness index and three indices as explanatory variables expressed on a linear specification is as follows:

$$HI = \alpha(ECI) + \beta(HEI) + \phi(PVI),$$

where HI stands for a happiness index; ECI represents an economic index; HEI is the health index; PVI is the personal values index; and α, β and ϕ are the parameters to estimate. This specification allows for complete substitutability, which means that any of the independent variables may assume a value of zero and still the result may have a positive value.

On the other hand, a multiplicative specification could be expressed as:

$$HI = (ECI)^{\alpha} (HEI)^{\beta} (PVI)^{\phi},$$

where the terms have the same meaning. This specification has the following characteristics: (i) a minimum level of each element is necessary to have a non-zero level of happiness; (ii) providing α is a positive number between 0 and 1, the marginal contribution of money (MCM) to the level of happiness follows a decreasing path; and (iii) the greater the levels of HEI and PVI the greater MCM, meaning that money is more productive in the generation of happiness when other factors are at high levels. Of course, this behavior is also true for the other two factors.

5. Results

General findings

An analysis of variance was carried out to identify differences in average happiness between groups of people with diverse characteristics. The first variables considered were those pertaining to demographics (Table 19.1). According to the results, the difference in average happiness between groups of different economic levels and of different sex is not statistically significant. However, education appears to make a difference; people with no education are on average unhappier. Note that compared with those who are single or widowed, and especially compared with those who are divorced or separated, married people are on average happier. These results

Table 19.1   Analysis of variance: demographics

(1)	(2)	Mean difference (1–2)	Std error	Sig.
Economic level				
High	Low	1.18	6.88	0.86
	Low-Medium	5.21	6.51	0.42
	Medium	4.18	6.47	0.52
	Medium-High	3.10	6.72	0.64
Education level				
No education	Elementary	−11.01	4.75	0.02
	Secondary	−10.67	4.66	0.02
	High school	−11.19	4.71	0.02
	Technical career	−12.38	4.75	0.01
	Bachelor	−11.46	4.74	0.02
	Graduate	−12.69	5.75	0.03
Martial status				
Married	Not married	2.77	1.25	0.03
	Divorced	9.70	3.84	0.01
	Widowed	8.12	2.98	0.01
	Living with someone	2.25	3.71	0.55
Marriage is				
Very happy	Not very happy	22.68	3.51	0.00
	Happy	12.85	3.71	0.00
Age				
70 years and older	15–20 years old	−11.82	3.75	0.00
	21–30 years old	−12.78	3.73	0.00
	31–40 years old	−14.36	3.80	0.00
	41–50 years old	−13.69	3.86	0.00
	51–60 years old	−11.33	3.94	0.00
	61–70 years old	−11.78	4.21	0.01

Note: Dependent variable: happiness.

concur with findings by Myers (1983). Moreover, a large significant difference in mean happiness arises from the comparison among those individuals who described their marriage as very happy and those who described it as not very happy. Difference on mean happiness between people of different ages is only statistically significant between those 70 years old and above and the rest.

Further analysis was carried to explore the relationships between happiness and variables associated with economic aspects (Table 19.2). Those who report having fewer material goods compared with significant others

Table 19.2   Analysis of variance: economic aspects

(1)	(2)	Mean difference (1–2)	Std error	Sig.
Material possessions compared to others				
Many less than others	Many more than others	−19.50	7.61	0.01
	More than others	−21.67	7.58	0.00
	Same as others	−22.25	6.98	0.00
	Less than others	−15.84	7.16	0.03
Income compared to others				
Inferior	Very superior	−4.84	3.93	0.22
	Superior	−5.53	2.19	0.01
	Same	−7.79	1.90	0.00
	Very Inferior	−1.15	6.54	0.86
Change in economic situation				
Economic situation	Situation improved	−4.68	2.12	0.03
worsened	No change	−3.62	2.19	0.10
Monthly family income				
Less than $1,200 pesos	$1,250–$2,400	−5.45	2.82	0.05
	$2,450–$3,600	−7.96	2.54	0.00
	$3,650–$4,800	−6.34	2.62	0.02
	$4,850–$6,000	−4.34	2.60	0.10
	$6,650–$7,200	−6.04	3.04	0.05
	$7,250–$8,500	−4.48	3.19	0.16
	$9,000–$10,000	−7.00	3.43	0.04
	$10,500–$15,000	−2.87	3.31	0.39
	$16,000–$20,000	−4.51	3.74	0.23
	$20,000–$30,000	−3.84	3.52	0.28
	$30,000–$50,000	−6.90	5.82	0.24
	$50,000 and over	−5.15	5.22	0.32

Note: Dependent variable: happiness.

are on average unhappier. The same situation arises if one looks at how people perceive their income level compared with others in groups close together. Findings suggest that people's evaluation of their present economic situation with respect to that in the past is relevant. Average happiness is higher among the group considering their economic situation to have improved in the last five years.

In order to explore the relationship between health and happiness, two tests were performed (Table 19.3). Results clearly indicate that people reporting having excellent health are on average the happiest. It was also found that the group of people who visited the doctor more than five times in the last three months are the least happy.

Table 19.3   Analysis of variance: health

(1)	(2)	Mean difference (1–2)	Std error	Sig.
Health				
Bad	Excellent	−24.34	3.63	0.00
	Good	−21.75	3.51	0.00
	More or less	−17.39	3.62	0.00
	Very bad	−19.50	10.25	0.06
Visits to doctor in past 3 months				
Five and more	None	−7.05	3.36	0.04
	1 or 2	−6.70	3.45	0.05
	3 or 4	−4.23	3.73	0.26

Note: Dependent variable: happiness.

Special emphasis was placed on differences in mean happiness and the importance assigned to certain values (Table 19.4) as studying the relationship between values and happiness is one of the main objectives of this chapter. In general, results indicate that those who consider being fair, respectful, honest, helpful and sincere with others to be very important values are on average happier; similar results arise when one looks at values such as being a hard worker, having time for leisure, partaking in country politics, and environmental protection. A very interesting result emerges with regard to the importance assigned to being helpful with others. The largest difference in average happiness derives from the comparison between those who consider being helpful to be a very important value and those who consider it not important at all. Regarding the issue of religiosity (Table 19.5), a statistically significant difference on mean happiness appears from the comparison of those who attend religious services more than once a week and those who do not attend religious services at all. A significant measure also derives from the comparison between individuals who believe in God and have no doubts about His existence and those who believe in God but have occasional doubts.

Regression results
Further analysis was carried out to explore the relationship between happiness and other variables using simple and multiple regressions. Models with different specifications were tested in order to compare statistical results. Some indices were built as suggested in previous studies while others were constructed using information derived from a factorial

Table 19.4   Analysis of variance: values

(1)	(2)	Mean difference (1–2)	Std error	Sig.
Being fair				
Is very important	Not very / Not important at all	8.33	3.29	0.01
	Important	2.56	1.29	0.05
Being respectful				
Is very important	Not very / Not important at all	6.43	3.43	0.06
	Important	4.50	1.39	0.00
Being honest				
Is very important	Not very / Not important at all	2.11	3.02	0.48
	Important	2.83	1.42	0.05
Being helpful				
Is very important	Not very / Not important at all	7.90	2.84	0.01
	Important	5.06	1.30	0.00
Being a hard worker				
Is very important	Not very / Not important at all	3.09	3.74	0.41
	Important	3.15	1.40	0.03
Being sincere				
Is very important	Not very / Not important at all	1.58	3.67	0.67
	Important	3.69	1.44	0.01
Being free				
Is very important	Not very / Not important at all	−0.19	2.87	0.95
	Important	3.98	1.43	0.01
Having time for leisure				
Is very important	Not very / Not important at all	5.23	1.85	0.00
	Important	4.54	1.35	0.00
Partaking in country politics				
Is very important	Not very	4.48	1.90	0.02
	Not important at all	4.56	1.86	0.01
	Important	5.51	1.98	0.01
Environment protection				
Is very important	Not very / Not important at all	5.81	2.11	0.01
	Important	4.73	1.35	0.00

Note: Dependent variable: happiness.

Table 19.5   Analysis of variance: religion

(1)	(2)	Mean difference (1–2)	Std error	Sig.
Attendance at religious services				
Less than once a year / never	More than once a week	−5.44	2.56	0.03
	Once a week	−3.25	1.96	0.10
	Once a month	−1.32	2.13	0.53
	Special occasions	−3.38	2.30	0.14
	Once a year	−0.79	2.93	0.79
Frequency of prayer				
Special occasions / never	Many times a day	−1.52	2.07	0.46
	Once a day	−1.26	1.72	0.47
	Twice a week	0.82	2.23	0.71
	Once a week	2.60	2.54	0.31
	Less than once a week	−3.64	3.58	0.31
Believes in God and has no doubts	Does not believe in God	6.60	5.09	0.19
	Believes in a higher power	0.81	3.34	0.81
	Believes in God but has occasional doubts	4.14	2.05	0.04

Note: Dependent variable: happiness.

analysis. The latter performed better in most cases. Results derived from a simple regression analysis (Table 19.6) concur with those derived from the variance analysis previously described. Demographic variables such as education, income, sex, number or persons living in the household, and marital status are poor predictors of happiness ($R^2 = 0.01$). Variables associated with health and attendance at religious services account for a slightly larger percentage in the variance of happiness ($R^2 = 0.07$). The grouping of aspects with the highest explanatory power ($R^2 = 0.24$) includes variables related to demographics, health, religious variables, domain importance and satisfaction, and being helpful with others.

The use of indices significantly improved the explained percentage in the variance of happiness. Indices (Table 19.7) were constructed based on results from a factorial analysis. For instance, the happiness index comprises results from questions such as: How happy are you? How happy were you yesterday? How happy have you felt in recent days? How satisfied are you with your happiness? How happy are you compared to those around you? The personal values index includes aspects such as being respectful, being helpful to others, importance assigned to family, and

Table 19.6   Regression results using single variables

Model	Variables included	Relationship with happiness	Significant at the 5% level	R^2
Demographics	Economic level	Neg	No	
	Married	Pos	No	
	Education level	Pos	No	0.01
	Age	Neg	No	
	Being female	Pos	No	
	No. of persons living at home	Pos	No	
Demographics– health–religion	Married	Pos	No	
	Education level	Pos	No	
	Age	Neg	No	0.07
	Being female	Pos	No	
	Self-reported health	Pos	Yes	
	Attendance at religious services	Pos	Yes	
Demographics–health– religion–importance	Married	Pos	Yes	
	Education level	Neg	No	
	Age	Neg	No	
	Being female	Pos	No	
	Self-reported health	Pos	Yes	
	Attendance at religious services	Pos	No	0.17
	Importance of health	Pos	No	
	Importance of happiness	Pos	Yes	
	Importance of education	Pos	No	
	Importance of government	Neg	Yes	
	Importance of media	Pos	Yes	
Demographics–health– religion–importance– satisfaction–values	Married	Pos	Yes	
	Economic level	Neg	No	
	Age over 70	Neg	Yes	
	Self-reported health	Pos	Yes	
	Attendance at religious services	Pos	No	
	Importance of happiness	Pos	Yes	0.24
	Importance of government	Neg	Yes	
	Importance of media	Pos	Yes	
	Satisfaction with own goals	Pos	Yes	
	Satisfaction with own family	Pos	Yes	
	Importance of being helpful	Pos	Yes	

Note: Dependent variable: happiness.

Table 19.7   Regression results using indices

Model	Variables included	Relationship with happiness	Significant at the 5% level	R^2
Previously proposed indices	Satisfaction with life scale	Neg	No	
Dependent variable is a subjective	Bradburn scale	Pos	Yes	
happiness scale developed by	Domain satisfaction scale	Pos	Yes	0.07
Lyubomirsky	Psychological index	Neg	No	
Previously proposed indices with	Satisfaction with life scale	Neg	No	
demographic variables	Bradburn scale	Pos	Yes	
	Domain satisfaction scale	Pos	Yes	
	Psychological index	Pos	No	0.08
	Married	Pos	No	
	Economic level	Neg	No	
	Age over 70	Neg	Yes	
Indices derived from factorial analysis with	Married	Pos	No	
demographic variables	Economic level	Neg	No	
	Age over 70	Neg	Yes	
(additive specification)	Personal values index	Pos	Yes	0.33
	Religiosity index	Pos	Yes	
	Emotional index	Pos	Yes	
	Health-related index	Pos	Yes	
	Economic index	Pos	Yes	
Indices derived from	Personal values index	Pos	Yes	
factorial analysis with no	Religiosity index	Pos	Yes	
demographic variables	Emotional index	Pos	Yes	0.28
(multiplicative	Health-related index	Pos	Yes	
specification)	Economic index	Pos	Yes	
Indices derived from	Personal values index	Pos	Yes	
factorial analysis with no	Health-related index	Pos	Yes	0.15
demographic variables (multiplicative specification). Limited to three indices and interception equal to zero	Economic index	Pos	Yes	

Note: Dependent variable: happiness index.

having time for leisure. The religious index considers importance given to God and to religion, frequency of prayer and of attendance at religious services, and satisfaction with one's religion. Satisfaction with life, achieved goals, material possessions, and accomplishment of one's wishes constitute the emotional index. The health index comprises information regarding self-reported health, number of visits to the doctor and importance of and satisfaction with personal health. Finally, the economic index considers the importance of and satisfaction with income and material possessions. Indices as suggested in previous works were tested, but results indicated those parameters to be not highly significant.

An additive specification was estimated with the use of indices as suggested in the literature. This specification takes happiness as the dependent variable[7] and life satisfaction,[8] positive and negative affect,[9] domain satisfaction and a measure of psychological behavior[10] as explanatory variables. This combination explains a very small percentage in the variance of happiness ($R^2 = 0.07$) as only two parameters were significant. Demographic variables were incorporated but results did not improve significantly ($R^2 = 0.08$).

Five indices were constructed for this study and a model following an additive specification was estimated. Built indices were tested along with some demographic variables and results improved considerably ($R^2 = 0.34$). All estimated parameters were significant at the 5 per cent level. The relationship among health, emotions, values, religion and the economic factor with happiness appears to be positive; the higher the value of an index, the greater the happiness. The factors contributing more to happiness are the health and the emotional indices.

In order to test the multiplicative specification, a model was estimated by taking the natural logarithms of the indices. The first model considered the five indices and an interception term. This combination accounts for 28 per cent of the variance of happiness and all parameters are statistically significant. The factor contributing the most was heath followed by the economic factor. When tried with no interception term, the R^2 fell to 0.28; however, all parameters remained significant. Finally, in order to analyse the substitutability among values, health and money, a model with only the these indices and no interception term was tested obtaining an R^2 of 0.15, again with all estimated parameters being significant.

Considering the model that incorporates the economic, the health and the personal values indices, it is possible to describe the relationship as follows:

$$HI = ECI^{0.27}HEI^{0.44}PVI^{0.31},$$

Where HI stands for happiness index; ECI for economic index; HEI represents the health index; and PVI is a personal values index. This specification shows an interdependence of factors in the generation of happiness. No factor can be zero or happiness would be zero as well. The factor contributing most to happiness is health, followed by the values, and then the economic factor. Marginal contribution (MC) to happiness for each factor may be represented as:

$$MCEC = 0.27(HEI^{0.44}PVI^{0.31})/ECI^{0.73}$$

$$MCHE = 0.44(ECI^{0.27}PVI^{0.31})/HEI^{0.56}$$

$$MCPV = 0.31(HEI^{0.44}ECI^{0.27})/PVI^{0.69}.$$

Given that all indices have a positive non-zero value, the three factors show a positive, decreasing marginal contribution to happiness. The higher an index is, the more happiness individuals get but in a decreasing fashion. Also, each marginal contribution depends on other indices' level. The higher level the other indices have, the greater the marginal contribution will be for each factor. Table 19.8 contains simulation results that show how the marginal contribution to happiness of a factor decreases as the level of its index increases.

6.   Discussion

Regression results were very consistent with those obtained from the analysis of variance. Demographic variables are poor predictors of happiness, obviating the necessity to include other aspects such as personality characteristics. The combination resulting from having certain demographic characteristics, and health and religious habits appeared significant. Variables associated with the importance assigned to certain aspects of life correlated positively with happiness. For instance, the importance placed on being happy and on the information provided by the media have a positive and significant relationship with subjective well-being. Possibly, those concerned with their happiness are more likely to look for ways to be happy. An interesting result indicated that those who consider having a good government as important tend to be unhappier. It is likely that corruption, poverty and recent currency devaluations in Latin America have engendered disappointment among the people. Thus, those who wish for a good government might feel frustrated and unhappy when governments fail to meet their expectations.

Table 19.8   Marginal contribution simulation results

If the	And the	MC
Economic index is 30	Health and values indices are 20	Money is 0.21
	Health and values indices are 80	Money is 0.60
Economic index is 70	Health and values indices are 20	Money is 0.11
	Health and values indices are 80	Money is 0.32
Health index is 30	Economic and values indices are 20	Health is 0.37
	Economic and values indices are 80	Health is 0.83
Health index is 70	Economic and values indices are 20	Health is 0.23
	Economic and values indices are 80	Health is 0.52
Personal values index is 30	Health and economic indices are 20	Personal values is 0.25
	Health and economic indices are 80	Personal values is 0.67
Personal values index is 70	Health and economic indices are 20	Personal values is 0.14
	Health and economic indices are 80	Personal values is 0.37

Domain satisfaction is a better predictor of happiness. Satisfaction with personal goals and one's family accounts for a greater percentage in the variance of happiness. This should come as no surprise as people from Latin American nations tend to assign much importance to family.

One of the main objectives of this chapter was to explain happiness with the use of indices. In this study a first attempt was made in this direction. Results are preliminary and further research is necessary in order to build indices that better adjust to the characteristics of the Mexican reality. The use of indices explained more variance in happiness. Previously tested indices were not very significant, except for the Bradburn scale. During the survey interviews, some respondents expressed difficulties understanding some of the questions used in traditional indices, which could perhaps explain their lack of significance. This issue allows for the conclusion that what works in some countries does not necessarily work in others; however, it is possible that further applications may bring better results. A different set of indices was built using a combination of information drawn from previous studies and results from a factorial analysis. A high percentage of the variance in happiness (0.33) was explained by a combination of these indices and demographic variables. Indices related to religiosity, personal values, emotions, health and economic factors resulted in a positive and significant relationship.

The model specified as a multiplicative function that incorporates only three indices: economic, health and values deserves special attention. A regression with no interception term was carried out in order to isolate the role these factors play on happiness and the substitution that exists among them. Although the specification imposes a constant elasticity restriction for the three factors along their different levels, it is worth looking at the MCs to happiness of each factor. (See Table 19.8.) For instance, since all the parameters estimated are less than one, all MC factors decrease the higher the level of the index. Hence, MCs of money can fall from 0.21 to 0.11 if other indices are constant at 20 and the economic index rises from 30 to 70. On the other hand, if the value of the other indices increase, the MC of money increases too. Based on the simulation results, if the economic index is constant at 30, but other indices grow from 20 to 80, the MC of money can increase from 0.21 to 0.60. These results support the idea that money can buy happiness, but not by itself. Money needs the interaction of other factors like health and personal values. The paradox of more money and less happiness can be explained by arguing that those who have enough money but are in poor health and/or have low personal values may not be as happy as those who enjoy good health and have high personal values. Even more, those who enjoy excellent health and have high personal values may not need much money to be happy.

The income paradox is perhaps the most intriguing for economists, as economic prosperity in this field is directly associated with general well-being. The fact that certain societies have experienced an important increase in their national income level that has not been accompanied by greater average happiness is certainly puzzling. Several possibilities have been suggested in order to account for this phenomenon. An appealing possibility for solving this paradox derives from the values approach. Possibly the lack of a strong relationship between money and happiness could be explained by the role played by culture and values in people's lives. The effect of income on happiness might depend on an individual's beliefs and on the importance he/she assigns to economic affluence. Thus if limited importance is given to money then its influence on happiness should be limited too. It is probable that having or following certain personal values allows individuals to put up with difficult times, that is, economic hardship. Maybe the phenomenon of getting richer but not happier can be explained by the fact that the increase in money and consumption has been accompanied by a loss of spirituality and religiosity and this loss negatively compensates for the rise in income. These possibilities are appealing and motivate further research, especially in a country like Mexico, where religion and other values play a key role in education both within and outside the home. Further research should explore whether the income paradox is relevant for the case of Mexico and should thoroughly analyse the role culture and values play in the Mexican society.

7. Conclusions

The following are the main findings of this investigation:

- It is possible to conclude that happiness is not a characteristic of economic level, as no significant differences in average happiness of people from different economic status were found.
- Compared to those who are single or widowed, and especially compared to those who are divorced, married people are on average happier. Moreover, being happily married positively contributes to happiness; whereas being unhappily married negatively influences SWB.
- Perceptions regarding how many material possessions one has compared to others around matters. Those who report having less material goods compared to significant others are on average unhappier. Results are similar if one looks at relative income.
- People who consider being fair, respectful, honest and helpful with others to be very important values are on average happier.
- Those who attend religious services more than once a week tend to be happier than those who rarely or never attend services.
- The use of single variables to try to account for the variance in happiness resulted in poor explanatory power.
- The use of indices significantly improved the explained percentage in the variance of happiness.
- In an additive specification, the factors contributing the most to happiness were the health and the emotional indices.
- In the multiplicative specification, the factors contributing the most to happiness were the health and the values indices.
- A decreasing marginal contribution to happiness was found. People become happier as one of the indices increases; however, the rise in happiness decreases at the margin.
- Values and health can help to become happier even if money is not at a high level, at least in this region of Mexico.
- Following this work in Monterrey, Mexico, the research should be extended to other parts of Mexico and Latin America to see whether the findings are consistent.

Notes

1. In this chapter, 'happiness' and 'subjective well-being' are used interchangeably.
2. These variables are: is R happy? top of the world, things going my way, life satisfaction, financial satisfaction and home satisfaction.

3. The basic QOL index includes seven variables: purchasing power, homicide rate, fulfillment of basic physical needs, suicide rate, literacy rate, gross human rights violations and deforestation.
4. The advanced QOL index includes seven variables: physicians per capita, savings rate, per capita income, subjective well-being, percent attending college, income equality and environmental treaties signed.
5. Data on countries like the United States and the United Kingdom show important increments in real national income accompanied by a virtually flat level of subjective well-being (Diener and Oishi 2000).
6. Designed by the Centro de Estudios sobre el Bienestar located at the University of Monterrey.
7. In this case happiness is measured as defined in the Subjective Happiness scale (Lyubomirsky and Lepper 1999).
8. Measured as suggested in the Satisfaction with Life scale (Diener et al. 1985).
9. Bradburn scale (Bradburn and Caplovitz 1965).
10. Adapted from the Psychological Well-being scales by Ryff and Keyes (1995).

References

Bradburn, N.M. and Z. Caplovitz (1965), *Reports on Happiness*, Chicago: Aldine.
Diener, E. (1984), 'Subjective well-being', *Psychological Bulletin*, **95**, 542–75.
Diener, E. (1995), 'A value based index for measuring national quality of life', *Social Indicators Research*, **36**, 107–27.
Diener, E. (2002), 'Will money increase subjective well-being?', *Social Indicators Research*, **57**, 119–69.
Diener, E. and S. Oishi (2000), 'Money and happiness: income and subjective well-being across nations', in Diener and Suh (eds), pp. 185–218.
Diener E. and M. Suh (2000) (eds), *Subjective Well-Being Across Cultures*, Cambridge, MA: MIT Press.
Diener, E., R.A. Emmons, R.L. Larsen and S. Griffin (1985), 'The satisfaction with life scale', *Journal of Personality Assessment*, **49** (1).
Frey, Bruno S. and Alois Stutzer (2002), 'What can economists learn from happiness research?', *Journal of Economic Literature*, **15**, 402–35.
Headey, Bruce (1993), 'An economic model of subjective well-being: integrating economic and psychological theories', *Social Indicators Research*, **28**, 97–116.
Headey, Bruce, Elsie Holmstrom and Alexander Wearing (1985), 'Models of well-being and ill-being', *Social Indicators Research*, **17**, 211–34.
Kasser, T. and R.M. Ryan (1996), 'Further examining the American dream: differential correlates of intrinsic and extrinsic goals', in P. Schmuck and K.M. Sheldon (eds), *Life Goals and Well-being*, Lengerich, Germany: Pabst Science Publishers.
Larson, R.J., E. Diener and R.A. Emmons (1985), 'An evaluation of subjective well-being measures', *Social Indicators Research*, **17**, 1–17.
Lyubomirsky, Sonja and Heidi S. Lepper (1999), 'A measure of subjective happiness: preliminary reliability and construct validity', *Social Indicators Research*, **46**, 137–55.
Mallard, Alison G.C., E. Charles Lance and C. Alex Michalos (1997), 'Culture as moderator of overall life satisfaction-life facet satisfaction relationships', *Social Indicators Research*, **40**, 259–84.
Mullis, Randolph (1992), 'Measures of economic well-being as predictors of psychological well-being', *Social Indicators Research*, **26**, 119–35.
Myers, David G. (1983), *The Pursuit of Happiness*, New York: Avon Books.
Ormel, Johan, Siegwart Lindenberg, Nardi Steverink and Lois M. Verbrugge (1999), 'Subjective well-being and social production functions', *Social Indicators Research*, **46**, 61–90.
Ryff, C.D. and C.L.M. Keyes (1995), 'The structure of psychological well-being revisited', *Journal of Personality and Social Psychology*, **69**, 719–27.

Schwartz, S.H. (1994), 'Beyond individualism-collectivism: new cultural dimensions of values', in U. Kim, H.C. Triandis, C. Kagitcibasi, S.C. Choi and G. Yoon (eds), *Individualism and Collectivism: Theory, Method, and Application*, Newbury Park, CA: Sage, pp. 77–119.

Stones, M.J. and A. Kozma (1991), 'A magical model of happiness', *Social Indicators Research*, **25**, 31–50.

Tepperman, Lorne and James Curtis (1995), 'A life satisfaction scale for use with national adult samples from the USA, Canada and Mexico', *Social Indicators Research*, **35**, 255–70.

Veenhoven, Ruut (1984), *Conditions of Happiness*, Dordrecht and Boston, MA: Kluwer Academic.

Veenhoven, Ruut (1997), 'The utility of happiness', *Social Indicators Research*, **20**, 333–54.

Appendix 19A

Table 19A.1   Descriptive statistics

	Mean	Std Dev.	Min.	Max.
Happiness[1]	91.13	13.86	0.00	100.00
Happiness index	87.09	10.73	23.00	100.00
Value index	91.10	9.95	25.00	100.00
Health index	83.77	10.68	35.83	100.00
Economic index	57.20	11.15	12.50	92.50
Age	36.18	17.08	15	85
Sex (1 = male; 2 = female)	1.49	0.50	1	2
Feeling happy[1]	89.80	17.59	0	100
Feel happy yesterday[1]	89.06	19.10	0	100
Satisfaction with your happiness[1]	90.12	17.21	0	100
Comparative happiness[2]	2.20	0.94	1	5
Material satisfaction[1]	78.01	21.82	0	100
Income satisfaction[1]	77.88	23.51	0	100
Comparative material possessions[2]	3.02	0.57	1	5
Comparative income[2]	2.87	0.67	1	5
Perceived health[3]	2.09	0.78	1	5
Visits to the doctor	1.05	1.69	0	15
Health satisfaction[1]	90.28	16.62	0	100
Importance given to health[1]	92.80	14.81	0	100
Justice[4]	3.61	0.56	1	4
Respect[4]	3.71	0.51	1	4
Honesty[4]	3.71	0.51	1	4
Service to others[4]	3.59	0.59	1	4
Work[4]	3.72	0.48	1	4
Sincerity[4]	3.70	0.52	1	4
Freedom[4]	3.63	0.60	1	4
Family[4]	3.85	0.43	1	4
Time[4]	3.27	0.76	1	4

Notes:
1. These variables have a range of 0 to 100, where 0 is the lowest level of satisfaction or importance given to the mentioned factor and 100 is the maximum.
2. Comparison variables like these have a response scale from 1 = much less (worse) than the rest, to 5 = much more (better) than the rest.
3. Perceived health scale goes from 1 = very poor, to 5 = excellent.
4. Importance given to values has a response scale from 1 = not important at all, to 4 = very important.

20 Happiness, satisfaction and socioeconomic conditions: some international evidence
Amado Peiró

1. Introduction

The pursuit of happiness and satisfaction underlies most human actions and creations. This is also true with regard to the role of the economy in human life. Nevertheless, economics has not always given these issues the importance they deserve. The roots of this neglect trace back to the discredit and fall of utilitarianism. In spite of being an influential trend in economic analysis, it lost most of its prestige at the beginning of the twentieth century due basically to two reasons: the problem of measuring utility, and the development of ordinal theories of utility that eradicated the approaches based on cardinal theories (see, for example, Lewin 1996; Kahneman et al. 1997).

Nowadays, the paradoxes, anomalies and refutations of ordinal theories of utility have motivated a reassessment of cardinal theories from different approaches. With respect to measurement of utility, numerous surveys have been carried out in the last decades where individuals quantify their happiness and satisfaction. Although there may be an initial reluctance to accept these measures of subjective well-being, psychological and sociological studies sanction them (Argyle 1987; Myers 1993; Pavot and Diener 1993). They are consistent with alternative evaluations (Frank 1997), and they may be superior to rival concepts (Sumner 1996; Holländer 2001).

In this context, economic research has recently begun to analyse the information contained in these surveys from its own perspective. This line of research should help to achieve several important goals: (i) a firmer establishment of foundations of economics; (ii) a reconsideration of economics in its relationship with psychology, sociology and other fields; (iii) to elucidate several important aspects of economics (see, for example, Di Tella et al. 2001); and (iv) to propose alternative economic policies based on the results obtained (Ng 1987; Frank 1997).

Recent empirical research has focused on different factors associated with happiness and satisfaction. In agreement with psychological and sociological studies, economic research has identified a number of personal and social characteristics associated with happiness and satisfaction. Some of the most important are the following: (i) health (Veenhoven 1991); (ii) age (Oswald 1997); (iii) social relationships and, in particular, marital status (Argyle and Martin 1991; Lee et al. 1999, Blanchflower and Oswald 2000); and (iv) political stability and development (Argyle 1987; Frey and Stutzer 2000a and 2000b).

Two economic factors have also been considered in their relationship with subjective well-being: unemployment and income. With regard to the first, most studies point to unemployment, beyond the consequent loss of income, as a significant source of unhappiness and dissatisfaction (Clark and Oswald 1994; Winkelmann and Winkelmann 1995; Gerlach and Stephan 1996). With regard to the second, income level seems to be associated with happiness (Veenhoven 1989). Nevertheless, the evidence on this last issue is mixed, depending on several points. Already in the pioneering contributions of Easterlin (1973 and 1974), individuals of a given country showed a positive relationship between income and happiness, but this relationship disappeared when considering different countries or time-series data. Today, there is a certain consensus in that: (i) over time, happiness does not increase significantly with per capita income, at least in developed countries (Easterlin 1995; Blanchflower and Oswald 2000); and (ii) people in richer countries are happier than people in poorer ones, though the relationship does not seem to be linear (Veenhoven 1989).

The purpose of this chapter is to provide new evidence on the relationship between socioeconomic conditions of individuals from different countries and their degree of happiness and satisfaction, paying special attention to the role of income. To achieve this objective, Section 2 presents the data used in this study. Section 3 analyses these relationships and, in particular, examines the relationship between income, on the one hand, and happiness and satisfaction, on the other. Finally, Section 4 summarizes the main conclusions.

2. Data

The source of data used in this study is the World Values Survey, 1995–96, which includes representative surveys of basic values in many societies on all inhabited continents. It grew out of surveys carried out in ten western European societies. In 1990–91, there was a second wave, and in 1995–96 the survey covered 54 independent countries. From these countries, information was available for 26 societies, and, among these, 15 were selected according to the basic criteria of quality and availability of information, and geographic diversity. The countries selected, with their sample sizes in parentheses, are the following: Argentina (1,079), Australia (2,048), Chile (1,000), China (1,500), Dominican Republic (417), Finland (987), Japan (1,054), Nigeria (2,769), Peru (1,211), Russia (1,961), Spain (1,211), Sweden (1,009),

Taiwan (1,452), USA (1,542) and Venezuela (1,200); they cover a considerable proportion of the world's population and present very different economic, social and political characteristics.

The surveys conducted include questions on happiness and satisfaction of individuals, as well as on their socioeconomic characteristics. Some of the most relevant questions are detailed in Appendix 20A.1. In particular, questions 2, 20 and 21 examine individuals' happiness, financial satisfaction and life satisfaction, respectively. These are the main variables that will be studied here. The answers to 20 and 21 range from 1 (completely dissatisfied) to 10 (completely satisfied). The possible answers to 2 range from 1 (very happy) to 4 (not at all happy), but in order to get an ordering analogous to the other questions, these answers have been recoded from 1 (not at all happy) to 4 (very happy).

Table 20.1 shows some basic statistics on happiness, financial satisfaction and life satisfaction. There are clear differences in these statistics across countries; Russia presents the lowest mean in happiness (2.50), very far from that of Venezuela (3.48), which presents the highest. Russia also has

Table 20.1   Basic statistics

	Happiness (H)		Financial satisfaction (FS)		Life satisfaction (LS)		Correlations		
	Mean	Std dev.	Mean	Std dev.	Mean	Std dev.	H, FS	H, LS	FS, LS
Argentina	3.10	0.72	4.96	2.50	6.93	2.31	0.27	0.50	0.40
Australia	3.37	0.62	6.40	2.39	7.58	1.88	0.24	0.51	0.48
Chile	3.07	0.70	5.91	2.27	6.92	2.14	0.29	0.39	0.48
China	3.05	0.66	6.11	2.45	6.83	2.42	0.38	0.45	0.71
Dominican Rep.	3.05	0.78	5.74	2.92	7.13	2.47	0.12	0.29	0.51
Finland	3.15	0.57	6.65	2.20	7.78	1.55	0.24	0.51	0.47
Japan	3.23	0.63	6.33	2.02	6.61	1.90	0.37	0.43	0.67
Nigeria	3.23	0.84	5.92	2.84	6.82	2.62	0.28	0.33	0.56
Peru	2.91	0.82	5.12	2.52	6.36	2.43	0.16	0.27	0.43
Russia	2.50	0.73	3.30	2.26	4.45	2.52	0.34	0.47	0.58
Spain	3.05	0.59	5.64	2.04	6.61	1.97	0.25	0.36	0.50
Sweden	3.34	0.60	6.26	2.43	7.77	1.81	0.30	0.57	0.43
Taiwan	3.14	0.63	6.33	2.15	6.89	2.03	0.32	0.40	0.63
USA	3.40	0.63	6.56	2.51	7.67	2.01	0.28	0.49	0.53
Venezuela	3.48	0.64	5.00	3.11	6.72	3.00	0.14	0.19	0.47

Note: Basic statistics on happiness, financial satisfaction and life satisfaction. All the correlations are significant at the usual significance levels.

the lowest means in the two other variables while the highest correspond to developed countries (Finland and the USA, in financial satisfaction, and Finland and Sweden, in life satisfaction). The anomalous statistics obtained for Russia are common to other studies, and are discussed in Veenhoven (2001). Table 20.1 also shows that all correlations between these measures of subjective well-being are positive and clearly significant. They are always lower between happiness and financial satisfaction, and are usually higher between financial satisfaction and life satisfaction than between happiness and life satisfaction. Very similar results were obtained with other non-parametric measures of association, like Kendall's or Spearman's rank correlations. In the interpretation of these results, it is important to bear in mind two points. First, although the concepts of happiness and life satisfaction may seem very similar, they present differences; according to psychological studies, happiness would be an emotional or affective state, while satisfaction would entail a cognitive process. Second, the questions on financial and life satisfaction were consecutive, and were both quite distant from the question on happiness. This fact could also affect subsequent results that will be analysed later.

3.   Happiness, satisfaction and socioeconomic conditions

To elucidate the causes and factors that underlie happiness and satisfaction of people in the different countries, ordered logit models were estimated. The dependent variables in these models are reported happiness, financial satisfaction and life satisfaction. Among the explanatory variables, several personal, demographic and economic characteristics were included. Appendix 20A.2 details these variables. Not all of them were available in the same way for all countries; this issue is also briefly commented on in the appendix.

Tables 20.2–4 show the results of these regressions in the different countries for happiness, financial satisfaction and life satisfaction, respectively. The analysis of the particular influence of each of the 26 variables in each of the three dependent variables and in each of the 15 countries would be a prolix task. Instead, the analysis will focus on those results that are common to several countries. While the results for each country are reported below, the practice of focusing on common results has the advantage of studying general facts, rather than analysing specific or peculiar features of one country.

In most regressions the coefficients of age and its square are negative and positive, respectively, and in many these coefficients are significant. This implies a convex shape in the relationship of happiness or satisfaction with age. Happiness and satisfaction decrease with age to reach a minimum, increasing afterwards. The minimum is reached at different ages depending on the countries, but typically it occurs in the forties for happiness and life satisfaction and in the mid-thirties for financial satisfaction. Thus, for example, the coefficients of age and its square are always negative and positive, respectively, for Australia. They are also always significant at the 1 per cent significance level. These values imply a 'U' shape in the relationship of happiness or satisfaction with respect to age. The minimums are obtained at 46, 34 and 40 years for happiness, financial satisfaction and life satisfaction, respectively. It is interesting to note the ubiquity of this feature across countries. These results are in accordance with many contributions that also find this same pattern (see, for example, Oswald 1997).

Bad health is strongly associated with unhappiness and dissatisfaction. In all cases the coefficient is negative, and in only three is it not significant. Having bad or very bad health substantially lowers well-being. This result is perfectly intuitive and agrees wholly with many studies conducted from very different fields that point to health as one of the main sources of happiness and satisfaction (Veenhoven 1991).

In six countries women declare a significantly higher happiness than men, and in five countries a significantly higher life satisfaction. Therefore, there is some evidence of differences in happiness and life satisfaction according to sex, but it is not general. With regard to financial satisfaction, the results are not significant: in only one country is the difference in financial satisfaction between women and men significant at the 1 per cent level; in the other countries the differences are of either sign.

The number of children does not seem to be an important factor of happiness or life satisfaction. However, in several countries, it seems to affect satisfaction negatively, especially financial satisfaction, due, perhaps, to the lower per capita income that children may imply in most households.

The marital status displays a strong association with happiness and satisfaction. In roughly half of the cases the variable MARRIED is significant, but, interestingly, in all these cases the sign of the coefficient is positive. It must be born in mind that people who are single form the reference category. Therefore, the evidence indicates that married people are often happier and more satisfied than bachelors. The difference frequently becomes stronger between married and widowed or between married and separated. This result is also in line with many contributions (see, for example, Argyle and Martin 1991).

Apart from a few exceptions, size of town and the education level do not seem to affect happiness or satisfaction significantly.

Only UNEMPLOYED, among the variables that reflect labor characteristics has a significant effect on the dependent variables. Unemployment has a negative and significant effect on financial and life satisfaction in almost half of the countries, but, very surprisingly, has no significant influence on

Table 20.2   Ordered logit models for happiness

	Argentina	Australia	Chile	China	Dominican Rep.	Finland	Japan
AGE	−0.059*	−0.067**	−0.044	−0.056*	−0.066	−0.170**	−0.063
AGE^2 (%)	0.050	0.072**	0.041	0.075*	0.132	0.168**	0.067
BADHEALTH	−0.990**	−1.270**	−1.281**	−1.245**	−3.930**	−1.964**	−1.430**
WOMAN	−0.074	0.402**	−0.262	0.404**	−0.070	0.474**	0.467**
1CHILD	−0.117	0.022	0.302	0.220	−0.068	−0.287	0.054
2CHILDREN	0.145	0.012	−0.095	0.320	−0.897	−0.057	−0.168
3CHILDREN	0.214	−0.016	0.151	−0.015	−0.542	0.063	0.154
>3 CHILDREN	−0.228	0.053	0.529	−0.237	−1.716**	0.096	0.275
MARRIED	0.666**	0.788**	0.355	0.078	0.117	0.533*	1.402**
WIDOWED	0.434	−0.416	−0.331	0.299	0.488	−0.252	1.194*
SEPARATED	−0.015	−0.277	−0.656*	−0.749	−0.562	−0.391	0.674
TOWN2		−0.105		−0.130	0.189		−0.068
TOWN3		−0.240	0.055	0.123	−0.032		
TOWN4		−0.178		0.478**	−0.290		
PRIMARY			−0.005	−0.275		0.234	
SECONDARY	−0.368	0.502*	−0.417	0.176	−0.262	0.227	
UNIVERSITY	−0.005	0.126	−0.553	0.009	0.065		
PARTTIME	0.195	−0.077	0.276	−0.396*	0.135	−0.354	−0.319
SELF-EMPLOYED	−0.124	−0.334	−0.099	0.245	−0.088	−0.213	−0.305
HOUSEWIFE	−0.068	−0.085	0.128	−0.391	0.070	0.407	0.453
STUDENT	0.054	0.737*	0.309	0.057	−0.116	0.590	−0.441
UN-EMPLOYED	0.079		−0.354	−0.115	−0.636	−0.243	1.430
IQ2	0.449*	0.140	0.340	0.714**	−0.302	0.236	0.234
IQ3	0.504*	0.504**	0.745**	1.349**	−0.389	0.851**	0.604**
IQ4	0.385	0.413*	1.112**	1.921**	−0.256	0.565	0.741**
IQ5	0.443	0.515**	0.994**	1.704**	0.256	1.187**	1.108**
N	757	1715	922	1473	295	885	833
Pseudo-R^2(%)	3.4	5.4	5.9	8.0	5.0	10.7	7.6

Note: Estimates of coefficients in ordered logit models for happiness. * and ** denote significance at the 5% and 1% significance levels, respectively. N denotes the sample size. See Appendix 20A2 for more details on the explanatory variables.

happiness in any country, though the estimates are mostly negative. This result is in sharp contrast to the evidence reported by many authors that point to unemployment as one of the main sources of unhappiness or dissatisfaction (Clark and Oswald 1994; Gerlach and Stephan 1996; Winkelmann and Winkelmann 1998).[1]

Besides the variables examined above, the variables IQ2, IQ3, IQ4 and IQ5 have also been included in the regressions shown in Tables 20.2–4. As

Nigeria	Peru	Russia	Spain	Sweden	Taiwan	USA	Venezuela
−0.060*	−0.026	−0.097**	−0.079**	−0.058	0.012	−0.013	0.007
0.071*	0.046	0.093**	0.082**	0.051	−0.027	0.018	−0.013
−1.659**	−0.949*	−1.286**	−1.174**	−1.783**	−0.961**	−1.294**	−0.809**
0.246*	0.245	−0.019	0.073	0.387*	0.183	0.040	−0.212
0.148	−0.392	0.141	−0.298	0.138	0.945*	−0.077	−0.165
0.386	−0.426	0.213	0.024	0.346	0.575	−0.275	−0.515*
0.656*	−0.787**	0.733**	−0.264	0.408	0.761	−0.497*	−0.343
0.460	−0.998**	0.680*	−0.315	0.729	0.926*	−0.391	−0.379
−0.187	0.229	0.581**	0.688*	0.549*	−0.209	0.877**	0.218
−0.888	0.457	−0.333	−1.021*	−0.837	−0.912	0.234	−0.449
−0.903*	−0.727*	−0.433	−0.645	−0.775*	−0.631	−0.068	−0.056
0.021	0.206	0.222	0.145	0.099	−0.170	−0.226	−0.829**
0.231	1.160	0.220	−0.022	0.302	−0.323	−0.132	−0.496*
0.230	0.960	0.185	−0.157			−0.428*	−0.291
−0.236		0.822	0.516		0.419		0.011
−0.107	0.053	0.903	0.621	−0.084	0.977**	−0.317	0.067
0.142	0.130	1.053	0.663	0.432	1.294**	−0.336	0.040
−0.072	0.060	0.130	−0.026	−0.184	0.092	−0.414*	0.023
0.102	−0.322	−0.375	−0.004	0.297	0.157	0.370	−0.029
−0.149	0.117	0.328	−0.147	−1.008	0.253	0.466*	0.380
0.049	−0.447	0.833*	−0.401	0.458	−0.111	−0.149	−0.141
0.032	−0.046	−0.375	−0.206	−0.360	−0.772	−0.127	−0.118
−0.108	0.235	0.368**	0.177	0.587*	0.351	−0.141	0.147
−0.038	−0.002	0.422**	0.359	0.753*	0.374	0.333	0.173
0.222	0.116	0.842**	0.013	0.716*	0.459*	0.289	0.143
0.566*	0.929	1.213**	0.628	0.931*	0.677**	0.474	0.129
1416	952	1881	871	796	1027	1244	1119
3.2	2.7	10.7	5.2	6.9	9.3	5.3	2.8

the reference category is composed of those who report being in the first quintile of income, positive (negative) significant coefficients of IQ2, IQ3, IQ4 and IQ5 reflect higher (lower) happiness or satisfaction of being in the second, third, fourth and fifth income quintiles, respectively, with respect to being in the first quintile. In addition to the comparison between the first and each of the other quintiles, it would be interesting to examine all the different pairs of quintiles. The results of these comparisons are presented in Tables 20.5–7, which report the results of the tests of equal coefficients of the different quintiles in the equations of happiness, financial satisfaction and life satisfaction.

Table 20.3   Ordered logit models for financial satisfaction

	Argentina	Australia	Chile	China	Dominican Rep.	Finland	Japan
AGE	−0.063*	−0.096**	−0.042	−0.068**	−0.353**	−0.071**	−0.100**
AGE²(%)	0.072*	0.140**	0.042	0.080**	0.459**	0.121**	0.122**
BADHEALTH	−0.464	−1.011**	−0.709**	−1.004**	−2.479	−0.897**	−0.792**
WOMAN	−0.317*	−0.106	−0.210	0.187	−0.538*	0.214	0.032
1CHILD	−0.358	−0.314	0.119	0.487	−0.297	−0.512*	0.048
2CHILDREN	−0.250	−0.380*	−0.203	0.555	0.106	−0.430*	−0.266
3CHILDREN	−0.458	−0.425**	−0.238	0.316	0.096	−0.646**	−0.148
>3 CHILDREN	−0.694*	−0.282	−0.244	0.688*	0.532	−0.586*	0.000
MARRIED	0.239	0.467**	0.363	−0.303	0.566	0.013	0.085
WIDOWED	0.448	−0.013	−0.050	0.064	−1.446	0.205	0.904
SEPARATED	−0.224	−0.404*	0.009	−0.226	0.200	−0.332	−0.644
TOWN2		−0.006		−0.053	−1.059		0.198
TOWN3		−0.079	−0.251	0.060	0.489		
TOWN4		−0.308*		0.278	−0.571		
PRIMARY			0.734	0.105		0.253	
SECONDARY	−0.344*	−0.410	0.750	0.121	−0.930	0.261	
UNIVERSITY	0.045	−0.428	0.520	0.324	0.286		
PARTTIME	0.291	−0.017	0.165	−0.021	−0.208	−0.033	−0.140
SELF-EMPLOYED	−0.127	0.048	−0.234	0.050	−0.645	0.392	−0.196
HOUSEWIFE	−0.278	0.097	0.010	−0.276	0.211	−0.026	0.528*
STUDENT	0.259	0.045	0.206	−0.168	−0.579	−0.238	−0.501
UN-EMPLOYED	−0.013		−0.777**	−0.189	−0.411	−0.622**	−0.683
IQ2	0.667**	0.525**	0.669**	1.203**	−0.337	0.578**	0.186
IQ3	1.281**	1.137**	0.819**	2.201**	0.592	1.061**	0.861**
IQ4	1.352**	1.294**	1.245**	2.968**	0.445	1.192**	1.137**
IQ5	1.686**	1.898**	2.273**	3.655**	1.481**	2.008**	1.890**
N	761	1713	924	1478	295	892	822
Pseudo-R²(%)	3.8	5.5	4.5	6.1	7.7	6.1	4.2

Note: Estimates of coefficients in ordered logit models for financial satisfaction. * and ** denote significance at the 5% and 1% significance levels, respectively. N denotes the sample size. See Appendix 20A2 for more details on the explanatory variables.

Not surprisingly, the estimates accompanying IQ2, IQ3, IQ4 and IQ5 are positive in the models for financial satisfaction (see Table 20.3), and almost all of them are significant. Very similar results were obtained in the comparison of the other quintiles (see Table 20.6); in fact, almost 80 per cent of the comparisons yield significant differences. Therefore, income seems to be an important source of financial satisfaction. More interestingly, Tables 20.5 and 20.7 report the results of the tests of equal coefficients in the

Nigeria	Peru	Russia	Spain	Sweden	Taiwan	USA	Venezuela
−0.011	−0.082*	−0.061**	−0.043	−0.077*	0.055	−0.044*	−0.034
0.018	0.086*	0.077**	0.050*	0.111**	−0.049	0.080**	0.034
−1.392**	−1.227**	−0.731**	−0.658**	−1.113**	−0.940**	−0.624*	−0.830**
0.323**	−0.093	−0.130	0.149	−0.130	0.266*	0.034	−0.109
−0.201	−0.135	0.006	0.080	−0.360	−0.129	−0.699**	−0.330
0.070	0.044	−0.146	0.090	−0.688**	−0.330	−0.568**	−0.396*
−0.029	−0.125	−0.448*	0.070	−0.903**	−0.158	−0.594**	−0.378
−0.070	−0.458	0.275	−0.013	−0.178	−0.197	−0.835**	−0.254
−0.138	0.023	−0.129	−0.085	0.641**	−0.011	0.616**	0.317*
−0.418	−0.190	0.069	−0.553	0.474	−0.335	0.197	0.042
−0.213	−0.445	−0.203	−1.453**	0.098	−0.521	−0.224	0.183
−0.724**	0.362	0.116	−0.048	0.075	0.799**	−0.116	0.902**
−0.579**	0.071	0.178	0.265	−0.127	0.651**	−0.153	0.391*
−0.540**	0.814	0.015	−0.233			−0.462**	0.608**
−0.202		1.198	0.033		0.020		0.322
−0.088	−0.232	1.445*	0.206	0.027	0.609*	−0.097	0.170
0.372	−0.080	1.642*	0.334	1.584	0.750*	−0.083	0.296
−0.168	−0.158	0.100	−0.273	0.042	−0.110	−0.033	−0.173
0.310*	0.183	0.213	0.060**	−0.183	0.076	−0.294	−0.167
0.190	0.299	−0.023	−0.231	0.724	0.475**	0.246	−0.240
0.324	0.052	0.059	−0.014	0.026	0.146	−0.520	−0.068
0.343	−0.216	−0.491**	−0.676**	−0.994**	−0.751*	0.149	−0.278
0.593**	0.452**	0.416**	0.234	0.796**	0.133	0.436	0.171
0.785**	0.770**	1.115**	0.820**	1.340**	0.397*	1.134**	0.520**
1.599**	1.309**	1.417**	1.092**	1.728**	0.434*	1.459**	1.017**
2.469**	1.444*	2.149**	1.814**	2.529**	0.897**	2.150**	0.675
1416	935	1911	873	801	1027	1248	1123
4.6	2.4	4.9	3.4	5.8	3.8	6.2	2.0

models for happiness and life satisfaction, respectively. With regard to this last variable, these tests also clearly indicate that income level is associated with life satisfaction. In most countries and for most income levels, richer individuals declare a higher life satisfaction. Nevertheless, the results for happiness are rather different. Roughly one-third of the tests detect significant differences at the 5 per cent significance level. Therefore, the differences in happiness associated with income, though existing, are not so overwhelming as in financial or life satisfaction. In particular, striking differences across countries are obtained. While countries like China and Russia present many significant differences, this is not observed, for any

Table 20.4   Ordered logit models for life satisfaction

	Argentina	Australia	Chile	China	Dominican Rep.	Finland	Japan
AGE	−0.064*	−0.076**	0.011	−0.064**	−0.126	−0.116**	−0.096**
AGE²(%)	0.060*	0.095**	−0.016	0.077**	0.161	0.129**	0.108**
BADHEALTH	−1.266**	−1.791**	−0.486	−1.143**	−2.379*	−1.842**	−0.925**
WOMAN	0.035	0.328**	−0.238	0.200*	−0.297	0.776**	−0.017
1CHILD	0.109	0.179	0.098	0.376	−0.050	−0.461*	−0.011
2CHILDREN	−0.038	−0.065	−0.379	0.489	−0.104	−0.238	−0.293
3CHILDREN	−0.096	0.032	−0.221	0.285	0.251	−0.190	−0.270
>3CHILDREN	0.305	0.309	0.030	0.536	−0.336	−0.068	−0.087
MARRIED	0.501*	0.719**	0.448*	−0.020	0.310	0.237	0.456
WIDOWED	0.402	0.210	0.223	0.516	0.463	−0.044	0.852
SEPARATED	0.153	−0.354	−0.154	−0.232	−0.106	−0.240	−0.206
TOWN2		0.066		−0.039	0.355		0.003
TOWN3		−0.212	−0.182	0.176	1.353*		
TOWN4		−0.131		0.182	−0.169		
PRIMARY			0.636	0.185		0.142	
SECONDARY	−0.458**	−0.274	0.415	0.306	−1.445*	0.209	
UNIVERSITY	−0.231	−0.401	0.314	0.430	−0.860		
PARTTIME	0.106	−0.173	0.433	−0.147	0.012	−0.274	−0.080
SELF-EMPLOYED	−0.091	−0.353	0.071	0.198	−0.321	0.027	−0.177
HOUSEWIFE	0.073	−0.118	0.019	−0.250	−0.339	0.112	0.490*
STUDENT	0.501	0.197	0.376	−0.013	−0.201	0.439	−0.329
UN-EMPLOYED	0.258		−0.577*	0.220	−1.064	−0.395*	−0.089
IQ2	0.506*	0.299*	0.576**	0.995**	−0.254	0.415*	0.332
IQ3	0.535**	0.625**	0.645**	1.634**	−0.040	0.888**	1.037**
IQ4	0.467*	0.652**	0.853**	2.229**	0.261	0.415	1.023**
IQ5	0.526*	0.735**	1.270**	2.438**	0.420	1.493**	1.447**
N	762	1712	922	1481	297	844	828
Pseudo-R²(%)	2.0	3.9	2.4	4.0	3.3	5.8	3.0

Note: Estimates of coefficients in ordered logit models for life satisfaction. * and ** denote significance at the 5% and 1% significance levels, respectively. N denotes the sample size. See Appendix 20A2 for more details on the explanatory variables.

income level, in countries like Peru, Spain or Venezuela. On the other hand, the number of rejections of the null hypothesis decreases when medium and high levels of income are compared; thus, the comparisons between quintiles 3 and 4, 3 and 5, and 4 and 5, yield only five rejections. This can be interpreted as evidence in favor of a lower degree of association between income and happiness once a medium level of income is reached.

This last point is related to a traditional result of international research. Many researchers agree that individuals are happier in richer countries, but

Nigeria	Peru	Russia	Spain	Sweden	Taiwan	USA	Venezuela
−0.008	−0.038	−0.094**	−0.102**	−0.089**	0.017	−0.041*	−0.024
0.016	0.060	0.098**	0.100**	0.092**	−0.010	0.056**	0.017
−1.101**	−1.413**	−0.788**	−0.821**	−2.096**	−0.982**	−0.778**	−0.746**
0.317**	0.061	−0.095	0.126	0.129	0.338*	0.191	0.017
−0.319	−0.307	0.054	−0.075	0.312	0.105	−0.259	0.269
−0.456	−0.641**	−0.010	0.059	0.131	−0.385	−0.434*	−0.243
−0.463	−0.597*	0.163	0.084	0.117	−0.212	−0.433*	−0.092
−0.510	−0.650*	0.603*	−0.166	0.524	−0.425	−0.248	−0.057
0.256	0.549**	0.059	0.498*	0.152	0.462	0.769**	0.413**
−0.666	−0.220	−0.207	−0.390	0.045	−0.554	−0.085	0.515
−0.312	−0.026	−0.351	−0.140	−0.768**	−0.219	−0.294	0.148
−1.022**	0.582**	0.193	0.300	−0.042	1.020**	−0.222	−0.450*
−0.461**	−0.172	0.162	0.053	−0.238	0.674**	−0.372*	−0.718**
−0.542**	−0.485	0.147	0.020			−0.577**	−0.150
0.025		0.758	−0.110		0.110		−0.417
0.320	0.178	0.985	−0.079	−0.083	0.486	−0.160	−0.544
0.646**	0.274	1.127	0.121	0.368	0.389	−0.052	−0.559
−0.182	−0.153	−0.015	−0.528*	−0.129	−0.053	−0.199	−0.191
0.149	−0.174	0.189	0.078**	0.335	−0.012	0.137	−0.193
−0.350	0.141	0.182	−0.038	0.186	0.328	−0.007	−0.150
−0.026	−0.002	0.661*	−0.009	0.076	−0.315	−0.038	−0.204
0.257	0.077	−0.457*	−0.651**	−0.877**	−1.220**	−0.460*	−0.670**
0.491**	0.395**	0.332**	0.165	0.101	0.437*	0.164	0.160
0.474**	0.229	0.588**	0.416*	0.566*	0.527**	0.648*	0.384*
0.813**	0.689*	0.899**	0.395	0.396	0.480**	0.630*	0.287
1.344**	0.586	1.279**	0.836	0.966**	0.583**	1.010**	1.418*
1413	946	1897	870	801	1026	1243	1117
2.9	1.7	3.7	2.2	3.7	4.4	3.7	1.6

that this relationship is not linear. Once a country reaches a certain economic level, the importance of economic conditions hardly affects happiness of individuals. The results here obtained suggest a similar 'intra-country' phenomenon. In the light of the results for 15 countries, the importance of income in happiness seems to diminish as income levels of individuals in a certain country attain medium and high levels.

Another important point that follows from Tables 20.2 and 20.4 is related to the differences in happiness and life satisfaction. As said above, the question on life satisfaction immediately followed the question on financial satisfaction, and, therefore, the response on life satisfaction could be conditioned by financial satisfaction. But, while non-economic conditions similarly affect

Table 20.5   Tests of equal coefficients of income quintiles in ordered logit models for happiness

	1–2	1–3	1–4	1–5	2–3	2–4	2–5	3–4	3–5	4–5
Argentina	0.03*	0.01*	0.13	0.10	0.79	0.80	0.98	0.62	0.81	0.84
Australia	0.36	0.00**	0.01*	0.00**	0.03*	0.10	0.03*	0.58	0.95	0.52
Chile	0.09	0.00**	0.00**	0.00**	0.04*	0.00**	0.01*	0.06	0.33	0.63
China	0.00**	0.00**	0.00**	0.00**	0.00**	0.00**	0.02*	0.00**	0.38	0.60
Dominican Rep.	0.37	0.25	0.50	0.58	0.80	0.90	0.22	0.71	0.14	0.26
Finland	0.24	0.00**	0.08	0.00**	0.00**	0.27	0.00**	0.34	0.32	0.11
Japan	0.29	0.01**	0.00**	0.00**	0.08	0.03*	0.00**	0.55	0.03*	0.14
Nigeria	0.54	0.83	0.25	0.01*	0.63	0.03*	0.00**	0.07	0.00**	0.08
Peru	0.12	0.99	0.68	0.18	0.18	0.67	0.32	0.69	0.19	0.27
Russia	0.01*	0.00**	0.00**	0.00**	0.68	0.00**	0.00**	0.00**	0.00**	0.08
Spain	0.37	0.14	0.97	0.22	0.35	0.60	0.36	0.29	0.59	0.25
Sweden	0.04*	0.01*	0.02*	0.02*	0.42	0.56	0.30	0.85	0.58	0.50
Taiwan	0.09	0.08	0.03*	0.00**	0.92	0.62	0.12	0.70	0.16	0.30
USA	0.60	0.23	0.30	0.10	0.01*	0.02*	0.00**	0.80	0.43	0.24
Venezuela	0.30	0.41	0.70	0.85	0.89	0.99	0.98	0.94	0.95	0.98

Note: *P*-values corresponding to the Wald tests of equal coefficients of the income quintiles indicated in the headings of the columns. * and ** indicate the rejections of equal coefficients at the 5% and 1% significance levels, respectively.

Table 20.6   Tests of equal coefficients of income quintiles in ordered logit models for financial satisfaction

	1–2	1–3	1–4	1–5	2–3	2–4	2–5	3–4	3–5	4–5
Argentina	0.00**	0.00**	0.00**	0.00**	0.00**	0.00**	0.00**	0.74	0.09	0.20
Australia	0.00**	0.00**	0.00**	0.00**	0.00**	0.00**	0.00**	0.28	0.00**	0.00**
Chile	0.00**	0.00**	0.00**	0.00**	0.41	0.00**	0.00**	0.02*	0.00**	0.00**
China	0.00**	0.00**	0.00**	0.00**	0.00**	0.00**	0.00**	0.00**	0.00**	0.05*
Dominican Rep.	0.30	0.06	0.22	0.00**	0.00**	0.03*	0.00**	0.65	0.03*	0.01*
Finland	0.00**	0.00**	0.00**	0.00**	0.01**	0.01**	0.00**	0.58	0.00**	0.01*
Japan	0.33	0.00**	0.00**	0.00**	0.00**	0.00**	0.00**	0.17	0.00**	0.00**
Nigeria	0.00**	0.00**	0.00**	0.00**	0.16	0.00**	0.00**	0.00**	0.00**	0.00**
Peru	0.00**	0.00**	0.00**	0.02*	0.05	0.00**	0.12	0.06	0.30	0.84
Russia	0.00**	0.00**	0.00**	0.00**	0.00**	0.00**	0.00**	0.01*	0.00**	0.00**
Spain	0.16	0.00**	0.00**	0.00**	0.00**	0.00**	0.00**	0.31	0.03*	0.12
Sweden	0.00**	0.00**	0.00**	0.00**	0.00**	0.00**	0.00**	0.03*	0.00**	0.00**
Taiwan	0.44	0.03*	0.02*	0.00**	0.15	0.10	0.00**	0.85	0.01*	0.01**
USA	0.08	0.00**	0.00**	0.00**	0.00**	0.00**	0.00**	0.04*	0.00**	0.00**
Venezuela	0.17	0.00**	0.00**	0.23	0.03*	0.00**	0.37	0.11	0.78	0.58

Note: *P*-values corresponding to the Wald tests of equal coefficients of the income quintiles indicated in the headings of the columns. * and ** indicate the rejections of equal coefficients at the 5% and 1% significance levels, respectively.

Table 20.7   Tests of equal coefficients of income quintiles in ordered logit models for life satisfaction

	1–2	1–3	1–4	1–5	2–3	2–4	2–5	3–4	3–5	4–5
Argentina	0.01*	0.00**	0.05*	0.03*	0.88	0.87	0.93	0.75	0.97	0.82
Australia	0.03*	0.00**	0.00**	0.00**	0.03*	0.02*	0.00**	0.85	0.46	0.54
Chile	0.00**	0.00**	0.00**	0.00**	0.71	0.14	0.00**	0.25	0.01**	0.06
China	0.00**	0.00**	0.00**	0.00**	0.00**	0.00**	0.00**	0.00**	0.02*	0.56
Dominican Rep.	0.43	0.90	0.46	0.30	0.51	0.14	0.10	0.36	0.23	0.69
Finland	0.01*	0.00**	0.12	0.00**	0.01*	0.01*	0.00**	0.07	0.05*	0.00**
Japan	0.08	0.00**	0.00**	0.00**	0.00**	0.00**	0.00**	0.94	0.05*	0.05
Nigeria	0.00**	0.01**	0.00**	0.00**	0.91	0.03*	0.00**	0.01**	0.00**	0.00**
Peru	0.01**	0.17	0.01*	0.37	0.32	0.28	0.77	0.10	0.59	0.88
Russia	0.01**	0.00**	0.00**	0.00**	0.03*	0.00**	0.00**	0.01**	0.00**	0.03*
Spain	0.33	0.04*	0.17	0.06	0.13	0.37	0.11	0.93	0.32	0.34
Sweden	0.67	0.03*	0.14	0.01**	0.01**	0.12	0.00**	0.34	0.15	0.04*
Taiwan	0.01*	0.00**	0.01**	0.00**	0.63	0.81	0.42	0.81	0.76	0.56
USA	0.51	0.01*	0.01*	0.00**	0.00**	0.00**	0.00**	0.91	0.02*	0.01**
Venezuela	0.20	0.03*	0.38	0.03*	0.18	0.69	0.05	0.77	0.11	0.10

Note: *P*-values corresponding to the Wald tests of equal coefficients of the income quintiles indicated in the headings of the columns. * and ** indicate the rejections of equal coefficients at the 5% and 1% significance levels, respectively.

happiness and life satisfaction, economic conditions show a rather different relationship. Unemployment presents a strong and negative association with life satisfaction, but not with happiness. Income has a much more intense association with life satisfaction than with happiness. These findings point to happiness and life satisfaction as two distinct spheres of well-being. While the first would be independent of economic factors, the second would clearly be conditioned by them. As a result, we can conclude that changes in economic conditions (employment or income) decisively affect a certain sphere of subjective well-being (satisfaction), but have a much more limited effect on another (happiness).

There are two further points to be noted. First, the ordered models that have been estimated above are very robust to alternative specifications. The conclusions hardly change when non-significant variables are excluded in the estimations for the different countries. Nor do they change when probit models are used instead of logit ones. Second, the relationships here analysed must be understood as association relationships, not as causal relationships. It could be that some explanatory variables do not cause happiness and satisfaction of individuals, but, conversely, it is happiness and satisfaction of individuals that affect these explanatory variables. Although it seems improbable, the statistical methods that have been used do not exclude this possibility.

4. Conclusions
Economic research has traditionally developed in a framework of revealed preferences and, consequently, has largely ignored the individuals' evaluations of their own satisfaction. This ignorance contrasts with the abundance of surveys where individuals quantify their happiness or satisfaction.

By using the World Values Survey conducted in 1995 and 1996, this chapter examines self-reported happiness, financial satisfaction and life satisfaction of individuals from 15 countries, relatively diverse from a socioeconomic perspective, from five continents. Some differences across countries are observed in these variables and there is some evidence that these differences are partially explained by the economic development of each country. The correlations between the different pairs of these three variables are clearly significant in all countries, and those between financial satisfaction and life satisfaction are often the highest.

To identify the socioeconomic factors associated with these variables, ordered logit models were estimated for each country. In spite of the socioeconomic, geographic and cultural differences across countries, there are sound similarities in the results of these estimations. The main conclusions are the following: (i) age is an important factor in almost all countries, though not in a linear form; happiness and satisfaction typically present a parabolic shape with respect to age, and reach their minimum about the age of 40 years; (ii) health shows a deep relationship with happiness and satisfaction; (iii) marital status is also an important factor; married people are, usually, happier and more satisfied than those who are widowed or separated; (iv) unemployment is significantly associated with financial and life satisfaction, but, surprisingly, does not seem to be so with happiness; and (iv) as expected, income holds a strong relationship with financial satisfaction; its relationship with life satisfaction and happiness is somewhat weaker, especially with this last variable, and presents differences both across countries and for levels of income. These results suggest the existence of two distinct spheres of well-being: happiness and satisfaction. Both are affected in a similar way by social conditions, but rather differently by economic conditions.

Note
1. Although these three contributions use the words 'unhappiness' or 'unhappy' in their titles, it is important to note that none of these papers uses reported happiness. Clark and Oswald (1994) use 'mental distress', and Gerlach and Stephan (1996) and Winkelmann and Winkelmann (1998) use 'life satisfaction'.

References

Argyle, M. (1987), *The Psychology of Happiness*, Methuen, New York.
Argyle, M. and M. Martin (1991), 'The psychological causes of happiness', in F. Strack, M. Argyle and N. Schwarz (eds), *Subjective Well-Being*, Pergamon Press, Oxford, 77–100.
Blanchflower, D. and A.J. Oswald (2000), 'Well-being over time in Britain and the USA', mimeo.
Clark, A.E. and A.J. Oswald (1994), 'Unhappiness and unemployment', *Economic Journal*, **104**, 648–59.
Di Tella, R., R.J. MacCulloch and A.J. Oswald (2001), 'Preferences over inflation and employment: evidence from surveys of happiness', *American Economic Review*, **91**, 335–41.
Easterlin, R.A. (1973), 'Does money buy happiness?', *Public Interest*, **30**, 3–10.
Easterlin, R.A. (1974), 'Does economic growth improve the human lot?', in P.A. David and M.W. Reder (eds), *Nations and Households in Economic Growth: Essays in Honor of Moses Abramovitz*, Academic Press, New York, pp. 89–125.
Easterlin, R.A. (1995), 'Will raising the incomes of all increase the happiness of all?', *Journal of Economic Behavior and Organization*, **27**, 35–47.
Frank, R.H. (1997), 'The frame of reference as a public good', *Economic Journal*, **107**, 1832–47.
Frey, B.S. and A. Stutzer (2000a), 'Happiness, economy and institutions', *Economic Journal*, **110**, 918–38.
Frey, B.S. and A. Stutzer (2000b), 'Maximizing happiness?', *German Economic Review*, **1**, 145–67.
Gerlach, K. and G. Stephan (1996), 'A paper on unhappiness and unemployment in Germany', *Economics Letters*, **52**, 325–30.
Holländer, H. (2001), 'On the validity of utility statements: standard theory versus Duesenberry's', *Journal of Economic Behavior and Organization*, **45**, 227–49.
Kahneman, D., P.P. Wakker and R. Sarin (1997), 'Back to Bentham? Explorations of experienced utility', *Quarterly Journal of Economics*, **112**, 375–405.
Lee, D.Y., S.H. Park, M.R. Uhlemann and P. Patsula (1999), 'What makes you happy? A comparison of self-reported criteria of happiness between two cultures', *Social Indicators Research*, **50**, 351–62.
Lewin, S.B. (1996), 'Economics and psychology: lessons for our own day from the early twentieth century', *Journal of Economic Literature*, **34**, 1293–323.
Myers, D.G. (1993), *The Pursuit of Happiness*, Aquarian, London.
Ng, Y.K. (1987), 'Relative-income effects and the appropriate level of public expenditure', *Oxford Economic Papers*, **39**, 293–300.
Oswald, A.J. (1997), 'Happiness and economic perfomance', *Economic Journal*, **107**, 1815–31.
Pavot, W. and E. Diener (1993), 'Review of the satisfaction with life scales', *Psychological Assessment*, **5**, 164–72.
Sumner, L.W. (1996), *Welfare, Happiness and Ethics*, Clarendon Press, Oxford.
Veenhoven, R. (1989), 'National wealth and individual happiness', in K.G. Grunert and F. Ölander (eds), *Understanding Economic Behaviour*, Kluwer Academic Publishers, Dordrecht, 9–32.
Veenhoven, R. (1991), 'Questions *on happiness: classical topics, modern answers, blind spots*', in F. Strack, M. Argyle and N. Schwarz (eds), *Subjective Well-Being*, Pergamon Press, Oxford, 7–26.
Veenhoven, R. (2001), 'Are the Russians as unhappy as they say they are?', *Journal of Happiness Studies*, **2**, 111–36.
Winkelmann, L. and R. Winkelmann (1998), 'Why are the unemployed so unhappy? Evidence from panel data', *Economica*, **65**, 1–15.

Appendix 20A1   Sample survey questions

2.   Taking all things together, would you say you are:

1.   Very happy
2.   Quite happy
3.   Not very happy
4.   Not at all happy

20.   How satisfied are you with the financial situation of your household? If '1' means you are completely dissatisfied on this scale, and '10' means you are completely satisfied, where would you put your satisfaction with your household's financial situation?

  1. Dissatisfied
  2.
  . . .
  9.
  10. Satisfied

21.   All things considered, how satisfied are you with your life as a whole these days?

  1. Dissatisfied
  2.
  . . .
  9.
  10. Satisfied

101.   Here is a scale of incomes. We would like to know in what group your household is, counting all wages, salaries, pensions and other incomes that come in. Just give the letter of group your household falls into, before taxes and other deductions.

  1. Lowest decile
  2.
  . . .
  9.
  10. Highest decile

Appendix 20A2

Explanatory variables

AGE: Age of the individual in years.

AGE^2: Square of AGE.

BADHEALTH: Dichotomous variable that takes value equal to 1 if the individual declares a poor or very poor state of health, and 0 otherwise.

WOMAN: Dichotomous variable that takes value equal to 1 if the individual is a woman, and 0 otherwise.

1CHILD, 2CHILDREN, 3CHILDREN, >3CHILDREN: Dichotomous variables that take value equal to 1 if the individual has 1, 2, 3, or more than 3 children, respectively, and 0 otherwise.

MARRIED: Dichotomous variable that takes value equal to 1 if the individual is married, and 0 otherwise.

WIDOWED: Dichotomous variable that takes value equal to 1 if the individual is widowed, and 0 otherwise.

SEPARATED: Dichotomous variable that takes value equal to 1 if the individual is separated or divorced, and 0 otherwise.

TOWN2, TOWN3, TOWN4: Dichotomous variables that take value equal to 1 if the individual lives in a town whose population is between 10,000 and 100,000, between 100,000 and 500,000, or of more than 500,000 inhabitants, respectively, and 0 otherwise.

PRIMARY, SECONDARY, UNIVERSITY: Dichotomous variables that take value equal to 1 if the highest educational level that the individual has attained is primary school, secondary school, and university, respectively, and 0 otherwise.

PARTTIME: Dichotomous variable that takes value equal to 1 if the individual works part-time, and 0 otherwise.

SELFEMPLOYED: Dichotomous variable that takes value equal to 1 if the individual is self-employed, and 0 otherwise.

HOUSEWIFE: Dichotomous variable that takes value equal to 1 if the individual is a housewife not otherwise employed, and 0 otherwise.

STUDENT: Dichotomous variable that takes value equal to 1 if the individual is a student, and 0 otherwise.

UNEMPLOYED: Dichotomous variable that takes value equal to 1 if the individual is unemployed, and 0 otherwise.

IQ2, IQ3, IQ4, IQ5: Dichotomous variables that take value equal to 1 if the individual is in the second, third, fourth, or fifth quintile of income, respectively, and 0 otherwise.

Limitations of data

The size of town was not available for Argentina and Finland. In Australia, Peru, the Dominican Republic, Sweden and the USA, as there were very few individuals without education, the reference category is formed by individuals without education or with primary school. In Chile, as no individual lived in a town with less than 10,000 inhabitants, and only two lived in towns with more than 500,000 inhabitants, the reference category is formed by individuals living in towns with less than 100,000 inhabitants, and TOWN4 was excluded. In Finland, as very few individuals had university-level education, UNIVERSITY was excluded. In Japan, the education level was not available, and, as no individual lived in towns with more than 100,000 inhabitants, TOWN3 and TOWN4 were excluded. In Sweden and Taiwan, as no individual lived in a town with more than 500,000 inhabitants, TOWN4 was excluded.

21 Happiness and the standard of living: the case of South Africa

*Nattavudh Powdthavee**

1. Introduction

An advert for Oxfam[1] appeals asks people in the UK, 'What do we dream for our children?'. If we were then to stop and think about the question for a minute, most of us would probably respond with success and health. However, according to Oxfam, a more natural response would have been happiness – or more simply, a 'good life' – for our children. The question then is what constitutes happiness? A review of research on well-being by Wilson (1967: p. 294) suggests that happiness comes from being young, healthy, well-educated, well-paid, religious, married with high self-esteem and job morale, modest aspirations, of either sex and of a wide range of intelligence. Oxfam, on the other hand, mentions none of the above in their list of possible answers. Rather, the things that constitute a good life for our children – at least in the developing countries that would receive aid – are more likely to be food, drinking water, and a shelter that they could call home.

The significant difference in the possible replies to Oxfam's happiness question, though it may seem predictable to many, raises some very important questions. If individuals' perception of what makes a good life depends crucially on how the normative framework for evaluation is formed, can we still then be reasonably satisfied with the conclusion that being married and young, highly paid with low aspirations, healthy and well-educated are all it takes to be global requirements for human happiness and well-being? Can we assume that happiness patterns are structually the same in the poorer countries as they are in the more affluent countries?

Recent economic studies on happiness, or subjective well-being, have given us some insights into what makes individuals – or our children for that matter – in wealthy nations satisfied with life. The results are found to be consistent and in keeping with Wilson's conclusion. Using the US and European data, researchers have been able to show how reported well-being is high among those who are married, employed, on a high income, women, white, healthy, highly educated with low aspirations, and looking after the home. Happiness is also apparently U-shaped in age, minimizing around the mid-40s (Deaton and Paxson 1994; Gerdtham and Johannesson 1997; Oswald 1997; Easterlin 2001; Frey and Stutzer 2000; Blanchflower and

447

Oswald 2004, among others). Economists have also found favorable comparison income to be a significant contribution to higher reported well-being for people in the developed world (Duesenberry 1949; Easterlin 1974, 1995; Morawetz et al. 1977; Frank 1985, 1989; van de Stadt et al. 1985; Tomes 1986; Clark and Oswald 1996; McBride 2001; Ferrer-i-Carbonell 2002; Stutzer 2002). The list of happiness research given above is not exhaustive by far, though it still suggests that the growing number of references are all converging towards establishing a unified theory that happy people – at least in the wealthy economies – are characterized by the same criteria.

The common patterns in happiness findings have led a number of economists to take an interest in the rarely available happiness survey data from transitional and developing economies. Using the US and European results as their benchmark, economists have so far been able to show how the effects of socioeconomic factors are similar in the poorer countries to those in the richer countries. For example, Graham and Pettinato (2001) find health, employment and marital status – with the addition of financial satisfaction and expectation in income mobility – to have significant marginal effects on overall happiness levels in Latin America, even after objective levels of wealth are controlled for. In other countries, Ravallion and Lokshin (1999, 2000) discover strong links between happiness levels and the changes in household income and health status, while relative income in the area of residence – as well as absolute income – matters to financial satisfaction in Russia. Namazie and Sanfey (2001) and Lelkes (2002) find evidence on socioeconomic variables such as age, gender, income, education levels, employment and marital status to have similar effects on the self-reported happiness levels in Kyrgyzstan and in Hungary to those in the more-developed economies, respectively.

This chapter follows the same line of research as other previous work on happiness in the less-developed economies, with particular focus on South Africa. We explore in detail the general relationships between the already identified socioeconomic variables and the newly introduced basic living indicator variables with the reported perceived quality of life in the post-apartheid South Africa in 1993, both at the individual and household levels. We begin by showing that subjective well-being regression equations on a set of household characteristics, and then later, on the personal attributes of the respondent and of other household members, have a generally similar pattern in South Africa to those that are expected in a more developed economy. The average educational level and occupational status of other individuals living in the same household are found to be significantly correlated to the reported well-being of the respondent. We also find basic living indicators such as durable assets ownership to be just as good a determinant as income in the assessment of subjective well-being, and that individuals care about relative income once the means of durable consumption in the area are controlled for in the regressions.

In Section 2, we discuss the motivation for subjective well-being research in a developing country framework. Section 3 looks at the background and dataset for South Africa. The empirical strategy and main findings are discussed in Section 4, and conclusions are set out in Section 5.

2. A good life in a less-developed environment

The impression as given by the existing work on subjective well-being is that it focuses only on wealthy nations. This is not far off the mark. Subjective well-being research has focused largely on the developed economies but only because adequate data are more readily available from these countries. Yet developing economies offer more opportunities for economists to also study poverty and inequalities, the volatility in various socioeconomic and macroeconomic factors, and their implications for the happiness of people living there.

Take Latin America, for example. Happiness in Latin America depends not only on the already identified individual and within-country variables, such as marital status, employment and inflation, but also on income mobility and inequality driven by technology-led growth. Apparently, the perception of past mobility and prospect of moving upwards on the economic ladder are positively correlated with happiness in Latin America, where the probabilities of moving up or down the income quintiles are much higher than in any advanced industrialized economy.[2] The majority of people in the developed world may rarely think about the prospect of moving up or down the economic ladder merely because they are less exposed to the same vulnerability than the people living in the emerging market economies. This leads to a possibility that a similar set of economic variables may or may not have the same significant effects on subjective well-being for those coming from a more advanced economy. It does not mean, however, that the same individuals from the developed countries will never respond to the perceived income mobility in the same manner as will the people living in Latin America, given a shock of the same volatile macroeconomic environment. Nevertheless, it can be argued that – given a higher standard of living – the weight regarding what makes us happy has been shifted towards some other factors. Given a high standard of living, contributions to higher happiness levels are more likely to result from individuals enjoying certain elements that are above that of the societal average, be that earning a higher income than our colleagues or owning a better-quality car than our neighbours, for example. Owning a car that has the characteristics of transportation when everybody else also owns one may not have the same marginal effects on happiness in the developed countries – providing, of course, that the car in question is not of a particular make or quality that is distinctively different from other cars on the road – as it would have in a less-developed country where car ownership is not considered a norm. However, it still does not necessarily mean that if a car – with its only use being to transport individuals – were to be taken away from the individual living in an advanced economy, then his/her standard of living, *vis-à-vis,* happiness will not drop, *ceteris paribus.* The same idea is put forward but in a slightly different context by Sen (1983) on bicycle ownership:

> If I am of a cheerful disposition and enjoy life even without being able to move around [as a result of owning a bicycle and have the ability to ride it], I am no doubt a happy person, but it does not follow that I have a high standard of living. A grumbling rich man may well be less happy than a contented peasant, but he does have a higher standard of living than that peasant. (p. 160)[3]

The issue is therefore, given different sets of living standards and providing that living standards are important in determining the level of reported happiness in some sense, the overall picture of what constitutes happiness at a single point in time may well be very different. A comparative-static analysis may find that a middle-income individual who believes that his/her prospect of moving up the economic ladder is high is happier living in a volatile macroeconomic environment than an upper-income individual who believes that his/her situation is deteriorating, even after controlling for the usual absolute and relative income. The influences of these unobservable features on happiness are probably more difficult to test using only developed country data. Nevertheless, recent work on happiness in developing countries argues that with enough controls of the surrounding environment, happy people are structurally the same across poorer countries as they would be in richer countries. And in this chapter, we take a step closer – through the use of South African cross-sectional data – to provide more evidence that will help to support such a claim.

3.   South Africa and data description
General background
According to the report by the Inter-ministerial Committee on Poverty and Inequality (ICPI) in 1998,[4] South Africa is classified as an upper-middle-income country with a per capita income higher than that of Poland and Thailand, and similar to that of Brazil and Malaysia.[5] Yet despite this relative wealth, South Africa still ranked behind most of the countries with a similar income per capita according to the Human Development Index (HDI) league table, where HDI represents a composite of the following

three factors: (i) longevity (as measured by life expectancy), (ii) educational attainment (as measured by adult literacy and enrolment rates), and (iii) real standard of living (as measured by real GDP per capita).[6]

In reality, the experience of around 50 per cent of the South African population is either one of outright poverty, or of continued vulnerability to becoming poor. Despite being classified as an upper-middle-income country, the nation holds to date one of the most unequal distributions in income and wealth in the world. This claim is supported by the following inequality indicators: the Gini coefficient and the income shares of households. According to the World Bank's 1996 *World Development Report*, the Gini coefficient – which measures the degree of income inequality – in South Africa is the second highest in the world in 1996 at 0.58 (behind Brazil's 0.63), where 0 signifies absolute equality and 1 indicates absolute concentration. The measurement of income shares of deciles of households tells us that the poorest 40 per cent of households – equivalent to about 50 per cent of the total population – has only 11 per cent of the total income, while the richest 10 per cent of households – 7 per cent of the total population – has over 40 per cent of the total income. Not surprisingly for a country where diversity is one of the key features, between-group inequality is also considered to be very large, with between-race inequality accounting for about 37 per cent of total inequality. As for the within-race inequality, the calculated Gini coefficients by race at the end of 1993 also display substantial values at 0.449, 0.412, 0.377 and 0.336 for blacks, coloureds, Indians and whites, respectively (see Deaton 1997: p. 157).

Looking more closely at the poor, a disaggregated analysis in the ICPI report on living standards has shown that there is a strong racial and regional dimension to poverty in South Africa. About 70 per cent of households classified as 'poor'[7] from a consumption-based poverty measure are found to be living in rural areas, while 61 per cent of the households from the same category come from the black African population. Most of the households classified as 'poor' living in rural areas are black Africans who have been deprived of access to basic services in their homes such as running water, electricity and telephone, as well as decent education and secure employment. There are also other clear relationships between poverty and other human development indicators such as ill-health and poor nutrition, as well as owning no material goods and having to live in a violent environment. Moving out of poverty is also considered to be extremely difficult for the majority of people. A panel study by Carter and May (1999) and a later summary compiled by Graham and Pettinato (2002) on income mobility suggest that a significant proportion of poverty in South Africa is much more chronic or permanent than in any other studied country, namely Peru, Russia and the USA, with about 66 per cent of those below the poverty line in 1993 still in the same place in 1998.

Other evidence on South Africa's poverty, which is more closely related to the analysis in this chapter, comes from a subjective measurement of poverty conducted by the South African Participatory Poverty Assessment (SA-PPA) team in 1997. The exercise was carried out by asking people from a number of participating communities to subjectively place themselves (or their households) on the community wealth ladder. The SA-PPA team found subjective responses to be correlated with many of the objective characteristics and other non-income variables of the respondents. For example, in the Nhlangwini community in the province of KwaZulu-Natal, people who had reported themselves to be in the poor category (38 out of 79 households) had all or some of the following criteria: their family members were not working for cash or were doing work that was poorly paid; they were in poor health; they had no parents; they were farm workers. The criteria for those in the average category (21 households) consisted of, for example, households with regular-wage workers or with some income coming from farming. The situation improves significantly for people who had classified themselves as rich (17 households). Some of these 'rich' households ran more than one business while others had a number of family members in salaried work. Other supporting work on subjective well-being in South Africa can also be found in Klasen (1997) and Møller (1998). However, the relationships between subjective well-being and socioeconomic factors established in these studies were made through general observations only, and not by econometric evaluation.

All in all, the evidence has provided us with the two main reasons for this study. The first is that the poverty and inequality problem represents a much more serious and widespread issue at the core of human development than general observations have made it out to be, and thus provides us with an interesting framework on which we can base our research. The second is the possibility that happiness responses can be correlated with various objective characteristics of households, as earlier studies suggest. Hence, the need for a more systematic survey involving a larger population, in order to corroborate any previous findings on subjective well-being in South Africa.

The South African integrated household survey
This chapter uses the household data from the South African Labour Research Unit (SALDRU) survey, which is a nationally representative, cross-sectional household survey which contains information on a series of subjects including – but not limited to – household composition, education, employment status and other income-earning activities, among others. The survey, carried out during the last five months of 1993 – shortly before the

election that made Nelson Mandela president in 1994 – consists of approximately 8,800 randomly selected households in as many as 360 communities. The data are collected by personal interview, and are made publicly available from the World Bank's Living Standard Measurement Study (LSMS) website.[8] One of the main reasons for choosing the SALDRU survey is because it contains a section – other than the information on objective household and personal characteristics – that asked households the perceived quality of life (PQOL) question: 'Taking everything into account, how satisfied is this household with the way it lives today?'. The five possible answers were 'very satisfied', 'satisfied', 'neither satisfied nor dissatisfied', 'dissatisfied' and 'very dissatisfied'. We rearranged these in order so that the highest level of happiness – 'very satisfied' – is recorded as a 5, 'satisfied' is a 4, 'neither satisfied nor dissatisfied' is a 3, 'dissatisfied' is a 2, and the lowest level of happiness – 'very dissatisfied' – is a 1.[9] Nevertheless, not all of the 8,800 households responded to the PQOL and relevant questions and had to be eliminated from the sample, leaving us with 7,499 observations (85 per cent from the original sample) for the analysis. The raw sample of PQOL distribution is given in Table 21.1. Data on the distribution of happiness responses in the United States, and the distribution of life satisfaction responses in Europe, respectively, are also shown.

The next section presents some empirical models that try to capture the relationship between PQOL and sociodemographic variables and outline our estimation procedures on cross-sectional data.

4. Empirical strategy and preliminary results
Basic models
We start this subsection by reintroducing a reported well-being function that has already been used by many with regard to US and European data, that is:

$$r = h[u(y, \bar{y}, z)] + \varepsilon, \tag{21.1}$$

where r is the self-reported well-being of an individual, $h(.)$ is a non-differentiable function that relates actual to reported well-being, $u(.)$ is the true well-being only observable to that individual, y is real income, $\bar{y}$ is a comparison income level against which the individual compares him- or herself (such a comparison could be made against the individual's cohorts' earning levels or past income), z is a set of demographic personal characteristics, and ε is an error term that subsumes the inability of human beings to communicate accurately their well-being levels. The reported well-being is assumed to be increasing with income, y, and reducing with comparison income level, $\bar{y}$. Using this simple happiness model as our benchmark, we can begin our empirical modelling on the reported perceived quality of life in South Africa.

Table 21.1   Distribution of PQOL responses

a.   *Distribution of PQOL responses in South Africa, 1993*

Whole sample	Observations	Percentage	Cumulation (%)
Very dissatisfied	1817	24.23	24.23
Dissatisfied	2431	32.42	56.65
Neither	707	9.43	66.08
Satisfied	1981	26.42	92.49
Very satisfied	563	7.51	100.00
Total	7499	100	100

b.   *Distribution of happiness responses in the United States, 1972–1994*

Happiness in USA	Percentage
Not too happy	11.55
Pretty happy	55.79
Very happy	32.66
Total	100

c.   *Distribution of life satisfaction responses in Europe, 1975–1992*

Life satisfaction in Europe	Percentage
Not at all satisfied	4.80
Not very satisfied	14.19
Fairly satisfied	53.72
Very satisfied	27.29
Total	100

Note: The PQOL question was 'Taking everything into account, how satisfied is this household with the way it lives today?'. There were five possible answers, with the lowest well-being response being 'very dissatisfied' and the highest being 'very satisfied'. Note also that the people from the US and European nations were more likely to give higher well-being responses (that is, a positive skew towards 'very happy' and 'very satisfied') than the South African population (that is, a negative skew of perception towards 'very dissatisfied' rather than 'very satisfied').

Source: The reported happiness levels in the USA and life satisfaction in Europe are taken from Di Tella et al. (2001).

Nevertheless, as the PQOL question was directed at how the respondent perceives the quality of life as it appears from the household's point of view, we first single out the individual characteristics (such as age and gender – normal variables in a general happiness equation) of the interviewees from the happiness regression equation and evaluate only the relationships between household-level characteristics and the reported well-being. Hence, we run an ordered probit regression with sampling weight on the PQOL data of the form:

$$H_{ihc} = \beta \sum_{j=1}^{J} a_{jh} + \gamma Y_h + \theta \bar{Y}_h + \lambda HH_h + \delta COM_c + \mu_{hc}, \quad (21.2)$$

where H_{ihc} is the reported well-being by individual i for household h in a community c, while a_{jh} represents a vector of durable goods from a set of durables J owned by household h. Y_h represents natural log of total household monthly income,[10] while $\bar{Y}_h$ includes two types of comparison income level: (i) comparison income level according to the people living in the same community, and (ii) comparison income level according to our past. For simplicity we shall call the first type 'external comparison income', and the second type 'internal comparison income'. External comparison income is calculated through dividing total household monthly income by the averaged household monthly income of other people within the same cluster area, and is allowed to vary between households.

Internal comparison income, on the other hand, comes from a dummy variable containing information on whether individuals *think* that their household financial situation today is better, the same, or worse off compared with that of their parents at the same point in the life cycle.[11] This parental wealth comparison variable would act as proxy for the individual's subjective assessment of the current household's status in comparison with its past experience, regardless of today's actual earning level. For example, an individual who grows up with wealthy parents will be likely to have a higher consumption standard than an individual who grew up in poverty (see McBride 2001).

HH_h includes a vector of other controlled household characteristics that include household race and location – rural or urban – while COM_c contains a vector of community controls that include the types of road, whether public transport is available within the area, and a cluster food–price index. Lastly, as it is a clustered sample – with clusters being mainly small communities or villages – households living in the same cluster are more likely to share not only the same infrastructure such as motorable roads but also the same climate, food prices, crime rate, or even the same local eccentric traits (Deaton 1997). As a result, homogeneity in a group dataset may lead to estimations with standard errors that are small. To correct for the underestimated standard errors then, cluster controls have been included in our estimations to capture any grouping effects present within the dataset. See Moulton (1990) for further discussion on potential pitfalls from estimating aggregate variables on micro units when standard errors are not corrected for.

The regression results at the household level shown in Table 21.2 provide some confidence in the structure of the responses in the subjective well-being question. We can see the interactions between household race and reported quality of life quite clearly: individuals living in an African household are more likely to report, on average, a relatively lower subjective well-being score than individuals living in either a coloured (non-white of mixed race), an Indian, or a white household, even after income and durable assets ownership are controlled for. Individuals from white households, on the other hand, have reported the highest level of PQOL score in general. The result is consistent with earlier findings on race and happiness in US and UK data (Oswald 1997; Di Telia et al. 2001). This is also in keeping with other results from Latin America where those individuals who self-reported their nationality (Peruvian or Chilean, for example) first rather than as a racial minority are happier than others (Graham and Pettinato 2001). One explanation for the depressed PQOL could therefore be the mind set shaped by years of discrimination during the apartheid years, despite the fact that the majority of the population are black. A supporting economic finding on the racial discrimination conjecture is provided, but only partially, in Schreiner et al.'s (1997) work on racial discrimination in hire/purchase lending in South Africa. Using a partial-observability model, he finds that black households are 13 percentage points more likely to demand a hire/purchase loan but not to have one supplied than are other households. Hence, the obtained result from the PQOL survey corresponds with other studies that suggest possible racial discrimination towards black households living in South Africa.

Controlling for income and durable ownership, household size is negatively associated with reported well-being. A plausible explanation for the negative correlation could be that, once we normalize for total income, an increase in the size of household will lead to a reduction in the income capita per household, and hence reduces the quality of life for everybody in the household. Running the same regression equation on per capita variables helps to support such a claim as the coefficient for household size has now been reduced to an insignificant value. Also, living in urban areas is negatively associated with the reported well-being. This could be explained partly by the stress-related and overcrowding problems normally found from urban living. Urban areas in many developing countries are also vulnerable to large inflows of migration from the rural population looking for a better life in the city, but often these people find themselves living in poor conditions with no access to either a job or healthcare in the city. In addition, the low PQOL scores recorded among the urban dwellers

Table 21.2   Life satisfaction equations with household variables for South Africa (ordered probit), 1993

	(1)	(2)	Per capita variables
Race of household			
Coloured	0.359 (2.74)***	0.355 (2.64)***	0.465 (3.50)***
Indian	0.428 (3.24)***	0.377 (3.02)***	0.560 (4.53)***
White	0.639 (4.76)***	0.648 (4.91)***	0.764 (5.76)***
Durable goods			
Motor vehicle	0.080 (2.73)***	0.084 (2.84)***	0.203 (2.24)**
Bicycle	0.024 (1.26)	0.020 (1.03)	0.133 (1.55)
Electric stove	−0.033 (−0.58)	−0.046 (−0.81)	−0.216 (−1.75)*
Electric kettle	0.027 (0.46)	0.005 (0.09)	−0.125 (−0.83)
Fridge	0.001 (0.03)	0.009 (0.28)	−0.055 (−0.56)
Gas cooker	0.010 (0.27)	0.002 (0.04)	−0.114 (−0.81)
Geyser	0.206 (3.32)***	0.189 (3.03)***	0.297 (1.86)*
Primus cooker	−0.008 (−0.27)	−0.012 (−0.45)	0.018 (0.17)
Radio	0.023 (1.33)	0.017 (0.99)	−0.030 (−0.61)
Telephone	0.153 (3.38)***	0.165 (3.74)***	0.302 (2.94)***
TV	0.045 (1.41)	0.026 (0.77)	0.231 (2.38)**
Rural/urban			
Urban (=1)	−0.195 (−2.60)***	−0.171 (−2.31)**	−0.154 (−2.01)**
HHSize (members)	−0.041 (−3.54)***	−0.035 (−3.23)***	0.006 (0.67)
Log of household monthly income	0.132 (6.54)***	0.114 (4.88)***	0.156 (4.84)***
Parental wealth comparisons			
PWealth: same as parents		0.498 (9.34)***	0.493 (9.41)***
PWealth: richer than parents		0.476 (10.68)***	0.486 (10.92)***
Relative income		−0.013 (−1.07)	−0.015 (−1.11)
N	7,499	7,499	7,499
Log likelihood	−10,082.028	−9,912.1554	−9,910.8806
Pseudo *R*²	0.0935	0.1088	0.1089

Note: * 10% CI (confidence interval), ** 5% CI , *** 1% CI (z-values in parentheses). Relative income = household monthly income/averaged community household monthly income. Cluster controls are types of community roads, public transports (yes/no), provinces (9), and cluster food prices. Reference variables are: Black (Race), Rural (Rural/urban), and PWealth – poorer than parents (parental wealth comparisons). Per capita variables replace underlined variables in (1) & (2) for log of household monthly income per capita, durable goods per capita and relative income per capita = household monthly income per capita/average community household monthly income per capita.

could to an extent have been the cause of some hidden political unrest in urban South Africa in the early 1990s, and which had not been captured in our model.

Consumer durables and quality of life   We test for the relationships between the different types of durable good consumption and the reported well-being for an average household in our first regression, in order to see which of the consumer durables, if any, is associated with higher PQOL responses. The data on durable goods come from the survey question that asks households how many of the listed durables are owned by someone in the household. These include the following items: (i) motor vehicle, (ii) bicycle, (iii) electric stove, (iv) electric kettle, (v) fridge, (vi) gas stove, (vii) geyser,[12] (viii) primus cooker, (ix) radio, (x) telephone and (xi) television. The average correlation is about 60 per cent between the quantity of each durable good, while none of the goods is correlated by more than 77.9 per cent (electric stove and kettle). The correlation is even lower between the quantity of each durable good and log household income (the maximum correlation being about 59 per cent) across the cross-sectional data.[13] As a result, we can base our analysis on the assumption that there are no two goods in the sample that are perfectly correlated with each other and with household income, which makes a further interpretation of the results plausible. We do not, however, have any relevant information on the quality and condition of the reported household durables. In other words, we do not know whether they are old or do not work, for example.

We find only some, but not all, of the household durables to be significantly associated with higher PQOL levels. Reported quality of life seems to improve with the number of motor vehicles, geysers and telephones owned by the household – including the ownership of televisions if per capita ownership is to be analysed instead. On the other hand, consumer durables such as electric kettles, gas cookers, primus cookers, bicycles, electric stoves, radios and refrigerators do not seem to register significantly in most people's evaluation of their life at all. The significance of the correlations seems plausible enough once each durable's ability to function are taken into account. For example, owning a motor vehicle or having a telephone in the household – both of which are rated widely as having a very high ability to function in themselves – is more likely to result in householders reporting a higher PQOL level than if they owned other durables with considerably less intrinsic use such as an electric kettle or a radio, *ceteris paribus*. None the less, despite the fact that durables such as motor vehicles and TVs are positively correlated with the reported quality of life of an average household, the positive findings on assets that are a necessity to everyday life, such as gas cookers or refrigerators, are not at all robust.

Although we do not have a conclusive answer to this issue, intuition tells us that durables such as gas and primus cookers are not the type of goods that are difficult to find substitutes for and as a result individuals may take their availability for granted. However, there is also the possibility that if they do not own these durables, their living standard, *vis-à-vis*, reported well-being would probably fall.

Comparison income   We also find strong evidence of people reporting high PQOL scores when they believe that the household is doing just as well financially – if not better – compared to its past, even after controlling for current income. The result is in keeping with the previous work on the effects of perceptions of past progress: the perception of one's present situation in a positive light compared to the past has positive and significant effects on subjective well-being (see McBride 2001 and Graham and Pettinato 2002). However, unlike the results obtained from the US and European data see Table 21.1, the coefficient of objective external comparison income is insignificant and has the wrong sign. In other words, we did not find objective external comparison income level to be significantly correlated with higher levels of reported well-being in South Africa under our first run of happiness regression equations.

> *Conclusion 1*   Reported perceived quality of life at the household level in South Africa is high among whites, households with a small number of family members, those living in rural areas, and among households with some durables ownership. A positive perception of past progress is also associated with higher levels of reported quality of life.

Personal attributes
In order to test for the influence of individual characteristics on the reported quality of life, the original model has been extended to the following form:

$$H_{ihc} = \beta \sum_{j=1}^{J} a_{jh} + \gamma Y_h + \theta \bar{Y}_h + \lambda HH_h$$

$$+ \delta COM_c + \Pi IND_{i/h}^{p=0,1} + \xi OHH_h + \mu_{ihc}. \quad (21.3)$$

The new variable, *IND*, represents a vector of personal characteristics such as gender, age, employment status, health status and education level. The subscripts *i* and *h* refer to the fact that personal variables can be run in the happiness regressions using the characteristics of the PQOL respondent alone or that of aggregated individual variables across all household members (for example, proportion of household members with higher education or in regular wage employment and so on), respectively.[14] The superscript p corresponds to the choices between the two alternatives ($p = 0$: personal characteristics of the PQOL respondent, $p = 1$: aggregated individuals variables).

OHH_h is a vector of individual characteristics of household members, *other than* the PQOL respondent from each household. It takes a similar form as the aggregated individual variables, IND_h, except that OHH_h includes only the aggregated personal characteristics taken from the people within the same household of the respondent but who did not answer the PQOL question. Let us assume for now that OHH_h can only be calculated from households with more than one member (or recorded as having household size greater than one). We also include a personal control, the relationship to the head of household, to differentiate between the roles held by the respondent within the household in our empirical model.[15]

We begin our analysis in Column 1 of Table 21.3 with a regression that includes only the personal characteristics of the PQOL respondent, $IND_{i|p=0}$ (leaving out for now the aggregated individual variables of other household members, OHH_h). The reported well-being is found to be significantly correlated with some of the already identified personal variables at the individual-level data, such as age and employment status of the respondent, even when the PQOL question is asked at the household rather than at the individual level. The results on employment status are consistent with the literature on employment and subjective well-being: employed individuals with a regular wage have reported a higher subjective well-being than the unemployed in general (Warr et al. 1988; Clark and Oswald 1994; Theodossiou 1998; Kingdon and Knight 2001). Individuals who look after the home or are in formal education still fared better than the unemployed, while the correlations are not as strong for the self-employed and the retired. There is also a non-linear relationship between age and happiness. Like individuals across the developed world, happiness in South Africa is U-shaped in age with a minimum around the middle of life (early to mid-40s).

The results on education do not appear to support the claim that well-educated individuals are happier than the less-educated ones, however. When controlling for wealth (durable assets ownership and income – both absolute and relative – included), a happiness regression equation with the respondent's personal characteristics for South Africa does not yield a positive correlation between education level and the reported well-being scores. Instead, the relationship between higher education and happiness is negative and significant for the responding individuals. One plausible

Table 21.3   *Life satisfaction equations with personal variables at individual and average household level for South Africa*

	Individual level	Household level
Gender		
Male (=1)	0.000 (0.01)	0.085 (0.67)
Race of household		
Coloured	0.347 (2.57)***	0.372 (2.76)***
Indian	0.384 (3.14)***	0.387 (3.23)***
White	0.644 (5.13)***	0.602 (4.69)***
Education level		
Std 1–3	0.040 (0.80)	0.122 (1.54)
Std 4–6	−0.112 (−2.09)**	−0.116 (−1.17)
Std 7–8	−0.087 (−1.58)	−0.002 (−0.02)
Std 9–10	−0.124 (−2.20)**	0.070 (0.79)
Std 10 or Higher	−0.009 (−0.13)	0.282 (2.63)***
Employment status		
Housewife/formal education	0.159 (3.93)***	0.282 (4.56)***
Regular wage employment	0.220 (3.54)***	0.387 (3.33)***
Casual wage employment	−0.091 (−1.13)	−0.021 (−0.19)
Self-employed	0.029 (0.45)	0.313 (3.44)***
Retired	0.117 (1.73)*	0.318 (3.78)***
Durable goods		
Motor vehicle	0.087 (2.91)***	0.076 (2.57)***
Bicycle	0.016 (0.82)	0.024 (1.14)
Electric stove	−0.040 (−0.71)	−0.042 (−0.77)
Electric kettle	0.002 (0.03)	−0.004 (−0.08)
Fridge	0.026 (0.89)	0.015 (0.51)
Gas cooker	0.017 (0.44)	0.002 (0.06)
Geyser	0.192 (3.12)***	0.188 (3.08)***
Primus cooker	0.002 (0.09)	−0.005 (−0.19)
Radio	0.016 (0.97)	0.018 (1.04)
Telephone	0.175 (3.78)***	0.158 (3.48)***
TV	0.037 (1.14)	0.035 (1.08)
Rural/urban		
Urban (=1)	−0.137 (−1.85)*	−0.139 (−1.89)*
HHSize (members)	−0.028 (−3.74)***	−0.024 (−3.34)***
Log of household monthly income	0.091 (4.30)***	0.065 (2.80)***
Parental wealth comparisons		
PWealth: same as parents	0.481 (9.36)***	0.480 (9.40)***
PWealth: richer than parents	0.469 (10.52)***	0.465 (10.71)***
Relative income	−0.009 (−0.82)	−0.008 (−0.64)
Age	−0.025 (−3.52)***	−0.011 (−2.19)**

Table 21.3   (continued)

	Individual level	Household level
Age^2/100	0.025 (3.39)***	0.016 (2.55)**
Sick during the last 2 weeks?		
Yes (=1)	−0.013 (−0.21)	0.004 (0.03)
N	7,499	7,499
Log likelihood	−9,866.9079	−9,854.8809
Pseudo R^2	0.1129	0.1140

Note: Relative income = household monthly income/average community household monthly income. Personal control is the relationship of the PQOL respondent to head of the household (48% of whom responded were resident heads, 33% were wives or husbands or partners, 13% were sons or daughters, and the rest were other family members). Cluster controls are the same as in Table 21.2. Additional reference variables are: Female (Gender), No Education (Education level), Unemployment (Employment status), No (Sick during the last 2 weeks?). Personal controls at the individual level represent personal variables for the PQOL respondents only, while personal controls at the household level represent average personal variables across all household members, including the PQOL respondent from each household (for example the age variable at the individual level now takes the form of an average age across all household members, or from no formal education to the proportion of household members with no formal education in the regression at the household level, and so on).

explanation for this is that the return to higher education in developing countries may be measured purely in terms of higher wealth. The correlation between education and income is probably higher in less-developed countries, whereas in more advanced economies more-educated people probably have the luxury or more security of working in lower-paying but more satisfying jobs, as in NGOs or universities, for example (Graham and Pettinato 2001). The theory of high aspiration levels found among people who are highly educated can also help to explain the negative relationship between education and happiness when wealth is being controlled for in the regression. The coefficient on the proxy for health status (whether the respondent has been sick during the previous two weeks), though it has the right sign, is insignificant.[16] In addition, there is no evidence of a significant relationship between gender and the reported PQOL scores at the individual level.

So far we have presented the results with the assumption that only the respondent's personal characteristics matter in the determination of the reported PQOL. Column 2 (Table 21.3) alters the assumption a little to allow for the idea that the PQOL data may correlate more with the personal characteristics taken from all household members, rather than from the respondent's attributes alone. The previous individual variables now take aggregate forms, $IND_{h/p=1}$, in our new regression.

With the aggregated personal variables data, we can see the proportion of household members in regular wage employment, and of those looking after the home and in formal education, are positively associated with higher reported PQOL in general. However, increasing proportions of household members in the self-employed and the retired categories – with the proportion of unemployed individuals in the household being the reference point – now correlate significantly with higher reported PQOL scores. This makes sense as, holding everything else constant, a 50 per cent self-employed and 50 per cent unemployed household would still be more preferable to an individual than a 0 per cent self-employed and 100 per cent unemployed household, given the fact that unemployment is the single most detrimental factor to lower well-being.

An increase in the proportion of household members with a Standard 10 education level or higher is associated positively with PQOL scores, where the coefficient for the same education level for PQOL respondents was previously negative and insignificant. The result on the aggregated education level variable is of some interest, and will be analysed in more detail below.

Average age and age-square are significant at the household level – the average age across all household members has a non-linear relationship with the reported well-being for South Africa – while a regression on the proportion of male members and of individuals having been sick in the last two weeks both yield positive and insignificant coefficients. The already identified household variables, such as household income and durable assets ownership, retain their significance in our happiness regression at the household level.

In Table 21.4 we integrate the assumptions on the effects of two different individual characteristics levels and run a regression with the respondent's personal characteristics, $IND_{i|p=0}$, and the aggregated individual variables of other members in the same household, OHH_h, in the model. We use only the households that have recorded more than one household member (HHSize > 1) in Column 1, so as to minimize the covariance between IND_i and OHH_h variables.

The first set of results are consistent with what have been found in both columns of Table 21.3. Both the respondent's personal characteristics and the aggregated individual variables of other household members are significant determinants of the reported PQOL, and not one or the other. For example, being regularly employed still associates positively with the reported well-being. There is a drop in the coefficient magnitude for employment with regular wage, from 0.202 to 0.164, which would only suggest that some of the positive effects picked up earlier come from the omission of other household members' personal characteristics. Increasing in the proportion of other people employed with a regular wage is also

Table 21.4   Life satisfaction equation with personal variables at the individual-level and controls for average household-level data for other members in the household

	(1)	(2)
Gender		
Male (=1)	−0.016 (−0.37)	−0.020 (−0.41)
Proportion of other male members in the HH	0.111 (1.84)*	0.064 (0.78)
Race of household		
Coloured	0.375 (2.71)***	0.374 (2.78)***
Indian	0.343 (2.80)***	0.398 (3.28)***
White	0.665 (5.27)***	0.619 (4.97)***
Education level		
Std 1–3	0.022 (0.37)	0.018 (0.35)
Std 4–6	−0.084 (−1.49)	−0.115 (−2.27)**
Std 7–8	−0.116 (−1.76)*	−0.112 (−1.98)**
Std 9–10	−0.147 (−2.18)**	−0.112 (−2.89)***
Std 10 & Higher	−0.046 (−0.56)	−0.058 (−0.80)
Prop. of other HH members with Std 1–3	0.091 (1.07)	0.102 (1.55)
Prop. of other HH members with Std 4–6	0.013 (0.14)	−0.009 (−0.11)
Prop. of other HH members with Std 7–8	−0.054 (−0.58)	0.081 (0.98)
Prop. of other HH members with Std 9–10	0.111 (1.16)	0.179 (2.30)**
Prop. of other HH members with Std 10 & Higher	0.141 (1.15)	0.210 (2.24)**
Employment status		
Housewife/formal education	0.137 (3.18)***	0.131 (3.27)***
Regular wage employment	0.164 (3.11)***	0.202 (3.61)***
Casual wage employment	−0.136 (−1.29)	−0.066 (−0.81)
Self-employed	−0.078 (−0.94)	−0.047 (−0.66)
Retired	0.098 (1.15)	0.090 (1.22)
Prop. of other housewife/ formal education in HH	0.157 (2.76)***	0.169 (3.44)***
Prop. of other regular wage employment in HH	0.075 (1.19)	0.147 (2.03)**
Prop. of other casual wage employment in HH	−0.086 (−0.76)	0.010 (0.12)
Prop. of other self-employed in HH	0.369 (3.29)***	0.319 (3.51)***

Table 21.4   (continued)

	(1)	(2)
Prop. of other retired members in HH	0.166 (1.95)**	0.174 (2.41)**
Durable goods		
Motor vehicle	0.062 (1.86)*	0.081 (2.76)***
Bicycle	0.027 (1.40)	0.032 (1.56)
Electric stove	0.037 (0.62)	−0.042 (−0.75)
Electric kettle	−0.033 (−0.59)	−0.001 (−0.02)
Fridge	0.033 (1.09)	0.026 (0.90)
Gas cooker	0.050 (1.33)	0.011 (0.30)
Geyser	0.209 (3.56)***	0.193 (3.17)***
Primus cooker	0.004 (0.16)	0.001 (0.04)
Radio	0.023 (1.20)	0.014 (0.85)
Telephone	0.137 (2.86)***	0.172 (3.71)***
TV	0.034 (1.01)	0.040 (1.27)
Rural/urban		
Urban (=1)	−0.196 (−2.60)***	−0.131 (−1.76)*
HHSize (members)	−0.016 (−2.20)**	−0.013 (−2.01)**
Log of household monthly income	0.108 (4.15)***	0.073 (3.23)***
Parental wealth comparisons		
PWealth: same as parents	0.390 (9.17)***	0.476 (9.42)***
PWealth: richer than parents	0.469 (10.69)***	0.462 (10.65)***
Relative income	−0.004 (−0.36)	−0.007 (−0.58)
Age	−0.012 (−1.55)	−0.027 (−3.59)***
Age^2/100	0.011 (1.27)	0.025 (3.23)***
Average age of other HH members	−0.007 (−1.24)	−0.000 (−0.08)
Average age^2/100 of other HH members	0.013 (1.91)*	0.006 (0.98)
Sick for the last 2 weeks?		
Respondent: Yes (=1)	−0.088 (−0.99)	−0.026 (−0.34)
Other members in the HH: Yes (=1)	−0.175 (−1.37)	0.016 (0.18)
N	5,209	7,499
Log likelihood	−6,703.016	−9,835.0735
Pseudo R^2	0.1307	0.1157

Note: Personal and cluster controls as in Table 21.2. Household-level average data for 'other' household members consist of averaged personal variables taken from all household members, excluding the PQOL respondent from each household. Column (1) consists only of HHSize > 1 sample, while Column (2) includes also the household-level average data taken from PQOL respondents from households with HHSize = 1.

positively correlated with the reported PQOL, controlling for the respondent's employment status.

Having more of other male members in the household is also good for the quality of life, even though being a male respondent has a negative – though insignificant – sign on the reported happiness. Respondents' education levels (namely, Standards 9–10) retain their significance with negative values, even after controlling for the education levels of other household members which remain positive (though are now slightly insignificant) at the highest education level.

In Column 2 we add in the remaining households with only one household member (HHSize = 1) into the regression, and this accounts for about 15 per cent of the full sample (1,127 observations). For these households, the PQOL question acts more like a normal happiness question asked at the individual level. To apply these observations to our model we assume, for example, an employed PQOL respondent living in a one-member household to automatically have a 100 per cent 'employment with regular wage' in the OHH_h variable set.

The results are remarkably similar to those obtained in Column 1, where almost all of the identified variables in Column 2 still retain their significance and signs. Personal variables such as age and age-squared are now significantly correlated with the reported well-being, while average age and average age-squared have remained largely insignificant. The reported PQOL is found to be high among households with a high proportion of other self-employed members, looking after the home and in formal education, and the retired members, *ceteris paribus*. A paradox emerges, however, between the respondent's and the aggregated education variables when we incorporate the remaining 1,127 households. The coefficients of the aggregated education variables at the higher levels are positive and statistically significant, while the respondent's education at the higher levels (namely at Standards 7–10) is still associated negatively with the reported well-being. This is an interesting result which suggests that own education, and not the aggregated household education level, is the only source for high aspirations which is used to reduce subjective well-being in South Africa. We nevertheless need to make the same analysis using the individual's earnings data rather than those at the household income level, and possibly on a panel dataset to see whether well-educated individuals who are unhappy will remain in the same job through time, in order to make the finding on education conclusive.

Conclusion 2   Both the respondent's personal attributes and aggregated individual variables across household members matter in the assessment of well-being. Unemployment at the individual and household levels is detrimental to the reported happiness levels. Own education levels are negatively associated with well-being, but the aggregated education variable has an opposite effect. Happiness is also U-shaped with regard to age.

Compensation variation and selected marginal effects   In Tables 21.5 and 21.6 we use the estimated coefficients from Column 2 in Table 21.4 to

Table 21.5   Valuations in household monthly income of life events

Income = R100 per month	Compensation income per month
Unemployment to reg. wage emp.	R1,491.28
Poorer to richer than parents	R55,946.52
Black to white	R481,381.09

Income = R2,064 (Avg. HH income)	Compensation income per month
Unemployment to reg. wage emp.	R30,780.00
Poorer to richer than parents	R1,154,736.14
Black to white	R9,935,705.74

Note: £1 = R4.89 on average in 1993.

Source: Quinn Consultant FX rate: www.quinns. com.au/accountant/tax_table/foreign.

Table 21.6   Selected marginal effects

	Dissatisfied	Neither	Satisfied
Increase motor vehicle by 1	−2.52%	+0.59%	+1.93%
Increase motor vehicle by 2	−5.18%	+1.15%	+4.02%
Increase motor vehicle by 3	−7.96%	+1.69%	+6.27%
Increase telephone by 1	−5.49%	+1.22%	+4.27%
Increase telephone by 2	−11.54%	+2.31%	+9.24%
Increase telephone by 3	−18.04%	+3.19%	+14.86%
Increase household size by 1	+0.40%	−0.10%	−0.30%
Increase household size by 2	+0.78%	−0.19%	−0.59%
Increase household size by 3	+1.17%	−0.29%	−0.88%
Increase income by Y*exp^1 (= +R1,658.61)	−2.25%	+0.53%	+1.72%
Increase income by Y*exp^2 (= +R6,167.18)	−4.61%	+1.04%	+3.57%
Increase income by Y*exp^3 (= +R18,422.74)	−7.08%	+1.53%	+5.55%

Note: The marginal effects are calculated at the sample means of all variables estimated in Table 21.4. The figures represent shifts in the probability between people reporting to be in (i) dissatisfied (1, 2), (ii) neither (3), (iii) satisfied (4, 5) category as a result of changes in values of the selected variables. The (absolute) average motor vehicle ownership in the sample = 0, average telephone ownership = 0, average household size = 4, average log of income = 6.87241 (or about R965.27).

calculate the 'compensation variations' for different life states and the 'marginal effects' of some selected variables, respectively. The first calculates how much extra household income per month is required to compensate for a bad occurrence in life, for instance, how much extra income will be needed to compensate an unemployed respondent so that he/she obtains the same level of reported well-being as people who are employed. Let us say, for example, that λ_1 represents a coefficient for the employed respondent with regular wages and λ_0 be the reference coefficient of being unemployed, our generalized compensation equation (*CP*) with log of income will depend upon Y and can be expressed in the following form:

$$CP = Y \cdot \left\{ \exp \frac{\lambda_1 - \lambda_0}{\gamma \ln Y} - 1 \right\}. \tag{21.4}$$

This is equivalent to saying that an unemployed individual will require a compensation income of *CP* to achieve the same level of well-being as an employed individual with the same monthly income, *Y*. Thus, *CP* represents the measurement of unpleasantness in unemployment.

Results in Table 21.5 tell us that a household monthly income of about R1,491 (or about £305) per month is required in order to compensate for being unemployed, for an average individual with a monthly income of R100. The compensation premium rises to about R30,780 or £6,295 per month for people earning at the average household income level of R2,064. The value goes up much higher for other life events: from no education to completing a university degree, from perceiving that you are richer than your parents, and from being black to being white. Some figures seem implausible: for instance, it requires a large sum of money to compensate an average individual earning R100 per month for being black (approximately R481,381.09 or a 4,813 per cent increase from the original income level), in terms of PQOL level. This supports our earlier hypothesis on the possible 'scaring effects' that racial discrimination during the apartheid years have had on the black population.

Table 21.6 follows the same method used by Lydon and Chevalier (2001) in calculating marginal effects from the sample means of all the other estimated variables. Starting from the sample average, we calculate by how much a unit would increase in a selected variable for everybody, change the percentage of people reporting to be in a (i) dissatisfied (1, 2), (ii) neither (3), or (iii) satisfied (4, 5) category. With an average of zero motor vehicles owned by the household, a unit increase in motor vehicles owned is associated with an increase of 1.93 per cent of the population in the satisfied category. The effect is non-monotonic as an increase in the motor vehicles owned by threefold is associated with a rise in the proportion satisfied of 6.27 per cent. The marginal effects are greater for unit increases in telephones, and smaller – with an opposite direction – for the household size. The increase in household income is based on the average log of income of 6.87 (or about R965.27). A proportionate increase in household income (by 1 point in the natural log, or an increase in income of R1,658.61 per month) is associated with 1.72 per cent, while a 1,800 per cent increase (a 3-point rise in the natural log scale) leads to a rise in the proportion of 5.55 per cent. The results from Tables 21.5 and 21.6 thus suggest that the relationship between income and well-being may be very weak when compared to other factors such as employment status and racial differences.

With the happiness equation used in Table 21.4 firmly established, we can now move on to subsample analysis. We begin in Table 21.7a by separating the data to be examined by race (black/non-black), location (rural/urban), gender (male/female), and age group (under/over 30 years old). This yields some interesting patterns in the reported PQOL responses. Looking at the black sample, the highest level of education of the respondent (Standard 10 or higher) is now significantly associated with lower well-being. This is particularly interesting as it suggests that black workers may be earning less relative to those with lower education (less than Standard 10), but were probably employed more favourably because of the possible racial discrimination. The correlations between employment status and some of the already identified durable assets ownership disappear for the non-black sample. The significance of the coefficient for health status (negative sign) has improved, however, for the non-black population.

The non-linear relationship between age and happiness disappears when the regression is run on the rural sample, while remaining well-defined for the urban South African. Generally, urban male respondents are reported to be less satisfied with life than females. Self-employment and employment with regular wage with reference to being unemployed have insignificant relationships with the recorded well-being in the rural area, although this could be because employment is defined differently in the two geographical settings. The idea of unemployment in the rural area is probably not as clearly defined as in the urban areas. Unemployed individuals may have things to do in the rural setting, even if they are not working on a farm. It is perhaps not surprising for an average employed person not to feel more relatively secure or socially superior than those who are unemployed in the rural areas, once income is controlled for in the regression.

The happiness structures are very similar between male and female subsamples. Being employed with regular wage is positively associated with well-being for both genders, with the coefficient being larger for males at 0.210 (2.60) than females at 0.154 (2.55). Looking after the home or studying in a

Table 21.7a *Life satisfaction equations with controls for other members in the household for different groups of people in South Africa*

	Black	Non-black	Rural	Urban	Male	Female	Age<30	Age≥30
Gender								
Male (=1)	-0.035	-0.010	0.086	-0.112			-0.125	0.030
	(-0.61)	(-0.13)	(1.27)	(-1.95)*			(-1.86)*	(0.53)
Race of household								
Coloured		-0.133	-0.010	0.347	0.511	0.267	0.531	0.309
		(-0.85)	(-0.04)	(2.40)**	(3.07)***	(1.77)*	(2.80)***	(2.05)**
Indian		-0.041	0.903	0.307	0.617	0.245	0.360	0.366
		(-0.30)	(1.17)	(2.37)**	(3.58)***	(1.78)*	(2.18)**	(2.68)***
White		(Reference)	0.423	0.512	0.728	0.539	0.755	0.518
			(1.24)	(3.61)***	(4.99)***	(3.44)***	(3.81)***	(3.90)***
Education level								
Std 1-3	0.011	-0.145	-0.019	0.058	0.058	-0.001	0.191	-0.000
	(0.21)	(-0.91)	(-0.31)	(0.65)	(0.63)	(-0.02)	(1.54)	(-0.01)
Std 4-6	-0.132	-0.145	-0.058	-0.191	-0.156	-0.086	-0.000	-0.119
	(-2.34)**	(-1.24)	(-0.95)	(-2.32)*	(-1.65)*	(-1.58)	(-0.00)	(-2.09)**
Std 7-8	-0.107	-0.156	0.033	-0.211	-0.145	-0.106	0.069	-0.152
	(-1.56)	(-1.41)	(0.40)	(-2.47)**	(-1.46)	(-1.65)*	(0.57)	(-2.31)**
Std 9-10	-0.146	-0.238	-0.196	-0.192	-0.242	-0.128	0.032	-0.216
	(-1.95)**	(-2.31)**	(-2.11)**	(-2.18)**	(-2.41)**	(-1.86)*	(0.28)	(-2.97)***
Std 10 or Higher	-0.395	-0.002	-0.238	-0.055	0.001	-0.124	0.052	-0.072
	(-3.33)***	(-0.22)	(-1.62)	(-0.59)	(-0.01)	(-1.32)	(0.37)	(-0.89)
Employment status								
Housewife/formal education	0.143	0.019	0.122	0.413	0.041	0.132	0.043	0.185
	(3.27)***	(0.50)	(2.57)***	(3.55)***	(0.32)	(2.88)***	(0.65)	(3.30)***
Regular wage employment	0.502	0.052	0.137	0.309	0.1370	0.154	0.194	0.220
	(3.70)***	(0.43)	(1.29)	(3.07)***	(2.60)***	(2.55)**	(1.76)*	(3.84)***

Casual wage employment	−0.105 (−1.08)	0.045 (0.25)	−0.151 (−1.18)	0.151 (1.12)	−0.122 (−0.89)	0.026 (0.26)	0.031 (0.17)	−0.056 (−1.58)
Self-employment	0.049 (0.56)	−0.323 (−2.30)**	−0.190 (−1.76)*	0.333 (3.31)***	−0.109 (−0.86)	0.014 (0.15)	0.278 (1.71)*	−0.108 (−1.36)
Retired	0.027 (0.32)	0.222 (1.27)	0.114 (1.14)	0.345 (2.68)***	0.115 (0.83)	0.118 (1.32)		0.128 (1.65)*
Durable goods								
Motor vehicle	0.142 (3.28)***	0.026 (0.67)	0.013 (0.29)	0.106 (2.91)***	0.056 (1.22)	0.086 (2.12)**	0.030 (0.52)	0.100 (3.13)***
Bicycle	0.037 (0.94)	0.061 (2.49)**	−0.033 (−0.88)	0.057 (2.44)**	0.029 (0.88)	0.035 (1.22)	−0.012 (−0.27)	0.048 (2.20)**
Electric stove	−0.048 (−0.67)	0.054 (0.70)	−0.023 (−0.25)	−0.039 (−0.58)	−0.016 (−0.20)	−0.049 (−0.70)	−0.078 (−0.90)	−0.023 (−0.37)
Electric kettle	0.032 (0.37)	−0.007 (−0.10)	0.072 (0.52)	−0.014 (−0.22)	−0.057 (−0.69)	0.024 (−0.33)	0.008 (−0.09)	−0.008 (−0.13)
Fridge	0.011 (0.25)	0.016 (0.39)	0.045 (0.97)	0.035 (1.01)	−0.003 (−0.06)	0.032 (0.89)	−0.002 (−0.03)	0.033 (0.98)
Gas cooker	0.051 (0.93)	0.008 (0.15)	0.068 (1.24)	−0.006 (−0.12)	−0.025 (−0.40)	0.048 (0.99)	0.051 (0.63)	0.007 (0.18)
Geyser	0.198 (1.51)	0.204 (3.85)***	0.367 (2.49)**	0.153 (2.34)**	0.301 (3.64)***	0.104 (1.30)	0.443 (3.97)***	0.133 (2.05)**
Primus cooker	0.002 (0.08)	−0.008 (−0.08)	0.009 (0.29)	−0.036 (−0.78)	−0.047 (−1.08)	0.030 (1.01)	0.031 (0.65)	−0.005 (−0.19)
Radio	−0.015 (−0.57)	0.031 (1.33)	0.017 (0.51)	−0.006 (−0.31)	0.026 (0.95)	0.006 (0.25)	0.008 (0.22)	0.012 (0.66)
Telephone	0.059 (0.67)	0.204 (4.21)***	−0.127 (−0.90)	0.210 (4.67)***	0.225 (3.59)***	0.132 (2.52)**	0.213 (2.65)***	0.173 (3.39)***
TV	0.119 (2.48)**	−0.005 (−0.12)	0.055 (0.96)	0.041 (1.03)	−0.00 (−0.00)	0.089 (2.09)**	0.086 (1.44)	0.042 (1.21)
Rural/urban								
Urban	−0.058 (−0.72)	−0.165 (−1.19)			−0.023 (−0.23)	−0.222 (−2.73)***	−0.156 (−1.55)	−0.117 (−1.55)

Table 21.7a (continued)

	Black	Non-black	Rural	Urban	Male	Female	Age<30	Age≥30
HHSize	-0.013	-0.046	-0.007	-0.032	-0.020	-0.016	0.012	-0.023
	(-1.75)*	(-2.41)**	(-0.77)	(-3.22)***	(-1.37)	(-2.29)**	(0.78)	(-3.05)***
Log of household monthly income	0.049	0.213	0.065	0.084	0.107	0.077	-0.005	0.105
	(1.75)*	(3.87)***	(2.15)**	(2.65)***	(2.85)***	(3.04)***	(-0.14)	(4.06)***
Parental wealth comparisons								
PWealth: same as parents	0.536	0.374	0.495	0.455	0.441	0.460	0.504	0.465
	(8.54)***	(6.14)***	(7.05)***	(8.63)***	(6.24)***	(9.78)***	(7.14)***	(8.89)***
PWealth: richer than parents	0.460	0.413	0.415	0.483	0.412	0.490	0.480	0.465
	(7.97)***	(7.37)***	(6.17)***	(9.16)***	(6.10)***	(9.58)***	(7.42)***	(9.40)***
Relative income	0.01	-0.025	0.008	-0.009	-0.022	0.006	-0.020	-0.008
	(0.27)	(-2.74)***	(0.72)	(-0.39)	(-2.15)**	(0.31)	(-0.56)	(0.71)
Sick during the last 2 weeks? (Yes = 1)	0.042	-0.244	-0.002	-0.066	-0.035	-0.077	-0.099	-0.003
	(0.43)	(-1.73)*	(-0.02)	(-0.63)	(-0.29)	(-0.79)	(-0.56)	(-0.03)
Age	-0.016	-0.066	-0.013	-0.036	-0.035	-0.018	0.109	-0.006
	(-1.95)**	(-4.03)***	(-1.35)	(-3.31)***	(-2.72)***	(-2.28)**	(0.89)	(-0.61)
Age²/100	0.015	0.064	0.012	0.035	0.039	0.013	-0.304	0.005
	(1.75)*	(3.71)***	(1.18)	(2.92)***	(2.93)***	(1.51)	(-1.20)	(0.61)
N	5,479	2,020	3,575	3,924	2,674	4,825	2,056	5,443
Log likelihood	-7,178.3271	-2,500.9554	-4,763.7128	-4,931.3974	-3,424.7554	-6,277.0526	-2,663.8340	-7,104.4972
Pseudo R^2	0.0563	0.1023	0.0627	0.1616	0.1467	0.1125	0.1142	0.1238

Note: Cluster and personal controls as in Table 21.4. Controls for other household members include proportion of other males in the household, proportion of people in each of different classified education level and employment status, proportion of household members who have been sick during the last two weeks, average age and average age-squared/100. The results on the controls of other household members on different groups of people are shown separately in Table 21.7b.

472

formal education category has no significant bearing on the reported well-being for males, while the coefficient for the same employment status is both positive and well-defined in the female subsample. Female respondents are reported to be happier if they come from a rural area or if there are television sets in the household, *ceteris paribus*.

The last two columns of Table 21.7a look at the age of the respondents. Being young and male is apparently worse than being young and female, while household size and household income have an insignificant relationship with the happiness responses for the young age group. Higher education levels, however, have a positive correlation with the reported well-being for the young, although the coefficients are not well-defined.

Table 21.7b shows the average household-level data of other household members, OHH_h, for different groups of people. In contrast to the non-black sample, the correlations between the proportion of household members in higher education and the reported well-being – although having the correct sign – are insignificant for the black households. Nevertheless, the proportion of household members with regular wage employment in an average black family is associated positively with the PQOL scores. The other significant finding from the subsample analysis comes from the proportion of male members in the household. The number of males in a household enters positively in the well-being equation providing that you are from the rural area. This could be explained partly by the fact that an increase in the number of male members leads to greater household security and greater productivity for household consumption from working on the farms.

In summary, it can be seen how different groups of people have fared differently in terms of subjective well-being responses. Non-financial variables such as gender, education and employment status can have different influences on human welfare, depending on the social norms of the respondents. One other possible variable that could have some effect on individuals' well-being is marital status: married people claim to be happier than the singletons (Oswald 1997; Alesina et al. 2004; Clark and Oswald 2002). However, the survey did not include a question on marital status (that is, married, divorced, widowed). A survey with the additional dummy of whether the individual is living with a spouse, however, yields an insignificant coefficient, and since it did not change the nature of our results we have decided not to include the spouse variable in our specification.

Relative income and durable consumption
None of the tables reveals an external comparison income variable that could be entered significantly and positively into the well-being equation in any of the subsamples or the full sample. This is in contrast to the relative

Table 21.7b   Life satisfaction equations and household-level average data for different groups of people in South Africa

	Black	Non-black	Rural	Urban	Male	Female	Age<30	Age≥30
Gender								
Proportion of other males in the HH	0.107	−0.003	0.276	−0.036	0.140	0.024	0.126	0.023
	(1.06)	(−0.04)	(2.13)**	(−0.57)	(1.57)	(0.38)	(1.05)	(0.29)
Education level								
Prop. of Std 1–3	0.055	0.272	0.059	0.142	0.211	0.020	0.067	0.121
	(0.78)	(1.68)*	(0.68)	(1.54)	(2.16)**	(0.24)	(0.50)	(1.76)*
Prop. of Std 4–6	−0.073	0.151	−0.028	−0.010	0.020	−0.012	0.104	−0.039
	(−0.86)	(1.13)	(−0.25)	(−0.11)	(0.19)	(−0.13)	(0.63)	(−0.54)
Prop. of Std 7–8	0.080	0.228	0.058	0.089	0.156	0.013	0.287	0.018
	(0.80)	(1.78)*	(0.45)	(0.92)	(1.48)	(0.12)	(1.80)*	(0.20)
Prop. of Std 9–10	0.011	0.434	0.026	0.214	0.211	0.204	0.222	0.148
	(0.11)	(3.14)***	(0.21)	(2.06)**	(1.83)*	(1.95)**	(1.68)*	(1.63)*
Prop. of Std 10 or Higher	0.148	0.335	0.169	0.217	0.291	0.187	0.291	0.189
	(0.82)	(2.17)**	(0.67)	(1.91)*	(1.86)*	(1.49)	(1.56)	(1.69)*
Employment status								
Prop. of housewife/formal education	0.139	0.204	0.147	0.242	0.224	0.122	0.263	0.131
	(2.73)***	(1.36)	(2.31)**	(2.74)***	(2.32)**	(2.14)**	(2.43)**	(2.25)**
Prop. of regular wage employment	0.200	−0.041	0.278	0.060	0.156	0.094	0.352	0.065
	(2.35)**	(−0.33)	(2.37)**	(0.82)	(1.52)	(1.37)	(2.83)***	(0.92)
Prop. of casual wage employment	0.043	0.034	−0.053	0.079	−0.051	0.012	0.086	−0.025
	(0.46)	(0.17)	(−0.39)	(0.70)	(−0.36)	(0.11)	(0.50)	(−0.24)
Prop. of self-employment	0.332	0.142	0.414	0.247	0.264	0.300	0.253	0.335
	(3.26)***	(0.65)	(2.98)***	(2.04)**	(1.58)	(2.55)**	(1.55)	(3.29)***
Prop. of retired	0.160	0.099	0.119	0.227	0.198	0.150	0.414	0.101
	(2.00)**	(0.53)	(1.33)	(1.85)*	(1.30)	(1.76)*	(2.59)***	(1.29)

Sick during the last 2 weeks?								
Prop. of other HH members:								
(Yes = 1)	0.042	0.057	0.041	0.005	0.124	−0.027	0.175	−0.028
	(0.43)	(0.36)	(0.29)	(0.04)	(0.86)	(−0.26)	(0.91)	(−0.28)
Average age	0.003	−0.002	0.000	−0.000	−0.001	−0.004	0.007	−0.004
	(0.54)	(−0.21)	(0.05)	(−0.00)	(−0.14)	(−0.66)	(0.72)	(−0.71)
Average age^2/100	−0.001	0.005	0.006	0.004	0.003	0.009	−0.008	0.010
	(−0.19)	(0.40)	(0.65)	(0.51)	(0.26)	(1.32)	(−0.58)	(1.59)
N	5,479	2,020	3,575	3,924	2,674	4,825	2,056	5,443
Log likelihood	−7,178.3271	−2,500.9554	−4,763.7128	−4,931.3974	−3,424.7554	−6,277.0526	−2,663.8340	−7,104.4972
Pseudo R^2	0.0563	0.1023	0.0627	0.1616	0.1467	0.1125	0.1142	0.1238

Note: Household-level average data are taken from all household members, excluding the PQOL respondent from each household, if HHSize > 1. For households with HHSize = 1, the household-level average data are taken from PQOL respondents themselves.

income findings from developed country data where objective external comparison income enters positively into the happiness equation: an increase in own income over the community earning level leads to higher reported welfare levels (Clark and Oswald 1996; McBride 2001; Stutzer 2002; Blanchflower and Oswald 2004).

Nevertheless, we find that income is not the only determinant of individual well-being, but that the number of durable assets owned by a household also matters significantly in the individual's assessment of quality of life. We also find through comparative–static analysis that durable assets ownership is not highly correlated with household income. What happens then if people also care about relative consumption as much as relative income? If that is the case then it would simply suggest that high household income across the community does not necessarily lead to a higher standard of living, if we do not allow for controls of relative durable consumption in the regression as well.

Running a correlation matrix between relative income and the averaged consumption levels of different durable goods in the community gives us a first glance at the relationship. The average consumption levels, which are allowed to vary between households, all appear to correlate negatively with relative income, except for primus cooker.[17] An increase in the average consumption level of a durable good reduces the probability of individuals reporting a higher relative income and, providing that the probability generated from such a good is significant, its average consumption level also has to be taken into account in the relative income analysis.

In Table 21.8 we include into the happiness regression the average consumption levels of different durable assets in the community for different groups of people. Controlling for relative consumption, we can see that relative income now enters positively and significantly into the well-being regression for the full sample. Absolute income still matters significantly in the evaluation of well-being. The average variables, on the other hand, are significant and positive (negative) for motor vehicles, radios and telephones (gas cookers and televisions) in the full sample regression. Looking across the columns, it can be seen that a higher level of relative income is associated significantly with higher reported PQOL scores for black, urban and female samples, while absolute income variable retains its significance in all except the urban sample and the under 30 age group. The results support our earlier hypothesis on the relationship between external comparison income and subjective well-being, and are consistent with previous work on relative income in the more developed economies.

Conclusion 3   Relative income enters positively into the individual's assessment of well-being. Relative consumption also matters *per se*.

Table 21.8 Life satisfaction equations with controls for relative durable consumption and relative income

	Full sample	Black	Non-black	Rural	Urban	Male	Female	Age<30	Age≥30
Average no. of motor vehicles	0.312	0.501	0.081	0.213	0.227	0.206	0.245	0.334	0.309
	(2.12)**	(1.99)**	(0.58)	(0.65)	(1.48)	(1.12)	(1.53)	(1.52)	(2.13)**
Avg. no. of bicycles	0.169	0.271	0.251	0.011	0.214	0.257	0.141	0.177	0.201
	(1.59)	(1.64)*	(2.11)**	(0.05)	(1.52)	(1.64)	(1.19)	(0.98)	(1.83)*
Avg. no. of electric stoves	−0.124	−0.019	−0.212	−0.587	−0.237	−0.109	−0.067	−0.455	−0.109
	(−0.50)	(−0.06)	(−0.57)	(−1.31)	(−0.74)	(−0.31)	(−0.25)	(−1.39)	(−0.43)
Avg. no. of electric kettles	0.311	0.227	0.549	1.478	0.017	0.413	0.105	1.021	0.136
	(0.89)	(0.48)	(2.03)**	(2.08)**	(0.05)	(0.79)	(0.34)	(2.20)**	(0.41)
Avg. no. of fridges	0.150	−0.322	0.449	−0.087	0.234	0.092	0.255	−0.006	0.196
	(0.82)	(−1.12)	(2.55)**	(−0.25)	(1.09)	(0.40)	(1.25)	(−0.02)	(1.02)
Avg. no. of gas cookers	−0.313	−0.353	−0.003	0.578	−0.549	−0.052	−0.320	−0.495	−0.245
	(−1.79)*	(−1.54)	(−0.02)	(1.89)*	(−2.39)**	(−0.23)	(−1.79)*	(−1.81)*	(−1.40)
Avg. no. of geysers	−0.005	−0.265	−0.084	−0.014	−0.016	0.400	−0.180	0.382	−0.104
	(−0.03)	(−0.95)	(−0.63)	(−0.02)	(−0.09)	(1.91)*	(−0.95)	(1.52)	(−0.61)
Avg. no. of primus cookers	0.121	0.158	−0.364	0.143	−0.065	0.250	0.068	0.253	0.078
	(1.06)	(1.27)	(−1.24)	(0.92)	(−0.33)	(1.62)	(0.60)	(1.55)	(0.69)
Avg. no. of radios	0.207	−0.038	0.109	0.218	0.105	0.066	0.319	0.042	0.247
	(2.09)**	(−1.48)	(0.98)	(1.24)	(0.75)	(0.50)	(3.17)***	(0.25)	(2.46)**
Avg. no. of telephones	0.460	1.193	0.023	−0.036	0.629	0.353	0.514	0.611	0.439
	(2.14)**	(3.32)***	(0.15)	(−0.05)	(3.29)***	(1.31)	(2.45)**	(2.00)**	(2.06)**
Avg. no. of TVs	−0.548	−0.293	−0.770	−0.856	−0.352	−0.861	−0.328	−0.822	−0.439
	(−2.75)***	(−1.05)	(3.53)***	(−2.23)**	(−1.41)	(−3.74)***	(−1.48)	(−3.05)***	(−2.16)**
Log of household monthly income	0.055	0.048	0.178	0.062	0.025	0.093	0.048	−0.031	0.086
	(2.43)**	(1.88)*	(3.26)***	(2.06)**	(0.79)	(2.46)**	(2.03)**	(−0.80)	(3.40)***

Table 21.8 (continued)

	Full sample	Black	Non-black	Rural	Urban	Male	Female	Age<30	Age≥30
Relative income	0.017	0.025	-0.011	0.014	0.056	-0.002	0.036	0.034	0.014
	(1.82)*	(1.74)*	(-1.34)	(1.28)	(2.44)**	(-0.22)	(2.90)***	(0.93)	(1.63)
N	7,499	5,479	2,020	3,575	3,924	2,674	4,825	2,056	5,443
Log likelihood	-9,715.6728	-7,033.8054	-2,481.5927	-4,727.2829	-4,849.5685	-3,393.0698	-6,184.3257	-2,617.7536	-7,014.7138
Pseudo R^2	0.1265	0.0753	0.1093	0.0699	0.1755	0.1546	0.1256	0.1296	0.1349

Note: Relative income = household monthly income/averaged community household monthly income. Personal, household, cluster, and other household members controls as in Table 21.6.

5. Conclusion

This chapter has attempted to answer the question of what are the global requirements for a good life, and whether happy people are the same across rich and poor countries. We examined the pattern of happiness responses in a developing economy framework via estimations of ordered probit well-being equations on a set of microeconomic variables for South Africa in 1993. Our main findings have been that there are similar patterns in the effects of already identified factors in the individual's assessment of happiness in South Africa as there are in the more-developed countries,[18] which can be summed up as follows.

First, we find that household variables correlate well with the perceived quality of life responses at the household level. The log of household income enters positively into the well-being equation, while household size has a negative relationship with the reported happiness levels. Black respondents appear to be much less satisfied with the quality of life than whites, despite comprising the majority of the population. This, however, is to be expected from a country where the majority has for generations been subject to apartheid. Past perception of financial well-being at the household level is also important in the evaluation of subjective well-being: if a respondent considers his/her current household situation to be the same or better in comparison with his/her parents at the same age, then the respondent is more likely to report a relatively higher well-being. Geographical setting of the household matters: urban dwellers are generally happier than those in the country. We also find basic living-standard indicators such as ownership of selected goods – namely, motor vehicles, geysers, telephones and television sets – to be positively correlated with the recorded welfare at the household level.

Second, the already identified individual characteristics correlate well with the reported perceived quality of life at the household level. Controlling for personal attributes of other members in the household, we find the reported well-being of the respondent to be significantly correlated with age, employment status and education level. People who receive a regular wage are more likely to be satisfied with life, *ceteris paribus*, than the unemployed, those looking after the home or in formal education, the self-employed and the retired. Like people in the richer countries, age has a U-shaped relationship with individual well-being, with the minimum being around the early to mid-40s. Contrary to many studies on happiness, education levels are negatively associated with the respondent's quality of life for South Africa. One interpretation of this is that higher education also leads to higher aspiration levels, and if these aspirations are not met by current incomes – as is often the case for many of the black employees – then the respondent is likely to report a lower subjective well-being, *ceteris paribus*. Education of other household members, however, enters positively into the happiness equation.

Third, our calculations of compensation variations and selected marginal effects suggest that non-economic factors, such as race and employment status, probably matter more psychologically than income. To compensate for a state of unemployment compared to receiving a regular wage would take a rise in household income of approximately R1,495 (£305) per month, while an extra R481,000 (£98,400) per month is required to compensate for being black, given that a household's monthly income is R100 (£21).

Fourth, we find that individuals care about their relative income standing in the community, all else being equal. Relative consumption of durables also matters in the evaluation of subjective well-being *per se*.

The overall finding on the well-being structure in South Africa does not offer us a completely new set of results in this field, and yet some economists may consider that to be a good thing. It signifies that there could be some merit in the study of subjective well-being responses in the less-developed nations. The results also support the idea that, subconsciously, people are the same everywhere. For example, employment keeps individuals happy because it provides security for people everywhere, both in the developed and less-developed countries. Education, on the other hand, may be negatively related to well-being in places like South Africa, *ceteris paribus*. However, we cannot conclude from the results that education is purely detrimental to well-being, but rather that the given developing economy environment does not allow for the variable to fulfil its purposes, that is to provide social status and stability for individuals. Socioeconomic factors are associated with individual happiness levels if the surrounding conditions allow individuals to satisfy their basic physical and psychological needs. In other words, it may be plausible to say that happy people are structurally similar everywhere, providing that their living standards are also similar, and that Wilson may be right in drawing his conclusions on what makes a happy person happy – all those years ago.

Notes

*   I am grateful to Andrew Oswald, Jeff Round, Carol Graham, Peter Law, Norman Ireland, Robin Naylor, Rea Lydon, Jonathan Gardner, Pedro Martins, Alexandros Zangelidis and Maureen Pauls. Helpful comments were also received during presentations at Warwick University, the Royal Economic Society Easter School in Birmingham (2002), and The Paradoxes of Happiness conference in Milan (2003). The usual disclaimer applies.
1.   Oxford Committee for Famine Relief, a non-governmental organization (NGO).
2.   See Graham and Pettinato (2002) for a summary on income mobility and its implication on happiness in Latin America.
3.   Sen's message emphasizes the observable difference in the standard of living between two people from opposite ends of the income quintile but possessing very different unobserved personal traits (that is, one was born happy, and the other was not) that may offset

the true effects of having a low standard of living on the reported subjective well-being. In a cross-sectional analysis such as this, it is virtually impossible to control for the omitted inborn dispositions. However, as other papers, and later our results on the correlations between well-being and different sets of personal and household variables suggest, the structure of the reported well-being data for South Africa is very similar to what would be obtained if the same regressions were to be run from panel data elsewhere. See also Clark and Oswald (2002) on comparing fixed-effects equations and cross-section equations in running a well-being regression.

4. The complete report can be downloaded from the South African government webpage at www.welfare.gov.za/Documents/2000/Docs/1998/Pov.html.

5. GNP per capita US$ (1994): Poland ($2,410), Thailand ($2,410), Brazil ($2,970), South Africa ($3,040), Malaysia ($3,480). Source: Inequality and Poverty Report, South Africa (1998).

6. HDI for selected middle-income countries in 1992 (rated out of 1): Poland (0.815), Thailand (0.798), Malaysia (0.794), Brazil (0.756), South Africa (0.677). Source: United Nations Development Programme (UNDP).

7. Defined in the ICPI report as the poorest 40 per cent of households.

8. See the LSMS website at www.worldbank.org/html/prdph/lsms/index.htm.

9. To our knowledge, the PQOL data have been studied in part by Kingdon and Knight (2001), who conclude using the South African survey that individuals in high unemployed households have generally reported lower life satisfaction than individuals residing in low unemployed households.

10. The reason for using log of household monthly income is because it is a proportionate rather than a unit increase in income, that is associated positively with happiness (Easterlin 2001). The income, which was calculated by the World Bank Group, includes all household income-earning activities and any money in-takes from non-employment sources.

11. The question is phrased as follows: 'When you compare your situation today with that of your parents, do you think you are richer, about the same, or poorer than they were? – 1. Poorer, 2. The same, 3. Richer'.

12. That is, a domestic gas water heater.

13. See Appendix 21A1 for the full summary of the correlation matrix for durable goods and income. In addition, why, if durable goods are important to an individual's standard of living, do high-income households not automatically imply to durable assets ownership. One plausible explanation could be that these durable assets are passed down intergenerationally, irrelevant to today's earning levels (Carter and May 1999). Moreover, living under apartheid rules may have reduced access to the assets market for the non-white population living in a relatively well-off household (Schreiner et al. 1997).

14. A similar model using averaged household-level data has been used in a paper by Kingdon and Knight (2001) to test for the unemployment effects on reported well-being in South Africa. As a result, they found household unemployment rate to be significantly correlated with low PQOL scores, controlling for household income per capita and other factors.

15. The life satisfaction equation (21.2) is closest to the equations used in US/UK happiness data:

$$H_i = \alpha Y_i + \beta Y_i^* + \Sigma Personal_i + \varepsilon_i,$$

where H_i represents happiness for individual i, Y is real income, Y^* is relative income, *Personal* is a set of sociodemographic and personal characteristics, and ε is the error term.

16. Our proxy for an individual's health status is different from the usual self-rated health status on a 4-point scale (from 'very poor health' to 'excellent health', for example) and takes into account only the respondent's health status in the previous two weeks. This may help to explain the insignificancy between the health variable and the reported well-being.

17. See Appendix 21A2 for the summary of correlation matrix for the average consumption levels for different durable goods and relative income.

18. See Appendix 21A3 for a summary of conclusions on the UK and US well-being data.

References

Alesina, A., R.Di Tella and R. MacCulloch (2004), 'Inequality and Happiness: are Europeans and Americans different?', *Journal of Public Economics*, **88**, 2009–42.

Blanchflower, D. and A. Oswald (2004), 'Well-being over time in Britain and the USA', *Journal of Public Economics*, **88** (7–8), 1359–86.

Carter, M. and J. May (1999), 'One kind of freedom: poverty dynamics in post-Apartheid South Africa', Department of Agricultural and Applied Economics, University of Wisconsin, mimeo.

Clark, A. and A. Oswald (1994), 'Unhappiness and unemployment', *Economic Journal*, **104**, 648–59.

Clark, A. and A. Oswald (1996), 'Satisfaction and comparison income', *Journal of Public Economics*, **61**, 359–81.

Clark, A. and A. Oswald (2002), 'Well-being in panels', Department of Economics, University of Warwick, mimeo.

Deaton, A. (1997), *The Analysis of Household Surveys: A Microeconometric Approach to Development Policy*, World Bank, Johns Hopkins University Press, Baltimore, MD.

Deaton, A. and C. Paxson (1994), 'Intertemporal choice and inequality', *Journal of Political Economy*, **102**, 437–67.

Di Tella, R., R. MacCulloch and A. Oswald (2001), 'The macroeconomics of happiness', Department of Economics, University of Warwick, mimeo.

Duesenberry, J. (1949), *Income, Saving and the Theory of Consumer Behavior*, Harvard University Press, Cambridge, MA.

Easterlin, R. (1974), 'Does economic growth improve the human lot? Some empirical evidence', in P.A. David and M.W. Reder (eds), *Nations and Households in Economic Growth: Essays in Honor of Moses Abramovitz*, Academic Press, New York and London, pp. 89–125.

Easterlin, R. (1995), 'Will raising the income of all increase the happiness of all?', *Journal of Economic Behaviour and Organization*, **27**, 35–47.

Easterlin, R. (2001), 'Income and happiness: towards a unified theory', *Economic Journal*, **111**, 465–84.

Ferrer-i-Carbonell, A. (2002), 'Income and well-being: an empirical analysis of the comparison income effect', Tinbergen Institute Discussion Paper, mimeo.

Frank, R. (1985), *Choosing the Right Pond: Human Behaviour and the Quest for Status*, Oxford University Press, Oxford.

Frank, R. (1989), 'Frames of reference and the quality of life', *American Economic Review*, **79** (2), 80–85.

Frey, B. and A. Stutzer (2000), 'Happiness, economics, and institutions', *Economic Journal*, **110**, 918–38.

Gerdtham, U. and M. Johannesson (1997), 'The relationship between happiness, health and socio-economic factors: results based on Swedish micro data', Department of Economics, Stockholm School of Economics, mimeo.

Graham, C. and S. Pettinato (2001), 'Happiness, markets, and democracy: Latin America in comparative perspective', *Journal of Happiness Studies*, **3**, 237–68.

Graham, C. and S. Pettinato (2002), *Happiness and Hardship: Opportunity and Insecurity in New Market Economies*, Brookings Institution Press, Washington, DC.

Inter-Ministerial Committee for Poverty and Inequality (ICPI) Report in South Africa (1998), www.welfare.gov.za/Documents/2000/Docs/1998/Pov.htm.

Kingdon, G. and J. Knight (2001), 'Unemployment in South Africa: the nature of the beast', Centre for the Study of African Economies, University of Oxford, mimeo.

Klasen, S. (1997), 'Poverty, inequality, and deprivation in South Africa: an analysis of the 1993 SALDRU Survey', *Social Indicators Research*, **41**, 51–94.

Lelkes, O. (2002), 'Tasting freedom: happiness, religion and economic transition', Centre for Analysis of Social Exclusion, London School of Economics, mimeo.

Living Standard Measurement Surveys (LSMS), World Bank, http://www.worldbank.org/html/prdph/lsms/lsmshome.html.

Lydon, R. and A. Chevalier (2001), 'Estimates of the effect of wages on job satisfication', Centre for Economic Performance Discussion Paper No. 0531, London School of Economics.

McBride, M. (2001), 'Relative income effects on subjective well-being in the cross-section', *Journal of Economic Behaviour and Organization*, **45**, 251–78.

Møller, V. (1998), 'Quality of life in South Africa: post-Apartheid trends', *Social Indicators Research*, **43**, 27–68.

Morawetz, D., E. Atia, G. Bin-Nun, L. Felous, Y. Gariplerden, E. Harris, S. Soustiel, G. Tombros and Y. Zarfaty (1977), 'Income distribution and self-rated happiness: some empirical evidence', *Economic Journal*, **87**, 511–22.

Moulton, B. (1990), 'An illustration of a pitfall in estimating the effects of aggregate variables on micro units', *Review of Economics and Statistics*, **72** (2), 334–8.

Namazie, C. and P. Sanfey (2001), 'Happiness and transition: the case of Kyrgyzstan', *Review of Development Economics*, **5**, 392–405.

Oswald, A. (1997), 'Happiness and economic performance', *Economic Journal*, **107**, 1815–31.

Ravallion, M. and M. Lokshin (1999), 'Subjective economic welfare',World Bank, Washington, DC, mimeo.

Ravallion, M. and M. Lokshin (2000), 'Identifying welfare effects from subjective questions', World Bank, Washington, DC, mimeo.

Schreiner, M., D. Graham, M. Cortes-Fontcuberta, G. Coetzee and N. Vink (1997), 'Racial discrimination in hire/purchase lending in apartheid South Africa', American Agricultural Economics Association Selected Papers, mimeo.

Sen, A. (1983), 'Poor, relatively speaking', *Oxford Economic Papers*, **35**, 153–69.

Stutzer, A. (2002), 'The role of income inspirations in individual happiness', Institute for Empirical Research in Economics, University of Zurich, mimeo.

Theodossiou, I. (1998), 'The effects of low pay and unemployment on psychological well-being: a logistic regression approach', *Journal of Health Economics*, **17**, 85–104.

Tomes, N. (1986), 'Income distribution, happiness and satisfaction: a direct test of the inter-dependent preferences model', *Journal of Economic Psychology*, **7**, 425–46.

van de Stadt, H., K. Arie and S. van de Geer (1985), 'The relativity of utility: evidence from panel data', *Review of Economics and Statistics*, **67**, 179–87.

Warr, P. (1990), 'The measurement of weil-being and other aspects of mental health', *Journal of Occupational Psychology*, **63**, 193–210.

Warr, P.B., P.R. Jackson and M. Banks (1988), 'Unemployment and mental health: some British studies', *Journal of Social Issues*, **44**, 47–68.

Wilson, W. (1967), 'Correlates of avowed happiness', *Psychological Bulletin*, **67**, 294–306.

Appendix 21A1

Table 21A1.1   Correlation matrix for different durable goods and log household income

	Motor	Bicycle	EStove	EKettle	Fridge	Gas
Motor	1.000	–	–	–	–	–
Bicycle	0.403	1.000	–	–	–	–
Electric stove	0.492	0.253	1.000	–	–	–
Electric kettle	0.547	0.285	0.746	1.000	–	–
Fridge	0.620	0.332	0.665	0.687	1.000	–
Gas	0.167	0.113	0.125	0.149	0.196	1.000
Geyser	0.637	0.355	0.640	0.685	0.649	0.140
Primus cooker	−0.294	−0.148	−0.455	−0.443	−0.368	−0.117
Radio	0.545	0.383	0.384	0.438	0.480	0.133
Telephone	0.628	0.335	0.621	0.664	0.649	0.136
TV	0.576	0.337	0.613	0.644	0.677	0.212
Log HH income	0.549	0.311	0.570	0.596	0.588	0.168

	Geyser	PCooker	Radio	Telephone	TV	Log income
Motor	–	–	–	–	–	–
Bicycle	–	–	–	–	–	–
Electric stove	–	–	–	–	–	–
Electric kettle	–	–	–	–	–	–
Fridge	–	–	–	–	–	–
Gas	–	–	–	–	–	–
Geyser	1.000	–	–	–	–	–
Primus cooker	−0.417	1.000	–	–	–	–
Radio	0.485	−0.137	1.000	–	–	–
Telephone	0.691	−0.366	0.490	1.000	–	–
TV	0.606	−0.322	0.514	0.618	1.000	–
Log HH income	0.583	−0.310	0.462	0.582	0.580	1.000

Appendix 21A2

Table 21A2.1   *Correlation matrix for the community means of different durable goods and relative income*

	MMotor	MBicycle	MEStove	MEKettle	MFridge	MGas
MMotor	1.000	–	–	–	–	–
MBicycle	0.802	1.000	–	–	–	–
MElectric Stove	0.709	0.514	1.000	–	–	–
MElectric Kettle	0.810	0.622	0.941	1.000	–	–
MFridge	0.868	0.699	0.907	0.937	1.000	–
MGas	0.260	0.249	0.275	0.308	0.303	1.000
MGeyser	0.886	0.697	0.804	0.885	0.889	0.283
MPrimus Cooker	−0.633	−0.500	−0.762	−0.785	−0.725	−0.190
MRadio	0.880	0.774	0.619	0.714	0.778	0.225
MTelephone	0.906	0.693	0.842	0.899	0.917	0.280
MTV	0.860	0.710	0.887	0.914	0.949	0.368
Relative income	−0.019	−0.014	−0.019	−0.022	−0.024	−0.010

	MGeyser	MPCooker	MRadio	MTelephone	MTV	Relative Y
MMotor	–	–	–	–	–	–
MBicycle	–	–	–	–	–	–
MElectric Stove	–	–	–	–	–	–
MElectric Kettle	–	–	–	–	–	–
MFridge	–	–	–	–	–	–
MGas	–	–	–	–	–	–
MGeyser	1.000	–	–	–	–	–
MPrimus Cooker	−0.720	1.000	–	–	–	–
MRadio	0.781	−0.515	1.000	–	–	–
MTelephone	0.908	−0.709	0.810	1.000	–	–
MTV	0.873	−0.697	0.789	0.913	1.000	–
Relative income	−0.017	0.001	−0.019	−0.020	−0.020	1.000

Note: Relative income = household monthly income/average community household monthly income. M(.) is the community means of (.) good, and is allowed to vary between households.

**Appendix 21A3   Summary of conclusions on the US and
UK well-being data**

1. Black people in the US are much less happy, *ceteris paribus*, than
    whites. One interpretation comes from the possible existence of racial
    discrimination in America.
2. Higher income is associated with higher happiness.
3. Reported well-being is greatest among women, healthy and married
    people, the highly educated, and those whose parents did not divorce.
4. Unemployed people are very unhappy.
5. To 'compensate' men for unemployment would involve a rise in income
    at the mean of approximately $60,000 per annum, and to 'compensate'
    for being black would involve an extra $30,000 per annum.
6. Relative income matters *per se*.
7. Happiness and life satisfaction are U-shaped in age. In both Britain
    and the US, well-being reaches a minimum, other things held constant,
    around the age of 40.

Sources: A. Oswald (1997), 'Happiness and economic performance', *Economic Journal*,
107, 1815–31; D. Blanchflower and A. Oswald (2004), 'Well-being over time in Britain and
the USA', *Journal of Public Economics*, **88** (7–8), 1359–86.

22 Federalism versus social citizenship: investigating the preference for equity in health care

*Luca Crivelli, Gianfranco Domenighetti and Massimo Filippini**

1. Introduction

Switzerland does not have a National Health Service like Italy and Great Britain, nor is its system based on a public insurance scheme such as in France and Canada. The Swiss health-care system is based upon a mixed insurance model. On the one hand, competing private non-profit companies are responsible for health insurance, and on the other hand, the system incorporates some elements that are normally adopted within the context of a social insurance, such as mandatory insurance for all residents, regulated and risk-independent premiums, public subsidies to the less wealthy for the payment of the insurance premiums. In an unusual health-care context such as the Swiss one, the decision-making autonomy of the single cantons, reinforced by fiscal federalism, has led to a highly heterogeneous system. This heterogeneity applies both to the production capacity and to the specific weight which each canton attributes to the various forms of health-care provision (for example to public versus private hospitals or nursing homes). Instead of being a single health-care system, Switzerland can therefore be considered an ensemble of 26 subsystems, connected to each other by the Federal Law on Health Insurance (FLHI).

In contrast to the majority of European countries, where the financial contribution of the state to health-care expenditure is significant, the Swiss system provides for a rather limited public participation. Moreover, the mandatory health insurance premiums are independent of income, and citizens finance 42 per cent of total health expenditure directly or by means of private insurances. This situation leads to a highly regressive financing of health care expenses. Moreover, the financial contribution of the State to the health-care sector in form of subsidies to public hospitals and to low-income households varies a great deal between the 26 cantons. The differences between the cantonal subsidy systems create, therefore, territorial inequity in the financing of the health-care sector in Switzerland. In general, the Swiss are fairly happy with the quality of health care in their country. However, satisfaction on the health-care delivery front is offset by the growing concern regarding the constant increase of health expenditure and in particular the share of costs financed by the regressive premiums of the mandatory health insurance.

In recent years many proposals have been formulated in the political arena, all aimed at reforming the financing of the mandatory health insurance. Among others, a popular vote, which was rejected by more than 70 per cent of voters in May 2003, invited the population to support the introduction of income- and wealth-derived health insurance premiums.

Switzerland therefore, represents a very interesting context to address questions that are linked with recent literature on the paradoxes of economics and happiness. From this stream of research we can learn, among many other things, the following three lessons:

- first, Frey and Stutzer (2002) found that direct democratic participation possibilities and federalism exhibit a statistically significant impact on reported happiness. Their empirical estimate shows that more 'local autonomy' is associated with a higher level of people's subjective well-being, due to better fulfillment of the voters' preferences in small jurisdictions;
- second, as illustrated by Banting and Corbett (2002) and Swank (2001), decentralization of decision-making power has generally a negative impact on the social welfare (redistributive) effort of the State;
- third, as shown by Alesina et al. (2004) people tend to declare themselves less happy when inequality (measured, for example, by the Gini coefficient) is high, although aversion to inequality seems to be concentrated among different ideological and income groups across the USA and Europe, according to the different perceptions of the degree of social mobility in the two areas.[1]

Combining the three lessons, a paradoxical situation emerges. On the one hand, more federalism and more direct democracy seem to be responsible for higher reported happiness of the population. On the other hand, decentralized decision-making and fiscal autonomy of local governments might lead to a lower level of vertical equity and raise issues of territorial equity. In countries like Switzerland, where the strength of federalism and direct democracy is very high, while social mobility is rather limited, inequalities among regions and individuals are expected to increase in time, with the final result of partially crowding out well-being provided by a decentralized political system.

The goals of the study presented here are: (i) to briefly describe the Swiss health-care system, paying particular attention to the issue of equity in the financing of health care; (ii) to show the consequences of federalism and wide-ranging cantonal autonomy in a particular health insurance context such as the Swiss one, in terms of interregional inequalities in per capita health care expenditure and in production capacity; (iii) to investigate the willingness of Swiss citizens to foster more equity in the financing of health care; and (iv) to empirically test the theory of Margolis (1982), whose fair-share model suggests that spending in group interest should behave as a superior good (that is, willingness to pay for collective interests – as in the case of a mandatory health insurance system – should rise as the income of individuals increases).

This chapter is structured as follows: in Section 2 we introduce some considerations on the nature of the patient's utility functions and we briefly describe the fair-share model developed by Margolis in 1982; in Section 3 we present the main features of the Swiss health-care system and show the consequences of federalism on the organization of the health-care sector; Section 4 is devoted to a short presentation of the reform proposals, which aim at achieving more equity in the financing of health care, presently under discussion; in Section 5 the specification of the model is discussed, while the dataset and the empirical estimation results are presented in Section 6; conclusions are drawn in Section 7.

2. Some considerations on the utility of spending for merit goods like health care

Some experimental and empirical evidence has been collected on the fact that people are more cooperative than assumed by standard rational choice theory and that fairness motives or affects the behaviour of many real people. In some circumstances individuals spontaneously contribute to the financing of public goods, although free-riding is a viable option, the return appears inconsequential and the effect of one's personal contribution to society's well-being is minimal (see, for example, Fehr and Gächter, 2000b; Andreoni and Scholz, 1998; and Andreoni, 1995). In a vast cross-cultural behavioural experiments project, Heinrich et al. (2004) recently approached, from an interdisciplinary perspective, the question whether the violation of the selfishness axiom seen in experiments can be interpreted as evidence of universal social preferences or rather if social preferences are shaped by economic, cultural, and social environments (the main result of the ambitious project being that the selfishness axiom is violated in every society studied, but in rather different ways). As shown for example, by Fehr, Fischbacher and Gächter (2002), if in the real world there are people who exhibit strong reciprocity, their existence might contribute to stabilizing human cooperation and to enforcing norms that prescribe participation in collective actions.

Looking only at the economics literature, in recent years we see that some scholars developed a bulk of new theories with the aim of explaining empirical and experimental observations better than standard self-interest models do. At the core of these new models we find hypotheses about preferences such as 'a sense of fairness' (Rabin, 1993), 'doing his/her fair share' (Margolis, 1982), 'morality of cooperation' (Sugden, 1984), 'strong reciprocity' (Fehr and Gächter, 2000a), 'self-centered inequity aversion' (Fehr and Schmidt, 1999), 'a concern for relative payoffs' (Rabin, 2002), and 'a taste for punishment' (Bolton and Ockenfels, 2000).

We rely in this chapter on the theoretical model developed by Margolis in the 1980s, which suggests treating differently individual preferences regarding private goods on the one hand, and group-interest spending on the other hand. Margolis assumes that the utility function of individuals includes two components that comply with two different logics.[2] Individuals value the consumption of private goods and services in a selfish way, but at the same time they value collective spending on merit or public goods from a group point of view. As members of a given community, they derive well-being from the amount of resources which are devoted to group-interest issues, but subject to the condition that they are personally 'doing their fair share' and contributing in such a manner that everyone enjoys equal access to group-interest services.

The logic of the utility maximization model is the following: each member of the community has an initial endowment of financial resources that should be divided into two spending alternatives: the maximization of the utility from the point of view of pure self-interest, and the maximization of the utility from the point of view of pure group-interest. The allocation decision depends on two factors: the ratio between the marginal utility of spending in group interest and the marginal utility of spending in self-interest and a weighting function, which varies positively with the participation ratio of the individual (in other words, the likelihood of spending an additional euro for self-interest rather than for group interest increases as the participation ratio grows).[3]

The fair-share model developed by Margolis has a simple theoretical implication: spending in group interest should behave as a superior good. As the endowment of a given individual increases spending for group interest should increase more than proportionally.

Margolis's model can be useful for the analysis of health-care services, which are generally considered to be merit goods.[4] In particular, the objective of granting all citizens equal access to basic health-care services by collectively financing the health-care system can be interpreted as one of the most relevant examples of group-interest spending. The demand for health care broadly reflects the utility that individuals draw from their health, whereby health represents a prerequisite for most human activities. For this reason many societies consider health-care services as merit goods.

Generally, the state promotes two dimensions of equity through the health-care system: horizontal equity (citizens with the same medical needs should receive the same treatment, even if they belong to different age and sex classes or ethnical groups) and vertical equity (the demand for basic health-care should not depend on the patients' ability to pay). In most OECD countries the emphasis given to equity has two major consequences: a significant public participation in the financing of health-care and the development of a package of medical services which should be granted to the entire population. In order to guarantee that social citizenship is offered to everybody, citizens participate (through taxes or through social health insurance contributions) to the financing of health-care services. In the case of federal states like Switzerland, the two dimensions of equity should be attained in the same way in all the country's regions.

Banting and Corbett (2002) illustrated that federal states offer a parti–cularly intriguing context. In federal states, the central government faces a trade-off between two social values: (i) a commitment to social citizenship, to be achieved through a common set of public health-care services for citizens across the entire country, and (ii) respect for regional communities and cultures, to be achieved through decentralized decision making and significant room for manoeuvre at the regional level in the health-care sector. Using the case study approach, the authors have proved that the regional variations in health-care supply (for example, the number of hospital beds or doctors per 1,000 inhabitants) and in per capita health-care spending are not very large in the five federative countries analysed (Belgium, Germany, Australia, the United States and Canada). The result is fairly surprising because it holds even in federal states where the decision-making power in the health-care sector has been delegated to regional authorities to a great extent or where the resort to interregional redistribution by means of financial transfers is very low. It seems that policy makers in the five countries are committed to granting comparable access to health services and to limiting interregional inequalities in health-care spending despite the importance of diversity embedded in the logic of federalism. However, as we shall illustrate in the next section, in Switzerland the situation is different. In fact, there is a marked heterogeneity between cantons in terms of vertical equity. Moreover, two features of the Swiss health-care system distinguish it from those of other European countries: (i) highly regressive health-care financing (due to the very limited public financial participation and income-independent insurance premiums) and (ii) the existence of significant differences among cantons in per capita health-care spending and in production capacity.

One of the objectives of this chapter is to assess whether Swiss citizens would favour a more equitable financing system and in particular whether they are willing to introduce income-dependent health insurance premiums.

According to Margolis's fair-share model we should expect growing willingness to pay for socialized health-care expenditure as income increases, since health-care services are usually considered merit goods. In our case we were not able to test directly the relationship between income and the desire to contribute to social health-care spending. However, the willingness of the higher-income classes to adopt income-dependent insurance premiums can be interpreted as a proxy for their higher willingness to contribute to the financing of health-care services.

3.   The Swiss health-care system
The main features of the health-care system are the following:

- the system is based on a private insurance model, with about 100 competing insurance companies on the one hand and some social characteristics on the other;
- since 1996 health insurance has been mandatory for all residents;
- the rights of the insured are laid down in individual insurance contracts; since 1996 the basic contract has been the same for all residents by law;
- both public and private hospitals as well as nursing homes offer inpatient health care, which (in most cases) is still reimbursed on a per diem base;
- ambulatory health-care services provided by freelance general practitioners and specialists are reimbursed according to a fee-for-service scheme;
- the insured can freely choose the service provider (general practitioner, specialist);
- the service fees are regulated and defined according to agreements concluded between the service provider's association, the health insurance companies and the state; and
- the financial contribution of the state (Swiss Confederation, cantons and local authorities) to the health-care system is very limited (subsidies to public-interest hospital structures, subsidies to the low-income classes for the payment of the mandatory health insurance premiums).

The financing model and the allocation of competences between the Confederation and the cantons
In 2000 a meagre 25 per cent of the total health-care expenditure was covered by general taxation.[5] Moreover, public contribution was predominantly provided by cantons and municipalities, whereas the Confederation contributed only 20 per cent to the public health-care budget. The rest

was financed by the mandatory (income and risk-independent) health insurance premiums (26 per cent), by contributions to other forms of social insurance (6.5 per cent) such as income-proportional deductions from salary for accidents. Citizens finance 42 per cent of the health-care costs directly (cost-participation and deductible amount from the invoices covered by the mandatory insurance, additional private insurance premiums and insurance-exempted services).

Switzerland's peculiarity is highlighted in the triangle of health-care financing depicted in Figure 22.1. The closer a country is to the triangle's hypotenuse, the higher the health-care expenditure share financed according to the citizens' paying ability (progressive general taxation or proportional payroll taxes). The closer it is to the right angle, the greater the use of private financing schemes.

Switzerland's position is in clear contrast with all the other European countries (which are all within a range of public financing between 65 per cent to 80 per cent of health-care expenditure) and shows some similarities with the situation in the United States. This particular structure of the health-care financing scheme has two main consequences:

1. The Swiss health-care system does not give much importance to the principle of equity of financing. In fact, the larger the share of progressive or at least income-proportional financing of health-care

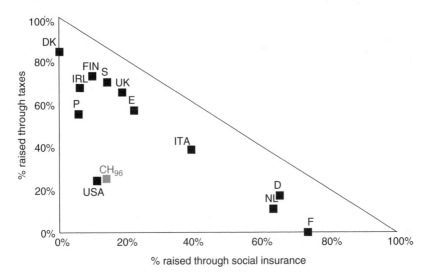

Source: Wagstaff et al. (1999).

Figure 22.1   Health-care financing triangle

costs, the greater the equity of health-care system financing. The fact that the mandatory health insurance premiums are independent of income and that citizens have to finance directly (or through private insurances) 42 per cent of total expenditure, leads to a highly regressive financing model.[6] This has negative repercussions especially on the medium-income class, which does not benefit from subsidies for the payment of insurance premiums.

2.   The presence of a large number of third-party payers makes it extremely complex to follow the financial flows, which in turn makes it more difficult to manage the health-care expenditure in general, and leads to a 'cost-shifting' problem in particular. Since nobody is responsible for the global health-care budget, it is sometimes easier for a single financing body to obtain a reduction in its own financial share than to engage in a more rational use of total health-care spending. This encourages shifting costs at the expense of another payer, rather than searching for solutions which would allow an effective rationalization of expenditure.

Although the state's presence in the health-care system cannot be considered to be very strong in financial terms, it is definitely stronger in terms of regulatory activity. As far as allocation of competences is concerned, the cantons are legally entitled to legislate on all health-care matters except for a few issues that explicitly fall within the competence of the Confederation. Almost all cantons have drawn up cantonal health-care laws and some provisions that regulate the application of the Federal health-care legislation. According to the Constitution, each canton enjoys decision-making autonomy in the planning of health-care institutions (in particular hospitals and nursing homes), in deciding which competences are to be delegated to the local authorities and with regard to vocational training. Since 1996, when the FLHI was introduced, the Confederation has played a more active role in the health-care sector. However, the additional decision-making powers of the central body were not supported by a formal devolution of competences from the cantons to the Confederation (which would have required a change in the Constitution) or by a redistribution of public health-care expenditure towards a greater engagement of the Confederation (see Crivelli and Filippini 2003).

The organizational autonomy granted to the cantons in the last 90 years has created a very heterogeneous picture both in the provision of health-care services and in the level of public health financing (direct contributions to public hospitals and health insurance premiums subsidies), giving rise to relevant issues of social and territorial inequity.

Such a marked decentralization of financing and of the provision of health care does not have any term of comparison in other countries with a federal setting such as Canada or Germany. In these countries, the central governments play a more active role in the financing of the health-care sector. Moreover, since the regional entities these are much larger than the Swiss cantons, the regional differences are not as marked and the problems connected to the presence of mini-systems are not as significant.

Consequences of federalism on the organization of the health-care system in Switzerland
Decentralization of competences and of expenditure and the strong autonomy of the 26 cantonal health-care subsystems has led to a series of significant inter-cantonal differences with regard to public financing and the regulatory settings as well as to production capacity.

The first sign of wide-ranging disparities among the cantons can be found in the per capita public health expenditure (Figure 22.2), which can be calculated by adding two fundamental elements: (a) the cantonal and

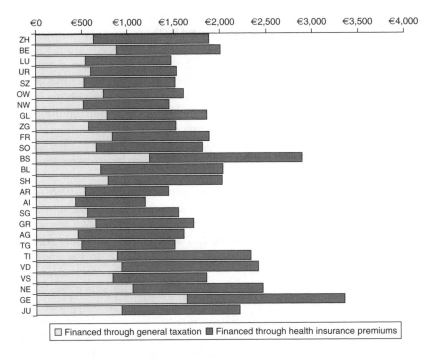

Source: Swiss Federal Statistical Office (2002), *Coûts du système de santé*, Neuchâtel; Swiss Federal Office for Social Security (2002), *Statistiques de l'assurance-maladie 2000*, Berne.

Figure 22.2   *Per capita public health expenditure and expenses covered by the mandatory insurance in Swiss cantons, 2000*

local direct financing for the provision of health-care services to the population (in particular the subsidies to public and private, public-interest hospitals, the participation in hospitalizations outside the home canton, the subsidies to nursing homes and to home-care services) and (b) the contributions to the less wealthy in the form of subsidies for the payment of the health insurance premiums (it is important to stress that each canton is entitled to develop its own model for the granting of subsidies and, within a framework set by the Confederation, they can also decide how many public funds should flow in this direction).

In 2000, per capita public health expenditure[7] ranged from €431 per capita in Appenzell Inner-Rhodes[8] to €1,641 in Geneva. It is important to remember that this indicator (financial contributions from the Confederation, the canton and the local authorities) represents only one part of the total expenditure for basic health-care services. The expenses covered by the mandatory insurance, which is financed by means of income-independent insurance premiums, have to be added.

The notable differences registered in the public health expenditure are to be found once again in the expenses covered by the mandatory health insurance, as shown in Figure 22.2. By adding the two expenditure items the socialized health expenditure is obtained, which ranged from a peak of €3,356 per capita in Geneva to a low of €1,192 in Appenzell Inner-Rhodes in the year 2000.[9] By combining these first two indicators we obtain interesting data concerning the socialized health expenditure financed by general taxation rather than by income-independent premiums. The highest percentage can be measured in Geneva (with 46 per cent), the lowest in Thurgovia, where only 26 per cent of the socialized health expenses were financed by tax revenues.

Therefore, a second source of variation across cantons regards equity of financing. Because health insurance premiums are based on community rating at cantonal level, the differences in expenses covered by the mandatory health insurance shown in Figure 22.2 signify a proportional variation in average premiums across the 26 cantons (Figure 22.3) and at the same time disparities within the single cantons (the basic health insurance is offered by several insurance companies, which calculate their premiums on a cantonal basis). The box-plot shows the median, maximum and minimum premium values for each canton and the concentration of the distribution of the premiums paid by 50 per cent of the cantonal population (the box-plot rectangle shows the dispersion between the first and the third quartile). The highest premium of all (more than €270 per month) was paid in Canton Geneva, the lowest (less than €90) was paid in Valais.

The real burden borne by citizens with a low income corresponds to the difference between the premiums and the State subsidies. Financing of

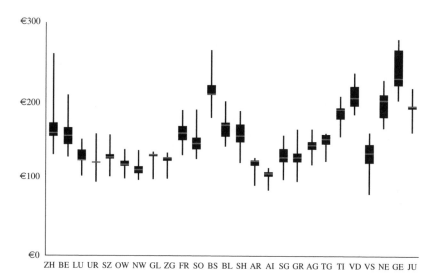

Source: Swiss Federal Office for Social Security (2002), *Statistiques de l'assurance-maladie 2000*, Berne.

Figure 22.3   Inter-cantonal and infra-cantonal differences in adult premiums, 2002

these subsidies is ensured to the extent of two-thirds by the Confederation and one-third by cantons. The distribution of the Confederation's funds and the financial participation of the cantons are established on the basis of an equalizing allocation system, depending on the financial strength of each canton. However, out of respect for the federalism that distinguishes the institutional order in Switzerland, the task of implementing the distribution system of subsidies lies with the cantons. The 26 cantonal systems greatly differ one from the other, in terms of technical profile as well as effectiveness. Looking at a representative household of 4 people (2 adults and 2 children) with a gross income of €45,000 and choosing the health insurer offering coverage at the average cantonal premium, the share between net premiums and disposable income ranged from 1.5 per cent of Valais to 14 per cent of Geneva in 2002.

There are also very marked differences between cantons with regard to production capacity in the health-care sector. The first aspect we would like to consider is the density of acute beds (Table 22.1). The national average is 4.5 acute beds per 1,000 inhabitants, but there are three cantons that exceed this average by over 35 per cent (Ticino: 6.4 beds; Appenzell Inner-Rhodes: 7.3 beds and Basle-Town: 8.1 beds), and four cantons that have a

Table 22.1   Density of acute beds per 1,000 inhabitants and density of medical practices per 10,000 inhabitants, 2000

Canton	Density of acute beds per 1,000 inhabitants	Density of medical practices per 10,000 inhabitants	Canton	Density of acute beds per 1,000 inhabitants	Density of medical practices per 10,000 inhabitants
Argovia (AG)	4.2	13.9	Nidwalden (NW)	2.5	10.6
Appenzell Inner-Rhodes (AI)	7.3	11.0	Obwalden (OW)	3.5	9.9
Appenzell Outer-Rhodes (AR)	3.2	15.2	St Gall (SG)	3.8	15.3
Berne (BE)	4.7	19.8	Schaffhausen (SH)	3.6	18.7
Basle-Country (BL)	3.6	18.6	Solothurn (SO)	4.1	15.3
Basle-Town (BS)	8.1	35.7	Schwyz (SZ)	2.9	11.5
Fribourg (FR)	4.0	14.2	Thurgovia (TG)	2.9	12.6
Geneva (GE)	4.5	32.2	Ticino (TI)	6.4	18.8
Glarus (GL)	3.6	12.5	Uri (UR)	4.9	13.0
Grisons (GR)	4.6	16.6	Vaud (VD)	5.3	23.8
Jura (JU)	4.7	14.9	Valais (VS)	4.1	16.8
Lucerne (LU)	3.8	14.1	Zug (VS)	2.9	16.5
Neuchâtel (NE)	4.3	20.1	Zurich (ZH)	4.6	21.9
Swiss average	4.5	19.3			

Sources: Swiss Federal Statistical Office, Informations sur le projet 'Statistiques des établissements de santé (soins intra-muros)', StatSanté 1/2002, 29 and *Bollettino dei medici svizzeri*, 2001, **82** (21).

density lower than the national average by over 35 per cent (Zug, Schwyz and Thurgovia: 2.9 beds; Nidwalden: 2.5 beds).

There is a real gap with respect to the density of medical practices. The data range from more than 30 medical practices per 10,000 inhabitants in Basle-Town and Geneva to 10–11 practices per 10,000 inhabitants in Obwalden, Nidwalden, Appenzell Inner-Rhodes and Schwyz, whereas the national average is 19.3. In Switzerland all doctors who have obtained a Swiss university degree in medicine and have at least two years' hospital experience are automatically entitled to practise independently and to invoice their services at the expense of the mandatory health insurance according to a fee-for-service scheme (the fees are fixed on a cantonal basis in a specific price list for medical services).[10] This easily leads to a phenomenon of supply-induced demand.

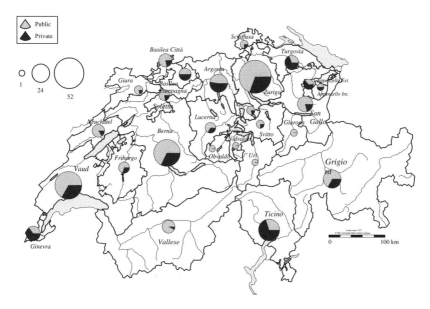

Source: Swiss Federal Statistical Office, Informations sur le projet 'Statistiques des établissements de santé (soins intra-muros)', StatSanté 1/2002, 17.

Figure 22.4   Comparison between public or subsidized, private acute hospitals and private clinics in the different Swiss cantons, 2000

Another difference that emerges among the Swiss cantons is the frequency of the institutional forms in the hospital sector. In Figure 22.4 a pie chart has been drawn within each canton. The pie surface corresponds to the total number of hospitals operating in a specific canton, whereas the 2 pie slices represent the relative weight of public and private subsidized hospitals in comparison with non-subsidized private institutions. The public–private mix has a strong impact on the financing model of mandatory health care. The higher the percentage of private beds in a canton, the higher the share covered by means of the health insurance premiums (which are income independent).

Consequently the cantons contribute less to the total expenditure, as they have to subsidize beds only in public and public-interest hospitals. Therefore the cantons can reduce the revenues of general taxation (and taxes are collected progressively according to the tax-payers' income). More private beds thus imply, *ceteris paribus*, a greater iniquity of financing. In this sense the hospital situation in Ticino, Thurgovia, Geneva and Appenzell Outer-Rhodes is unusual, as it is characterized by a clear prevalence of private non-subsidized hospitals.

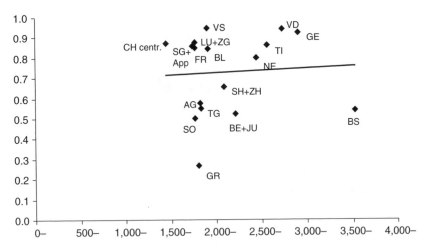

Figure 22.5   Correlation between average satisfaction and per capita expenditure of the mandatory health insurance in Swiss cantons, 2002

All the indicators presented in this chapter concern the expenditure, organizational levels and schemes of the health-care sector in the various cantons. This analysis clearly fails to consider the effectiveness factor (outcome indicators), which would make it possible to determine whether such different expenditure and activity levels lead to a proportional difference with regard to the population's health conditions and degree of satisfaction. In the light of the difficult task of measuring the effectiveness of a health-care system, on the basis of few simple indicators such as mortality amenable to medical intervention, the population's degree of satisfaction concerning the cantonal health-care system (see Figure 22.5) and the subjective rationing perception (like the indicator of waiting lists, virtually non-existent in all cantons),[11] it is possible to conclude that there are no significant effectiveness gaps in Switzerland at present.[12]

This conclusion emphasizes the wide-ranging differences with respect to each cantons' performance in terms of the cost-effectiveness ratio. In fact, the per capita health-care expenses are much higher in some cantons than in others, even though the effectiveness level is very much the same. The differences in these expenses could be partially caused by an excessive production capacity (high density of medical practices and hospital beds) and therefore they could be the consequence of a situation of supply-induced demand.

In conclusion, the Swiss health-care system seems to guarantee a satisfying level of equity of access to the health-care services, while lacking

Table 22.2   Summary of the disparities existing at the cantonal level

	Situation	Possible reasons
Horizontal equity	No significant differences (the *outcome* is fairly homogeneous)	The central government defines the package of health-care services that ought to be granted to the whole population
Mandatory health insurance premiums	Differences among cantons and, within the same cantons, between the insurance companies	Federalism, lack of competition in the health insurance system, limited planning on the supply side, inappropriate incentives
Public subsidies for the payment of health insurance premiums	Marked differences among cantons	Federalism
Per capita 'socialized' health-care expenditure	Marked differences among cantons	Federalism, limited planning on the supply side, inappropriate incentives
Production capacity and regulatory settings	Marked differences among cantons	Federalism, limited planning on the supply side, inappropriate incentives

equity both at the individual and the territorial level with regard to the system's financing. In Table 22.2 a summary of the differences between the Swiss cantons is presented and an attempt is made to explain the reasons.

4.   Proposals for a reform

People in Switzerland are, in general, fairly satisfied with the way the health system in their country is run.[13] In a survey carried out in September 2002 among a sample of 1,128 respondents, 21 per cent said they were 'very satisfied' and 45.1 per cent 'fairly satisfied' with the way health care is run. On a European scale these percentages – see Table 22.3 – can be compared with the figures gathered in 1996 by the Eurobarometer survey of citizens' views on health-care systems (see Mossialos 1997). Only in Denmark was the rate of 'very satisfied' respondents higher than in Switzerland. By adding the percentages of the 'very satisfied' and 'fairly satisfied', Switzerland (with 66.93 per cent) would drop from the second to the seventh place in a hypothetical European ranking; it would be passed not only by Denmark (90.0 per cent) but also by Finland (86.4 per cent), Holland (72.8 per cent), Luxemburg (71.1 per cent), Belgium (71.1 per cent) and Sweden (67.3 per cent). The main

Table 22.3   Satisfaction regarding the health-care system in Switzerland, 2002

	Answer percentage	Cumulative percentage
Very satisfied	21.81	21.81
Fairly satisfied	45.12	66.93
Neither satisfied nor dissatisfied	15.43	82.36
Fairly dissatisfied	10.90	93.26
Very dissatisfied	3.99	97.25
Do not know	2.75	100.00

limitation of these comparisons lies in the fact that people voice their opinions on the basis of their personal experiences (which are in general limited to their own health-care system) and of the expectations they place in the system, whereby expectations are endogenous, that is, they tend to increase as the perceived quality of the health system itself improves.[14]

This satisfaction on the health-care delivery front is offset by the Swiss population's growing concern regarding the constant increase of health expenditure and in particular the share of costs financed by the premiums of the mandatory health insurance. Indeed, between 1996 – the year in which universal health insurance became compulsory under federal law – and 2002, premiums rose in Switzerland on average by 62 per cent. The population's growing concern with respect to these massive increases is reflected in the difficulty that many families experience nowadays when it comes to paying health insurance premiums. As an example, Table 22.4 displays the situation of two representative households (a couple without children and a couple with two children), both earning the Swiss median income of about €5,000 and living in the Canton Ticino. For the year 2002 we have calculated the amount that each household would pay in income taxes (including federal, cantonal and local taxes) and the amount it would pay in terms of the mandatory health insurance premiums for all family members.

In the case of the couple without children, the health insurance premiums sum up to 78 per cent of the amount spent on taxes, whereas in the case of the couple with two children premiums equal 1.8 times the amount spent on income taxes. This situation could undermine the social fabric and has ultimately prompted the political forces to work out proposals to amend current laws, with a view to introducing greater control and planning on the supply side (thus directly influencing the cost pattern), to enforcing more competition among insurance plans and to providing for a more equitable financing mechanism.

Table 22.4   Proportion between spending on income taxes and health insurance premiums in the case of a representative household, 2002 (€)

	Couple without children	Couple with two children
Family's gross income	65,000	65,000
Family's taxable income	45,333	34,667
Federal income taxes	681	308
Cantonal income taxes	2,743	1,538
Local income taxes	2,331	1,307
Total taxes	5,755	3,154
Yearly health insurance premiums	4,480	5,680

Swiss citizens voted on 18 May 2003 on a citizens' initiative launched by the left wing and supported by labour unions and consumer organizations, whose most important aim was to challenge the way health insurance premiums are currently financed. Instead of income-independent flat premiums, the following financing rule for the compulsory health insurance expenditure was suggested: 60 per cent of total health insurance cost based on personal income, 15 per cent based on the personal wealth stock and 25 per cent by means of a general value added tax (VAT) increase. Such a system would be, according to the proponents, more in line with the models adopted by the other European countries and would contribute to maintaining the already existing equal access to health care guaranteeing at the same time a fair financing method. The proposal was rejected by a strong majority of the population (72.9 per cent), in all 26 cantons (however, the participation at the ballot remained below 50 per cent).

Two surveys conducted during the second half of the year 2002, among them the one that provided the data for the analysis presented in Sections 5 and 6, have shown that a substantial majority (63 per cent) are willing to pay health insurance premiums that depend proportionally on their income, though they are rather sceptical when it comes to supporting a VAT increase to finance the health sector. It should be noted that the proposal of income-dependent premiums illustrated in the questionnaire of the surveys, was quite different from the proposal of the initiative rejected in May 2003. For instance, the initiative proposed to calculate the premiums on the basis of a person's personal wealth stock. Moreover, the initiative proposed a general VAT increase to finance the health sector. These differences have to be kept in mind when interpreting the following empirical analysis.

Table 22.5   Percentage of people favouring income-dependent health insurance premiums by income class, 2002

Income per month (€)	In favour	Against	Do not know
Less than 2,000	79.3	13.8	6.9
2,000–3,000	72.9	19.9	7.2
3,000–4,000	67.5	20.7	11.8
4,000–6,000	57.6	33.2	9.2
6,000–9,000	42.5	54.5	3.0
More than 9,000	23.1	69.2	7.7

Table 22.5 illustrates the percentage of people in favour of income-dependent insurance premiums according to six income classes. However, these results could also be influenced by factors other than income, for example, family size or age. In the regression analysis, which we shall present in Sections 5 and 6, these factors will be taken into account.

The government and a majority of parliament are opposed to making health insurance premiums directly dependent on income and wealth and to shifting a part of the burden to indirect taxation. Both the parliament and the federal government advocate maintaining the current health insurance system where premiums are not related to criteria such as the risk of the insured and the individual's financial resources. They suggest solving the social issue by simply resorting more frequently to the subsidies the Confederation and the cantons are already paying to the less wealthy in order to help them finance their health insurance premiums. Current legislation, which grants cantons large autonomy in the organization of subsidy distribution, should be amended in favour of a more homogeneous regulation. The new law will require that health insurance premiums paid by very poor families (by very poor single persons) do not exceed a maximum threshold of 2 per cent (4 per cent) of their income. If income becomes sufficiently high, premiums can account for a greater percentage of income (4 per cent, 6 per cent or 8 per cent), but at the most reach 10 per cent of the income in the case of families and 12 per cent in the case of singles. Accordingly, if premiums paid by a family (a single) exceed the limit defined by the law, the family becomes automatically eligible for subsidies, while cantonal governments are obliged to provide the corresponding financial means. The only freedom left to cantons concerns the definition of the five income classes associated with the maximum ratios.

The analysis we have presented here is based on data gathered in September 2002 and thus takes into account the inital willingness of the citizens to accept income-related premiums, that is, their stance prior to the start of the political and media campaign leading up to the voting on this issue.

5. Model specification

The binomial logit model was used in this study.[15] The resort to this model is especially appropriate when working with dependent binary qualitative variables, built up from qualitative data obtained through surveys containing a wide range of questions concerning individual attitude, characteristics and behaviour. In our case we are interested in identifying the most important factors that can explain the choice to support (dependent variable = 1) or not to support (dependent variable = 0) the introduction of income-dependent health insurance premiums in Switzerland.

Several factors could potentially influence a person's decision with respect to this proposal. Household income is an obvious candidate. We hypothesize, following Margolis's thesis, that in the case of people with a higher income, the probability of an affirmative answer to the proposal of income-dependent health insurance premiums will increase or remain the same. This means that the high-income classes are more likely to support the proposal than the low-income classes because of their willingness to do their fair share. A competing theoretical explanation for high-income classes giving stronger support to redistribution than poor people could be a high degree of perceived social mobility, as explained, for example, by Piketty (1995).

In this analysis, we have also considered the following socioeconomic factors that could influence an individual's behaviour: age, gender, household size, employment and level of education. The probability that an individual falls within the group of people in favour of the proposal concerning the introduction of income-dependent health insurance premiums is defined by the following model:[16]

$$
\begin{aligned}
L_i = \beta_0 &+ \beta_1\,DY_1 + \beta_2\,DY_2 + \beta_3\,DY_3 + \beta_4\,DY_4 + \beta_5\,DY_5 + \beta_6 \\
&DY_6 + \beta_7\,DHS_1 + \beta_8\,DHS_2 + \beta_9\,DHS_3 + \beta_{10}\,DGENDER + \beta_{11} \\
&DACA + \beta_{12}\,DPRE + \beta_{13}\,AGE + u_i,
\end{aligned} \tag{22.1}
$$

where:

L_i = unobserved dependent variable which takes on the value 1 if the household chooses to support the income dependent health insurance premium and zero if it does not;

DY_a = dummy variable indicating whether the person belongs to the income class a, with $a = 1, \ldots, 6$; therefore, in our analysis, the income level of a person is measured using a series of dummy variables for different income classes;

DHS_1 = dummy variable indicating whether the person is living in a one-person household;

DHS_2 = dummy variable indicating whether the person is living in a two-person household;

DHS_3 = dummy variable indicating whether the person is living in a three-person or more household;

$DGENDER$ = dummy variable indicating the gender;

$DACA$ = dummy variable indicating whether the person has an academic degree;

$DPRE$ = dummy variable indicating whether the person is living in a canton where the level of the health insurance premiums is higher than the Swiss average;

AGE = age of the person; and

u_i = stochastic error term.

6. Data and estimation results

The household micro data used in this study has been compiled through a special survey carried out in Switzerland in 2002 by a private market research company. The questionnaire used for this survey was developed by the Department of Health and Social Affairs of the Canton Ticino in cooperation with the Istituto Mecop of the University of Lugano. The data were collected by phone interviews using a pre-coded questionnaire. The total sample consisted of 1,128 households living in Switzerland. After correcting for missing values, the sample was reduced to a total of 819 individuals. This dataset contains socioeconomic information on the individuals, as well as preferences from a list of proposals for a reform of the Swiss health system. The questionnaire included a specific question on the proposal concerning the introduction of income-dependent health insurance premiums.

Tables 22.6 and 22.7 give some statistical details on the variables employed in the estimation of the model (22.1).

In Table 22.8 we report the estimation results for the logit model specification (22.1). The statistical results are significant regarding most of the important coefficients.[17] Moreover, the value of the count R^2, a fit measure for the estimated model, is within the acceptable range. Therefore, our model performs quite well in predicting the individual's choice.

The main aim of this empirical study is to identify the effect of income and income classes on the choice to support or not to support the proposal of income-dependent health insurance premiums.[18] Most coefficients of the dummy variables for the different income classes (DY_2, DY_3, DY_4, DY_5, DY_6) are significantly different from zero and have a negative sign. These coefficients have to be interpreted with respect to the first income class (DY_1), taken as a reference, which does not appear in the table. The absolute

Table 22.6   Descriptions of the dummy variables

Variable	Condition for which the variable value = 1	Frequency (%)
DY_1	Individual in income class 1 (< 3,000 CHF)	9.2
DY_2	Individual in income class 2 (3,000–4,500 CHF)	18
DY_3	Individual in income class 3 (4,500–6,000 CHF)	28.3
DY_4	Individual in income class 4 (6,000–9,000 CHF)	28.1
DY_5	Individual in income class 5 (9,000–15,000 CHF)	15.1
DY_6	Individual in income class 6 (> 15,000 CHF)	1.3
DHS_1	One-person household	23.6
DHS_2	Two-person household	35.5
DHS_3	Three- and more person household	40.9
DGENDER	Male	44.9
DACA	Individual with an academic degree	20.3
DPRE	Individual living in a canton with high premiums	52

Table 22.7   Descriptive statistics on AGE

Variable	Min	Median	Mean	Max
AGE	18	44	46	74

Table 22.8   Estimated coefficients for the logit model

Variable	Coefficients	*t*-ratio
Constant	1.438***	2.860
DY_2	−0.599	−1.471
DY_3	−0.774**	−1.991
DY_4	−1.521***	−3.908
DY_5	−2.316***	−5.576
DY_6	−2.983***	−3.796
DHS_2	0.785***	3.401
DHS_3	0.464**	2.080
AGE	0.002	0.335
GENDER	−0.359**	−2.161
DACA	−0.279	−1.391
DPRE	0.429**	2.627

Notes:
a. *t*-test of whether the coefficient is zero $*p < 0.10$, $**p < 0.05$, $***p < 0.01$.
b. count $R^2 = 0.704$.

value of the coefficients of these variables increases with an increase of the income class. These negative coefficients suggest that, *ceteris paribus*, an increase in income is associated with a lower probability of an affirmative answer to the proposal of income-dependent health insurance premiums. Therefore, these results show that the willingness to have a higher degree of equity in financing the health-care system decreases as income increases. This result is confirmed by the analysis of the marginal effects for the income class dummy variables, which give the change in the probability of a yes (dependent variable=1) that results from changing a single dummy variable from zero to one, holding all other variables at some fixed values, for example, at their mean values.[19]

In order to estimate the magnitude of the effect of the income class on the decision to support or not to support the proposal of income-dependent premiums, we have set the explanatory variables to values that should represent a 'typical individual' of the sample, for example, a 50-year-old man with family, without an academic degree and living in a canton with high health insurance premiums. If an individual with these characteristics belongs to the third income class (DY_3), there is a probability of supporting the proposal of 0.87. If this individual belongs to the fourth income class (DY_4), the probability decreases to 0.75.

The coefficients of the two-person and three-person household dummy variables are positive and significant. This result implies that, *ceteris paribus*, small households are less likely to accept health insurance premiums dependent on income than three or more person households. Moreover, men appear, *ceteris paribus*, to be significantly less interested in increasing the degree of equity in financing the health services. Finally, people living in cantons characterized by high health insurance premiums are more likely to accept the proposal of income-dependent premiums.

7. Conclusions

The main goal of this chapter was to verify empirically the underlying hypothesis of Margolis (1982), namely that spending in group interest is a superior good. We tested the fair-share model in the context of health-care services, which in the most OECD countries are considered merit goods. After presenting the main features of the Swiss health-care system, we emphasized the strongly regressive financing of health care in Switzerland, which is due to the limited public participation in health-care spending and to income-independent premiums for the mandatory health insurance. The willingness of the population to favour more vertical equity has been assessed with regard to the principle of introducing income-dependent premiums in the mandatory health insurance. We applied the binomial logit model using micro data collected through a special survey carried out in 2002. It should be noted that people participating in the survey gave their opinion not on the basis of a precise proposal (that is, being aware of marginal benefits and costs) but only on the general principle of promoting vertical equity through income-dependent health insurance premiums. For this reason, the results could vary by submitting a more precise proposal of income-dependent premiums. In this case the results of the econometric analysis reject the Margolis hypothesis of group-interest spending behaving as a superior good. Indeed, as household income increases, the likelihood of accepting a more equitable financing of health insurance decreases. However, it is intriguing to note that many individuals who earn more than the median income (that is, people who will suffer a financial loss through a reform of the system) favour the more equitable financing system. Since perceived social mobility in Switzerland is quite limited, this result can be interpreted as suggestive evidence that fairness, inequality aversion or reciprocity play a role in the preferences of at least a part of the high-income population in Switzerland. Finally, the econometric analysis shows that women are significantly more interested than men in increasing the degree of vertical equity, while small households (which are affected more by taxation and less by individual premiums) and people living in cantons characterized by low health insurance premiums are less likely to accept income-dependent health insurance financing.

Notes

*   We would like to thank the Department of Health and Social Affairs of Ticino for providing us with the dataset used in this study, Karen Ries, Mary Ries and Ranjit De Sousa for proofreading the final version of the text and an anonymous referee for many useful remarks on a previous version of the paper. The views expressed in this chapter are strictly personal. Responsibility for any remaining errors lies solely with the authors.

1.   In Europe, the poor and the left wing respondents show a strong aversion to inequality, while in the USA the only group displaying aversion to inequality is the rich. This puzzle is explained by the authors as follows: the American rich dislike inequality since they perceive their chance of moving down the income ladder as higher, whereas the European poor feel their chances of moving up the income ladder are lower than in the USA and, therefore, their dislike of inequality is stronger. What matters for this potential explanation to hold are, of course, perceived and not real social mobility differences.

2.   It is worth mentioning that other relevant studies rely, analogously, on two different components of individuals' objective function, such as Harsanyi's (1955) well-known distinction between personal and ethical preferences and, within the literature on private provision of public goods, the distinction between agents driven by 'pure altruism' and agents driven by 'impure altruism'/ 'warm glow' motives.

3.   'The larger the share of my resources I have spent unselfishly, the more weight I give to my selfish interests in allocating marginal resources. On the other hand, the larger benefit I can confer on the group compared with the benefit from spending marginal resources on myself, the more I will tend to act unselfishly' (Margolis 1982: 36).

4.   It is important to recognize the particular nature of the commodity 'health care' (see Arrow 1963). Health-care *per se* has little utility. If any satisfaction is associated

with medical services, this occurs with higher likelihood in the case of people who are ill, the productivity of health care being state dependent (see Zweifel and Breyer 1997).

5. This quota is divided into shares of 15.4 per cent for public financing of hospitals and nursing homes, 8.7 per cent for subsidies to the less wealthy citizens in form of a public contribution to the payment of the mandatory health insurance premiums and of the nursing homes' daily rates, and 1.5 per cent for public subsidies to other social insurances that participate in the health-care expenditure.

6. Wagstaff et al. (1999) have published a comparative study on the equity of financing in OECD countries, where Switzerland ranked last.

7. Including direct public health expenditure and subsidies to the low-income classes for the payment of the mandatory health insurance premiums.

8. A list of the cantons and their abbreviations can be found in Table 22.1.

9. For an empirical analysis of the determinants of the socialized health-care expenditure at cantonal level, see Crivelli et al. (2006).

10. The health insurance companies are obliged to cooperate with all the medical practitioners entitled to practise independently within the framework of the coverage provided for by the FLHI. Service providers can be excluded from the reimbursement of the mandatory health insurance only in the case of citizens who have voluntarily joined a managed care insurance scheme.

11. For a more complete illustration of some of these indicators for six groups of cantons, see Crivelli and Domenighetti (2003).

12. The figure highlights the results of a survey carried out in September 2002 on 1,128 households based in Switzerland. Among others the following question was asked: 'In general, would you say that you are very satisfied, fairly satisfied, neither satisfied nor dissatisfied, fairly dissatisfied or very dissatisfied with the way health care is run in your canton?'. The satisfaction index was constructed by weighting the five possible answers with 2, 1, 0, –1 and –2 points, respectively. Some small cantons had to be aggregated in order to achieve a sufficient number of observations.

13. Switzerland can be regarded as the world's greatest 'health shopping centre' because there are almost no barriers to the access to medical and/or health services.

14. The theory of *hedonic treadmill*, developed by Brickman and Campbell (1971), and that of *satisfaction treadmill*, illustrated in Kahneman et al. (1999), could explain the evolving aspirations in the field of health-care service delivery and provide us with a theoretical framework for interpreting countries' results from surveys on the satisfaction with their own health care system.

15. For a general presentation of the logit model, see Grene (2000).

16. To recall that the sign of an estimated coefficient of the model (22.1) gives the direction of the effect of a change in the explanatory variable on the probability to accept the proposal of income dependent health insurance premiums.

17. For the econometric estimation we used LIMDEP, version 8.

18. The variables DY_1 and DHS_1 do not appear in the table because they are taken as the reference levels, in order to avoid the dummy variable trap.

19. The values of the marginal effects are: -0.132 for DY_2; -0.169 for DY_3; -0.34 for DY_4; -0.521 for DY_5; -0.602 for DY_6.

References

Alesina, A., R. Di Tella and R. MacCulloch (2004), 'Inequality and happiness: are Europeans and Americans different?', *Journal of Public Economics*, **88**, 2009–42.

Andreoni, J. (1995), 'Cooperation in public-goods experiments: kindness or confusion?', *American Economic Review*, **85** (4), 891–904.

Andreoni, J. and J.-K. Scholz (1998), 'An econometric analysis of charitable giving with interdependent preferences', *Economic Inquiry*, **36** (3), 410–28.

Arrow, K. (1963), 'Uncertainty and the welfare economics of medical care', *American Economic Review*, **53** (5), 941–73.

Banting, G. and S. Corbett (2002), *Health Policy and Federalism. A Comparative Perspective on Multi-Level Governance*, Montreal & Kingston: McGill-Queen's University Press.

Bolton, G.E. and A. Ockenfels (2000), 'ERC: a theory of equity, reciprocity, and competitions', *The American Economic Review*, **90** (1), 166–93.

Brickman, P. and D.T. Campbell (1971), 'Hedonic relativism and planning the good society', in M.H. Apley (ed.), *Adaptation-level Theory: A Symposium*, New York: Academic Press, 287–302.

Crivelli, L. and G. Domenighetti (2003), 'Influence de la variation des densités médicales régionales en Suisse sur la mortalité, les dépenses de santé et la satisfaction des usagers', *Cahiers de Sociologie et de Démographie Médicales*, **43** (3), 397–426.

Crivelli, L. and M. Filippini (2003), 'Il federalismo nel settore sanitario', in A. Ghiringhelli (ed.), *Il Ticino nella Svizzera*, Locarno: Dadò, 353–79.

Crivelli, L., M. Filippini and I. Mosca (2006), 'Federalism and regional health care expenditures: an empirical analysis for the Swiss cantons', *Health Economics*, **15** (5): 535–41.

Fehr, E., U. Fischbacher and S. Gächter (2002), 'Strong reciprocity, human cooperation and the enforcement of social norms', *Human Nature*, **13**, 1–25.

Fehr, E. and S. Gächter (2000a), 'Fairness and retaliation: the economics of reciprocity', *Journal of Economic Perspectives*, **14**, 159–81.

Fehr, E. and S. Gächter (2000b), 'Cooperation and punishment in public goods experiments', *American Economic Review*, **90**, 980–94.

Fehr, E. and K.M. Schmidt (1999), 'A theory of fairness, competition, and cooperation', *Quarterly Journal of Economics*, **114**, 817–68.

Frey, B.S. and A. Stutzer (2002), *Happiness and Economics. How the Economy and Institutions affect Well-Being*, Princeton, NJ: Princeton University Press.

Greene, W. (2000), *Econometric Analysis*, New York: Prentice-Hall.

Harsanyi, J. (1955), 'Cardinal welfare, individualistic ethics, and interpersonal comparisons of utility', *Journal of Political Economy*, **63**, 309–21.

Heinrich, J., R. Boyd, S. Bowles, C. Camerer, E. Fehr and H. Gintis (eds) (2004), *Foundations of Human Sociality. Economic Experiments and Ethnographic Evidence from Fifteen Small-Scale Societies*, Oxford: Oxford University Press, 55–95.

Kahneman, D., E. Diener and N. Schwartz (eds) (1999), *Well-being: The Foundations of Hedonic Psychology*, New York: Russell Sage Foundation.

Margolis, H. (1982), *Selfishness, altruism and rationality*, Cambridge: Cambridge University Press.

Mossialos, E. (1997), 'Citizens' view on health care systems in the 15 member states of the European Union', *Health Economics*, **6**, 109–16.

Piketty, T. (1995), 'Social mobility and redistributive politics', *The Quarterly Journal of Economics*, **110** (3), 551–84.

Rabin, M. (1993), 'Incorporating fairness into game theory and economics', *American Economic Review*, **83**, 1281–302.

Rabin, M. (2002), 'A perspective on psychology and economics', *European Economic Review*, **46**, 657–85.

Swank, D. (2001), 'Political institutions and welfare state restructuring: the impact of institutions on social policy change in developed democracies', in P. Pierson (ed.), *The New Politics of the Welfare State*, Oxford: Oxford University Press.

Sugden, R. (1984), 'Reciprocity: the supply of public goods through voluntary contributions', *The Economic Journal*, **94**, 772–87.

Wagstaff A., E. van Doorslaer, H. van der Burg, S. Calonge, T. Christiansen, G. Citoni, U.-G. Gerdtham, M. Gerfin, L. Gross, U. Hakinnen, P. Johnson, J. John, J. Klarus, C. Lachand, J. Lauritsen, R. Leu, B. Nolan, E. Peran, J. Pereira, C. Propper, F. Puffer, L. Rochaix, M. Rodriguez, M. Schellhorn, G. Sundberg and O. Winkelhake (1999), 'Equity in the finance of health care: some further international comparisons', *Journal of Health Economics*, **18**, 263–90.

Zweifel, P. and F. Breyer (1997), *Health Economics*, Oxford and New York: Oxford University Press.

23 Happiness and sustainability: a modern paradox
Silva Marzetti Dall'Aste Brandolini

1. Introduction

Sustainability is a social construct, and non-sustainability is considered a consequence of social actions. As we read in *Our Common Future* (WCED 1987, pp. 11, 63) 'an environment adequate for health and well-being is essential for all human beings – including future generations'. Therefore, if we have to pass from economic growth to human sustainable development, we need a moral evolution which must help humankind 'cope with rapidly changing social, environmental, and development realities'.

Economists are directly involved in this change, because material prosperity is still the main worry of human beings. They speak of welfare economics in the awareness that the link between what is valuable and what is right is welfare. However, the nature of value and its nexus with welfare and morality is a source of controversy in ethics and this disagreement is also reflected in economics. Philosophers, in fact, distinguish different ethical doctrines, and welfare economics has to a large extent been influenced by these. We believe that not only do the utilitarian and the neo-Humean views have to be kept in mind in the discussion about values in welfare economics, but also idealism and specifically the idealism of George Edward Moore. Therefore we distinguish four different theories of economic welfare, each one based on a different picture of values: the 'classical' theory[1] based on the utilitarian view; the new welfare economics (NWE) based on the neo-Humean view; John Harsanyi's rule utilitarianism based on Benthamism and the neo-Humean view; and John Maynard Keynes's macroeconomics inspired by Moore's idealism.

The choice between the different ethical doctrines does not depend on logic alone, but is mainly a matter of personal attitudes (Moore 1903; Russell 1954; Harsanyi 1958). Generally speaking, according to Lamont (1955, pp. 39–40), each member of a community can be thought to be engaged in the pursuit of the 'total conception of good' in a situation of scarce resources. In addition, each person expresses a scale of the goods included in his/her system of values; for example a social end may be compared with a personal end to attribute to each of them a degree of value. These brief considerations beg the following questions: if we focus on sustainability and sustainable development, what things considered as good should a person include in his/her total conception of good? Consequently, are the aforesaid economic welfare theories consistent with the values involved in sustainable development? We shall try to reply to these questions. Therefore, after presenting in Section 2 the basic concept of sustainability and sustainable development, in Section 3 we shall analyse the different welfare theories according to the relation between value and morality, and discuss which of them are consistent with the relatively new concept of sustainable development. We shall explain why, from the point of view of moral values, traditional utilitarianism is not consistent with sustainability, while Pareto efficiency is not fully consistent with this concept although it is intended as weak sustainability. Only rule utilitarianism and Keynes's view of welfare are consistent with sustainable development: rule utilitarianism with weak sustainability; Keynes's approach to welfare with strong sustainability. Because Keynes's view of good and happiness is not always well known to economists, special attention is devoted to Keynes's point of view. In particular, we shall show that the Keynesian view of goodness admits all kinds of values, not only instrumental but also intrinsic ones. In addition, recognizing that public good and private interest may compete, Keynes admits situations in which it is morally acceptable that sacrifice is uncompensated; and, if we pursue sustainable development, the sacrifice of the present generation could be unavoidable.

2. Moral values, sustainable development and welfare theories
Sustainability moral values: nature and intergenerational justice
Sustainability is a product of the human mind, a social construct.[2] Its different aspects, given by renewable resources, non-renewable resources, ecosystem services and biological diversity, contribute to human welfare. The question of 'the maintenance or improvement of the integrity of the life-support system on Earth' – in other words, biogeophysical sustainability (Holdren et al. 1995, p. 7, box 1.1) – has in itself an important philosophical aspect. It is first of all based on the value of nature, intended as the total system of things. Every process of development has to be sustainable to attain the integrity of the life-support system; so what has to be promoted is a sustainable development, which ought to satisfy the needs of the present generation without reducing the possibility that future generations can satisfy their own needs. The definition of sustainable development, therefore, highlights another value: intergenerational justice. In other words, other than the present generation, two new actors have to be considered: future generations and non-human things.

Nature and justice in philosophical literature are judged as intrinsic values or as instrumental values. In particular, in environmental ethics we can distinguish different currents of thought. With regard to nature, non-anthropocentrism claims that nature has instrumental value and objective intrinsic value independent to human value. According to Hans Jonas (1974a, p. 10), 'it would mean to seek not only human good but also the good of things extra-human, that is, to extend the recognition of "ends in themselves" beyond the sphere of man'. Anthropocentrism, instead, considers nature as instrumental value and as subjective intrinsic value dependent on human value.[3] As regards justice, instead, we particularly highlight that, in general, justice expresses an idea of interaction, and the pursuit of justice limits the pursuit of welfare. According to Gauthier (1993, pp. 198–206), justice is an entity existing independently of specific actions and things, and just social relationships relate persons as ends in themselves. Justice has not only an instrumental value, for in general:

> [I]ndividuals can flourish, can realize their goals whatever those goals may be, only in association with their fellows. A characteristic, such as the sense of justice, that fits them for such association, is then of value whatever their particular aims and concerns. And it is because justice is of value in this way that it is a genuine moral disposition . . . .

A person who has justice among his/her values has 'a concern or a range of concerns directed at the distribution of benefits and costs viewed as requirement for and products of social interaction'. With reference to sustainable development, justice can thus be intended as a moral disposition of a person towards not only the other persons of the same generation but also towards all the generations of the infinite future. Every person of the present generation who has justice in his/her total conception of good has to prevent future generations from being worse off than the present generation.

Because it is not possible to choose rationally between these different philosophical points of view, the concept of sustainability cannot specify to which of them we have to refer. In environmental economic literature, therefore, sustainability is considered in both a strong and a weak sense, and the focus is mainly on the different ethical points of view about the values on which sustainability is based and the different ways of considering the capital stock. When nature and intergenerational justice are recognized only as anthropocentric instrumental values, and natural capital and human-made capital are supposed to be substitutable, we speak of weak sustainability and its aim is non-decreasing total capital stock from one generation to the next; when nature and intergenerational justice are also considered as intrinsic values, and at least a part of the natural capital is considered unsubstitutable or critical, we speak of strong sustainability whose aim is non-decreasing critical natural capital stock (Turner 1999).

The responsibility principle

'Why is the distant future of mankind and the planet important?' (Vogel 1955). This question raises the issue as to whether or not a good end justifies a bad means.

In fact, given a future result (the end of nature and intergenerational justice) which is considered good, there is the immediate result (the means) to pay for the maintenance of the life-support system, which can be considered bad. Following Karl Popper (1952, vol. I, pp. 286–7), we have to consider three different questions about this: (i) Can we be really confident about the assumed causal connection between means and ends? (ii) Supposing that we are reasonably certain of the causal relation, should the present generation be condemned to suffer for the advantage of the future generations and non-human things? (iii) Is the final result (the end) more important than the intermediate result (the means)? Since there will always be doubtful cases, Popper claimed that recourse to critical discussion is justified.

It is not our task to enter into this philosophical debate, but I am struck by the thought of Hans Jonas who replies to these questions by referring to the responsibility principle, and justifies and develops the idea that humanity needs a new ethics which takes into account that the modern technological revolution has changed the nature of human action. The dominant scientific view of nature in the modern era (mechanistic materialism) considers nature only as matter in motion. Nature has no ends; only human beings are the source of all value in nature:

> [In traditional ethics] the ethical universe is composed of contemporaries . . . No one was held responsible for the unintended later effects of his well-intentioned, well-considered and well-performed act. The 'neighbour' ethics – of justice, charity, honesty, and so on – still hold . . . for the nearest, day by day sphere of human interaction.
>
> [Instead] the critical vulnerability of nature to man's technological intervention [is showing] that a new object – no less than the whole biosphere of the planet – has been added to what we must be responsible for because of our power over it. . . . Nature as a human responsibility[4] is surely a novum to be pondered in ethical theory. (Jonas 1974a, pp. 7–10)

Jonas seems to go beyond the distinction between anthropocentrism and non-anthropocentrism, because he recognizes that nature commands the reverence of humanity, but humans have special dignity as moral agents, since they are in sympathy with ends beyond their own essential ones (Vogel 1995).

The responsibility principle, thus, binding humanity to pursue a sustainable development, should be considered a constituent of the economic sphere in the same way as (by general admission) 'self-interest' or 'need' (Jonas 1974b, p. 93).[5] The exercise of responsibility about other human beings, through the care of parents for children, and non-human objects perpetuates the capacity for responsibility; therefore nature and intergenerational justice constitute nothing but perpetual values always stated by the wisdom of ancients. In particular, in the last decades, the application of the contingent valuation method for valuing environmental public goods such as forests and beaches has given support to the belief that important motives of willingness to pay for their conservation are their existence and bequest values (Loomis et al. 1993). In other words, a non-negligible part of agents are willing to sacrifice a part of their own happiness for the conservation of environmental goods just because they exist and for the happiness of the future generations.

3.   Welfare theories compared with sustainability: weak and strong sustainability
In spite of the different philosophical views about the relation between human beings and nature, the awareness of the need to preserve and improve the environment is unanimous. Therefore, in describing and comparing the different economic welfare theories, I shall also refer to their practical capability to pursue sustainability. In social science, in fact, where organic relations exist, a theory must satisfy conditions not only of consistency but also of realism, and the criterion of choice between alternative theories ought to be their comparative usefulness in relation to the specific problem considered (see, for example, Meek 1964; Myrdal 1969).

Utilitarianism and the neo-Humean view: two ethics of motive
From the considerations made above, it is clear that welfare theories exclusively based on individualism are in difficulty in the light of sustainable development: people do not always act following their own self-interest.

Traditional utilitarianism   This view greatly simplifies ethics and moral decisions, because it considers only one kind of thing as good. It identifies happiness with pleasure (a natural quality), and pleasure is the only *summum bonum*, the fundamental motive of human conduct. Because welfare is considered in terms of pleasure alone, things such as freedom, truth, justice and nature are only means to reach the greatest happiness. In particular, according to Bentham (1948, pp. 151–4), the value of any pleasure and pain is measurable, and morality claims the maximization of welfare intended as the exact balance between pleasure and pain with respect to the total number of individuals in a community. In addition, this calculus considers statistical probability. Utilitarianism is based on the atomism hypothesis – methodological individualism in human sciences – and an aggregative conception of interpersonal impartiality (agent neutrality). Because it is not rational to prefer the happiness of one person to that of another, the sole rational object of conduct is the greatest pleasure of the greatest number, without regard to its distribution. The moral importance is attributed to the pleasure alone, and not to whoever has pleasure (Brink 1993, p. 253). This interpretation of the egalitarian principle is considered to be an important reason for utilitarianism's appeal.

This doctrine has been subjected to much criticism. For the purpose of this work we highlight that the simplification of a sole kind of good is not corroborated by the facts of experience; pleasure cannot be considered the sole good. Below it is shown that Harsanyi's rule utilitarianism, as a modern version of utilitarianism, maintains cardinal measurability but does not identify utility only with pleasure. Second, the fact that utilitarianism avoids considering an important moral phenomenon such as distributive justice, and also intergenerational justice, could suggest following an action which impoverishes future generations, if it maximizes the social utility of the present generation. In particular, Rawls (1971, pp. 3–9, 266) rejects the utility maximization principle as theory of justice and, inspired by Kantian moral thought, establishes a different theory of justice based on two principles that govern society:

> 1) Each person is to have an equal right to the most extensive total system of equal basic liberties compatible with a similar system of liberty for all; 2) social and economic inequalities are to be arranged so that they are both a) to the greatest benefit of the least advantaged, consistent with the just savings principle, and b) attached to offices and positions open to all under conditions of fair equality of opportunity.

As regards justice between generations, Rawls specifically claims that the maximum level of expectations of those with least advantages (the max–min criterion) is connected with the sharing of the burden of capital accumulation between generations. Amongst sustainable growth models, the Hartwick-Solow rule is based on this view.

The Humean view   In this view, instead, no single *summum bonum* emerges, but qualities are approved or preferred for their utility. More specifically, according to Hume, the fact of considering that a thing is good means that people approve or prefer or desire it. Feeling and reason are equally involved in morals: feeling is the fundamental motive of conduct; reason is an instrument in the service of our feeling of preference. This conception of rationality is at the basis of the new welfare economics. Welfare is built on an idea of impartiality to the ends: morality requires every one of us to be impartial to the ends of one person over another, and to maximize welfare by pursuing autonomous projects. The NWE admits the Pareto interpretation of efficiency which affirms that a situation is Pareto optimum if no consumer can be made better off without making another consumer worse off.[6] However a Pareto non-optimal situation can be considered optimal if the distributional constraint that a sacrifice (measured in terms of utility) requires a compensation (*SRC*), at least potentially, is satisfied[7] (Brink 1993, pp. 252–8). Therefore, uncompensated sacrifices are morally unacceptable. So a distribution is morally acceptable only if it does not impose an uncompensated or a net loss of welfare to one person in order to provide benefits to others.

The so-called Pareto sustainability is based on the Pareto interpretation of efficiency. It is claimed to characterize the so-called 'very weak' sustainability when social losses are only potentially compensated, and 'weak' sustainability when social losses are instead really compensated (Turner et al. 1994; Munda 1996). Nevertheless, from a philosophical point of view, Pareto sustainability is not adequate to pursue a sustainable development because of the SRC distributional constraint. The Pareto interpretation of SRC constraint not only raises the issue of compensating future generations, if actions of the present generation impose losses on the future generations, but it also raises the issue of compensating the losses of the present generation when their behaviour favours the future generations. About this last issue, for example, Derek Parfit (1982) presents the 'non-identity problem',[8] which we consider in the version given by Temkin (1993, pp. 294–5):

> Let A represent a generation contemplating two policies. On the live-for-today policy, they have children immediately, and deplete the natural resources for current uses. B would result: they would be better off, but their children would fare less well. On the take-care-of-tomorrow policy, they postpone having children a few years, and conserve their resources. C would result; they would fare slightly less well than they do now, but the children they have would fare as well as they.

The take-care-of-tomorrow policy satisfies intergenerational justice, but it is incompatible with the Pareto criterion of efficiency. 'If the take-care-of-tomorrow policy is adopted there will be someone for whom it is worse, namely the parents.' In this case nobody can compensate the present generation, and the SRC principle cannot be respected. As regards the compensation of the future generations, some authors include in the sustainable growth model 'faith' in technological progress: future generations will be compensated by financing new research in technology for substituting the natural capital depleted today with new human-made capital stock (Gutés 1996; Victor 1991). Nevertheless, the 'neoclassical economist' has still left open the philosopher's issue of the present generation compensation.

Rule utilitarianism   According to this view, nature and intergenerational justice, considered only as means, could be included in the moral code that maximizes social utility, if they satisfy the individual preferences of all utilitarian individuals.

Rule utilitarianism combines Benthamism with the Humean view of preferences. A moral value judgement is a judgement of preference, intended in the narrow sense of want and taste, and the consequences of a moral act are computable in all situations because not only probability but also preferences are supposed to be cardinally measurable and comparable. 'The ultimate logical basis for interpersonal utility comparisons lies in the postulate that the preferences and utility functions of all human individuals are governed by the same basic psychological laws' (Harsanyi 1976, p. 50). In particular, from a formal point of view, Harsanyi's rule utilitarianism is a theory of the social welfare, built on Bayesian rationality postulates together with an individualism axiom and a symmetry axiom (which assigns the same weight to each of the different agents' utility functions). Every agent expresses his/her own preferences not only in his/her personal utility function (personal preferences), but also in his/her social welfare function (moral preferences). In this way social good is dependent on individual preferences. In particular, moral preferences are intended as the hypothetical preferences that each agent 'would entertain if he forced himself to judge the world . . . from an impersonal and impartial point of view' (ibid., p. ix).[9] On the assumption that each agent assigns the same strategy to every utilitarian agent, rule utilitarianism asks all utilitarian agents together to choose that social system, or moral code, which maximizes the expected social utility, always intended as the sum of the individual utilities, or which yields the higher average utility level to the individual members of society (ibid., p. 45).

More specifically, a moral action is chosen in two steps. First, all the utilitarian agents choose the moral rule or code which maximizes the expected social utility out of the set of all possible moral rules, where the act utilitarian moral code is a special case;[10] in this step the ultimate criterion of morality is the consequentialist criterion of social welfare maximization. Second, each agent chooses a personal act consistent with the socially optimal code, but it is admitted that a code may evaluate individual acts by a non-consequentialist criterion, 'if such a moral code is judged to yield higher social utility' (Harsanyi 1986, p. 59). The social role of a moral code is 'to enjoin people to do certain things and not to do some other things'; therefore individual rights and special obligations are established without requiring the respect of the SRC principle. In particular, a moral code can satisfy the demand of justice (Harsanyi 1976, p. 74) and also of intergenerational justice. In this way, rule utilitarianism is compatible with the concept of sustainable development, but only in the weak sense.

Even if this doctrine is built with great care for logical coherence, it cannot be considered a general theory of welfare because, admitting preferences only in the narrow sense of want, it does not recognize intrinsic values which instead are admitted about nature. Like the NWE, therefore, rule utilitarianism does not escape the more general criticism regarding welfare as preference satisfaction, and Harsanyi's optimal moral code cannot be considered the sole dominant criterion of choice.[11] In addition, with regard to practical applicability, Harsanyi (1953, 1976; 1986, p. 60) himself highlights that 'rule utilitarianism . . . is not a criterion always easy to apply in practice', because in the real world value judgements concerning social welfare are not of the moral preference kind: an agent in practice is unlikely to choose a particular action in complete ignorance of his personal position. Harsanyi (1976, pp. 82–3) also seems aware that a part of John Maynard Keynes's criticism to traditional utilitarianism is valid also for his theory: 'it deals with the present without any consideration for the fact that agents know very little about the future; so it is very difficult to make predictions about future facts (Keynes, CW IX, p. 284).[12] In many statistical problems, in fact, 'the existence of an a priori distribution cannot be postulated, and, in those cases where the existence of an a priori distribution can be assumed, it is usually unknown to the experimenter and therefore Bayes' solution cannot be determined' (Wald 1950, p. 16). In these situations of limited rationality it is rational to act with criteria different from that of maximization of the expected utility function. Environmental economists seem not to use game theory models in order to represent the intergenerational dynamic of a sustainable economic system, perhaps because intergenerational interaction is difficult to organize. Nevertheless, Harsanyi's idea of moral preferences has inspired the ethical social choice theory, where ethical preferences are included in sustainable development models as moral duties (Asheim, 1996, p. 56).

John Maynard Keynes's view of moral value
Keynes is not taken in by the fallacy about preferences. He has very deep philosophical foundations and he believes in the impossibility of arriving at a satisfactory theory of economic welfare by combining preference with an atomistic hypothesis, and admitting Bayes's rationality. The ethical theory of the mathematical expectation makes two assumptions that Keynes does not share: 'first, that degrees of goodness are numerically measurable and arithmetically additive, and second, that degrees of probability also are numerically measurable' (CW VIII, p. 343). About the consequences of a rational act, in fact, an important Keynesian conclusion is that 'the doctrine that the "mathematical expectations" of alternative courses of action are the proper measures of our degrees of preference is open to

doubt' (CW VIII, p. 344). This belief is justified by two reasons: Keynes does not share the utilitarian and the Humean view of happiness because he adheres to the idealism of Moore, and he has a logical conception of probability. With regard to moral values, Keynes (1904a, 1905, 1971–89) is aware of the need to specify what things are good. He does not consider economic science as a natural science, but a moral science because it deals with 'introspection and with values' (Keynes, CW XIV, p. 300); therefore economists are to be involved in the question about the nature of goods.[13] Keynes shares Moore's idealism, according to which two theorems define the nature of the ideal intended as ultimate good.[14] (i) good is an objective reality which can be perceived by intuition (Moore's first theorem); and (ii) its value as a whole 'must not be assumed to be the same as the sum of the values of its parts' (Moore's second theorem) because an organic relation between part and whole is admitted (Moore 1959, pp. 27–8). Moore's idealism is a pluralistic view of good, an ethics of ends. For knowledge, beauty, love, justice and nature can also have intrinsic value; they are not only good as means (ibid., p. 63 and chap. VI).[15] In particular, admitting organic relations, Keynes admits also that quantities of goodness are not always subject to the laws of arithmetic (CW VIII, p. 344):

> The atomic hypothesis which has worked so splendidly in physics breaks down in psychics. We are faced . . . with the problems of organic unity, of discreteness, of discontinuity – the whole is not equal to the sum of the parts, comparisons of quantity fail us, small changes produce large effects, the assumptions of a uniform and homogeneous continuum are not satisfied. (CW X, p. 262)

With regard to probability, in 1921 Keynes published his *Treatise on Probability* in which he expresses his doctrine of rational intuition and his theory of logical or inductive probability. Here our aim is not to present Keynes's theory of probability, though it does play a very important role in Keynes's thought about rational economic conduct. We highlight only that Keynes's probability is not a degree of belief in the same sense of Ramsey's probability (later developed by De Finetti 1938, and Savage 1954), because it is established objectively in the sense that every agent in the same circumstances establishes the same probability. Keynes searches for rational objective principles to justify inductive judgements, because science needs a concept of probability that is not merely dependent on a valuation which may be different from subject to subject.[16] He deals with 'probability in its widest sense' and does not 'adopt a definition of probability which presupposes its numerical mensurability' (CW VIII, pp. 36–7): given our knowledge, probability is a degree of rational belief in a proposition, perceived by intuition. As knowledge changes, probability also changes relatively to this new knowledge (CW VIII, pp. 9–37) and, as experience shows, sometimes this intuitive judgement is represented by a number, sometimes not, because 'our knowledge of the future is fluctuating, vague and uncertain' (CW XIV, p. 113). Therefore, not all probabilities are measurable and comparable. In addition, when knowledge is scarce for logical intuition, probability exists but is unknown.

Because of these reasons, in rational conduct affecting the future, the basis for computing a mathematical expectation does not always exist. Keynes discards 'the calculus and the mensuration and the duty to know exactly what one means and feels' (CW X, p. 442) and he admits the resorting to intuition when we cannot apply the maximization principle. 'If, therefore, the question of a right action is under all circumstances a determinate problem, it must be in virtue of an intuitive judgment directed to the situation as a whole, and not in virtue of an arithmetical deduction derived from a series of separate judgments directed to the individual alternatives each treated in isolation'. More specifically, mathematical expectation theory first 'ignores . . . the "weight" of the arguments, which is defined as the amount of evidence upon which each probability is founded'. The problem is posed in the following way: 'if two probabilities are equal in degree, ought we, in choosing our course of action, to prefer that one which is based on a greater body of knowledge?' (CW VIII, p. 345). Keynes's reply is affirmative, because expectations are a function of the state of confidence, which is in turn a function of uncertainty, and uncertainty depends on 'weight'. Second, mathematical expectation ignores the element of risk. In particular, the question is: 'is it certain that a larger good, which is extremely improbable, is precisely equivalent ethically to a smaller good which is proportionately more probable? We may doubt whether the moral value of speculative and cautious actions respectively can be weighted against one another in a simple arithmetical way' (CW VIII, p. 347). Therefore Keynes claims: 'If one good is greater than another, but the probability of attaining the first less than of attaining the second, the question of which it is our duty to pursue may be indeterminate, unless we suppose it to be within our power to make direct quantitative judgments of probability and goodness jointly' (CW VIII, p. 345).

Keynes's macroeconomics: Sacrifice does not require compensation   Moore's idealism, intuition and organicism in Keynes's thought justify the building of a completely new welfare economic theory: Keynes's macroeconomics.

In Keynes's macroeconomics the principle of organic unities plays a very important role. From the awareness that the structure of ethical action is organic, it follows that the structure of social and economic action also has an organic component. The relevance of this conviction is also highlighted by Popper (1957 [1985, p. 30]), who claims that a social group is something more than the simple total sum of its members, and it is also something more than the simple total sum of the purely personal relations existing between the single members at some given time. In *Miscellanea Ethica* (1905, pp. 20–21), Keynes had already included utility among those things to which the principle of organic unities is applicable, clearly highlighting that this leads to difficulties in traditional economics.[17] The macroeconomic level cannot be reduced to the microeconomic one, just because the whole is not equal to the sum of its parts;[18] therefore, if we want to control the economic system, we must also study the laws that govern the behaviour of the economic system as a whole. Specifically these laws are not totally atomistic laws, but psychological laws with an organic component. In addition, organicity justifies situations of real uncertainty, and for this reason Keynes admitted even before Tinbergen (1952) and Simon (1955) the existence of situations of limited rationality (Marzetti 1999): the Keynesian economic agents are not always well informed, and in spite of this they have to act rationally.

The belief that economics is a moral science goes well beyond the admission that interpersonal comparisons are unavoidable. There is the need to give a reply to the following question: if the duty to behave right conflicts with personal interest, has this to be sacrificed? The question is very important and is about the possibility, admitted by Moore, that private advantage and social good may be in conflict. The objective nature of the ideal justifies the fact that private interest, according to the situation, can be sacrificed to pursue social good (Keynes, CW IX, p. 295; CW XXI, p. 375).

Specifically Keynes is sensitive to a particular form of justice: distributive or social justice. Justice needs the discipline of wants, and he is worried about the cost of *laissez-faire*. This view about the relation between private interest and social good, admitting situations in which someone has to sacrifice himself in order that others may benefit for social purposes without any compensation, not only denies the utilitarian harmony between private good and social good and the fact that no kind of loss is intrinsically more significant than another, but it also conflicts with the Paretian criterion which is valid only if, because of a change, nobody suffers a loss. In this way a personal sacrifice may be moralized by pursuing a social good.

Because Keynes 'prefers the good to the useful', in his macroeconomic theory he does not mention welfare in terms of maximum social utility. According to Keynes, a logical nexus between economic welfare and ultimate good does not exist; just as it does not exist between private interest and social good. The nexus is imprecise, for the passage from economic welfare to ultimate good is an art, the art of life, which not all people know. Material welfare is only an intermediate good, a means of facilitating the reaching of ultimate happiness (Marzetti 1999, 165–8). More specifically, Keynes's macroeconomics is a theory of economic welfare in which maximization rationality has been substituted by intermediate objectives like full employment, monetary stability, and redistribution of wealth and income. Their achievement is the right solution for economic problems, and Keynes's macroeconomics is connected with the general theory of the ultimate good because intermediate objectives are fit objects to favour its pursuit (Keynes 1905, p. 5). In other words, the actual achievement of the greatest happiness does not belong to the realm of formal theory: ethical rationality indicates the way and the measure to use the possibilities offered by economic welfare to reach the greatest good (Marzetti 1999). We call Keynes's sacrifice of the economic welfare function the Keynesian simplification about welfare; it avoids not only all the difficulties which can arise when a theory makes reference to the concept of preference, but also the duty to calculate exactly the consequences of a moral action.

For these reasons Keynes attributes the task of achieving the intermediate moral goals to the state: 'when great decisions are to be made, the State is a sovereign body of which the purpose is to promote the greatest good of the whole'(CW IV, p. 56).[19]

Policy makers, given uncertainty about future consequences, can act according to an intuitive judgement on the specific situation considered as a whole.[20] The resort to intuition, as an original and independent source of knowledge, is justified when it is not possible to obtain knowledge from other sources, like inference and observation; therefore it is considered 'a reason for holding' that any choice is correct (Moore 1959, p. 144).

In this theoretical context, given the practical situation at Keynes's time, his prime concern was for the ultimate good of contemporaries and he mainly suggested short-term economic policy.[21] Nevertheless his awareness of the link between the economic future and the present, and of the need to pursue intergenerational justice as well is expressed about the intermediate objective of employment. Even if a present full employment is secured, 'it would remain for separate decision on what scale and by what means it is right and reasonable to call on the living generation to restrict their consumption, so as to establish in course of time, a state of full investment for their successors' (Keynes, CW VII, p. 377). In this way, Keynes admits that painful choices must be made, and therefore sustainable development must rest on political will.

Strong sustainability and sustainable economic welfare   The spirit of Keynesian thought seems present in the *Report of Human Development* (UNDP 1992, pp. 11–22), in which we read that:

> social orders have to be judged according to the extent to which they promote
> human good; income and wealth should not have intrinsic value, but should be

considered means to achieve ultimate objectives, because welfare depends on the usage that a society makes of them and not on their level; nobody can guarantee happiness to a person and his choices are a personal issue, but a development process should, at least, create the individual and collective conditions by which he is able to lead a productive and a creative life according to his needs and interests; economic policy has the difficult and weighty task of favouring the process by which economic growth turns into human development; the way in which economic growth is administrated is important; and a well organised public expenditure and a distributive policy of income are adequate means to favour human development.

In modern terms, Keynes had already distinguished between economic growth and human development and he was concerned with the latter (Marzetti 1999, p. 175). More specifically, in Keynes's view of economic science as moral science, nature and intergenerational justice, in particular non-anthropocentric intrinsic values and non-human rights, can be taken as *summa bona* that government has to promote. Since the principle of organic unity can also be valid through time, goodness, supposed to be organic, can be 'composed of simultaneous or successive parts' (Keynes, CW VIII, pp. 342–3); therefore, considering sustainability, perpetual moral values can be thought of as an organic whole between generations. Admitting intrinsic values as well, Keynes's view of welfare is compatible with strong sustainable development which requires that intrinsic values ascribed to nature have to be considered when a decision about management is to be made. Keynes's view of moral value, just because it does not exclude intrinsic values, can be considered a general theory of welfare. Traditional utilitarianism, the NWE and rule utilitarianism, instead, seem to be special cases of the Keynesian view of welfare: every one of them excludes some kind of moral value. The Keynesian view of moral value is shared by a number of environmental economists and ecologists who invoke the recognition of intrinsic value for the preservation of nature. For example, Kerry Turner (1999, pp. 33–4) claims:

> [B]ecause the range of secondary values (use and non-use) that can instrumentally derive from an ecosystem is contingent on the prior existence of such a healthy and evolving system, there is in a philosophical sense a 'prior value' that could be ascribed to the system itself. Such a value would, however, not be measurable in conventional economic terms and is non-commensurate with the economic (secondary) values of the system. The continued functioning of a healthy ecosystem is more than the sum of its individual components.

For this reason the health of the ecosystem can be taken as an 'intuitive guide' for sustainable policies.

In the new technological dimension of action, in pursuing sustainable development, we need to be guided by an adequate economic welfare theory which recognizes as actors not only present generations but also future generations and non-human things. Keynes's macroeconomics is conceived with the specific aim of being useful for the solution of practical problems, but to pursue a sustainable development requires adaptation. As Daly (1991, pp. 256–7) claims, in Keynesian macroeconomics the goal of the 'optimal scale of the whole economy relative to the ecosystem' can be introduced and the economic system can be represented as an 'open subsystem of the finite natural ecosystem'. In particular, government's economic policies should not be based on GNP but on sustainable economic welfare.[22] In addition, technology today has also changed the state of knowledge about the future; this is certainly incomplete, but certainly superior to every previous knowledge (Jonas 1973). This superior knowledge together with the responsibility for nature and, therefore, the fear of dramatic future consequences should be a valid justification, on one hand, for renouncing profitable but environmentally damaging short-term economic policies and, on the other, for trying to adopt those long-term economic policies that a sustainable development requires, such as, for example, the safe minimum standards (a habitat is conserved unless the social cost is unacceptably high) and the precautionary principle (future generations have to inherit no less than the present level of biodiversity (Turner 1999)).

4.   Final considerations

We have shown that, from the moral value point of view, traditional utilitarianism considers nature only as instrumental to happiness, and it avoids considering distributive justice; therefore it is not consistent with sustainability. Pareto sustainability, instead, seems not completely adequate to pursue a weak sustainable development, because excluding any view that recognizes duties of mutual aid in which benefactors are totally or in part uncompensated, also excludes that the sacrifice of the present generation is uncompensated. Rule utilitarianism, instead, admits that nature and intergenerational justice can take part of the moral code that maximizes social utility, without any reference to the compensation principle, but does not admit intrinsic values; therefore this doctrine is adequate to pursue a weak sustainable development. Keynes's view of moral value, instead, admits all the possible situations: it recognizes intrinsic values and, believing that private interest and public good may compete, admits uncompensated sacrifice. Therefore it is the only view of happiness consistent with strong sustainability among those we have considered.

Economists, today, mainly claim that an action to conserve or deplete the natural environment is economically rational if benefit is higher than cost. Some of them have introduced in the theory of optimal growth sustainability as a binding constraint, such as non-declining consumption or utility path; some others have used growth models in order to compute an environmental life-support multiplier (Kaufmann 1995). Nevertheless, when economists pass from the theoretical model to the practical experience, the complexity of the relations between human beings and nature, and also human concern for the destiny of future generations cannot be represented only by a certain number of axioms introduced in the maximization model (Pezzey 1997).

Sustainability, therefore, claims that our philosophy of economic life is modified. In a cosmopolitan perspective, poverty in developing countries must still be reduced and the standard of living of their population must still be improved to reach that level of 'decent consumption' for every person which also permits energies to be occupied in the non-economic interests of life (Keynes, CW XXI, p. 393). Nevertheless the economic growth should be defined in terms of sustainable development. This requires the recognition not only of environmental intrinsic values and of the impossibility of fully substituting human-made capital for the life-support system, but also of what we call the paradox of sustainability: individuals ought to sacrifice themselves today in order to be happy in the future, to allow future generations to be happy and also to preserve non-human things; therefore sacrifice is good.

Notes

1. The term 'classical' theory is used not only in the sense of J.M. Keynes, that is, of the English traditional economic theory, which also includes the neoclassical theory, but in a wider sense because rule utilitarianism is also included.
2. Social issues are important to establish what is to be sustained, in what way and for how long, who are the beneficiaries from what is being sustained and in what measure, and when we have to change our unsustainable behaviour (Munasinghe and Shearer 1995, pp. xvii–xx).
3. As regards the different main currents of thought about environmental ethics see, for example, Hargrove (1992) and Bartolomei (1989).
4. Responsibility means the possibility of foreseeing the consequences of an action and correcting the action itself according to the prediction. Therefore responsibility is based on the notion of choice and on limited freedom.
5. Economics is thus considered an art 'designed precisely and basically to subserve these two basic drives: hunger and reproductive love' (Jonas 1974b, p. 93).
6. Hicks (1939, pp. 700–701) highlights: 'movements, which make some people better off and some people worse off, cannot be reckoned as involving an increase in "social satisfaction" . . . But movements, which benefit some people without damaging others . . . represent an increase in economic welfare – or better, an increase in the efficiency of the system as a means of satisfying wants, that is to say, in the efficiency of the system *tout court*'.
7. The SRC constraint is justified by the hypothesis of *separateness of persons*, which is satisfied by Pareto-superior or Pareto-indifferent outcomes. An alternative B is Pareto superior to another A, if at least one person is better off in B than in A and no one is better off in A. A and B are Pareto indifferent if no one is better off in A than in B and vice versa. The separateness of persons hypothesis is an objection to the person-neutrality characteristic of utilitarianism.

8. The 'non-identity problem' about future generations arises because it is not clear to whom the rights must be attributed. Future generations, in fact, could not exist; they are only *possible* individuals.

9. This hypothesis of *impersonality* and *impartiality* satisfies the need to introduce in the model some form of objectivity, and is based on the principle 'Treat other people in the same way as you want to be treated yourself' (Harsanyi 1958, pp. 311–13).

10. Harsanyi (1955, 1977, 1986) was inspired by R. Harrod (1936) and R.B. Brandt (1959). Harrod conceived the idea on which rule utilitarianism is based, and Brandt distinguished between act utilitarianism and rule utilitarianism. Harsanyi represents them mathematically by the games theory: when the fundamental motive of conduct is supposed to be preference and not pleasure, traditional utilitarianism is intended as *act utilitarianism*. Society thus takes the form of a non-cooperative game: each agent acts independently, but all agents have the common objective of reaching the greatest expected social utility intended as the *sum* of the *n* individual utilities or their arithmetical mean. According to rule utilitarianism, instead, the society can be represented by a cooperative game requiring full *commitment* by the agents to a moral code and by prohibiting any deviation from it. It provides a full solution, for it simultaneously determines all the *n* strategies of the utilitarian agents.

11. In particular, Amartya Sen (1973) suggests considering not only the mean utility value to the individual members of the society but also a measure of inequality among the different utility levels of agents.

12. On this topic, see also Binmore (1989).

13. Regarding the method, economic science is considered a branch of logic, and logic is intended in the broad sense of science of thought (CW VIII, p. 3). Specifically Keynes (CW XIV, pp. 296–7) considers economics 'a science of thinking in terms of models joined to the art of choosing models which are relevant to the contemporary world'. But choosing good models requires 'a vigilant observation of the actual working of the [economic] system'.

14. The first authoritative exponents of idealism were Plato and Aristotle.

15. Regarding what is good conduct, Moore, instead, accepts the maximization criterion and also the Benthamite calculus: an action is right if it produces the greatest possible *amount of good* in the Universe. This theory of conduct is therefore called 'ideal utilitarianism'.

16. In other words, Keynesian probability is concerned with 'objective relations between propositions' (Keynes, CW X, p. 339). One of the main criticisms of Keynesian probability comes from Ramsey, who takes from Keynes the idea of degree of belief, but denies that there is evidence for the ability of intuition to establish objective degrees of belief. Nevertheless, in 'Ramsey as a Philosopher' (CW X, pp. 338–9) Keynes claims: 'Ramsey argues, as against the view which I had put forward, that probability is concerned not with objective relations between propositions but (in some sense) with degrees of belief, and he succeeds in showing that the calculus of probability simply amounts to a set of rules for ensuring that the system of degrees of belief which we hold shall be a *consistent* system. Thus the calculus of probabilities belongs to formal logic. But the basis of our degrees of belief – or the *a priori* probabilities . . . – is part of human outfit, perhaps given us merely by natural selection, analogous to our memories rather than to formal logic. So far I yield to Ramsey – I think he is right. But in attempting to distinguish "rational" degrees of belief from belief in general he was not yet, I think, quite successful. It is not getting to the bottom of the principle of induction merely to say that it is a useful mental habit'. In other words, Keynes believes that induction belongs to the realm of logic and that it would be too subjective to consider induction as only a useful mental habit.

17. If laws can be atomic or organic, and if the inductive method is useless in organic situations and prediction impossible, we cannot be surprised that Keynes, passing from epistemological study to moral and specifically economic study, considers the inductive method – inference from past particulars to future generalizations – partially useless for economic science (Pasquinelli and Marzetti 1994).

18. This is one reason why the attempts to establish the microfoundations of Keynes's macroeconomics are doubtful. See, for example, Janssen (1993).
19. Edmund Burke provides Keynes with a logically consistent political philosophy to justify the intervention of the state as a means to promote the greatest good of the community (Keynes 1904b).
20. The task attributed to the state is very complex. Keynes (CW IX, p. 311; XIX, p. 639) claims that the political problem of mankind is to combine 'economic efficiency, social justice, and individual liberty'. We emphasize that the Keynes concept of efficiency is different from that considered by Pareto. The former is a criterion of order; for example, Keynes considers it is rational to substitute the unproductive distribution of subsidies to unemployed persons with the partially unproductive distribution of funds for public investments. Instead, as Roberto Scazzieri (1981, pp. 15–28) highlights, the latter is a criterion of classification, for it considers efficient only that productive system which satisfies some specific conditions.
21. The distinction between short and long periods is very important to Keynes. He shares Burke's and Moore's belief that the limits of knowledge permit the choice of only the best alternative in the immediate future, and therefore shares Burke's government precept, according to which the sacrifice of current benefits for very uncertain future benefits should generally be avoided.
22. Daly and Cobb (1989), for example, attempt to consider a compensation of the future generations' losses by building an index of sustainable economic welfare (ISEW). The compensation takes the form of an amortization of the natural capital. See also Faucheux et al. (1991). ·

Bibliography

Asheim, G.B. (1996), 'Ethical preferences in the presence of resource constraints', *Nordic Journal of Political Economy*, **23**, 55–67.
Bartolomei, S. (1989), *Etica e Ambiente.Il rapporto uomo-natura nella filosofia morale contemporanea di lingua inglese*, Guerini, Milan.
Bentham, J. (1948), *A Fragment on Government and an Introduction to the Principles of Morals and Legislation*, Basil Blackwell, Oxford.
Binmore, K.G. (1989), 'Social contract I: Harsanyi and Rawls', *Economic Journal*, **99**, 84–102.
Brandt, R.B. (1959), *Ethical Theory*, Prentice-Hall, Englewood Cliffs, NJ.
Brink, D. (1993), 'The separateness of persons, distributive norms, and moral theory', in R.G. Frey and C.W. Morris (eds), *Value, Welfare and Morality*, Cambridge University Press, Cambridge, pp. 252–89.
Daly, H.E. (1991), 'Towards an environmental macroeconomics', *Land Economics*, **67** (2), 255–9.
Daly, H.E. and J.B. Cobb jr (1989), *For the Common Good*, Beacon Press, Boston, MA.
De Finetti, B. (1938), 'Probabilisti di Cambridge', *Supplemento statistico ai nuovi problemi di politica, storia ed economia*, **4**, II, no. I, Ferrara, pp. 21–37.
Faucheux, S., E. Muir and M. O'Connor (1997), 'Neoclassical natural capital theory and "weak" indicators for sustainability', *Land Economics*, **73** (4), 528–52.
Gauthier, D. (1993), 'Value, reasons, and the sense of justice', in R.G. Frey and C.W. Morris (eds), *Value, Welfare and Morality*, Cambridge University Press, Cambridge, pp. 181–208.
Gutés, M.C. (1996), 'The concept of weak sustainability', *Ecological Economics*, **17**, 147–56.
Hargrove, C. (1992), 'Weak anthropocentric intrinsic value', *The Monist*, **75** (2), 183–207.
Harrod, R.F. (1936), 'Utilitarianism revised', *Mind*, **45**, 137–56.
Harsanyi, J.C. (1953), 'Cardinal utility in welfare economics and in the theory of risk-taking', *Journal of Political Economy*, **61**, 434–5. Reprinted in Harsanyi (1976), pp. 3–5.
Harsanyi, J.C. (1955), 'Cardinal welfare, individualistic ethics, and interpersonal comparisons of utility', *Journal of Political Economy*, **63**, 309–21.
Harsanyi, J.C. (1958), 'Ethics in terms of hypothetical imperatives', *Mind*, **15**, 289–316.

Harsanyi, J.C. (1976), *Essays on Ethics, Social Behaviour, and Scientific Explanation*, Reidel, Dordrecht.
Harsanyi, J.C. (1977), 'Rule utilitarianism and decision theory', *Erkenntnis*, **11**, 25–53.
Harsanyi, J.C. (1986), 'Utilitarian morality in a world of very half-hearted altruists', in W.P. Heller, R.M. Starr and D.A. Starrett (eds), *Social Choice and Public Decision Making*, Cambridge University Press, Cambridge, 57–73.
Hicks, R. (1939), 'Foundations of welfare economics', *Economic Journal*, **49**, 696–712.
Holdren, J.P., G.C. Daily and P.R. Ehrlich (1995), 'The meaning of sustainability. Biogeophysical aspects', in M. Munasinghe and W. Shearer (eds), *Defining and Measuring Sustainability. The Biogeophysical Foundation*, World Bank, Washington, DC, pp. 3–17.
Janssen, M.C.W. (1993), *Microfoundations. A Critical Inquiry*, Routlege, London.
Jonas, H. (1974a), 'Technology and responsibility: reflections on the new tasks of ethics', in H. Jonas (ed.), *Philosophical Essays: From Ancient Creed to Technological Man*, The University of Chicago Press, Chicago, pp. 3–20.
Jonas, H. (1974b), 'Socio-economic knowledge and ignorance of goals', in H. Jonas (ed.), *Philosophical Essays: From Ancient Creed to Technological Man*, The University of Chicago Press, Chicago, pp. 81–104.
Kaufmann, R.K. (1995), 'The economic multiplier of environmental life support: can capital substitute for a degraded environment', *Ecological Economics*, **12**, 67–79.
Keynes, J.M. (1904a), *Ethics in Relation to Conduct*, J.M. Keynes Papers, UA/19/2, King's College Library, Cambridge.
Keynes, J.M. (1904b), *The Political Doctrine of Edmund Burke*, J.M. Keynes Papers, UA/20/3, King's College Library, Cambridge.
Keynes, J.M. (1905), *Miscellanea Ethica*, J.M. Keynes Papers, UA/21, King's College Library, Cambridge.
Keynes, J.M. (1971–89), *The Collected Writing of J.M. Keynes* (CW), vols I–XXX, edited by E. Johnson and K. Moggridge, Macmillan, London.
Lamont, W.D. (1955), *The Value Judgement*, Edinburgh University Press, Alva, Scotland.
Loomis, J., M. Lockwood and T. DeLacy (1993), 'Some empirical evidence on embedding effects in contingent valuation of forest protection', *Journal of Environmental Economics and Management*, **24**, 45–55.
Marzetti, S. (1999), 'Bene morale e condotta giusta: la politica economica di J.M. Keynes', in Marzetti and R. Scazzieri (eds), *La probabilità in Keynes: Premesse e influenze*, CLUEB, Bologna, pp. 139–88.
Meek, R.L. (1964), 'Value-judgements in economics', *British Journal for the Philosophy of Science*, **15** (58), 89–96.
Moore, G.E. (1903 [1959]), *Principia Ethica*, Cambridge University Press, Cambridge.
Munasinghe, M. and W. Shearer (1995), 'An introduction to the definition and measurement of biogeophysical sustainability', in Munasinghe and Shearer (eds), *Defining and Measuring Sustainability. The Biogeophysical Foundation*, World Bank, Washington, DC, pp. xvii–xxxiii.
Munda, G. (1996), 'Cost–benefit analysis in integrated environmental assessment: some methodological issues', *Ecological Economics*, **19**, 157–68.
Myrdal, G. (1969), *Objectivity in Social Research*, Duckworth, London.
Parfit, D. (1982), 'Future generations: further problems', *Philosophy and Public Affairs*, **2**, 113–72.
Pasquinelli, A. and S. Marzetti Dall'Aste Brandolini (1994), 'Introduzione', to *Trattato sulla probabilità* (Italian translation) by J.M. Keynes, CLUEB, Bologna, pp. ix–xxvi.
Pezzey, J.C.V. (1997), 'Sustainability constraints versus "optimality" versus intertemporal concern, and axioms versus data', *Land Economics*, **73** (4), 448–66.
Popper, K.R. (1945 [1952]), *The Open Society and Its Enemies*, Routledge & Kegan Paul, London, Vols I and II.
Popper, K.R. (1957), *The Poverty of Historicism*. Italian translation: *Miseria dello storicismo*, Feltrinelli, Milan, 1985.
Rawls, J. (1971), *A Theory of Justice*, Harvard University Press, Cambridge, MA.
Russell, B. (1954), *Human Society in Ethics and Politics*, Allen & Unwin, London.
Savage, L.G. (1954), *Foundations of Statistics*, Wiley, New York.

Scazzieri, R. (1981), *Efficienza produttiva e livelli di attività*, il Mulino, Bologna.

Sen, A.K. (1973), *On Economic Inequality*, Clarendon Press, Oxford.

Simon, H.A. (1955), 'A behavioural model of rational choice', *The Quarterly Journal of Economics*, **LXIX**, 99–118.

Temkin, L. (1993), 'Harmful goods, harmless bads', in R.G. Frey and C.W. Morris (eds), *Value, Welfare and Morality*, Cambridge University Press, Cambridge, pp. 290–324.

Tinbergen, J. (1952), *On the Theory of Economic Policy*, North-Holland, Amsterdam.

Turner, R.K. (1999), 'The place of economic values in environmental valuation', in I.J. Bateman and K.G. Willis (eds), *Valuing Environmental Preferences*, Oxford University Press, Oxford, pp. 17–41.

Turner, R.K., D.W. Pearce and I. Bateman (1994), *Environmental Economics. An Elementary Introduction*, Hemel Hempstead, Harvester Wheatsheaf.

United Nations Development Programme (UNDP) (1992), *Report of Human Development 1*. *Italian translation: Rapporto sullo sviluppo umano 1. Come si definisce, come si misura*, Rosemberg & Sellier, Turin.

Victor, P.A. (1991), 'Indicators of sustainable development: some lessons from capital theory', *Ecological Economics*, **4**, 191–213.

Vogel, L. (1995), 'Does environmental ethics need a metaphysical grounding?', Hastings Center, The Hastings Center Report, Hastings on Hudson, Hastings Center, **25** (7), 30–40.

Wald, A. (1950), *Statistical Decision Functions*, J. Wiley & Sons, New York.

World Commission on Environment and Development (WCED) (1987), *Our Common Future*, Oxford University Press, Oxford.

24 Ideals, conformism and reciprocity: a model of individual choice with conformist motivations, and an application to the not-for-profit case

Lorenzo Sacconi and Gianluca Grimalda*

1. Introduction

Studies dealing with the economic and social function of the nonprofit enterprise can be traced back to two major strands of literature. The first emphasizes peculiar failures – mainly median voter and asymmetry of information – of both political and market systems in providing public or welfare goods (respectively, Weisbrod 1988; Hansmann 1980), thus arguing for the necessity of new organizational forms of production in those sectors. However, these models do not actually explain what in the peculiar institutional nature of a nonprofit should help to solve this kind of inefficiency.

The second approach does offer a 'positive' explanation for the nonprofit firm, which draws on the idea that agents involved in the nonprofit sector are ideologues – that is, they have other-regarding motivations such as altruism, are ready to conform to an established system of norms, and are disposed to reciprocate the perceived fairness of others' action (for a review, see Rose-Ackermann 1987). However, in our view this approach does not provide a sound theoretical foundation for these attitudes, which risks making the whole explanation void. Moreover, such a theory is at odds with evidence on extensive conflicts of interests that also affect the agents involved in the nonprofit activity, as highlighted by the frequent practice of self-imposing norms involving fiduciary duties and codes of conduct even in the nonprofit sector. In fact, the reality of the nonprofit sector appears much more variegated than what would result from this approach.

The model we develop in this chapter seeks to address both shortcomings that we perceive in the received theory. First, it takes on the question of individual motivations to choose, providing a general model of choice in which a variety of possibly conflicting motives to action is weighed up by an agent. In this setting, a seemingly altruistic behaviour is not a mere attitude of the individual, but is one of the possible outcomes emerging from a process of rational evaluation of different motives to action. In the application of this model to the case of the nonprofit enterprise, we shall assume that agents' preferences are represented by a comprehensive utility function, in which two basic motives to action are considered: the first is a (standard) self-interested motivation, whereas the second is a conditional willingness to conform to an ideology, with the content of a moral principle, which for brevity we call a conformist, or ideal, motive to action. Ideology is shaped as a normative criterion of evaluation for collective modes of behaviours, which provides the agents with a ranking of states of affairs based on their greater or lesser fulfilment of this normative principle. Ideology is seen as the result of a (possibly hypothetical) contract between agents involved in interaction in an *ex ante* phase. This rests on a normative principle that offers an assessment of social outcomes in an *ex post* phase, broadly described in terms of fulfilment of the principle itself; that is to say, the normative principle boils down to a social welfare function that measures the correspondence of any outcome with the normative prescriptions provided by a given ideology. Agents, therefore, use such a shared principle in order to measure their own and any other's degree of conformity with it; and we assume that one's own motivation to act in conformity with the principle increases with others' (expected) conformity. In other words, individual compliance with ideology is conditional on others' compliance with it, as perceived by the agent. This peculiar feature of reciprocity contingent over others' behaviour calls for an extension of the usual equipment of decision theory, which is provided by the theory of psychological games (Geanakoplos et al. 1989).

Second, we propose a possible way in which the model is capable of accommodating the piece of evidence mentioned above, namely the possibility of a conflict of interests within the nonprofit firm. In fact, a nonprofit firm is one of the possible outcomes in a 'game of production' where some relevant agents setting up the productive activity, ideally an entrepreneur and a worker, determine the nature of the organization through their decisions. Since the structure of interaction turns out to be that of a coordination game, then codes of ethics and self-imposed rules of conduct can be justified as devices extending the structure of the game in order to select an outcome corresponding to the nonprofit organization. Or, as we suggest for future extensions of the work, investments made to 'reveal' the 'true' type of the firm to external stakeholders, for example, donors, in a context of asymmetric information.

Overall, there are two features that are needed to turn the nature of the firm from profit to nonprofit in the production game. First, agents must attach a sufficiently high weight to the conformist motive to action in comparison with the material loss that this may bring about. Second, the ideology that agents incorporate into their system of ends is shaped as a result of a (possibly hypothetical) 'social contract' between the relevant figures participating in the venture. In particular, ideology is inclusive in that it takes into account not only the interests of agents active in the productive enterprise, but also the interests of beneficiaries and stakeholders of the good produced. This additional category is represented in the model by a third agent, the consumer, who does not have any active role in the post-constitutional phase; that is, he/she is a dummy player in the stage game of production. By conforming to the ideology, therefore, the active players are aware that they are giving 'voice' to some categories otherwise excluded from social consideration. Moreover, the ideology is assumed to consist of a fair and efficient criterion for distribution of a surplus, in accordance with the contractarian, since the interests of each participant – consumer included – are symmetrically accounted for (Brock 1979; Sacconi 1991, 2000). Given such an impartial perspective that characterizes the *ex ante* stage of agreement over the set of distributive principles, the resulting choice can also be said to embody a peculiar moral ideal. Operationally, the Nash bargaining solution is taken as the function representing this ideology. Overall, the nonprofit organizational form is seen as the result of a – possibly hypothetical – internal social contract agreed upon by the relevant figures setting up the enterprise, which assesses the interests of external stakeholders in an equitable manner. Therefore, ideology stands out as a crucial asset for the nonprofit organization.

The first part of the chapter (Sections 2 and 3) is devoted to the development of a model of individual choice. Section 2 introduces the distinction between consequentialist and conformist individual preferences. Material and ideal games are then presented as representations of the same interaction though assessed from different standpoints, which adopt the self-interested consequentialist and the conformist attitudes, respectively. Finally, a general version of the comprehensive utility function is presented. Section 3 offers a specification of the conformist motive to action, introducing a peculiar notion of reciprocity in compliance with the ideology, which is based on an extension of Rabin's model of fairness (1993).

The second part (Sections 4 and 5) aims to apply such a model of behaviour to the account of the nonprofit enterprise as a peculiar organizational form. Section 4 illustrates the setting of the 'production game', where both the active players have one action improving the quality of a good and another one that leaves it unaltered with respect to a market standard. The consumer surplus is directly linked to how many agents perform the quality-improving action. It is then shown how this stage game leads to different solutions depending on whether it is evaluated from the self-interested standpoint (material game) or from the ideal one (ideal game).

Section 5 explores a solution to the production game when the two conflicting attitudes are blended into a comprehensive utility function. We show how an equilibrium is possible that leads both active agents to perform the quality-improving solution, provided that the weight attributed to the ideological motivation is sufficiently high. However, we observe that under the same conditions there is another equilibrium in which agents perform the non-quality-improving action, besides a third equilibrium in mixed strategies. Since the structure of such a psychological game resembles that of a coordination game, we suggest that the issuing of a code of ethics by the firm may act as a cognitive device able to generate determinate expectations over the quality-improving equilibrium. We finally interpret this result as a main underpinning for the nonprofit firm. Section 6 concludes.

2. An agent's system of choice

Self-regarding and other-regarding motives to action: an overview
The idea that individuals take into account a large number of reasons to action when making decisions, which extend well beyond the stereotypical self-interested motive, is now largely accepted among rational choice theorists. As Binmore puts it (1994: 19), 'not even in Chicago are the views [that homo economicus strictly abides by his/her own self-interest] given credence any more'. This set of supplementary motivations may include altruism, the willingness to act in accordance with the received sense of morality, or the want to conform to the behaviour or the expectations of the other members of a given community. In principle, every type of motivation, even those dictated by a person's whims, or by self-destructive and anti-conformist desires, can be included in one's system of ends.

Therefore, according to this view, the range of the agent's possible motives to action is left as wide as possible. In other words, there is no constraint on the set of ends that the agent may like to pursue, but the correspondent choices need to satisfy requirements of internal consistency in order to be called rational. In particular, when a sequence of choices made under different circumstances – that is, under different values of the 'parameters' that frame the context of choice – fulfils the basic axioms of transitivity, completeness, reflexivity, and possibly some others, then internal consistency and thus rationality of the action can be said to hold. A utility function does not have any intrinsic meaning but its working as a formal device to represent such a coherent system of choice.[1] In particular, individual rationality is not assessed on the grounds of an agent's effectiveness in pursuing some notion of self-interest, but rather on the logical internal coherence of his/her choices with respect to his/her ends: even the behaviour of a saint can be assessed in terms of rationality in much the same way as that of a homo economicus.[2]

Ben Ner and Putterman (1998) provide a theoretical underpinning for such a model of individual choice, by distinguishing between self-regarding, other-regarding and process-regarding motivations. The difference between them depends on whether agents are concerned with the consequences of their action on themselves, on others, or on the way outcomes are brought out, respectively. We shall expand on this point in the next section. Another way of representing these ideas has been put forward by Copp (1997), who associates different reasons to act with different standpoints that can be adopted in assessing a particular social outcome. In particular, a self-regarding motivation stems from the adoption of a standpoint that is internal to the individual, where the standard of assessment is some form of his/her well-being. In the case of other-regarding motivations, the agent uses a perspective external to that of his/her own self. In this case, the agent may adopt the standpoint of a single agent different from him/her, which may lead to altruism, or that of the 'team' of which he/she is a part (Sugden 2000), or the point of view of an impartial observer sympathetic to each member of the group of agents (Harsanyi 1977).

Only recently have some contributions been put forward that build on this background theoretical framework to provide working models of choice. In particular, Bernheim (1994) and Sugden (1998a, 1998b) add to the self-interested motivation a second one given by the desire to obtain others' commendation and avoid their disapproval with respect to one's own actions. In these models the other-regarding motive is thus associated with the desire to live up to others' expectations, which is the reason why these approaches are generally referred to as normative expectations models (Sugden 1998a, b).

Another strand of contributions is connected with the flourishing body of literature in experimental economics, where evidence gathered in laboratory experiments on individual behaviour, somewhat unaccountable by relying only on self-interested motivations, have spurred the elaboration of new hypotheses in choice models. Fehr and Schmidt (2001) distinguish theories where agents are endowed with 'social preferences' – that is, their utility function also depends in some way on the payoff distribution among them – and theories where agents are motivated by 'intentions-based' reciprocity; that is, the individual is spurred to replicate the 'intention' perceived in others' actions.

In particular, social motives taken into account in the first approach include aversion to inequality in surplus distribution, or some form of altruism, or concern for individual position within the payoff ranking. The second approach builds on Rabin's seminal model of fairness (1993). Its main idea is that an agent may assign a different value to others' actions depending on how he/she perceives their intentions in bringing them out. For instance, an action may be deemed as kind when it brings about an extra utility with respect to what was expected in relation to some standard of behaviour, or it may be perceived as nasty when it leads to an unexpected loss. According to investigations in psychology, a key trait in human behaviour is to reciprocate the intention perceived in others' behaviour with an action of the same sign. On this view, Rabin's model is a formal device to incorporate these observations into individual choice theory.

The theory of psychological games provides us with some tools to embody these considerations into a formal analysis. In fact, it introduces beliefs, of every possible order, on each other behaviour into the utility function (Geneakoplos et al. 1989). In this fashion, it is possible to model the idea that an agent can be more or less satisfied depending on how others' actual actions correspond to his/her initial expectations. In particular, for simplicity restricting the analysis to the case of two-person interactions, Rabin considers a pair of 'kindness functions', which measure the extent to which the agent's and his/her counterpart's actions increase or diminish one another's expected payoff. This estimate is used by each agent to appraise other parties' kindness to him/herself, on the grounds of his/her second-order expectation, and the kindness of the subject towards the other agent, as perceived on the basis of his/her first-order expectation. The way in which these functions are constructed is to consider the best and the worst payoff that each agent can cause to the other on the basis of the reciprocal expectations, and then to consider how the payoff actually brought about lies between those two extremes.[3]

Other models have been developed in which agents' social preferences and intention-based reciprocity attitudes are both present in individual motivations. For instance, in Charness and Rabin (2000) the 'weight' that each individual attaches to each other individual in his/her own social preference depends on the disesteem with which the agent thinks of the others, which is appraised in terms of the 'distance' of others' behaviour from a purely disinterested one. Likewise, in Falk and Fischbacher (1999) each agent computes a 'benevolence term' for any other agent, which depends on the degree to which any other agent's action has increased or diminished inequality in the overall distribution. This term is then multiplied by a 'reciprocity term' that is positive or negative in relation to the other agent's action being perceived as kind or hostile. Finally, another parameter measures the relative weight attached to material utility with respect to that of reciprocity on the social distribution.

Our model is similar to those now illustrated in that reciprocity is related to some form of normative evaluation of the social states. However, as we shall argue in Sections 3 and 5, it differs from them in the content of the normative function.

Conformist preferences
Consequentialist preferences versus deontological reasons to prefer   In this chapter we shall embrace the view outlined in the previous subsection that the number of motivations that agents consider extends beyond the standard self-interested reasons to action. However, we believe that prior to the distinction between self-regarding and other-regarding reasons to action there exists an even deeper distinction between consequentialist and conformist types of preferences of the individual, on which our model will be grounded. Given the importance of the matter, we devote this subsection to putting forward in detail the theoretical underpinnings of this individual system of preference.

Simply stated, preferences can be said to be consequentialist when they are defined in terms of the consequences of agents' actions. Consider a situation of strategic interaction involving many agents. Each combination of individual actions generates a state of affairs that can be given a different description according to the list of characteristics taken as relevant. If these characteristics are understood as consequences, states of affairs are what happens to the decision maker in that state – that is, outcomes to the decision maker him/herself – or what happens to any subset of individuals or to every individual – that is, outcomes to anyone in the same state. In the first case, characteristics under consideration would be the attributes of a single agent – such as his/her wealth, leisure, effort and so on. In the second case, characteristics under consideration would be attributes of some set of individuals (possibly all of them). The distinction between self-regarding and other-regarding consequentialist preferences thus depends on whether the list of characteristics comprises only self-referred consequences, or also consequences to other agents. In the former case we have self-regarding consequentialist preferences. When instead the agent takes account of the consequences of social interaction on other individuals, other-regarding consequentialist preferences obtain. Note that this definition does not necessarily imply a benevolent disposition towards other people, but just that each individual's preferences are affected by the outcomes occurring to other people as well as by those occurring to him/herself.

Second type preferences are called 'personal conformist preferences' as opposed to personal consequentialist preferences. Like first type preferences, conformist preferences are defined over states of affairs, but these latter are no longer described in terms of the consequences occurring to any individual. Rather they are seen as patterns of interdependent or collective behaviours, and as beliefs about such modes of behaviour. We find a deontological element at their basis, since these preferences are grounded on intrinsic characteristics of agents' actions rather than on their extrinsic characterization – that is, their consequences or the outcomes they produce for agents. In other words, agents are motivated to act by the awareness that their pattern of actions satisfies as such some formal properties, not by some value attached to the outcomes of their actions. For instance, agents may attach value to the knowledge that a decision procedure they follow is 'fair' according to some definition, or that their acts respect 'rights' or allocate benefits according to some rule that they deem 'just' or which is simply such that they accept it as a source of obligation.[4] Again, it is possible to draw a secondary distinction between self-regarding and other-regarding conformist preference, where the former refers to the case in which the agent cares only about an intrinsic characteristic of his/her own action, whereas the latter points to the characteristics of both his/her own and the others' participants actions.

In order to better understand the distinctions between these two basic concepts of preference, the following elements are to be considered in sequence: the relevant description of states of affairs; the preference ordering over states of affairs as it depends on the relevant description of the states; the induced preferences ordering over the actions set of each individual player; and the numerical representation of such preferences by an utility index that we call ideal utility.[5]

The relevant description of states of affairs   States of affairs are now primarily described as sets of interdependent actions (vectors of acts) to which each player's beliefs about the others' actions are appended. These are considered with respect to their coherence (or lack of coherence) with a given abstract principle of justice. Under this description, states are modes of joint behaviour by the players. We can identify a pattern of behaviours (a vector of strategies) as perfectly deontological when it fully complies with an abstract principle of fairness or with a fair criterion of benefits distribution among the concerned parties. We call this state the 'ideal'. We may then look for degrees of compliance with the ideal displayed by each state of affairs resulting from individual choices actually made by all the players. We call this degree of compliance with the principle displayed by all participants in the interaction 'joint conformity', and we take it to be the basic notion of value underlying conformist preferences. In other words, we allow for the possibility that agents experience different levels of 'preference' – that is, different degrees of motivational strength – in relation to the extent to which a normative principle can be said to be fulfilled.

A point arises here which warrants some comment. The principle of justice with which agents want their actions to conform may well be a principle of distributive justice, and this will indeed be the case in our model. Therefore, outcomes have to be taken into account in order to check the extent to which the distribution of something of value to each individual is fair. However, this does not reduce the second type of preferences to the first. First-type utilities are no more than rough materials of the second type. We must know about outcomes where utilities for consequences are allocated among the players if we are to describe whether they correspond to the ideal distribution defined according to an abstract principle. A principle of fairness (that is, a given fair bargaining solution to a social contract model) accounts for each state according to a distribution criterion. This enables us to say whether the occurring vector of actions complies with the abstract principle of fairness because it determines a payoff distribution that instantiates that distributive criterion. But what matters for the relevant description of states of affairs are not consequences or material payoffs as such, but the fulfilment of a distributive property of payoffs. Under this description there is no individual to whom the relevant characteristic of the state of affairs happens as a consequence. We simply have a distribution displaying a ratio according to which a pie, which provides the largest possible amount of benefits, is partitioned among different players. For example, one player may receive, as an outcome, a very high payoff that none the less results from a very unfair distribution – which shows that what is certainly a 'wrong' under the state description we are considering may none the less be a 'good' under the state description focusing on consequences. Hence, we may say that the concern for outcomes is in this case only indirect, because it lies primarily in compliance with the ideal principle of justice rather than in the consequences that this brings about. Content and features of such a principle will be specified in more detail below and in Section 5.

Another important feature of our approach is that, despite the deontological element posited as the basis of conformism, we cannot gainsay the ultimately subjective nature of preferences for states of affairs, construing this as some sort of subjective affection of the players (Gauthier 1986); put otherwise, the reasons to act remain 'agent relative'.[6] In fact there are no grounds for concluding that the preference criterion should be based on some objective value with an ontological reality 'out there' and completely independent from the affections or the judgement of those who are asked to express their preference. Note that while conformist preferences depend on degrees of compliance – which are an objective measure of the levels of deontology built into the description of states – deontology is defined as the conformity of actions with a fair distribution principle that has simply been rationally agreed to, as will be further argued in Section 4.

To clarify matters, we summarize the hierarchy within which different components of the argument thus far should be understood. First, for each player it is taken for granted that there exists some first-order utility function defined on states initially described in terms of the consequence that each player gets from feasible benefit allocations. Second, players accept some terms of agreement concerning benefit distributions. This agreement is worked out according to a fundamentally subjective notion of unanimous rational choice under ideally symmetrical bargaining conditions. Moreover, it defines a principle for distributing benefits in any game situation of the kind under consideration. Third, this principle is adopted as the ideal term of reference in order to measure the compliance of states of affairs – described as vectors of interdependent actions – with a principle of fairness, and this introduces a deontological assessment of the states of affairs.

The result is a preference ordering defined over states of affairs which holds not merely because of primitive psychological desires for material payoffs or preferred consequences, but because it complies with a rationally agreed abstract principle. That conformist preferences are based on a principle derived in turn from a rational bargaining model (over payoff distributions) does not make the reason for preference at this second level of the argument less deontological. None the less the deontological nature of these second-order preferences does not make them dependent on values (ontologically) objective in nature or completely independent of the decision maker's affectivity or judgement. Duties are simply those that we have rationally agreed upon in a hypothetical bargaining situation.

Mutual conformity   We now give a more specific characterization to the way in which individuals attach value to conformity with an accepted moral principle: the relevant characteristics are joint conformity, conditionality and reciprocity.

First, the preference ordering of states depends ultimately on an objective measure of compliance of each vector of actions with the abstract principle of fairness as it is built into the description of each state of affairs (as seen through the players' beliefs concerning the others' actions). The less distance there is between a state of affairs and the ideal, the more this is said to fulfil the principle and thus motivates players. Therefore, joint conformity is a characteristic that we assume to be considered by players in order to say how desirable a state is. Contrary to a simplistic understanding of deontological reasoning, this means that the value underlying conformist preference is not individual compliance with a principle in isolation. We assume, on the contrary, that fulfilment of the moral principle depends on the joint pattern of actions carried out by all the agents involved in the interaction. In other words, with the principle of justice defined as a function of the actions of all the players involved, its full attainment would require their unanimous compliance. This is in fact the other-regarding characteristic of conformist preferences that we mentioned above.

Second, although the fulfilment of a principle is understood in terms of joint agents' actions, this is not to rule out that an agent may assess the degree of fulfilment from his/her own personal perspective as well – conditionally on the expected actions performed by the other agents. In other words, provided that it is possible to measure the distance between various states of affairs in terms of degrees of fulfilment of the moral principle, an individual may ask him/herself whether his/her own action helps to get closer to the ideal, given the pattern of actions of the other agents. Therefore, while we can define an absolute idea of fulfilment of the moral principle, when this is defined according to the joint set of actions performed by every agent, we are also enabled to define a conditional notion of fulfilment of the moral principle when an agent observes the degree to which his/her own action helps to improve fulfilment of the overall moral principle, conditionally on actions expected from the other players. In fact, we assume that individual conformist preferences reflect how much each individual choice by the agent helps to generate a state of affairs as near to the ideal as possible, given (an expectation over) the other players' choices. Thus conditional conformity is what is properly involved in conformist personal preferences defined on the action set of each player. This illustrates a further aspect of how deontological reasoning takes place in our model: conditional conformity clearly presupposes an 'agent-relative' point of view of the subject of preference. The agent values his/her own contribution to attainment of a state of affairs which complies as closely as possible with the principle, which can be clearly distinct from the 'neutral point of view' according to which he/she may understand the measure of joint conformity defined on states of affairs (vector of strategies).

Third, how do players come to attach value to conditional conformity? Our main assumption with regard to this aspect is that the preference for individual conditional conformity with the moral principle is mediated through a hypothesis (expectation) about the reciprocal degree of conditional conformity by other agents. That is, the conditional willingness to comply depends on the (expected) compliance of other agents with morality (given their expectations of the first player's action). We take this to be a natural feature of human nature, somehow analogous to what Robert Sugden calls the 'resentment hypothesis' (2000). In other words, we do not try to justify this aspect in terms of any other underlying aspect, as some game theorists have instead done in their attempt to account for cooperation in terms of some variant of a tit-for-tat story. More precisely, we model mutuality by assuming that the closer the (expected) compliance of other members with morality, the greater the motivational force for an agent to comply with it as well. This view then presupposes that each agent is able to form expectations concerning other agents' actions, to evaluate their degree of fulfilment of the moral principle, and then to condition his/her own conformity with morality on this degree of fulfilment. In the next section we show how these considerations can be given formal treatment using the tools of psychological game theory.

The role played by 'reciprocity in individual compliance with the prescriptions of the principle of justice' in determining the kind of preference we are defining is a strong reason for calling them conformist. In fact when a common pattern of behaviour abiding with the principle of justice has become established and is mutually expected among the players, then individual preferences, according to our view, reflect a willingness to conform with a generally accepted pattern of behaviour. Although this view applies 'in equilibrium' especially, that is, when a norm can be said to have been established, the conditional desire to conform with others' compliance with the principle of justice can be seen as a trait of agents' preferences even 'off-equilibrium', thus making the labelling appropriate. The type of conformism we are describing is none the less moral, in that the principle whose general observance triggers utility is, in our model, the result of an *ex ante* unanimous and impartial rational choice.[7]

Preference orderings and ideal utility   In the end, what really matters are each player's preferences over his/her own actions. As consequentialist preferences induce personal preferences over the actions' sets of every player, this must also be true for conformist preferences. Simply, these are induced by conformist preferences over the states described so far. If a player thinks that a strategy combination conforming to a principle of fairness is currently the most probable state of affairs, then he/she will prefer his/her action that conforms to the duty – call it the deontological action – exactly because it contributes to bring about a state of affairs conforming to the duty.

To state it more formally, agent A conformistically prefers action X_1 over action X_2 if A observes an action Y by the other player B that would bring about a state of affairs S (a strategy vector) that conforms to the principle P if chosen in response to action X_1 more than in response to action X_2.

This definition, however, hides how important beliefs are to the definition of personal conformist preferences. We must account for the fact that a player, while he/she does not observe vectors of actions as such, on the contrary holds beliefs over other players' actions and over other players' beliefs over his/her own action. Thus a player holds preferences over actions according to whether these actions, along with what he/she believes other players will do and what he/she believes other players will believe about what he/she does, contributes to bring about states of affairs that conforms to a rationally agreed principle of fairness.

To give again a formal definition, agent A conformistically prefers action X_1 over action X_2 if A believes that agent B will adopt the action Y, given that B believes that A chooses action X_1, so that by choosing action X_1 (together with act Y) agent A believes that a state of affairs S will ensue that conforms to principle P more than by choosing action X_2. This definition makes it natural to explain personal conformist preferences of agent A as resting upon a hierarchy of mutual beliefs, within which any layer of beliefs of each party is justified by a higher-order layer of beliefs.[8]

Since conformist preferences are also two-place relationships, by assuming that they satisfy the usual conditions of completeness and transitivity, we can derive a standard preference ordering over the strategy set of an agent.[9] Thus, even if conformist preferences are defined over characteristics of joint actions, rather than on their consequences, this does not prevent us from representing them by means of a utility function, which would satisfy in addition the usual axioms of expected utility. We call it individual ideal utility of actions as it is based on the agent's conformist preference ordering on actions.

In what follows, we shall provide an example of a utility function that additively compounds the self-interested consequentialist motive to act and the deontological–conformist one. The two will be associated with what we call a material and a conformist, or ideal, (source of) utility, which, under a reasonable assumption of separability, make up the individual comprehensive utility function. The existence of this pair of different attitudes calls for two different types of analysis, descending from two different concepts of solution of the same basic game situation under scrutiny. We call the first type of analysis the 'material game', in which the self-interested attitude is dominating and agents are only concerned with their material utility: this will be given a formal illustration in the next subsection. The second is the 'ideal game', where instead a deontological source of preference is the relevant one and agents are concerned with their ideal utility, as shown in the subsequent subsection. The agent's final choice will be based on how these two prompts to action are combined in a comprehensive utility function, and in particular on the weight that the agent assigns to one rather than to the other prompt to action.

Material game

It is given a game G, made up as usual by a triplet of elements: a set I of players, a set of strategies S_i and a utility function U_i for each agent. Formally, $G = \{I, S, U\}$, where $S = \underset{i \in I}{\times} S_i$ defines the set of feasible strategies profiles, and likewise U is the set of vectors of utilities. Allowing for the use of mixed strategies by the agents, we can further introduce the operator $\Delta(X)$ to express the randomizations over a set of elements X. We can thus define the set of possible randomizations over the strategy sets of the agents: $\Sigma_i := \Delta(S_i)$; finally, we can consider the vector including a randomization for each agent: $\Sigma: = \underset{i \in I}{\times} \Sigma_i$, where the generic element is indicated with $\sigma \in \Sigma$.

In the game G, utility functions represent a measure of agents' self-interest, thus reflecting the first type of motivations illustrated above. They are defined, as customary, first over the outcomes of the games – that is over the consequences to any player attached to a given way of playing the game, such that they are functions of profiles of pure strategies: $\bar{U}_i(S)$.[10] Furthermore, taking on standard assumptions regarding expected utility, we introduce Von Neumann–Morgenstern utility functions defined over mixed strategy profiles, $U_i(\Sigma)$, where $U_i(\sigma): = \Sigma_{s \in S} P_\sigma(s) \bar{U}_i(s)$. $P_\sigma(s)$ represents the probability that any pure strategy profile s is played according to the mixed strategy profile σ. Provided that the nature of this game does not differ from the standard, the relevant concept of solution would be the Nash one.

Ideal game

The ideal game differs from the previous one in that agents evaluate social situations from a different standpoint with respect to the self-interested consequentialist one, possibly including an evaluation of other agents' material payoffs who are affected by their actions but cannot affect the final outcome. Hence, we introduce an ideal game G^* as an extension of the material game G, in which the set of players is possibly larger than in the material game thus modifying the corresponding set of utilities. Formally, this game is defined by the triplet: $G^* = \{I^*, S, U^*\}$, with $I \subseteq I^*$ and $U^* = \underset{i \in I}{\times} U_i$. Note that the set of actions S is left unaltered with respect to the material game: by definition the players now included in the game are dummy players in the original one.

Resting on this construction, we can now introduce the notion of a normative principle used to appraise social state of affairs resulting from strategic interaction. This generates a ranking over strategy combinations made on the grounds of the ideology, or the moral principle, which is *ex ante* accepted by agents. Note that this ranking is established according to the level to which vectors of material utilities (the standard payoff vectors) satisfy a given formal distributive property, that is whether, attached to any outcome, a distribution of the material utilities does materialize that satisfies a normative property T. Consequently, we are assuming that it is possible to measure on some scale the correspondence of social states of affairs to an ideal norm of assessment, which is represented by a function of social outcomes. This is analogous to an individualistic social welfare function in that it is dependent on the material utilities of agents involved in the interaction and establishes a certain formal property of the material utilities' distribution among agents themselves:

$$\bar{T}: = \underset{i \in I^*}{\times} \bar{U}_i(S) \to R.$$

Therefore, such a normative principle permits the creation of an ordering over possible states of affairs (strategy vectors like $s \in S$), which represents the assessment that an impartial spectator would give to different social situations on the basis of the relevant normative criterion of distribution. A higher value of function T, defined over outcomes, implies that the associated social state of affairs satisfies to a higher degree the normative criterion.

Of course, taking the structure of the game as granted, it is possible to make the function directly dependent on the pure strategy profile set S, and, also, on the mixed strategies of the game: $T(\sigma): = \Sigma_{s \in S} P_\sigma(s) \bar{T}[\bar{U}(s)]$.

In analogy with individual expected utility, the expected normative function is simply a weighed sum of the indices of welfare distribution under all possible pure strategies profiles, with weights given by the probabilities that each outcome is actually played.

Comprehensive utility function
As already pointed out, we allow for an agent having various, possibly conflicting, motives to act in his/her own system of deliberation. The first is given by the usual self-interested motivation, whereas the second hinges upon the ordering of the social outcomes that is carried out by means of the normative principle T introduced in the previous subsection. It consists in the utility derived from the knowledge that the action performed by the agent, given his/her expectation on others players' action, satisfies, to some extent, the normative principles T with respect to the assessment of the social states of affairs based on the ranking of the corresponding outcomes.

We now introduce what we call a 'comprehensive utility function', whose components are given by material and ideal utility. In what follows we shall assume that agents are able to fully compare this pair of reasons to act and to take a decision, thus leaving aside the issue of commensurability of different sources of value.[11]

The comprehensive utility function will then have the following form:

$$V_i(\sigma) = U_i(\sigma) + \lambda_i f[T(\sigma)] \quad i \in I^*.$$

The first term U_i represents the material utility and is shaped in accordance with the agent's self-interested consequentialist preferences. The second term is the ideal utility and reflects the agent's concern with other types of reasons to act, meant in general as the degree of conformity of the social state of affairs – the agent's and the other participants' behaviour – to the normative principle of welfare distribution T. This is expressed as a function f, shared by all agents, of the social normative criterion T. For simplicity, the two components enter the function additively, and the parameters λ_i, possibly different for the agents, measure the weight attributed to their ideal rather than material source of utility. The function f may be specified in different ways in order to account for various possible forms of the morality-grounded motive to act. In the following section we shall provide a particular specification based on an idea of expected mutuality in conforming to the normative prescriptions.

3. Mutual conformism
A reciprocity-based account of the ideological motive
The model that we wish to develop understands reciprocity as acting in accordance with a shared normative principle embodying an ideology, which is represented by the welfare distribution function T. In particular, the idea we want to capture by means of our model is germane to a common approach in the literature on moral philosophy that sees agents as ready to perform a 'just' action, possibly detrimental in terms of their self-interest, only in so far as they expect other agents are doing the same. Indeed, this is a restatement of the usual notion of reciprocity, where this is now intended in generalized terms and with respect to a normative principle, rather than as a two-side relationship where agents are concerned with each other's payoffs.

We model this account of reciprocity by building on Rabin's model of fairness (see Section 2). In particular, Rabin's kindness functions are substituted by functions of expected conformity to the normative principle, so that each agent's incentive to perform an action satisfying the moral principle, and possibly contrasting the self-interested reason to act, is positively linked with the extent to which the opponent is expected to perform an action consistent with the same normative principle. In this way, we model the idea that agents derive utility from their expected reciprocal conformity to a shared normative principle, rather than from an expectation about how kind they are one towards the other in terms of the satisfaction of their own consequentialist preferences.

Expected conformity to ideology

To model these ideas, we need a further extension of the analytical structure of individual preferences, derived from this approach of psychological games (Geneakoplos et al. 1989). In principle, this formal apparatus requires the construction of hierarchies of beliefs of infinite order, but this aspect is much simpler here since, for our purposes, beliefs of first two orders are all is needed in order to account for reciprocity.

A first-order belief for player i is a probability measure over the other players' mixed strategy set, namely $B_i^1 := \Delta(\Sigma_{-i})$; thus a generic element $b_i^1 \in B_i^1$ indicates the probability with which i believes that other players are going to implement the profile of strategies σ_{-i}. In the same fashion we can define $B_{-i}^1 := \times_{j \neq i}(B_j)$. Obviously, when there are just two active players, we have $B_i^1 := \Delta(\Sigma_j)$ and $B_{-i}^1 := B_j$. A second-order belief for player i is a conjecture over the belief of j over i's strategies. Therefore, it consists of a probability measure over the Cartesian of other players' beliefs of first order: $B_i^2 := \Delta(B_{-i}^1)$. Thus a generic element of this set, $b_i^2 \in B_i^2$, represents i's probability that the belief of j over i's strategies is b_j^1.[12] We shall indicate with $b_i = (b_i^1, b_i^2, \ldots)$ the infinite-dimension vector collecting the beliefs of each order for player i.

We now restrict our attention to a two-person game (where players are denoted by i and j respectively), even though a generalization to the case of n players would be straightforward. In analogy with Rabin's pair of kindness functions, measuring the mutual impact of one's actions on the other's individual utility, we can now introduce functions computing degrees of conformity to the ideal – that is, to a moral principle (we continue to call it thereafter 'ideology'). We first define i's conditional conformity to the ideology in the following way:

$$f_i(\sigma_i, b_i^1) = \frac{T(\sigma_i, b_i^1) - T^{MAX}(b_i^1)}{T^{MAX}(b_i^1) - T^{MIN}(b_i^1)},$$

where

$$T^{MAX}(b_i^1) = \arg \max_{\Sigma_i} T(\sigma_i, b_i^1) \text{ and } T^{MIN}(b_i^1) = \arg \min_{\Sigma_i} T(\sigma_i, b_i^1).$$

In other words, $T^{MAX}(b_i^1)$ and $T^{MIN}(b_i^1)$ are, respectively, the maximum and minimum value that the welfare distribution function, representing normative principle or ideology, can assume, depending on i's action, given i's first-order belief b_i^1 over the action that j is going to perform.[13] Therefore, if $T^{MAX}(b_i^1)$ $[T^{MIN}(b_i^1)]$ is obtained, then agent i is maximizing (minimizing) the welfare function given his/her first-order belief. $T(\sigma_i, b_i^1)$ is instead the value of the welfare function corresponding to i's actual choice σ_i, given what he/she expects from player j.

Hence, $f_i(\sigma_i, b_i^1)$ is an index varying between -1 and 0 expressing the extent to which i's action satisfies the normative criterion associated with the function T. When $f_i(\sigma_i, b_i^1)$ is equal to 0 (-1) it means that i is exactly performing the strategy maximizing (minimizing) the welfare function, given i's first-order belief, and this proves that his/her action is consistent with the normative prescriptions at the maximum (minimum) degree. In other words, conformity to an agreed-upon normative principle is measured by the extent to which one's action reduces the distance between the actual state of affairs and the ideal one, that is the state where the value of the welfare distribution function is maximized over the agent's strategy set, given the expected choice by the counterpart.

To model the concept of reciprocity in individual motivational systems, we need to introduce a function symmetric to the one set out above. This is the esteem that player i forms about j's compliance with the ideology:

$$\tilde{f}_j(b_i^1, b_i^2) = \frac{T(b_i^1, b_i^2) - T^{MAX}(b_i^2)}{T^{MAX}(b_i^2) - T^{MIN}(b_i^2)},$$

where

$$T^{MAX}(b_i^2) = \arg \max_{\Sigma_j} T(b_i^2, \sigma_j) \text{ and } T^{MIN}(b_i^2) = \arg \min_{\Sigma_j} T(b_i^2, \sigma_j).$$

Therefore, $T^{MAX}(b_i^2)$ and $T^{MIN}(b_i^2)$ are the value that the welfare function takes when player j respectively maximizes or minimizes it, given the second-order belief of player i. In other words, those functions indicate the maximum and minimum values that player j can attribute to the welfare function, given the belief he/she has about i's action as perceived by i him/herself. In fact, recall that such a function measures the esteem of j's compliance to the ideology as measured from i's standpoint. Thus, if player i has formed a belief b_i^2 about player j's belief over i's action, i will judge j's actions from this point of view. Player i will then consider the best and the worst value that j can do with respect to the welfare function, and then compare these values with $T(b_i^1, b_i^2)$, which is the actual value that i expects the welfare function to take according to his/her beliefs. Alike the twin function $f_i(\sigma_i, b_i^1)$, a value of $\tilde{f}_j(b_i^1, b_i^2)$ equal to 0 (-1) indicates the maximum (minimum) degree of conformity by player j to the ideology as embodied in the welfare function T.

The comprehensive utility function
We can now introduce the final version of the utility functions. Note that, as in every psychological game, the utility of an agent depends on his/her beliefs over different possible outcomes (strategy vectors). We assume the following representation, which blends the two functions of compliance to the ideology:

$$V_i(\sigma_i, b_i^1, b_i^2) = U_i(\sigma_i, b_i^1) + \lambda_i[1 + \tilde{f}_j(b_i^2, b_i^1)][1 + f_i(\sigma_i, b_i^1)].$$

The fact that b_i^1 now substitutes σ_j depends on the fact that only in equilibrium are the two assumed to coincide. The ideal utility, again weighted by the coefficient λ_i, consists of the product of the two conformity functions augmented by 1.

The idea we wish to capture through this specification is twofold. On the one hand, an agent's utility depends positively on the realization of the 'best' social state of affairs, in terms of satisfaction of a normative criterion; indeed, the ideal utility is increased when an agent performs an action increasing the value of T, whoever he/she is. The second aspect is 'reciprocity' in compliance with the normative criterion: in fact, (esteemed) conformity of the other player, as expressed by $\tilde{f}_j(b_i^1, b_i^2)$, may be seen as a 'marginal incentive' that the subject has in pursuing his/her ideal motivations, as represented by $f_i(\sigma_i, b_i^1)$. Therefore, ideal utility increases as the counterpart's action is perceived as more consistent with the ideology, thus eliciting a similar behaviour from the agent him/herself. In the extreme case, where $\tilde{f}_j(b_i^1, b_i^2)$ is equal to –1, which denotes the worst action that agent j can perform in terms of the normative principle, the coefficient of the ideological motive gets equal to zero, thus leaving self-interest as the only relevant motive to action.[14] Conversely, when $1 + \tilde{f}_j(b_i^1, b_i^2)$ is positive and sufficiently 'large', then agent i may accept to perform an action that is contrary to his/her self-interest but conforms to the normative principle.[15] In general, evaluating the opponent's conformity to the normative principle magnifies or shrinks the individual motivation to act in accordance with the normative principle itself.

Psychological Nash equilibrium
The peculiar innovation introduced in the comprehensive utility function, that is the inclusion of beliefs in the arguments of the function, calls for an extension of the standard concept of solution of games, namely the Nash equilibrium. We shall adopt the original notion of Nash psychological equilibrium put forward by Geanakoplos et al. in their seminal contribution, although some refinements of this notion have been suggested (Kolpin 1992) and others appear possible.

The underlying idea of this concept is that, if we are in equilibrium, then rational players' beliefs must be coherent with strategies that are there being played. As an example, if in equilibrium I observe my opponent playing the (possibly mixed) strategy $\sigma_j \in \Sigma_j$, then my first-order belief must assign probability one to that particular strategy and 0 to all of the others. This is tantamount to saying that once an equilibrium has been reached, all of the first-order beliefs must be single-point distributions assigning probability one to the equilibrium strategy. The higher-order beliefs are then generated upon a condition of coherence with this initial condition (Geanakoplos et al. 1989: 64). We shall call $\beta_i(\sigma)$ the distribution of beliefs associated with the distribution that is coherent with assigning probability 1 to the strategy σ, and with $\beta(\sigma) = [\beta_1(\sigma), \ldots \beta_n(\sigma)] \in B$ the profile of such beliefs for the n players.

Recalling the definition of b_i as the vector collecting the beliefs of each order for player i, and consequently of $b = (b_1, \ldots, b_n)$ as the profile of beliefs for each of the n players, we are now able to provide the definition of psychological Nash equilibrium (ibid.: 65):

A psychological Nash equilibrium for an n-person normal form psychological game G is a pair $(\hat{b}, \hat{\sigma}) \in B \times \Sigma$ such that:

(i) $\hat{b} = \beta(\hat{\sigma})$
(ii) for each $i \in I$ and $\sigma_i \in \Sigma_i$, $V_i[\hat{b}_i, (\sigma_i, \hat{\sigma}_{-i})] \leq V_i(\hat{b}_i, \hat{\sigma})$.

Condition (ii) is a simple restatement of the standard Nash equilibrium condition, affirming that for each player the equilibrium strategy must confer a payoff no smaller than could be attained by any other feasible strategy, given the opponents' strategies and the beliefs.[16] Condition (i) restrains the beliefs to be coherent with the equilibrium strategy. Note that if beliefs are not part of the utility function then condition (i) becomes redundant and the definition boils down to the standard Nash equilibrium definition.

4. The game of production

After the philosophical and analytical underpinnings of the agents' system of choice have been set out, we can now apply this model of choice to analysing the nonprofit enterprise (NPE). First, we depict a situation of interaction in the production of a good, whose outcomes correspond to a variety of different behaviour of a firm corresponding in turn to different organizational form. This game is analysed in accordance with the two attitudes that make up the utility functions of the players. In Section 5, the Nash social welfare function is adopted as the normative principle used by the agents, and we analyse the conditions under which a nonprofit organizational form can be an equilibrium of the game.

Setting of the game

We suppose that three players are involved in the production game: a worker (W), an entrepreneur (E) and a consumer (C).[17] The last is actually a dummy player, whose actions do not have any impact on the others' payoffs, though her payoff is affected by the others' actions. The worker and the entrepreneur work together in a firm, and are to decide the degree of their commitment to the organization, which is supposed to be measurable along some scale. Their different degree of involvement brings about different organizational forms for the firm. More specifically, each of the active agents has two available strategies; one prescribes performing an action that would be standard in a market, profit-orientated context (notice that no assumption of perfect competitive market is made here). The second action permits an improvement in quality of the supplied good with respect to such a for-profit, free market, standard, but triggers an extra cost that is to be sustained by the agent. For instance, the entrepreneur may decide to adopt a productive practice, or a technology, which permits an increase in the good's quality, whereas, this technology is more costly with respect to that adopted in a competitive context. Analogously, the entrepreneur may renounce a part – or all – of her profits in order to reinvest them in the productive process either by improving the quality or increasing the quantity of the good supplied at the same price. We shall indicate with h_E and l_E the adoption of the good's quality-improving action and that leaving the quality of the good unaltered with respect to the market with-profit-orientated-firms standards, respectively. Letters h and l refer to the high or low quality-enhancing purpose of the action, and the subscript E stands for the entrepreneur.

Likewise, the worker may decide to work at a lower wage than that fixed in a market context, thus partially – or totally – supplying his labour contribution on a voluntary basis. Similarly, he may increase his effort in the provision of the good at the same wage. In both cases, either the quality of the good is improved, or this is offered in a larger amount at the same price. We shall indicate this pair of actions with h_W and l_W. The consumer does not have actions affecting the utility of the other two agents, but the surplus derived from the consumption of the good depends on its quality, thus on the level of effort put in by the producers.

Following the formalization introduced above, we distinguish between the set $I = \{W, E\}$ of the active players and the set $I^* = \{W, E, C\}$ that includes the dummy player C. A strategy set for the two agents can easily be introduced by considering that both have an action that improves the quality of the good and another that leaves it unaltered with respect to a competitive context. We indicate this with $S_i = \{h_i, l_i\}, i \in I$. Also recall that $S = \underset{i \in I}{\times} S_i$, where the generic element $s \in S$ indicates a vector of pure strategies for the two players, and that $\Sigma := \underset{i \in I}{\times} \Sigma_i$ is the set of mixed strategy profiles, with generic elements $\sigma \in \Sigma$.

The game representing the interaction depicted so far is then as follows:

	h_E	l_E
h_W	$\underline{w}, R - \underline{w} - c, s$	$\underline{w}, R - \underline{w}, \frac{s}{2}$
l_W	$\bar{w}, R - \bar{w} - c, \frac{s}{2}$	$\bar{w}, R - \bar{w}, 0$

The first, second and third terms in each box represent material payoffs for the worker, the entrepreneur and the consumer, respectively. c stands for the extra cost that must be paid for by the entrepreneur if she wants to engage in the quality-enhancing action of the good, namely h_E. R indicates the revenues from selling the good, which is assumed to be constant in all of the four possible outcomes, and w is the wage, which enters as a cost for the entrepreneur and as the only source of material utility for the worker.[18] There are two possible levels of the wage: $\bar{w}$ is a comparatively high level that obtains when the worker supplies a level of labour in accordance with a market standard (strategy l_W), whereas $\underline{w}$ is a lower level that the worker can earn when engaged in the good's quality-enhancing action (strategy h_W). Therefore, the difference between $\bar{w}$ and $\underline{w}$ is the cut in the real wage that the worker can accept in order to improve the quality of the good.

The consumer's utility is given by the surplus gained in the four possible outcomes. This depends on the effort put in by the other agents in improving the quality of the good. In particular, we normalize to 0 her level of surplus in the outcome where neither the worker nor the entrepreneur engage in the quality improving action, that is (l_W, l_E). We then assume that when both agents agree to enhance the quality of the good, the surplus gained by the consumer is comparatively higher, equal to the level s, whereas when only one of the two agents contributing to production provides such an activity the surplus reaches an intermediate level, for simplicity equal to $s/2$.[19]

We identify the outcome in which both agents perform the quality-improving actions that lead to the constitution of a nonprofit venture. The intuition is quite simple: provided that by construction the outcome (l_W, l_E) is associated with the level of effort supplied in a with-profit-orientated-firms market context, (h_W, h_E) takes on all the relevant characteristics of a nonprofit-orientated enterprise; that is, the entrepreneur gives up her profits to invest in a quality-enhancing technology, or simply to increase the quality or the quantity of the good, while the worker supplies a larger amount of effort or some voluntary work. The surplus of the consumer is then as high as possible. The other pair of outcomes represent different situations: (h_W, l_E) gives the best payoff for the entrepreneur as she can count on the worker giving his maximum effort while not performing any quality-increasing action; conversely (l_W, h_E) provides the worst payoff for the entrepreneur as the extra costs that she sustains cannot be compensated by the provision of some extra work by the worker.

If the game were played by the two active players without any concern for the dummy player, then the game depicted in the previous matrix would degenerate to the following standard game, where only the payoffs of agents representing their self-interest are depicted, as they are only relevant to the solution of the game:

	h_E	l_E
h_W	$\underline{w}, R - \underline{w} - c$	$\underline{w}, R - \underline{w}$
l_W	$\overline{w}, R - \overline{w} - c$	$\overline{w}, R - \overline{w}$

It is apparent how a unique Nash equilibrium in dominant strategies exists, in which both agents perform the low-quality action. In fact, neither agent has any incentive to perform the quality-enhancing action, given that the consumer's utility is neglected in this game. One could say that a nonprofit form of enterprise could emerge only if some other-regarding attitude towards the beneficiary is sufficiently developed among the active agents. However, in what follows this attitude is not directly modelled as altruistic towards the dummy player, but as a conformist preference for mutual compliance with an accepted principle of fairness or towards the nonprofit ideology. How this ideology can be selected is the argument of the next section.

5.   Psychological equilibria of the game

Contractarianism and ideology of the nonprofit enterprise (NPE)
As already pointed out, the set of normative criteria moulding the conformist motive to act (see Sections 2 and 3) has not yet been attributed a specific shape. In fact, to the purpose of building up a model of choice, our main point was to emphasize the existence of a prompt to action different from the self-interested one, which emphasizes the conditional willingness of the agents to abide by some general moral or ideological principle. But the question of the exact shape of such a general principle had been somehow left on the backstage of the argument. To be sure, this is nothing

but a secondary question, which conveys other relevant matters like the convergence of every agent to embrace the same general principle as a reference point in the evaluation of their actions. Needless to say, seeking a general answer to those questions lies beyond the scope of this chapter.

However, we suggest here a conjecture that we take as reasonably suitable for an account of the NPE, both from the positive and normative standpoints, which is based on the consideration that both the NPE's entrepreneur and worker are 'ideologues' (Rose-Ackerman 1996). We make this point by introducing two assumptions in sequence. These are meant to capture two distinct roles of morality in the NPE: first is the 'rational justification giving' role that we capture in terms of contractarian ethics. Second is the 'motivational role', which we model by a particular interpretation of the ideal utility of the NPE members. It is a basic tenet of this chapter that these two roles must be considered as both indispensable but irreducible to each other, so that both should be squarely faced by any endeavour to explain how morality can play a role in economic organizations.[20]

> H1 The NPE internal players' ideology states that the NPE is grounded on a hypothetical 'social contract' among all the players – the consumer included – affirming a principle of fairness.

The situation has to be understood as if, before playing the actual game, a hypothetical cooperative bargaining game among all the players were played. This game captures the *ex ante* perspective according to which players could agree to join the organization in the different roles of entrepreneur, worker and consumer. In doing this they look for a justification for their joining the organization. Thus, they take an impartial or moral point of view, which means that the decision to join must be rationally acceptable from whichever point of view. In other words, terms of agreement must be rationally acceptable under the permutation of personal or role-relative points of view, so that an agreement must be invariant when it is considered under two apparently distinct perspectives: the perspective of each particular player, choosing according to his/her best payoff, and the perspective of 'anyone' – that is, the perspective of whichever player would consider the problem of finding an acceptable agreement without any knowledge of his/her name and personal role in the game (Sacconi 1991).

In fact the impartial perspective is adopted in order to settle the mission and the conjoint strategy of the organization, which is intended as the one that would be agreed upon among all the internal members and the external stakeholders of the NPE as well. In particular, this perspective is taken in order to identify a reasonable and acceptable balancing among the claims of all the interested participants, from which internal players derive the fiduciary duties that the NPE must discharge towards beneficiaries (consumer). Thus the 'social contract' works as a 'constitutional' ideology legitimating the enterprise as an institution from the *ex ante* perspective.

At the very core of the contractarian approach lies the idea that a fair distribution can be worked out through a rational agreement for mutual advantage of all the interested parties. Inclusion also of the consumer within the set of bargaining players is due to the impartial perspective taken in this justificatory exercise. As it is an example of the justificatory role of ethics, it disregards the effective influence of the dummy players in the actual game. On the contrary it considers the *ex ante* perspective in which the consumer would also have a voice about the terms of agreement on the cooperative venture in which the beneficiary essentially contributes, as he/she agrees to consume the organization's output. A rational agreement in this hypothetical game thus requires an efficient production of the surplus and its fair distribution among both the internal and the external players.

Formally this can be modelled as the requirement that the NPE distributes the surplus according to the Nash bargaining solution for cooperative bargaining games, that is, we pick up the distribution maximizing the product of the three players' payoffs net of the status quo (Nash 1950). Note that the Nash bargaining solution always selects an outcome reflecting the degree of symmetry of the payoff space, which means that if the payoff space is symmetric hence the solution must be perfectly symmetric among players (that is, it splits the pie in equal parts). Consequently the solution is covariant with any asymmetry in the utility representation of the outcome space. This solution excludes any discrimination against any player (of course the utilities' product becomes zero if any factor in the multiplication is zero) and always selects equality in so far as equality is represented in the shape of the payoff space. In sum, we adopt the Nash bargaining solution as a normative criterion for defining a moral preference over the outcomes of the original game, which orders outcomes according to 'fairness'.[21]

With respect to the non-cooperative game of the foregoing section, the constitutional ideology is what can be called the result of a 'pre-play communication' phase, an agreement that players endorse before the beginning of the actual non-cooperative game on surplus allocation. However the underlying game is non-cooperative. This means that commitments on the ideological principle are not binding *per se*, and there is nothing in the rules of the game capable of ensuring that the precepts of the ideology will be enforced or put into practice by the players. Moreover, due to the payoff structure of the actual game and its Nash equilibrium, we know that players do not have the appropriate incentives to put into practice the precepts of the constitutional ideology. Why then do active players, the entrepreneur and the worker, comply with their constitutional ideology? This brings us to our second hypothesis.

> H 2   Internal players of the NPE take the expectations of reciprocity in conformity to the constitutional ideology as a source of utility *per se*.

In other words, there is an intrinsic source of utility in acting according to the ideology as far as you believe that, while you act according to the ideology, other players are also conforming to the same ideology, and you also believe that they in fact expect you to act according to the ideology while they act according to it. This is where ideal utility based on conformist preferences enters the production game, but now the resulting comprehensive utility function of the players is specified by the contractarian form of the NPE members' ideology.

The nonprofit enterprise as a psychological equilibrium
Recall that the expression of the Nash welfare function is as follows:

$$N(U_1, \dots, U_N) = \prod_{i=1}^{N} (U_i - d_i),$$

where d_i represents the reservation utility that agents can get when the process of bargaining breaks down, that is when they refuse to act in mutual cooperation. In the present context, it is appropriate to set all of these reservation utilities to the level of zero.[22]

Applying this function to our model, and expressing it with respect to the pair of the relevant agents' actions, we obtain the following values:

$$N_{hh} \equiv N(h_W, h_E) = \underline{w}(R - \underline{w} - c)s$$

$$N_{hl} \equiv N(h_W, l_E) = \underline{w}(R - \underline{w})\frac{s}{2}$$

$$N_{lh} \equiv N(l_W, h_E) = \overline{w}(R - \overline{w} - c)\frac{s}{2}$$

$$N_{ll} \equiv N(l_W, l_E) = 0.$$

For a significant set of the parameters, we can assume that the Nash function is maximized in (h_W, h_E).[23] Recalling the previous section, this would be the allocation obtained in the process of bargaining among the three agents.

It is now straightforward to show how agents can view this outcome as optimal when their conformist utility is sufficiently high with respect to the material. Specifically, we want to prove that (h_W, h_E) can be sustained as a Nash psychological equilibrium, as defined above. Let us first consider the position of the worker and compute his level of utility associated with such an outcome. His material utility is clearly the lower wage; what about his conformist utility? Recalling the two functions measuring conformity to ideology, we can note that, provided that in N_{hh} the Nash bargaining function is at a maximum, both compliance functions will be equal to zero, thus attributing the maximum value to the ideological source of utility: $V_W(h_W, b_W^1 = h_E, b_W^2 = h_W) = \underline{w} + \lambda$. Note that in the computation of this value we have used the definition of the Nash psychological game equilibrium, which implies that agents' beliefs must be confirmed by agents' actual choice. Accordingly, these beliefs assign probability one to the equilibrium strategies.

Let us now test whether the worker finds this allocation optimal or whether he has any incentive to deviate. In psychological games, a deviation from a certain allocation consists of a change in the agent's strategy, given the set of beliefs held in that allocation. In other words, when deviating, an agent must take into account what the expectations of other agents on his/her behaviour are, and then compute the possible change in his/her own comprehensive utility deriving from not conforming to such expectations. In our case, we shall generically indicate with $\sigma_W < 1$ a probability with which the worker plays h_W in a mixed strategy adopted to deviate. Estimation of the entrepreneur's compliance to ideology is unaffected by this deviation, since by construction the worker knows that she still believes that he is going to perform h_W.

However, the worker's very conformity to the normative principle must change. Given that the entrepreneur is still going to perform with probability one h_E, the resulting value for the Nash function is: $N(\sigma_W, h_E) = \sigma_W N_{hh} + (1 - \sigma_W)N_{lh}$. Given the worker's belief, his action that maximizes (minimizes) the Nash function is to play $h_W(l_W)$. Formally: $N^{MAX}(b_W^1 = h_E) = N_{hh}$, and $N^{MIN}(b_W^1 = h_E) = N_{lh}$. Substituting these values into the function measuring the conformity of the worker with the normative principle, we obtain:

$$f_W(\sigma_W, b_W^1 = h_E) = \frac{(1 - \sigma_W)(N_{lh} - N_{hh})}{N_{hh} - N_{lh}} = -(1 - \sigma_W).$$

Hence, the comprehensive utility of the deviation is:

$$V_W(\sigma_W, b_W^1 = h_E, b_W^2 = h_W) = \sigma_W \underline{w} + (1 - \sigma_W)\overline{w} + \lambda \sigma_W.$$

The ideal source of utility is now smaller: the worker is paying because he is not reciprocating the action of the counterpart. Knowing that the entrepreneur is doing her best to act in accordance with the normative principle, the fact that the worker is partly failing in doing the same causes a lesser satisfaction deriving from the conformist motive. A different but related interpretation is that the worker feels guilty for not having conformed to the counterpart's expectations. On the other hand, the expected value from material utility is certainly higher. To ensure optimal choice of the quality improving action for the worker, we therefore need a further condition:

$$V_W(h_W, b_W^1 = h_E, b_W^2 = h_W) > V_W(\sigma_W, b_W^1 = h_E, b_W^2 = h_W) \Leftrightarrow \lambda_W > \overline{w} - \underline{w}.$$

This condition states that the weight attributed to the ideological source of utility must be sufficiently large so as to compensate for the loss in material utility caused by not performing the best action in terms of self-interest.

An analogous condition ensuring the pursuing of the quality-improving action holds for the entrepreneur:

$$V_E(h_E, b_E^1 = h_W, b_E^2 = h_E) > V_E(\sigma_E, b_E^1 = h_W, b_E^2 = h_E) \Leftrightarrow \lambda_E > c.$$

We therefore have a simple intuition of how the presence of a conformist motivation in an individual system of preferences helps the emergence of an equilibrium associated with what we can identify as the NPE's behaviour. When the importance attributed to this is sufficiently high in comparison with the material gain that must be given up when acting in conformity with the normative principle, then the outcome in which both agents perform their best action in terms of the interests of the third party involved in the interaction, going against the pursuit of their mere self-interest, does emerge as an equilibrium of the game. Hence, the presence of two agents motivated to act in accordance with a normative principle, which we identify with the NPE constitutional ideology, emerges as a necessary condition for the emergence of an equilibrium state where we observe the typical behaviour of the NPE.

Up to now this result seems fairly natural: whenever two agents are sufficiently concerned with conformity to the normative criterion, and when they entertain reciprocal expectations that both will abide by such a criterion, then a conformist equilibrium emerges as a solution of the game. However, there are some questions still unanswered: is the presence of 'ideology-motivated' agents a sufficient condition to ensure the emergence of this outcome? As we shall argue in the next subsection, the answer is negative: even when the agents have conformist preferences, the type of interaction resembles a coordination problem, where the outcome corresponding to the for-profit behaviour of the firm can emerge as an equilibrium too as well.

Multiple equilibria and codes of ethics as devices for selection
We now want to investigate whether other types of solutions are feasible in this game. First, let us examine whether the 'opposite' outcome to that until now considered, in which both agents perform the best action in terms of self-interest (l_W, l_E) can be sustained as a psychological equilibrium. The answer is in fact positive. Consider the worker's situation. Since each agent is performing the worst action in terms of the maximization of the normative function given the belief on the other's action, the worker derives utility only from the material component: $V_W(l_W, l_E) = \bar{w}$. However, the worker cannot gain any benefit from deviation from this outcome: in fact, esteem accorded to his counterpart is at the minimum level, namely $\tilde{f}_E(b_W^1 = l_E, b_W^2 = l_W) = -1$. Therefore, he does not have any incentive to perform an action going against his self-interest and somehow respecting the moral principle. Every other strategy cannot but do worse than the current outcome.

Obviously, similar considerations hold for the entrepreneur, thus making (l_W, l_E) a psychological Nash equilibrium of the game. This is indeed a relevant fact: even when agents are inclined to act in accordance with moral principles reigning in a society, that is their λs are sufficiently high, and this is known to them, there exists an equilibrium where agents do not care about such morality-grounded motivations and perform actions just pursuing their own self-interest. This may be indeed be seen as a sort of 'non-profit failure': even when the necessary conditions to build an NPE are present, a self-interested outcome can none the less emerge.

The situation is therefore similar to a coordination problem, where the existence of a multiplicity of equilibria leaves open the problem of the selection of one of these. That this is indeed the case can be shown more generally: the problem of the choice of each agent's best reply to the opponent's is represented in Figure 24.1.

It is noticeable that there is a threshold level in the best reply functions such that each agent performs the 'good' action only if the action of the counterpart is sufficiently 'good' and vice versa. This gives rise to a third equilibrium, this time in mixed strategies.

Therefore, the presence of a significant agents' disposition to perform actions prescribed by the fairness principle to a full extent is a necessary

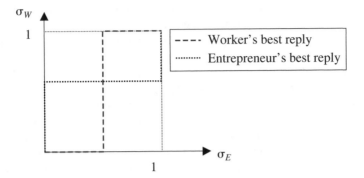

Figure 24.1   Best reply functions in the production game

condition in order that the NPE be derived as an equilibrium of the game. Nevertheless, this condition is not sufficient: even when agents assign a large 'weight' to their conformist motive to act, a failure in signalling their attitude to their counterpart may lead to the selection of the for-profit organizational form as the equilibrium outcome of the game.

This observation points to the importance of some characteristics of possible coordination equilibria that may be 'external' to the inner structure of the game, and that can act as focal points to make one of the equilibria 'salient' with respect to the others. As suggested extensively in the literature (Schelling 1960; Lewis 1969; Sugden 1986), the ability of recognizing the salience of one outcome within a set of available results rests on the sharing of some common cultural traits that makes convergence to that outcome common knowledge for all the agents. Codes of ethics can be thought of as an effective device to signal agents' disposition to coordinate on the socially more efficient outcome in the context of a coordination game or, more generally, in a situation of contract incompleteness. In the present context, a code of ethics would signal the agents' mutual disposition to comply with the moral principles in a pre-play phase; this would make it common knowledge that they give large importance to the ideology-grounded motivation within their individual system of choice. This may take the form of an announcement by both the entrepreneur and the worker directed to the other party concerning the main goals that the partnership in the productive activity should attain. Indeed, this type of announcement is exactly what is embedded in a code of ethics. Thus, codes of ethics can act as focal point generators in solving the coordination problem and in attracting agents with 'good' dispositions to the equilibrium associated with the setting up of a nonprofit firm.

Whereas in the context of a purely coordination game, such as the psychological game under scrutiny, the present argument does not seem too problematic, the consideration of the most realistic situation of incomplete information on each other's types raises some concerns as to whether the announcement of the constitutional ideology through a code of ethics is sufficient to create the appropriate reciprocal expectation system leading to the NPE. This would be a situation in which the conformist disposition of agents is a private hidden characteristic, namely a type; in other words, each weight λ_i would be unknown to the counterpart. It is clear that in such a situation, viewing a code of ethics as a cost-free announcement would not help to solve the coordination problem between players with a high disposition to conform to the ideology. In fact, the possibility that such an announcement is used strategically by a profit-orientated entrepreneur in order to attract the collaboration of non profit-orientated workers, thus bringing about extra profits for the entrepreneur, would make this device ineffective. In other words, agents with low λ have an incentive to 'cheat' in the pre-play phase, thus leading to the well-known result of a pooling equilibrium in a signalling game.

However, a code of ethics can be seen as a substitute for the commitments within a game of reputation under unforeseen contingencies, where standard commitments on specific and concrete strategies of the game (the standard 'types' of the reputation game literature) are made void because of the impossibility of specifying *ex ante* their requirements contingently upon unforeseen states of the world that will be revealed *ex post* (Sacconi 2000, 2006). In a related work, Sacconi (2004) suggests that a code of ethics may therefore work as a basis for introducing reputation effects in a repeated trust game between an NPE as a whole and its external consumers and stakeholders in general, modelled as a game under unforeseen contingencies and incompleteness of contracts. This is in fact the typical context within which an institutional form like an NPE can be expected to be constituted, so that the firm is endowed with some authority towards the beneficiaries under the condition that it discharges some fiduciary duties towards the beneficiaries themselves. In this case the existence of strong complementarities between the game of production (the interaction between entrepreneur and worker, with the consumer as a dummy player) and a game involving the NPE as a whole and its external stakeholders can be proved. On the one hand the existence of ideology and conformist preference provides a basis for assuming that the 'type' of enterprise which discharges its duties according to a commitment (the 'type' coinciding with the code of ethics) has positive prior probability. On the other, reputation model's belief dynamics, which proves the existence of an equilibrium of reputation such that the firm complies with its code, also makes salient the outcome of the internal game where active players give up some of their material utility to the advantage of the consumer. This leads to the formation of an expectations system that supports the emergence of a psychological equilibrium of the internal game in which the ideal utility of agents plays the main role in guiding their strategy choices (l_W, l_E).

6. Conclusions

The goal of this chapter was to offer a characterization of the nonprofit enterprise to some extent different from others put forward in the literature so far. Our main point has been to emphasize the importance of the sharing of a common ideology by the participants in the productive venture, whose main feature is the inclusion of all relevant stakeholders in the distribution of the surplus. In order to attain this goal, we introduced an individual model of choice encompassing a self-interested and a mutually conformist prompt to action. We then developed a specification of the latter to bring in the simple intuition that the disposition to comply with moral principles is greater when other participants to the social interactions are also doing the same.

Through this model of reciprocity in individuals' system of choice, we have been able to account for the constitution of the NPE as an equilibrium in a psychological game where the weight assigned to the morality-grounded motivation is sufficiently high compared with the self-interested one. The role of codes of ethics was then emphasized as a helpful device to solve the coordination problem that arises in this type of interaction.

Of course, our analysis is not complete in that some other important aspects of the NPE have been overlooked. First, the question of efficiency of the nonprofit firm has been somehow neglected, although it is apparent how its constitution can help to reduce transaction costs in the 'market' of the demand and supply of welfare goods. This aspect has been elaborated in a different work (Sacconi 2004). Moreover, the extension of the model to the case of incomplete information, which was sketched in Section 5, opens the analysis to the relevant issue of the 'external' relation of the NPE with stakeholders other than the consumers, such as donors, where reputation effects become relevant. Nevertheless, we believe that focusing on the 'internal' framework of the constitution of the nonprofit venture is a helpful starting-point in order to develop a comprehensive understanding on this subject.

Notes

*   Support received by the MIUR (Italian Ministry for University and Research) under the national research project 'Economic comparative analysis of institutions and institutional complexity of governance forms, in the perspective of incomplete contracts' is gratefully acknowledged.

1. For the evolution of the concept of 'utility' in economic theory, see Broome (1999: ch. 2).
2. Despite this change in the perspective and scope of rational choice theory, this approach cannot be said to be immune from various types of criticism, both of an empirical and a theoretical nature. On the one hand, critics stress the bulky informational assumptions that are needed in order that such a logically coherent set of choices be made. On the other hand, experimental economics single out the existence of systematic violation of the axioms underlying the standard theory of rational choice, especially under conditions of uncertainty, in the individuals' actual choices. See, for instance, Hogarth and Reder (1986) and Hargreaves-Heap (1989). For a review, see North (1990: ch. 3). Also, Nelson and Winter (1982) are among the first authors who have argued extensively on this subject.
3. In particular, the threshold level that Rabin thinks is appropriate in order to classify an action as kind or hostile is what he calls the 'equitable payoff', which consists of the middle point between the best and the worst payoff the agent can obtain, provided that both of the associated outcomes are Pareto efficient.
4. Our approach to the description of 'states of affairs' resembles Scanlon's (2001) discussion of Sen's consequentialism (2001), by which is meant an all-encompassing description of *outcomes*, including such considerations as whether individual rights are respected or violated in consequence of individual actions. Scanlon calls this 'representational consequentialism', because it deems rights and duties to be intuitively relevant, but seeks to account for them in terms of whether they give rise to better or worse consequences – that is, it is an attempt to represent everything that may be relevant as part of the set of consequences. Scanlon contrasts this form of mild consequentialism with what he calls 'foundational consequentialism', whose basic tenet is that the *deontic* values of actions – their *rightness* or *wrongness* – should have *no* part in the assignment of value even in these all-encompassing descriptions of consequences. Scanlon, however, finds 'representational consequentialism' objectionable in that simply *representing* rights and duties as parts of consequences is not meaningful unless these may be explained in terms of some independent, clearer and more basic notion of value. He suggests that contractualism, rather than foundational consequentialism, is the appropriate evaluation of states of affairs, including the description of any level of respect for rights or their violation. We agree with Scanlon in not endorsing the idea of an 'enriched' description of *outcomes*, for we maintain the separation between the description of states as consequences and the deontological description of them as sets of actions in relation to the fulfilment of a principle. We shall draw on this distinction in the development of a 'comprehensive' utility function in Section 3. Verbeek (2001) makes a point in favour of our position when he says that there is an inconsistency between some basic postulates of consequentialism and a description of outcomes (which nevertheless he calls 'states of affairs') that includes any information about the fairness of the procedures of choices followed in producing those outcomes. Far from contradicting our approach, this is consistent with it, for we admit that at the basis of the agent's comprehensive utility function there may be two completely distinct descriptions of states of affairs, one according to the idea of consequences (the final outcomes of a game or a decision tree), the other as a set of actions (characterized in terms of their fairness). In the end we assume that the two preference orderings can be treated as separable but commensurable, so that they can be combined additively, notwithstanding the completely different nature of the motive that underlies the two kinds of partial preference ordering. In so far as fairness may be seen as a *reason* for preferring states of affairs, Verbeek would be correct to say that conformist preference goes beyond the simple idea that 'reason' consists in no more than the 'consistency' of a primitive un-interpreted preference relation leading to choice of the best consequence.
5. For more on this, see Sacconi (2004).
6. Note that arguing that the reasons why players are attracted to a principle are ultimately the invariance or agreement among their 'agent-relative' reasons to act, is entirely consistent with the idea of deontology (see Scanlon 2001).

7. This aspect comprises the main difference between Sugden's normative expectations approach and ours: in Sugden (2000) there is no independent normative condition shaping the rule with which agents are required to conform: in fact, agents pay a disutility (a penalty) for not living up to anyone else's expectation. This implies that virtually any outcome of the game may emerge as an ethical rule to be followed, since every convention may find support in the motivational force engendered by community members' expectations. In our model, the rule must reflect an abstract principle of justice whose only requirements are that it should be rationally acceptable and fair in an *ex ante* perspective. In other words, not all patterns of mutual conformity, but only those satisfying *ex ante* properties of rational acceptability, are embraced by the agents.

8. Hierarchies of beliefs are typical game-theoretical constructions built on David Lewis's seminal account of common knowledge (Lewis 1969); see Mertens and Zamir (1985) and Tan and Werlang (1988). They are also basic for the theory of psychological games (Geanakoplos et al. 1989).

9. As long as conformist preferences are assumed to satisfy the formal conditions for being represented by a utility function, we suggest that this is an example of the 'betterness relationship' proposed by Broome (1999), which is a binary relation expressing whichever reason for saying that in one state of affairs or action there is 'more good' (it is better) than in another. Therefore, these preferences can be represented by a utility function, even if it does not correspond in any sense to the typical 'desire' or 'revealed' interpretation of preference.

10. Outcomes are here intended as what happen to each single player in consequence of the result of a certain way of playing the game by the participants (see Harsanyi 1977, p. 90); see also Binmore (1992, p. 27): 'Each terminal node [of a game tree] must be labelled with the consequences for each player if the game ends in the outcome corresponding to that terminal node'. In this sense outcomes are the relevant description of a state of affairs resulting from strategic interaction, which are required by consequentialist preferences. However, the same state of affairs can be described also directly in terms of characteristics of actions *per se*. We have suggested in the foregoing subsection that the relevant characteristic is fairness of the strategy combination, but we also argued that this can be detected by a property of the utility distribution attached to outcomes as compared to an abstract principle of fair distribution.

11. Indeed, that agents are able to fully compare different values frees us from a troubling question. For the question of incommensurability of values, see Broome (1999, chs 8 and 9). For a sceptical view, doubtful as to the possibility of comparing various reasons to act in an individual's system of practical choice, see Copp (1997).

12. Although beliefs are probability distributions iteratively defined over probability distributions, the associated probabilities over pure strategies can easily be obtained by means of the following formulae:

$$P_{b_i^1}(s_j) = \int_{\Sigma_j} P_\sigma(s_j) P_{b_i^1}(\sigma_j) d\sigma_j; \quad P_{b_i^2}(s_i) = \int_{B_j^1} P_{b_j^1}(s_i) P_{b_i^2}(b_j^1) db_j^1.$$

Thus the first formula indicates the overall probability that player j is going to play s_j, according to the belief b_i^1 held by player i, and the second the overall probability that player j holds about i's performing s_i, according to the second-order belief b_i^2.

13. Note the dependence of $T^{MAX}(b_i^1)$ and $T^{MIN}(b_i^1)$ on the belief b_i^1. Indeed the belief is necessary in order to determine the probabilities for the expected value of the welfare function, which is:

$$T(\sigma_i, b_i^1) = \sum_{S_j} \sum_{S_i} \bar{T}(s_i, s_j) P_{\sigma_i}(s_i) P_{b_i^1}(s_j),$$

where the probability $P_{\sigma_i}(s_i)$ is what is prescribed by the mixed strategy σ_i, and $P_{b_i}(s_j)$ is the probability computed in accordance with the formula of the previous note.

14. Indeed, if agent i performs his/her worst action in terms of conformity to the normative principle, the fact that agent j acts contrarily or in favour of the same normative principle does not affect i's overall utility function. Therefore, we can interpret the situation where one or both the agents perform the action leading to the worst outcome according to the welfare distribution function as one in which the social contract between the agents breaks down.

15. Of course this is only one of the possible models of the ideological motive to action. Another one, which, *mutatis mutandis*, coincides with Rabin's specification is the following:

$$V_i(\sigma_i, b_i^1, b_i^2) = U_i(\sigma_i, b_i^1) + \lambda_i \left[\frac{1}{2} + \tilde{f}_j(b_i^2, b_i^1) \right] \left[\frac{3}{2} + f_i(\sigma_i, b_i^1) \right].$$

An 'equitable' payoff in the normative function is here identified with half of the difference between T^{MAX} and T^{MIN}. Hence, agent i will experience a positive incentive to perform an action increasing the social welfare only when the opponent performs an action above this level. However, if agent j executes an action below this equitable level, then agent i would be subjected to an incentive to act *contrarily* to the normative criterion. This specification seems to emphasize the aspect of reciprocity *per se* partly neglecting the other aspect of the will to contribute to the normative principle satisfaction. We think, however, that this emphasis would be somehow inappropriate in the present context, thus opting for a specification in which the incentive provided by the opponent in acting according to the normative principle is always non-negative, and nil only in the extreme case of him/her inflicting the least value to the social welfare function. A specification in which the agent is not concerned with the action of the counterpart would be the following:

$$V_i(\sigma) = U_i(\sigma) + \lambda_i[T(\sigma)].$$

This account captures the idea that agents are interested in fulfilling the normative principle of distribution through the materialization of appropriate social outcomes, without any concern for the other agents' commitment to the same principles. This specification can be taken as a useful reference point with respect to the more elaborated version of the next section.

16. The refinements of such a notion of equilibrium deal with the possibility that the beliefs of the player is 'deviating' from the equilibrium can vary as well, reflecting the 'direction' of this deviation.

17. As customary, we attribute different sexes to the players: E and C are both females, whereas W is a male.

18. For simplicity the material utility of both worker and entrepreneur is assumed to be linear in the monetary revenue.

19. The game of production is meant to incorporate in a schematic model the essentials of the economic situations in which typically nonprofit organizations are seen to emerge: production and delivering of welfare goods and services, characterized by strong asymmetries of information and incompleteness of contracts, such that an individual consumer is unable to observe, verify or make legally enforceable any specific levels of quality of goods provided by the productive organization. What we have in mind are situations wherein the consumer's demand for the good is completely rigid with respect to various levels of quality not because she is not interested in it, but just because she doesn't know it. She also cannot negotiate an incentive contract with the firm, based on expected quality of outcomes, simply because she cannot even observe it, and such a sales contract would be so incomplete in a number of contingencies that the firm would have no clear commitment to the consumer under all these *ex ante* indescribable situations. In situations like these, decisions concerning the quality level are in practice discretionary to the

firm (and its internal players), whereas the consumer is unable to influence this choice, even though she receives the effects on decisions made by internal players. In a sense the productive organization's results are insulated from the demand side and they depend essentially on the internal interaction among producers. This justifies the assumption that the consumer is a dummy player. Moreover it also explains the apparently questionable assumption that the revenue R is invariant under all the end-states of the game, which means that revenue is independent of the quality choice and parallels the assumption that quality is discretionary. In this situation a business strategy of the entrepreneur who would charge a higher price for higher quality, in order to create incentives, would be a non-starter. Higher quality may depend only on non-self-interested behaviour by both the internal players of the productive organization.

20. For a similar point, see Gauthier (1986), who makes the basic distinction between *internal rationality* of social contract, that is, it can be solved in terms of rational bargaining theory, and *external rationality* of social contact, that is, the compliance problem, a point that we face in a completely different way by introducing conformist preferences.

21. The idea of basing the social contract on Nash's bargaining solution was first put forward by Horace Brock (Brock 1979); see also (Sacconi 1986, 1991, 2000). It is also adopted in a somewhat different way by Ken Binmore (Binmore 1997). Using the words 'social welfare function' (SWF) can be misleading, because they lead us to think that there is a sort of super-individual decision maker whose objective function is defined according to the SWF. That is not the case, however. By SWF we mean an ethical criterion of fairness useful to judge the outcomes of the game. It is not a consequence that a decision maker would bring about for him/herself. This is clear given the underlying contractarian account of the Nash bargaining solution.

22. This choice calls for some justification. Many authors would argue that the proper choice for the 'exit option' would be the Nash solution of the material game played non-cooperatively. However, this choice is not immune from criticism as a possible situation of prevarication of one party over the other in the status quo would carry over to the final 'moral' solution. This is the reason why other authors have proposed the notion of a 'moralized' status quo, in which some minimal form of reciprocal respect is already in place. Therefore, one may consider our choice equivalent with a, perhaps naive, notion of moralization of the status quo from which the 'bargaining' starts.

23. In particular,

$$N_{hh} > N_{hl} \Leftrightarrow R - \underline{w} > 2c$$

and

$$N_{hh} > N_{lh} \Leftrightarrow 2\frac{R - \underline{w} - c}{R - \bar{w} - c} > \frac{\bar{w}}{\underline{w}}.$$

The first condition implies that the extra cost required for the quality improving technology is not too large in comparison with the profits of the firm when the worker accepts the lower wage. The second condition ensures that the increase in the consumer's and entrepreneur's utility when the worker partly acts voluntarily compensates the loss in the earnings of the worker himself.

Bibliography

Ben Ner, A. and L. Putterman (eds) (1998), *Economics, Values, and Organization* , Cambridge: Cambridge University Press, pp. 3–69.

Bernheim, B. (1994), 'A Theory of Conformity', *Journal of Political Economy*, **102** (5), 841–77.

Binmore, K. (1992), *Fun and Games*, Lexington, MA: Heath and Company.

Binmore, K. (1994), *Game Theory and the Social Contract, Vol. 1: Playing Fair*, Cambridge, MA: MIT Press.

Binmore, K. (1997), *Game Theory and the Social Contract, Vol. 2: Just Playing*, Cambridge, MA: MIT Press.
Brock, H. (1979), 'A game theoretical account of social justice', *Theory and Decision*, **5** (11), 239–65.
Broome, J. (1999), *Ethics out of Economics*, Cambridge: Cambridge University Press.
Charness, G. and M. Rabin (2000), 'Social preferences: some simple tests and a new model', mimeo, University of California at Berkeley.
Copp, D. (1997), 'The ring of Gyges: overridingness and the unity of reason', *Social Philosophy and Policy*, **14** (1).
Falk, A. and U. Fischbacher (1999), 'A theory of reciprocity', Working Paper no. 6, Institute for Empirical Research in Economics, University of Zurich.
Fehr, E. and K. Schmidt (2003), 'Theories of fairness and reciprocity – evidence and economic applications', in M. Dewatripont, L.P. Hansen and S. Turnovsky (eds), *Advances in Economic Theory: Eighth World Congress of the Econometric Society*, Cambridge: Cambridge University Press.
Gauthier, D. (1986), *Morals by Agreement*, Oxford: Clarendon Press.
Geanakoplos, J., D. Pearce and E. Stacchetti (1989), 'Psychological games and sequential rationality', *Games and Economic Behavior*, **1**, 60–79.
Grimalda, G. (2001), 'A survey on the nature, reasons for compliance and emergence of social norms', *LIUC* Papers no. 92, Supplement, Cattaneo University of Castellanza, October.
Grimalda, G. and L. Sacconi (2005), 'The constitution of the not-for-profit organisation: reciprocal conformity to morality', *Constitutional Political Economy*, **16** (3), September, 249–76.
Hansmann, H. (1980), 'The role of nonprofit enterprise', *Yale Law Journal*, **89**, 835–901.
Hansmann, H.B. (1987), 'Economic theory of nonprofit organisation', in Walter W. Powell (ed.), *The Nonprofit Sector*, New Haven, CT: Yale University Press, pp. 27–42.
Hansmann, H.B. (1988), 'Ownership of the firm', *Journal of Law, Economics and Organisation*, **4**, 267–304.
Hargreaves-Heap, S. (1989), *Rationality in Economics*, New York: Blackwell.
Harsanyi, J. (1977), *Rational Behavior and Bargaining Equilibrium in Games and Social Situations*, Cambridge: Cambridge University Press.
Hogarth, R. and M. Reder (eds) (1986), 'The behavioural foundations of economic theory', *Journal of Business* (supplement).
Kolpin, V. (1992), 'Equilibrium refinements in psychological games', *Games and Economic Behavior*, **4** (2), 218–28.
Kreps, D.M. (1990), 'Corporate culture and economic theory', in J. Alt and K. Shepsle (eds), *Perspectives in Positive Political Economy*, Cambridge: Cambridge University Press, pp. 90–143.
Lewis, D. (1969), *Convention: A Philosophical Study*, Cambridge, MA: Harvard University Press.
Mertens, J.F. and S. Zamir (1985), 'Formulation of Bayesian analysis for games with incomplete information', *International Journal of Game Theory*, **14** (1), 1–29.
Nash, J. (1950), 'The bargaining problem', *Econometrica*, **18**, 155–62.
Nelson, R. and S. Winter (1982), *An Evolutionary Theory of Economic Change*, Cambridge, MA: Harvard University Press.
North, D.C. (1990), *Institutions, Institutional Change and Economic Performance*, Cambridge: Cambridge University Press.
Rabin, M. (1993), 'Incorporating fairness into game theory', *American Economic Review*, **83** (5), 1281–302.
Rose-Ackerman, S. (1987), 'Ideals versus dollars: donors, charity managers, and government grants', *Journal of Political Economy*, **95** (4), 810–23.
Rose-Ackerman, S. (1996), 'Altruism, nonprofits, and economic theory', *Journal of Economic Literature*, **34**, 701–28.
Sacconi, L. (1986), 'Teoria dei giochi un approccio adeguato al problema della giustizia sociale', *Teoria Politica*, **II** (3), 73–96.

Sacconi, L. (1991), *Etica degli affari, individui, imprese e mercati nella prospettiva dell'etica razionale*, Milan: Il Saggiatore.

Sacconi, L. (1997), *Etica, economia ed organizzazione*, Bari: La Terza.

Sacconi, L. (2000), *The Social Contract of the Firm*, Berlin: Springer.

Sacconi, L. (2004), 'Efficiency of the non-profit enterprise: constitutional ideology, conformist preferences and reputation', in B. Hodgson (ed.), *The Invisible Hand and the Common Good*, Berlin: Springer-Verlag, pp. 207–56.

Sacconi, L. (2006), 'Incomplete contracts and corporate ethics' a game theoretic model under fuzzy information', in F. Cafaggi, A. Nicita and U. Pagano (eds), *Legal Orderings and Economic Institutions*, London: Routledge (in press).

Scanlon, T.M. (2001), 'Symposium on Amartya Sen's philosophy: 3 Sen and consequentialism', *Economics and Philosophy*, **17**, 39–50.

Schelling, T.C. (1960), *Strategy of Conflict*, Cambridge, MA: Harvard University Press.

Sen, A. (1985), 'Well-being, agency and freedom', *Journal of Philosophy*, **82**, 169–221.

Sen, A. (2000), 'Consequential evaluation and practical reason', *Journal of Philosophy*, **97**, 477–502.

Sen, A (2001), 'Symposium on Amartya Sen's philosophy: 4 Reply', *Economics and Philosophy*, **17**, 51–66.

Sugden, R. (1986), *The Economics of Rights, Co-operation and Welfare*, Oxford: Basil Blackwell.

Sugden, R. (1998a), 'The motivating power of expectations', mimeo, University of East Anglia.

Sugden, R. (1998b), 'Normative expectations: the simultaneous evolution of institutions and norms', in Ben-Ner and Putterman (eds), pp. 73–100.

Sugden, R. (2000), 'Team preferences', *Economics and Philosophy*, **16**, 175–204.

Tan, T. and S.R. Werlang (1988), 'The Bayesian foundation of solution concepts in games', *Journal of Economic Theory*, **45**, 370–91.

Verbeek, B. (2001), 'Consequentialism, rationality and the relevant description of outcomes', *Economics and Philosophy*, **5** (17), 181–205.

Weisbrod, B. (1988), *The Non Profit Economy*, Cambridge, MA: Harvard University Press.

Index